A Photographic Review of Creativity '79

Edited by
DON BARRON

Displayed at
the New York Coliseum
New York, September 18, 19, 20, 1979

ART DIRECTION BOOK COMPANY New York, NY 10016

Advertising Directions, Volume 13

Designed by Al Lichtenberg

ISBN: 0-910158-55-X
ISBN for Creativity Annuals Standing Orders: 0-910158-10-X
Library of Congress Catalog Card #74-168254

Printed in the United States of America.

Distributors:
USA and Canada: Art Direction Book Company
Foreign Distributor: Fleetbooks, c/o Feffer & Simons, Inc.
100 Park Avenue, New York, N.Y. 10017

CONTENTS

TELEVISION / FILM

CONCEPT / DESIGN

...the Art Director is the genre artist of our times. His talent is his eye and mind for the contemporary scene, and his skill the ability to depict his client's product in terms of the immediate moment.

FROM THE ANNOUNCEMENT FOR THE FIRST CREATIVITY SHOW, 1970

This CREATIVITY Show dramatized the marked improvement in art directing that has been taking place over the past five years. The change has been gradual, somewhat like a tide coming in over a long, flat beach. Often, during the period, it was difficult to pinpoint the differences. Now it is quite clear that art directors are working under much better conditions.

Budgets have improved substantially. The demand for long copy has decreased. White space is no longer a crime. Art illustration is possible. It is also possible to change layouts. You don't have to do the same thing for every assignment. In short, flexibility is replacing rigidity. The prime responsibility isn't always saving money now; it's also coming up with good art directing.

The show and this Annual document the transition. You will see visual freedoms here, a factor that has been long absent from Award shows. The looseness is evident in the imaginative use of white space in combination with such other elements as irregularly shaped photographs; big, bold headlines; insets; borders and color. The flood of new treatments overshadows the neatness and cleanliness of past years. Tidy styling still remains, but it no longer seems as important. This is particularly true for fashion advertising, which tended towards opulence and flamboyance.

Humor has become a noticeable fixture of advertising. It is somewhat on the quiet side, and it is not unusual for it to be almost biting. Visually, it's not quite punk art, although there's a certain air of ''tackiness'' about it.

Illustrative photography is very strong in this show. It has been a factor for several years, and this year it dominates advertising design. Much of this must be due to art director efforts to transfer the drama that is so much a part of TV commercials into print ads. In fact, some camera work attempts to go beyond illustration and tell a story in a photo. As has happened so often in the past, photography had another outstanding year.

Art illustration, at the same time, keeps on gaining strength, and had by far its best year since the early 1960s. Assignments for trade and business paper ads were substantial.

••••

Here is the rundown in visual developments by design category.

Consumer ads. Visual treatments now range over a wide area and include: white space, borders, insets, intense colors, excessive cropping, multi-model layouts, massive product shots, illustrative photography. The handling of type is becoming somewhat less than excellent, but when the type is well directed, it is superb. For the first time in the Creativity shows, consumer ads have become one of the star sections. They continue to show the biggest improvements, as they have for the last two years.

•••

Magazine covers. Here, too, the improvement was impressive. Despite the demands, competition, and frustrations magazine cover art directors put up with the covers this year were the best we've seen for a long time. There is a marked trend towards simplicity and a better use of color. The handling of type also improved markedly.

••••

Annual Reports. Many b/w photos of ordinary people rather than usual 4 color, smiling executives shots emphasize the drift away from the slick in this category. Also, the reports came down in number of pages, increased the use of printing papers other than the cast coateds, and there was less color. Annual reports can hardly be expected to ever be models of modesty, but this year's reports were refreshingly simpler. The photography and offset printing was outstanding.

••••

TV commercials. Slowly, very slowly, humor is returning to this now worldwide art form. As slowly, also, the Tv AD is assuming stronger control. While far too few commercials seem worth airing, there is, at the same time, an increasing amount with good story lines, propping, casting, music, and overall execution. Biggest improvements are showing up not in the United States, but elsewhere. Brazilian TVcs, for example, are superb.

••••

3
Herb Lubalin Art Director
Heather Cooper Illustrator
Burns, Cooper, Hynes Limited Studio
Aspen Design Conference Client

2
Jim Crawford Art Director
David Haggerty Photography Photographers
Ross Roy N.Y./Compton Agency
Bacardi Imports Client

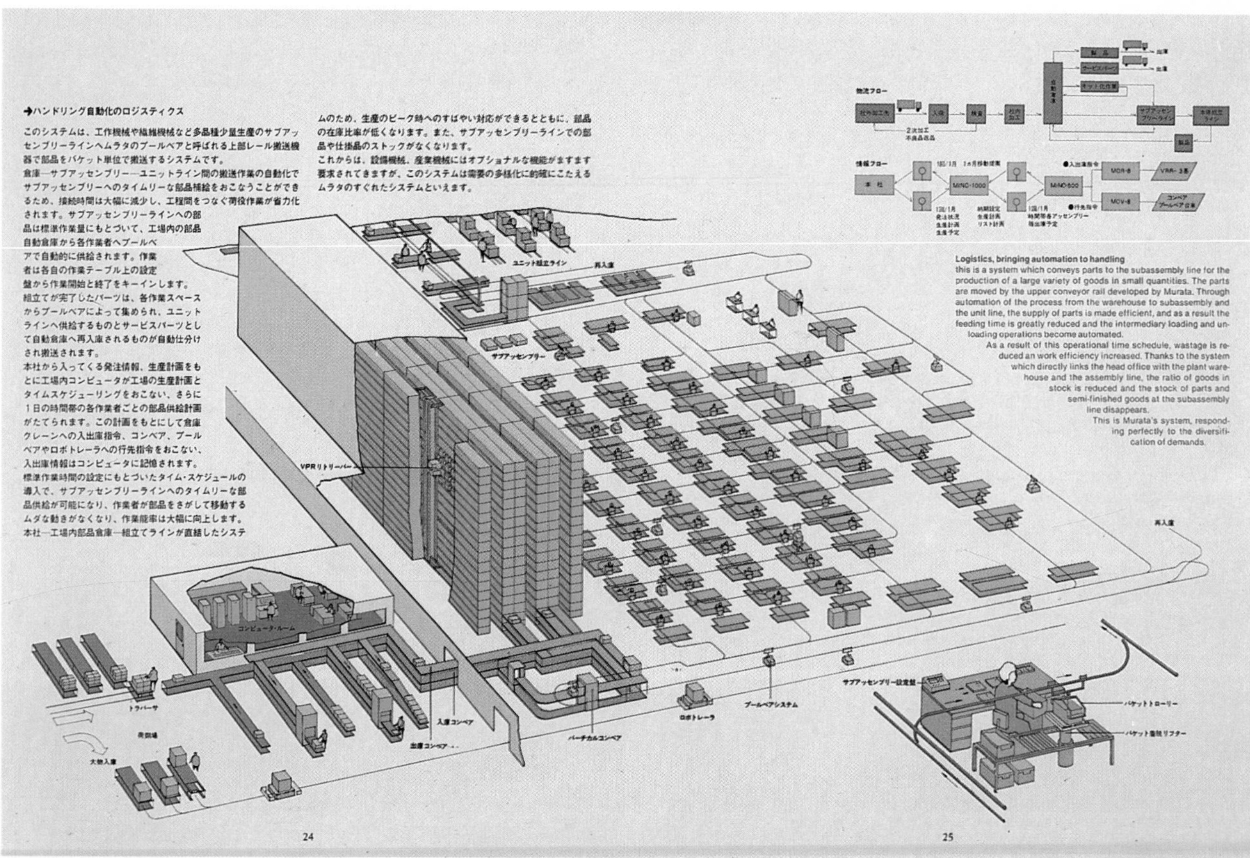

➔ハンドリング自動化のロジスティクス

このシステムは、工作機械や繊維機械など多品種少量生産のサブアッセンブリーラインへムラタのプールベアと呼ばれる上部レール搬送機器で部品をバケット単位で搬送するシステムです。
倉庫—サブアッセンブリー—ユニットライン間の搬送作業の自動化でサブアッセンブリーへのタイムリーな部品補給をおこなうことができるため、接続時間は大幅に減少し、工程間をつなぐ荷役作業が省力化されます。サブアッセンブリーラインへの部品は標準作業量にもとづいて、工場内の部品自動倉庫から各作業者へプールベアで自動的に供給されます。作業者は各自の作業テーブル上の設定盤から作業開始と終了をキーインします。
組立てが完了したパーツは、各作業スペースからプールベアによって集められ、ユニットラインへ供給するものとサービスパーツとして自動倉庫へ再入庫されるものが自動仕分けされ搬送されます。
本社から入ってくる発注情報、生産計画をもとに工場内コンピュータが工場の生産計画とタイムスケジューリングをおこない、さらに1日の時間帯の各作業者ごとの部品供給計画がたてられます。この計画をもとにして倉庫クレーンへの入出庫指令、コンベア、プールベアやロボトレーラへの行先指令をおこない、入出庫情報はコンピュータに記憶されます。
標準作業時間の設定にもとづいたタイム・スケジュールの導入で、サブアッセンブリーラインへのタイムリーな部品供給が可能になり、作業者が部品をさがして移動するムダな動きがなくなり、作業能率は大幅に向上します。
本社—工場内部品倉庫—組立てラインが直結したシステムのため、生産のピーク時へのすばやい対応ができるとともに、部品の在庫比率が低くなります。また、サブアッセンブリーラインでの部品や仕掛品のストックがなくなります。
これからは、設備機械、産業機械にはオプショナルな機能がますます要求されてきますが、このシステムは需要の多様化に的確にこたえるムラタのすぐれたシステムといえます。

Logistics, bringing automation to handling
this is a system which conveys parts to the subassembly line for the production of a large variety of goods in small quantities. The parts are moved by the upper conveyor rail developed by Murata. Through automation of the process from the warehouse to subassembly and the unit line, the supply of parts is made efficient, and as a result the feeding time is greatly reduced and the intermediary loading and unloading operations become automated.
As a result of this operational time schedule, wastage is reduced an work efficiency increased. Thanks to the system which directly links the head office with the plant warehouse and the assembly line, the ratio of goods in stock is reduced and the stock of parts and semi-finished goods at the subassembly line disappears.
This is Murata's system, responding perfectly to the diversification of demands.

24 25

4

KÖP VITA LEE OCH FÄRGA SJÄLV MED DYLON!

I år blir det sköna overallmodet ännu festligare!
Med färg! Nu kommer de klara, glada kulörerna med solgult i spetsen. Och med Dylon Wash'n Dye kan du välja vilka som helst av regnbågens färger. Och allt är lätt som en plätt – du färgar i tvättmaskinen!
Lev skönt och visa färg i år!

DYLON
Wash'n dye

GRIPEN · LINKÖPING

5

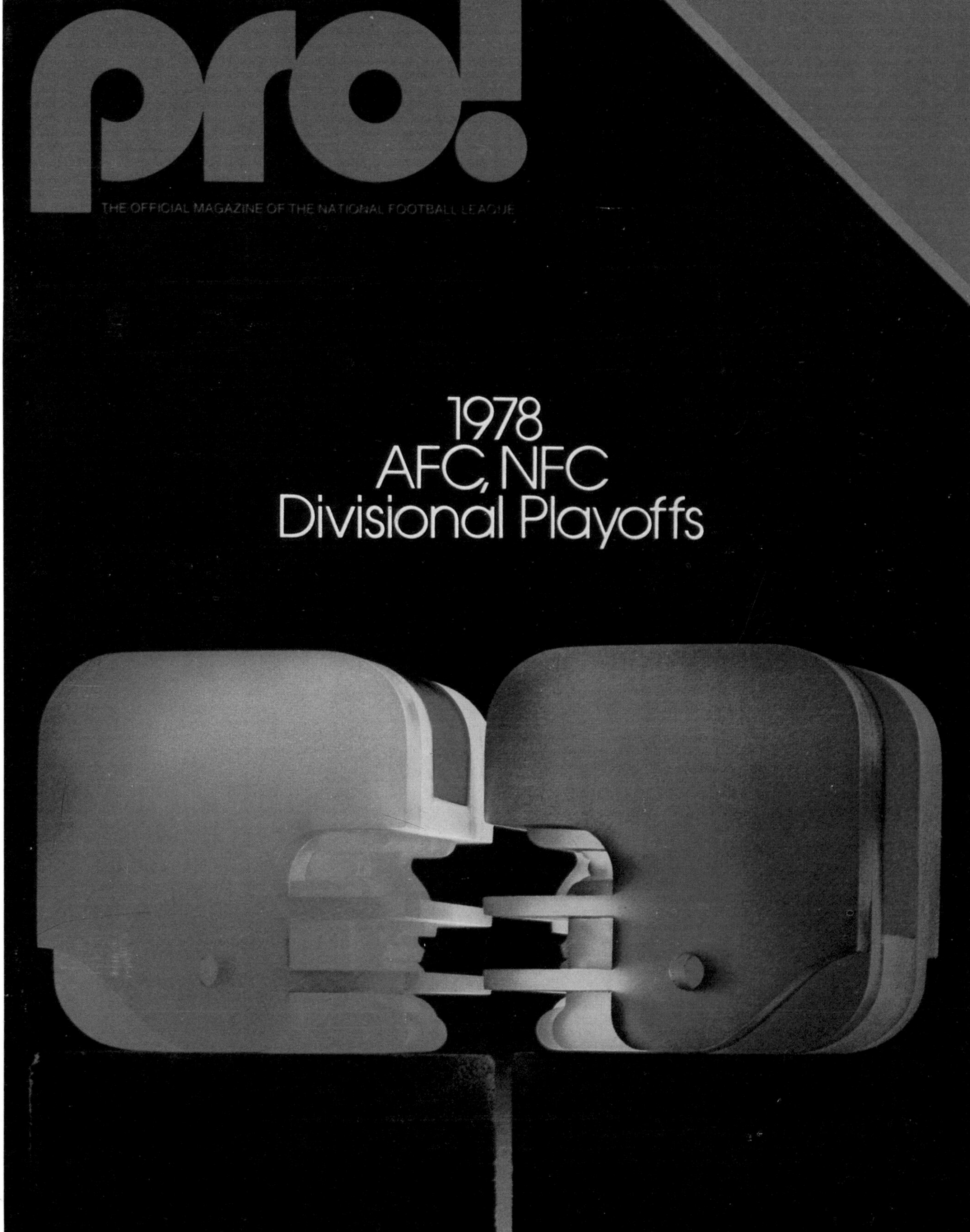

pro!
THE OFFICIAL MAGAZINE OF THE NATIONAL FOOTBALL LEAGUE
1978
AFC, NFC
Divisional Playoffs

6

4
Yutaka Matsushita Art Director
The Design House, Inc. Agency
Murata Machinery Ltd. Client

5
Ingemar Jacobson Art Director
Svante Fischerstrom Photographer
Sven O. Blomquist Adv. Agency Agency
Tekniska Fabriken Gripen Client

6
Dave Boss Art Director
Stan Caplan Photographer
Don Weller Illustrator
The Weller Institute for the Cure of Design Agency
National Football League Properties Client

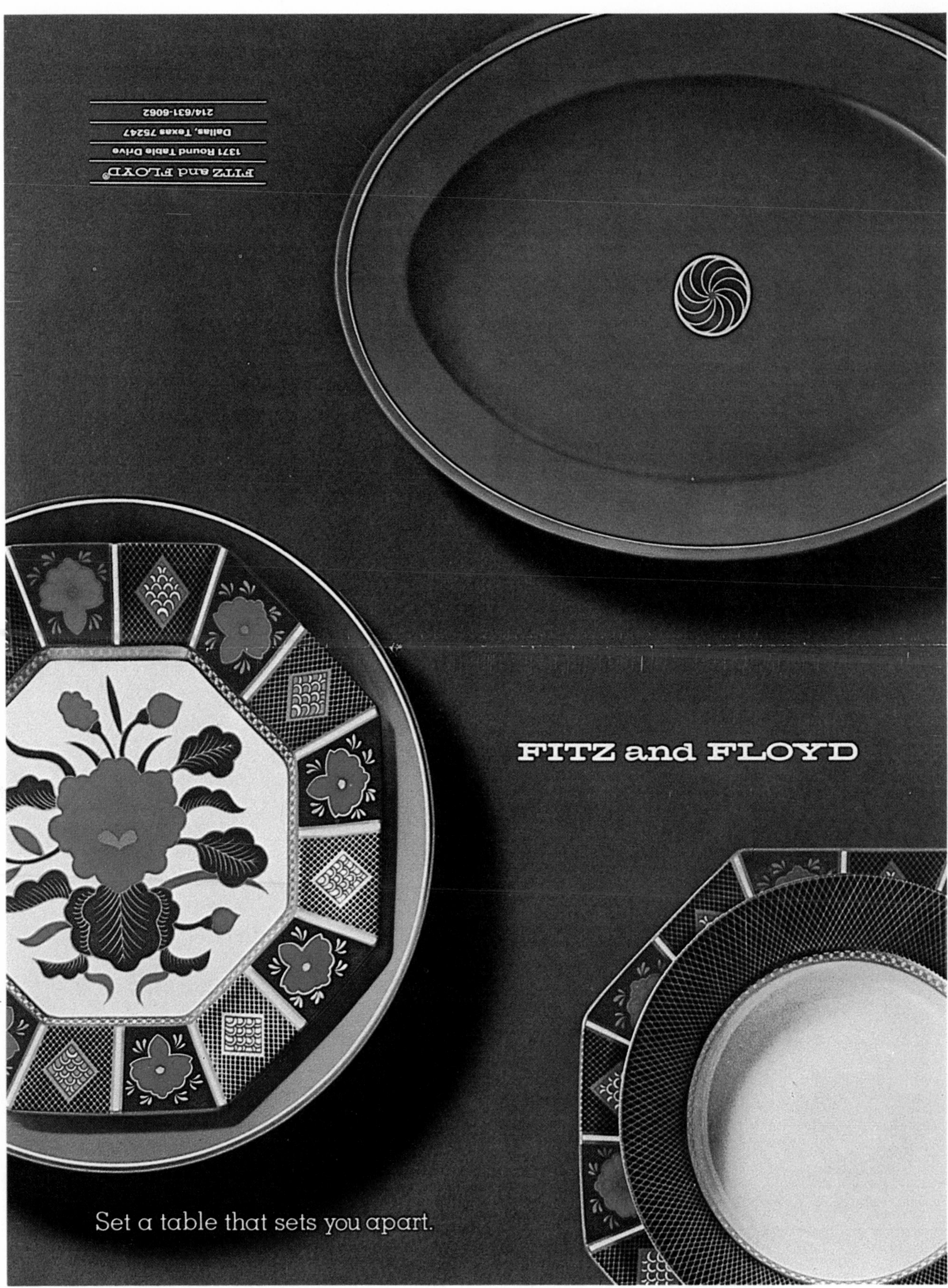

7
Kay Sabinson Art Director
Irene Stern Photographer
Burson-Marsteller Agency
Fitz & Floyd Client

8
Yukiko Inuzuka Art Director
Masami Hagiwara Photographer
Hisao Takehana Designer
CDP Japan Limited Advertising Agency
Harveys of Bristol Ltd. Client

Harveys Sherry

HARVEYS BRISTOL CREAM

IMPORTED BY SUNTORY

9
Doug Fisher Art Director
Mathew Brady Photographer
Lord, Sullivan & Yoder Agency
Nevamar Client

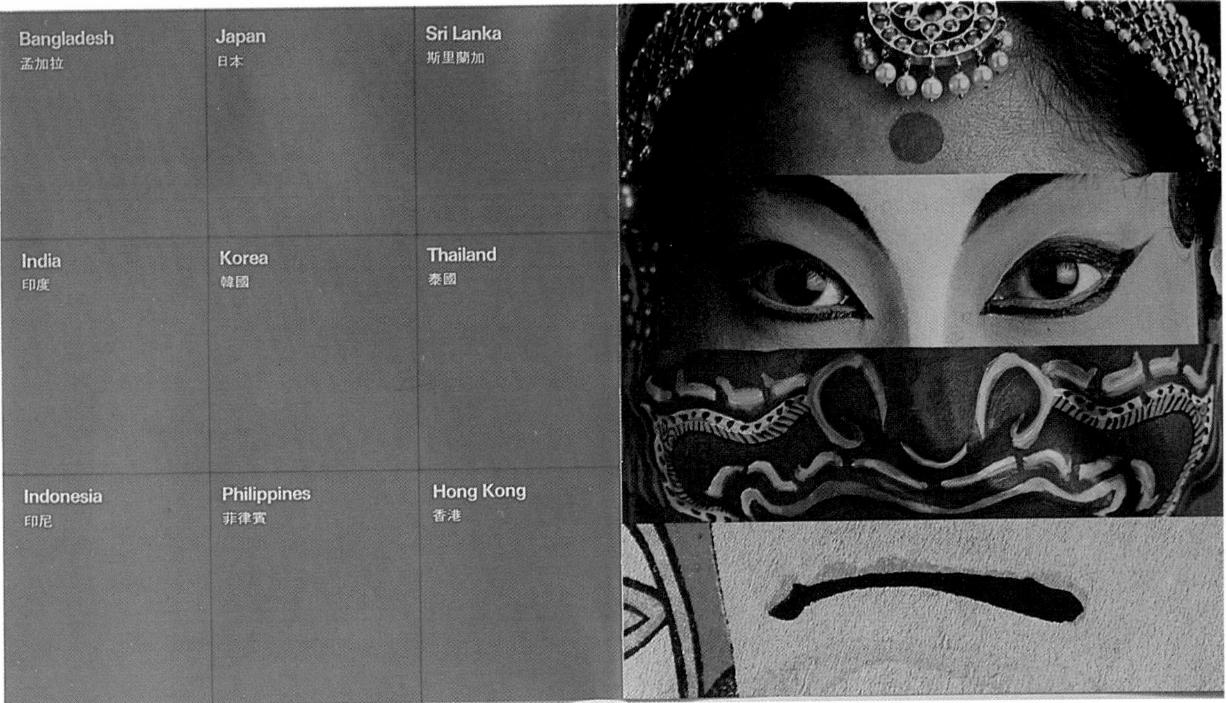

10
Kan Tai-Keung, Cheung Shu-Sun Art Directors
SS Design & Production Agency
The Urban Council, Hong Kong Client

11
Richard M. Ference Art Director
Jeremiah Chechik Photographer
Bomac Batten Production House
Chatelaine Magazine Client

A SLAVE OF LOVE
directed by Nikita Mikhalkov
starring Rodion Nakhapetov and Elena Solovei
from Cinema 5
American Premiere August 14 Plaza Theatre

13
Ed Brodkin Art Director
Walter Glinka Designer
Diener/Hauser/Bates Agency
Cinema 5 Client

12
John Clayton Art Director
John Clayton Photography Studio

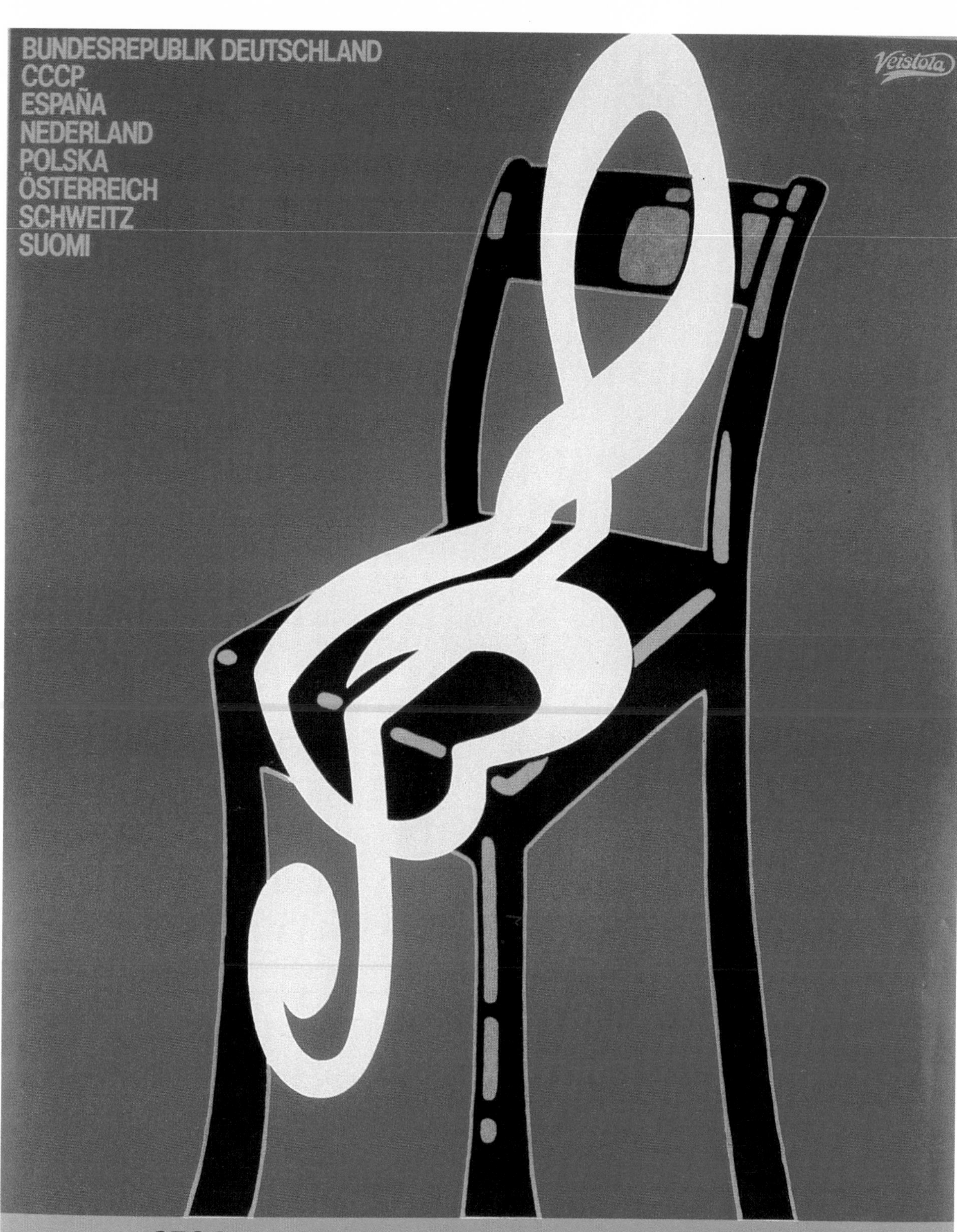
BUNDESREPUBLIK DEUTSCHLAND
CCCP
ESPAÑA
NEDERLAND
POLSKA
ÖSTERREICH
SCHWEITZ
SUOMI
Veistola
SECOND EBU
INTERNATIONAL STRING
QUARTET COMPETITION
IN HELSINKI 10.-14.10.1978
EBU
EBUN TOINEN
KANSAINVÄLINEN
JOUSIKVARTETTIKILPAILU
HELSINGISSÄ 10.-14.10.1978
Alku- ja välierät 10.-13.10.
Finaali Sibelius-Akatemiassa 14.10.
OY YLEISRADIO AB · YLE · FINNISH BROADCASTING COMPANY

15
William A. Sloan Art Director
Cunard Ltd. Client

14
Jukka Veistola Art Director
Varis-Poteri-Veistola Agency
Finnish Broadcasting Company Client

USA Film Festival
March 30~April 8, 1979·Bob Hope Theatre/SMU·Dallas·214 692-2979

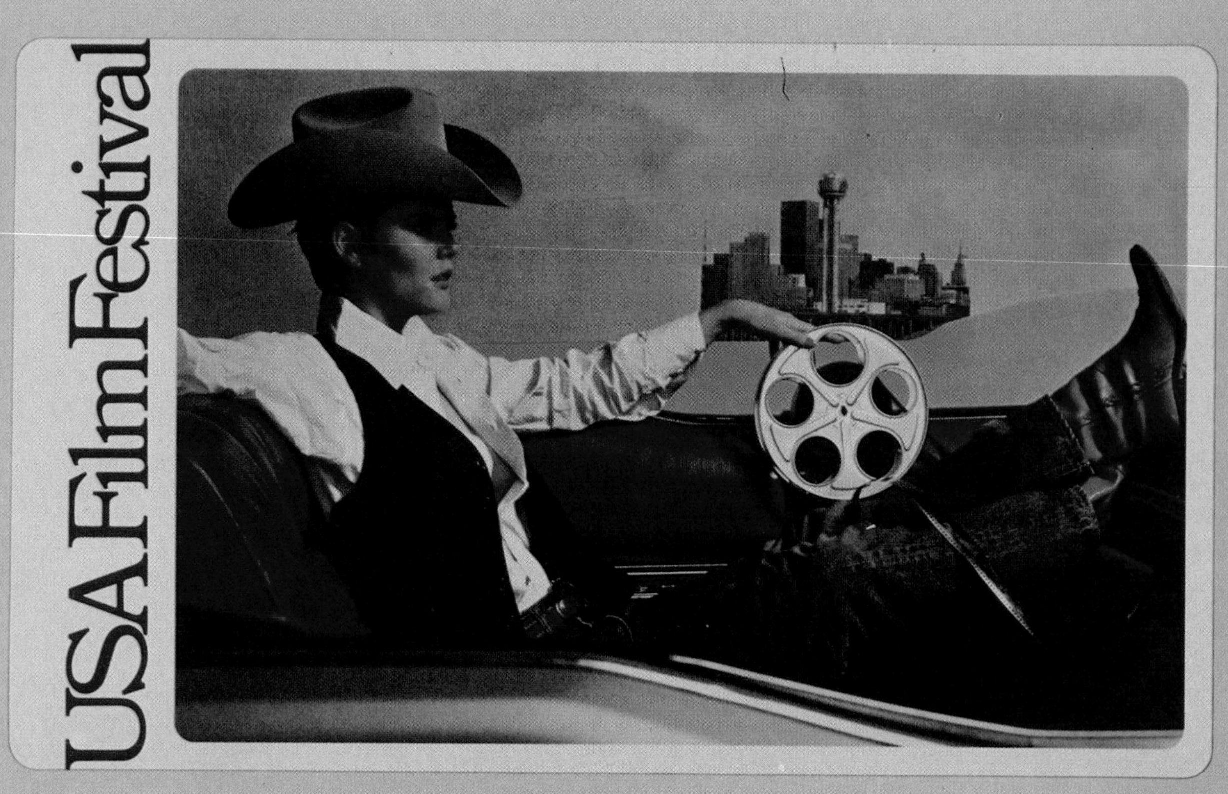

16

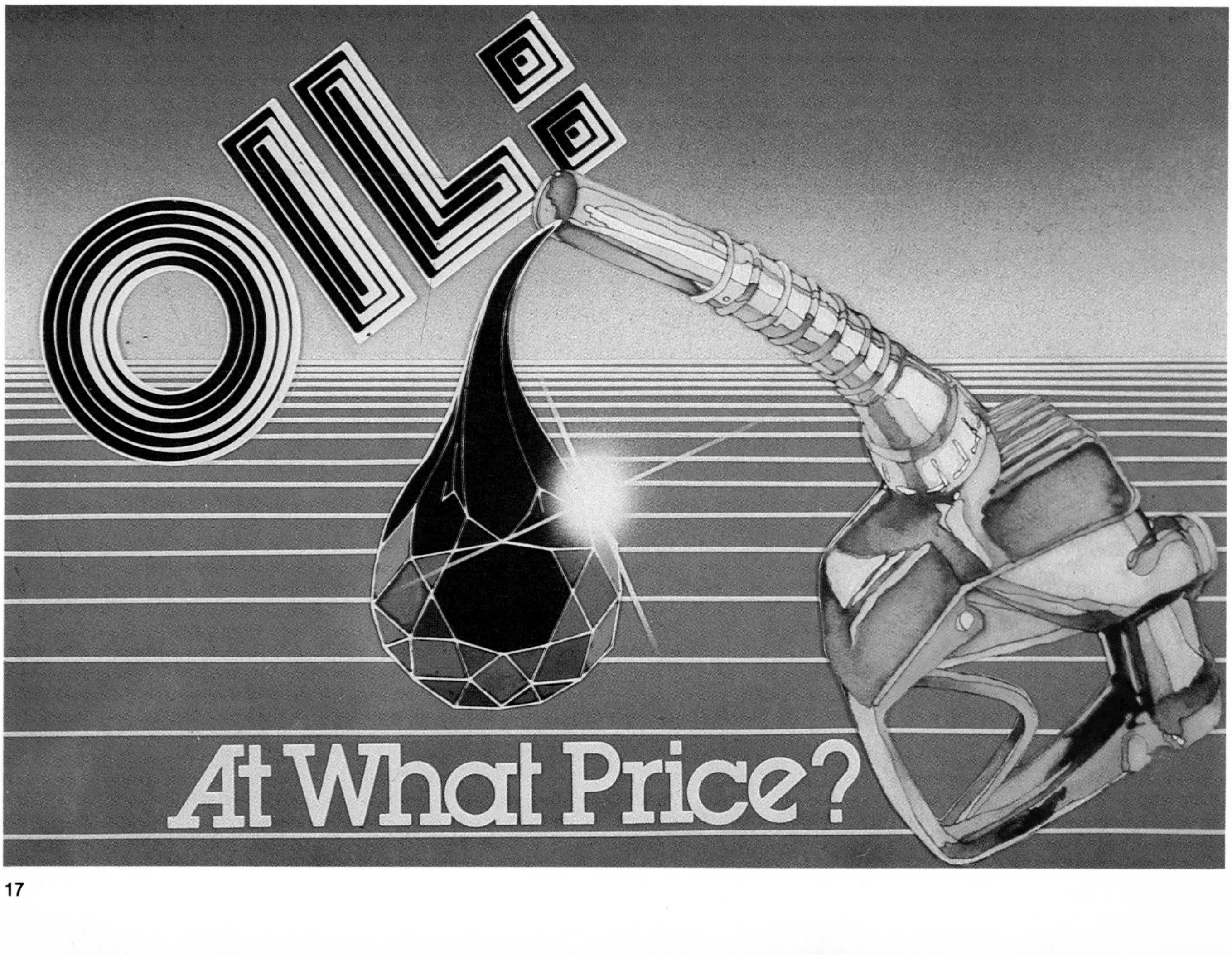

OIL:
At What Price?

17

18

16
Mickey Stuart, Tom Henvey Art Directors
Michael Morris Photographer
Abigail Stewart Model
Rita Barnard Designer
USA Film Festival Client

17
Beverly Littlewood Art Director
James Gayles Illustrator
NBC NewsCenter 4 Client

18
Dennis Thompson, Jody Thompson Art Directors
Coming Attractions Agency
Somerset Wine Company Client

ZIM
ZIM
ZIM
ZIM
ZIM
ZIM
ZIM

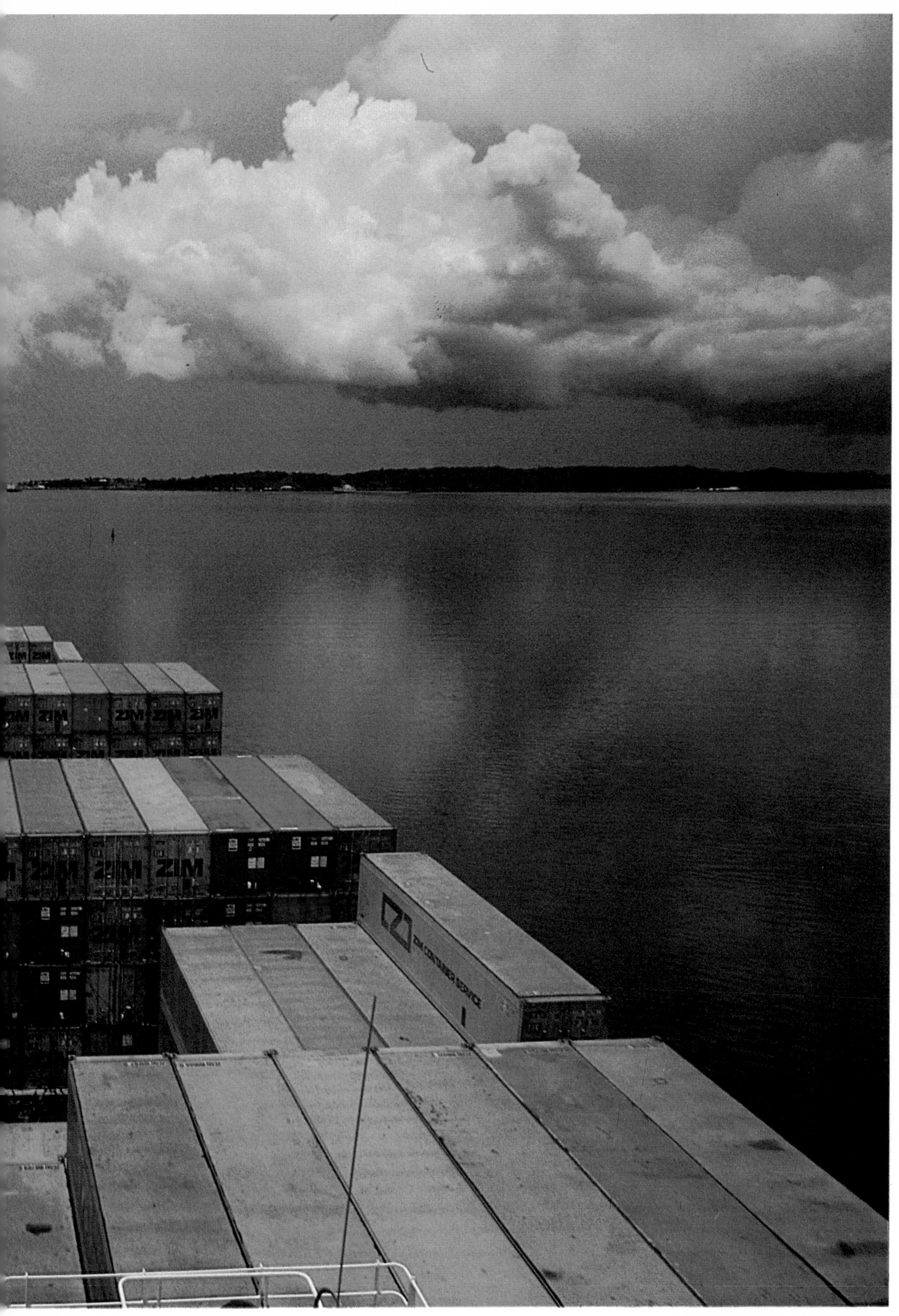

19
Roy Tuck Art Director
Tom Zimberoff Photographer
Gilbert Felix & Scharf Agency
Ehrenreich Photo/Nikon Client

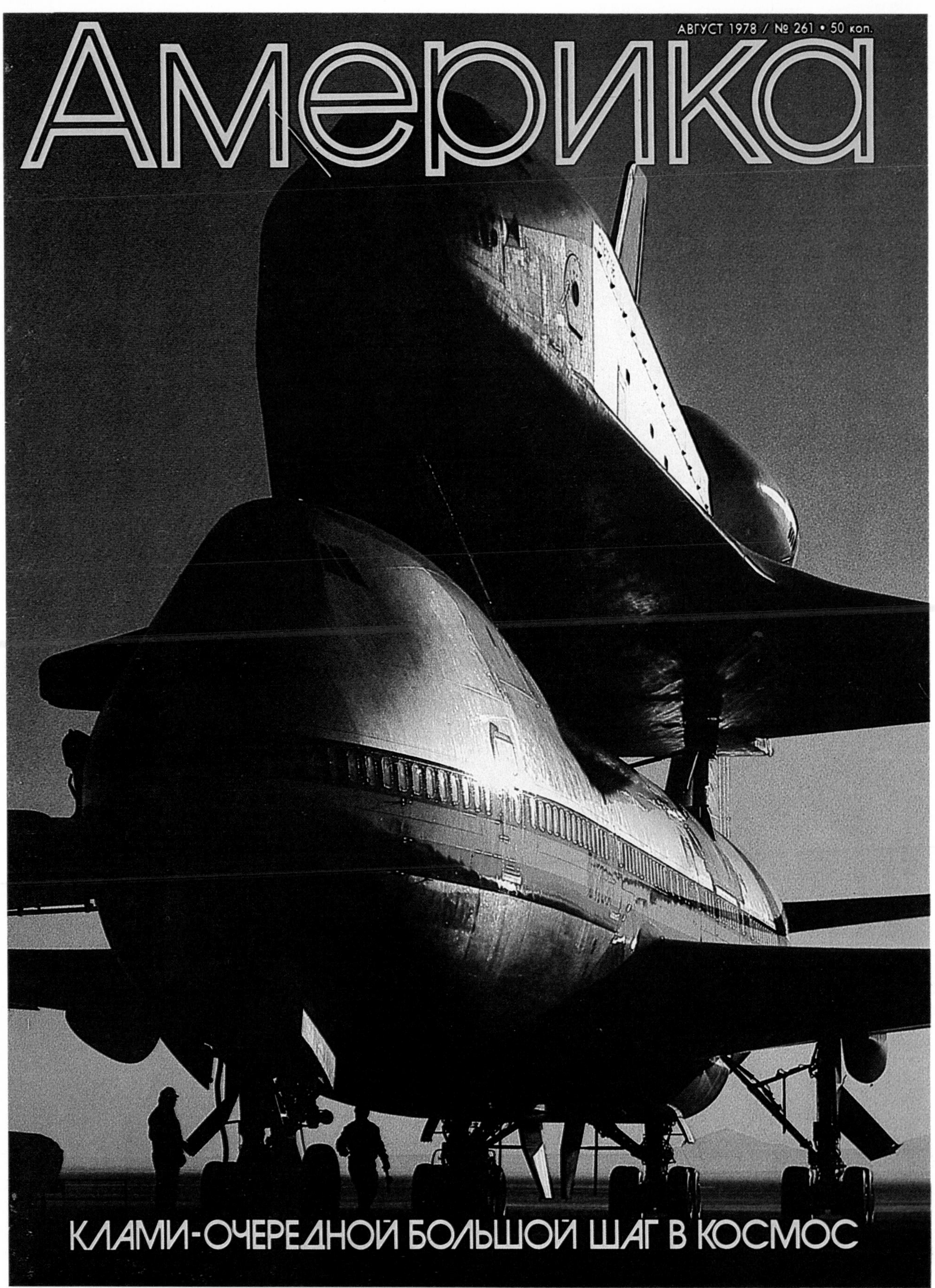

20
Dorothy Fall, David Moore Art Directors
Christopher Springmann Photographer
Dorothy Fall Designer
U.S. International Communication Agency Agency
America Illustrated Magazine Client

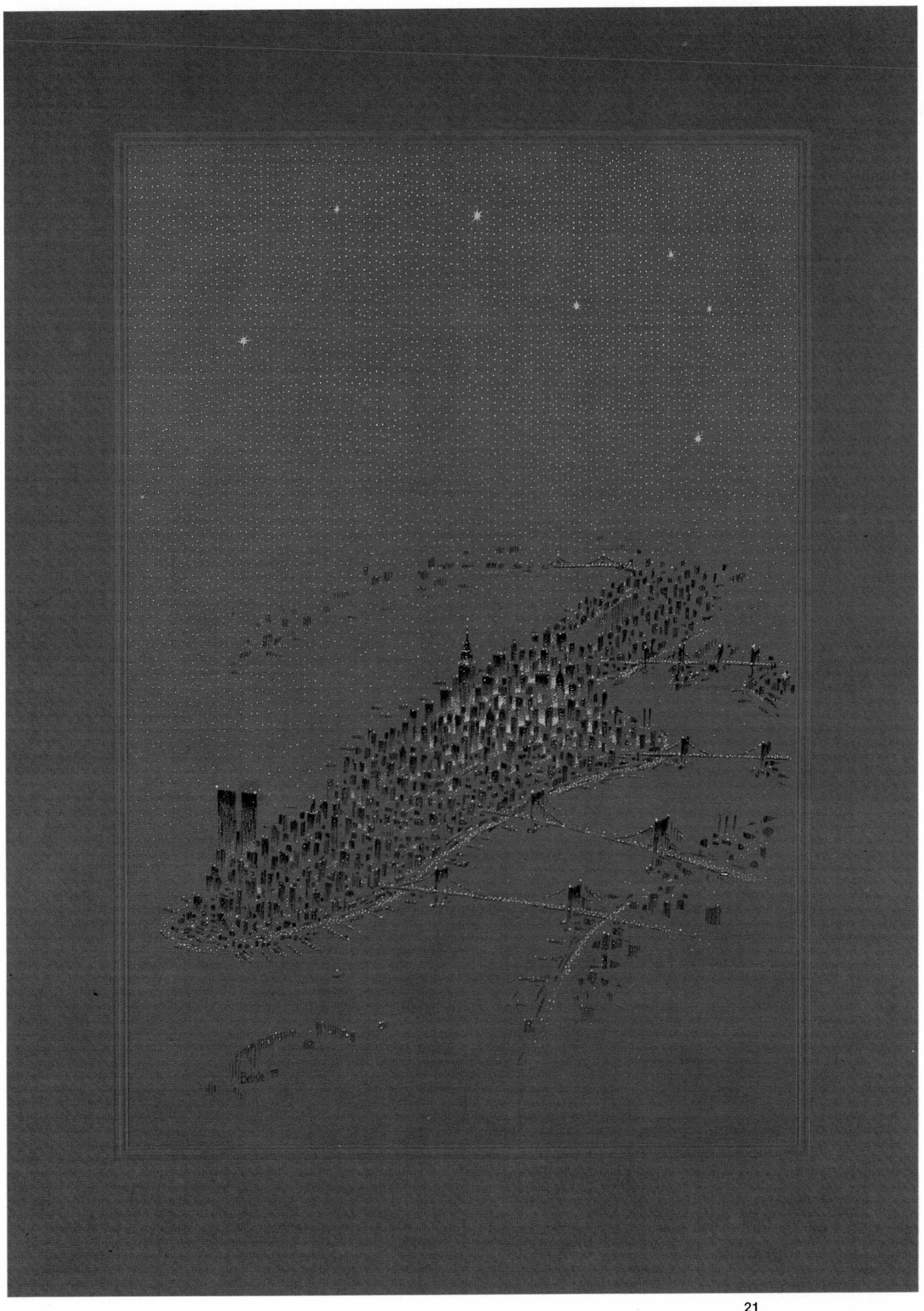

21
Brice Belisle Art Director
Redler, Inc. Client

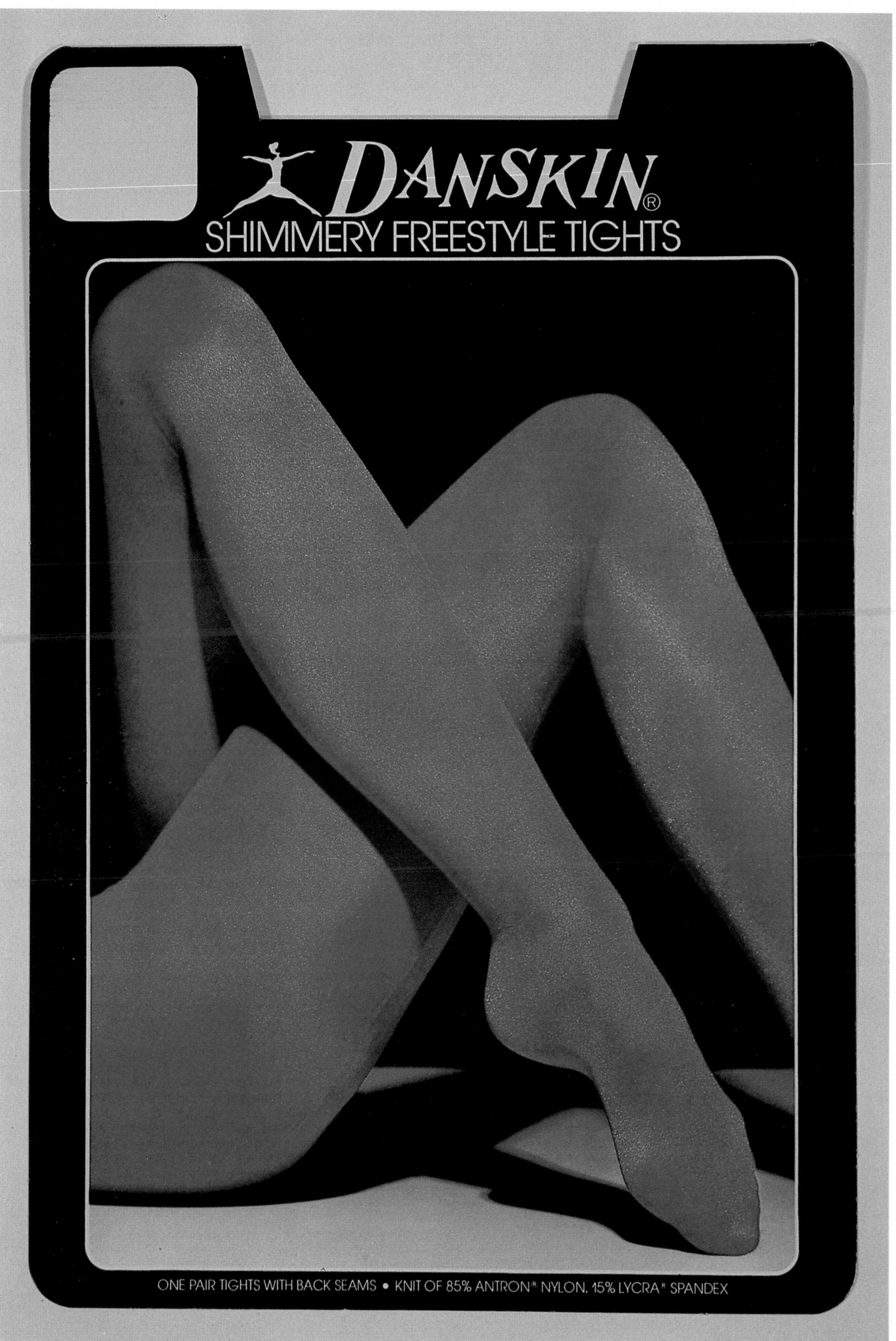

DANSKIN®
SHIMMERY FREESTYLE TIGHTS
ONE PAIR TIGHTS WITH BACK SEAMS • KNIT OF 85% ANTRON® NYLON, 15% LYCRA® SPANDEX

22
Sarah Melvin, Sky Underwood Art Directors
Gordon Munro Photographer
Susan Johnson Designer
Danskin, Inc. Client

23
Joseph Morgan Art Director
Dan McCoy Photographer
Ellen Toomey Picture Editor
International Communication Agency Agency
Horizons USA Client

24
Kay Sabinson Art Director
Ed Lindlof Illustrator
Burson-Marsteller Agency
St. Regis Client

28

29

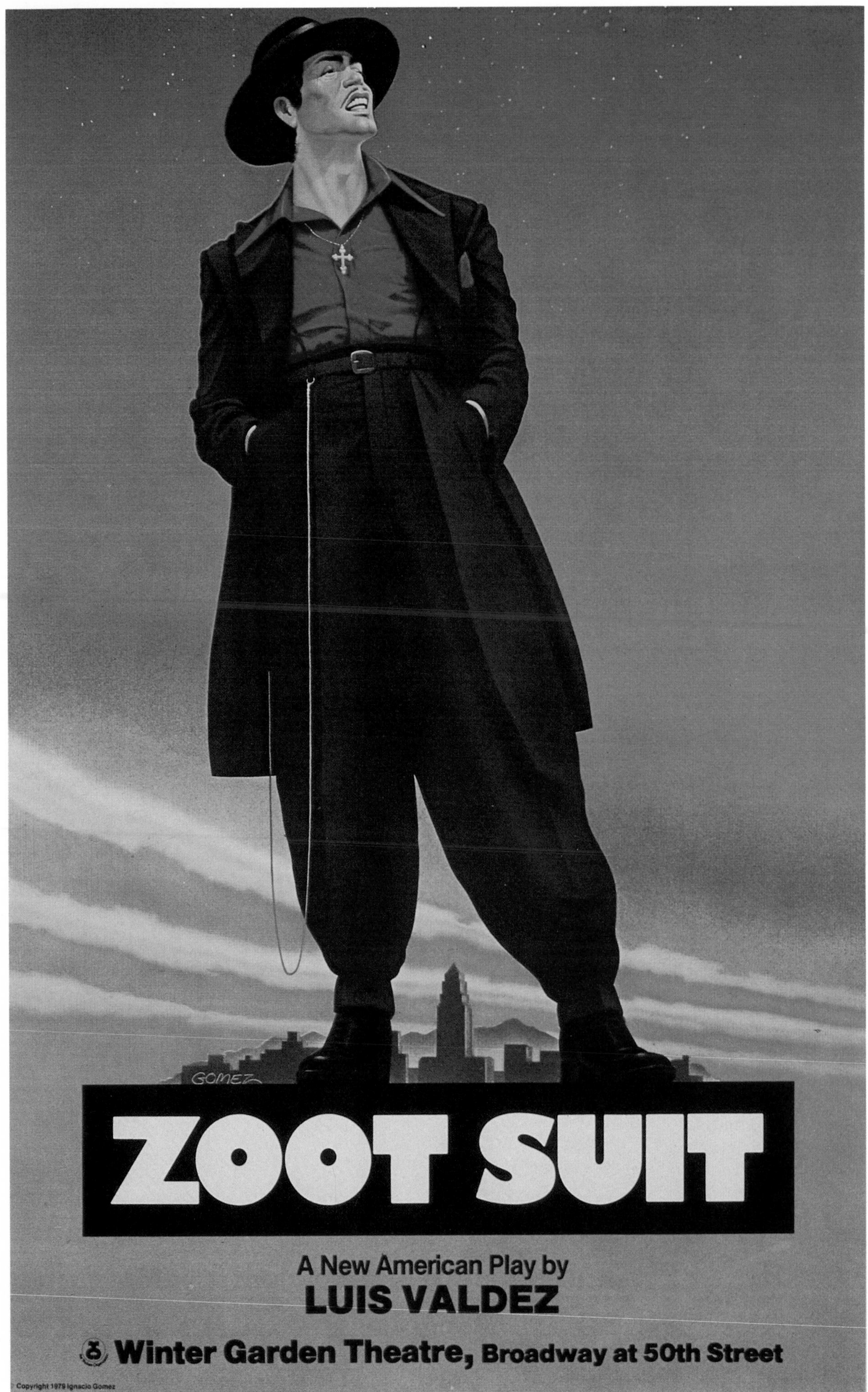
GOMEZ
ZOOT SUIT
A New American Play by
LUIS VALDEZ
Winter Garden Theatre, Broadway at 50th Street
© Copyright 1979 Ignacio Gomez

30
John Follis Art Director
Ignacio Gomez Illustrator
Elizabeth Kooker, Elizabeth Baird Designers
John Follis & Associates Agency
Center Theatre Group/Mark Taper Forum Client

31
Ken Kimura, Ethan Revsin Art Directors
Ethan Revsin Copywriter
Lee King & Partners Agency
Frye Shoe Co. Client

Photograph and makeup design by Serge Lutens. Model wears Brun Rythme Lipstick, Beige Bop Nail Enamel, Brown and Mauve Matte et Brillant Duo Eyeshadows.

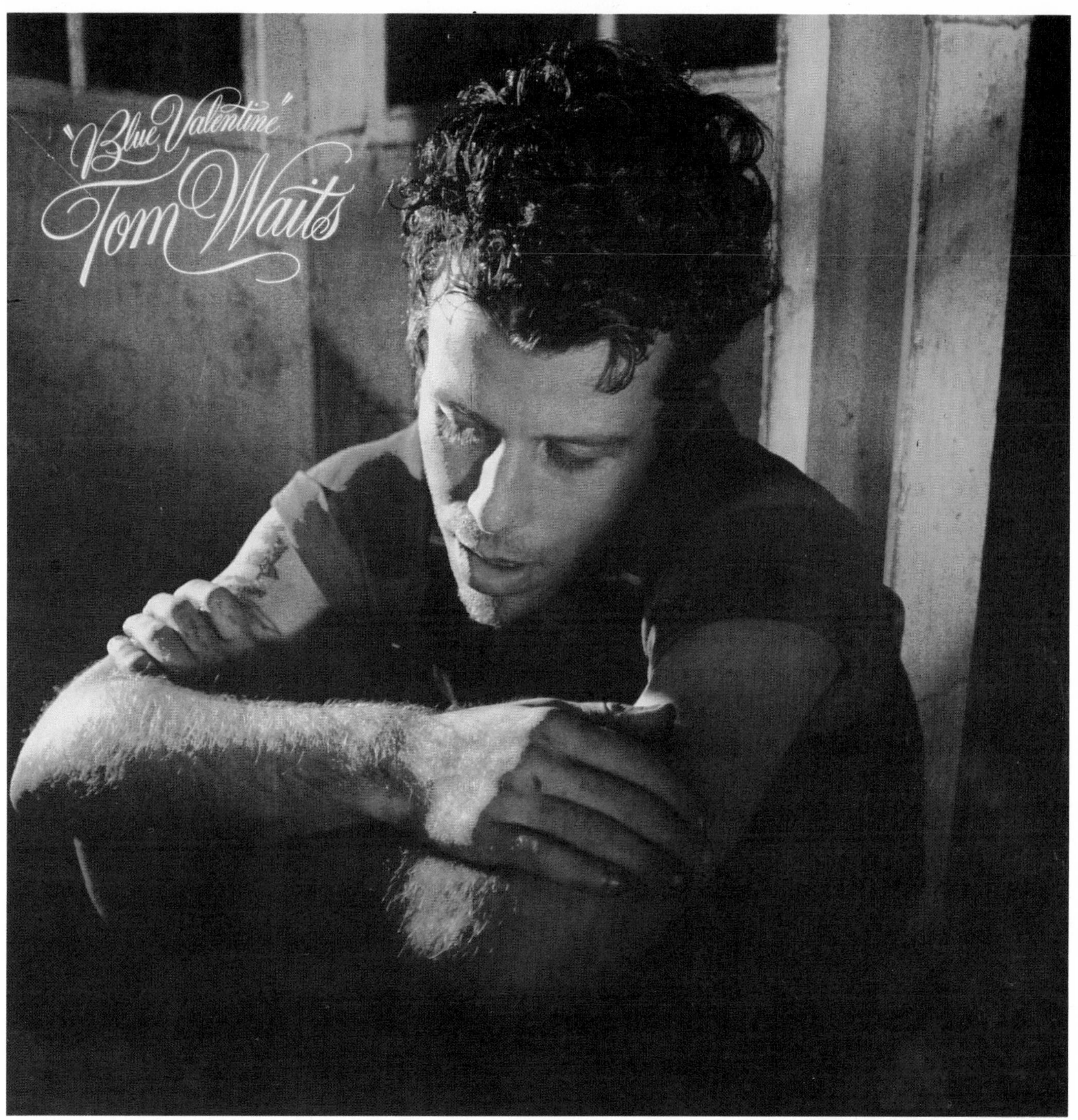

33
Ron Coro Art Director
Elliot Gilbert Photographer
Elektra/Asylum Records Client

32
Kuhn Caldwell Art Director
Serge Lutens, Shig Ikeda Photographers
Christian Dior Perfumes, Inc. Client

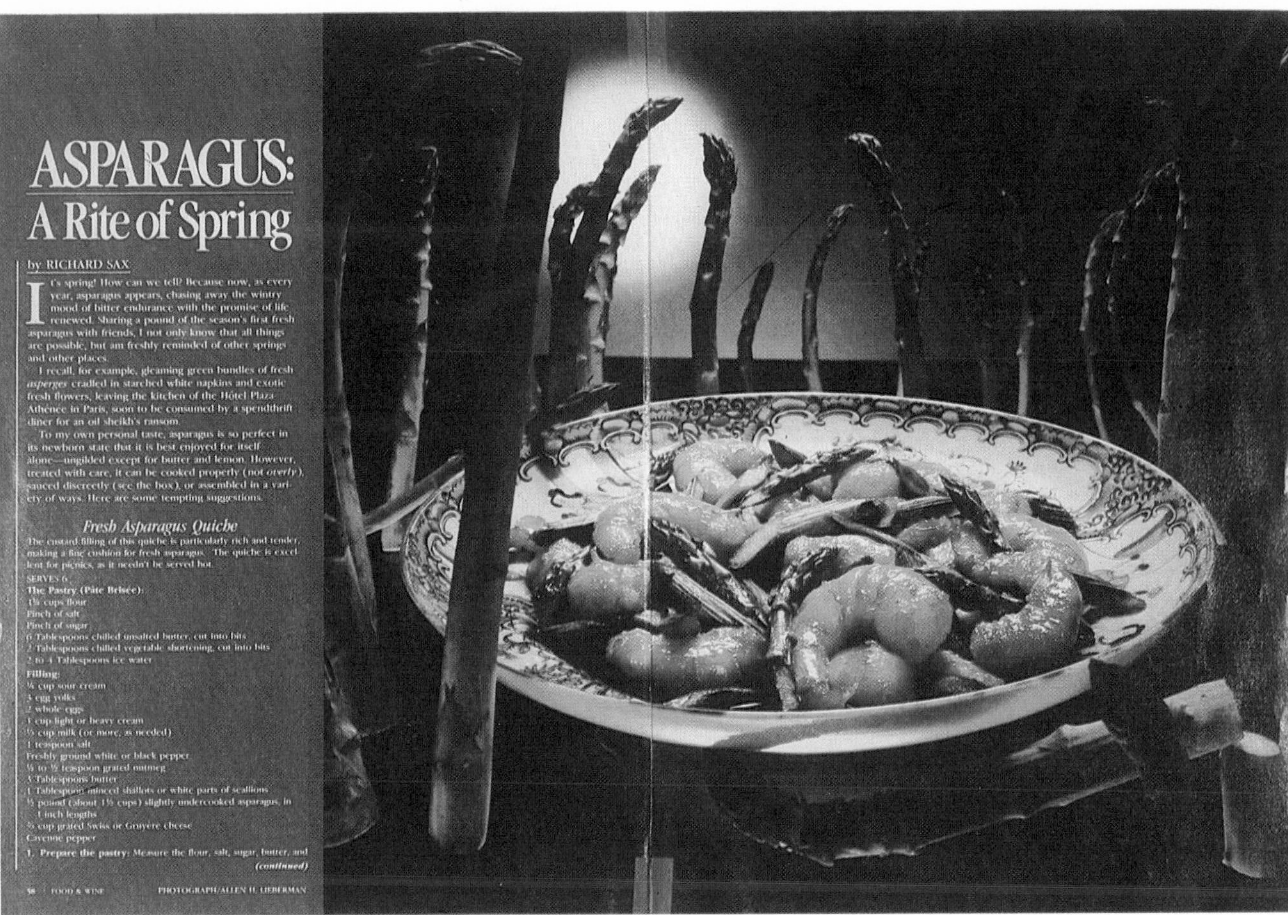

ASPARAGUS: A Rite of Spring

by RICHARD SAX

It's spring! How can we tell? Because now, as every year, asparagus appears, chasing away the wintry mood of bitter endurance with the promise of life renewed. Sharing a pound of the season's first fresh asparagus with friends, I not only know that all things are possible, but am freshly reminded of other springs and other places.

I recall, for example, gleaming green bundles of fresh *asperges* cradled in starched white napkins and exotic fresh flowers, leaving the kitchen of the Hôtel Plaza Athénée in Paris, soon to be consumed by a spendthrift diner for an oil sheikh's ransom.

To my own personal taste, asparagus is so perfect in its newborn state that it is best enjoyed for itself alone—ungilded except for butter and lemon. However, treated with care, it can be cooked properly (not *overly*), sauced discreetly (see the box), or assembled in a variety of ways. Here are some tempting suggestions.

Fresh Asparagus Quiche

The custard filling of this quiche is particularly rich and tender, making a fine cushion for fresh asparagus. The quiche is excellent for picnics, as it needn't be served hot.

SERVES 6

The Pastry (Pâte Brisée):

1½ cups flour
Pinch of salt
Pinch of sugar
6 Tablespoons chilled unsalted butter, cut into bits
2 Tablespoons chilled vegetable shortening, cut into bits
2 to 4 Tablespoons ice water

Filling:

¼ cup sour cream
3 egg yolks
2 whole eggs
1 cup light or heavy cream
⅓ cup milk (or more, as needed)
1 teaspoon salt
Freshly ground white or black pepper
⅛ to ¼ teaspoon grated nutmeg
3 Tablespoons butter
1 Tablespoon minced shallots or white parts of scallions
½ pound (about 1½ cups) slightly undercooked asparagus, in 1-inch lengths
⅔ cup grated Swiss or Gruyère cheese
Cayenne pepper

1. Prepare the pastry: Measure the flour, salt, sugar, butter, and

(continued)

PHOTOGRAPH/ALLEN H. LIEBERMAN

34

35

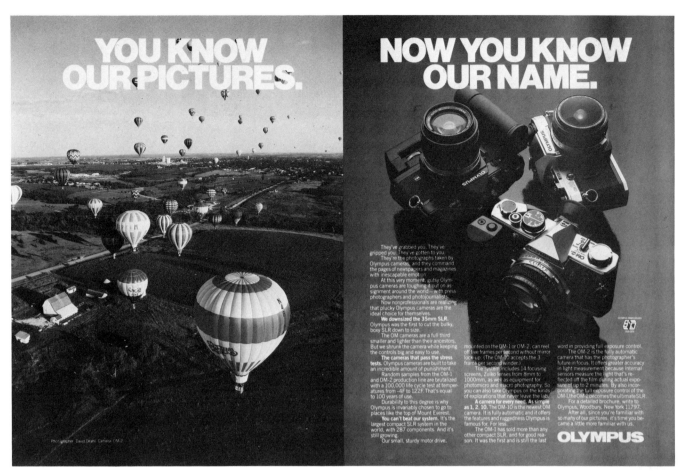

YOU KNOW OUR PICTURES.

Photographer: David Deahl. Camera: OM-2

NOW YOU KNOW OUR NAME.

They've grabbed you. They've gripped you. They've gotten to you.

They're the photographs taken by Olympus cameras, and they command the pages of newspapers and magazines with inescapable emotion.

At this very moment, gutsy Olympus cameras are toughing it out on assignment around the world—with press photographers and photojournalists.

Now nonprofessionals are realizing that plucky Olympus cameras are the ideal choice for themselves.

We downsized the 35mm SLR. Olympus was the first to cut the bulky, boxy SLR down to size.

The OM cameras are a full third smaller and lighter than their ancestors. But we shrunk the camera while keeping the controls big and easy to use.

The cameras that pass the stress tests. Olympus cameras are built to take an incredible amount of punishment.

Random samples from the OM-1 and OM-2 production line are brutalized with a 100,000 life cycle test at temperatures from -4F to 122F. That's equal to 100 years of use.

Durability to this degree is why Olympus is invariably chosen to go to places like the top of Mount Everest.

You can't beat our system. It's the largest compact SLR system in the world, with 287 components. And it's still growing.

Our small, sturdy motor drive, mounted on the OM-1 or OM-2, can reel off five frames per second without mirror lock-up. (The OM-10 accepts the 3 frame per second winder.)

The system includes 14 focusing screens, Zuiko lenses from 8mm to 1000mm, as well as equipment for photomicro and macro photography. So you can also take Olympus on the kinds of explorations that never leave the lab.

A camera for every need. As simple as 1, 2, 10. The OM-10 is the newest OM camera. It is fully automatic and it offers the features and ruggedness Olympus is famous for. For less.

The OM-1 has sold more than any other compact SLR, and for good reason. It was the first and is still the last word in providing full exposure control.

The OM-2 is the fully automatic camera that has the photographer's future in focus. It offers greater accuracy in light measurement because internal sensors measure the light that's reflected off the film during actual exposure of up to 2 minutes. By also incorporating the full exposure control of the OM-1, the OM-2 becomes the ultimate SLR.

For a detailed brochure, write to Olympus, Woodbury, New York 11797.

After all, since you're familiar with so many of our pictures, it's time you became a little more familiar with us.

OLYMPUS

45
Constance Kovar Art Director
Central Reproduction & Photography Photographers
Constance Kovar, Kate Thompson Designers
Lincoln, Pitt & Associates Agency
Garrard Products Client

44
Don Slater Art Director
David Deahl, Cailor-Resnick Photographers
Adam Hanft Copywriter
Wells, Rich & Green Agency
Olympus Camera Corp. Client

SCRATCH!

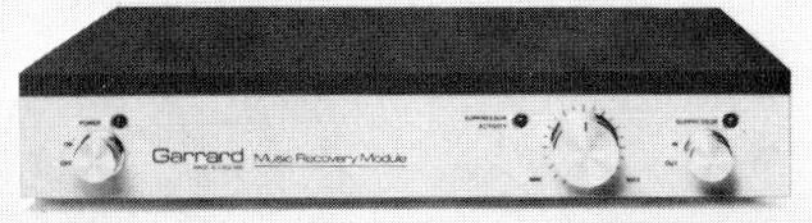

Somehow, no matter how careful we are, our records get scratched. To make matters worse, even brand new records give us pops and clicks that disturb our enjoyment of the performance. And, of course, when we make a tape for use in the car or on the beach, the scratches go right along with us.

Now there's the MRM, Garrard's Music Recovery Module. It suppresses impulse noise — the pops, clicks and scratches that plague almost all records, old or new.

The MRM works with the simple elegance of all great inventions. A detector is programmed to recognize the unique characteristics of a scratch. A suppressor functions only when those characteristics are present. There's no effect on the music at all.

Of course the MRM won't restore music where it has been literally worn away. But it will easily suppress those pops that come from "nowhere" and those scratches that come from everywhere.

We invite you to send for our free booklet. Meanwhile, visit your dealer and take along a record. The one you dropped the stylus on. Scraaatchhh...

Scratch? What scratch?

Garrard.

Garrard Division, Plessey Consumer Products, Dept. G, 100 Commercial Street, Plainview, N.Y. 11803.

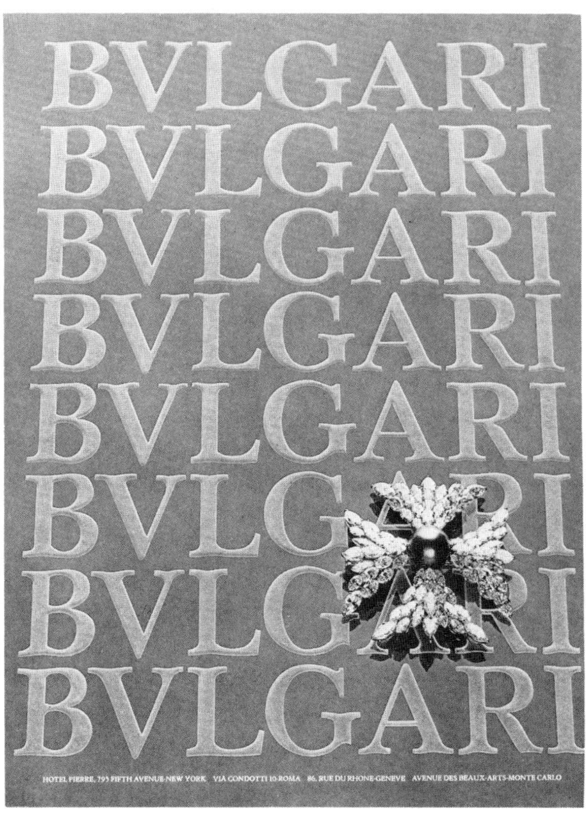

46
Len Favara, Peter Rogers Art Directors
Andrew Unangst Photographer
Peter Rogers Associates Agency
Bulgari Client

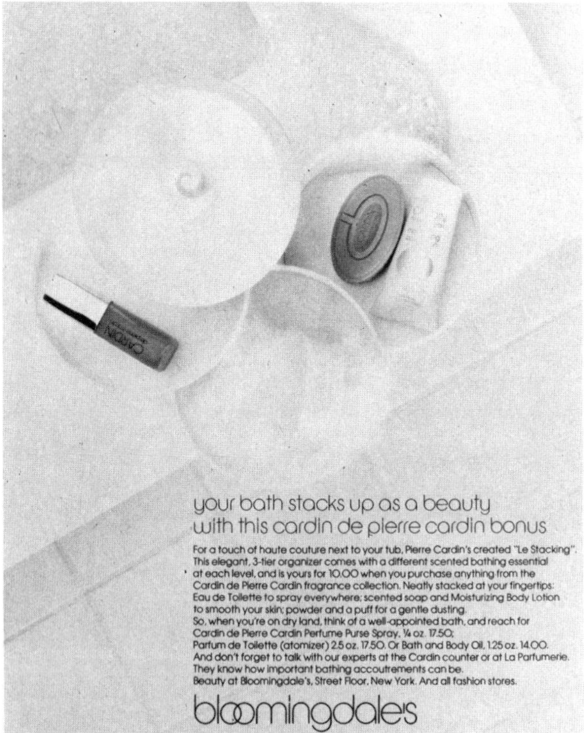

47
Benita Cassar-Torreggiani, Raina Domevich Art Directors
Gary A. Perweiler Photographer
Pierre Cardin Client

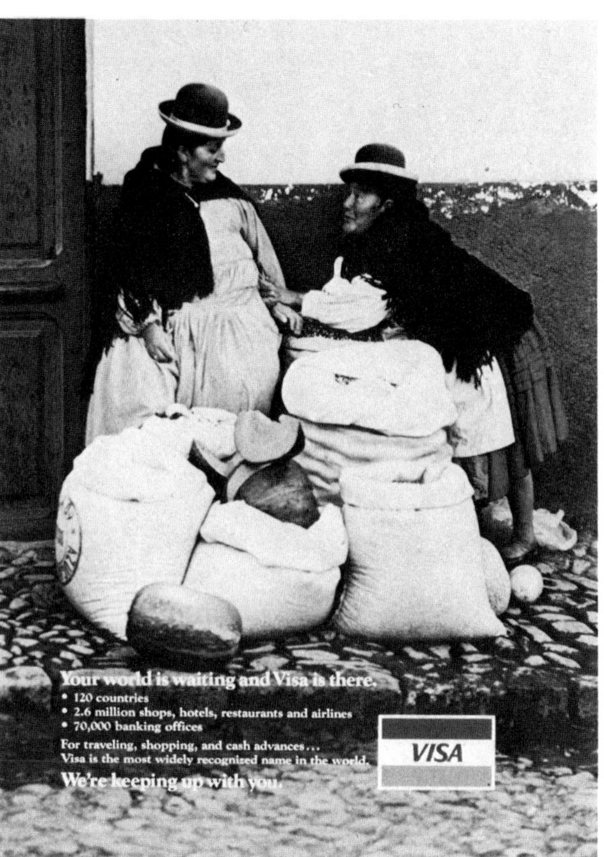

48
Roger Shelly Art Director
Jay Freis Photographer
Visa USA, Inc. Client

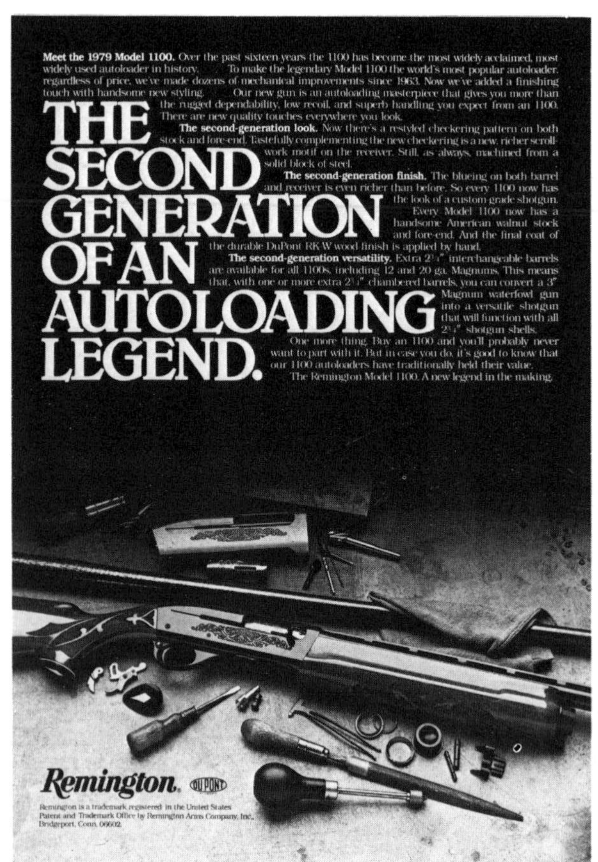

49
Michael Fountain, Tony Timov Art Directors
Dick Faust Photographer
John F. Connelly Copywriter
Rumrill-Hoyt, Inc. Agency
Remington Arms Co., Inc. Client

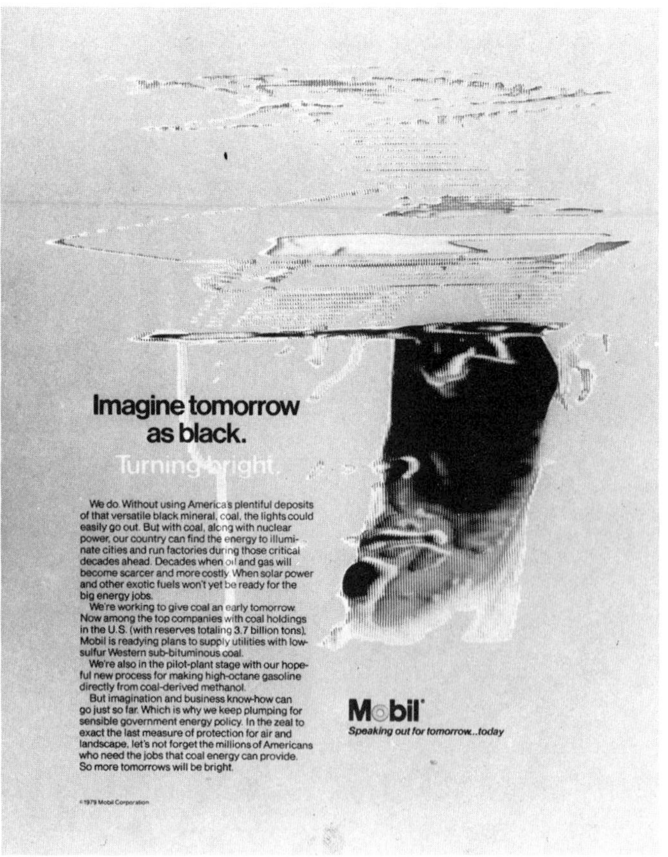

50
Jerry Demoney Art Director
Peter Angelo Simon Photographer
Mobil Corp. Client

51
Jim Crawford Art Director
David Haggerty Photography Photographers
Ross Roy N.Y./Compton Agency
Bacardi Imports Client

52
B. Montgomery Art Director
Patrick Russell Photographer
Batey Advertising Agency
Silvaroyal Pty Ltd. Client

TISSOT. THE FASHION MOVEMENT. DESIGNER CREATIONS, INCLUDING QUARTZ AND DIGITAL MODELS. GUARANTEED IN 150 COUNTRIES.

SHOWN HERE: "STYLIST" FROM THE TISSOT DRESS QUARTZ COLLECTION.

THE NEXT TIME.
TISSOT
BEST SELLING WATCH AMONG THE SWISS.

't Lijkt op een ballpoint, 't schrijft als een vulpen:

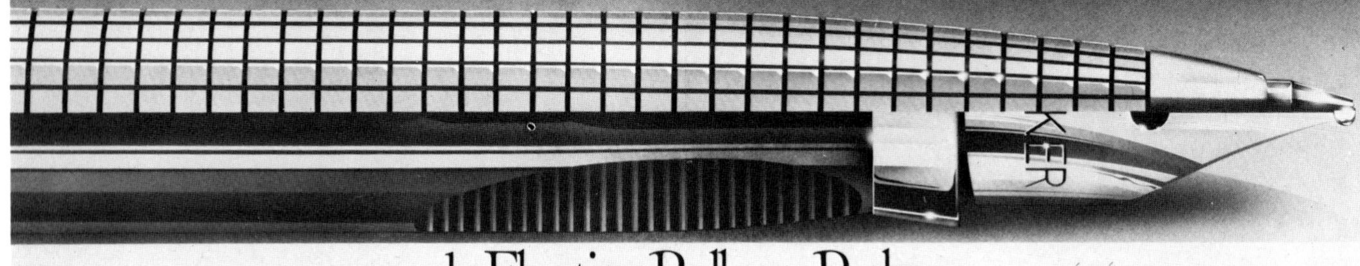

de Floating Ball van Parker.

Soms is een vulpen te deftig.
Soms schrijft zelfs de mooiste ballpoint nog wat te min.
Je zou dus eigenlijk een pen moeten hebben die de kwaliteiten biedt van beide: een adequate pen voor het luxe schrijfwerk, maar ook een pen die goed is voor de gewone alledaagse notitie.

Parker, de schrijfspecialist bij uitstek, vond na naarstig speurwerk een oplossing waar nog niemand aan had gedacht: de Floating Ball.
Een pen met het principe van de bekende, handige ballpoint, maar met de klasse en het karakter van het meest superieure schrijfinstrument: de vulpen.
De Floating Ball bevat, net als de ballpoint, een losse, vervangbare vulling, waarin een minuscuul kogeltje de inkt over het papier verdeelt.
Let wel: echte vulpeninkt. Een netwerk van ragfijne kanaaltjes verdeelt zorgvuldig de inkt fijntjes en gelijkmatig over het papier.
Op die manier schrijft u licht en soepel als een veertje en geeft de Floating Ball uw handschrift weer vulpen-klasse.

U krijgt trouwens ook weer plezier in schrijven, want de Floating Ball vlekt niet, krast niet en droogt niet uit.
U kunt er zelfs ondersteboven mee schrijven, of onder atmosferische druk, zoals b.v. in een vliegtuig.
Deze nieuwe Parker wordt geïntroduceerd in het slanke edelstalen model 180.

U vindt 'm bij uw Parker-winkelier; hij heeft de pen voor u klaarliggen. Stap bij 'm binnen en schrijf.
Dan merkt u vanzelf dat er heel wat is veranderd tussen ballpoint en vulpen: de Floating Ball, geboren uit het beste van twee.

Nieuw: Parker Floating Ball.
Uw handschrift is een Parker waard.

PARKER

53
Walter Schulte Art Director
Henk Brandsen Photographer
Pete Kelly Illustrator
Walter Schulte, Wim Ubachs Designers
McCann-Erickson (Nederland) BV Agency
Fortress Handelmaatschappij BV Client

54
Joel Gilman Art Director
Al Satterwhite Photographer
Hall & Levine Agency
Redken Laboratories Client

55
Bill Sweeney Art Director
David L. Simpson Photographer
Simpson/Flint, Inc. Studio
Cole Henderson & Drake Agency
Omni Client

56
John C. Jay Art Director
Horst Photographer
Lanny Udell Copywriter
Charles Banuchi Designer
Bloomingdale's Advertising Dept. Agency
Bloomingdale's Client

IS HER HAIR GETTING ALL THE PROTEIN IT NEEDS?

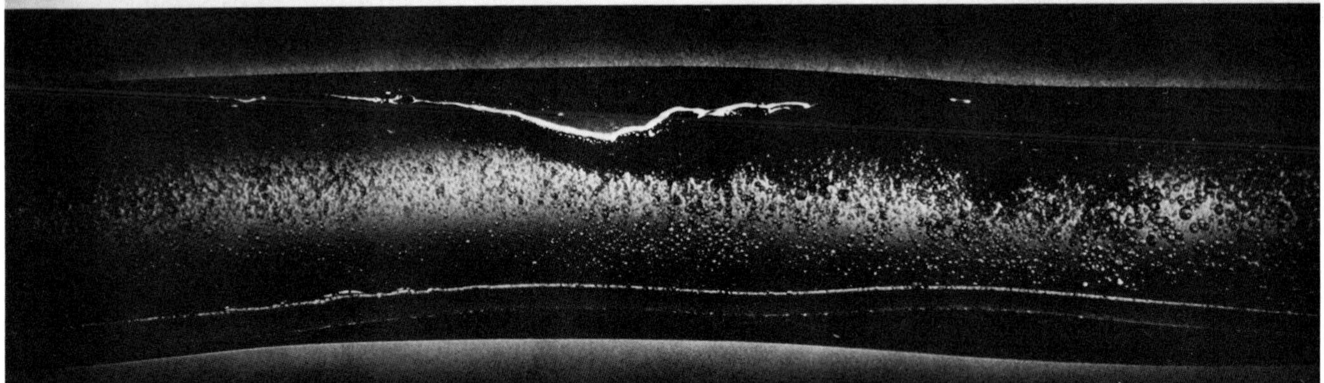

Imagine this is a shaft of hair.
■ Red represents the amount of protein that could be absorbed by the hair before CPP Catipeptide.™
■ Gold represents Redken's unique protein, CPP Catipeptide. It can be absorbed so much better than any protein we've ever used.

To look and feel its healthiest, hair needs protein. If it's bleached, tinted, permed, shampooed frequently or subjected to the sun or chlorine, chances are the hair needs protein. The question is how to get it.

Redken's spent 18 years researching hair just to come up with the answers. And during that time we learned a great deal about protein. How is it absorbed by hair in the first place? The hair's protein has a certain amount of electric charges (think of the static electricity you generate by brushing hair). So does our protein. Hair in need, especially damaged hair, happens to have more negative electric charges while protein has positive ones. And remember from your high school chemistry, opposites attract. These opposite charges naturally like each other. They act like little magnets.

Redken has manufactured a natural protein that's more attractive to hair. CPP Catipeptide is different because it averages two positive charges instead of just one like other proteins.

CPP Catipeptide is also specifically designed to the correct molecular size and weight. So it can get through to the inner core of hair and stay there.

CPP Catipeptide responds to the hair's protein needs, whether it's a little or a lot. CPP Catipeptide delivers.

Where can you find this incredible protein? In a group of Redken hair care and conditioning products: Amino Pon® Concentrate Ready-to-Use Shampoo, Climatress® Moisturizing Creme Protein Conditioner, P.P.T. "S-77"® Protein Conditioner and Bodimer+,® our body builder.

We'll be telling the American woman all about it. In magazines like Vogue, House & Garden, Cosmopolitan, Mademoiselle, Good Housekeeping, Glamour, Ladies' Home Journal, Seventeen and Redbook. Over 54 million women will learn about CPP Catipeptide and where to find it. We also have a Yellow Pages program directing them to you. So be ready for them.

Is her hair getting the protein it needs? Now you don't have to worry.

CPP CATIPEPTIDE.
FOR HAIR THAT NEEDS.

REDKEN®

OMNI

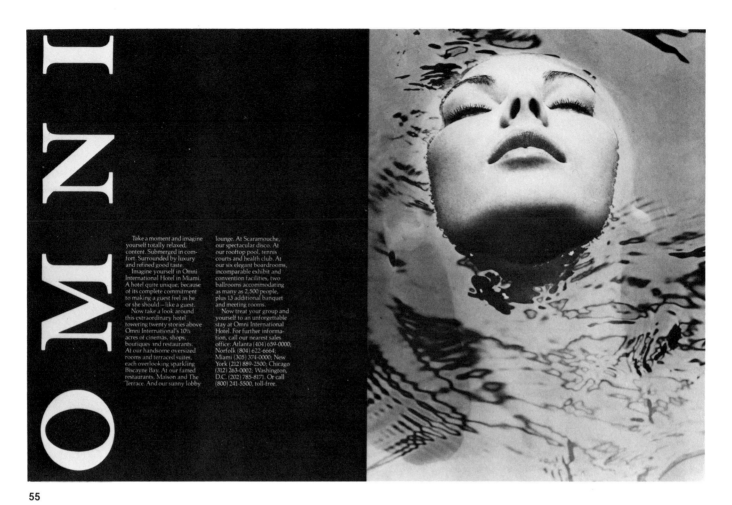

Take a moment and imagine yourself totally relaxed, content. Submerged in comfort. Surrounded by luxury and refined good taste.

Imagine yourself in Omni International Hotel in Miami. A hotel quite unique, because of its complete commitment to making a guest feel as he or she should—like a guest.

Now take a look around this extraordinary hotel towering twenty stories above Omni International's 10½ acres of cinemas, shops, boutiques and restaurants. At our handsome oversized rooms and terraced suites, each overlooking sparkling Biscayne Bay. At our famed restaurants, Maison and The Terrace. And our sunny lobby lounge. At Scaramouche, our spectacular disco. At our rooftop pool, tennis courts and health club. At our six elegant boardrooms, incomparable exhibit and convention facilities, two ballrooms accommodating as many as 2,500 people, plus 13 additional banquet and meeting rooms.

Now treat your group and yourself to an unforgettable stay at Omni International Hotel. For further information, call our nearest sales office: Atlanta (404) 659-0000; Norfolk (804) 622-6664; Miami (305) 374-0000; New York (212) 889-2500; Chicago (312) 263-0002; Washington, D.C. (202) 785-8171. Or call (800) 241-5500, toll-free.

55

56

57
Madeleine Kinel Art Director
Carson Pirie Scott & Co. Client

58
Aric Frons Art Director
Cosimo Photographer
Harvard Peskin & Edrick, Inc. Agency
Aurea Jewelry Creations Client

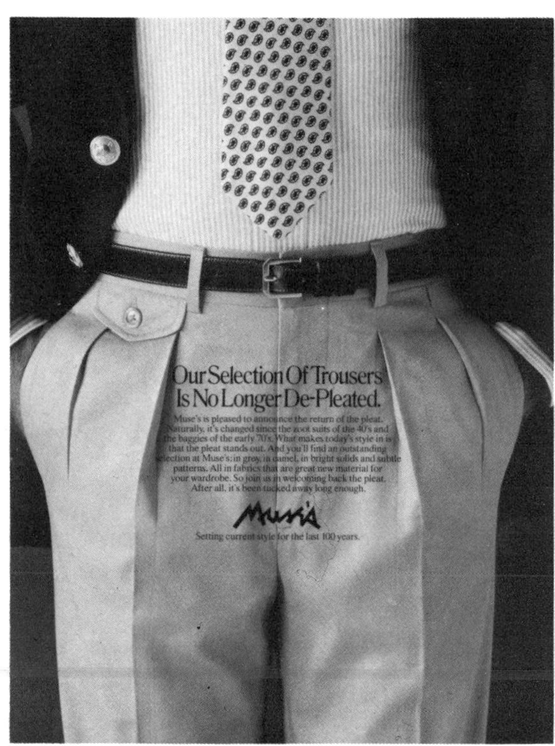

Our Selection Of Trousers Is No Longer De-Pleated.
Muse's
Setting current style for the last 100 years.

59
Michael Hutchinson Art Director
Allen Matthews Photographer
Pringle Dixon Pringle Agency
Muse's Clothing Store Client

60
Kuhn Caldwell Art Director
Serge Lutens, Shig Ikeda Photographers
Christian Dior Perfumes, Inc. Client

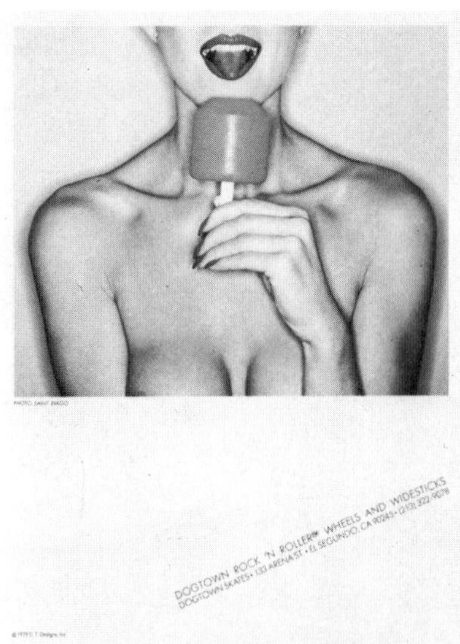

61
Saint-Jivago Desanges Art Director
Saint-Jivago Desanges Studio Studio
Dogtown Skates Client

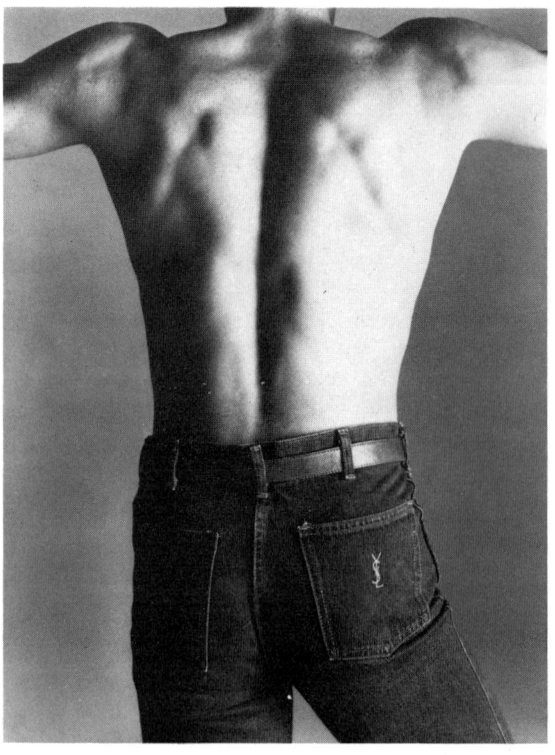

62
Yvon C. Dihe Art Director
Richard Avedon Photographer
Yvon C. Dihe Advertising Ltd. Agency
Yves St. Laurent Client

Have we got a winter for you.
SKI QUEBEC

63
Pierre Leduc Art Director
Gillian Proctor Photographer
Chales et Leduc Ltd. Agency
Tourisme Quebec Client

RABBIT AND COSTELLO.

How did photographer Marty Costello happen to opt for a VW Rabbit?

"I was shooting for the performance," answered Costello.

See, every day Rabbit and Costello travel the 35 miles round trip from Hammond, Indiana (where they live), to downtown Chicago (where they work). That's a lot of miles.

And a lot of driving in temperatures that plummet to a merciless 20° below in winter and climb all the way up to a sticky, not-so-terrific 100° in summer.

"So why a Rabbit?" we asked.

"Look," he said, "my Rabbit and I have been performing together for over a year now, and we're still going strong. Why? I'll tell you why. I get a lot for my dollar with it. I get a comfortable ride, great visibility, incredible road handling with front-wheel drive, and sensational service from people who are even friendlier than I am."

Nicely put, Mr. Costello.

"And don't forget," he added, "my work has me hopping around all over the place. I need a car that can get me everywhere quickly and comfortably. One that's rugged enough to be driven almost anyplace, anytime. With my Rabbit, I've got a lot more than just a car with enough room to pack all my cameras, props and lighting equipment. I've got a pretty good idea that everything will always arrive in one piece."

Then we asked Costello one final question.

"You seem to get a million calls a day. What determines which job you take?"

To which he replied, with an appropriately devilish grin:

"Who's on first."

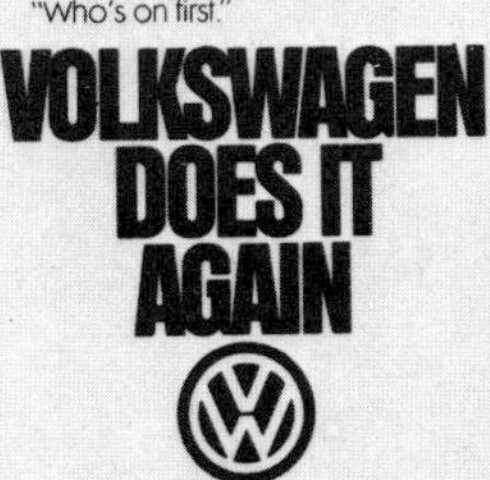

65
Michael Leon Art Director
Cosimo Photographer
Doyle Dane Bernbach Agency
Volkswagen Client

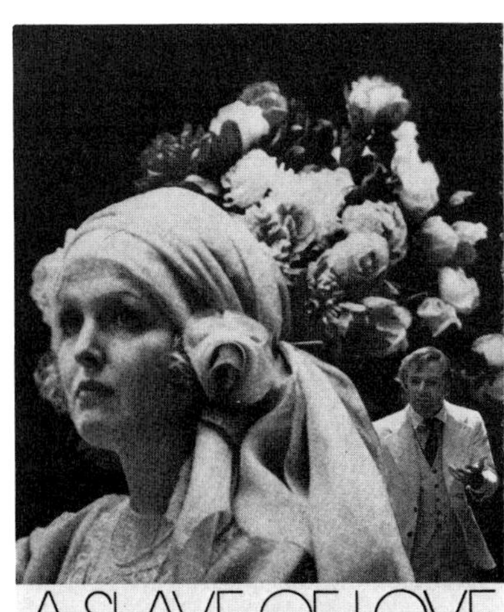

64
Ed Brodkin Art Director
Walter Glinka Designer
Diener/Hauser/Bates Agency
Cinema 5 Client

PIZ BUIN
Get your hands on the sensuous tan.

66
Roy Toma Art Director
Suzanne M. Nyerges Photographer
Suzanne M. Nyerges Studio Studio
Roy Toma & Associates Agency
Piz Buin Client

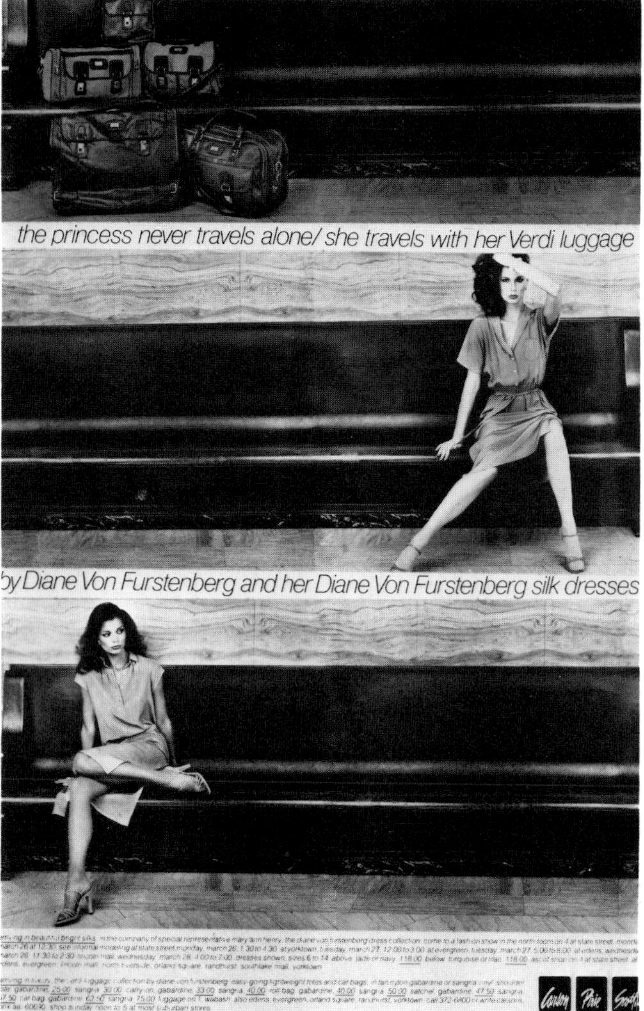

67

68

67
Madeleine Kinel Art Director
Carson Pirie Scott & Co. Client

68
Derek Szeto Art Director
Foote, Cone & Belding Agency
Bermuda Department of Tourism Client

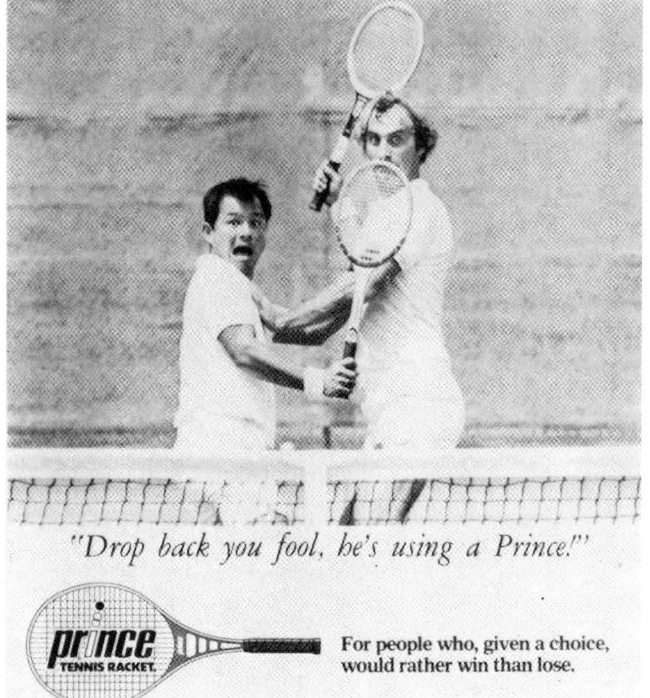

69
Don Schnably Art Director
David L. Simpson Photographer
Simpson/Flint, Inc. Studio
Richardson, Myers & Donofrio Agency
Prince Client

KÖP VITA LEE OCH FÄRGA SJÄLV MED DYLON!

70
Ingemar Jacobson Art Director
Svante Fischerstrom Photographer
Sven O. Blomquist Adv. Agency Agency
Tekniska Fabriken Gripen Client

71
Karen Brown Art Director
Tom Clayton Photographer
Dayton's Client

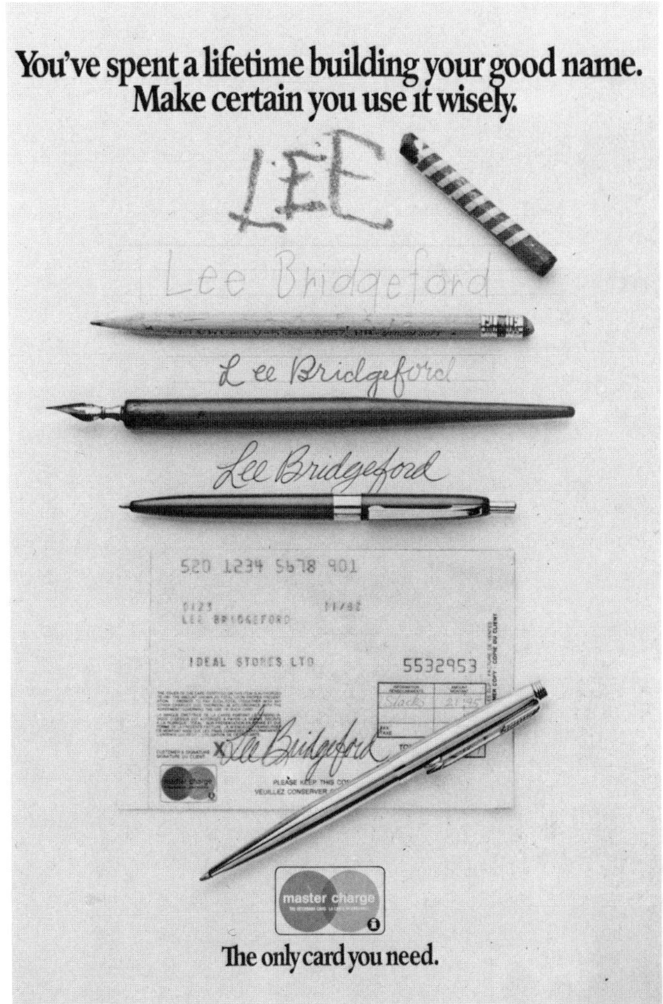

72
Bruce Dowad Art Director
Gillian Proctor Photographer
Oasis Studio
Vickers & Benson Ltd. Agency
Master Charge Client

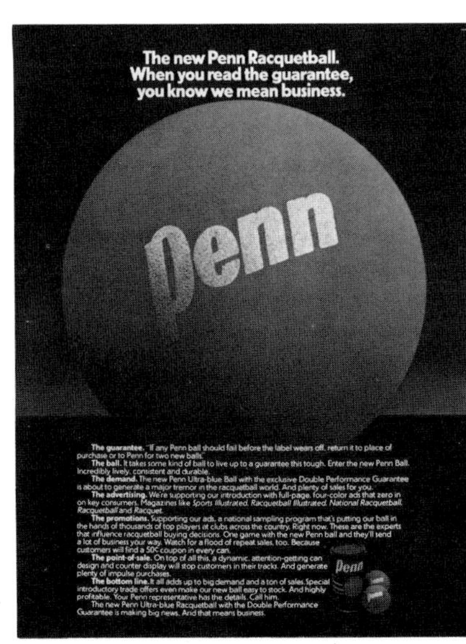

73
Linda Schweikert Art Director
Gary A. Perweiler Photographer
Perweiler Studio, Inc. Studio
Ketchum MacLeod & Grove, Inc. Agency
Penn Balls Client

74
Mark Kent Art Director
Ralph King Photographer
The Graphic Supermarket Agency
Cuoio Client

75
George R. Fugate Art Director
Whole Hog Studio Illustrators
Morgan & Associates Agency
Richmond Hyatt House Client

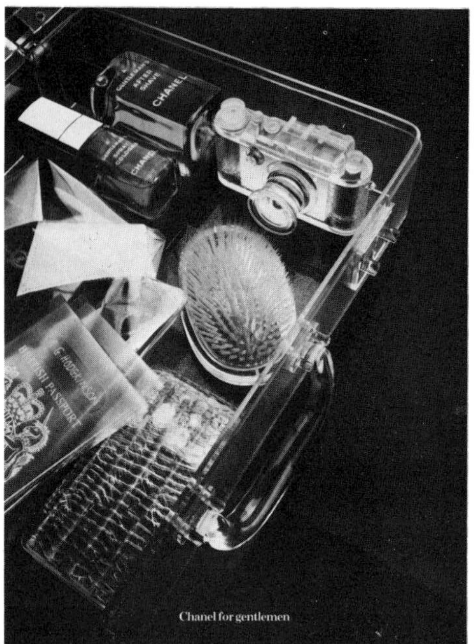

76
C. W. Vickers Art Director
Julian Cotrell Photographer
Ultima Studio
ABH International Agency
Chanel Client

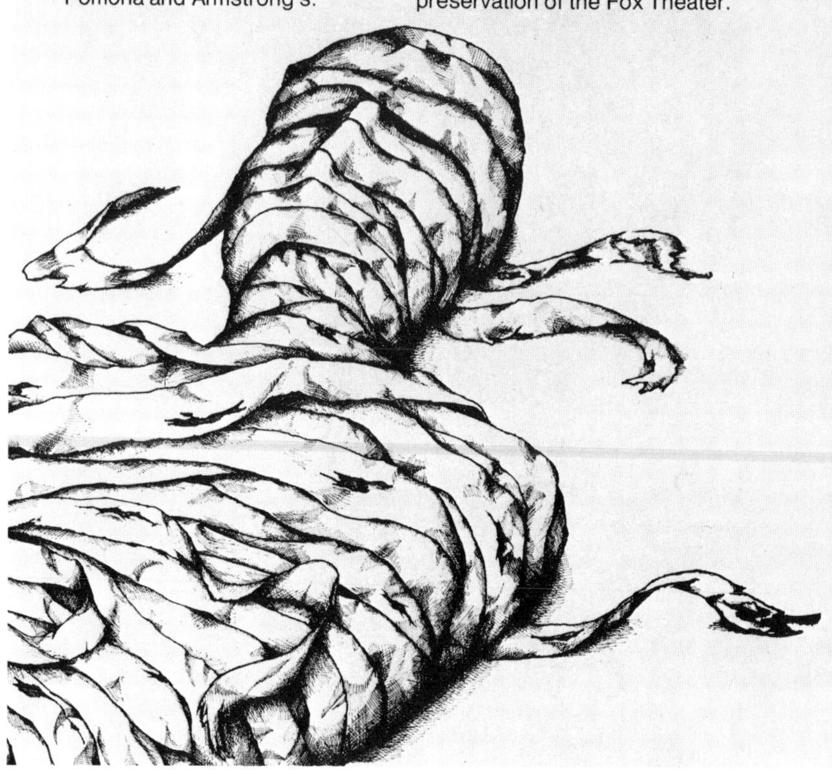

78
Michael Egan Art Director
Michael Egan, Rod Schenken Illustrators
Michael Egan Advertising & Graphic Design Agency
Armstrong's Gallery Client

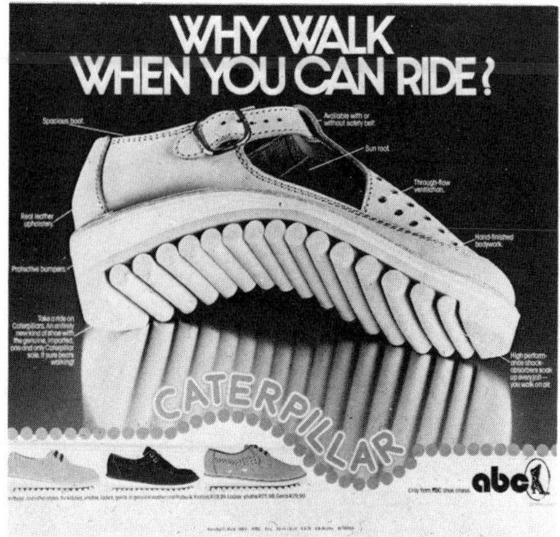

WHY WALK WHEN YOU CAN RIDE?
CATERPILLAR
abc

77
Jenny Groenewald Art Director
Horst Klem Photographer
Goodgoll Said Campbell-Ewald Agency
ABC Shoe Corporation Client

79 A-B
Dennis Brown Art Director
Brown, Christensen & Associates, Ltd. Agency
Fisher & Paykel Ltd. Client

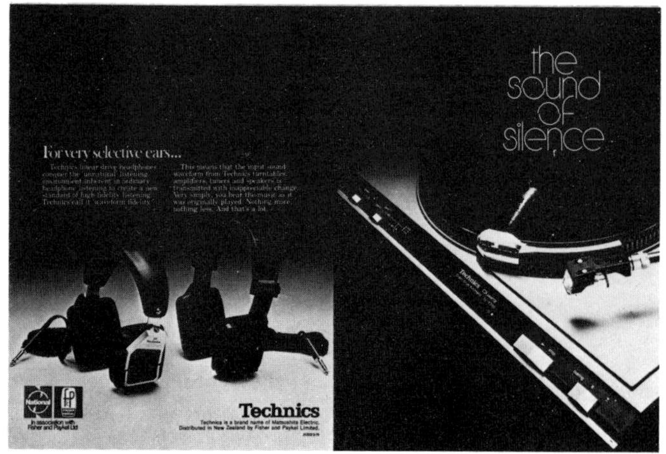

79A

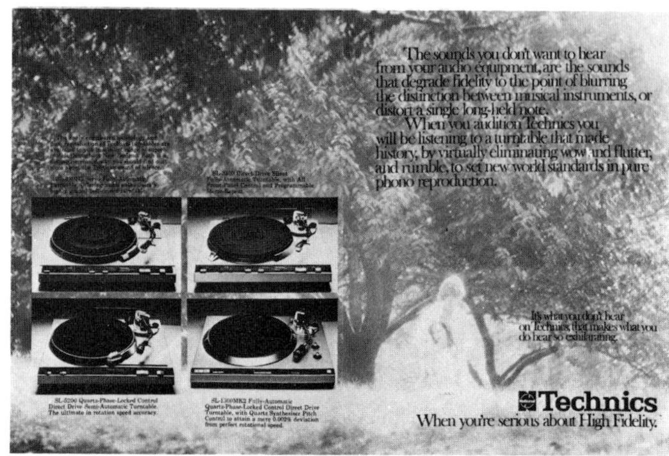

B

New Clear PAM.
4 Ways Better Than Ever!
100 vs 82 PORTIONS
1. Crystal-Clear Coverage
New PAM® is still crystal-clear. But now there's a glisten wherever it touches the pan. So you can *see* to spray the perfect amount every time!
And cleanup has never been better!
New PAM is the way to keep food from sticking... even caked-on casseroles practically sponge clean.
2. Environmental Formula
New clear PAM contains no heavy fluorocarbons. No water, either, like other cooking sprays. That's why PAM feels so light!
But don't let the ounces fool you. You get more PAM per can than ever before!
And don't forget—PAM adds less fat and less calories than oil or butter. Adds no cholesterol, either.
3. More For Your Money
Now you get more sprays per can. Our old 9 oz. can held 82 portions. Without fluorocarbons, our new 4 oz. can holds 100 portions. At the same price!
No matter how you spray it, new PAM is one of the best buys around!
4. No Unpleasant Fumes
PAM's change in propellants is a change for the better. No fluorocarbons. No unpleasant odor.
Try it once and you'll never cook without it again!
VEGETABLE COOKING SPRAY FOR ALL COOKWARE
NEW PAM
STOPS FOOD FROM STICKING
LOW CALORIE
NO CHOLESTEROL
100 PORTIONS
New. Crystal-Clear.
Better Than Ever!
© 1979 PAM/Boyle-Midway

80
Judith Savage Art Director
Gary Colby, Dennis Magdich, Ignacio Gomez Illustrators
Kathy Kleitz Copywriter
Arthur Meyerhoff/BBDO Agency
PAM/Broyle Midway Client

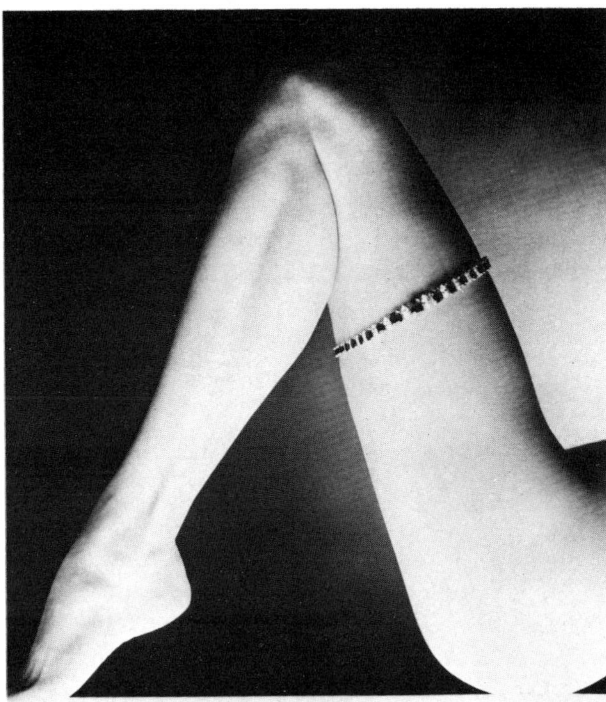

Harry Winston Inc.
Rare jewels of the world. Paris, Geneva, Monte Carlo. New York: 718 Fifth Avenue 10019

81
Ron Winston, Onofrio Paccione Art Directors
Paccione Photography, Inc. Photographers
Stan Merritt Agency
Harry Winston Inc. Client

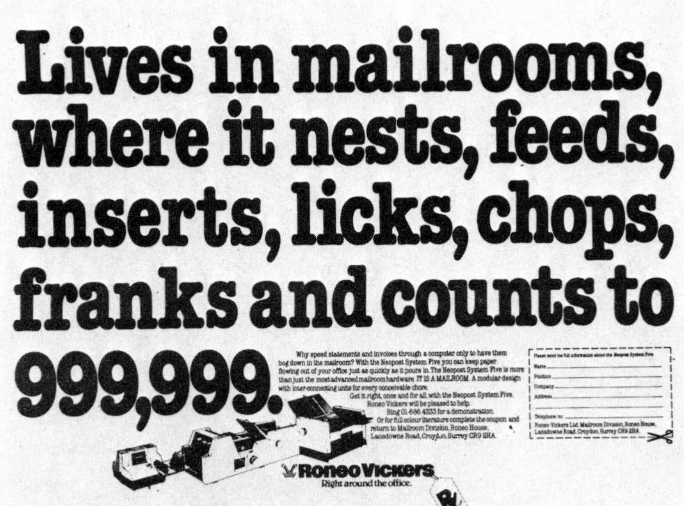

82
Martin Connolly, Ken Carter Art Directors
David Williams & Ketchum Ltd. Agency
Roneo Vickers Ltd. Client

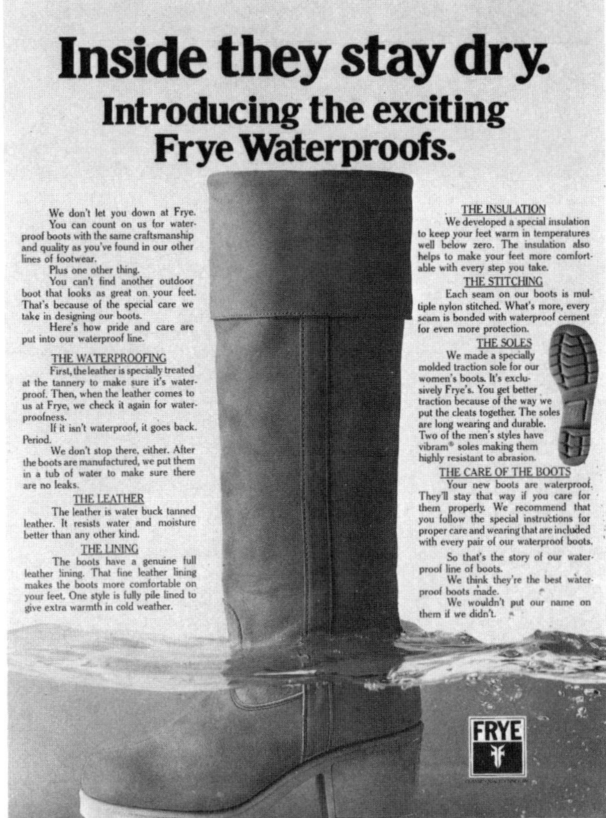

Supplement to FOOTWEAR NEWS
Inside they stay dry.
Introducing the exciting Frye Waterproofs.
We don't let you down at Frye.
You can count on us for waterproof boots with the same craftsmanship and quality as you've found in our other lines of footwear.
Plus one other thing.
You can't find another outdoor boot that looks as great on your feet. That's because of the special care we take in designing our boots.
Here's how pride and care are put into our waterproof line.
THE WATERPROOFING
First, the leather is specially treated at the tannery to make sure it's waterproof. Then, when the leather comes to us at Frye, we check it again for waterproofness.
If it isn't waterproof, it goes back. Period.
We don't stop there, either. After the boots are manufactured, we put them in a tub of water to make sure there are no leaks.
THE LEATHER
The leather is water buck tanned leather. It resists water and moisture better than any other kind.
THE LINING
The boots have a genuine full leather lining. That fine leather lining makes the boots more comfortable on your feet. One style is fully pile lined to give extra warmth in cold weather.
THE INSULATION
We developed a special insulation to keep your feet warm in temperatures well below zero. The insulation also helps to make your feet more comfortable with every step you take.
THE STITCHING
Each seam on our boots is multiple nylon stitched. What's more, every seam is bonded with waterproof cement for even more protection.
THE SOLES
We made a specially molded traction sole for our women's boots. It's exclusively Frye's. You get better traction because of the way we put the cleats together. The soles are long wearing and durable. Two of the men's styles have vibram® soles making them highly resistant to abrasion.
THE CARE OF THE BOOTS
Your new boots are waterproof. They'll stay that way if you care for them properly. We recommend that you follow the special instructions for proper care and wearing that are included with every pair of our waterproof boots.
So that's the story of our waterproof line of boots.
We think they're the best waterproof boots made.
We wouldn't put our name on them if we didn't.
FRYE

83
Jerry Fremuth Art Director
Peter Elliott Photographer
Peter Elliott Photography Studio
Lee King & Partners Agency
Frye Boots Client

The woman. The legend. The story. It unfolds in these excerpts from the new Stephen Birmingham book. His disclosures about her family will help reveal the truth about the woman herself.

Jacqueline Bouvier Kennedy Onassis

BOUVIER

"It was within this myth of huge genetic superiority that little Jacqueline Bouvier was born, and it was with it that she grew up. No one, certainly not she, ever supposed Grandpa Bouvier could have made it all up, that "Our Forebears" was, at best, a work of massive self-deception."

What was she really like? Where did she learn what made her so attractive to men? And how much did standing out in a crowd really cost?

Young Jacqueline and her sister were trapped. Caught in the middle of a bitter tug-of-war between divorced parents. And striking out for "something else." What effect did this have on the girls? Don't miss an excerpt.

"To Jack Bouvier, the name Kennedy was enough to make his entire face clench, and if anyone had told him that his daughter would one day marry Joe Kennedy's son, he would have knocked that person to the floor and kicked him."

KENNEDY

Read how the two met. Follow the aspirations of the woman whose husband was to become a driving and driven man aiming for the highest office in the land.

"At the dinner was Congressman John F. Kennedy, who was just beginning his campaign for election to the U.S. Senate and whose campaign manager had said of the handsome Irishman, 'Every woman wants to mother him or marry him.'"

It wasn't an easy role to play. It was wrought with tragedy, trouble, sickness and pain.

"For several hours after her dead baby was born, Jackie's own condition was listed as critical. Once more a priest was summoned."

How much more could the dream woman, the princess from the fairy tale, take? Perhaps the "Camelot" she was a part of in Washington was not as attractive as it seemed.

"Any romantic love that might have once existed between them had long since evaporated and all that was left was a need to put the best public face on things."

Not one chapter of her life is unexplored. Not one action unquestioned.

"On the plane she had been urged to change her dress, which was spattered with blood. She refused."

YOU MAY NOT LIKE HER BUT YOU'LL NEVER FORGET HER. STEPHEN BIRMINGHAM'S BIOGRAPHY OF JACKIE DAILY IN THE STAR.

STARTING TOMORROW. YOU CAN READ HER LIFETIME.

ONASSIS

What the name meant to her was someone to lean on, someone to guide and comfort her. What the name meant to the public was another story.

"When the world learned that the President's widow was about to marry an aging Greek shipping tycoon, the public reeled and gasped at the news."

What, in fact, was the statement Jacqueline Bouvier Kennedy Onassis was trying to make?

"I will show them I can do exactly as I want, thumb my nose at the slobs, go off to Greece where there's a man who wants me."

JACKIE

The schoolgirl whose yearbook ambition was "not to be a housewife" had certainly accomplished something. But what?

"At the same time the myth of John F. Kennedy was beginning to disintegrate. Reports were starting to appear in the press about lurid presidential goings-on. Camelot was over."

Was it a crushing blow to her? Or was the celebrity inside her still very much alive?

"In 1977, just two years after joining Viking Press, Jacqueline Onassis suddenly and angrily quit her job."

Whatever became of the girl who wanted to stand out in a crowd? How does Jackie live? And even more important, what is her style of life now?

"In certain circles of New York society, Jackie is regarded as not only a money-grubber but also a man-snatcher."

An explosive tale? Mildly sensational? It will be.

"Jackie runs through men the way she runs through clothes."

But how could a story with a subject like Jacqueline Bouvier Kennedy Onassis be any less than enthralling. You'll want to read every excerpt from the Stephen Birmingham biography.

"Jackie, they may not always understand you, but at least they'll come back for more."

Yours. Every day. Starting tomorrow in The Star.

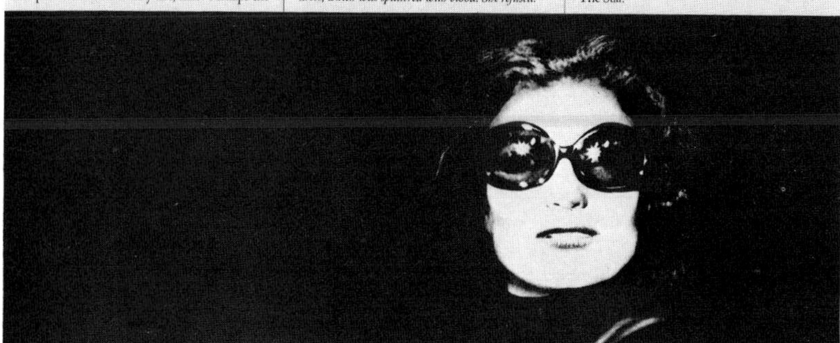

Special Stories. Because Toronto means a lot to The Star

84

A SIGHT FOR SORE WRISTS.

ACTUAL SIZE

TINY NEW LIGHTWEIGHT BINOCULARS BY PENTAX.

ASAHI PENTAX For a free leaflet describing the new Pentax roof prism binoculars, write or phone Hampo Systems, 41 Pim St., Newtown. P.O. Box 170, Johannesburg 2000, tel. 836-4041. Durban tel. 32-9944. Cape Town tel. 22-0330.

GREY-PHILLIPS, BUNTON, MUNDEL & BLAKE

86

84
Bruce Dowad Art Director
Vickers & Benson Ltd. Agency
The Toronto Star Client

85
Vince Aniano, Ed Sobel Art Directors
Susan Grossman, Kathie Broyles Designers
Nort Amerman Copywriter
CBS Television Network Client

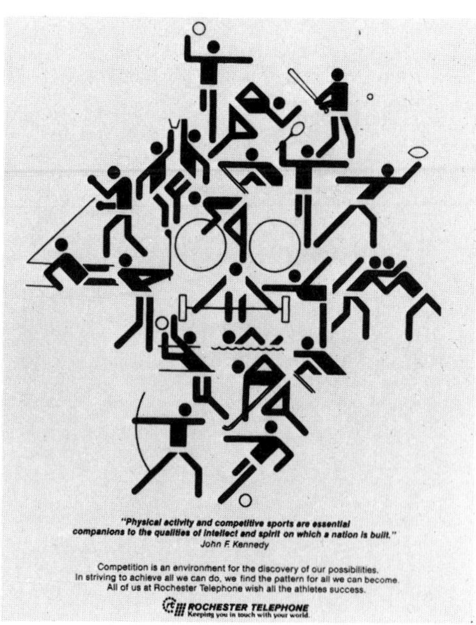

"Physical activity and competitive sports are essential companions to the qualities of intellect and spirit on which a nation is built."
John F. Kennedy
Competition is an environment for the discovery of our possibilities.
In striving to achieve all we can do, we find the pattern for all we can become.
All of us at Rochester Telephone wish all the athletes success.
ROCHESTER TELEPHONE
Keeping you in touch with your world.

86
Mark Simkins Art Director
Chris Marrington Copywriter
Grey-Phillips, Bunton, Mundel & Blake Agency
Hampo Trading Co. (Pty) Ltd. Client

87
John Kuchera Art Director
Steve Moscowitz Illustrator
Hutchins/Y&R Agency
Rochester Telephone Client

Consumer Campaigns

A

B

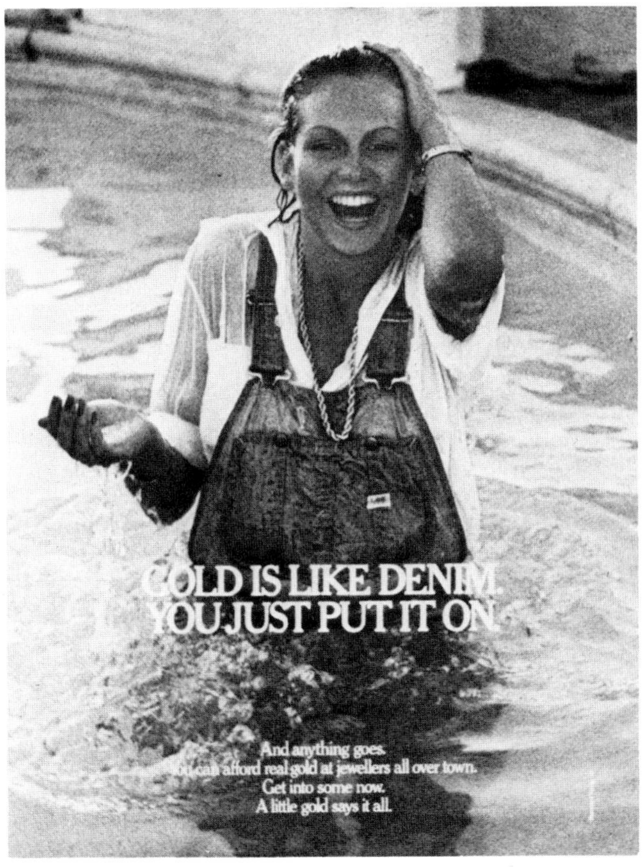

C

88 A-C
Roger Havercroft Art Director
Michael Golding Copywriter
Marchant Young Agency
Intergold Client

"Hey, look everybody,
I found where George keeps the Chivas."
Chivas Regal • 12 Years Old Worldwide • Blended Scotch Whisky • 86 Proof General Wine & Spirits Co., N.Y.

A

CHIVAS REGAL
Chivas Regal • 12 Years Old Worldwide • Blended Scotch Whisky • 86 Proof
General Wine & Spirits Co., N.Y.

B

"Your Chivas or mine?"
Chivas Regal • 12 Years Old Worldwide • Blended Scotch Whisky • 86 Proof General Wine & Spirits Co., N.Y.

C

89 A-C
Charles Abrams Art Director
Charles Saxon Illustrator
Doyle Dane Bernbach Agency
General Wine & Spirits Company,
Chivas Regal Clients

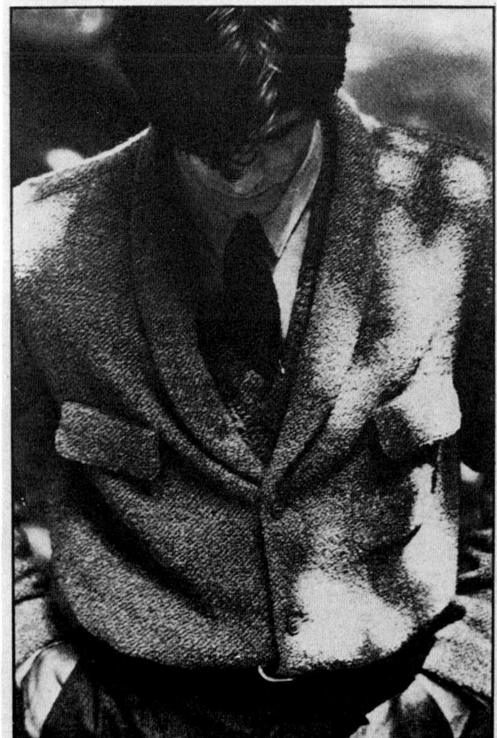

Bill Kaiserman/rafael
CHARIVARI
BROADWAY AT 85 STREET NEW YORK NY

A

90 A-B
Roberta Bendavid Art Director
Susan Shacter Photographer
Rafael Fashions, Inc. Client

Bill Kaiserman/rafael

SUSAN SHACTER

Jerry Magnin

Beverly Hills California

B

The Honda Civic. The car we designed around a shopping bag.

It's true. We had supermarket shopping bags flown to our factory when we designed the Honda Civic* Hatchbacks. Measuring the bags helped us determine the size of the rear cargo area.

This may seem like a lot of fuss over a small detail. But at Honda we do everything that way. For all its simplicity, the Honda Civic has been planned with meticulous care.

So you see? It's not by accident that four full-sized shopping bags fit inside our hatch.

Of course, four also happens to be the number of full-sized people that fit inside our Civic's passenger compartment. And if we went to all that trouble to make a shopping bag comfortable, just imagine what we must have done to make you comfortable.

HONDA
We make it simple.

A

Our engine sits sideways so you don't have to.

When people sit in a Honda Civic* 1200* or Civic CVCC* for the first time, they are often surprised at the amount of room inside.

They discover that despite their brief overall length our Civics have plenty of room for four adults. Plus luggage space behind the rear seat.

How do we do it? To help solve the mystery, we took the roof and hood off a Honda Civic CVCC Hatchback.

As you can now see, one reason for the Civic's roominess is the way the engine sits. Because it sits sideways, instead of lengthwise, the engine doesn't interfere with front-seat legroom. Instead, it is neatly tucked away up front, out of everybody's way.

Of course, the engine in our Civic CVCC 4-speed Hatchback is sitting pretty when it comes to fuel economy. This model got 42 mpg for highway driving, 36 mpg city, according to EPA estimates. The actual mileage you get will vary depending on the type of driving you do, your driving habits, your car's condition and optional equipment. Mileage estimates are lower for California and high altitude cars.

Getting back to roominess. We gave the Civic additional space by giving it front-wheel drive. This means there is no drive-shaft to the rear wheels, so the hump running through the passenger compartment is reduced.

So now when you sit in a Honda Civic, please don't be surprised that you're not cramped for space. And that you're not sitting sideways.

After all, it was a simple matter to make our engine sit that way instead.

HONDA
We make it simple.

B

Why we make it simple.

Honda set out to design one car that suited the basic transportation needs of the entire world.

So to help us discover that basic design we studied and analyzed data from 91 different countries. We collected information on everything from road conditions in Morocco to rainfall in Denmark to the dimensions of the average motorist in the United States.

In time the answer became clear. If Honda was to fill a universal need, we would have to build a simple car.

Simple to drive, simple to park, simple to understand, simple to own.

Today we offer three simple cars. The Honda Civic* 1200*, the Honda Civic CVCC*, and the Honda Accord*.

Consider for a moment how simplicity can help minimize just one of today's many automotive problems: the cost of gasoline.

All Hondas meet emissions requirements without a catalytic converter. So all Hondas run on regular as well as unleaded gasoline.

But don't be misled. A simple design is often the most difficult. For all their simplicity, Hondas are among the most sophisticated cars in their price range.

There is, of course, another reason why we make simple cars. The reason is you. We know that choosing a new car can be a complex problem.

It's a problem, however, that we can solve quite easily by giving you your choice of just three cars.

There. Now haven't we made your life simple?

HONDA
We make it simple.

C

94 A-C
Frank Kirk, Gale Napier Art Directors
Bob Cox Creative Director
Dick James Photographer
Gil Lumbard Copywriter
Needham, Harper & Steers Advertising, Inc. Agency
American Honda Motor Company, Inc. Client

Out of sight sound that's within your reach.
Ten years ago, Technics was just a gleam in an audiophile's eye. Now it is one of the fastest-growing hi-fi companies in the world.
Constant innovation and sound value are the reasons why.
For instance, the ST-9038 FM tuner has a digital readout frequency display instead of a dial scale. Push a button and its quartz synthesizer scanning device tunes in stations automatically.
Once a program time and station have been put into the memory of the SH-9038 microcomputer, they automatically take precedence. So while you're listening to one program the computer is keeping tabs on the time.
The computer can be programmed up to seven days ahead. Ready to turn on the cassette-slim RS-M85 quartz-locked DD cassette deck and switch to the station you want to tape. You can also arrange to make off-the-air recordings while you're away from home.
Providing the power for all this: the SU-8080 DC amplifier. A striking example of the audio engineer's art, it provides an ideal blend of high power and near-zero distortion.
Technics is part of Japan's largest consumer electronics group—Matsushita Electric.
This year, we're celebrating our 60th anniversary. Our founder started the business in 1918, making electric light fittings in his living room. We got where we are today because we believe in making what people want.
When it comes to hi-fi, that means state-of-the-art sound at old-fashioned prices.
Technics
National Panasonic and Technics are the brandnames of Matsushita Electric

A

C'est un"extra-plat" Technics, il est unique dans son genre.
Technics

B

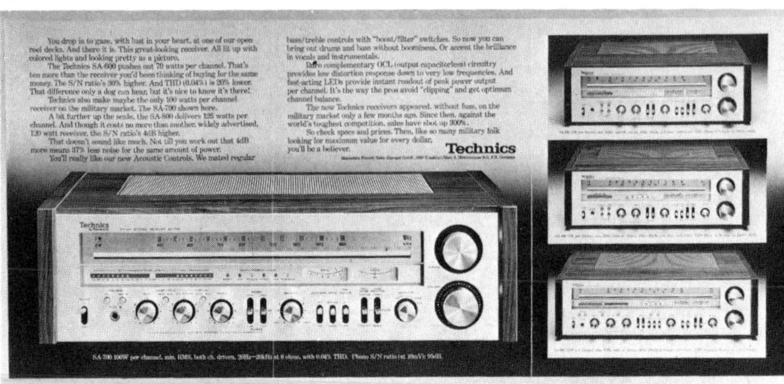

Technics

C

95 A-C
David Gribbin Art Director
Masayoshi Shimoda Photographer
Osamu Adachi, Takuya Yamaguchi Designers
CDP Japan Limited Advertising Agency
Matsushita Electric Client

96
Joseph Barbera, Steen Svensson Art Directors
Hoechst Fibers Industries Client

A

B

C

D

97 A-D
Hans Kramers Art Director
Terry Fincher, Clive Arrowsmith, Paul Huf, Jan Henderik, Cees Van Gelderen Photographers
ARA Marketing & Advertising Agency
Olympus Nederland BV Client

A

98 A-C
Paul Leeves Art Director
Willie Tang Photographer
Batey Advertising Agency
United Overseas Bank Client

B

C

The International Bank.

About the dollar's yen to be a yen.

Right now, the world's fastest rising currency might be from the land of the rising sun. Tomorrow, the Swiss Franc could soar, the Deutsche Mark reach a new high.

The dollar's yen to be a yen can change. As suddenly, and substantially, as exchange rates. The difference between one day and the next can be the difference between profit or disaster for a company.

How rock hard are currencies? Or how rocky? We have to know. For accurate assessment of the international currency climate is basic to our business.

Basic to the quality of advice we give you, our clients, on purchase and sale of foreign currencies — both spot and forward. On overseas finance on export and import contracts. Exchange control. Establishing overseas markets. International methods of payment.

We have to know what's happening in every money market of the world. And, what's likely to.

It's here we have an advantage. Size.

Because we are the largest banking organisation in the country, working closely with correspondent banks all over the world, we get first-hand financial information. Fast. We can act on it. First. And get the best rates. For ourselves. And you.

Rates are important. But, so is our specialist expertise. Our International team's knowledge of overseas markets. The trends and the tactics.

As an international businessman this is yours for the asking. Ask for it. Our team would be more than happy to discuss your business. And, the world.

Here's where you'll find our Senior Management team:

Business Development: Ted Jones, 3rd Floor, Carlton Centre, Johannesburg. Telephone 21-9154.

Foreign Exchange: Gerry Christy, 4th Floor, Alex Aiken House, Corner Kerk and Fraser Streets, Johannesburg. Telephone 833-4911.

Overseas Finance: Ian Robb, 2nd Floor, Alex Aiken House, Corner Kerk and Fraser Streets, Johannesburg. Telephone 833-4911.

There's a whole lot more to International Finance with the Professionals.

BARCLAYS
INTERNATIONAL DIVISION

Barclays National Bank Limited • Registered Commercial Bank

A

The Leasing Bank.

Does your Taxman's cup runneth over?

There's a whole lot more to Leasing with the Professionals.

BARCLAYS
BARCLAYS LEASING

B

The Insurance Broker.

There are times a broker has to stick his neck out, fast.

There's a whole lot more to Insurance with the Professionals.

BARCLAYS
BARCLAYS INSURANCE BROKERS·SA·LIMITED

C

99 A-F
John Cockle, Chris Casalena Art Directors
Sue Roytowski Concept/Copy
J. Walter Thompson SA Agency
Barclays Bank Client

The Insurance Broker.

Why Noah would have got our Marine cover. For nothing.

There's a whole lot more to Insurance with the Professionals.

BARCLAYS
BARCLAYS INSURANCE BROKERS·SA·LIMITED

D

The Factoring Bank.

When you feel growing pains.

There's a whole lot more to Factoring with the Professionals.

BARCLAYS
BARCLAYS FACTORS

E

The Insurance Broker.

THE LARGE PRINT GIVETH,
and the small print taketh away.

There's a whole lot more to Insurance with the Professionals.

BARCLAYS
BARCLAYS INSURANCE BROKERS·SA·LIMITED

F

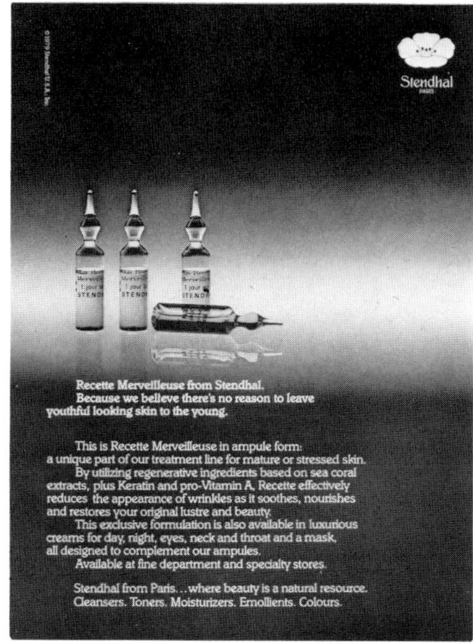

A

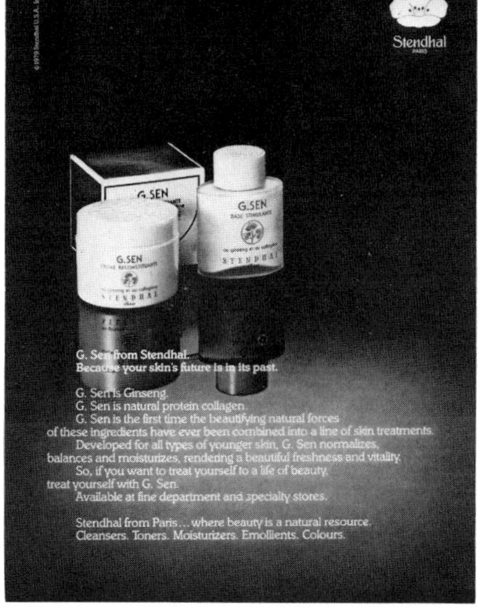

B

C

100 A-C
John Margeotes Art Director
Andrew Unangst Photographer
Margeotes/Fertitta Agency
Stendhal USA Client

101
Peter Rogers Art Director
Francesco Scavullo Photographer
Peter Rogers Associates Agency
Bill Blass Client

Blassport

Bill Blass as seen through the eyes of Scavullo

Expensive...By Design
Belle Stemware
Mouth blown crystal . . . designed by Jens Quistgaard
DANSK
Dansk International Designs
Mt. Kisco, New York 10549, Box 431
Write for free color brochure

A

102 A-B
Lou Dorfsman Art Director
Henry Wolf Productions Agency
Dansk Int. Client

Being an innocent bystander didn't stop the Douc Langur from paying the price of war.

Are you as vulnerable to violent change?

The war in Vietnam brought swift and harsh changes to the environment of the Douc Langur. Chemical defoliation and hungry soldiers seriously hurt this species' battle to survive.

The industrial environment is no less vulnerable to sudden and disruptive change. To protect yourself against risks created by factors beyond your influence, you should adopt a flexible system of loss control. And that's where Allendale can help. Allendale Mutual Insurance Company, Allendale Park, Johnston, Rhode Island, 02919.

Allendale Insurance

Printed in U.S.A.

A

Thanks to a forty-year conservation program the Trumpeter Swan just might survive.

What will it take to save your plant?

During the 18th and 19th centuries the reckless slaughter of the Trumpeter Swan nearly caused its extinction. Today, however, as a result of a long-term conservation effort, the Trumpeter Swan has a fighting chance for survival.

Within an industrial environment, too, effective conservation techniques cannot be implemented overnight. To avoid losses, a rigorous long-term loss control program is necessary. And that's where Allendale can help. Allendale Mutual Insurance Company, Allendale Park, Johnston, Rhode Island 02919.

Allendale Insurance

Printed in U.S.A.

B

The Spanish Lynx has already used up eight of its lives.

How many do you have left?

Having preyed once too often on domestic stock, this feline hunter became the victim of severe counterattacks from incensed farmers. Today, just a few dozen of these cats survive in the mountains of southern Spain.

Errors in judgement can have serious consequences in industry, too. But strict adherence to loss control procedures can minimize negative effects. And that's where Allendale can help. Allendale Mutual Insurance Company, Allendale Park, Johnston, Rhode Island, 02919.

Allendale Insurance

Printed in U.S.A.

C

103 A-C
Wayne Waaramaa Art Director
Bruce Coleman Photographer
Joe O'Brien Designer
Horton, Church & Goff Inc. Agency
Allendale Insurance Company Client

B

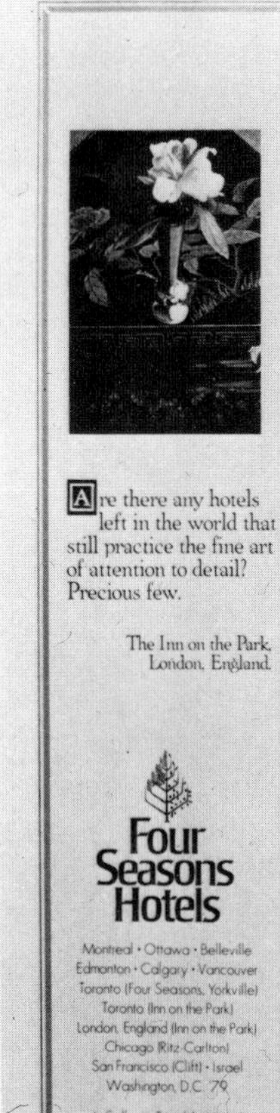

Are there any hotels left in the world that still practice the fine art of attention to detail? Precious few.
The Inn on the Park, London, England.
Four Seasons Hotels
Montreal • Ottawa • Belleville
Edmonton • Calgary • Vancouver
Toronto (Four Seasons, Yorkville)
Toronto (Inn on the Park)
London, England (Inn on the Park)
Chicago (Ritz-Carlton)
San Francisco (Clift) • Israel
Washington, D.C. '79
Call your Travel Agent or
Reserve Toll-Free: Toronto 445-5031
Elsewhere in Canada 800-268-6282

Everything to write home about.
The Four Seasons Montreal
Four Seasons Hotels
Montreal • Ottawa • Belleville
Edmonton • Calgary • Vancouver
Toronto (Four Seasons, Yorkville)
Toronto (Inn on the Park)
London, England (Inn on the Park)
Chicago (Ritz-Carlton)
San Francisco (Clift) • Israel
Washington, D.C. '79
Call your Travel Agent or
Reserve Toll-Free: Toronto 445-5031
Elsewhere in Canada 800-268-6282

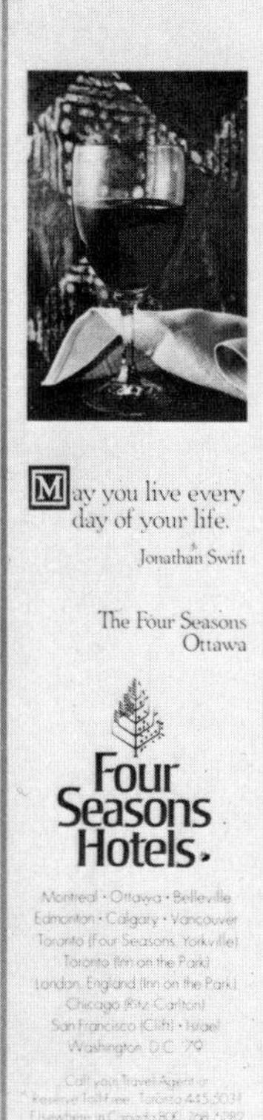

May you live every day of your life.
Jonathan Swift
The Four Seasons Ottawa
Four Seasons Hotels
Montreal • Ottawa • Belleville
Edmonton • Calgary • Vancouver
Toronto (Four Seasons, Yorkville)
Toronto (Inn on the Park)
London, England (Inn on the Park)
Chicago (Ritz-Carlton)
San Francisco (Clift) • Israel
Washington, D.C. '79
Call your Travel Agent or
Reserve Toll-Free: Toronto 445-5031
Elsewhere in Canada 800-268-6282

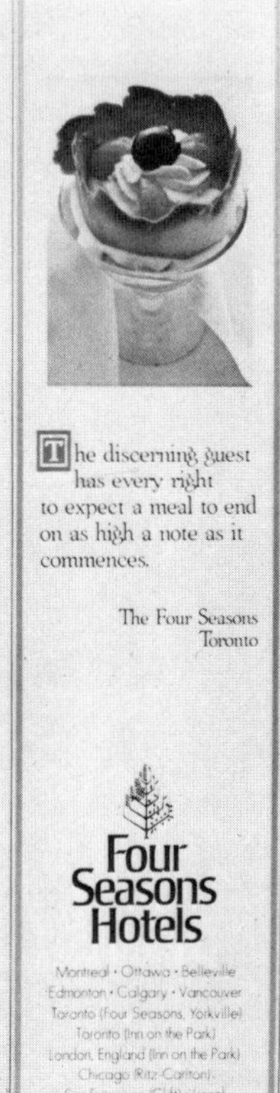

The discerning guest has every right to expect a meal to end on as high a note as it commences.
The Four Seasons Toronto
Four Seasons Hotels
Montreal • Ottawa • Belleville
Edmonton • Calgary • Vancouver
Toronto (Four Seasons, Yorkville)
Toronto (Inn on the Park)
London, England (Inn on the Park)
Chicago (Ritz-Carlton)
San Francisco (Clift) • Israel
Washington, D.C. '79
Call your Travel Agent or
Reserve Toll-Free: Toronto 445-5031
Elsewhere in Canada 800-268-6282

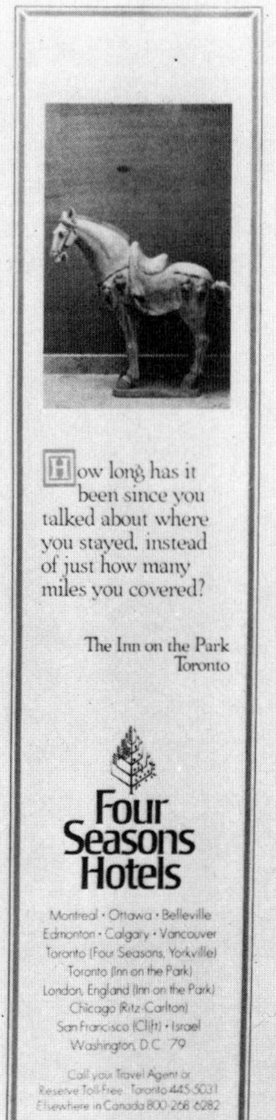

How long has it been since you talked about where you stayed, instead of just how many miles you covered?
The Inn on the Park Toronto
Four Seasons Hotels
Montreal • Ottawa • Belleville
Edmonton • Calgary • Vancouver
Toronto (Four Seasons, Yorkville)
Toronto (Inn on the Park)
London, England (Inn on the Park)
Chicago (Ritz-Carlton)
San Francisco (Clift) • Israel
Washington, D.C. '79
Call your Travel Agent or
Reserve Toll-Free: Toronto 445-5031
Elsewhere in Canada 800-268-6282

A

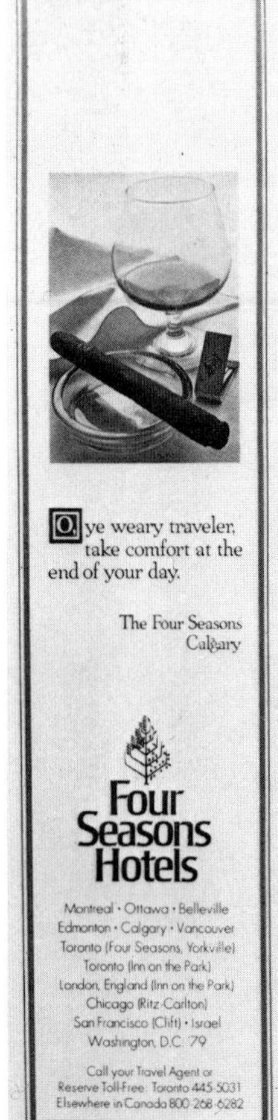

O, ye weary traveler, take comfort at the end of your day.
The Four Seasons Calgary
Four Seasons Hotels
Montreal • Ottawa • Belleville
Edmonton • Calgary • Vancouver
Toronto (Four Seasons, Yorkville)
Toronto (Inn on the Park)
London, England (Inn on the Park)
Chicago (Ritz-Carlton)
San Francisco (Clift) • Israel
Washington, D.C. '79
Call your Travel Agent or
Reserve Toll-Free: Toronto 445-5031
Elsewhere in Canada 800-268-6282

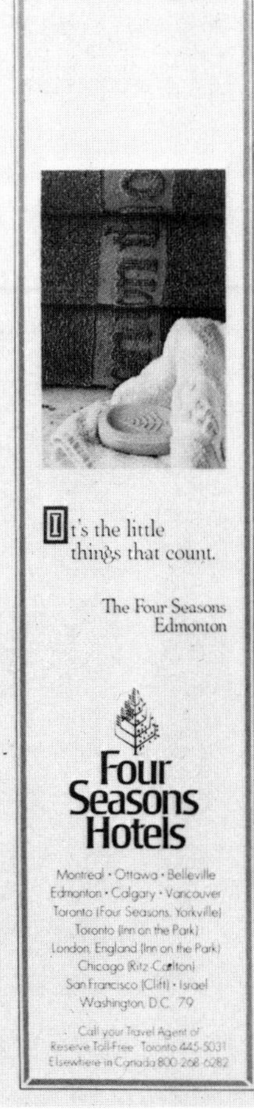

It's the little things that count.
The Four Seasons Edmonton
Four Seasons Hotels
Montreal • Ottawa • Belleville
Edmonton • Calgary • Vancouver
Toronto (Four Seasons, Yorkville)
Toronto (Inn on the Park)
London, England (Inn on the Park)
Chicago (Ritz-Carlton)
San Francisco (Clift) • Israel
Washington, D.C. '79
Call your Travel Agent or
Reserve Toll-Free: Toronto 445-5031
Elsewhere in Canada 800-268-6282

Farewell, plastic and computerized world. Good morning, elegance.
The Four Seasons Vancouver
Four Seasons Hotels
Montreal • Ottawa • Belleville
Edmonton • Calgary • Vancouver
Toronto (Four Seasons, Yorkville)
Toronto (Inn on the Park)
London, England (Inn on the Park)
Chicago (Ritz-Carlton)
San Francisco (Clift) • Israel
Washington, D.C. '79
Call your Travel Agent or
Reserve Toll-Free: Toronto 445-5031
Elsewhere in Canada 800-268-6282

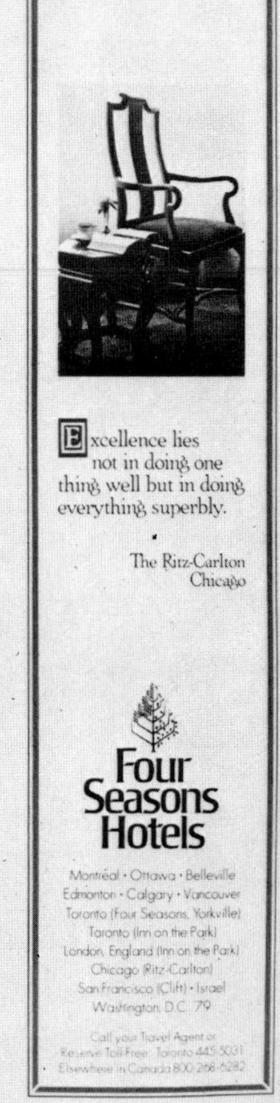

Excellence lies not in doing one thing well but in doing everything superbly.
The Ritz-Carlton Chicago
Four Seasons Hotels
Montréal • Ottawa • Belleville
Edmonton • Calgary • Vancouver
Toronto (Four Seasons, Yorkville)
Toronto (Inn on the Park)
London, England (Inn on the Park)
Chicago (Ritz-Carlton)
San Francisco (Clift) • Israel
Washington, D.C. '79
Call your Travel Agent or
Reserve Toll-Free: Toronto 445-5031
Elsewhere in Canada 800-268-6282

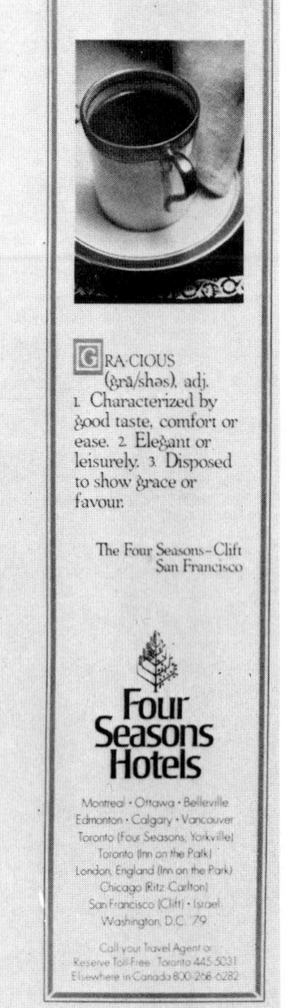

GRA·CIOUS (grā/shəs), adj.
1. Characterized by good taste, comfort or ease. 2. Elegant or leisurely. 3. Disposed to show grace or favour.
The Four Seasons–Clift San Francisco
Four Seasons Hotels
Montreal • Ottawa • Belleville
Edmonton • Calgary • Vancouver
Toronto (Four Seasons, Yorkville)
Toronto (Inn on the Park)
London, England (Inn on the Park)
Chicago (Ritz-Carlton)
San Francisco (Clift) • Israel
Washington, D.C. '79
Call your Travel Agent or
Reserve Toll-Free: Toronto 445-5031
Elsewhere in Canada 800-268-6282

B

104 A-B
John McDonnell Art Director
Young & Rubicam Ltd. Agency
Four Seasons Hotels Ltd. Client

SNAPPER,

tarragon sauce, zucchini florentine, avocado salad and Mirassou Monterey Riesling. The Mirassou Family recommends this crisp, refreshing white wine as the perfect complement for your intimate dining, fabulous feast or to merely sip alone.
Enjoy the fresh fruit taste, reminiscent of crisp apples – a flavor captured by a unique harvesting process. The grapes are crushed less than a minute after leaving their Monterey vines. Monterey Riesling, a delicate fine wine. It's young. It's ripe. It's ready for you and your snapper.
The Mirassou Family has been making the finest varietal wines for 125 years. Enjoy them in your home or at finer restaurants.
For more information and our newsletter, write to: Mirassou Vineyards, 3000 Aborn Road, San Jose, California 95121.

America's Oldest Winemaking Family

A

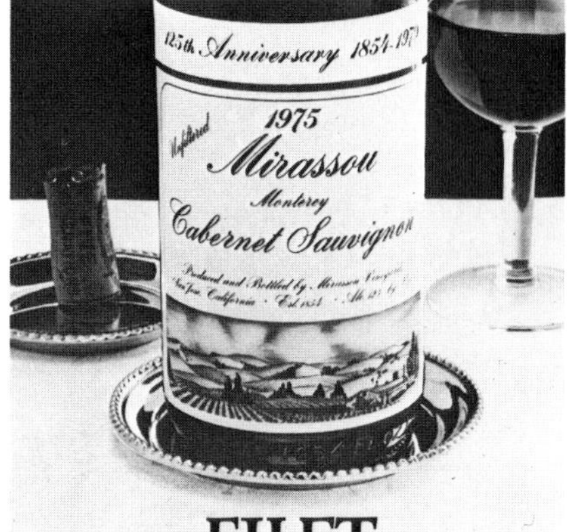

FILET

mignon, broccoli with hollandaise, a steaming baked potato and Mirassou Cabernet Sauvignon. Why is our Cabernet Sauvignon the perfect complement to this savory meal? Because the Mirassou taste strategy begins in the field. Just as the grape buds set in Spring, controlled irrigation stresses the vines forcing rich, intense, varietal character. Once crushed and fermented, the grapes are aged in the Mirassou tradition using small French oak barrels. Additional taste complexity results from further aging in the bottle. Enjoy it now or years from now. It's unique. It's well balanced. It's the perfect complement to you and your filet.
The Mirassou Family has been making the finest varietal wines for 125 years. Enjoy them in your home or at finer restaurants.
For more information and our newsletter, write to: Mirassou Vineyards, 3000 Aborn Road, San Jose, California 95121.

America's Oldest Winemaking Family

B

CRAB,

lemon slices, warm sourdough french bread, spinach salad and Mirassou Monterey Riesling. The Mirassou Family recommends this crisp, refreshing white wine as the perfect complement for your intimate dining, fabulous feast or to merely sip alone.
Enjoy the fresh fruit taste, reminiscent of crisp apples – a flavor captured by a unique harvesting process. The grapes are crushed less than a minute after leaving their Monterey vines. Monterey Riesling, a delicate fine wine. It's young. It's ripe. It's ready for you and your crab.
The Mirassou Family has been making the finest varietal wines for 125 years. Enjoy them in your home or at finer restaurants.
For more information and our newsletter, write to: Mirassou Vineyards, 3000 Aborn Road, San Jose, California 95121.

America's Oldest Winemaking Family

C

105 A-C
David Gauger Art Director
Peter Olgivie Photographer
David Gauger, Roger Takiguchi Designers
Gauger Sparks Silva Agency
Mirrasou Vineyards Client

106 A-C
Kurt Tausche Art Director
Fred Dingler, Richard Green, Warren Hanson Illustrators
James Anderson Copywriter
Paragon Companies Agency
Northern States Power Company Client

Wind and Electricity
What's Being Done?
Wind Power:
Today's Wind Turbine Generator
A concept from the past that could help meet tomorrow's energy needs.
NSP
The World is Changing

106 A

Many advanced technology programs continue to suffer from lower performance, later delivery, and higher cost than originally planned and promised.

Too often these delinquencies are tolerated in the mistaken belief that technology cannot be managed efficiently.

At Northrop we take a different view. To us advanced technology works successfully only when it results in fulfillment of all commitments for performance, for schedule, and for price.

For example, Northrop's George A. Fuller division is managing construction of the medical sciences school at the University of California, Irvine campus. This project is on schedule and is meeting all budget commitments.

In every part of our business—aircraft, electronics, communications, construction, and services—we make technology work. In every sense of the word.

NORTHROP

Making advanced technology work.

Exterior stairway of the medical sciences school, University of California, Irvine. George A. Fuller Company, construction manager.

107 A

Many advanced technology programs continue to suffer from lower performance, later delivery, and higher cost than originally planned and promised.

Too often these delinquencies are tolerated in the mistaken belief that technology cannot be managed efficiently.

At Northrop, we take a different view. To us, advanced technology only works successfully when it results in fulfillment of all commitments for performance, schedule, and price.

For example, Northrop has produced more than 3,000 aircraft in its series of F-5 and T-38 tactical jet fighters and trainers. Every one of these aircraft met or exceeded performance requirements. And each of them was delivered on time and within contract price.

In every part of our business—aircraft, electronics, communications, construction, and services—we make technology work. In every sense of the word.

NORTHROP

Making advanced technology work.

Aerodynamically contoured fuselage of Northrop F-5E Tiger II tactical fighter.

B

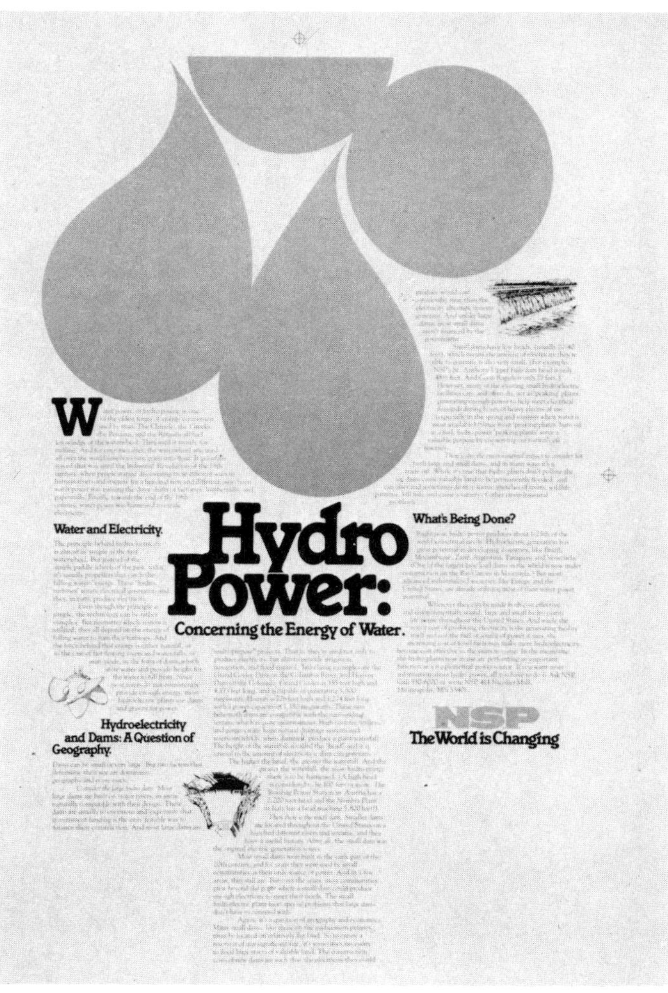

B

Photovoltaic Conversion (Solar Cells)

The Sun

Solar Heating

What's Being Done?

Solar Energy:

A gift from the sun.

Solar Thermal Power (Generation of Electricity)

NSP

The World is Changing

C

MANY advanced technology programs continue to suffer from lower performance, later delivery, and higher cost than originally planned and promised.

Too often these delinquencies are tolerated in the mistaken belief that technology cannot be managed efficiently.

At Northrop we take a different view. To us advanced technology works successfully only when it results in fulfillment of all commitments for performance, for schedule, and for price.

As an example, Northrop has produced more than 3,000 aircraft in its series of F-5 and T-38 tactical jet fighters and trainers. Every one of these aircraft met or exceeded performance requirements. And each of them was delivered on time and within contract price.

We are also at work on the F-18 strike fighter, being built for the U.S. Navy and Marine Corps by McDonnell Douglas together with Northrop. The innovative use of technology to increase performance and reliability has resulted in the most cost-effective expression of the multi-role fighter concept.

In every part of our business—aircraft, electronics, communications, construction, and services—we make technology work. In every sense of the word.

NORTHROP

Making advanced technology work.

Aerodynamically sculptured fuselage and wing of Northrop's prototype of the F-18 strike fighter for the U.S. Navy and Marine Corps.

C

107 A-C
Darion DuBois Art Director
Bob Cox Creative Director
Per Volquartz, Inc. Photographers
Gil Lumbard Copywriter
Needham, Harper & Steers Advertising, Inc. Agency
The Northrop Corporation Client

georges rech
homme

108 A

B

C

D

E

"Ultimately it's Marantz. Go for it!"

ON MARANTZ,

I've got a Marantz brochure here in the shop and on the inside front cover it says 'we sound better'. That's really some statement for a hi-fi company to make. Especially these days when there's really no bad hi-fi. There are literally 10—15 brands which are all good. So it's a bold statement to make 'we sound better'. But, you know, I think Marantz actually does sound better.

What's so different about Marantz? I believe they give extra special attention to detail ... to quality. Marantz is manufactured in the Far East, but it's American design.

And ... you ... know ... just as they were first made in California in the Californian sunshine not far from Hollywood. And just as Hollywood made movies bigger and better, I believe that's been Marantz's

aim. To be bigger and better than everybody.

And Marantz comes in a wide range. Prices from real budget levels right up to the most expensive you can get. But where Marantz specialise is in the separate pre-amp and power-amp units. And what we'll be showing at the fair is what I consider is 'state of the art' hi-fi. But at more everyday prices. We'll be looking, among other things, at the 3250 pre-amplifier — I don't want to go through all the heavy specs — but they're tremendous. And the 170 DC power-amplifier which matches it. With the 170 we talk about 85 watts per channel with very low THD — total harmonic distortion. In fact, into 4 ohm speakers we would really be talking about something like 140 watts per channel. But into the normal 8 ohm speakers it would be something like 85 watts per channel. That's a lot of power! But it's not there to give you noise. It's there to give you quality.

Doug Ramage. Manager, Etkind's Sandton City, Sandton. On Marantz & Ortofon.

You need pretty heavy speakers to handle power like that. So Marantz have come up with the HD 880, which is a 4-way system. Most hi-fi speakers tend to be two-way — a tweeter for the treble and a woofer for the base. Here with 880 we have a 4-way system. A woofer for your base, a mid range unit to cover those sounds in the mid range, a tweeter for the treble and a super tweeter to give you absolute purity in the higher notes. So you get a beautiful range of sound from those speakers, with 150 watts added power capacity. So you can take the big, heavy amps.

Speakers like the HD 880 can handle all the power you want — Certainly the 3250/170 DC combination I've spoken about.

Marantz have a wide range of turntables, from belt drive 6100 up to the top of the pops 6350 direct drive turntable, which one could put with this system as well.

ON ORTOFON,

But what's becoming more and more important these days is the cartridge. Sometimes the cartridge supplied with the turntable is not up to the same quality as the rest of the stuff we're talking about. So what have we got over here? Well, along with Marantz, we will be showing the Ortofon cartridges. Ortofon is a Danish company and they're the biggest selling imported cartridges in Japan. They've recently won a number of Japanese awards. They go right from a R19,95 cartridge right up to — and I kid you not — a moving coil cartridge with it's own transformer for around R1 000. On the other hand, Ortofon does have a moving coil cartridge which can be bought with or without its own head amplifier available for under half that.

AND ON PRICE.

With Marantz we're not talking cheap. We're talking outstanding quality. But, a Marantz system, complete with amplifier, turntable and speakers could start as low as R80 deposit and R40 a month for 24 months. Or just over R700 cash. The upper end Marantz ... well ... we're talking way above that. I believe, though, that if somebody has about R2 000 to spend and they're looking for real quality hi-fi, ultimately it's Marantz — go for it!

Your nearest Etkind's/Bermeister branch has at least one person just as knowledgeable on the 'State of the Art' as Doug Ramage. All our Managers and Salesmen are highly trained specialists. And they have the interest and the time to discuss any aspect of the 'State of the Art' with you. It's all part of our 'great deal more' promise.

A good price & a great deal more.

etkind's bermeister

111 A

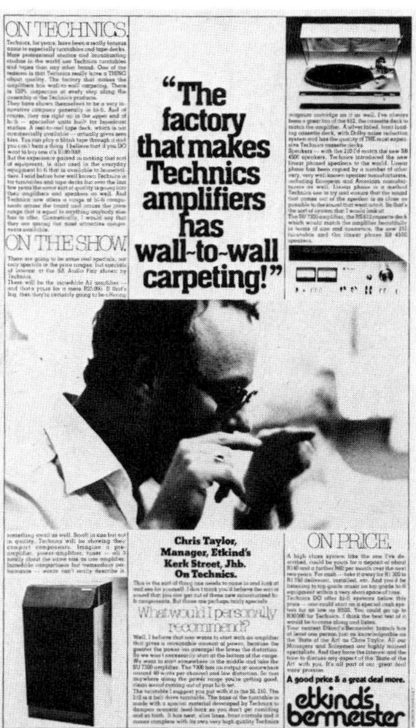

ON TECHNICS.
"The factory that makes Technics amplifiers has wall-to-wall carpeting!"
ON THE SHOW.
Chris Taylor, Manager, Etkind's Kerk Street, Jhb. On Technics.
ON PRICE.
A good price & a great deal more.
etkind's bermeister

B

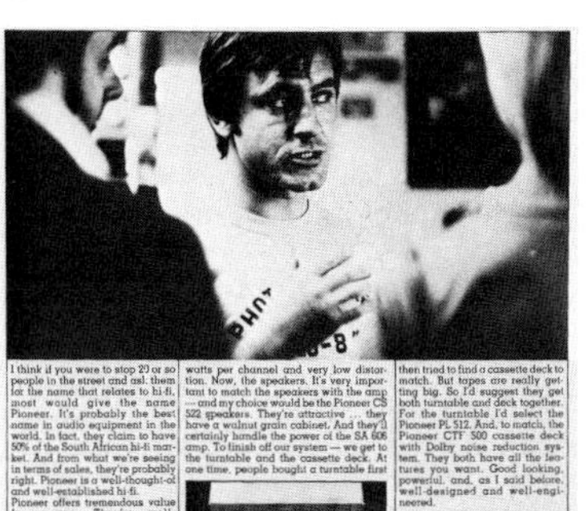

"Pioneer... everything you hear is true."

What would be my choice of an ideal Pioneer system?

And the cost?

On the show...

Allan Manley, Senior Salesman, Bermeisters, Eloff Street, Jhb. On Pioneer.

A good price & a great deal more.

etkind's bermeister

C

ON SONAB
& THORENS
"Nobody really believes the performance you can get from these speakers."
A good price & a great deal more.
etkind's bermeister

D

111 A-D
Linda-Jane Lee-Duncan Art Directors
Grey/2 Agency
Etkinds/Bermeister Client

C

D

Legal aids.

From dictation supplies to legal pads. All the assistance you need to keep your visit brief.

Banks'

Stationery and office supplies
929 State Street, Santa Barbara
966-4177

B

C

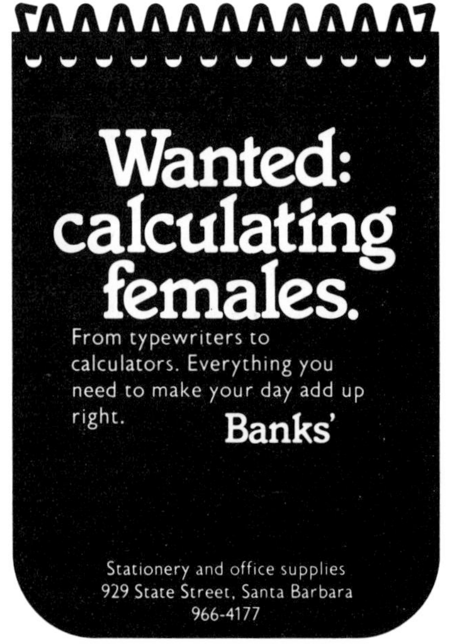

D

109 A

B

109 A-D
James Wilkins Art Director
James Wilkins, Don Trousdell Designers
William F. Finn & Associates, Inc. Agency
Citizens First National Bank Client

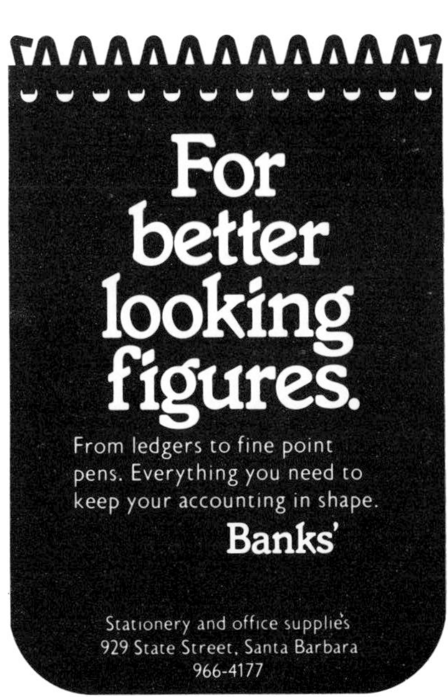

A

110 A-D
Mark Oliver Art Director
Mark Oliver Associates Studio
The Garth De Cew Group Agency
Bank's Stationery Client

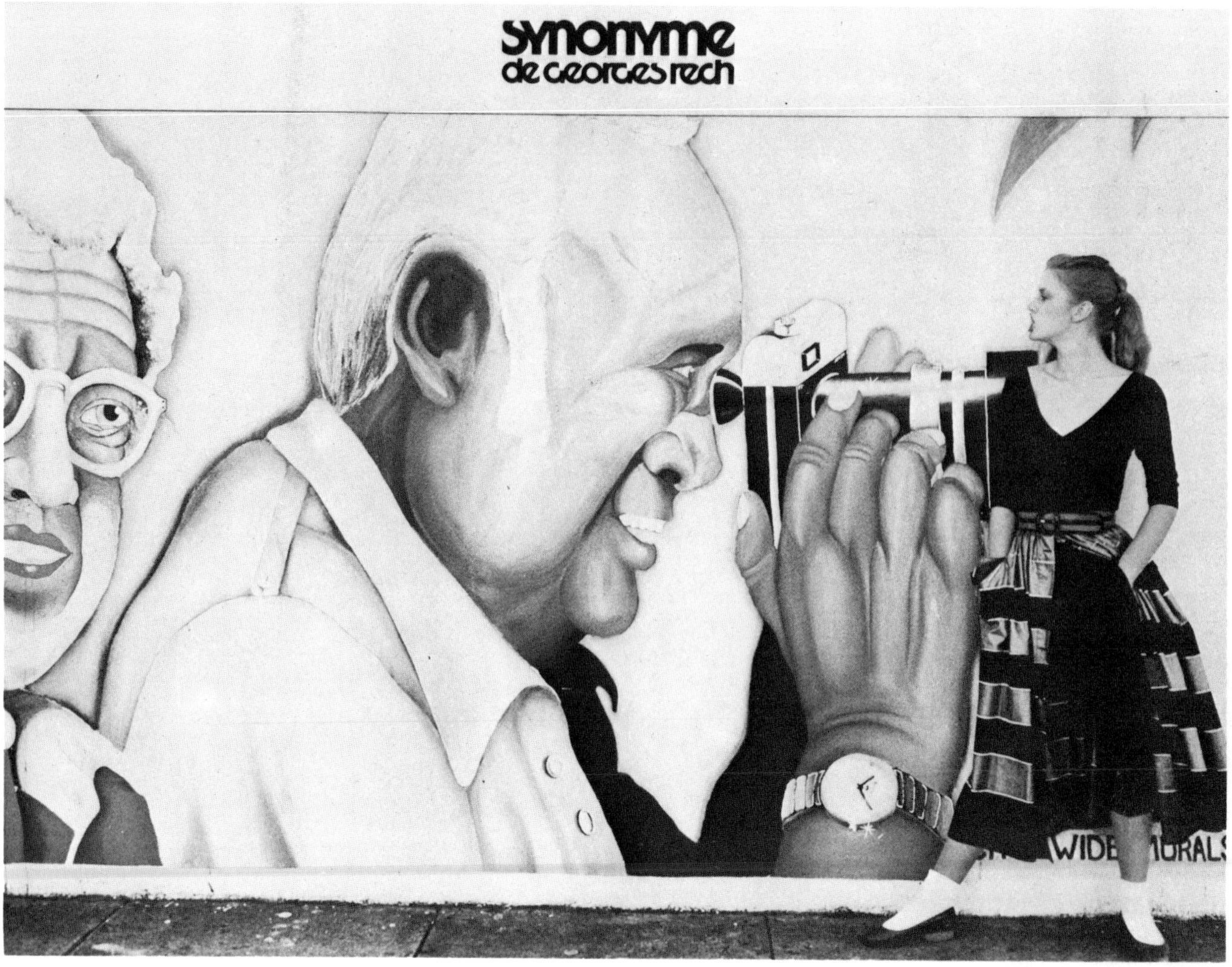

synonyme
de georges rech

F

G

H

108 A-H
Joel Desgrippes Art Director
Barry Lategan Studio Studio
Desgrippes Studio Agency
George Rech Client

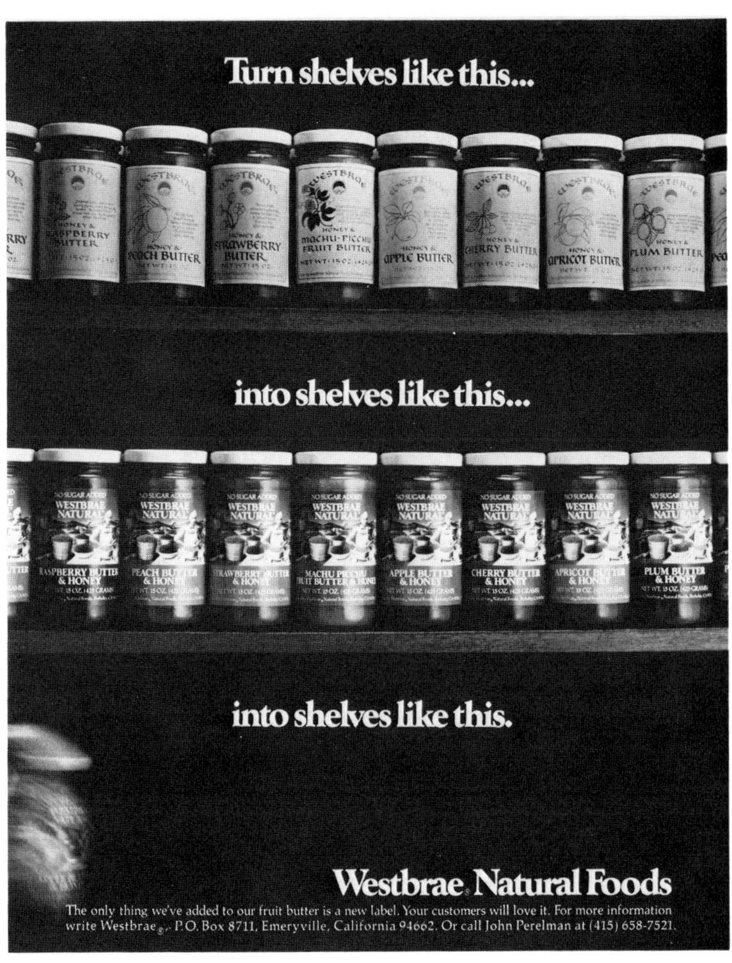

Turn shelves like this...
into shelves like this...
into shelves like this.
Westbrae Natural Foods
The only thing we've added to our fruit butter is a new label. Your customers will love it. For more information write Westbrae®, P.O. Box 8711, Emeryville, California 94662. Or call John Perelman at (415) 658-7521.

Trade Advertising

112
David Gauger Art Director
Peter Olgivie Photographer
David Gauger, Robert Takiguchi, Paulette Traverso Designers
Gauger Sparks Silva Agency
Westbrae Natural Foods, Berkeley Client

113
Jeff Cooper Art Director
Doug Johnson Illustrator
Al Merrin Copywriter
BBDO, Inc. Agency
Hammermill Papers Group Client

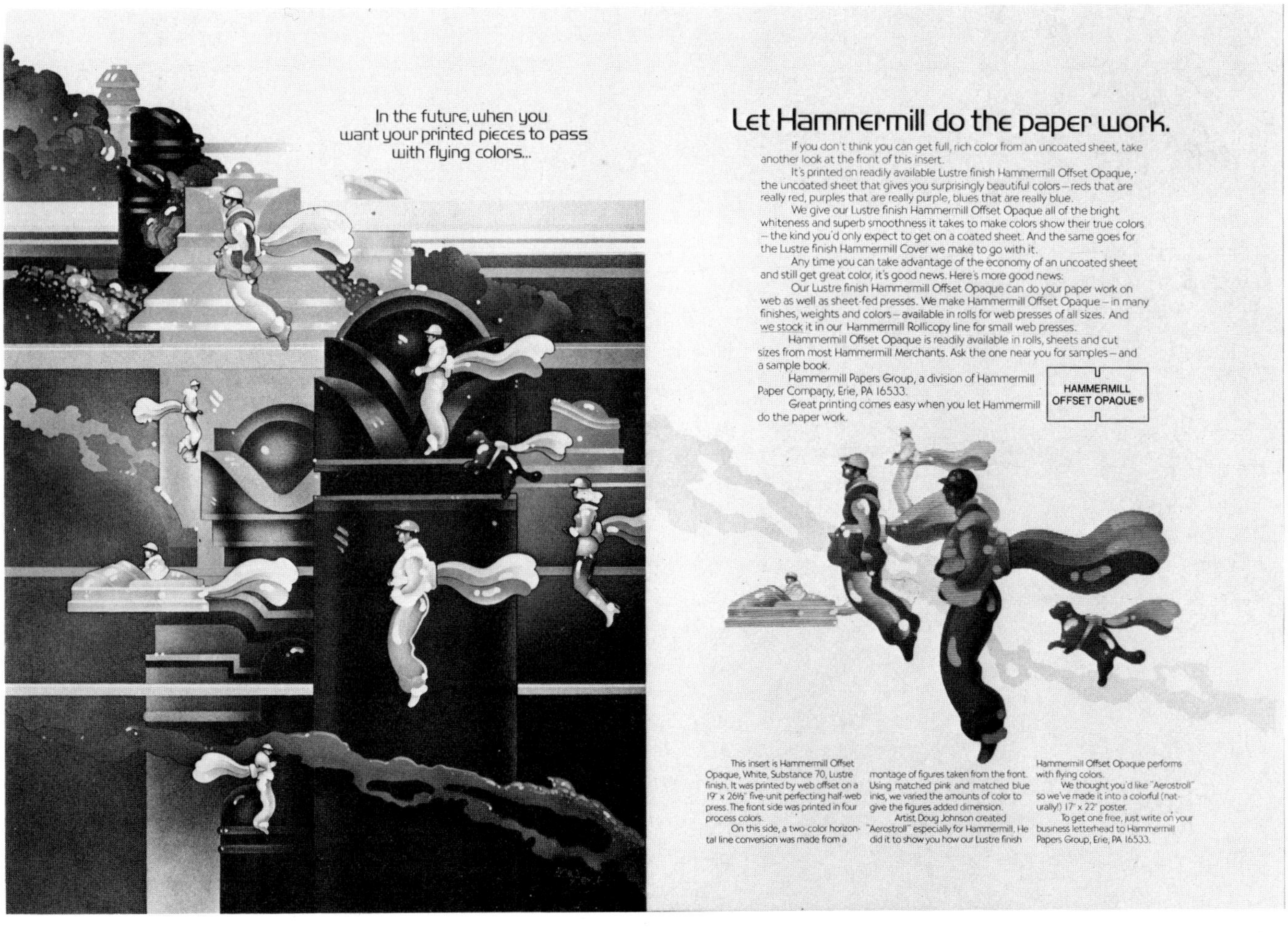

In the future, when you want your printed pieces to pass with flying colors...

Let Hammermill do the paper work.

If you don't think you can get full, rich color from an uncoated sheet, take another look at the front of this insert.

It's printed on readily available Lustre finish Hammermill Offset Opaque, the uncoated sheet that gives you surprisingly beautiful colors – reds that are really red, purples that are really purple, blues that are really blue.

We give our Lustre finish Hammermill Offset Opaque all of the bright whiteness and superb smoothness it takes to make colors show their true colors – the kind you'd only expect to get on a coated sheet. And the same goes for the Lustre finish Hammermill Cover we make to go with it.

Any time you can take advantage of the economy of an uncoated sheet and still get great color, it's good news. Here's more good news:

Our Lustre finish Hammermill Offset Opaque can do your paper work on web as well as sheet-fed presses. We make Hammermill Offset Opaque – in many finishes, weights and colors – available in rolls for web presses of all sizes. And we stock it in our Hammermill Rollicopy line for small web presses.

Hammermill Offset Opaque is readily available in rolls, sheets and cut sizes from most Hammermill Merchants. Ask the one near you for samples – and a sample book.

Hammermill Papers Group, a division of Hammermill Paper Company, Erie, PA 16533.

Great printing comes easy when you let Hammermill do the paper work.

HAMMERMILL OFFSET OPAQUE®

This insert is Hammermill Offset Opaque, White, Substance 70, Lustre finish. It was printed by web offset on a 19" x 26½" five-unit perfecting half-web press. The front side was printed in four process colors.

On this side, a two-color horizontal line conversion was made from a montage of figures taken from the front. Using matched pink and matched blue inks, we varied the amounts of color to give the figures added dimension.

Artist Doug Johnson created "Aerostroll" especially for Hammermill. He did it to show you how our Lustre finish Hammermill Offset Opaque performs with flying colors.

We thought you'd like "Aerostroll" so we've made it into a colorful (naturally!) 17" x 22" poster.

To get one free, just write on your business letterhead to Hammermill Papers Group, Erie, PA 16533.

114
Ralph DeLuca, Jeff Billig Art Directors
Arnold & Company Inc. Agency
Nabisco Confection Client

115
Carl Nelson Art Director
Brady Willette, Image Studios Photographers
Color Graphics Production House
J. MacLachlan & Associates Agency
Miller Electric Manufacturing Co. Client

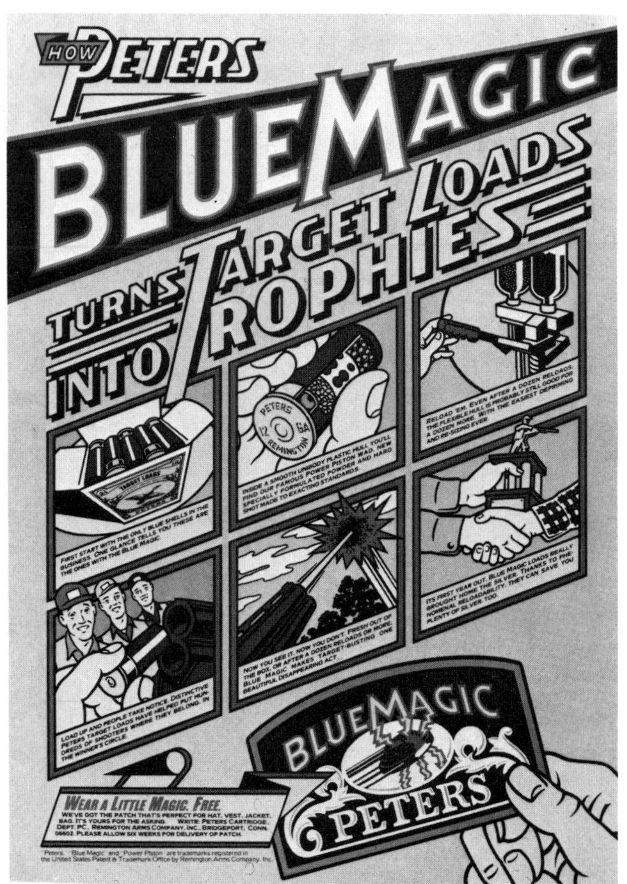

116
Michael Fountain Art Director
Lou Brooks Illustrator
John Connelly Copywriter
Michael Doret Designer
Rumrill-Hoyt, Inc. Agency
Peters Ammunition Client

117
Tom Haynes, Mark Rubin Art Directors
Hashi Photographer
Steve Abbruscato Copywriter
Sudler & Hennessey Agency
Stuart Pharmaceuticals Client

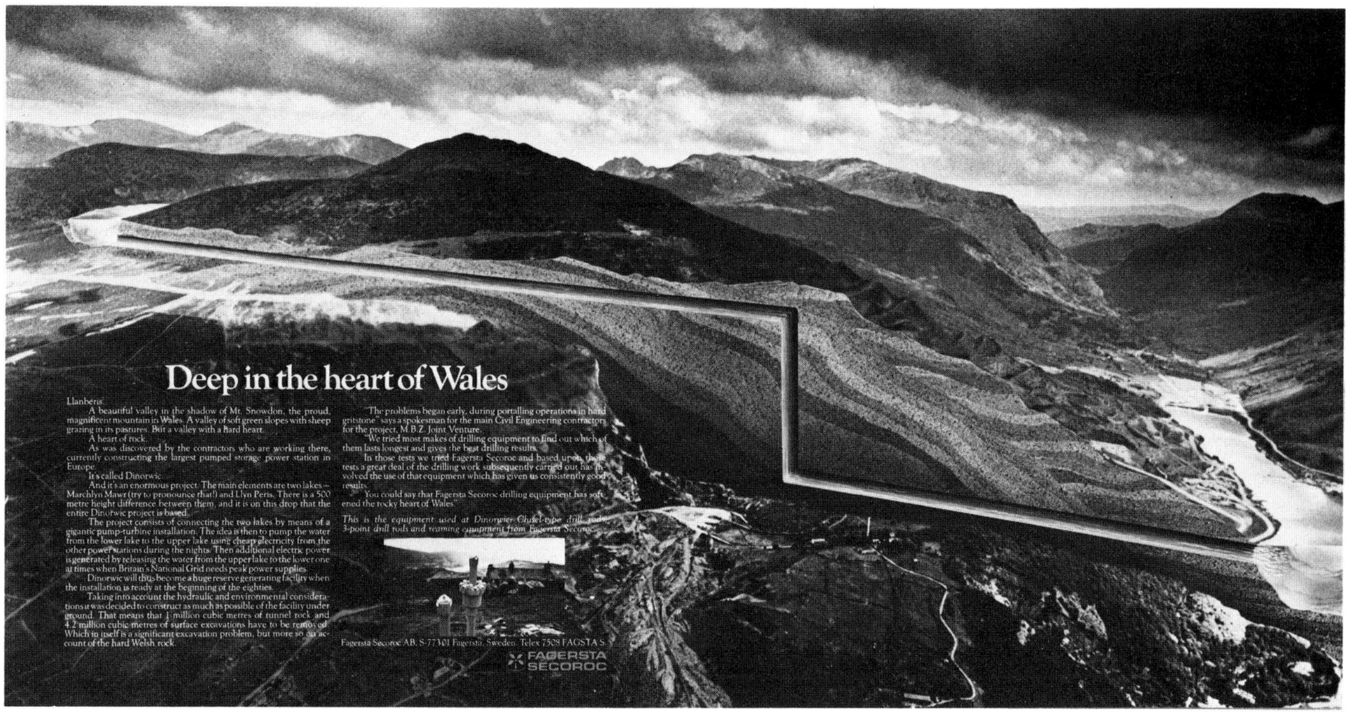

118
Christer Laurent Art Director
Ehrenstrahle & Co. Ltd. Agency
Fagersta Secoroc AB Client

119
Barry Vetere, Bill Nelson Art Directors
Arthur Fox Photographer
Ally Gargano Agency
Piper Aircraft Corporation Client

THE PIPER AEROSTAR. IT FLIES HIGHER, FASTER, FARTHER
AND MORE ECONOMICALLY THAN ANYTHING ELSE IN ITS CLASS.
WHEN THAT SITUATION CHANGES, WE'LL CHANGE THIS AD.

More airplane for the dollar. PIPER
Piper Aircraft Corporation, Lock Haven, Pa. 17745
A Bangor Punta Company Member of GAMA

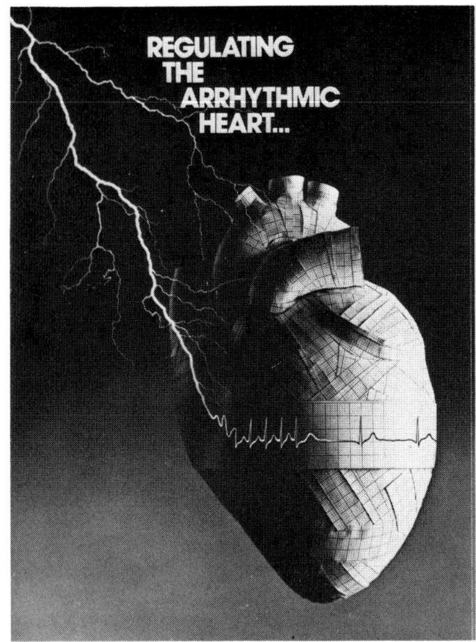

120
Dick Russinko Art Director
Blake Hampton Model Maker
Gemma Just Copywriter
Sudler & Hennessey Agency
Ayerst Laboratories Client

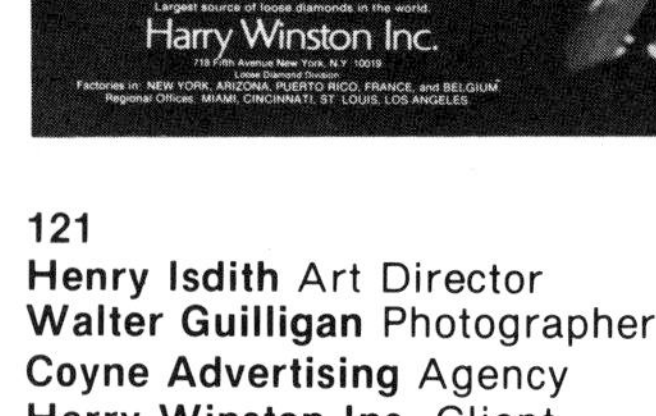

121
Henry Isdith Art Director
Walter Guilligan Photographer
Coyne Advertising Agency
Harry Winston Inc. Client

124
Stan Dornfest Art Director
Bernard Vidal Photographer
Wesson & Warhaftig, Inc. Agency
Schering Corporation Client

125
Howard Kates Art Director
Tom Atkinson Copywriter
Doremus Uptown Agency
Crane Corporation Client

122
Joe Phair Art Director
Robert Pryor Illustrator
Ketchum New York Agency
Westinghouse Lamp Commercial Division Client

123
Art Riser Art Director
Jamie Cook Photographer
John H. Harland Client

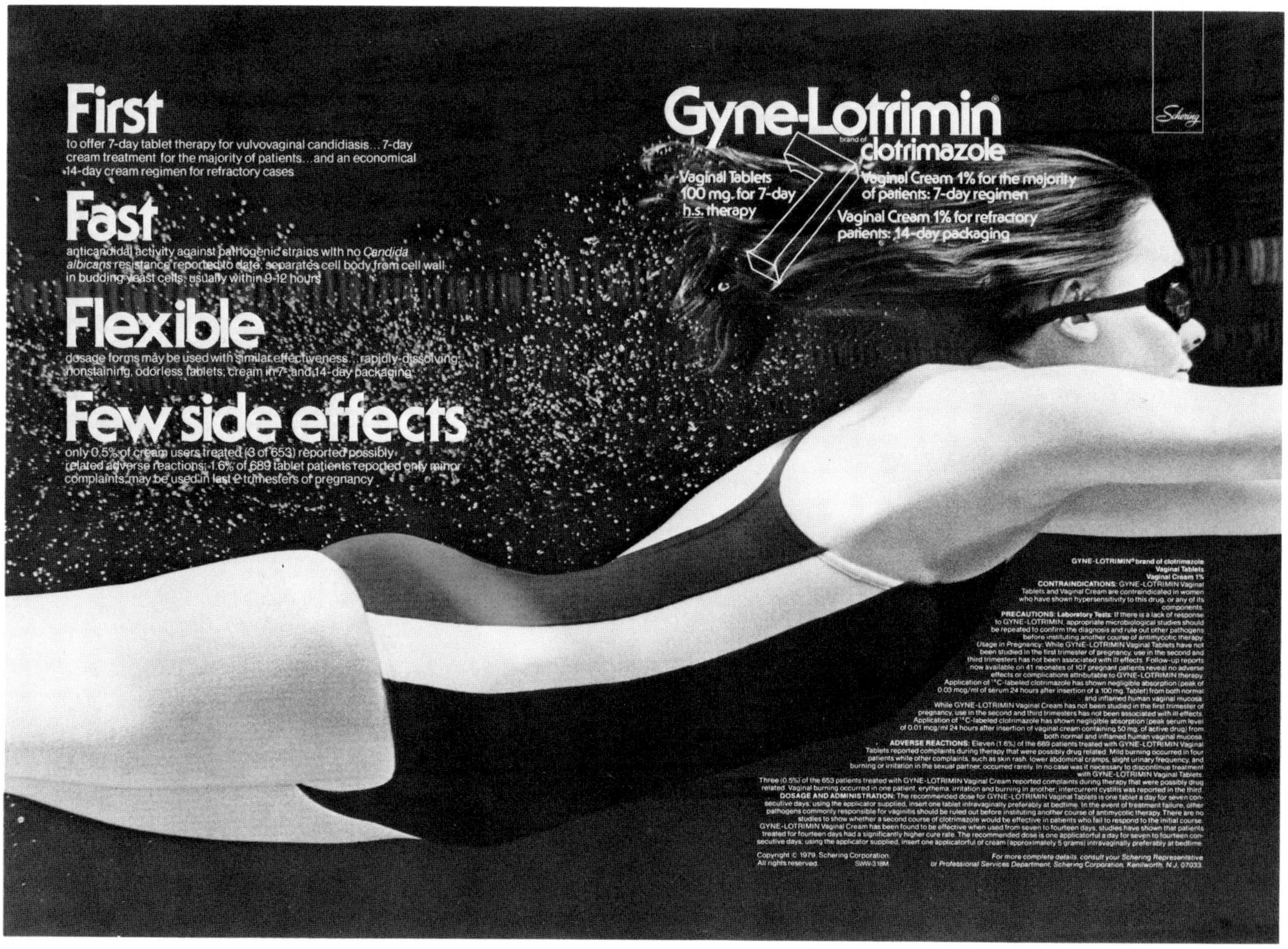

First

to offer 7-day tablet therapy for vulvovaginal candidiasis... 7-day cream treatment for the majority of patients... and an economical 14-day cream regimen for refractory cases

Fast

anticandidal activity against pathogenic strains with no *Candida albicans* resistance reported to date; separates cell body from cell wall in budding yeast cells, usually within 9-12 hours

Flexible

dosage forms may be used with similar effectiveness... rapidly-dissolving, nonstaining, odorless tablets; cream in 7- and 14-day packaging

Few side effects

only 0.5% of cream users treated (3 of 653) reported possibly related adverse reactions; 1.6% of 689 tablet patients reported only minor complaints; may be used in last 2 trimesters of pregnancy

Gyne-Lotrimin®

brand of clotrimazole

7

Vaginal Tablets 100 mg. for 7-day h.s. therapy

Vaginal Cream 1% for the majority of patients: 7-day regimen

Vaginal Cream 1% for refractory patients: 14-day packaging

Schering

GYNE-LOTRIMIN® brand of clotrimazole
Vaginal Tablets
Vaginal Cream 1%

CONTRAINDICATIONS: GYNE-LOTRIMIN Vaginal Tablets and Vaginal Cream are contraindicated in women who have shown hypersensitivity to this drug, or any of its components.

PRECAUTIONS: Laboratory Tests: If there is a lack of response to GYNE-LOTRIMIN, appropriate microbiological studies should be repeated to confirm the diagnosis and rule out other pathogens before instituting another course of antimycotic therapy.

Usage in Pregnancy: While GYNE-LOTRIMIN Vaginal Tablets have not been studied in the first trimester of pregnancy, use in the second and third trimesters has not been associated with ill effects. Follow-up reports now available on 41 neonates of 107 pregnant patients reveal no adverse effects or complications attributable to GYNE-LOTRIMIN therapy.

Application of ^{14}C-labeled clotrimazole has shown negligible absorption (peak of 0.03 mcg/ml of serum 24 hours after insertion of a 100 mg. Tablet) from both normal and inflamed human vaginal mucosa.

While GYNE-LOTRIMIN Vaginal Cream has not been studied in the first trimester of pregnancy, use in the second and third trimesters has not been associated with ill effects. Application of ^{14}C-labeled clotrimazole has shown negligible absorption (peak serum level of 0.01 mcg/ml 24 hours after insertion of vaginal cream containing 50 mg. of active drug) from both normal and inflamed human vaginal mucosa.

ADVERSE REACTIONS: Eleven (1.6%) of the 689 patients treated with GYNE-LOTRIMIN Vaginal Tablets reported complaints during therapy that were possibly drug related. Mild burning occurred in four patients while other complaints, such as skin rash, lower abdominal cramps, slight urinary frequency, and burning or irritation in the sexual partner, occurred rarely. In no case was it necessary to discontinue treatment with GYNE-LOTRIMIN Vaginal Tablets.

Three (0.5%) of the 653 patients treated with GYNE-LOTRIMIN Vaginal Cream reported complaints during therapy that were possibly drug related. Vaginal burning occurred in one patient, erythema, irritation and burning in another; intercurrent cystitis was reported in the third.

DOSAGE AND ADMINISTRATION: The recommended dose for GYNE-LOTRIMIN Vaginal Tablets is one tablet a day for seven consecutive days, using the applicator supplied, insert one tablet intravaginally preferably at bedtime. In the event of treatment failure, other pathogens commonly responsible for vaginitis should be ruled out before instituting another course of antimycotic therapy. There are no studies to show whether a second course of clotrimazole would be effective in patients who fail to respond to the initial course. GYNE-LOTRIMIN Vaginal Cream has been found to be effective when used from seven to fourteen days; studies have shown that patients treated for fourteen days had a significantly higher cure rate. The recommended dose is one applicatorful a day for seven to fourteen consecutive days, using the applicator supplied, insert one applicatorful of cream (approximately 5 grams) intravaginally preferably at bedtime.

 SWW-318M

For more complete details, consult your Schering Representative or Professional Services Department, Schering Corporation, Kenilworth, N.J. 07033.

124

We're down to earth.

When the Space Shuttle eased back to earth, automatic anti-skid brake controls manufactured by Crane's Hydro-Aire Division brought the historic test flight to a safe and successful conclusion. Just as they do on almost all commercial and military aircraft in service today. And have for 30 years.

Hydro-Aire. A division of Crane Co., where down-to-earth concentration on essential products for essential industries helps build a strong and growing business. In steel. In building products. In fluid and pollution control. And, of course, in aerospace and aircraft.

Crane Co., 300 Park Avenue, New York, NY 10022

CRANE®

125

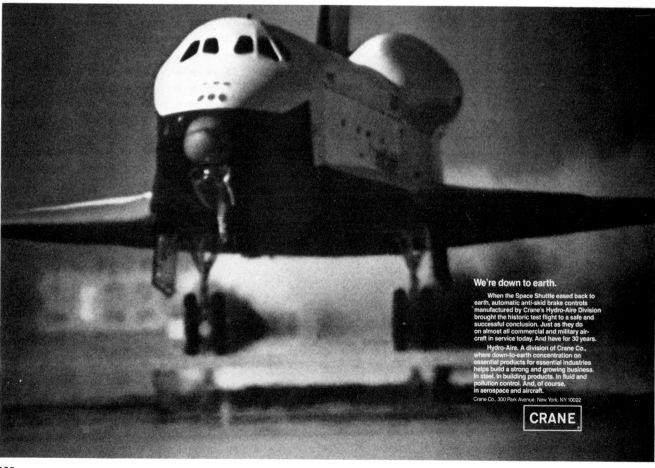

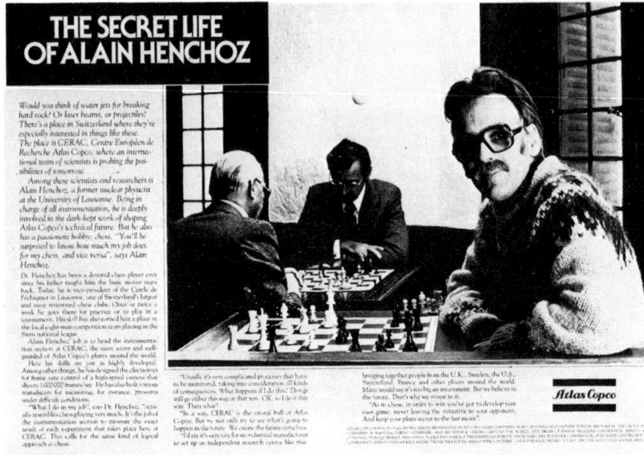

THE SECRET LIFE OF ALAIN HENCHOZ
Atlas Copco

126 A

THE MAN WHO BROUGHT WATER TO SKOPELOS.
Atlas Copco

B

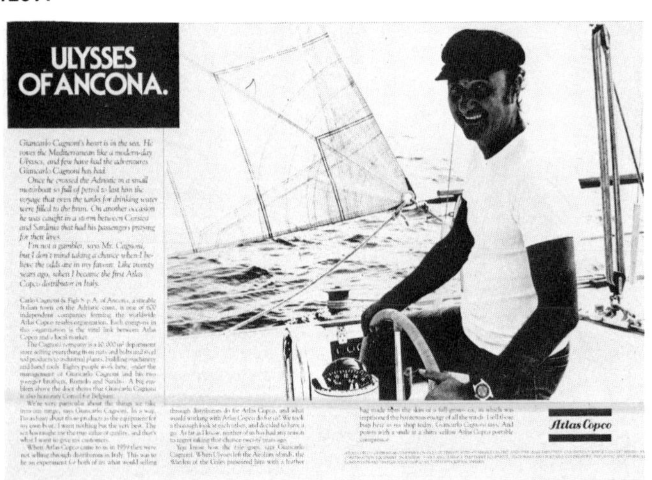

C

D

126 A-D
Kenneth Bodlund Art Director
Jan Bengtsson Photographer
Anderson & Lembke Vintergatan Agency
Atlas Copco AB Client

In the beginning was the word.
Help
Inland Steel

127
Frank McCallum Art Director
Guy Billout Illustrator
Jim Keithley Copywriter
Lee King & Partners Agency
Inland Steel Client

128
Vince Marrapodi Art Director
Robert Lewis Photographer
CBS Records, Inc. Client

129
Doris Fortino Art Director
Tom Bach Photographer
Marvy! Advertising Photography, Inc. Studio
Campbell-Mithun Agency
3M Client

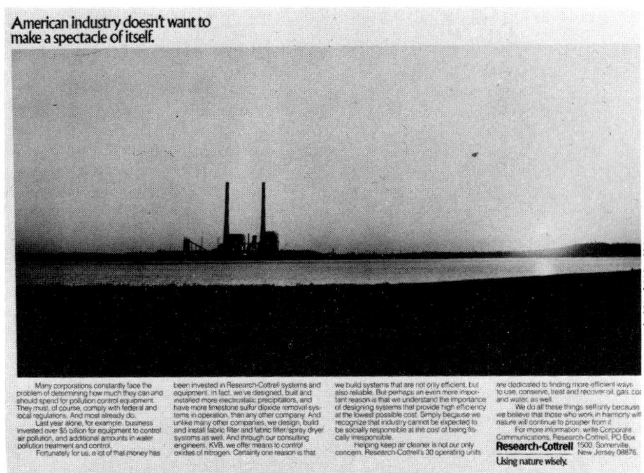

130
Mike Rosen Art Director
Hammond Farrell Inc. Agency
Research-Cottrell Client

131 A-E
Diane J. Hamel Art Director
Morton C. Tadder Photographer
Harry London Copywriter
Beck Engraving Production House
Eisner & Associates Agency
McCormick Flavor Division Client

131 A

B

C

D

E

"Min framtid är mina kunder och min personal.

Min framtid är helt enkelt så bra som butiken är, varken mer eller mindre.

Är det en bra butik kommer kunder och personalen att trivas.

Man ska naturligtvis ägna sig åt att planera för framtiden. Men det har jag inte tid med."

En butikschef måste fungera som försäljare, inköpare, lagerchef, personalman, till och med som springpojke.

En stor del av hans dag går åt till rutinsysslor.

HUR SKA HAN FÅ TID ÖVER?

Det finns kvalificerade hjälpredor som kan ta hand om åtskilliga av rutinsysslorna och mer därtill. Om du som är butikschef har en sådan får du mer tid över till väsentligheter.

Det finns idag speciella datorer för livsmedelsbutiker. En sådan butiksdator hjälper dig på många sätt.

Det blir enklare att ha ett lagom stort lager.

Det blir enklare att veta när det är dags att beställa nytt.

Kassorna ansluts till datorn och ger besked om vad som säljs. Du vet alltså hela tiden vad som finns i butiken av varje vara och hur mycket som går åt.

Det blir enklare att inventera, av samma anledning.

Det blir mindre svinn. En stor del av kassasvinnet kommer du åt genom att risken för felinslag i kassan i stort sett försvinner. Man slår in en varukod istället för priset och får uppgifterna från datorns minne.

Det blir enklare att bedöma hur sortimentet ska se ut. Du ser ju snabbt vilka varor som säljer bra eller dåligt.

Då kan du göra dig av med hyllvärmarna innan de har kostat för mycket, och satsa på lönsammare varor.

Det finns andra vinster att göra också. Du kan till exempel direkt avläsa resultatet av omplacering av varor och extrapriser.

Datorn ger dig möjligheten att hela tiden veta vad som händer.

Dina kunder märker det också direkt. De får kassakvitton som uttryckligen talar om vad de har köpt.

De märker det på ett annat sätt också. Det märks när man har tid att planera. Och du får mer tid. Tid till nytta för dig själv, din personal och dina kunder.

IBM har jobbat med det här i många år. Vi har en hel del erfarenhet. Vi har ett verkligt bra butiksdatorsystem som passar butiker i många olika storlekar.

Är du intresserad?

Du kan skicka efter mer detaljerad information om hur butiksdatorn kan hjälpa dig. Eller varför inte begära en demonstration.

Hör i så fall av dig till IBM, tel 08-7300000. Tala med Harry Gindin, Lars Malm eller Sune Tungström, eller skicka kupongen till IBM Svenska AB, Informationsavdelningen, 16392 Stockholm.

Ja tack, skicka mig mer detaljerad information om IBM:s butiksdatorsystem.

Namn ....

Företag ....

Adress ....

Postadress ....

.... Tel. ....

IBM

EN IBM BUTIKSDATOR GER MER TID FÖR FRAMTIDEN.

132

BUT STILL PUMPING.

This is not the kind of maintenance procedure we recommend for any piece of machinery. Not even our rugged Flygt pumps. But it happened. Through an oversight, the 4 inch Flygt Pump shown here somehow was left off the routine maintenance schedule. For nearly four years.

Eventually, an extension was added to the waste system and the plan called for a tie-in right where the old pump had been. Had been? Still was—covered with grime and muck, but still pumping away! The sturdy veteran was cleaned up, given its long overdue routine maintenance and at last report is still pumping away.

That kind of durability—and dependability under the worst of conditions—is the result of the quality of design and engineering Flygt builds into all of its pumps, big and little.

Flygt has the broadest range of submersibles available. Capacities to 19,500 GPM and discharge sizes to 24 inch. And every submersible backed up by Flygt's proven experience and performance—over 30 years experience and over a half million submersible installations around the world. That's more than all other manufacturers combined. Proven dependability, easy maintenance and the right pump for the job all add up to the best evaluated cost. Only Flygt Corporation has them all.

FLYGT ® A SUBSIDIARY OF ITT Flygt, Norwalk, Connecticut 06856.

133

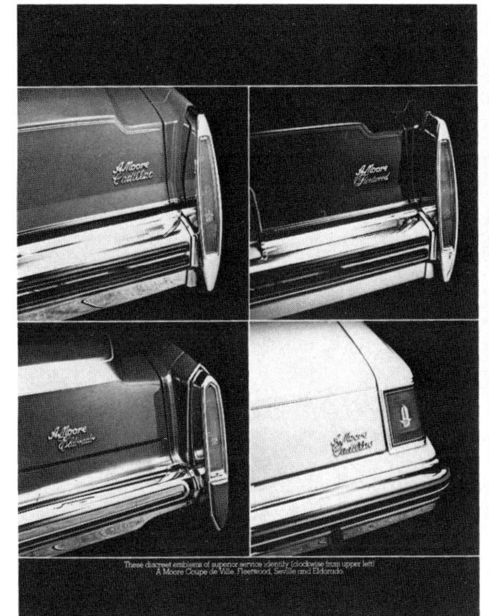

These discreet emblems of superior service identify (clockwise from upper left)
A Moore Coupe de Ville, Fleetwood, Seville and Eldorado.

You never had them so good.

The Moore Cadillac Company is founded on the idea that when you move up to one of the world's finest motorcars, you have a right to superior technical and personal attention. First, to match the quality of your automobile. Second, to match the quality of your life. It is an idea whose time has come. And it comes with an attractive choice—simply Moore or less.

The Moore Cadillac Company/8598 Leesburg Pike (Rt. 7) Tyson's Corner, Vienna, Va. 22180

142
Jim Kingsley Art Director
Dave Simpson Photographer
Demaine/Lambert Advertising Agency
Moore Cadillac Client

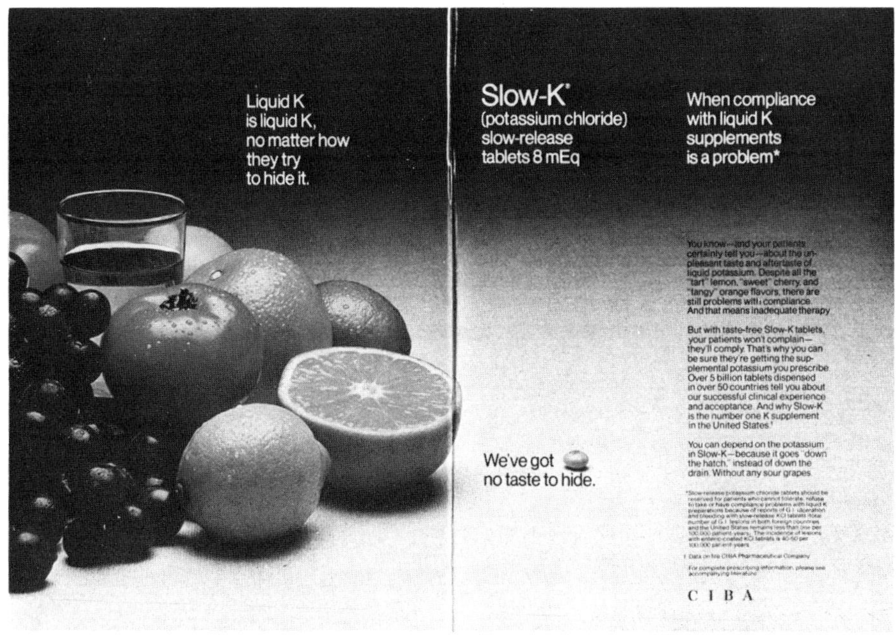

Liquid K
is liquid K,
no matter how
they try
to hide it.
Slow-K®
(potassium chloride)
slow-release
tablets 8 mEq
When compliance
with liquid K
supplements
is a problem*
You know—and your patients certainly tell you—about the unpleasant taste and aftertaste of liquid potassium. Despite all the "tart" lemon, "sweet" cherry, and "tangy" orange flavors, there are still problems with compliance. And that means inadequate therapy.
But with taste-free Slow-K tablets, your patients won't complain—they'll comply. That's why you can be sure they're getting the supplemental potassium you prescribe. Over 5 billion tablets dispensed in over 50 countries tell you about our successful clinical experience and acceptance. And why Slow-K is the number one K supplement in the United States.†
You can depend on the potassium in Slow-K—because it goes "down the hatch," instead of down the drain. Without any sour grapes.
We've got no taste to hide.
CIBA

143
John Kashiwabara Art Director
Ed Gallucci Photographer
Ciba-Geigy Client

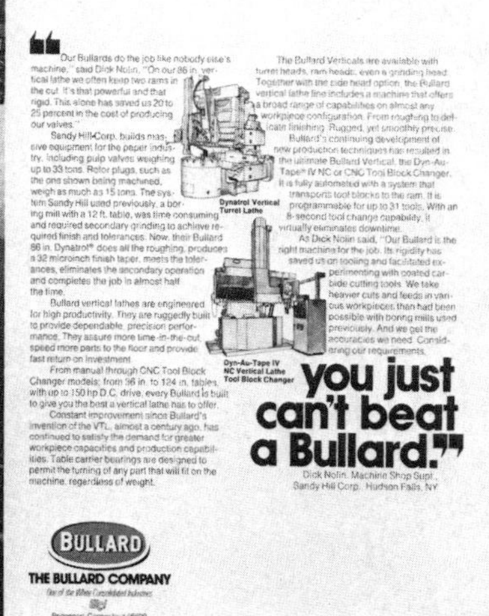

144
Herb Stricker Art Director
Richard Derling Photographer
Charles Berger Illustrator
Tom Gabrielli Designer
Communigraphics Inc. Agency
The Bullard Company Client

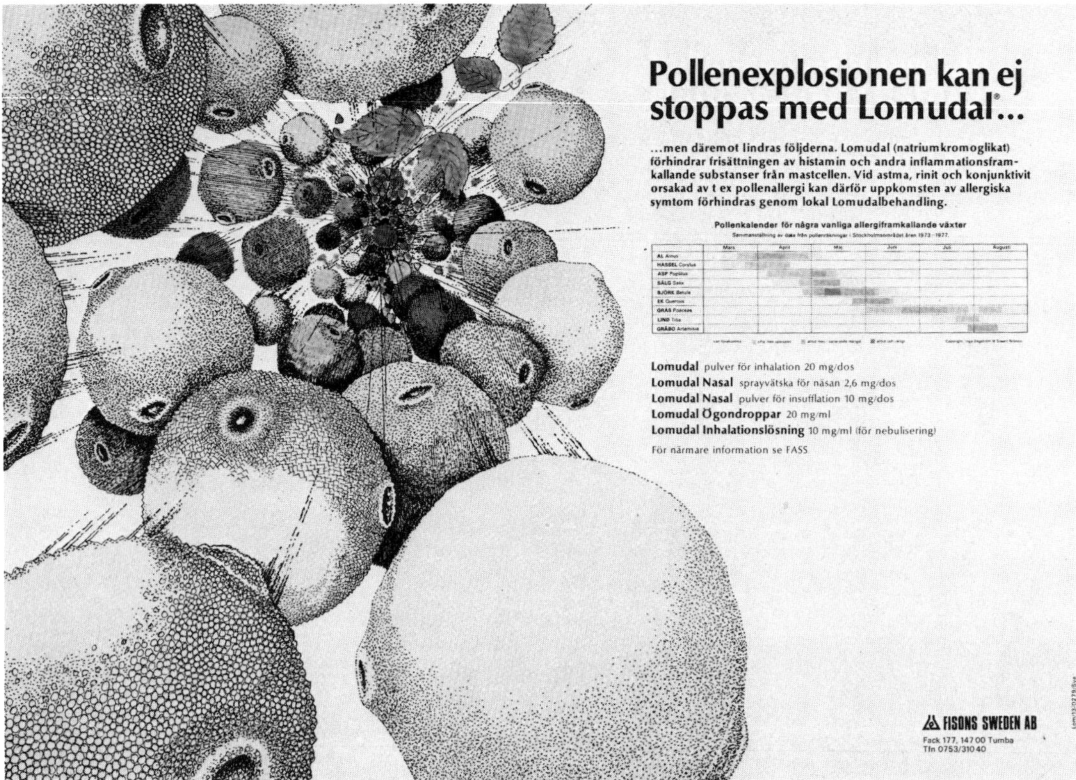

145
Toivo Blomgren Art Director
Studio 18 AB Agency
Fisons Sweden AB Client

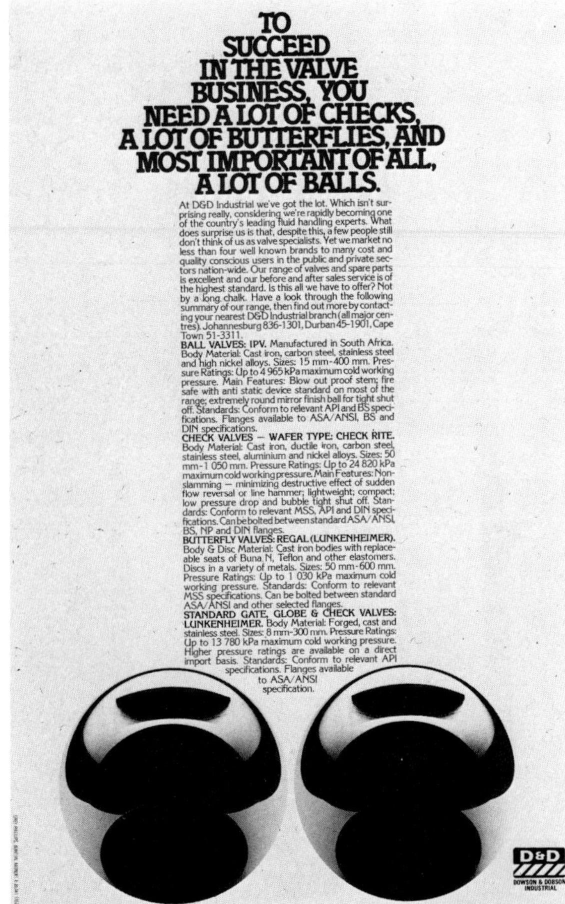

146
Mark Simkins Art Director
Iain Campbell Photographer
Chris Marrington Copywriter
Grey-Phillips, Bunton, Mundel & Blake Agency
Dowson & Dobson Engineering Limited Client

ARROW COMPOSITION HAS MANY GOOD POINTS 267-9724

147
Stavros Cosmopulos Art Director
Arnold & Company Inc. Agency
Arrow Composition Client

Trade Campaigns

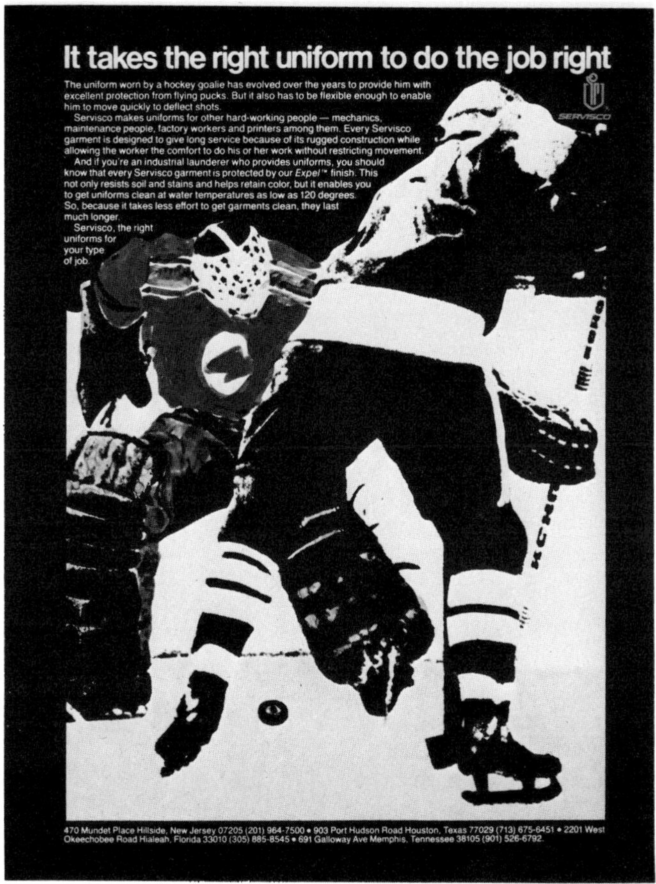

It takes the right uniform to do the job right
The uniform worn by a hockey goalie has evolved over the years to provide him with excellent protection from flying pucks. But it also has to be flexible enough to enable him to move quickly to deflect shots.
Servisco makes uniforms for other hard-working people — mechanics, maintenance people, factory workers and printers among them. Every Servisco garment is designed to give long service because of its rugged construction while allowing the worker the comfort to do his or her work without restricting movement.
And if you're an industrial launderer who provides uniforms, you should know that every Servisco garment is protected by our *Expel*™ finish. This not only resists soil and stains and helps retain color, but it enables you to get uniforms clean at water temperatures as low as 120 degrees. So, because it takes less effort to get garments clean, they last much longer.
Servisco, the right uniforms for your type of job.
SERVISCO
470 Mundet Place Hillside, New Jersey 07205 (201) 964-7500 • 903 Port Hudson Road Houston, Texas 77029 (713) 675-6451 • 2201 West Okeechobee Road Hialeah, Florida 33010 (305) 885-8545 • 691 Galloway Ave Memphis, Tennessee 38105 (901) 526-6792.

A

148 A-C
Irwin Schonhorn Art Director
GS & J Communications Inc. Agency
Servisco Client

It takes the right uniform to do the job right
In medieval times, each knight's suit of armor was especially crafted for him. It had to provide protection from the blows of opponents, yet give him freedom of action to press his own attack.
Today, Servisco carries on this tradition by making work uniforms for a wide variety of jobs that are also just right for the user. Whether they're for maintenance people, mechanics, printers, factory workers or any other use, they are made to provide comfort and freedom of action so that people can do their work without hindrance or irritation.
And if you're an industrial launderer who provides uniforms, you should know that every Servisco garment is protected by our *Expel*™ finish. This not only resists soil and stains and helps retain color, but it enables you to get uniforms clean at water temperatures as low as 120 degrees. So, because it takes less effort to get uniforms clean, they last much longer.
Servisco, the right uniform for your type of job.
SERVISCO
470 Mundet Place Hillside, New Jersey 07205 (201) 964-7500 • 903 Port Hudson Road Houston, Texas 77029 (713) 675-6451 • 2201 West Okeechobee Road Hialeah, Florida 33010 (305) 885-8545 • 691 Galloway Ave Memphis, Tennessee 38105 (901) 526-6792.

B

It takes the right uniform to do the job right
A deep-sea diver's outfit has to be created carefully to do the job he undertakes. Not only must it be completely waterproof, but it must provide the diver with the comfort and flexibility he needs to do his hazardous work.
At Servisco, we design work uniforms that are just right for a wide range of jobs — for maintenance people, mechanics, printers, factory workers — and many others. Each is designed to provide comfort and freedom of action, so that people can work at maximum efficiency without feeling cramped or restricted.
And if you're an industrial launderer who provides uniforms, you should know that every Servisco garment is protected by our *Expel*™ finish. This not only resists soil and stains and helps retain color, but it enables you to get uniforms clean at water temperatures as low as 120 degress. So, because it takes less effort to get uniforms clean, they last much longer.
Servisco, the right uniform for your type of job.
SERVISCO
470 Mundet Place Hillside, New Jersey 07205 (201) 964-7500 • 903 Port Hudson Road Houston, Texas 77029 (713) 675-6451 • 2201 West Okeechobee Road Hialeah, Florida 33010 (305) 885-8545 • 691 Galloway Ave Memphis, Tennessee 38105 (901) 526-6792.

C

WE'RE DOING OUR PART TO HELP KEEP BUILDING COSTS FROM SENDING YOU THROUGH THE ROOF.

At Burlington Northern we haul lumber and building products. And we do it at a darn good price. For example, the going rate for shipping a hundred pounds of shingles from Seattle to Chicago is about three dollars.

Why the surprisingly low price in a time of rampant inflation? There are a number of reasons.

Because lumber is our second largest commodity, we maintain a fleet of over 20,000 suitable lumber cars. So, in essence, we're continually geared up to transport wood products.

System wide, nearly half our main trackage is welded rail. Capital expenditures on this and other improvements exceeded $400 million last year, but it's well worth it in added efficiency.

And finally, we hauled over 300,000 car loads of lumber and wood products last year. Enough to build 600,000 homes.

Indications are that '79 will be another year of heavy capital expediture for Burlington Northern. Not only for the railroad, but for BN Transport, our trucking subsidiary, Burlington Northern Air Freight Inc., our air freight subsidiary, and our timber, coal and mineral operations as well. And the more we invest in our future the better we can do for you.

BURLINGTON NORTHERN

149 A

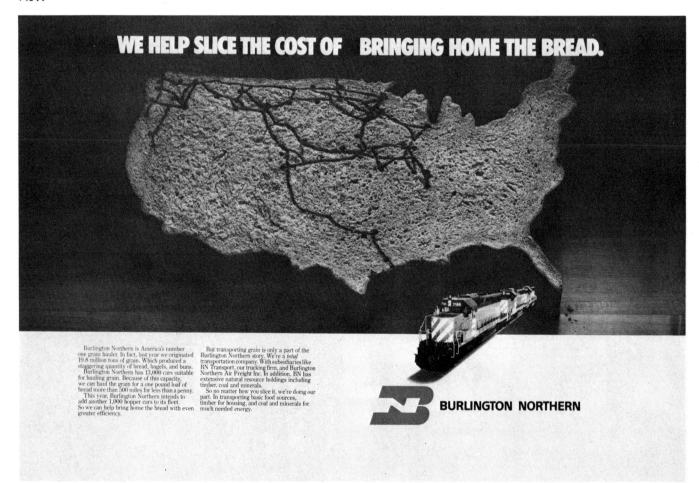

WE HELP SLICE THE COST OF BRINGING HOME THE BREAD.

Burlington Northern is America's number one grain hauler. In fact, last year we originated 19.8 million tons of grain. Which produced a staggering quantity of bread, bagels, and buns.

Burlington Northern has 13,000 cars suitable for hauling grain. Because of this capacity, we can haul the grain for a one pound loaf of bread more than 500 miles for less than a penny.

This year, Burlington Northern intends to add another 1,000 hopper cars to its fleet. So we can help bring home the bread with even greater efficiency.

But transporting grain is only a part of the Burlington Northern story. We're a *total* transportation company. With subsidiaries like BN Transport, our trucking firm, and Burlington Northern Air Freight Inc. In addition, BN has extensive natural resource holdings including timber, coal and minerals.

So no matter how you slice it, we're doing our part. In transporting basic food sources, timber for housing, and coal and minerals for much needed energy.

BURLINGTON NORTHERN

B

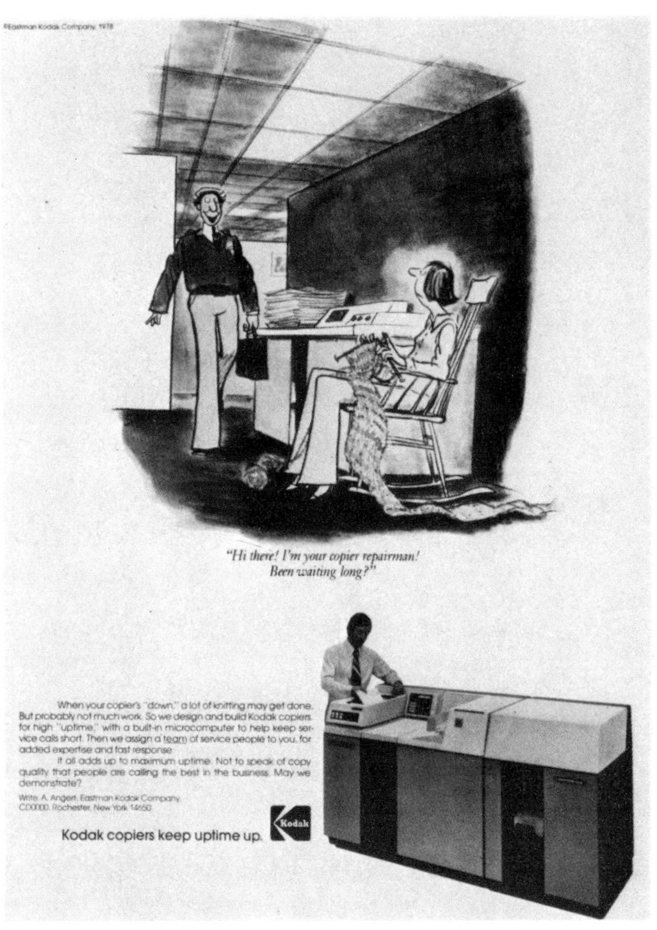

150 A **B**

149 A-B
Bruce Armstrong Art Director
Kerry Peterson Photographer
Barb Thornton, Brad Palm, Bob Heili, Steve Andrews Illustrators
Marvy! Advertising Photography, Inc. Studio
BBDO, Inc. Agency
Burlington Northern Client

150 A-E
Ozzie Hawkins Art Director
Charles Saxon Illustrator
Bill Irvine Copywriter
J. Walter Thompson Agency
Eastman Kodak Co.—Business Systems Client

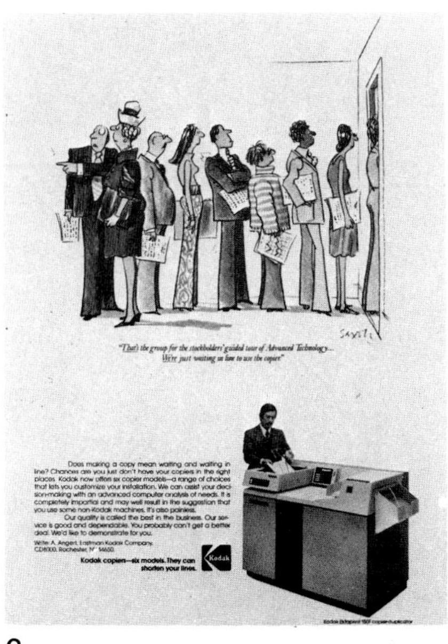

C

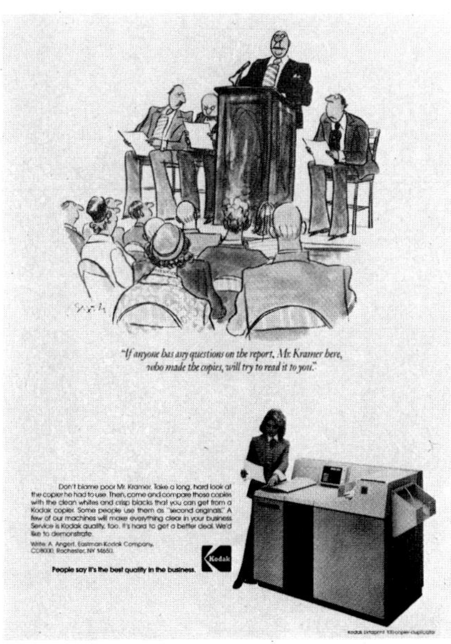

D

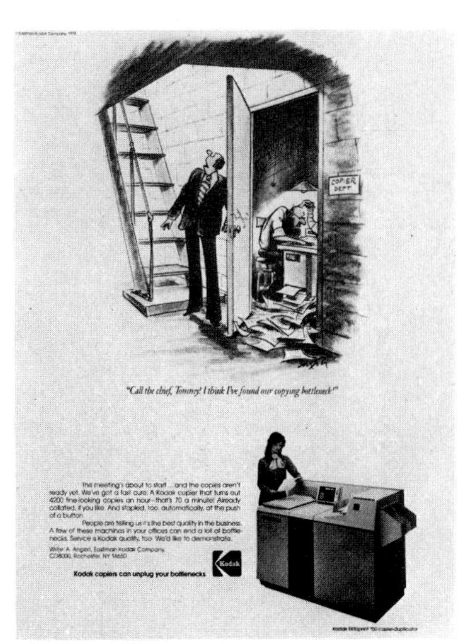

E

151 A

B

C

151 A-C
Doug Fisher Art Director
Mathew Brady Photographer
Lord, Sullivan & Yoder Agency
Nevamar Client

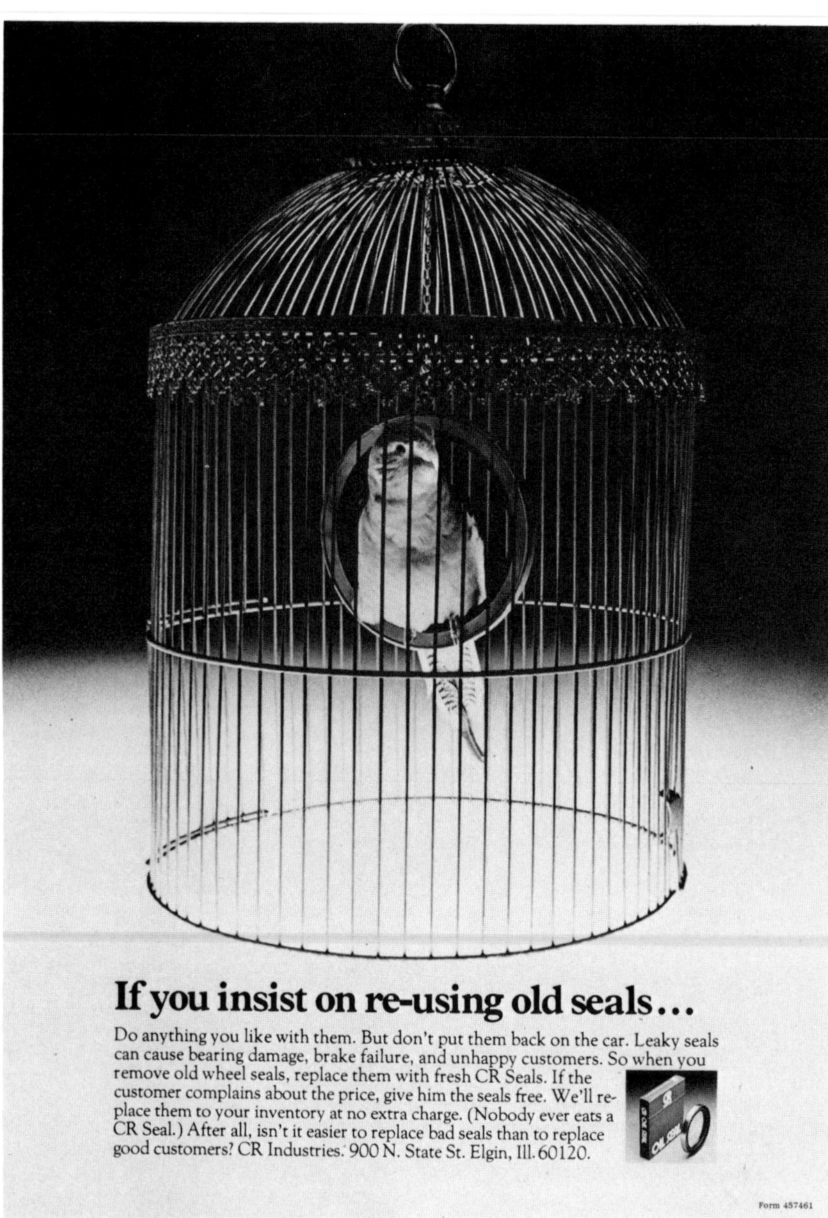

If you insist on re-using old seals...
Do anything you like with them. But don't put them back on the car. Leaky seals can cause bearing damage, brake failure, and unhappy customers. So when you remove old wheel seals, replace them with fresh CR Seals. If the customer complains about the price, give him the seals free. We'll replace them to your inventory at no extra charge. (Nobody ever eats a CR Seal.) After all, isn't it easier to replace bad seals than to replace good customers? CR Industries. 900 N. State St. Elgin, Ill. 60120.
Form 457461

152 A

B

C

152 A-C
Joe Giacalone Art Director
Michael Vollan Photographer
George Joseph & Associates, Inc. Studio
Brand Advertising, Inc. Agency
CR Industries Client

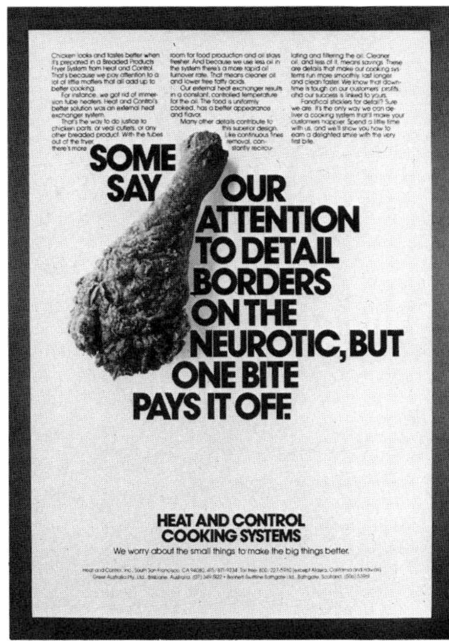

SOME SAY OUR ATTENTION TO DETAIL BORDERS ON THE NEUROTIC, BUT ONE BITE PAYS IT OFF.
HEAT AND CONTROL COOKING SYSTEMS
We worry about the small things to make the big things better.

THE MOST IMPORTANT THING WE'VE LEARNED IN 27 YEARS OF MAKING COOKING SYSTEMS: NITPICKING PAYS.

HEAT AND CONTROL COOKING SYSTEMS

We worry about the small things to make the big things better.

SHOP TALK. SHOP TALK. SHOP TALK. WE DRIVE OUR FAMILIES NUTS, BUT LOOK AT THE CONSISTENCY.
HEAT AND CONTROL COOKING SYSTEMS
We worry about the small things to make the big things better.

A B C

153 A-E
Debra Placzek Norby Art Director
Larry Kunkel Photographer
Fred Wickham Copywriter
Placzek & Haworth Design Studio
Bozell & Jacobs, Inc. Agency
Heat & Control Cooking Systems Client

OUR EXTREME FUSSINESS ACTUALLY BOTHERS SOME PEOPLE, BUT LOOK AT THE UNIFORMITY.

HEAT AND CONTROL COOKING SYSTEMS

We worry about the small things to make the big things better.

OK, WE ADMIT WE'RE PERFECTIONISTS, BUT LOOK HOW WE CONQUERED SHRINKAGE.

HEAT AND CONTROL COOKING SYSTEMS

We worry about the small things to make the big things better.

D E

154
Dieter F. Kaufmann Art Director
Adrian Jacobs Designer
Anderson Advertising Agency
Maison de Change Forexco Client

LA DOLCE LIRA
MILLE
Maison de Change Forexco Ltée

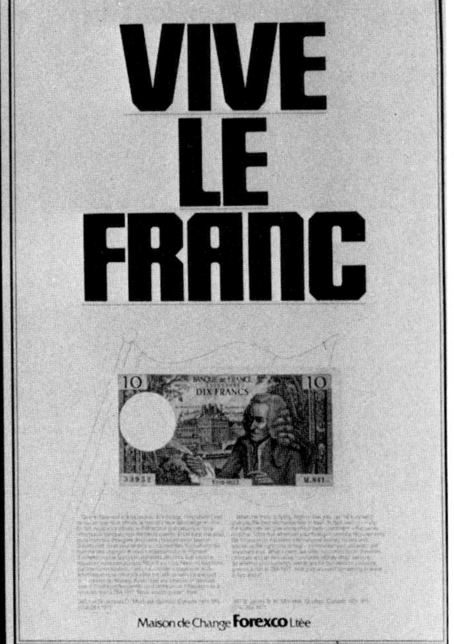

VIVE LE FRANC
DIX FRANCS
Maison de Change Forexco Ltée

A B C

"As an Industrial Engineer," says Kramer Weissenborn, *"my job at the Anheuser-Busch Williamsburg plant is to reduce costs, whether it be cans, beer, better use of people or more efficient use of fork lift trucks. We started out the plant with 23 trucks, using another gage and no lift interrupts. We had some problems with over-discharging and heating up of the bat-*

teries. We operate the trucks at maximum safe speed. The combination of safety and efficiency is important to keeping our plant operation at capacity. As a result, the battery could reach a discharge level too quickly and won't keep the fork lift going at the speed we want. The 933 lets us know when we're slowing up and we recharge as soon as we see the level going down. We've

got to keep the beer going out the door. The 933 is successful here. It's just a little dial on the truck that tells you how much juice you've got left. We've got good people here and they'll plan if we give them the opportunity to do it. Even new, inexperienced people who don't have a 'feel' can use the gage to tell them when they're near depletion. It's going to save

us some batteries. It's going to save money on the maintenance and the replacement of batteries. It's also a safety precaution for us and well worth the investment. When our expansion is completed in April 1980, we'll have twelve double-wide fork lifts in our plant, in addition to a large number of singles. They'll all have the 933 gage on them."

The CURTIS 933 "fuel gage"

The Curtis 933 is a "fuel" gage and battery controller for electric fork lift trucks. It displays continuously the state of charge of the battery, warns the operator of a low condition and eventually locks out the lift before any damage is done. Major plants throughout the world have found that the Curtis 933 lowers maintenance costs, extends battery life and saves energy costs. Contact us for complete information.

CURTIS

CURTIS INSTRUMENTS, INC.
200 Kisco Ave., Mt. Kisco, N.Y. 10549 • Tel. (914) 666-2971
P.O. Box 25, Northampton, England, NN40JF

A

"I don't mind beating the drum for the Curtis 933 'fuel gage,' it's been a very good thing for us," says Clarence Bauer, Maintenance Manager of the 2 million square foot J.C. Penney Catalog Distribution Center in Lenexa, Kansas. *"I know they're 99% accurate. We have facts and figures to prove that because we ran our own study here in the plant. The best*

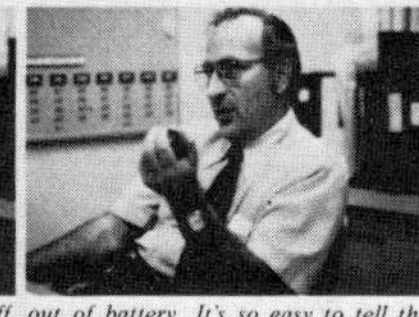

part about the 933 is that any man off the street can get on a fork lift truck and know at a glance when he's running out of battery. It's so easy to tell the operator, 'Look, when the needle goes into the yellow, watch it. When it goes into the red, bring it back in for a charge because you're going to lose your lift.' I just have to point to the gage and send

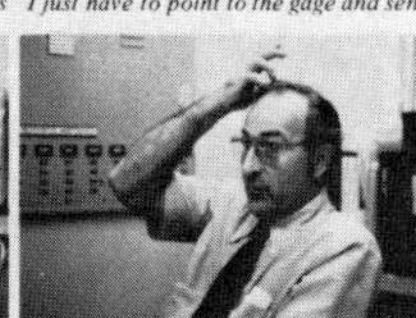

him on his way. I started out with about 100 material handling trucks. Fifty-five of them came in with the Curtis 933 fuel gage in them. We've only had one failure. Since then, we've replaced other units with the 933. It just makes sense to me to go with the unit with the best track record. Another important point is the ease of locating the 933 on the lift truck.

It fits right there in the open like a gas gage on your car, with no protrusions. It's flush mounted. I feel that Curtis has really come up with the answer. Batteries are expensive, and with the 933, you don't have to buy so many batteries. I have to say it's been a super tool in maintaining our equipment and I can't think of any other substitute."

The CURTIS 933 "fuel gage"

The Curtis 933 is a "fuel" gage and battery controller for electric fork lift trucks. It displays continuously the state of charge of the battery, warns the operator of a low condition and eventually locks out the lift before any damage is done. Major plants throughout the world have found that the Curtis 933 lowers maintenance costs, extends battery life and saves energy costs. Contact us for complete information.

CURTIS

CURTIS INSTRUMENTS, INC.
200 Kisco Ave., Mt. Kisco, N.Y. 10549 • Tel. (914) 666-2971
P.O. Box 25, Northampton, England, NN40JF

B

"Energy conservation is one of the vital factors at General Motors and Vauxhall Motors not only in Britain but in the whole of the world," says Bill Baines, General Supervisor of Plant Maintenance at the Vauxhall Motors/GM Luton plant in England. *"I am pleased, without a doubt, with the Curtis 933 unit because there is energy conservation in it and there is extended*

battery life in it. I have more than 6 million square feet here and 260 of my trucks are fitted with the 933. What we have noticed is a reduced amount of electrical breakdowns, and a reduced amount of traction motor burnouts and electrical circuitry in general. The 933 is a standard specification on all original equipment here. Material handling in my days has moved from

the man who was pushing a trolley with materials on it to the present day materials handling efficiency. I think it's advanced more than any other concept of industrial life in the last thirty years. This 933 instrument is the biggest innovation since the introduction of solid state controls on the trucks themselves. It closes the big gap on battery utilizatión. Batteries are my life

blood. I'm looking for economics on internal transport. I would like to say that looking through the whole of the concept of traction battery maintenance, we at Vauxhall/GM are as efficient or possibly more efficient than 99% of the battery users in the country. With the Curtis fitted, we can actually get more efficiency. We are really happy with the instrumentation."

The CURTIS 933 "fuel gage"

The Curtis 933 is a "fuel" gage and battery controller for electric fork lift trucks. It displays continuously the state of charge of the battery, warns the operator of a low condition and eventually locks out the lift before any damage is done. Major plants throughout the world have found that the Curtis 933 lowers maintenance costs, extends battery life and saves energy costs. Contact us for complete information.

CURTIS

CURTIS INSTRUMENTS, INC.
200 Kisco Ave., Mt. Kisco, N.Y. 10549 • Tel. (914) 666-2971
P.O. Box 25, Northampton, England, NN40JF

C

"The Curtis 933 has been fantastic as far as we're concerned," says Joe Lacasse, Warehouse Manager of Pfizer's Distribution Center in Atlanta, Georgia. *"Our greatest saving has been in the energy area. Before we installed the 933 on our fork lift trucks, we hooked up our lift trucks on a daily basis. We no longer do this. As a matter of fact, some of our trucks are*

being hooked up only twice a week. You know, if you're hooking up your fork lifts every night, whether they need it or not, that's wasting power. We'll be saving in the battery area too. I think you get better battery usage if you discharge it to the recommended level rather than going all the way down to the bottom or only discharging it 40%-50% and then charging

it back up again. The 933 gage makes it easy for us to discharge the batteries efficiently, and we feel this is a real savings. It's not a hit or miss type of operation. In a Corporate Improvement Plan report I submitted recently, I was able to show substantial dollar savings resulting from the use of the Curtis 933. The name of the game today is energy savings. We've

got a new sit-down dock-type vehicle coming in and we've ordered it with the 933 on it. I must be sold on the unit if I'm specifying it for our new trucks as well. Our lift drivers depend on the gage—they really use it to know what's happening with their batteries and we can keep track of the status of our lifts. I'm really willing to say the unit is good, because it is."

The CURTIS 933 "fuel gage"

The Curtis 933 is a "fuel" gage and battery controller for electric fork lift trucks. It displays continuously the state of charge of the battery, warns the operator of a low condition and eventually locks out the lift before any damage is done. Major plants throughout the world have found that the Curtis 933 lowers maintenance costs, extends battery life and saves energy costs. Contact us for complete information.

CURTIS

CURTIS INSTRUMENTS, INC.
200 Kisco Ave., Mt. Kisco, N.Y. 10549 • Tel. (914) 666-2971
P.O. Box 25, Northampton, England, NN40JF

D

155 A-D
Marc Dorian Art Director
Gail M. Ross Photographer
Marc Dorian, Inc. Agency
Curtis Instruments, Inc. Client

A

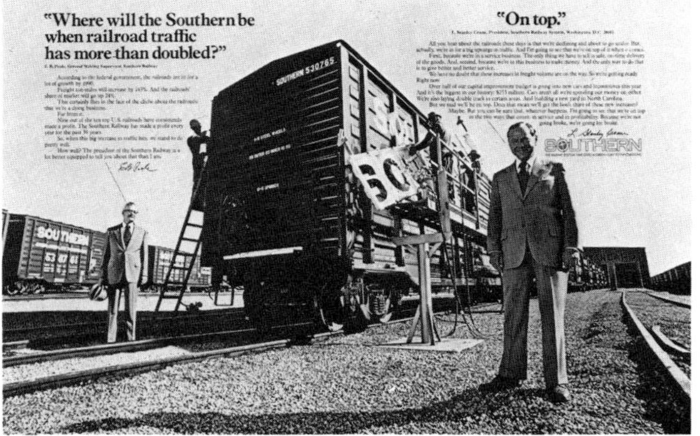

B

C

156 A-C
Herm Siegel Art Director
Carroll Seghers II, John Zoiner Photographers
Cunningham & Walsh, Inc. Agency
Southern Railway System Client

157
Vince Verrecchio Art Director
Pete Bastiansen Illustrator
Kamstra Communications, Inc. Agency
Neenah Division, Kimberly-Clark Client

158 A-C
Mike Rosen Art Director
Charles Gold Photographer
Mike Rosen, Bob Goetz Designers
Hammond Farrell Inc. Agency
General Electric Client

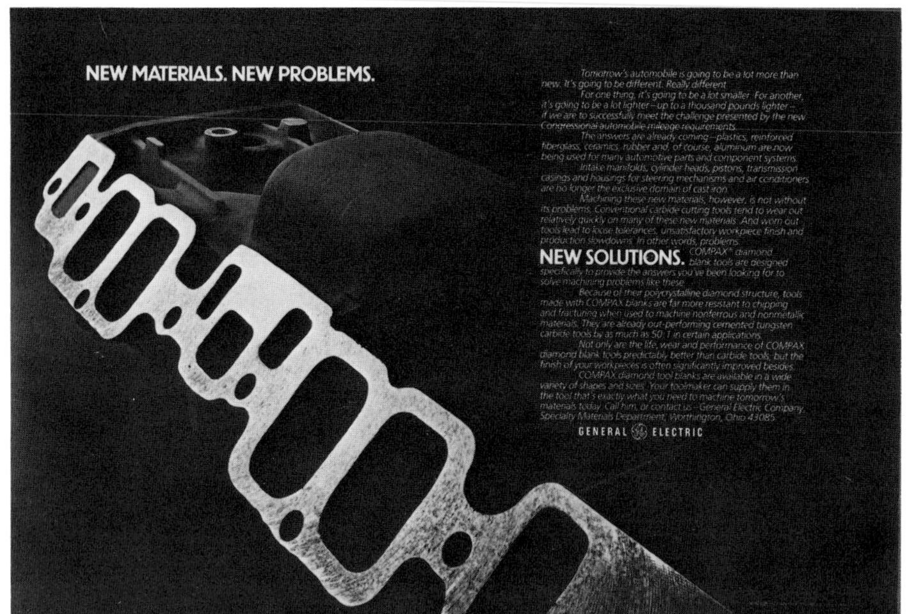

158 A

B

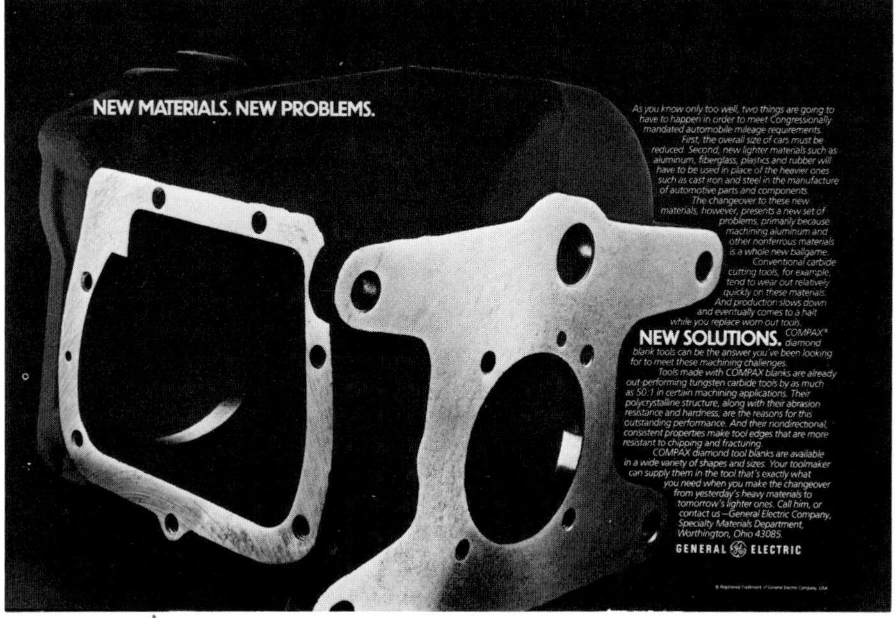

C

159 A-C
James Wilkins Art Director
Andy Wages, John Cook, Don Trousdell Illustrators
William F. Finn & Associates, Inc. Agency
IMCO Services Client

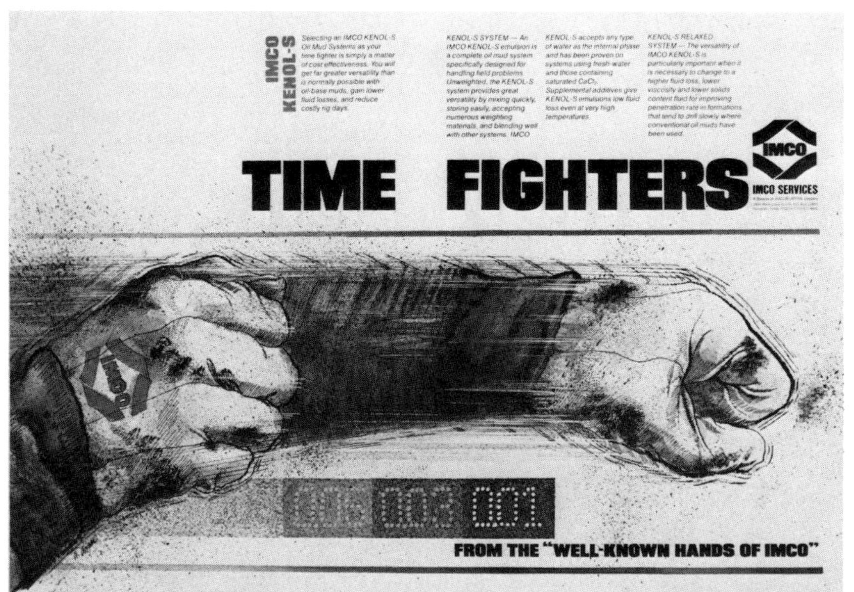

159 A

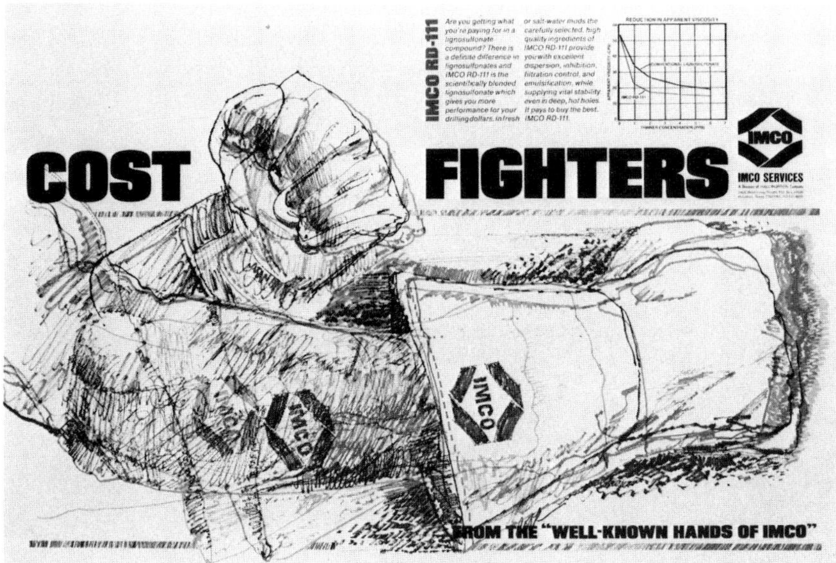

B

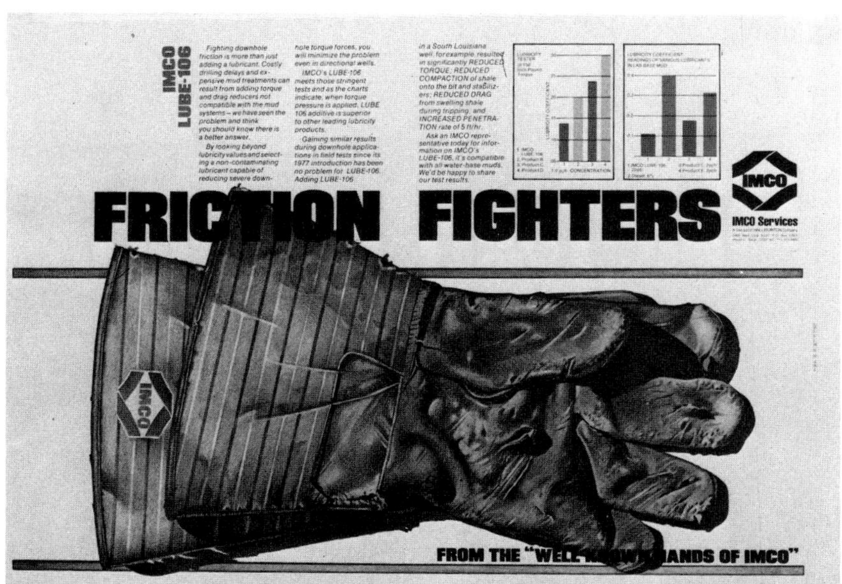

C

160 A

B

C

160 A-C
Charles Fillhardt Art Director
Rudy Legname Photographer
Bergthold, Fillhardt & Wright Agency
Memorex Corporation Client

Posters

161
David Rushlow, Bill Nelson Art Directors
Arthur Fox Photographer
Group 3 Agency
Piper Aircraft Corporation Client

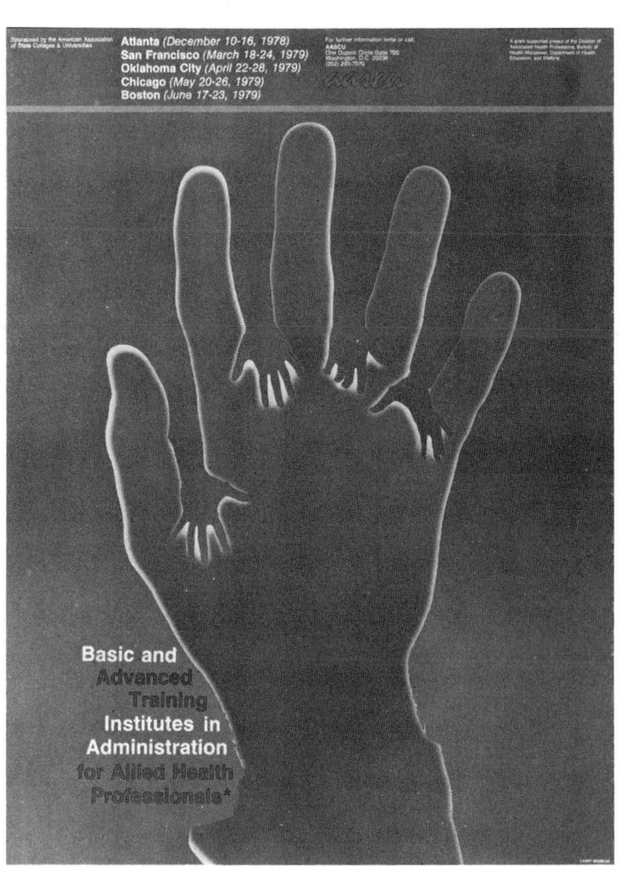

163
Lanny Sommese Art Director
Lanny Sommese Design Studio
Commercial Printing Production House
American Association of State Colleges & Universities Client

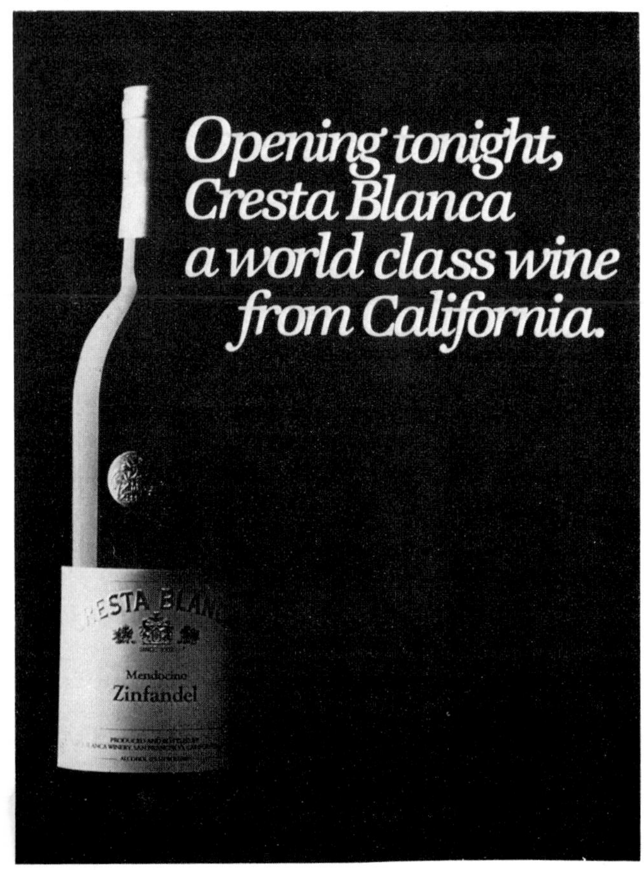

162
Dennis Thompson Art Director
Peter Thompson Photographer
Coming Attractions Agency
Cresta Blanca Winery Client

164
Sky Underwood, Susan Johnson Art Directors
Gordon Munro Photographer
Susan Johnson Designer
Danskin, Inc. Client

DANSKINS ARE NOT JUST FOR DANCING

A
dillar, a dollar, a ten o'clock scholar,
You're really not doing so fine;
The first registration has come and gone
So please make the second on time!
D
on't Be Dilatory.
Second Priority Registration
Winter Semester Deadline:
November 22nd.

A

M
ary, Mary, quite contrary,
How did your payment go?
Did you shell out on time,
Avoiding the fine,
Or do you have greenbacks to blow?
W
hy be contrary?
Avoid the $20 late fee.
Winter Semester Tuition
Deadline December 21st.

B

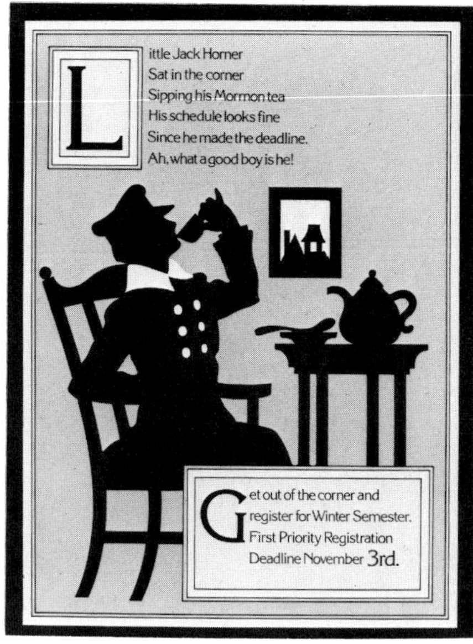
L
ittle Jack Horner
Sat in the corner
Sipping his Mormon tea
His schedule looks fine
Since he made the deadline.
Ah, what a good boy is he!
G
et out of the corner and
register for Winter Semester.
First Priority Registration
Deadline November 3rd.

C

165 A-C
McRay Magleby Art Director
Graphic Communications Agency
Brigham Young University Client

A Wedding

Released by 20th Century-Fox
Produced by Robert Altman
Directed by Robert Altman
Starring Carol Burnett, Lillian Gish, Geraldine Chaplin,
Mia Farrow, Lauren Hutton, Desi Arnaz Jr.,
Vittorio Gassman, Amy Stryker, Howard Duff
Color rated PG
Films Incorporated
"One of Altman's best films, at once one of his funniest and one of
his darkest visions of a crazy, contradictory America."
—Jack Kroll, Newsweek

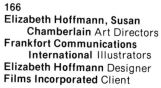

166
Elizabeth Hoffmann, Susan Chamberlain Art Directors
Frankfort Communications International Illustrators
Elizabeth Hoffmann Designer
Films Incorporated Client

St. Nicholas' Theater Company Presents
2851 North Halsted
Reservations 281-1202
little
Eyolf
Written By Henrik Ibsen
Directed By Steven Schachter
November 10—December 24

167
Peter Crockett Art Director
Burson-Marsteller/Design Group Agency
St. Nicholas Theater Client

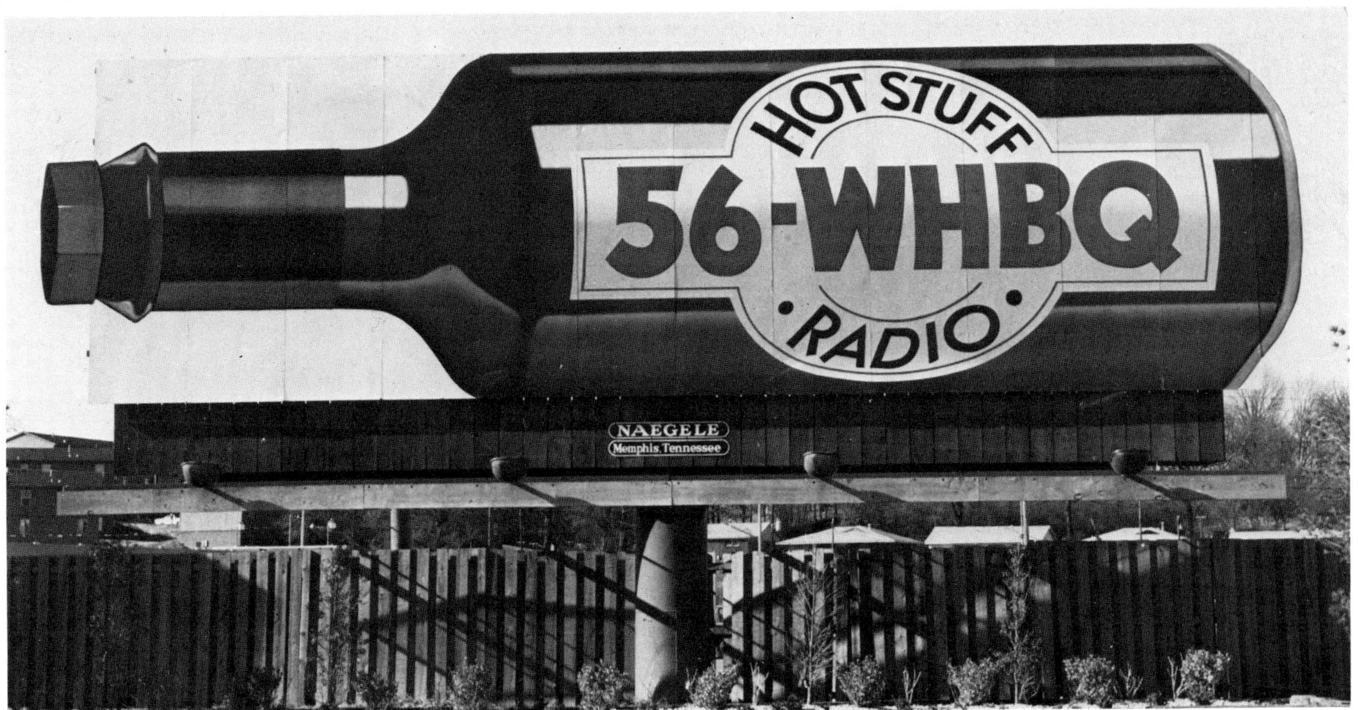

168
Bob Schiffer Art Director
John Boatright Illustrator
John Malmo Advertising Agency
WHBQ Radio Client

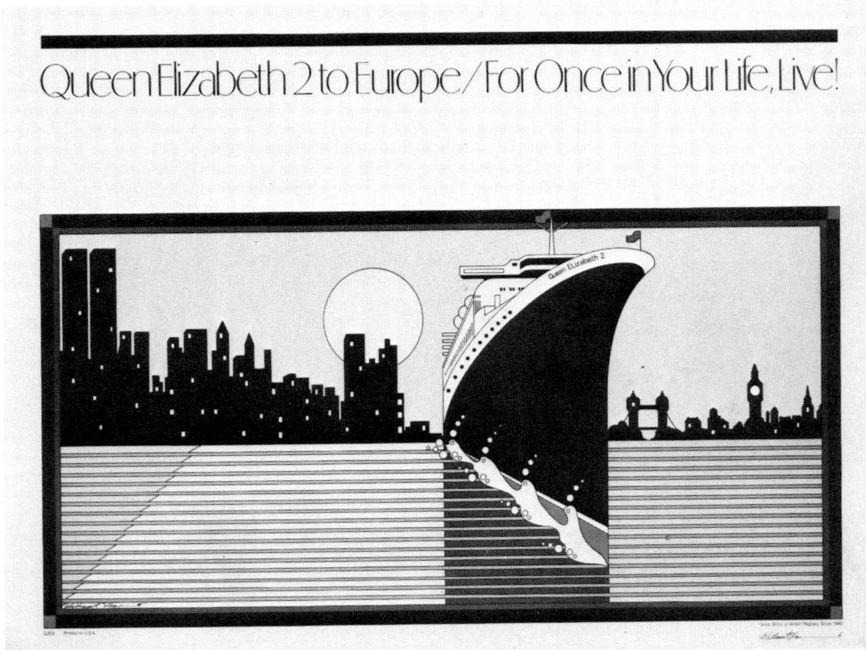

169
William A. Sloan Art Director
Apple Design, Inc. Studio
Cunard Ltd. Client

170
Ron Bergner Art Director
Tom O'Brien Photographer
Miriam Slater Illustrator
Ron Bergner & Assoc. Agency
Asahi Beer Client

171
Yukiko Inuzuka Art Director
Masami Hagiwara Photographer
Hisao Takehana Designer
CDP Japan Limited Advertising Agency
Harveys of Bristol Ltd. Client

172
Herb Lubalin Art Director
Heather Cooper Illustrator
Burns, Cooper, Hynes Limited Studio
Aspen Design Conference Client

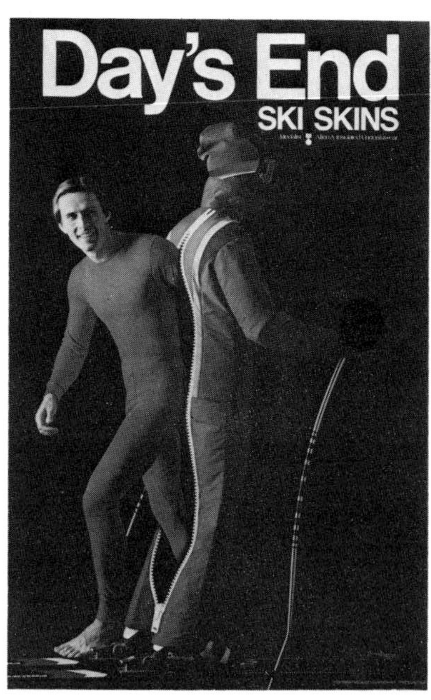

173
Doug Fisher Art Director
Pringle-Booth Photographers
Lord, Sullivan & Yoder Agency
Allen-A Client

174
Lisa Paperno Art Director
David Alexander Photographer
Graphitti Studio
GRT/Shadybrook Records Client

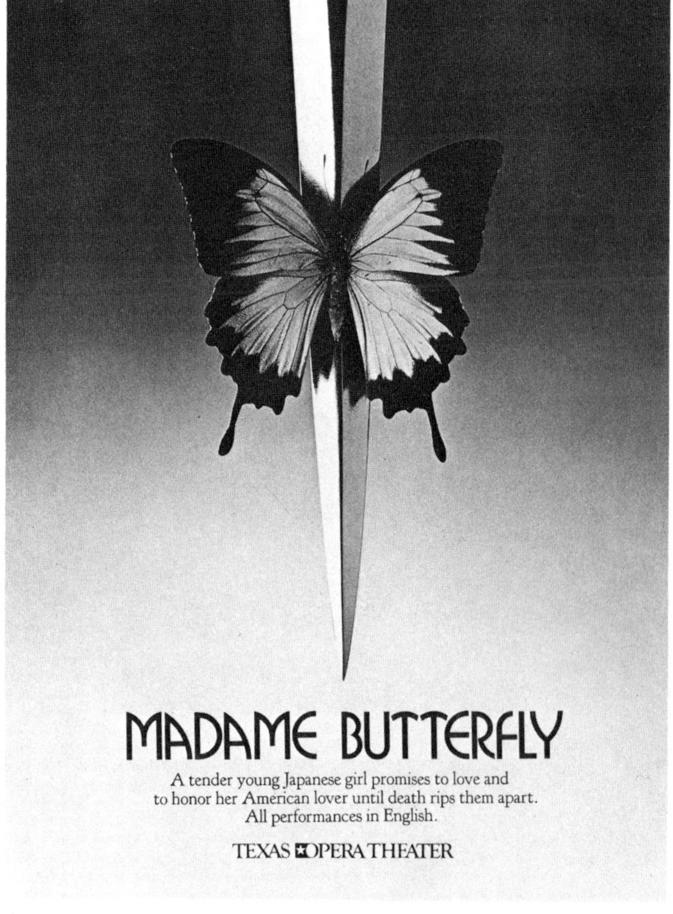

175
Dave Jenkins Art Director
John Katz Photographer
Ogilvy & Mather Agency
Texas Opera Theatre Client

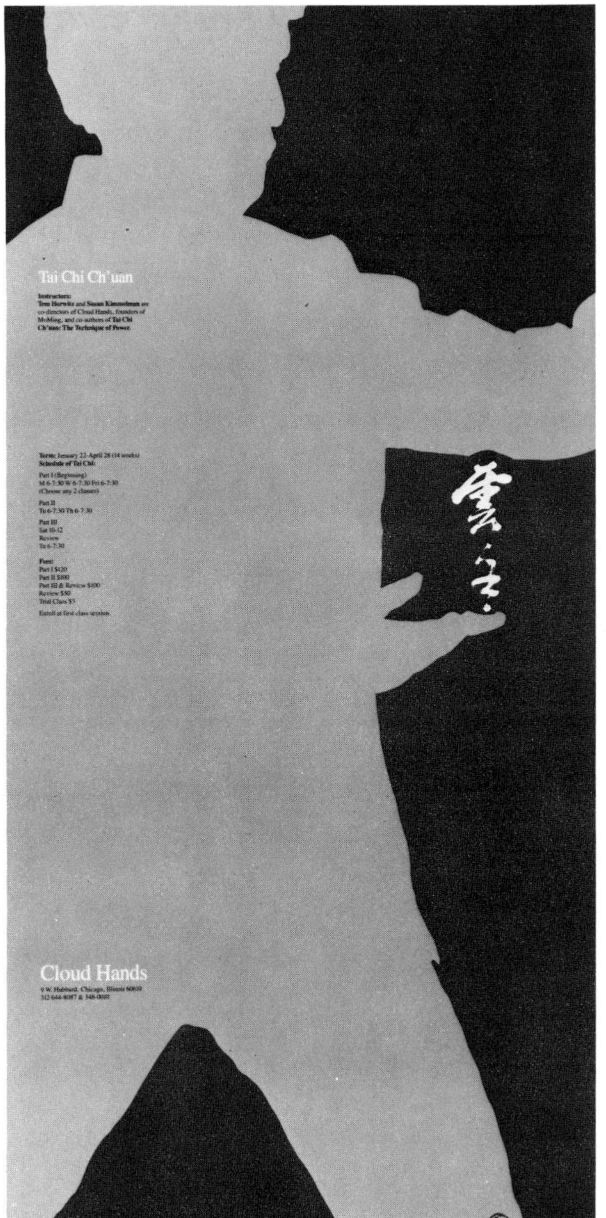

177

176
Joseph M. Essex Art Director
Burson-Marsteller / Design Group Agency
Cloud Hands Client

177
Richard Wilde Art Director
Nancy Ward, Laura Goodman, Susan Spivack Masks
Ken Ambrose Photographer
Diane Addesso Designer
Visual Arts Press Production House
School of Visual Arts Client

178
Mickey Stuart, Tom Henvey Art Directors
Michael Morris Photographer
Abigail Stewart Model
Rita Barnard Designer
USA Film Festival Client

179
Richard Sowa Art Director
Frank Maresca Photographer
Optyl Corp. Client

180
Douglas Hoppe Stone Art Director
George Jurij Zebot Illustrator
Douglas Stone & Associates Agency
AMF-Voit Client

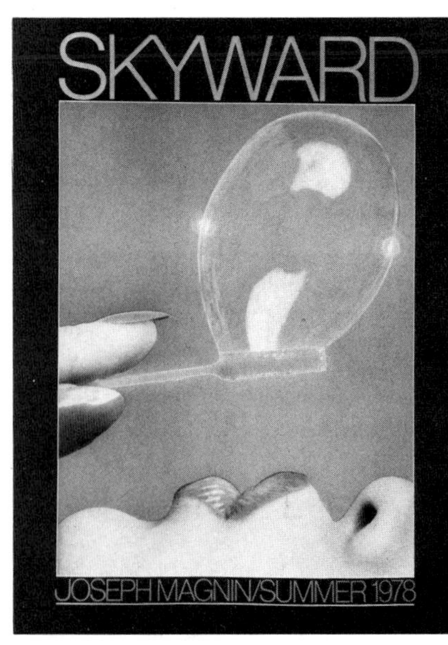

181
Don Clark Art Director
Robert Blakeman Photographer
Joel Ely Copywriter
Joseph Magnin Client

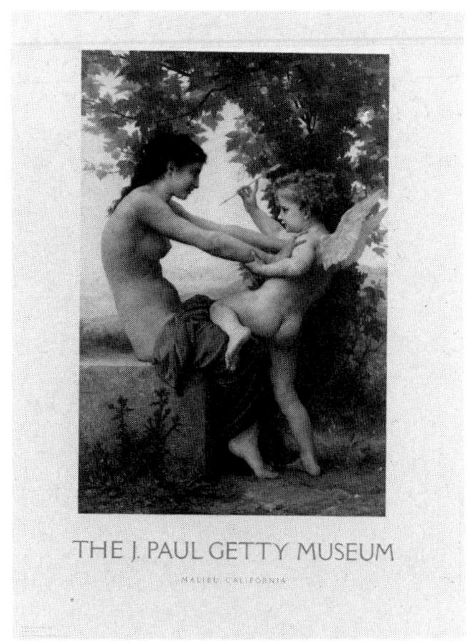

182
John Coy Art Director
Donald Hull Photographer
John Coy, Maryl Lavelle Designers
John Coy Design Agency
The J. Paul Getty Museum Client

183
Phil Carroll Art Director
Fantasy Records Client

192
Rick Cowan, Rick Fisher Art Directors
Cockfield Brown & Company Agency
Air Canada Client

193
David A. Knox Art Director
Bureau of Publications Agency
University Theatre, Arizona State University Client

194
John Follis Art Director
Ignacio Gomez Illustrator
Elizabeth Kooker, Elizabeth Baird Designers
John Follis & Associates Agency
Center Theatre Group/Mark Taper Forum Client

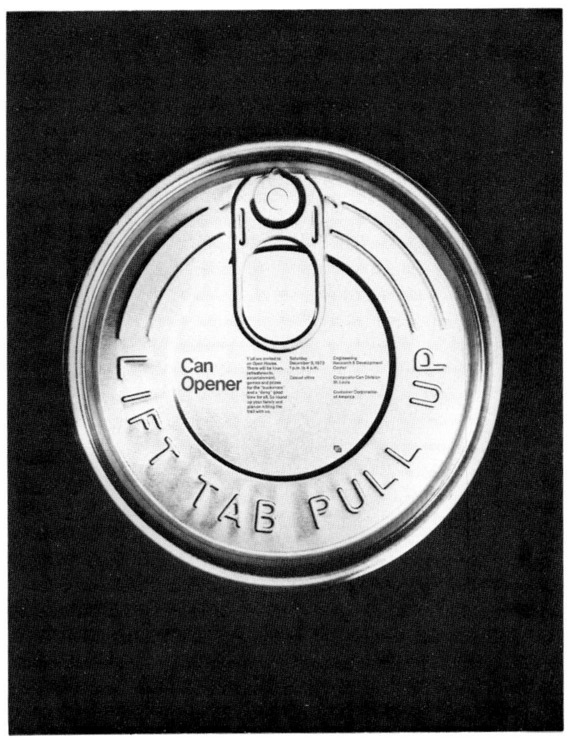

195
Jeff Barnes Art Director
Container Corporation of America Client

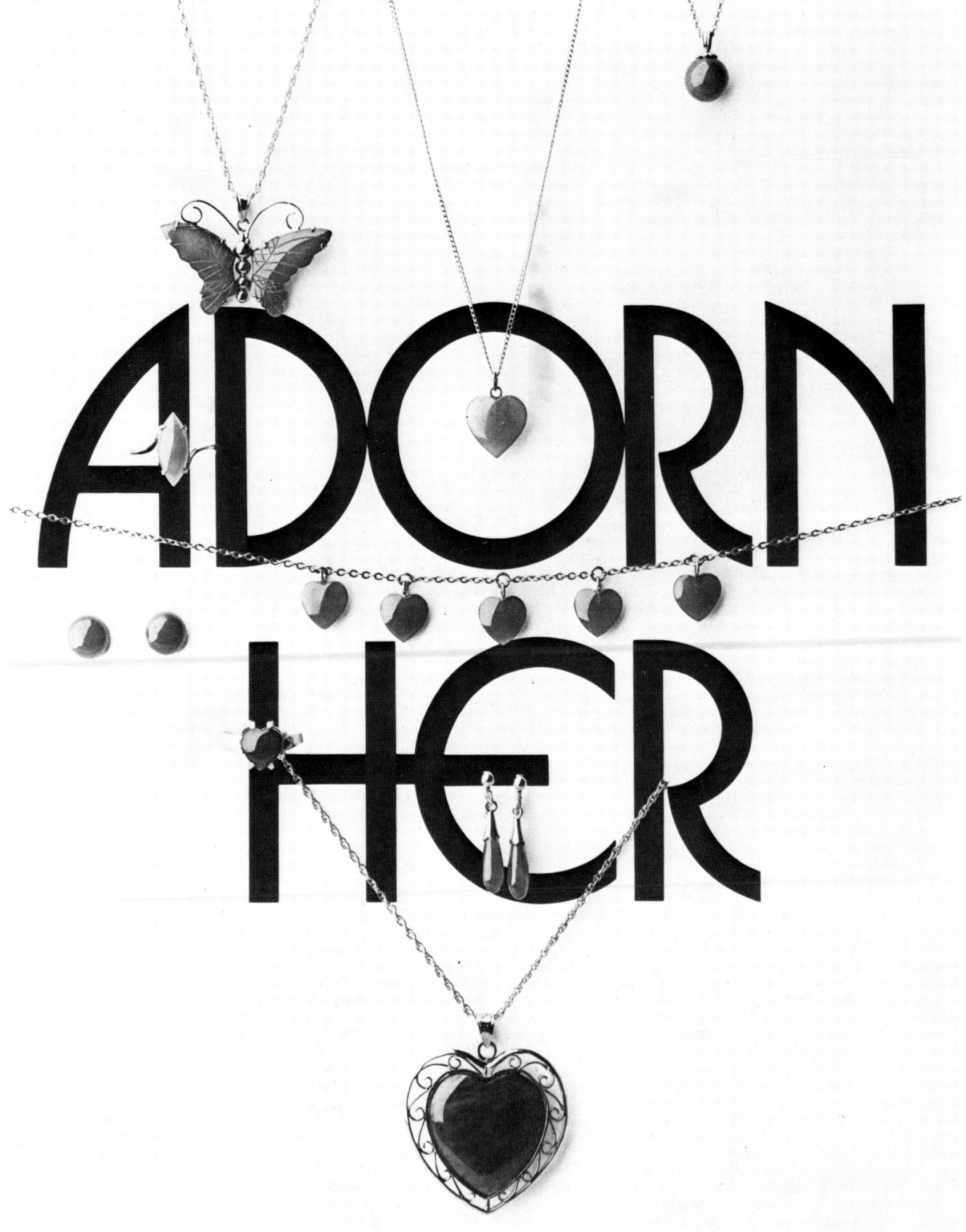

191
Michael Somers Art Director
Jamie Cook Photographer
John Malmo Advertising Agency
Dobbs House Client

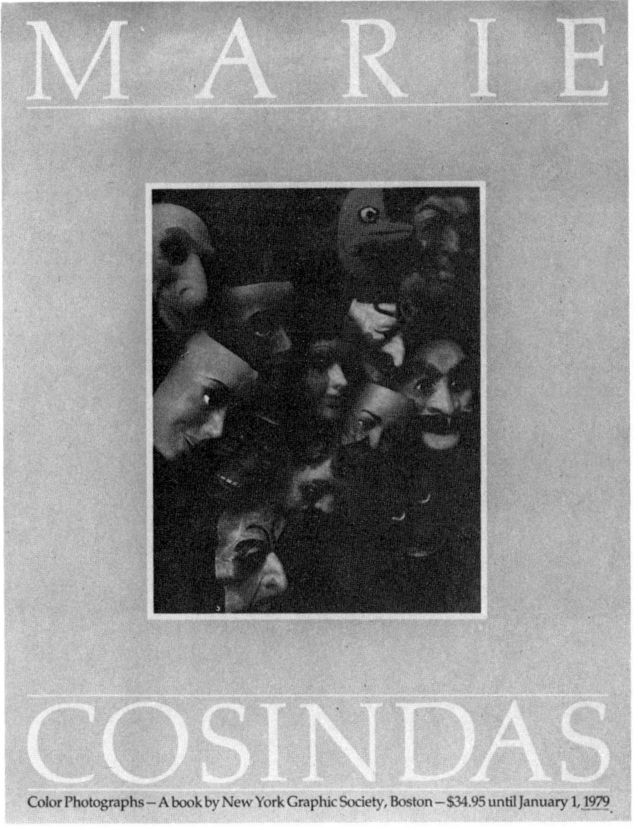

MARIE
COSINDAS
Color Photographs – A book by New York Graphic Society, Boston – $34.95 until January 1, 1979

188

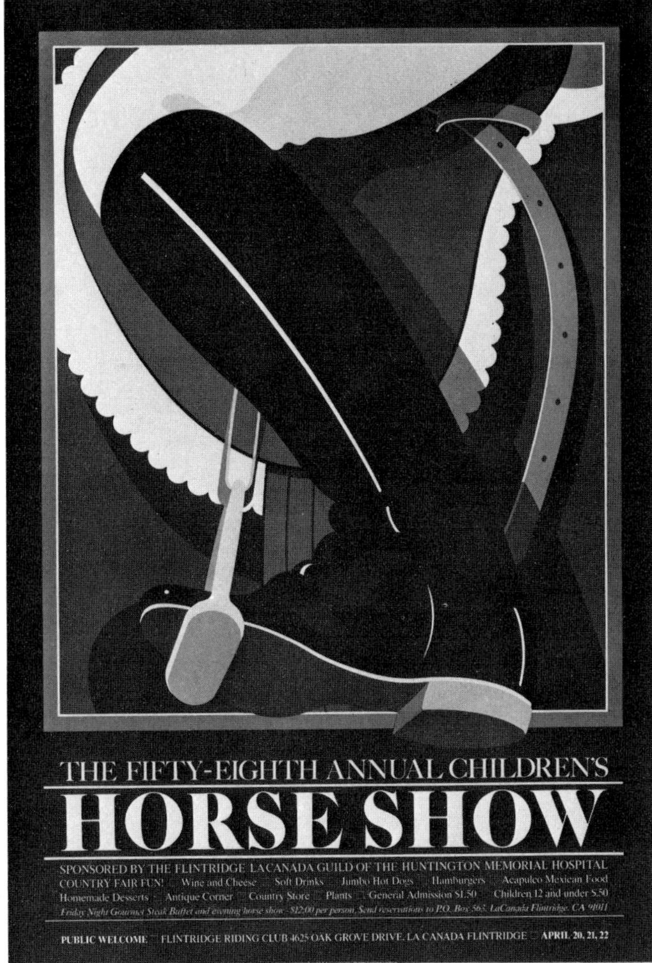

THE FIFTY-EIGHTH ANNUAL CHILDREN'S
HORSE SHOW
SPONSORED BY THE FLINTRIDGE LACANADA GUILD OF THE HUNTINGTON MEMORIAL HOSPITAL
COUNTRY FAIR FUN! Wine and Cheese Soft Drinks Jumbo Hot Dogs Hamburgers Acapulco Mexican Food
Homemade Desserts Antique Corner Country Store Plants General Admission $1.50 Children 12 and under $.50
PUBLIC WELCOME FLINTRIDGE RIDING CLUB 4625 OAK GROVE DRIVE, LA CANADA FLINTRIDGE APRIL 20, 21, 22

189

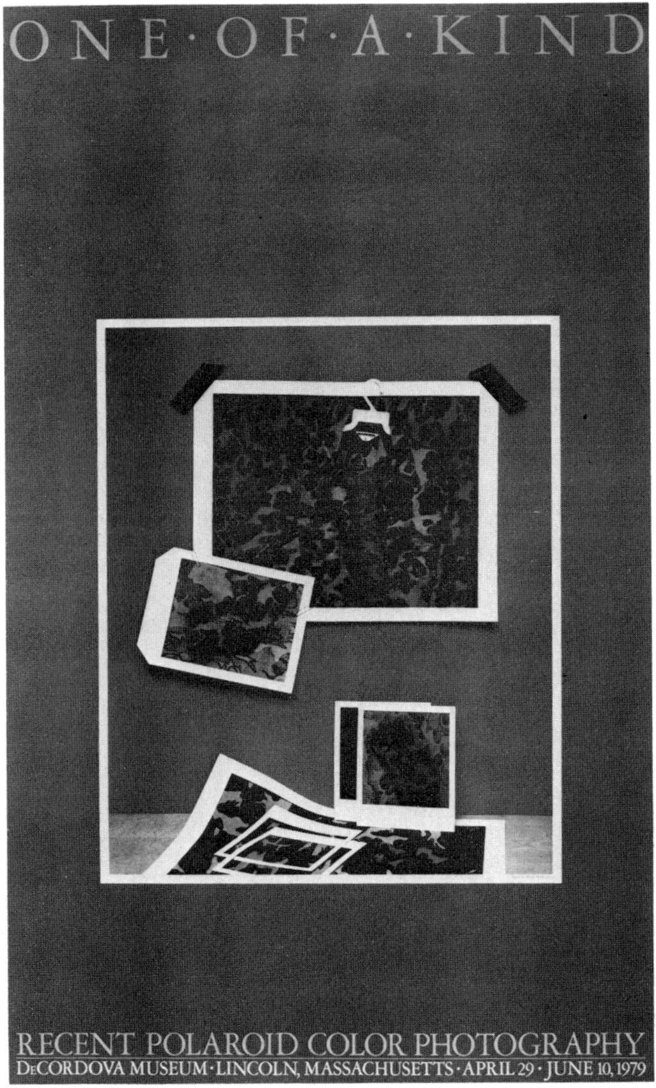

ONE·OF·A·KIND
RECENT POLAROID COLOR PHOTOGRAPHY
DeCORDOVA MUSEUM·LINCOLN, MASSACHUSETTS·APRIL 29·JUNE 10, 1979

188
Roy Alan Hughes Art Director
Marie Cosindas, Polaroid Corporation
Clients

189
Dennis S. Juett Art Director
Jeff Lawson Illustrator
Dennis S. Juett & Associates, Inc.
Agency
Elintridge La Canada Guild of the Huntington Memorial Hospital
Client

190
Victor Cevoli Art Director
Michael Bishop Photographer
Acme Printing Production House
Polaroid Corporation Client

186
Andy Malcolm, George Pastic Art Directors
National Tap Dance Company of Canada Client

184
John C. Jay Art Director
Shig Ikeda Photographer
Lanny Udell Copywriter
Charles Banuchi Designer
Bloomingdale's Advertising Dept Agency
Bloomingdale's Client

185
Len Favara, Peter Rogers Art Directors
Vincent Petragnani Illustrator
Peter Rogers Associates Agency
Salvatore Ferragamo Client

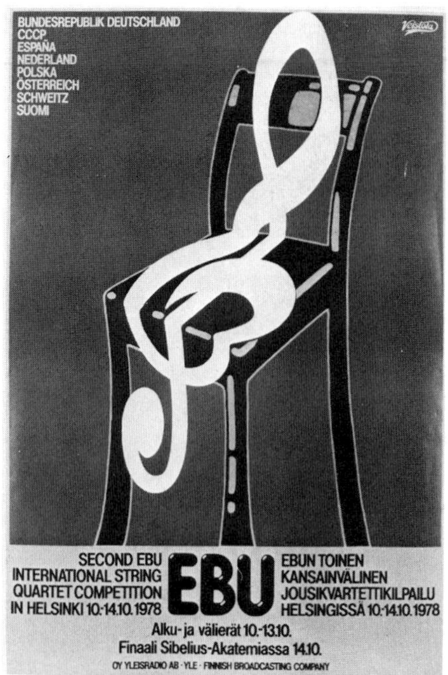

187
Jukka Veistola Art Director
Varis-Poteri-Veistola Agency
Finnish Broadcasting Company Client

Art-Director: BARBARA STICHER-DIBUE
ROBERT DIBUÉ
photographs people
1185 Avenue of the Americas
New York N.Y. 10036
Tel. (212) 490-0486
Frankfurt (0611) 616158

196
Barbara Sticher Dibue Art Director
Robert Dibue Photographer
Robert Dibue Associates Client

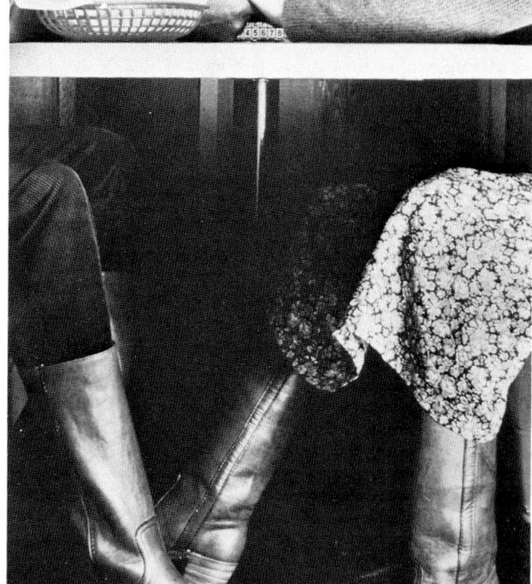

A

B

197 A-B
Ken Kimura, Ethan Revsin Art Directors
Ethan Revsin Copywriter
Lee King & Partners Agency
Frye Shoe Co. Client

YOU'RE INVITED TO BE IN THE RIGHT PLACE AT THE RIGHT TIME.

THE RIGHT PLACE:
NEW YORK COLISEUM.
THE RIGHT TIME:
MARCH 18-21, 1979.

The historic news: New York is the site and March 18-21 is the date for the first International Fur Fair ever to be held in America.

It will be the right time because it will be the season's first Fur Fair...your first opportunity to see and study everything from raw skins to finished products that exemplify the finest craftsmanship and styling in the world of fashion.

And it will be the right place, for as the United States' first city of glamour and home of the famed "Fur District," New York is the most appropriate host for America's first International Fur Fair.

Over 125 exhibitors from the U.S. and these 16 other countries will be represented: Argentina, Australia, Belgium, Brazil, Canada, England, Finland, France, West Germany, Greece, Israel, Italy, New Zealand, Spain, Sweden, and the U.S.S.R.

Make plans now to be there. In Europe, make arrangements and reservations through Andre Simon, 11 F.G. Poissonniere, 75009 Paris. For further information please contact American International Fur Fair, Inc., 855 Avenue of the Americas, New York, N.Y. 10001. Telephone: 212-564-5133. Telex: 62638. Cable: AMFURINDU New York.

The premiere Fur Fair of the 1979 season will also be America's inaugural show. A spectacular combination of "firsts," you'll have to agree.

Be there when history is made.

American International Fur Fair.
Be there when history is made.

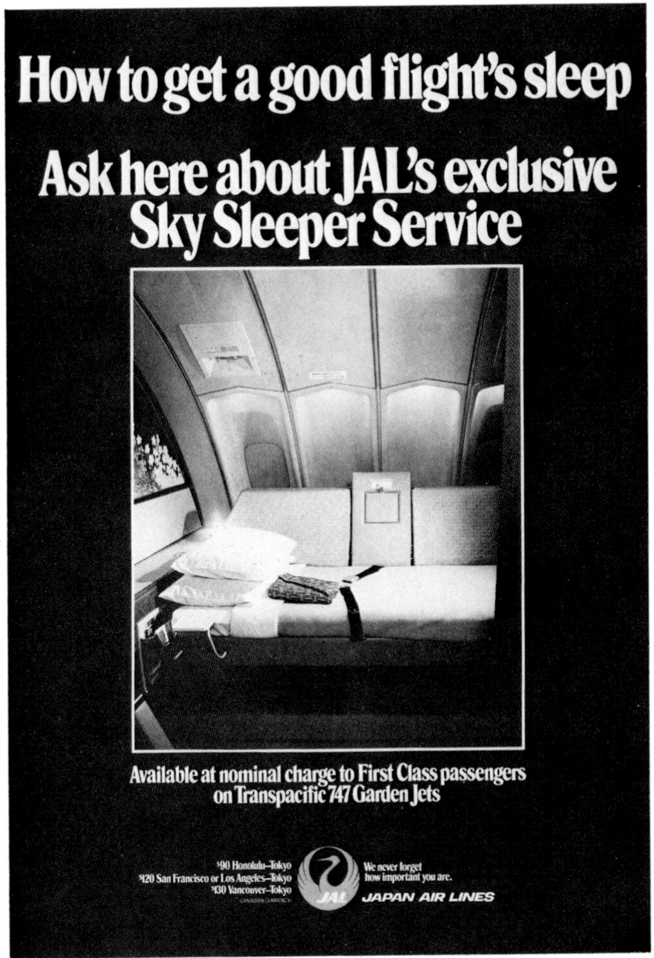

How to get a good flight's sleep
Ask here about JAL's exclusive Sky Sleeper Service
Available at nominal charge to First Class passengers on Transpacific 747 Garden Jets
$90 Honolulu–Tokyo
$120 San Francisco or Los Angeles–Tokyo
$130 Vancouver–Tokyo
JAL
We never forget how important you are.
JAPAN AIR LINES

199
Katsuji Asada Art Director
Ichio Hishitani Photographer
Ketchum New York Agency
Japan Air Lines Client

WHEN YOU WANT TO LOOK GOOD ON PAPER
MOHAWK

200
Robert Paige, Richard Loomis Art Directors
Wilson McLean Illustrator
Evans Garber & Paige Agency
Mohawk Paper Mills, Inc. Client

201
Jose Zaragoza Art Director
Duailibi, Petit, Zaragoza Propaganda Agency
Repro Photo Engravings Client

198
George Moy Art Director
Richard Rosenblum Illustrator
Leber-Katz Partners Agency
American Fur Industry Client

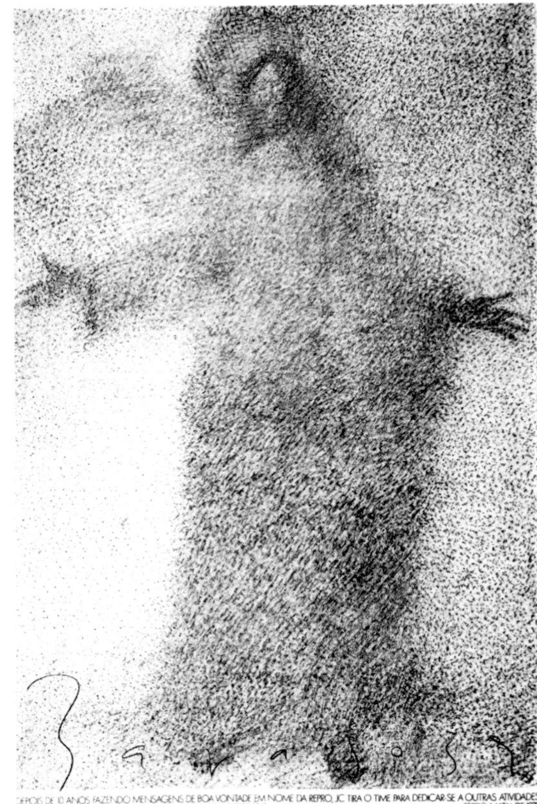

201

Annual Reports

202
Robert Meyer Art Director
Ted Kawalerski Photographer
Gannett Co. Inc. Client

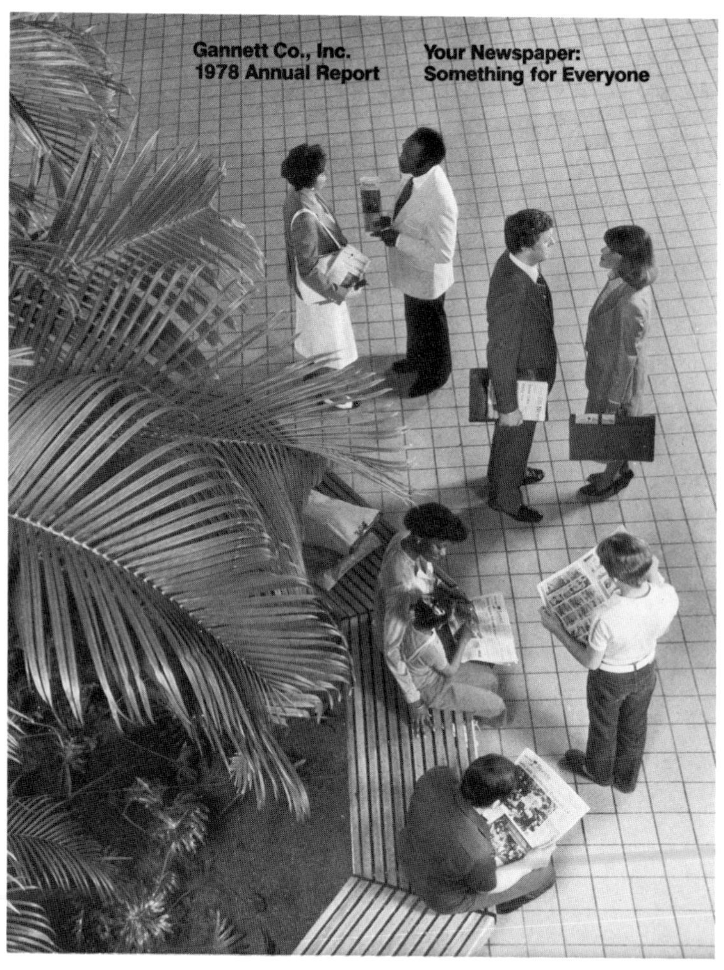

203
Ronald Rampley Art Director
David Barnes, Jon Brenneis Photographers
Linda Comb Illustrator
Logan, Carey + Rehag Agency
Dean Witter Reynolds Organization, Inc. Client

(l. to r.) Robert W. Swinarton, Robert M. Gardiner

most sophisticated in the industry and provides a daily detailed listing of the clients' positions, equity and other required information. This report is transmitted to the client's branch office each day.

UNIT TRUSTS

Unit investment trusts have become increasingly popular with investors and we offer more different trust funds than any other firm in the industry. Dean Witter Reynolds co-sponsors municipal and corporate income funds, both long and intermediate term, corporate preferred funds, corporate certificates of deposit funds, GNMA funds, and regional long-term municipal funds in three states. In addition, we are sole sponsor of the Dean Witter Reynolds Tax-Exempt Trust, both long and intermediate term. A total of 51 issues of these twelve different funds generated $360 million in sales during the first eight months of calendar 1978.

In addition, the GNMA Department is responsible for the sale of mortgage backed securities. This includes Government National Mortgage Association, Federal Home Loan Mortgage Corp. and pools of conventional mortgages. We have a growing participation in the public and private offering of these securities.

INTERNATIONAL

As a result of the merger, Dean Witter Reynolds has strengthened its position in the international markets. We now have ten sales offices, two each in Canada, Germany, Switzerland and the United Kingdom, and one each in Italy and the Netherlands. In addition, there is the Corporate Finance office in Paris and the Research office in Tokyo.

RESEARCH

The Research Department provides useful and pertinent investment information, on a timely basis, to a wide range of clients. The form this investment information takes varies according to the particular requirements of the user—retail investors, domestic institutional clients, international clients, and the Corporate Finance Department.

During the past year, the effectiveness of our research effort has continued to improve as measured by a number of objective surveys conducted among banks, insurance companies and other professional money management organizations. These rankings indicate that a growing number of institutions now consider Dean Witter Reynolds among their preferred sources of investment advice. The quality and competitiveness of the research effort has been enhanced by key additions to our analytical staff, which now has 39 professionals located domestically in New York and San Francisco, and overseas in Tokyo. Included are two economists, 23 fundamentalists who specialize in 28 major industry groups, seven special situations/generalists, one of whom covers corporate clients, two analysts covering foreign securities, and five technical/COMPARE analysts.

The work of the Research Department is directed toward developing general investment advice as well as specific stock recommendations. The risk of an investment opportunity is just as important as estimating the

A

AIRFREIGHT

Flying Tigers Revenue and Earnings Reach New Highs

In late 1974 Flying Tigers began adding 747 jetfreighters to improve and expand its international scheduled airfreight services and capacity. Since then scheduled service frequencies have been increased substantially, routes have been extended and international cargo capacity has been increased over 94 percent.

In the United States, air cargo deregulation became effective in January, 1978, and Flying Tiger Line moved swiftly to take advantage of its opportunities. We embarked on a five-year program to expand our route structure to all of the nation's key domestic markets.

In 1978, Flying Tigers introduced service to eight more cities in the United States as well as to Singapore. These new services increased our coverage to a total of 18 cities in the United States and nine in the Pacific.

Clearly established as the world's largest airfreight carrier, Flying Tiger Line logged an all-time high of 1.2 billion airfreight revenue ton miles in 1978, up 38 percent from 1977.

The Flying Tiger Line	1974**	1975**	1976**	1977**	1978

Operating Review

Scheduled Airfreight

Nearly 45 percent of the 1.4 million pounds of seafood Flying Tigers transported last year was fresh salmon from Anchorage to Seattle. At right, auto components bound for the West Coast are loaded onto a 747 jet freighter in Detroit.

B

204 A-B
Gretchin Groot Art Director
Jay Freis Photographer
Groot Organization Agency
Tiger International Client

205
Al Corchia Art Director
Stanley Seligson Photographer
Al Corchia, Ellen Woliner Designers
Al Corchia, Inc. Agency
Public Securities Association Client

206
Nathan Felde, Julius Friedman Art Directors
Jerry Poynter Photographer
Implement, Ltd. Studio
Texas Gas Transmission Corp. Client

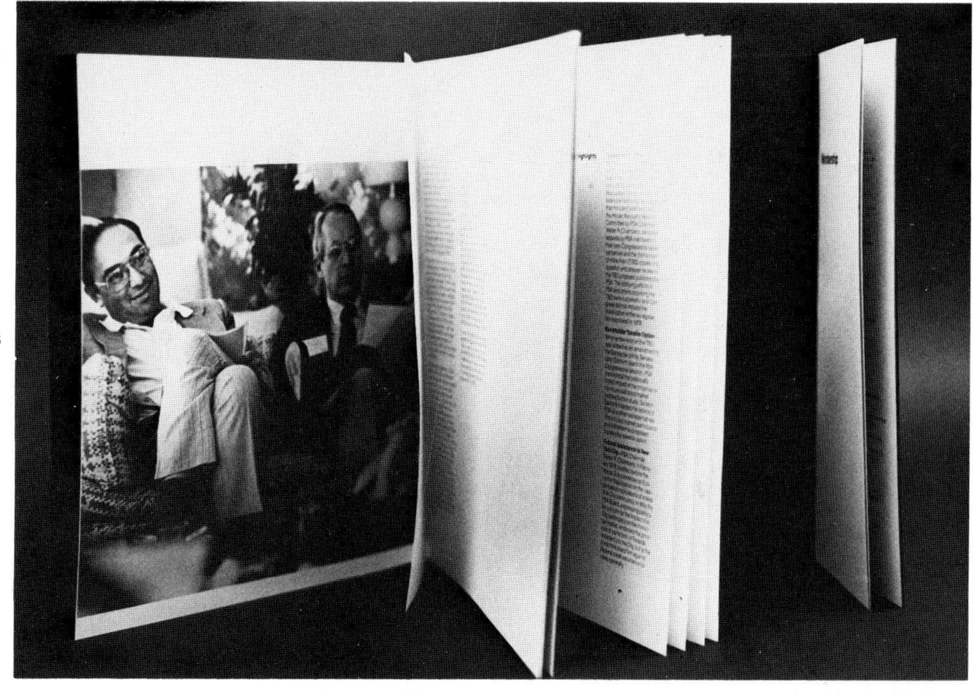

205

Inland Waterways Services Division

Dollars in Thousands, except as indicated	1978	1977	1976	1975	1974	1973
Income before interest, debt expense and income taxes, by quarter:						
March 31	$ 2.923	$ 2.156	$ 9.193	$ 7.693	$ 5.416	$ 5.526
June 30	11.066	7.323	11.107	7.910	9.398	4.063
September 30	9.798	6.930	6.949	7.551	6.185	4.418
December 31	10.767	8.034	8.042	8.291	8.517	8.243
Total	$ 34.554	$ 24.443	$ 35.291	$ 31.445	$ 29.516	$ 22.250
Interest and debt expense	11.499	9.098	6.484	7.084	8.275	5.737
Income taxes	9.769	6.608	13.818	12.029	10.308	7.884
Income from continuing operations	$ 13.286	$ 8.737	$ 14.989	$ 12.332	$ 10.933	$ 8.629
Identifiable assets, year-end	$304.427	$276.575	$224.953	$192.250	$185.526	$158.955
Number of employees, year-end	2.922	2.387	2.684	2.354	2.769	2.634
Barging Operations:						
Revenues, by category:						
Nonbulk (steel, newsprint, etc.)	$ 15.413	$ 10.867	$ 10.629	$ 7.912	$ 11.518	$ 7,951
Coal	31,556	31,473	27,195	25,590	21,672	16,815
Grain	25,014	20,275	19,355	12,981	12,775	11,492
Liquids (chemicals, food oils, etc.)	21,377	19,740	17,971	14,887	16,448	8,920
Other bulk, etc.	23,476	16,278	16,563	20,109	19,221	14,000
Total	$116,836	$ 98,633	$ 91,713	$ 81,479	$ 81,634	$ 59,178
Total tons of freight handled, millions	24.4	24.2	23.9	21.7	22.1	21.6
Total ton miles transported, billions	20.2	18.5	18.2	15.8	17.1	16.1
Owned equipment:						
Total barges loaded	15,626	15,310	15,054	13,844	14,073	14,294
Average tons per load	1,443	1,455	1,434	1,444	1,414	1,407
Average miles per load	808	769	756	692	765	735
At year-end:						
Towboats in fleet	56	53	52	49	48	44
Horsepower of fleet	222,700	205,300	196,270	184,790	171,950	152,650
Barges in fleet	1,367	1,333	1,258	1,141	1,127	1,114
Average age of towboats (years)	8.8	8.1	7.8	8.1	9.5	10.2
Average age of barges (years)	9.4	9.3	9.6	9.6	8.9	8.5
Capacity of barges in fleet, net tons	2,086,200	2,028,600	1,904,600	1,707,400	1,686,800	1,658,300
Shipyard Operations:						
Revenues:						
Public	$ 43,013	$ 19,895	$ 47,708	$ 53,641	$ 36,401	$ 32,196
Intercompany	$ 27,691	$ 34,526	$ 23,695	$ 8,382	$ 12,311	$ 16,899

Inland Waterways Services Division

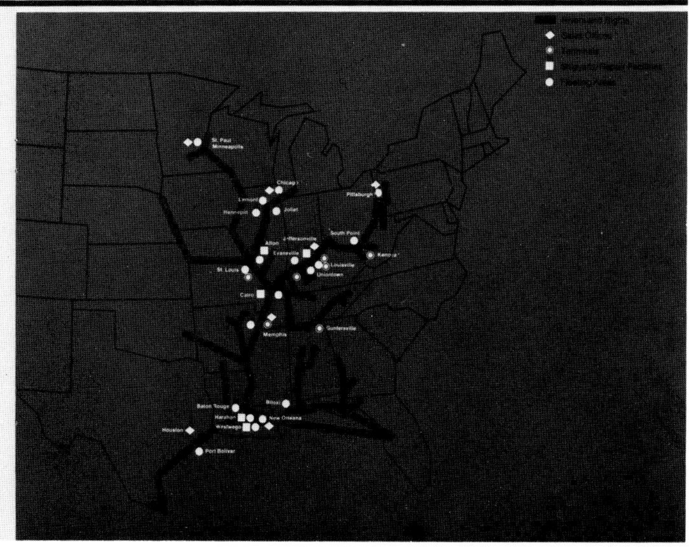

206

207
Gene Galasso Art Director
Gene Galasso, Phil Colprit Illustrators
Gene Galasso, Mary L. Frey Designers
Gene Galasso Associates Inc. Agency
Shipbuilders Council of America Client

209 A

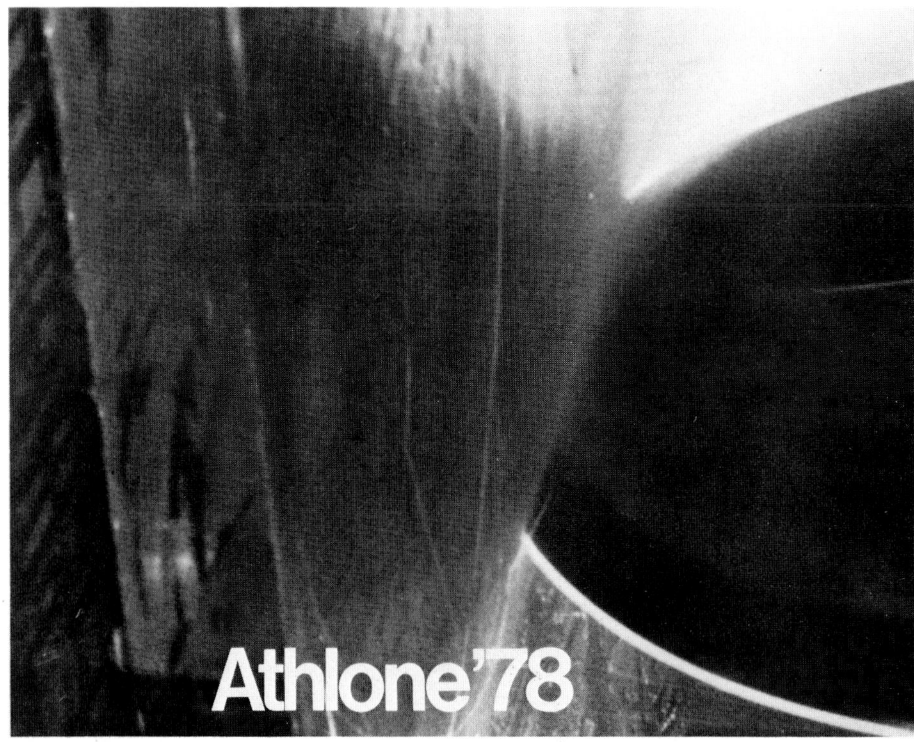

208
Jay Tribich Art Director
Arthur Lavine, Clifton Watts Photographers
J. Tribich Design Associates, Inc. Studio
Athlone Industries, Inc. Client

209 A-C
Sheldon Rysner Art Director
Christopher Gould, Shigeta-Wright Associates Photographers
John Olds Designer
Goldsholl Associates Agency
Bliss & Laughlin Industries Client

Construction Related Tools and Equipment and Metal Products —Continued Growth

Building owners and architects have increased the use of drywall construction through a preference for gypsum wallboard over lath and plaster. Ames Taping Tool, the number one company in the manufacture, rental and service of drywall taping tools, has benefitted from this development. Ames leases labor saving automatic taping and finishing tools. This proprietary product provides Bliss & Laughlin with a special niche serving the residential and commercial markets.

Another Bliss & Laughlin service to the construction market is Waco Scaffold and Shoring Co., one of the nation's important scaffolding and shoring companies. Waco furnishes equipment for rent and sale in high-rise, residential, commercial and industrial construction projects and also provides custom frames, weather enclosures and other equipment to meet specific customer requirements.

Above:
This section of Waco scaffolding is used for an interior purpose. On a larger scale, Waco scaffolding found use in constructing the interior of the Kennedy Center in Washington, D.C.

Tekform, the largest designer and supplier of metal packages for hybrid microelectronics, manufactures products for aerospace and missile programs, medical electronics instrumentation, airborne computers and commercial aircraft sound systems. Tekform packages have been custom designed for systems that activate aircraft anti-skid devices, check fighter plane readiness, guide laser missiles and operate the space shuttle vehicles. One of Tekform's platform packages was used in the Mariner Mission to Jupiter and Saturn.

Nestaway supplies plated and vinyl-coated racks and baskets for kitchen use. Among the products manufactured are dishdrainers, automatic dishwasher racks, as well as brackets for refrigerators and freezers. Customers include such quality home appliance manufacturers as Maytag, Hobart, Whirlpool and General Electric.

Faultless, one of the largest manufacturers of casters in the world, is responsible in great part for furniture mobility in the office and home. Products are found on beds, sofas, chairs, dressers, televisions and most other movable furniture. Faultless, using a die cast technique, also manufactures specialty decorative hardware.

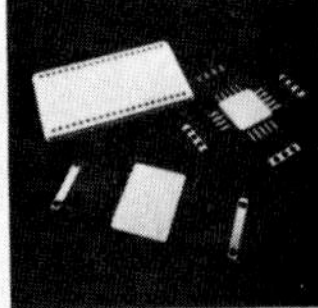

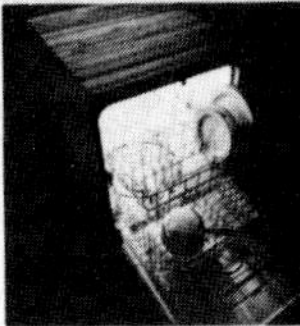

Top Right:
Tekform produces these miniature parts for microelectronic circuit packages. Highly flexible in its product offerings, Tekform will design parts to fit a specific purpose or application.

Middle Right:
Bliss & Laughlin's Nestaway Division produces for major appliance manufacturers the vinyl coated dishwasher rack shown here.

Bottom Right:
Bliss & Laughlin's Faultless Division manufacturers casters and wheels; the Faultless Doerner Division supplies chair bases and controls — and together they support a chair which is both functional and visually aesthetic.

Left:
The labor efficient Ames taping tool is shown with its construction accessories: drywall tape, produced by Bliss & Laughlin's Marco Division, and gypsum wallboard.

11

B

When Bliss & Laughlin acquires or develops a "niche business" company, total corporate resources are available to assist in the new division's operations. Diverse operations sometimes require a variety of management approaches. Bliss & Laughlin has refined the experience and controls to provide effective attention and direction to the demands of these various approaches. As a result, Bliss & Laughlin has been able to increase the size and scope of the niche businesses and improve their productivity.

Bliss & Laughlin invests carefully to achieve this goal. One such recent investment, the construction during 1978 of a new industrial caster plant in Blytheville, Arkansas, for the Faultless Division, supplements the production capacity for the Evansville, Indiana plant. The Harvey, Illinois, steel mill, the original division of the Company, constitutes another good example of our investment philosophy. The modernization of the Harvey mill, now complete, makes the mill the most efficient cold finished steel bar mill in the country and expands our ability to make and deliver high quality, lower cost products.

Consistent and profitable growth of the Company's portfolio of assets demands that each Bliss & Laughlin business receives attention as an asset to be employed. This recognition of potential leads to well balanced growth through internal improvement as well as select acquisitions. Assets are concentrated in areas demonstrating higher earnings potential, while cash produced from mature businesses is invested in enterprises with greater growth potential.

Bliss & Laughlin's direct mail industry catalog business, for example, represents a very rapid growth area, with the circulation of 8.7 million catalogs in 1978 producing 40% more revenue than last year. Along with increased sales, Bliss & Laughlin's record for improving efficiency and productivity is exemplified by the substantially reduced turnaround time from order to delivery.

The Bliss & Laughlin operating plan attempts to provide a focus for analyzing industry trends and yet remain flexible enough to accommodate tactical revisions to programs. A dramatic example occurred in 1975 when, as a result of careful planning, management instituted contingency plans that enabled Bliss & Laughlin to achieve a modest earnings increase despite a $38 million dollar decline in revenues.

In managing the Company's affairs, Bliss & Laughlin's management and its Board of Directors remain mindful of their ultimate responsibility to shareholders, employees, and the communities in which they reside. Responsibility to shareholders can be best demonstrated by the record earnings and 160 consecutive quarters in which dividends have been paid. Under present management, dividends have increased 96%.

Left:
Two recent additions to Bliss & Laughlin are the Duve Fischbein Co. and Metalart Buckle Co. Although serving very different markets, both of these companies are prime examples of Bliss & Laughlin's philosophy of acquiring major firms in specialty niche businesses.

Earnings Trends in Fully Diluted Earnings Per Share (1961-1978)

(in dollars)

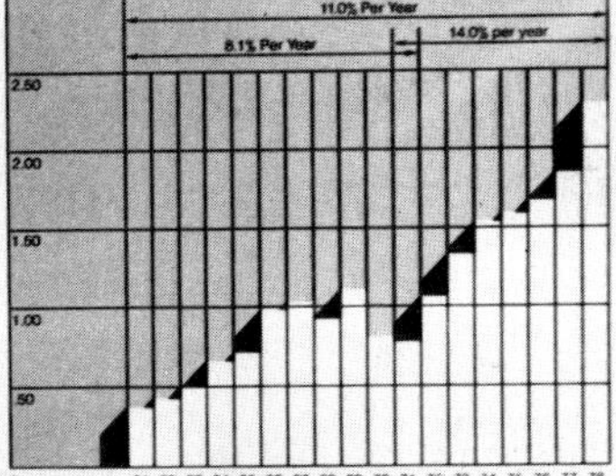

The growth trend of fully diluted earnings per share of 11% per year since Bliss & Laughlin's decision to diversify in 1961 and 14% under present management corroborates the wisdom of that decision.

Bliss & Laughlin Stock Price Comparison (1962-1978)

(index)

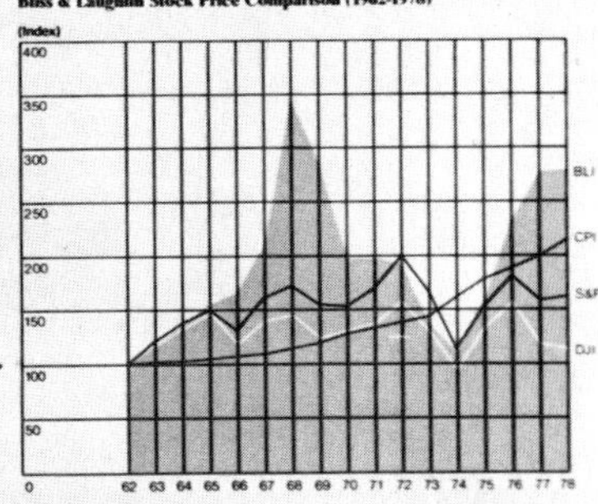

Bliss & Laughlin stock price has outperformed leading indices.

Comparing Bliss & Laughlin's year end stock price (BLI) to the Dow Jones and Standard & Poor's year end stock price averages and the Consumer Price Index for each year since 1962 confirms Bliss & Laughlin's long term outperformance of all these indices.

C

210
Richard L. Downes Art Director
Hayman Studios, David Frazee Photographers
Thomas A. Neilson, Richard L. Downes, Richard B. Douglas, S. R. Clark Designers
De Martin, Marona, Cranstoun, Downes, Inc. Agency
Hercules Incorporated Client

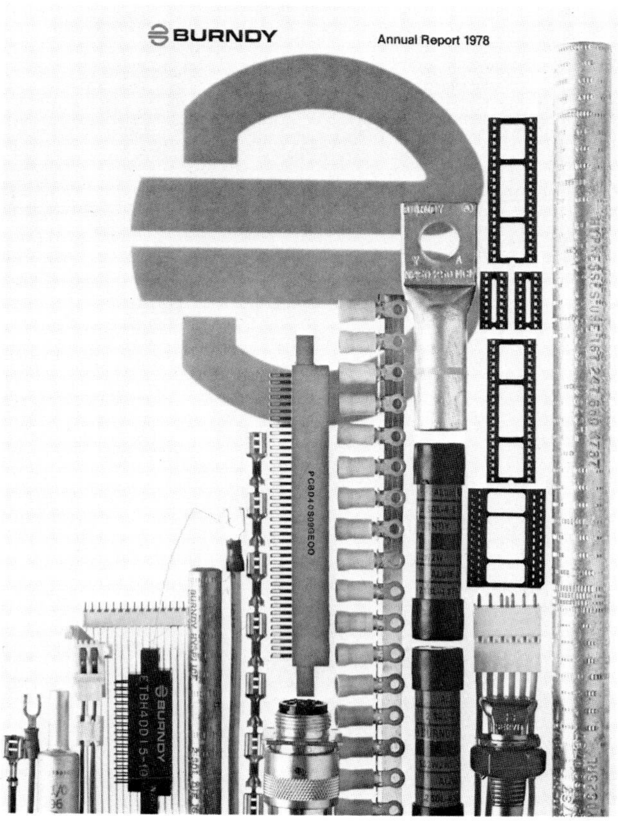

211
Ian Barrival Art Director
Michael Weiss Photographer
Greg Rudd Illustrator
Ted Colangelo Associates Agency
Burndy Client

SECURITY NEW YORK STATE CORPORATION 1978 ANNUAL REPORT

"the surprising heartland"

The heartland region in upstate New York—the service area of Security New York and its member banks. A region that continues to exhibit a surprising range of economic strengths.

High technology in the heartland: Rochester is the nation's number one exporter of high technology equipment—a major segment of the diversified manufacturing sector in the region.

Take the metropolitan center: Rochester-Monroe County. It has the highest value-added per worker of any U.S. city, and one of the lowest unemployment rates in the state.

Endowed with rich soil for pasture and produce, the heartland lists agribusiness as its number one industry. (Statewide impact: $7 billion.) And where else will you find a $150,000 Holstein?

Surprising resources? What about 6,500 producing gas and oil wells? Or 2.2 million acres of timber? Or the nearby Great Lakes, with 20 percent of the world's fresh water supply?

What's ahead? New growth industries like tourism. (Try the Soaring Festival at Harris Hill.) Plus a future with opportunity for manageable growth. ("The Surprising Heartland," page 10)

212
Bill Buckett Art Director
Ted Kawalerski Photographer
Saphar & Associates, Inc. Agency
Security New York State Corp. Client

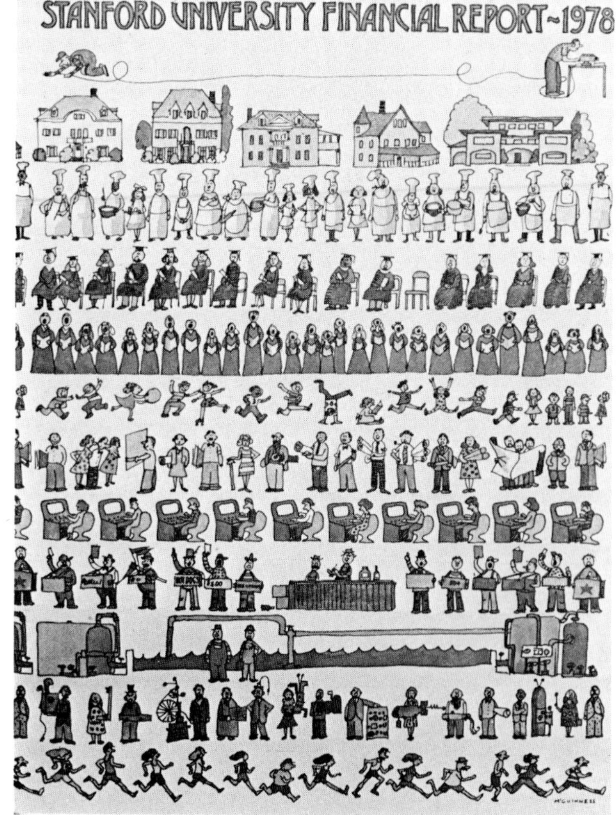

213
Jim M'Guinness Art Director
Stanford Publications Service Agency
Stanford University Client

214 A-B A
James Cross Art Director
Roger Marshutz Photographer
Jay Novak, Ken Rang Designers
James Cross Design Office, Inc. Studio

B **The Newhall Land and Farming Company** Client

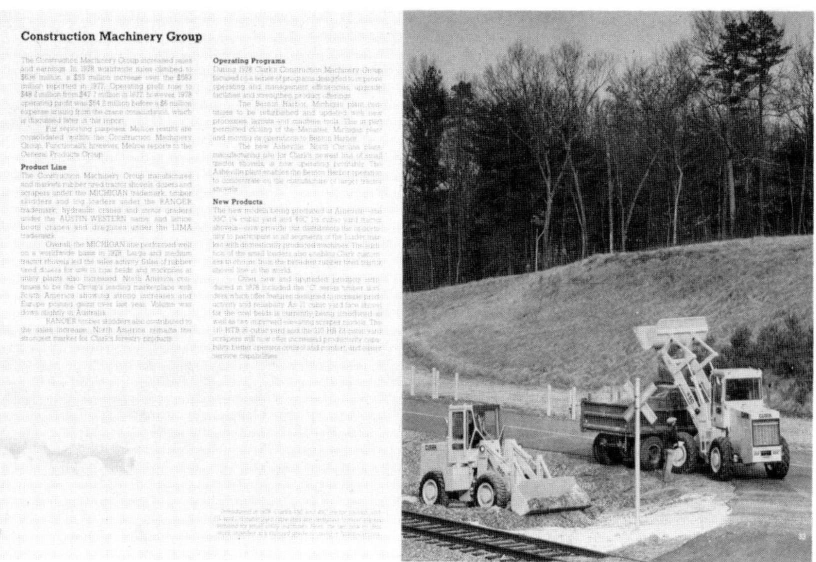

215 A-B A
Joseph M. Essex Art Director
Steve Feldman Photographer
Burson-Marsteller/Design Group Agency

B **Clark Equipment Co.** Client

216 A-B A
James Cross Art Director
Cheryl Rossum Photographer
James Cross, Carl Seltzer Designers
James Cross Design Office, Inc. Agency

B **The Northrop Corporation** Client

217 A-C
Marty Neumeier Art Director
James Chen Photographer
Robert Overby Designer
Marty Neumeier Design Studio
Oceaneering 1978 Client

217 A

218
Robert Burns Art Director
Bert Bell Photographer
Heather Cooper Illustrator
Ann Ames Designer
Burns, Cooper, Hynes Limited Agency
Dylex Limited Client

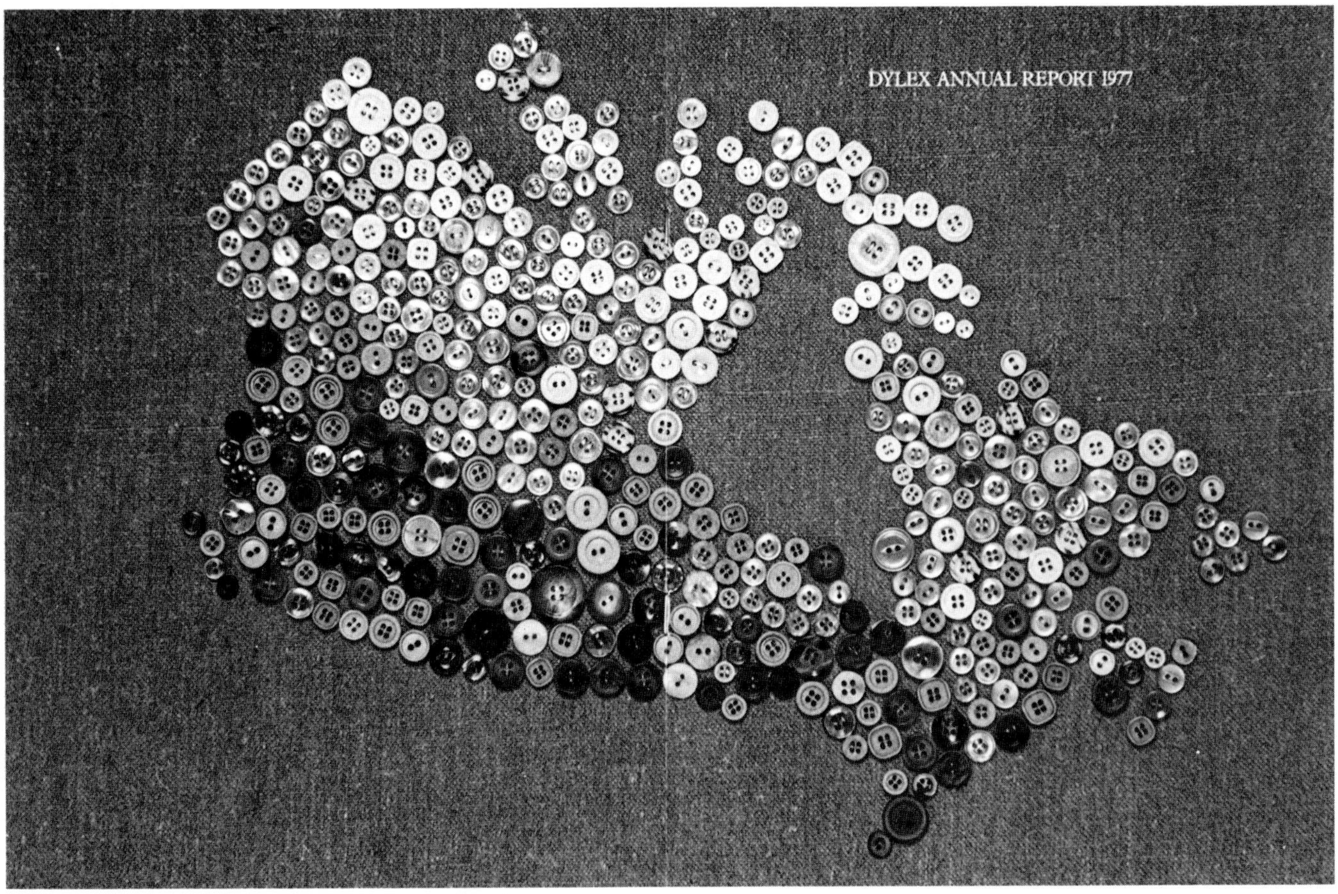

Miles off the coast of Brazil, Oceaneering divers are now working in more than 400 feet of water (also page 12). Sealed inside a one-atmosphere suit called JIM, our divers work comfortably at great depths without the need for decompression or expensive mixed gases. A dive in 1000 feet of water, for example, would take a total of 15 days using a traditional saturation diving team. Ten of those days would be needed for decompression. With JIM, the entire dive, in some cases, could be completed in a single day. A smaller support crew and far less deck space are required, affording JIM even further economic advantages over mixed-gas diving.

Diving bells like the one pictured are commonly used to support offshore drilling operations. Frequently, when oil companies contract for the use of deep-water rigs, they also hire diving services and systems which allow divers to work on the seabed for extended periods of time. Oceaneering's diving crews are normally stationed aboard the rig during the entire operation. Our ability to perform prompt underwater inspections and repairs allows the rig operator great economic savings by minimizing rig downtime and the need to abandon subsea equipment. This particular bell can be deployed to depths of 1000 feet for conducting a variety of rig diving tasks.

B

WASP is Oceaneering's newest one-atmosphere diving system which, like JIM, requires no diver decompression. Whereas JIM was engineered to work on the ocean floor, WASP is designed for off-the-bottom, mid-water tasks. Using foot-controlled thrusters, the WASP diver can maneuver in any direction and function comfortably in depths up to 2000 feet. Here WASP is shown inspecting platform anodes in the Gulf of Mexico. Direct television transmission and two-way voice communication allow the customer to thoroughly supervise the diver's activities from the surface. WASP's small support crew and deck space requirements, combined with fast mobilization, make the system an extremely economical alternative to mixed-gas diving for inspection and minor repairs.

Since its first working dive in 1974, JIM has established an outstanding reputation for deep-water work, making record dives to 1444 feet off the coast of Spain, and Canadian Arctic dives in 900 feet of freezing water. JIM, simply defined, is a one-atmosphere diving suit engineered to let its operator work in normal surface pressure at depths never before possible. In 1978, Oceaneering logged hundreds of successful JIM dives in offshore fields around the world, including several off Brazil during the first phase of a long-term project. Here JIM participates in the final series of tank tests on a prototype subsea completion "tree." JIM will assist in installing several similar systems, and then carry out a multi-year maintenance program on the production network.

C

A

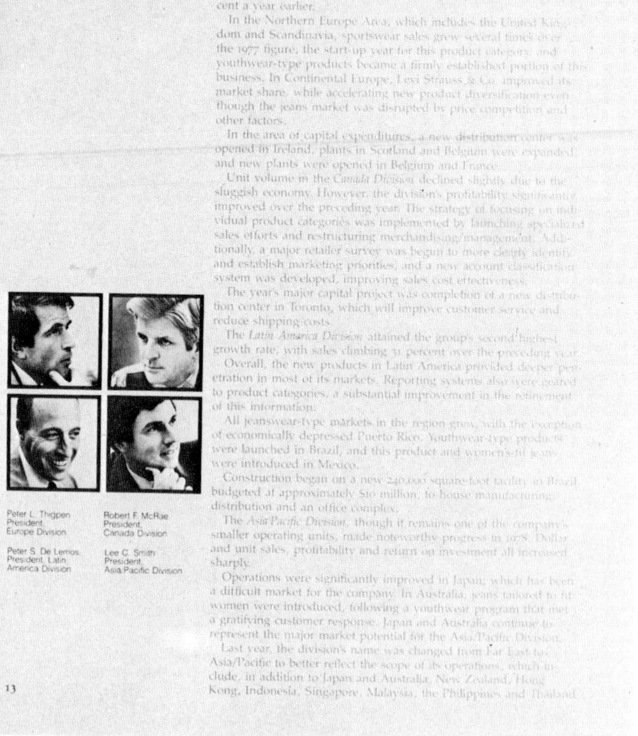

Advertising and promotion strategies remained varied among international divisions in 1978, ranging from a general lifestyle approach in some to specific product support in countries with more highly developed markets and broader product lines.

The *Europe Division* increased sales volume 33 percent and its contribution to total company dollar sales to 18.7 percent from 15.2 percent a year earlier.

In the Northern Europe Area, which includes the United Kingdom and Scandinavia, sportswear sales grew several times over the 1977 figure, the start-up year for this product category, and youthwear-type products became a firmly established portion of this business. In Continental Europe, Levi Strauss & Co. improved its market share, while accelerating new product diversification even though the jeans market was disrupted by price competition and other factors.

In the area of capital expenditures, a new distribution center was opened in Ireland, plants in Scotland and Belgium were expanded, and new plants were opened in Belgium and France.

Unit volume in the *Canada Division* declined slightly due to the sluggish economy. However, the division's profitability significantly improved over the preceding year. The strategy of focusing on individual product categories was implemented by launching specialized sales efforts and restructuring merchandising/management. Additionally, a major retailer survey was begun to more clearly identify and establish marketing priorities, and a new account classification system was developed, improving sales cost effectiveness.

The year's major capital project was completion of a new distribution center in Toronto, which will improve customer service and reduce shipping costs.

The *Latin America Division* attained the group's second highest growth rate, with sales climbing 31 percent over the preceding year.

Overall, the new products in Latin America provided deeper penetration in most of its markets. Reporting systems also were geared to product categories, a substantial improvement in the refinement of this information.

All jeanswear-type markets in the region grew, with the exception of economically depressed Puerto Rico. Youthwear-type products were launched in Brazil, and this product and women's-fit jeans were introduced in Mexico.

Construction began on a new 240,000 square-foot facility in Brazil budgeted at approximately $10 million, to house manufacturing, distribution and an office complex.

The *Asia/Pacific Division*, though it remains one of the company's smaller operating units, made noteworthy progress in 1978. Dollar and unit sales, profitability and return on investment all increased sharply.

Operations were significantly improved in Japan, which has been a difficult market for the company. In Australia, jeans tailored to fit women were introduced, following a youthwear program that met a gratifying customer response. Japan and Australia continue to represent the major market potential for the Asia/Pacific Division.

Last year, the division's name was changed from Far East to Asia/Pacific to better reflect the scope of its operations, which include, in addition to Japan and Australia, New Zealand, Hong Kong, Indonesia, Singapore, Malaysia, the Philippines and Thailand.

B

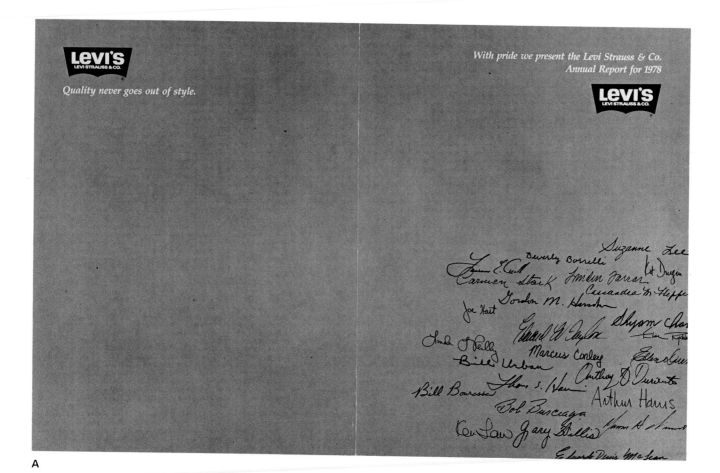

219 A-B
Robert Miles Runyan Art Director
Marvin Silver Photographer
Al Briggs Designer
George Rice & Sons Production House
Robert Miles Runyan & Associates Agency
Levi-Strauss & Co. Client

220 A-B
Patrick Soo Hoo Art Director
Jay Silverman Photographer
Patrick Soo Hoo, Phillip Komai Illustrators
Peter Langer, Mary Ann Beebe Copywriters
Patrick Soo Hoo/Designers Agency
Capital Research & Management Co. Client

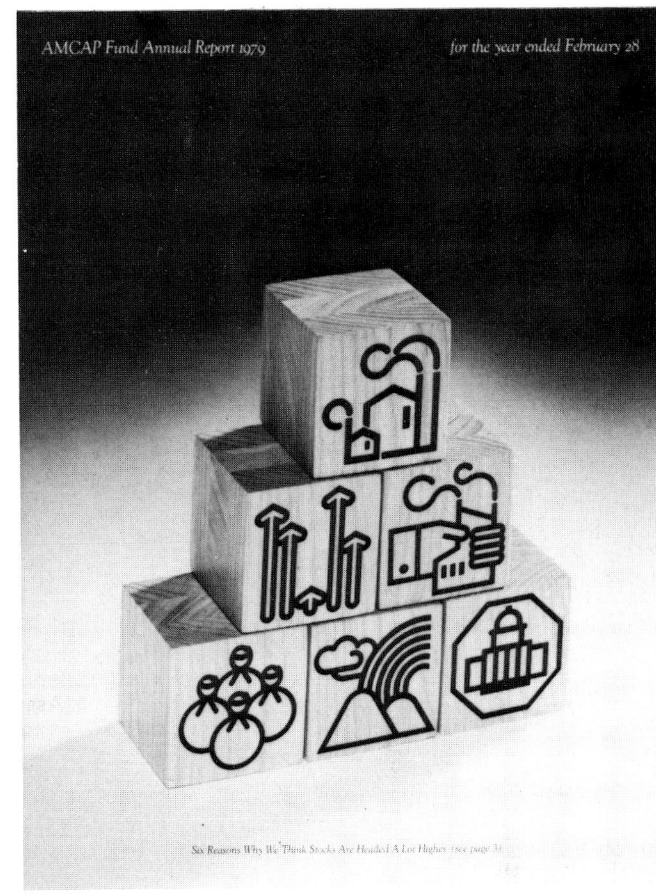

AMCAP Fund Annual Report 1979
for the year ended February 28
Six Reasons Why We Think Stocks Are Headed A Lot Higher (see page 3)

A

Other forms of investment have had such a run-up, they can hardly be called bargains. Stocks are and good bargains are hard to resist.

orders, you didn't really need the cash and you weren't particularly keen on selling a piece of your company.

Now it's ten years later and you've benefited handsomely from the boom in bicycles. Your firm is worth at least $4 million — four times as much as it was then — and you're now taking out four times as much money in salary and dividends. You've enlarged your plant, upgraded your production equipment and added a showroom. What's more, the value of the property on which your plant is built has increased substantially. Along comes that same man. He looks around and offers you only twice as much as before: $200,000 for 10% of your business!

As illogical as that sounds, it's precisely the sort of thing we've been seeing in the market. Many companies have chalked up impressive gains in earnings and dividends and expect to keep on doing so. Their underlying assets have grown significantly and continue to appreciate every day. Yet their stocks have gone up by much smaller amounts and are selling at prices that reflect only a fraction of their fundamental value. We think that stocks like these will soon be more fully recognized as investors find it increasingly difficult to pass up such bargains.

2. Stocks Are Big Bargains Compared To Other Investments

Over the past decade, people have rushed to buy real estate, precious metals, antiques, fine art and other collectibles as hedges against inflation. As a result, many of these investments have soared to lofty levels.

Stocks, on the other hand, are just about the only asset that has not increased in price during the last ten years. Today many of them represent bargains that are too good to go begging, especially when you consider their underlying value. But that's what many people tend to overlook. They see stocks as pieces of paper called stock certificates when in fact they are shares of ownership in very real enterprises which have tangible assets plus the ability to generate growing earnings and dividends.

3. The Gap Between Price And Value Continues To Attract Sophisticated Investors

A growing number of the bargains in the market are being recognized by sophisticated investors, judging from the rash of mergers and acquisitions over the past several years. Large corporations are willingly paying substantial premiums — often more than 50% over market price — for the companies they've set out to acquire. The logic here is simple. It can be illustrated with that same bicycle company.

This time let's assume that your company's shares are publicly traded.

With stock prices depressed, it's often cheaper for a corporation to buy existing assets than to build and equip new plants.

A larger bicycle manufacturer has plenty of cash and wants to expand its line and extend its markets. Although your company has grown at a far-above-average rate and has excellent prospects, the price of its stock has gone up far less than your company's real value. Since your shares are so underpriced, the larger manufacturer decides that it would be a lot cheaper to acquire your company — with its production facilities, trained personnel and established outlets — than to spend its money setting up new plants and marketing programs. The manufacturer makes a tender offer that represents a 40% markup over the current price of your stock, an offer that is accepted by most of your shareholders.

We've seen this happen a number of times in AMCAP's portfolio over the past few years. Since 1977, eight of the companies we owned were purchased by larger firms through attractive tender offers. As a result, the prices of all eight stocks rose significantly, thus benefiting you as an AMCAP shareholder.

4. Record Sums Of Money Are Available For Equity Investing

Thousands of investors with billions of dollars in cash equivalents and other fixed-income securities are watching for a sign that the time has come to buy stocks.

Institutional investors like banks, insurance companies and pension funds probably hold the biggest portion of those securities. Pension funds, the country's largest single source of investment capital, have an estimated $250 billion — nearly half of their total assets — in non-equity investments. And large sums of additional money are flowing into these funds regularly.

Foreign investors also represent a huge reservoir of buying power. For them, U.S. stocks are double-barreled bargains — first, because they represent such attractive values and, second, because the U.S. dollar is still severely depressed in relation to other currencies. The political unrest, economic uncertainties and investment restrictions that confront many of these investors in their own countries make U.S. investments even more attractive.

We have no way of knowing precisely when these institutional and foreign investors — as well as the millions of individual American investors who are also sitting on the sidelines — will move into the market, but we have every reason to believe they will. If just a small portion of their huge fixed-income investments were shifted into equities, it would have a significant impact on stock prices. If a sizeable portion were invested in equities, we would see vast amounts of money competing for a supply of stocks that is not much larger than it was ten years ago. In effect, a large crowd would be rushing for a small door. When we consider this probability, we're particularly glad that AMCAP's assets are already invested in reasonably priced stocks of strong, growing companies. In this environment, we would rather be a little early — even if we have to weather some temporary declines — than a little late.

Institutional, foreign and individual investors have [illegible] reserves.

B

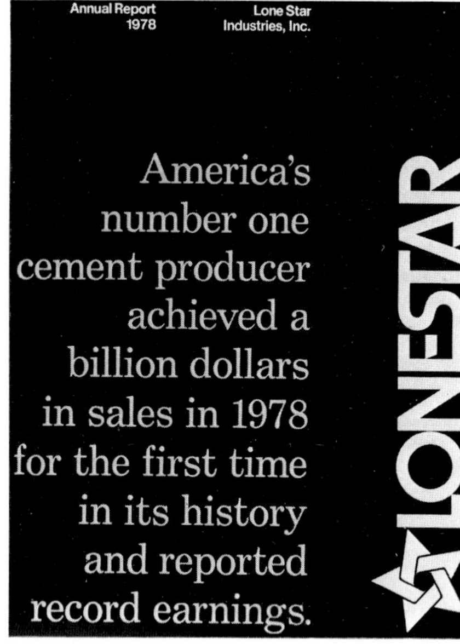

221
Bob Barber Art Director
Burk Uzzle Photographer
Hill and Knowlton, Inc. Agency
Lone Star Industries, Inc. Client

222
Barry Ostrie Art Director
Bill Farrell Photographer
John Heiney & Associates, Inc. Agency
Automatic Data Processing, Inc. Client

223
John F. Morrell Art Director
George Kamper Photographer
Roger Dimuth Illustrator
Rumrill-Hoyt, Inc. Agency
Fay's Drug Inc. Client

225
Pierre Nolin Art Director
Cabana, Seguin, Inc. Agency
Caisse de Depot et Placement du Quebec Client

224
Robert Bothell Art Director
Gary Gladstone, Marv Koner, Simon Nathan Photographers
Roland Des Combes Illustrator
Shareholder Reports, Inc. Agency
Moore McCormack Resources, Inc. Client

Moore McCormack Resources, Inc.

Annual Report
1978
Moore McCormack is Water Transportation and Natural Resources

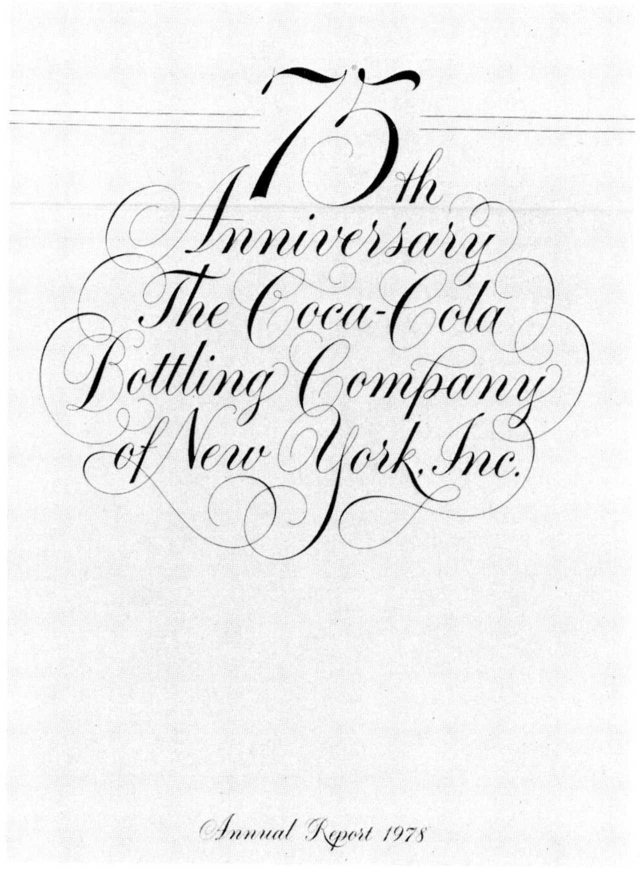

226 A-B
Wayne Roth Art Director
Barron Storey Illustrator
Corporate Annual Reports, Inc. Agency
The Coca-Cola Bottling Co. Client

226 A

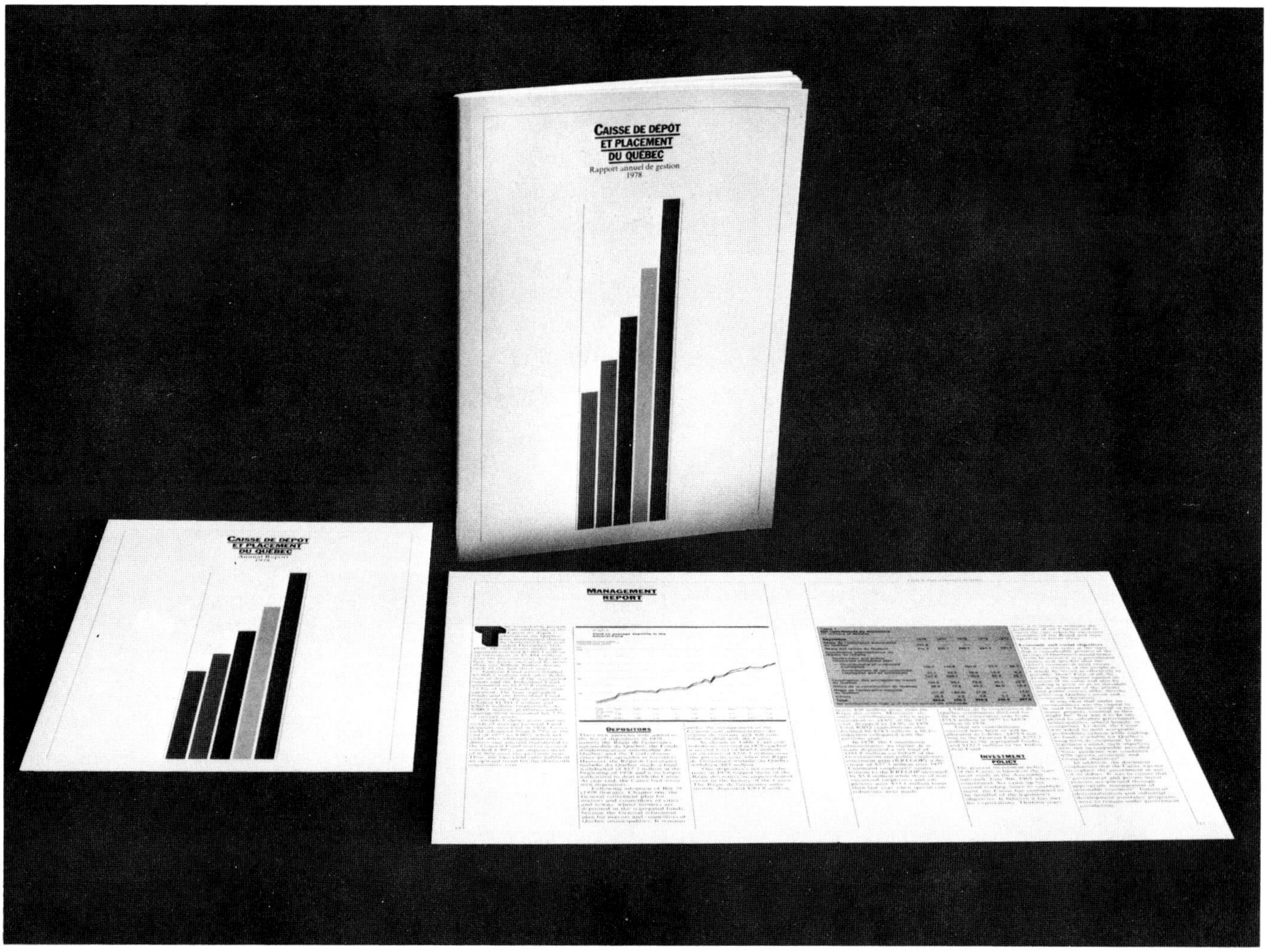

225

Observing the Pratts' operation in Newark and New York, Culpeper became convinced of the future of Coca-Cola in bottles. And so, with Candler's blessing, he resigned from Coke Atlanta to enter the bottling business, purchasing the Pratts' Newark company in 1917 and their New York operation in 1918. Culpeper was 43 years old at the time of the New York purchase, which cost him and his wife Daphne approximately $160,000.

The Culpepers were dynamic builders of the company, and under their guidance it rapidly assumed a position of industry leadership. Mr. Culpeper served as chairman and president, and Mrs. Culpeper was treasurer. Totally devoted to the company's affairs, they lived in an apartment on the roof of the Bronx plant and enjoyed a close, warm relationship with their employees.

The Culpepers spread Coca-Cola to new territories with the zeal of missionaries. They added Buffalo, New York in 1921 and Bridgeport, Connecticut in 1922, and expanded distribution in suburban communities around New York City.

They introduced important packaging innovations—such as the six-bottle open carton developed in 1926 by Claude Keith, superintendent of the company. This package subsequently was adopted by bottlers around the nation and was a key step in creating the at-home market for Coke.

In addition, they withstood the kinds of challenges faced by the owners of any young and growing enterprise, including difficult negotiations with Coke Atlanta for a perpetual franchise. As a result of these negotiations, a uniform, perpetual franchise was issued to all Coca-Cola bottlers in 1929.

The company's board of directors during the Culpeper years read like a "who's who" of the soft drink industry. Members included Raymond M. Brown, Sr., for many years owner of the Newport News Coca-Cola Bottling Company of Virginia, and Chapman J. Root, founder of the Root Glass Company, designer of the original Coca-Cola bottle, and founder of the Associated Coca-Cola Bottling Co. of Daytona, Florida.

When Charles Culpeper died in 1940 at age 65, the company was selling nearly 8.5 million cases of soft drinks annually and ranked among the largest soft drink bottling companies in the world. Although Mrs. Culpeper retired as treasurer the following year, she retained an active interest in the company until her death in 1977.

The Murray Years: 1940-1968

Culpeper was succeeded as chairman and president by James T. Murray, the company's 42-year-old general counsel. A native of New York City, Murray attended Harvard and was graduated with honors from Fordham Law School. He was a strong, aggressive, chief executive who demanded, and received, a great deal from the people who worked for him. He also was extremely generous and, without ever expecting anything in return, helped many employees finance their childrens' educations or pay unexpected medical bills.

Under Murray's leadership, the company:
• completed a large, modern bottling plant on East 34th Street in Manhattan in 1947;
• became the first Coca-Cola bottler to initiate product advertising on television in 1951;
• acquired the Coca-Cola Bottling Company of Stamford, Connecticut in 1953;
• listed its shares on the New York Stock Exchange in 1960;
• became the world's first Coca-Cola bottler to use more than 5 million gallons of syrup annually in 1961; and,
• introduced new soft drinks, including TAB in 1964 and Fresca in 1967.

The Delta Queen and the Mississippi Queen are unique—the only overnight passenger steamboats on U.S. inland waters. The boats were acquired by Coke New York in 1976.

10

11

B

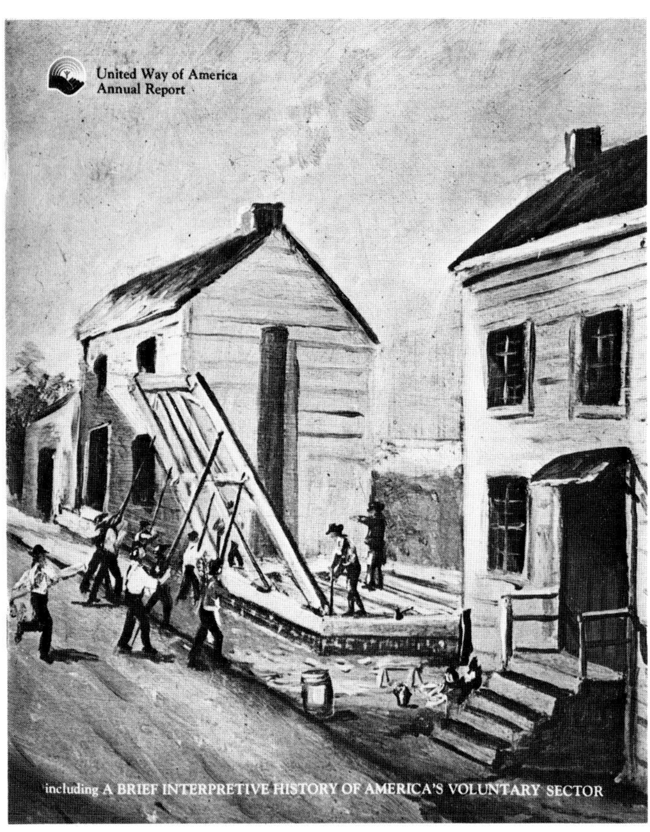

227
Gil Meekins Art Director
Mario Pellegrini Creative Director
Anthony Ripley, Richard Cornuelle Copywriters
United Way of America Client

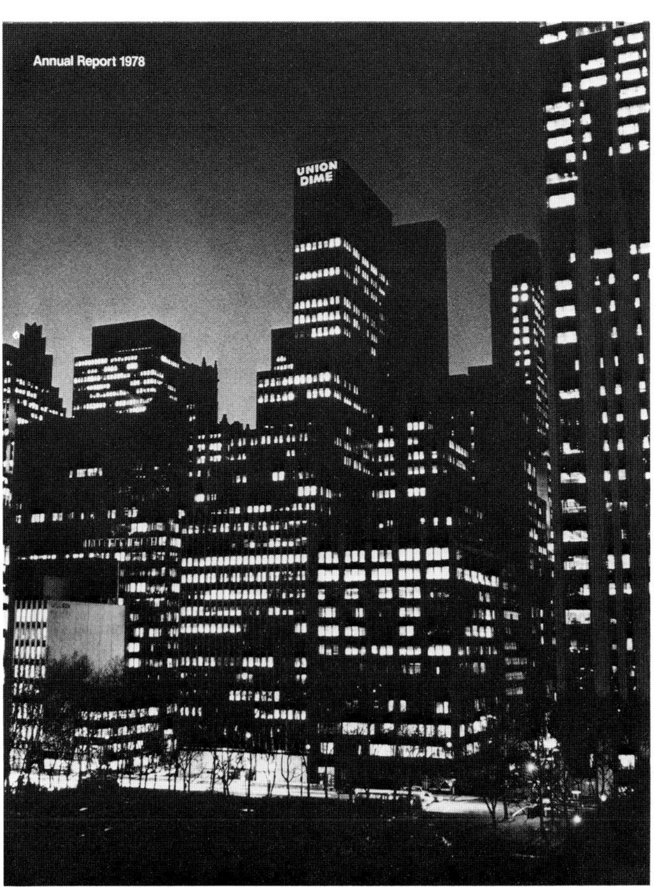

228
Wayne Roth Art Director
Michael Melford Photographer
Corporate Annual Reports, Inc. Agency
Union Dime Client

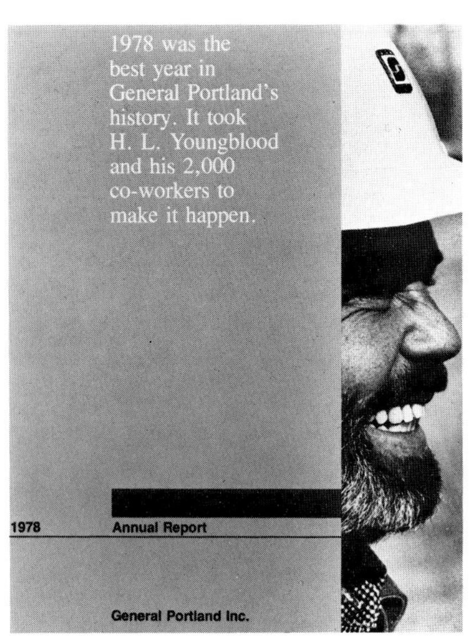

229
Bob Barber Art Director
Gary Bishop Photographer
Hill and Knowlton, Inc. Agency
General Portland, Inc Client

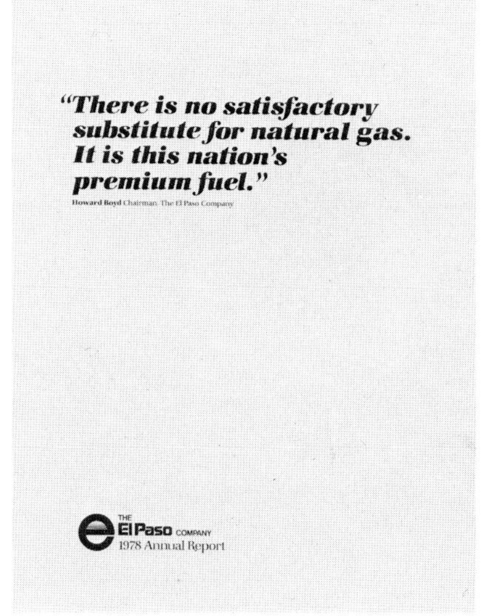

230
Debra D. Boetsch Art Director
Clifford G. Trussell Photographer
The El Paso Company Client

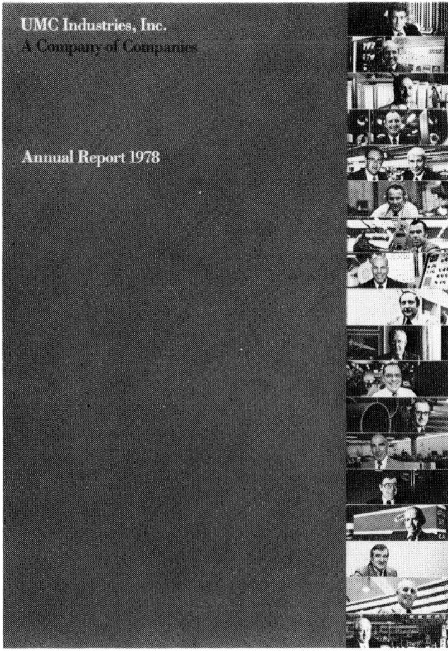

231
Dick Lopez, Sharon Reiter Art Directors
Bob Salpeter Creative Director
Lopez Salpeter, Inc. Agency
UMC Industries, Inc. Client

Standard Brands Paint Company Annual Report 1978

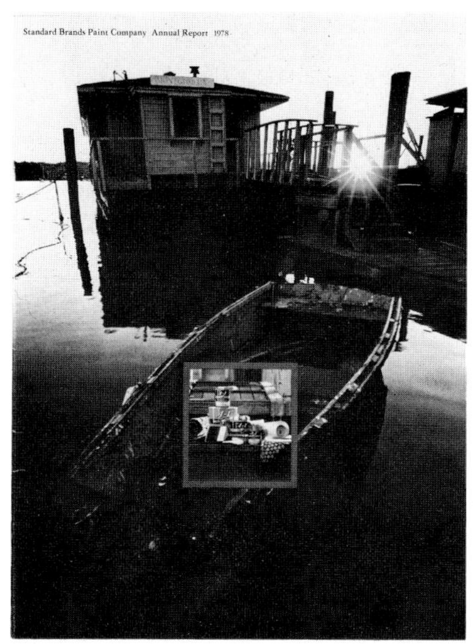

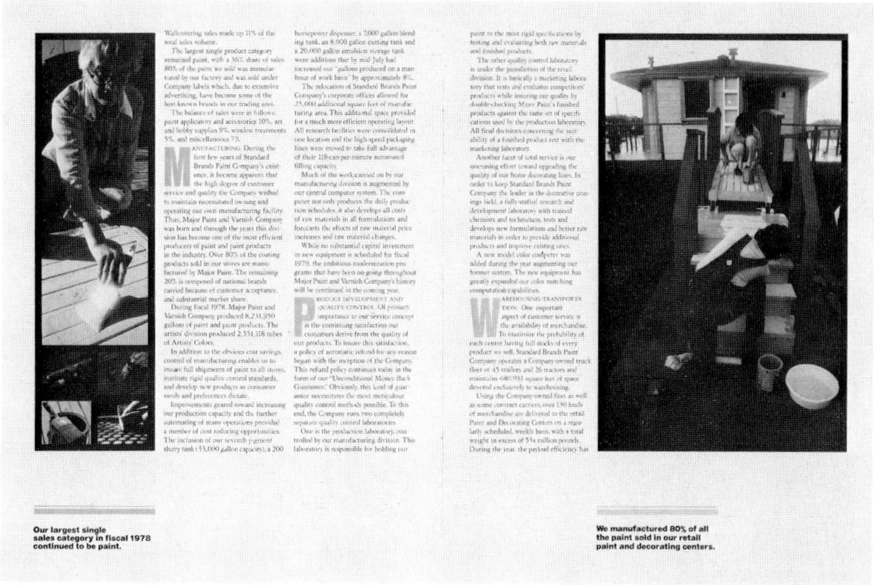

Our largest single sales category in fiscal 1978 continued to be paint.
We manufactured 80% of all the paint sold in our retail paint and decorating centers.

232 A-B
Don Weller Art Director
Ron Scott Photographer
Don Weller, Chikako Matsubayashi Designers
The Weller Institute for the Cure of Design Agency

A B

Standard Brands Paint Company Client

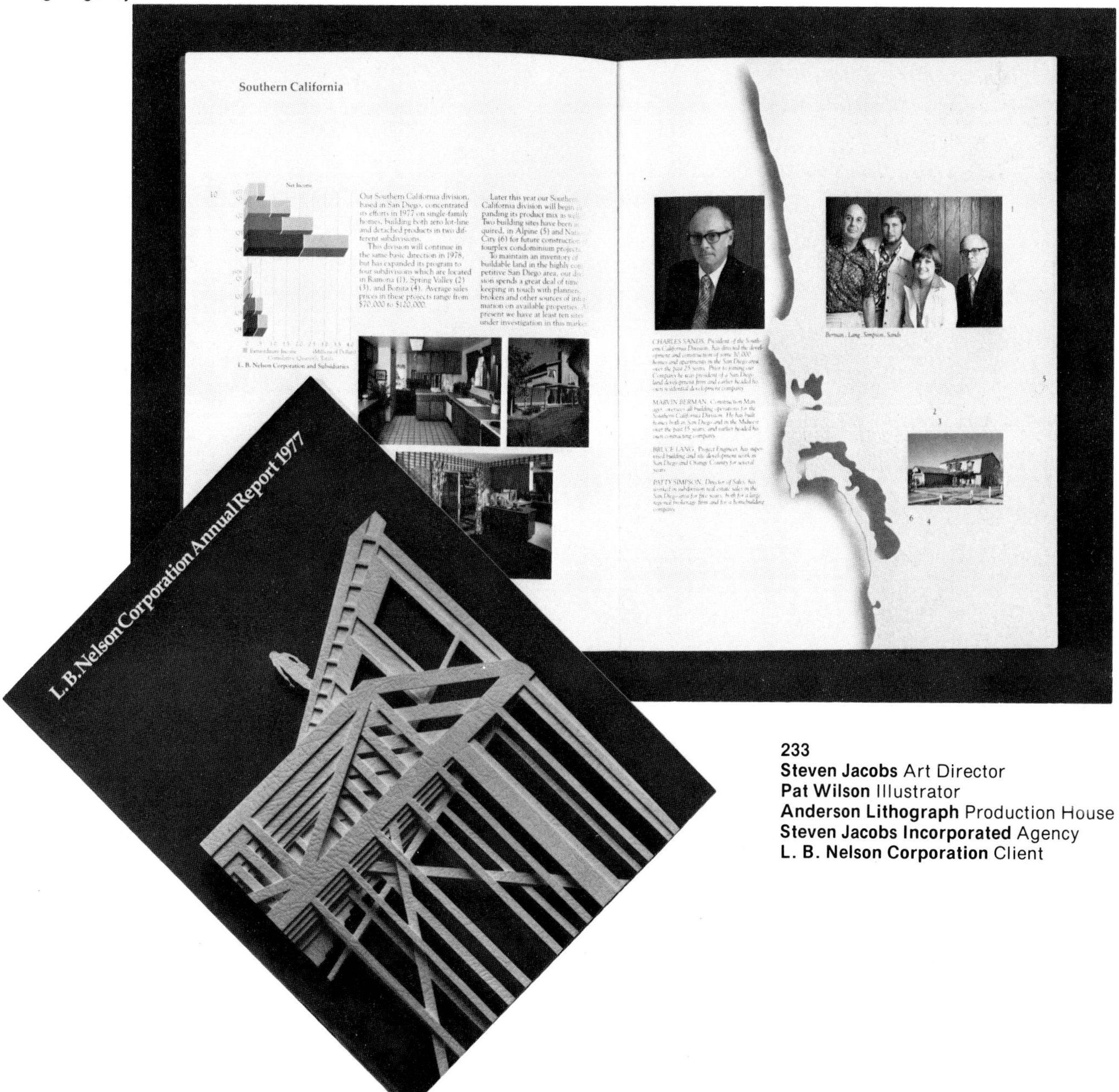

Southern California
L. B. Nelson Corporation Annual Report 1977

233
Steven Jacobs Art Director
Pat Wilson Illustrator
Anderson Lithograph Production House
Steven Jacobs Incorporated Agency
L. B. Nelson Corporation Client

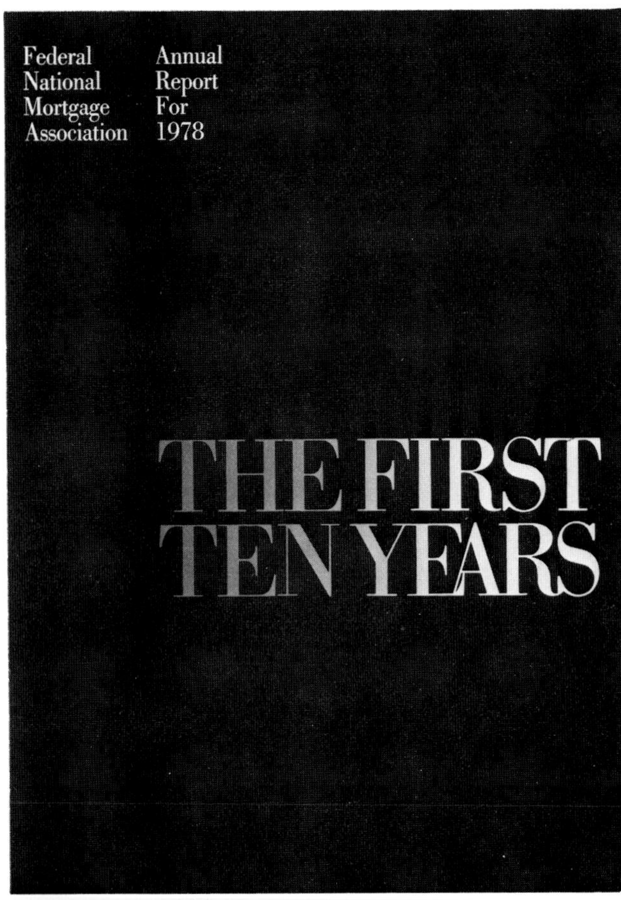

A

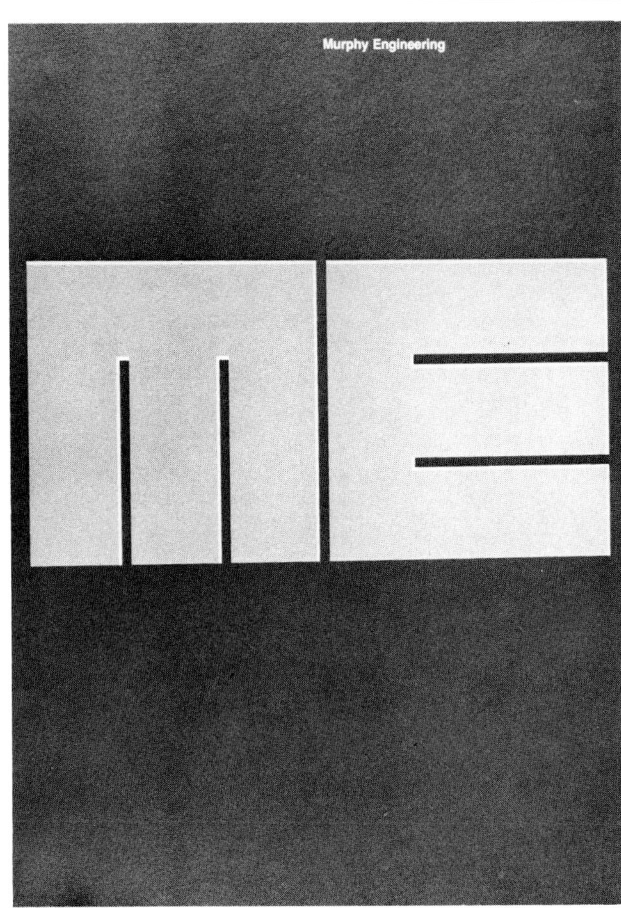

235 A

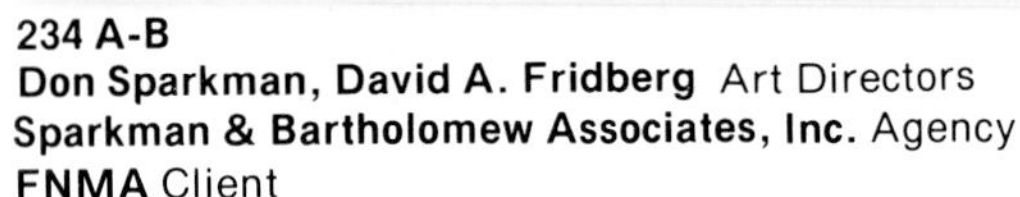

234 A-B
Don Sparkman, David A. Fridberg Art Directors
Sparkman & Bartholomew Associates, Inc. Agency
FNMA Client

THE FIRST TEN YEARS

12

high demand for credit, combined to create conditions calling for greater levels of support by FNMA in 1973 and 1974.

Consequently, FNMA mortgage purchases in 1973 were $6.3 billion, a record quickly eclipsed by the $7.0 billion purchased in 1974. As credit availability tightened, the proportion of total residential mortgage credit provided by FNMA increased. In 1973 the corporation contributed 8.2 percent of the nation's net new residential mortgage investment, compared with less than five percent in 1971 and 1972. In 1974 FNMA's share rose to 13.5 percent. The company ended 1974 with a mortgage portfolio of $29.7 billion.

The next three years constituted a period of relative credit ease, although interest rates began to rise in 1977. FNMA's mortgage purchases were modest and relatively stable in this period —$4.3, $3.6 and $4.8 billion in 1975, 1976 and 1977, respectively. But a jump in its issuance of purchase commitments—from $6.1 and $6.2 billion in 1975 and 1976 to $10.9 billion in 1977—was a portent of things to come.

Credit conditions worsened in 1978 until year-end when mortgage rates were at their highest in modern home-finance history. This environment produced unprecedented demand on FNMA to support the mortgage market. The company's $19.0 billion of commitments was nearly double the previous record set a year earlier, and mortgage purchases of $12.3 billion nearly equaled the total purchases of the three preceding years. FNMA contributed 8.6 percent of the nation's net new residential mortgage investment in 1978. And while the company's portfolio had increased by an average of only 5 percent a year in the previous three years, it showed a 26 percent increase in 1978—to $43.3 billion.

In its first ten years, FNMA's year-end mortgage portfolio had grown from $7.2 billion to $43.3 billion, a compound annual growth rate of 20 percent.

FNMA finances the net increase in its portfolio primarily by issuing long term (debentures) and short term (discount notes) debt.

Net borrowings by FNMA in any one year have ranged from a low of $0.6 billion in 1976 to a high of $9.1 billion in 1978. FNMA's indebtedness has increased in parallel with the growth of its mortgage portfolio, and at year-end 1978 totaled $41.0 billion.

The average term of FNMA's outstanding debt at the end of 1969 was 16 months—meaning that it had to refinance half of its total debt in little more than a year. This proved costly during the credit crunch of 1969-70, reducing FNMA's earnings per share to $.19 in 1970 from $.63 the previous year.

In 1970, the process of lengthening FNMA's debt was begun, and by the end of 1972, outstanding debt had an average maturity of 4 years 7 months.

13

HOUSING UNITS FINANCED
Thousands of units

1969	1970	1971	1972	1973	1974	1975	1976	1977	1978
266.7	302.3	210.8	224.3	333.0	326.7	171.7	120.2	147.8	311.9

MORTGAGE AND LOAN PORTFOLIO
Dollars in billions

1969	1970	1971	1972	1973	1974	1975	1976	1977	1978
11.1	16.1	18.5	20.3	24.5	29.7	31.9	32.9	34.4	43.3

B

People and Resources

Every project requires engineering services of the highest quality, but Murphy Engineering recognizes that quality alone is not sufficient. The work must be completed on-schedule, and with an emphasis on economy. Frequently, the most economical solution is not the most apparent, and a creative approach is required to identify and evaluate all of the feasible solutions to a given problem.

To best utilize the firm's broadly-based professional talent, Murphy Engineering employs a team approach. Each project is reviewed by the principals of the firm, who select a design team—the composition and size of which are dictated by the requirements of the particular job. Murphy Engineering's resources are extensive: with its affiliates in the Murphy Group, the firm can provide full planning, design, construction supervision and contract management services, together with many specialized services, including a well-equipped computer department, and a graphics and audio-visual team.

The first step in any project is the selection of an appropriate study or design team. In-house technical briefings and seminars are an important resource for keeping the professional staff abreast of new technologies.

B

235 A-C
Steve Keller Art Director
Roy Slowinski, Susan Johnson, Jim Vest, Wayne Sorce Photographers
Susan Johnson Designer
Rohner Printing Production House
Graphics Group Agency
Murphy Engineering Inc. Client

Transportation Systems
Airports

A major engineering challenge at Chicago's O Hare International Airport, relocating and rehabilitating taxiways and runways with minimum disruptions of traffic. Other large scale logistic problems were solved when Murphy Engineering was asked to provide engineering services for the roadways, approach ramps, and pedestrian tunnels for the 9300 space O Hare parking structure, one of the largest in the world.

The modern airport, with its large-scale, complex transportation activities, offers a particular challenge to the engineer. Design studies encompass an unusual array of operations, performance standards, and safety requirements, and must be based on highly accurate long-range projections of air and ground traffic. Expansion programs are frequent, but their implementation cannot interrupt service.

Murphy Engineering has an excellent background in airport development. The firm has completed a number of major projects for the world's busiest airport, O'Hare International. Murphy engineers have participated in every phase of the O'Hare expansion program and have provided continuous engineering services for the maintenance programs at both O'Hare and Midway airports. For the civil engineer, the challenge in airport work is to create a design that will both effectively meet today's needs and will easily accommodate future expansions and modifications.

C

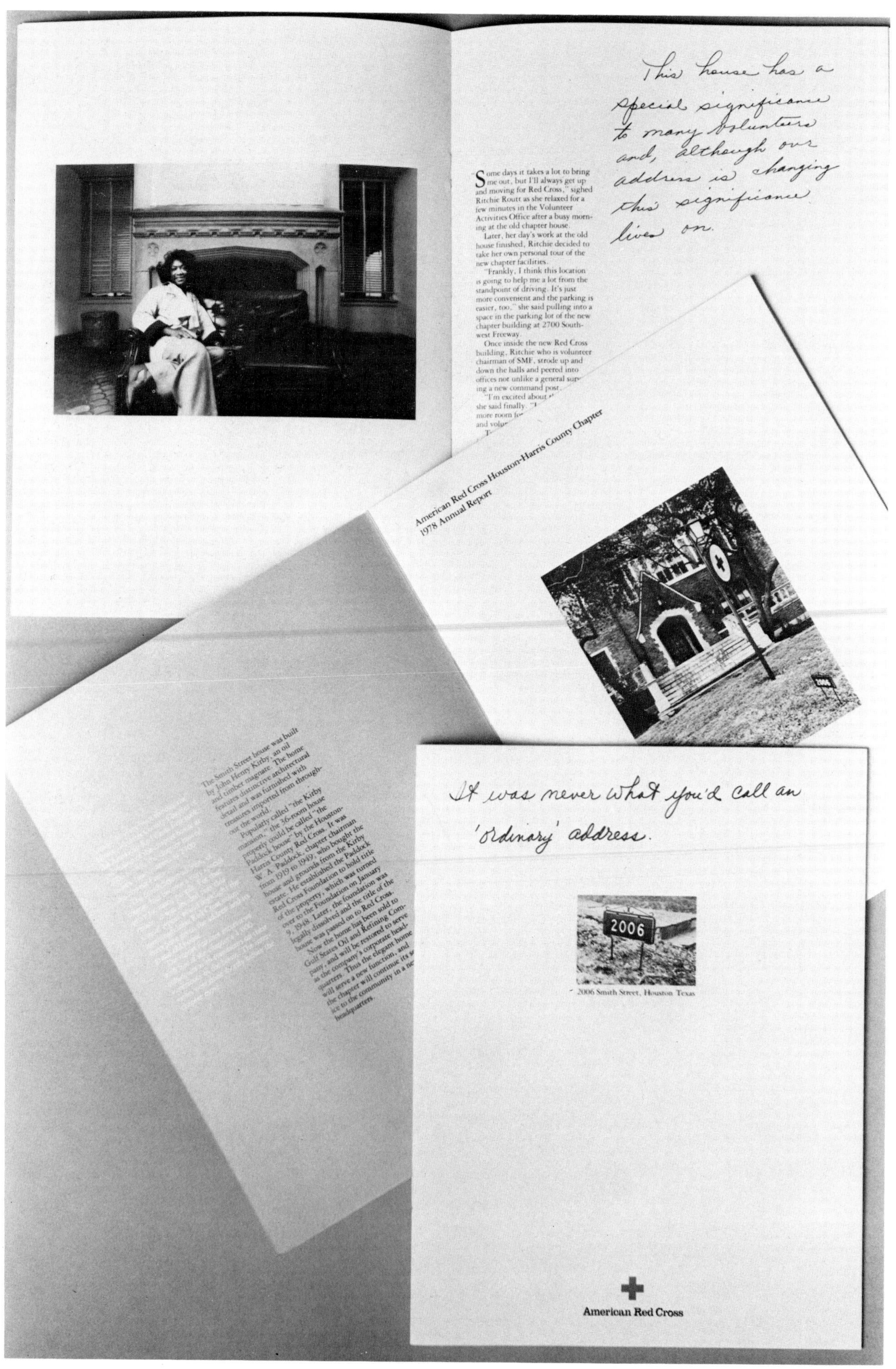
Some days it takes a lot to bring me out, but I'll always get up and moving for Red Cross," sighed Ritchie Routt as she relaxed for a few minutes in the Volunteer Activities Office after a busy morning at the old chapter house.
Later, her day's work at the old house finished, Ritchie decided to take her own personal tour of the new chapter facilities.
"Frankly, I think this location is going to help me a lot from the standpoint of driving. It's just more convenient and the parking is easier, too," she said pulling into a space in the parking lot of the new chapter building at 2700 Southwest Freeway.
Once inside the new Red Cross building, Ritchie who is volunteer chairman of SMF, strode up and down the halls and peered into offices not unlike a general sur
ing a new command post.
"I'm excited about
she said finally.
more room fo
and volu
This house has a special significance to many volunteers and, although our address is changing this significance lives on.
American Red Cross Houston-Harris County Chapter
1978 Annual Report
2006
The Smith Street house was built by John Henry Kirby, an oil and timber magnate. The home features distinctive architectural detail and was furnished with treasures imported from throughout the world.
Popularly called "the Kirby mansion," the 36-room house properly could be called "the Paddock house" by the Houston-Harris County Red Cross. It was W. A. Paddock, chapter chairman from 1919 to 1949, who bought the house and grounds from the Kirby estate. He established the Paddock Red Cross Foundation to hold title of the property, which was turned over to the Foundation in January 9, 1948. Later, the foundation was legally dissolved and the title of the house was passed on to Red Cross.
Now the home has been sold to Gulf States Oil and Refining Company, and will be restored to serve as the company's corporate headquarters. Thus the elegant home will serve a new function, and the chapter will continue its service to the community in a new headquarters.
It was never what you'd call an 'ordinary' address.
2006
2006 Smith Street, Houston Texas
American Red Cross

236
Steven Sessions Art Director
Joe Baraban Photographer
Joe Romano Retoucher
Baxter + Korge, Inc. Agency
American Red Cross, Houston Client

Cenikor has meant hope to me.

237 A-B
Jerry Herring Art Director
Joe Baraban Photographer
Herring Design Agency
Cenikor Foundation Client

A

The most thing I would expect
would be out of my self. To be able
to live by the law. And to
appreciate them. To become
a responseible person and stand
on my one two feet. And to
hold a job and appeaciate it.
and to develope my
character.

Jeannene, service crew
with Cenikor three months

B

A

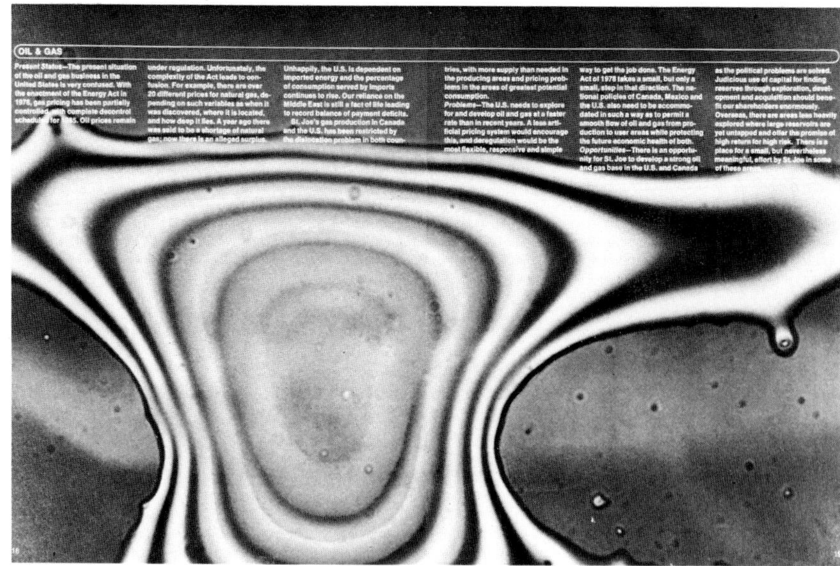

B

238 A-B
Len Fury Art Director
John Delly, John W. Alexanders Photographers
Corpcom Services, Inc. Studio
Corporate Annual Reports, Inc. Agency
St. Joe Minerals Client

239 A-B
Nathan Felde, Julius Friedman Art Directors
Implement, Ltd. Studio
Federal Intermediate Credit Bank of Louisville Client

239 A

B

240 A

B

Brochures & Catalogs

VOLKSWAGEN OF AMERICA ANNOUNCES A MAJOR BREAKTHROUGH IN REPLACEMENT PARTS:
Autobahn

244
Doug Morrall Art Director
Brand Advertising, Inc. Agency
Volkswagen of America Client

245
William A. Sloan Art Director
Cunard Ltd. Client

Queen Elizabeth 2 The 1980 World Cruise

SPECIAL TENTH ANNIVERSARY CELEBRATION

80 days from New York / 78 days from Florida / 60 days from Los Angeles

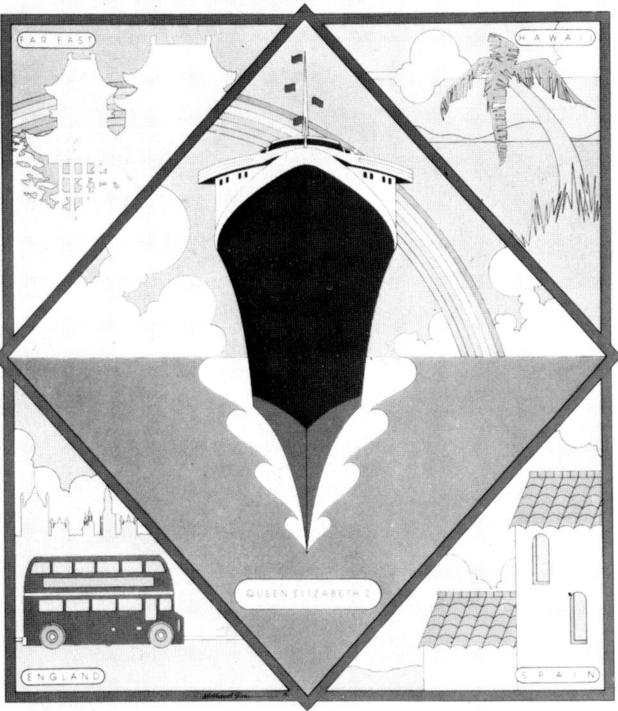

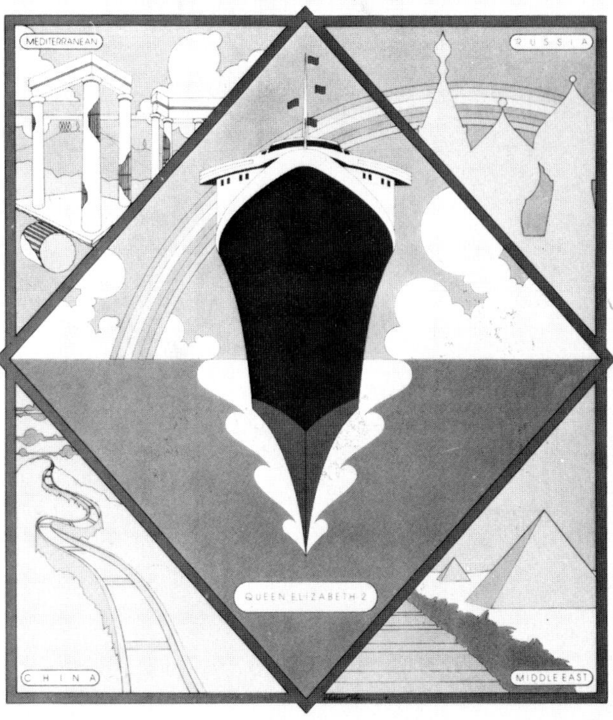

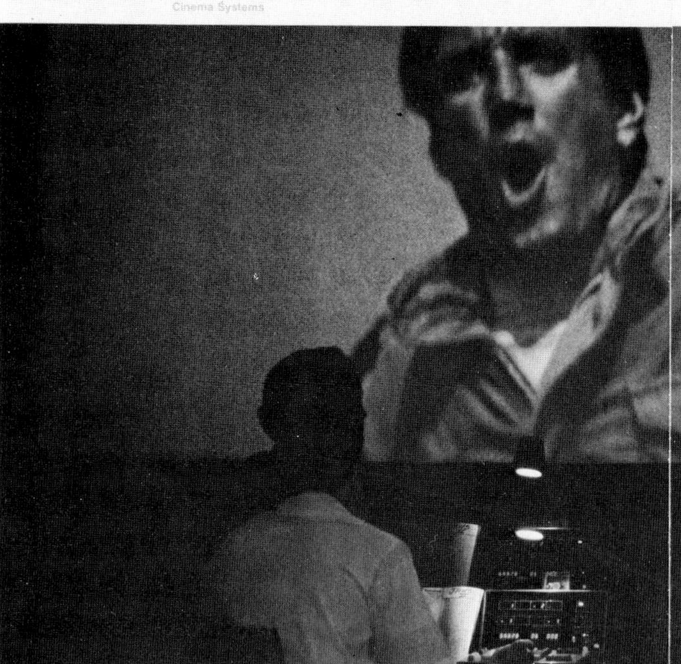

Technicolor Limited

Did You Know
The capacity of Technicolor's North Hollywood professional film laboratory exceeds the combined possible output of its two largest competitors in the world.

The Company's 70% owned subsidiary, Technicolor Limited, substantially completed the conversion to the color positive process on September 1, 1978 and achieved a significant reduction in personnel at the London laboratory at the time of the changeover. As a result of greater operating efficiencies and reduced labor costs associated with the color positive process, it is anticipated that the profitability of the London lab will improve significantly during the current fiscal year. Work is proceeding on new computer systems for this laboratory modeled on those in place in the North Hollywood facility, and it is expected that these systems will become fully operational in the final quarter of the current fiscal year. A thorough review of the London laboratory's pricing and markets will be undertaken during this fiscal year and it is expected that new aggressive sales direction and pricing structures similar to those successfully implemented in North Hollywood will result from this study. Ray Gaul, president of the Cinema Systems Division, has temporarily assumed the position of Managing Director of Technicolor Limited and will remain in London until an orderly transfer to the new color positive process has been accomplished and a permanent Managing Director of Technicolor Limited has been selected.

New York

The New York laboratory showed increased sales and satisfactory profits during the past year. Improved systems are being installed in the New York laboratory, and an expansion of that facility which is currently underway will permit the New York laboratory to handle a greater volume of business, while providing improvements in operating efficiencies, thus increasing the profitability of that laboratory.

Summary

As a result of the sales growth and improved operating efficiencies in all the Company's professional film processing laboratories, we anticipate continued major improvements in earnings and cash flow for our largest division. We now operate an international network of the most modern, efficient and customer responsive professional film laboratories in the world.

242 B

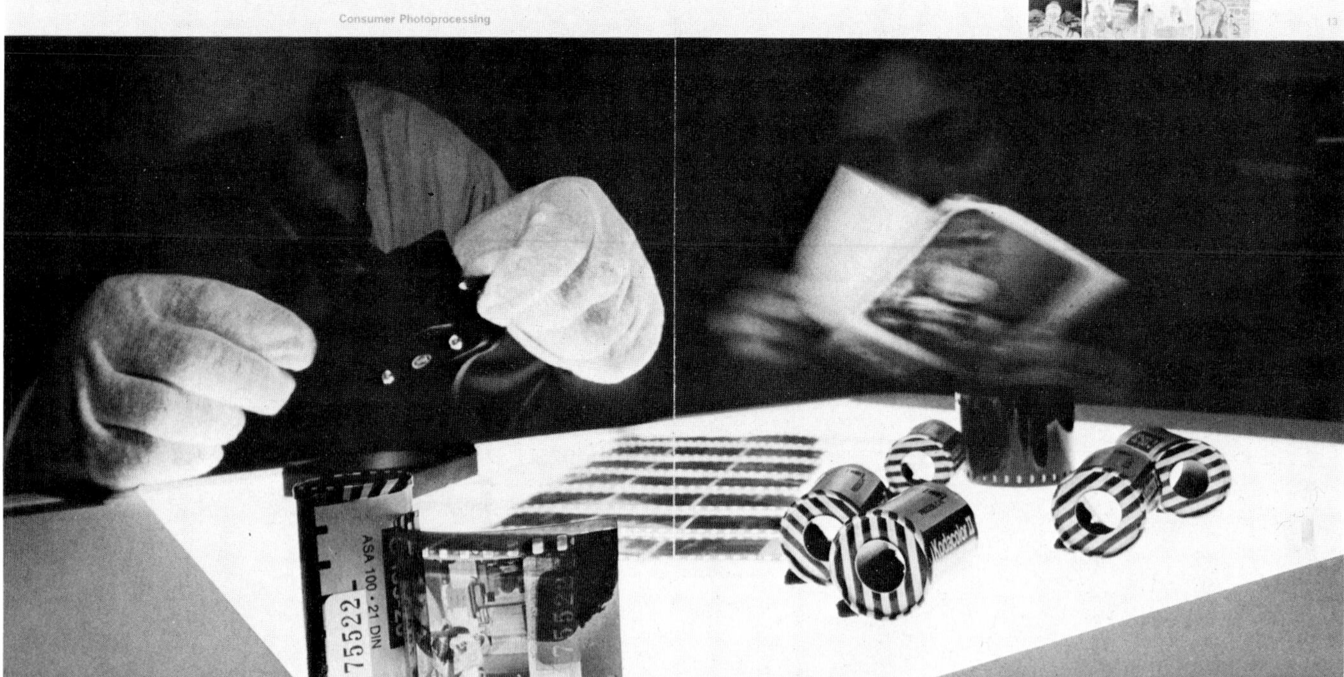

Did You Know
Technicolor's Standard Manufacturing is one of the leading manufacturers of consumer photoprocessing laboratory film splicing equipment and our equipment is used in the majority of all consumer film laboratories around the world.

China Project

Final testing of the equipment for a dye transfer process professional film laboratory for the Chinese Government near Peking was concluded in August, 1978. We expect that all unresolved matters will be satisfactorily concluded during the current fiscal year and that payment of the remaining balance on the contract will be received by and recognized in the accounts of Technicolor Limited in fiscal 1979.

Corporate Outlook

Despite the substantial write-offs in Italy, we enter fiscal 1979 with Technicolor in the strongest financial position in its history. We anticipate significant profit improvement in the near term, and we intend to take maximum advantage of the major cash flow expected to be generated by our existing operations by finding new areas of expansion for the Company where we can best capitalize on our expertise and the Technicolor reputation for quality services and products. Technicolor's future promises to be exciting — our executives and employees have eagerly joined us in accepting the challenges ahead and we look forward to reporting future results which reflect our present optimism.

Respectfully,

Morton Kamerman
Chairman of the Board
& Chief Executive Officer

Arthur N. Ryan
President and Chief
Operating Officer

C

242 A-C
Robert Miles Runyan Art Director
Marvin Silver Photographer
Jim Berte Designer
George Rice & Sons Production House
Robert Miles Runyan & Associates Agency
Technicolor, Inc. Client

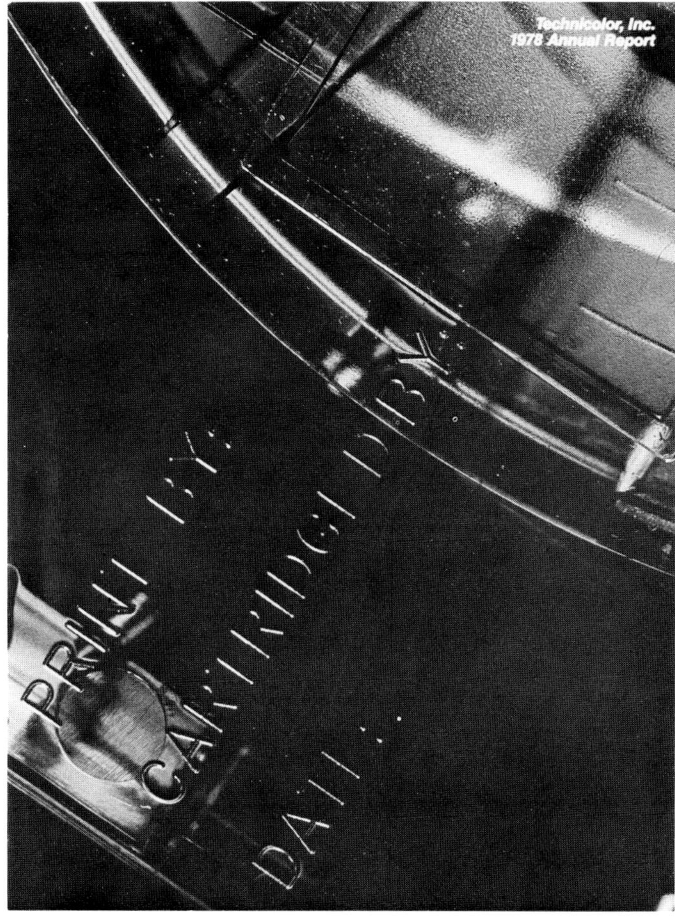

A

243
Guy Salvato Art Director
Jean-Claude Lejeune Photographer
Chris Fones Copywriter
Salvato & Coe Associates Studio
St. Joseph Hospital Client

"It's ironic, but sometimes we have to give people permission to show their feelings."

George Deming
Director of Social Services

George Deming was curious. As the director of Social Services in a hospital, he was constantly aware of the feelings and conflicts of those people who had their freedom, but not their health. When he volunteered his services as a clinical counselor to the residents of the local state penitentiary, he sought to find out how it felt for a person who had his health, but not his freedom. It became important for George to work out that balance.

George is deeply involved in a profession that helps people to honor their feelings and to make necessary decisions in moments of crisis—but he is also an individual with needs all his own. He is aware that in order to do his job well he must come to grips with his own feelings, explore his own sensitivities and search to answer his own questions.

"Discovering how we feel about something, and then venting—verbalizing the anger, guilt or frustration that is at the center of our emotions, is essential," George said. "It's ironic, but sometimes we have to give people permission to show their feelings."

One of George's current involvements is a group that

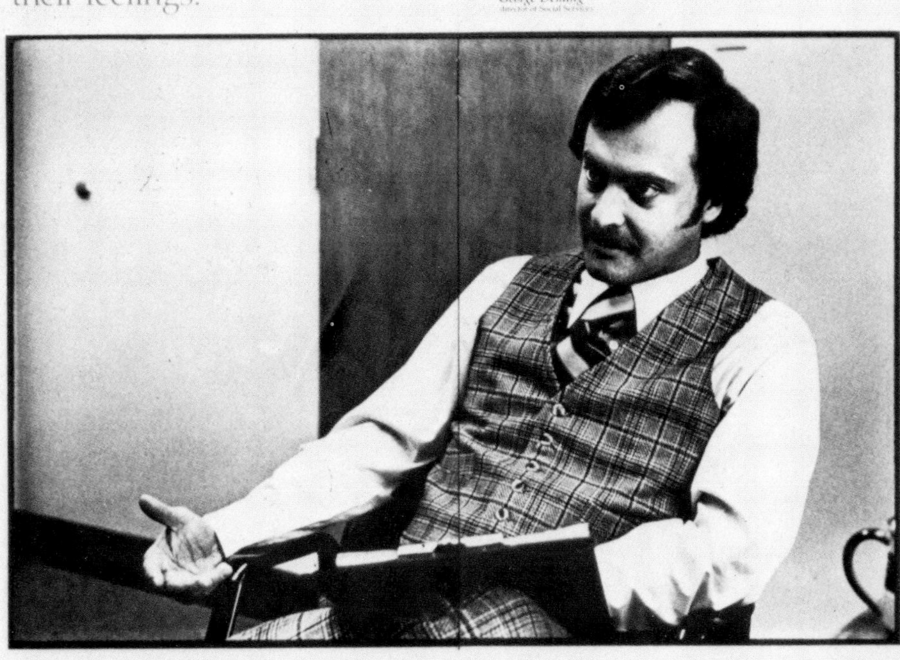

helps him answer his own questions—and gives others the "permission," the social and psychological framework in which they can deal with their feelings. The Compassionate Friends of Will County is a self-help group comprised of parents who have lost their children and are trying to resolve their grief. George is one of the co-sponsors of the group, but he describes his role as minimal. "The parents themselves are the foundation of the group," he said. "They identify with one another and can mirror and support each other's feelings. They're not learning from me—I'm learning from them."

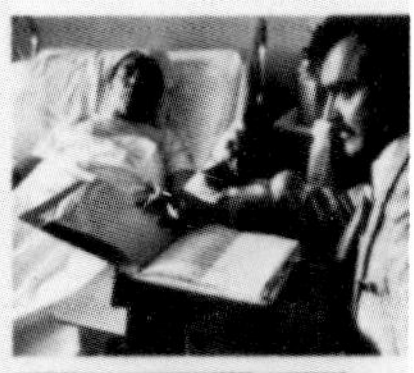

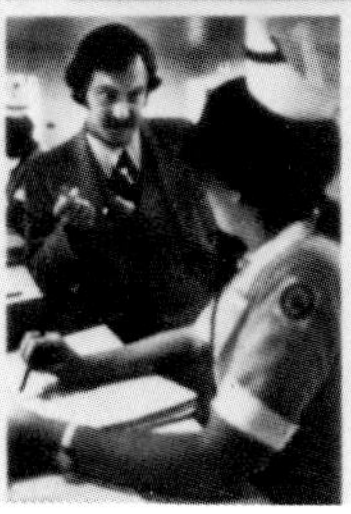

241 A-B
Jack Odette Art Director
John Batt, John Conn, Pat Guarasci Photographers
Francois Colos, Gene Calogero Illustrators
Mike Focar Designer
Citibank Client

240 A-B
John Anselmo, Tom Lombardi Art Directors
Brent Bear Photographer
John Anselmo Design Associates, Inc. Agency
Kennington Ltd. Client

A Young Texan's Guidebook to the Complete Education at Rice University

To help you in planning your higher education, Rice proudly presents ten excursions into the world of a university and its people. Read on, pardner.

246 A

EXCURSION I

Introduction

Reading time: approximately one minute.

There is a core of truth to Texas and Texans though to get to it you first have to slice through a lot of exaggerations. Take the case of the cowboy. Now, outside of a few culturally isolated spots, few people believe that everyone in Texas is a lariat-toting, shoot 'em-up cowpoke. But the flavor of mythic Texas lingers in that honest-to-God bowl of chili (that just can't be cooked in New Jersey) and in a genuine vitality of life here in the Lone Star State.

We in Texas are at home on the open range of human possibility. For that matter, Texans always have been, for the history of our state is not a history of staid contemplation or considered scholarly thought. Except, that is, at Rice University.

Rice is a unique place in the world of Texans – a university of international recognition and esteem. Only a handful of schools can match Rice as an undergraduate institution. Yet, folks tend to look askance at what's local, believing in the myth of distance and greener pastures, the notion that nothing can be too good if it's too nearby. Friend, Rice's reputation is peerless, and it's in Texas.

One of the tales heard by most Texas high school students is that Rice is a school with high academic standards and a long, recognized scholastic record, a school without "compare" in the region. This is true. The same students might be told that the entrance standards are so rigorous and the academic environment so severe that Rice is all work and no play. Pardner, this is one of those exaggerations.

Make no mistake about it, at Rice, standards are high, and the academics are challenging.

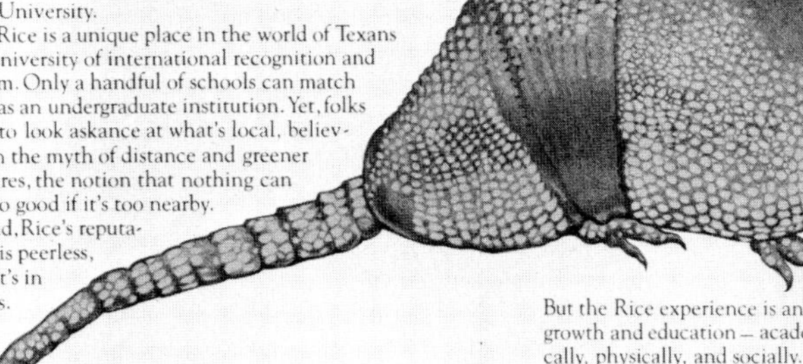

But the Rice experience is an experience in total growth and education – academically, philosophically, physically, and socially.

As Texas of today is an experiment in rapid growth, Rice is an experiment in human potential. By being the caliber of school it is and by being in the heart of the Houston area, Rice can offer educational and culturally cosmopolitan opportunities that very few schools can match. All that is missing is the catalyst – you, the promising student looking for a superb, well-rounded education.

B

246 A-B
Jerry Herring Art Director
Melissa Grimes Illustrator
Herring Design Agency
Rice University Client

247
Frank Pastorini Art Director
Manny Denner Photographer
Ted Colangelo Associates Studio
Xerox Corporation Client

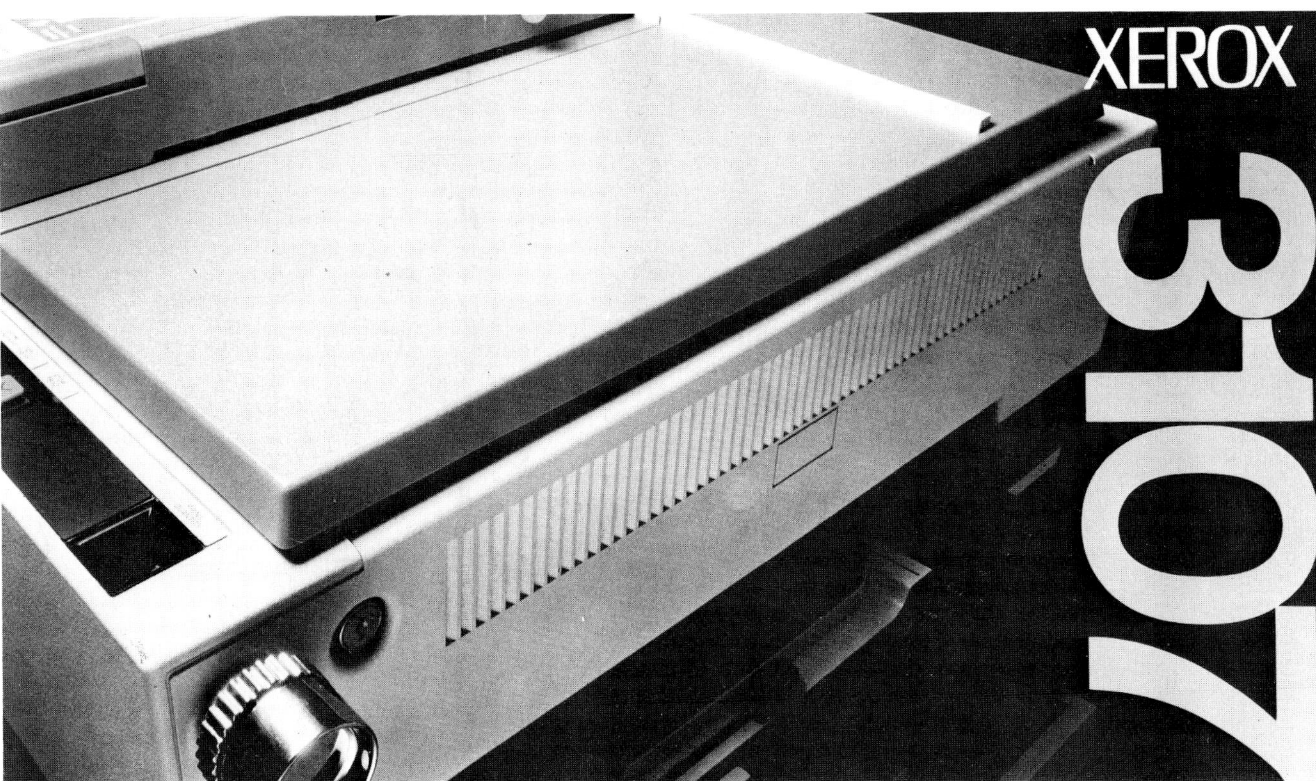

247

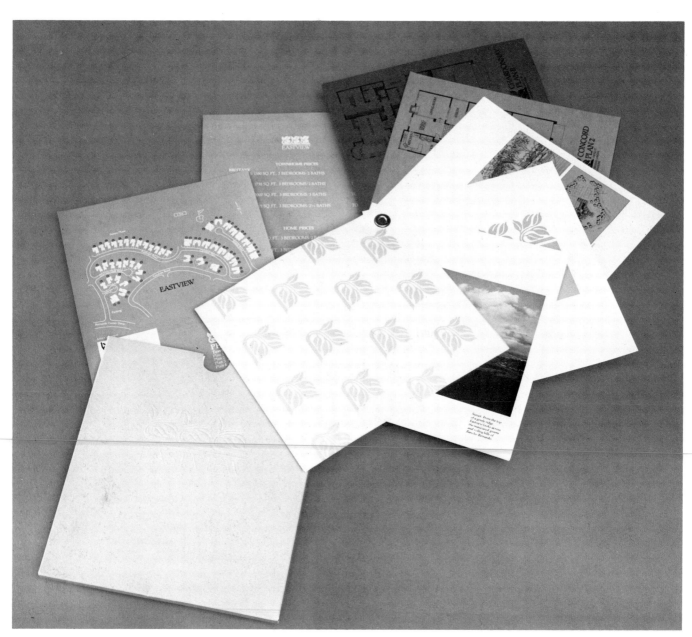

248
Jann Church Art Director
Lea Pascoe Designer
Jann Church Advertising & Graphic Design, Inc. Agency
Fujiken Kogyo Development Ltd. Client

249 A-B
Jackie Merri Meyer Art Director
Michael Bauman Photographer
Madelyn Black Copy Chief
Abraham & Straus Client

A

A

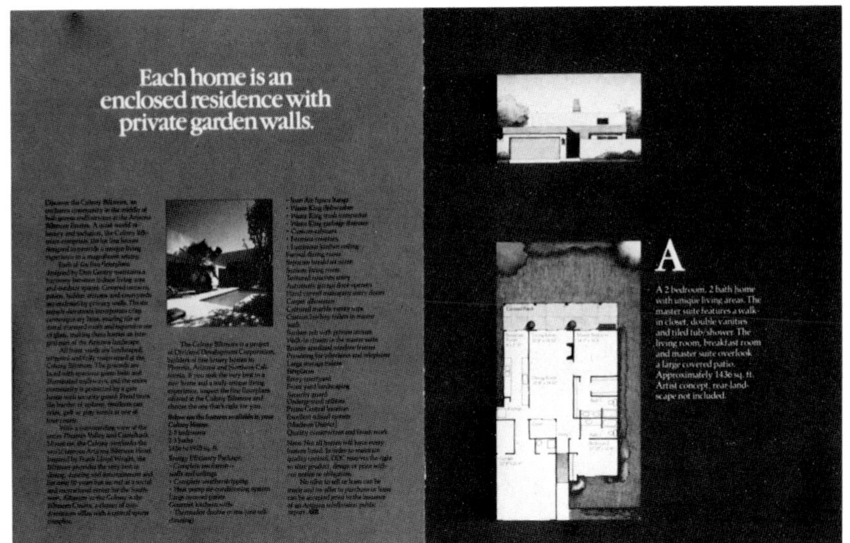

B

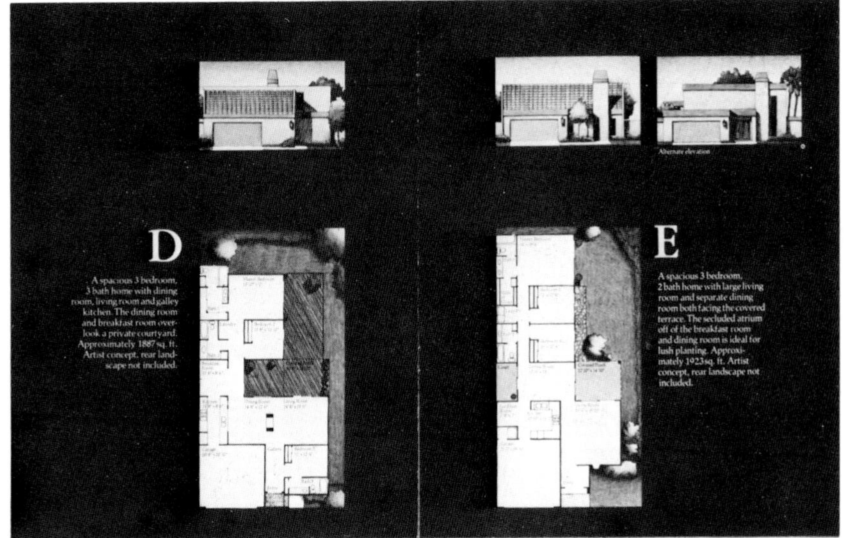

C

250 A-C
David Gauger Art Director
Barbeau Engh Photographer
Bob Johnson Illustrator
Greg Chew Designer
Gauger Sparks Silva Agency
Dividend Development Corp. Client

B

252 A-D
Joseph M. Essex Art Director
David Deahl Photographer
Burson-Marsteller/Design Group Agency
Society of Typographic Arts Client

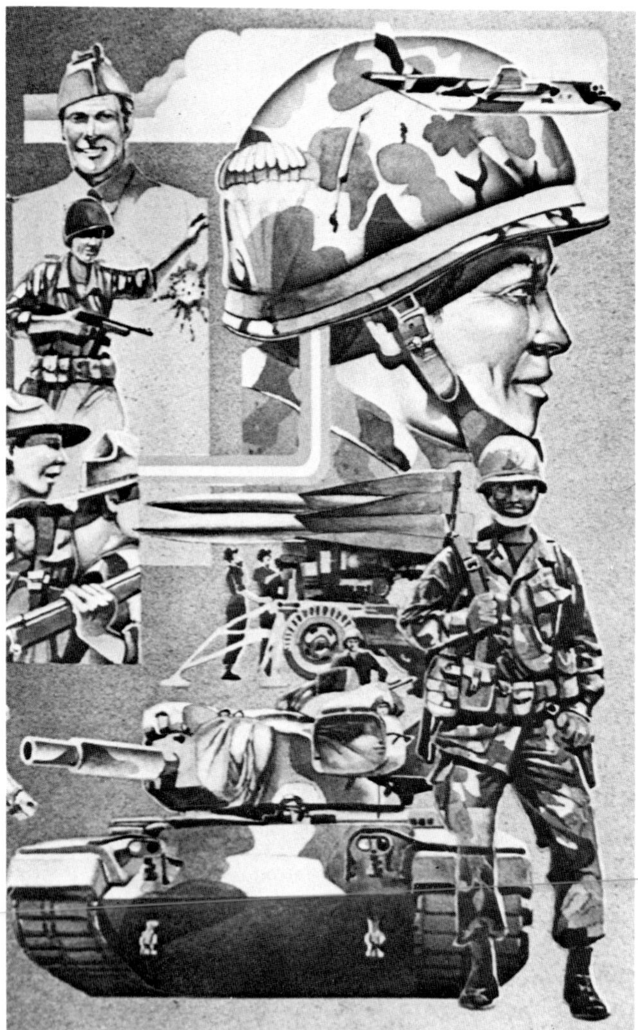

A

ARMOR

The arm of decision. Direct descendant of the horse-soldiers. Mission: move in swiftly. Disorganize, demoralize and destroy the opposition.

Scout vehicles dart in, spot the enemy. Report. Call in the heavyweights. Tanks. Big tanks. Up to 57 tons of steel and 750 horsepower come thundering in on each set of treads. Stop. Fire. Maneuver. Stand your ground. Slug it out. Mighty machines. But battles are won by men.

As an Armor soldier, you can be the brain, the heart and the muscle that make it happen. The machine will be an extension of yourself. As a gunner, loader or driver, you'll get to know your machine as you know your own mind. Your skill and courage will turn the rumbling giant into a fearful fighting machine.

Make it move, feint, throw punches. Then bring it home without a mark on it. That's the challenge of Armor. A big one. Big enough to test the best.

B

251 A-D
Paul DiMartino Art Director
Graphics Group Agency
U.S. Army Client

C

RANGERS

The go-anywhere soldiers. The best trained, most highly disciplined troops in the world. They have a tradition of physical challenge that came into being before the War of Independence. Volunteers all. They choose to live by a creed of honor and dedication that reads in part: "Surrender is not a Ranger word. I will never leave a fallen comrade to fall into the hands of the enemy, and under no circumstances will I ever embarrass my country."

As a Ranger, you'll learn to survive and function under the most extreme conditions. You'll accept danger as a constant companion. You'll act as the eyes of the Army, probing deep into unfriendly territory. You'll lead others on long range reconnaissance missions. And they'll follow, because your fellow soldiers know that the Ranger identification you wear means you've mastered the challenge of the toughest training the Army has to offer.

RANGER
"I will always endeavor to uphold the prestige, honor, and high esprit de corps of my Ranger Battalion."

D

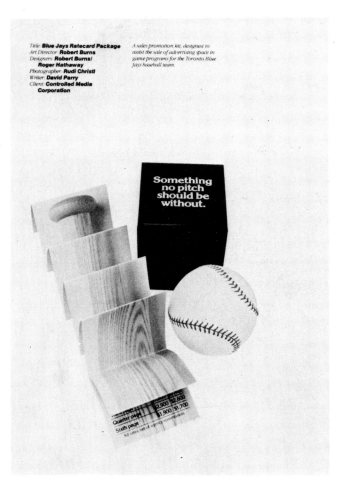

252 A

Title **Illini Union Poster**
Art Director **Gary Alfredson**
Designer **Gary Alfredson**
Writer **Christine Haxager**
Agency **Burson-Marsteller/ Chicago**
Client **University of Illinois**

The clubhouse referred to in the headline of this poster, is the Illini Union, a student center of the University of Illinois. The poster is sent to all first-time students as part of an introduction package the summer before the first term. It serves as an introduction to the building's services, its people and its tradition. Its main purpose is image-building: equating the rise of many campus activities and events with the push to build and maintain the Illini Union.

STA Member

B

Title **Blue Jays Ratecard Package**
Art Director **Robert Burns**
Designers **Robert Burns/ Roger Hathaway**
Photographer **Rudi Christl**
Writer **David Parry**
Client **Controlled Media Corporation**

A sales promotion kit, designed to assist the sale of advertising space in game programs for the Toronto Blue Jays baseball team.

Something no pitch should be without.

C

Title **St. Regis Annual Report 1976**
Art Directors **Roger Cook, Don Shanosky**
Designers **Roger Cook, Don Shanosky, Cook and Shanosky Assoc., Inc.**
Photographer **Arthur Beck**
Writer **Bruce McGhie, McGhie Associates**
Agency **McGhie Associates**
Client **St. Regis Paper Company**

Our three goals with the 1976 report:

To report on the year's operations with candor and clarity.

To feature in a compelling way a commitment to printing as a prime St. Regis market.

To make the report itself an example of conceptual simplicity and graphic excellence. Our technique was to present in parallel the business report—precisely organized and backed by useful statistics—and an illustrated story comprised of strongly composed still-lifes and tightly worded story captions.

1976 Annual Report
ST REGIS

D

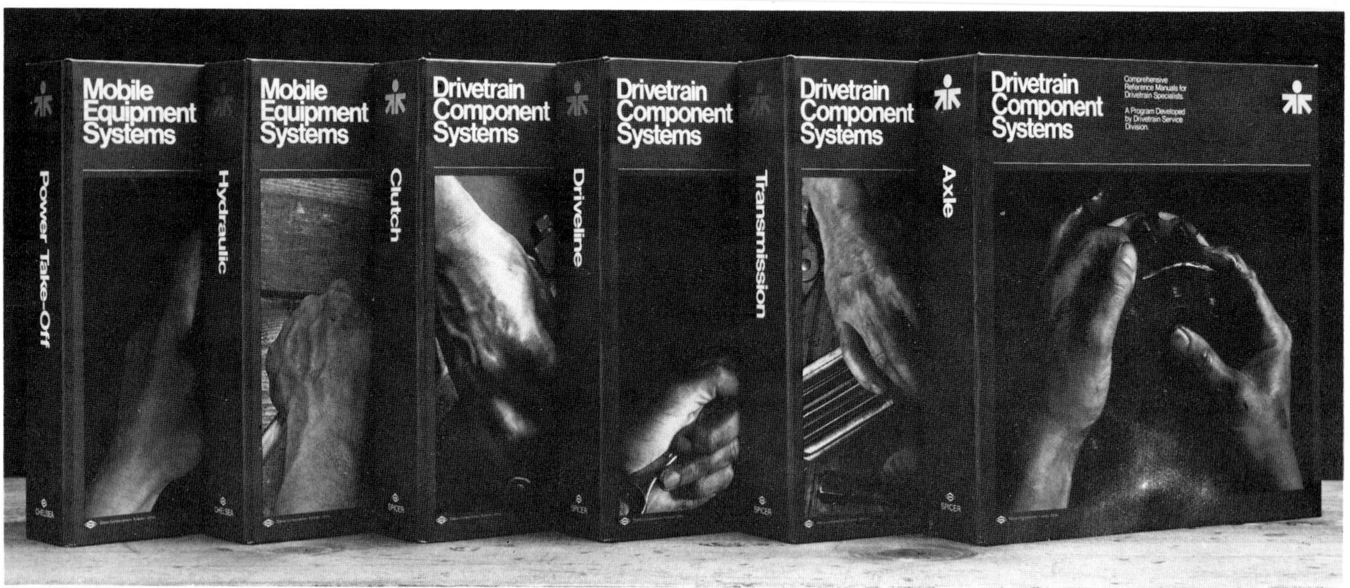

253
Terry Lesniewicz, Al Navarre Art Directors
Jim Rohman Photographer
Lesniewicz/Navarre Agency
Drivetrain Service Division, Dana Corporation Client

254
Hal Frazier Art Director
Bob Stevens Photographer
John Vince, Paul Hauge, Designers
Frazier Design Associates Studio
Neumarket Design Associates Agency
Cole-Haan Client

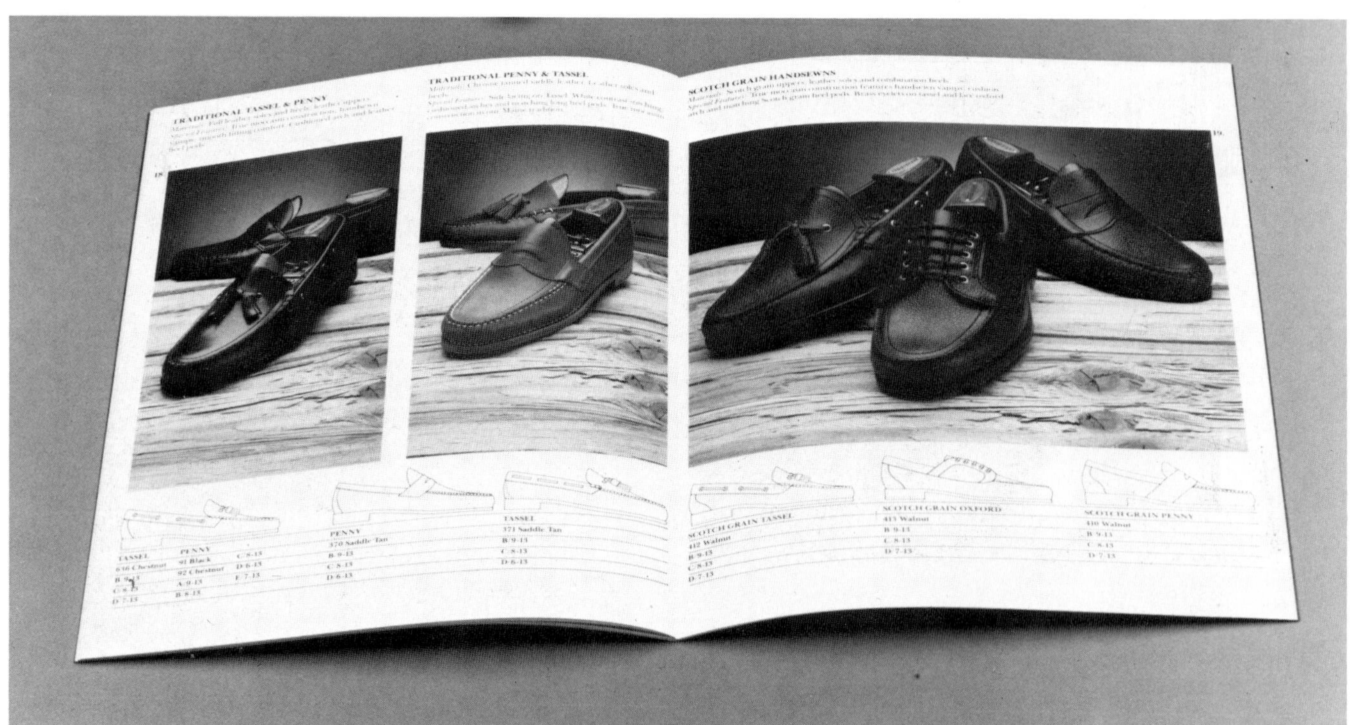

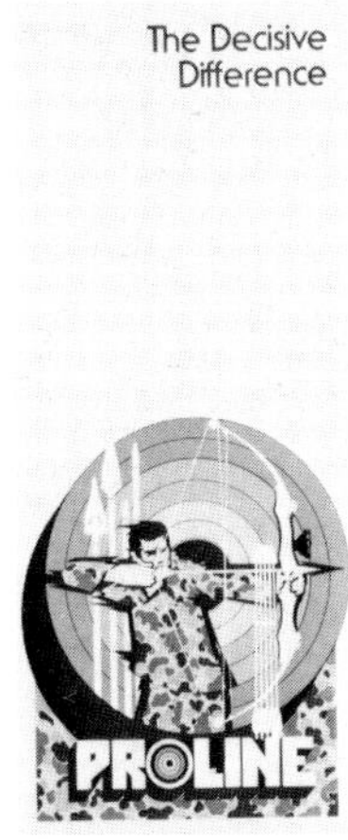

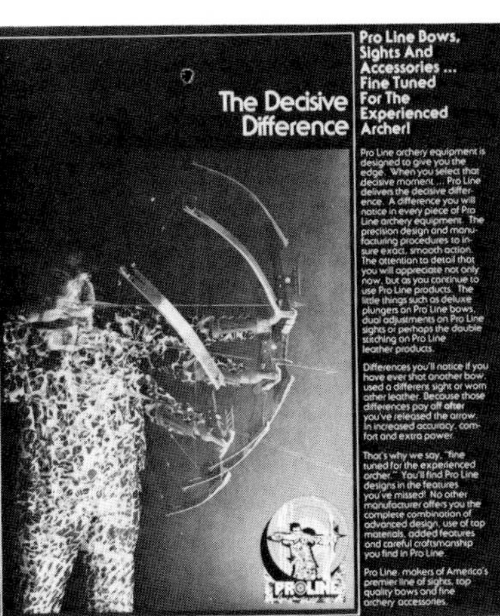

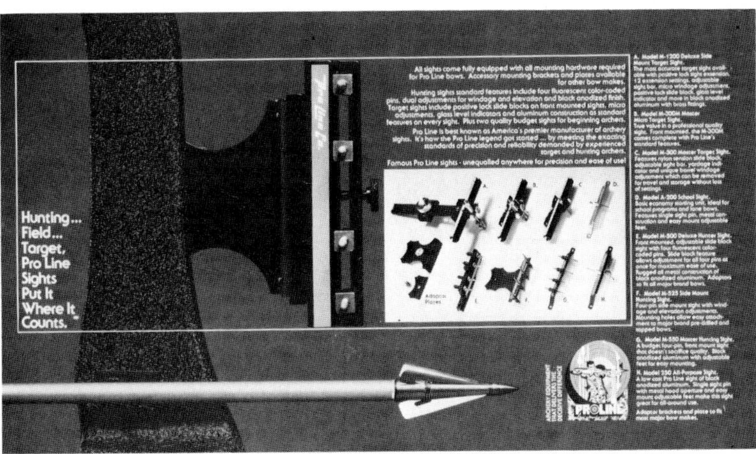

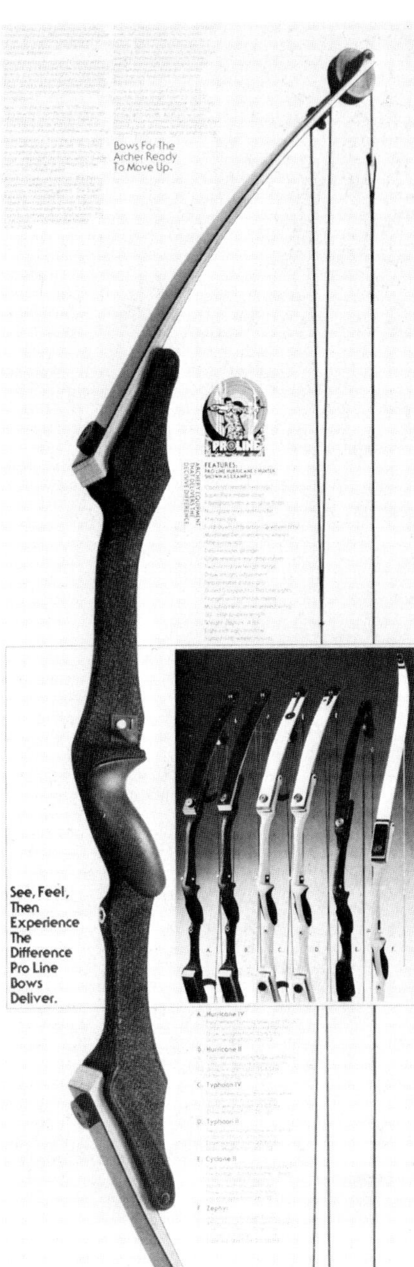

255
Marc A. Williams Art Director
Rick Everly, Marc A. Williams Photographers
Starr Advertising Agency
Pro Line Company Client

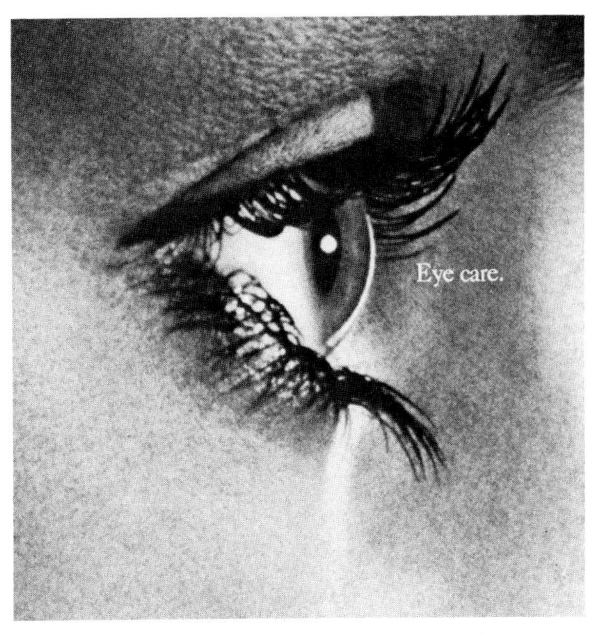

256
Bob Paganucci Art Director
Ed Gallucci Photographer
Bob Paganucci, Jane Cullen Designers
Ciba-Geigy Client

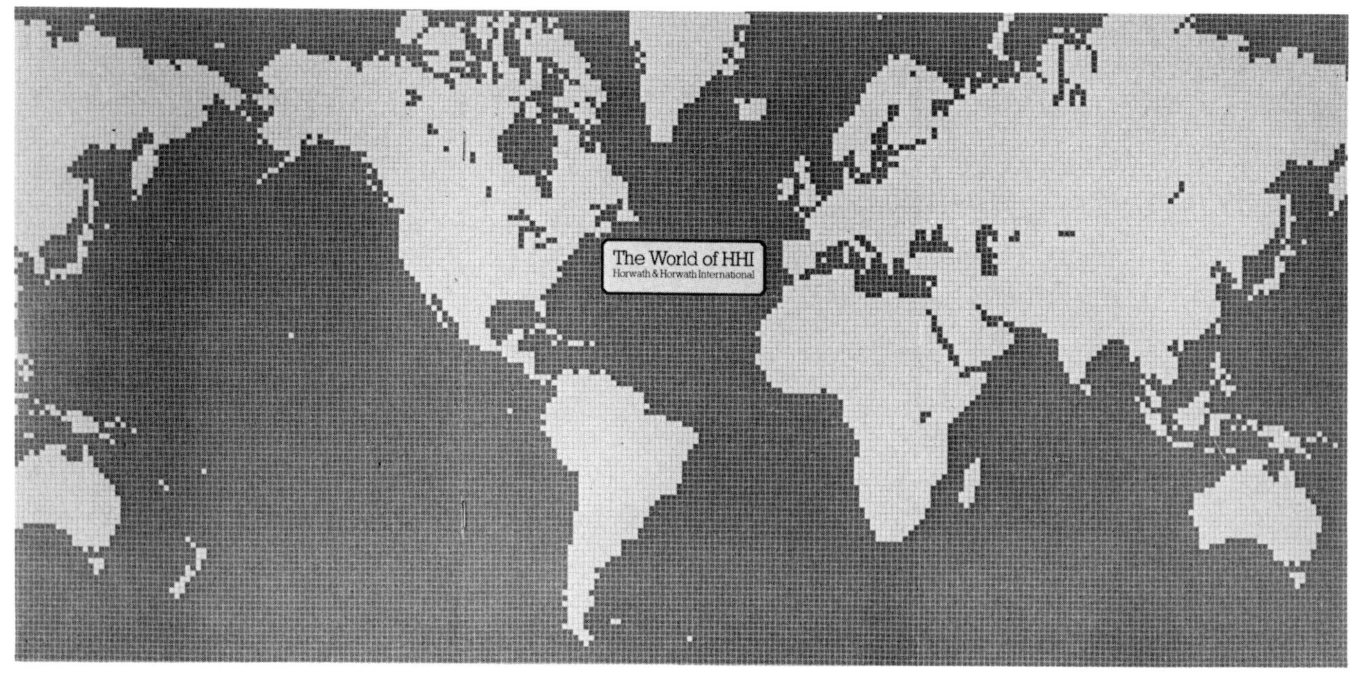

A

257 A-D
Robert Burns Art Director
Diane Dusseault Technical Artist
Ann Ames Designer
Burns, Cooper, Hynes Limited Agency
Horwath & Horwath International Client

"Horwath & Horwath International was deliberately created to provide something extra for its clients."

A common thread links all these stories. In each case, a growing client was assisted in realizing its goals by a firm of auditors, accountants and advisers that was equally growth-oriented itself. Each company found contacts, resources, experience and expertise to help chart a safe and sound course through unfamiliar waters.

The services they used came from an international network of independent accounting firms called Horwath & Horwath International. It was deliberately created to provide something extra for its clients.

In the Horwath & Horwath International network, each member firm is an independent entity in its own country, owned and operated by local professionals. Each firm is well established as a leader in its national business community.

The benefits of this particular structure are considerable.

First, it allows the network to include firms of the highest calibre in each country. Since each firm retains its autonomy, there is a "home office" in every country.

Second, because each firm is solidly rooted in its own national environment, each possesses contacts, experience and an intimate knowledge of local customs, laws and business conditions that only nationals can acquire. The result is a pool of practical commercial expertise on a world wide scale that is truly comprehensive.

Third, because the member firms frequently work together on behalf of clients, there are abundant opportunities for the development, extension and sharing of specialized expertise in such areas as tax planning, foreign exchange controls, and management information systems.

B

"Client relationships are personal, not institutional, and services are designed to meet each client's individual requirements."

The network includes major firms in each of the leading industrial nations. But it is by no means confined to these regions; there are more than 60 HHI member firms in over 50 countries around the world.

Apart from its comprehensive international coverage, the HHI network has another notable characteristic – a highly personal, entrepreneurial approach to client service. This means that the needs and ambitions of growth-oriented businessmen are uppermost in the minds of HHI accountants and consultants at all times. It also ensures that even among the largest member firms, client relationships are personal, not institutional, and services are designed to meet each client's individual requirements.

Of course, providing something extra is only practicable when the basic requisites are already there. Auditing, accounting and tax services of the highest quality are the prime products of the HHI network, and the foundation upon which everything else rests. To maintain superior standards in these areas, all HHI members participate in regular international reviews to keep abreast of technical developments and changes in auditing and accounting methods, procedures and controls around the world. Formal programs also assist members in recruiting fully-qualified personnel and in providing advanced education for existing staff.

HHI firms offer additional services which provide each client with specialized expertise and assistance to fit its particular needs.

Tax planning has become an extremely important aspect of international business management, and constitutes a major field of specialized service. As world trade has expanded, so have the complexities of tax legislation, sometimes compounded by drastic differences of both principle and practice between countries.

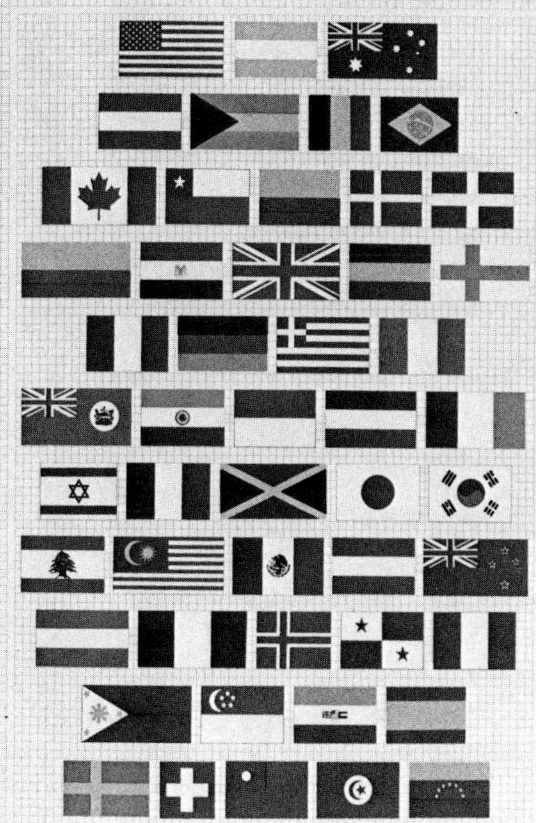

C

"The Horwath & Horwath International network offers a variety of management advisory services that is as broad and sophisticated as the network's clientele."

Although fraught with potential hazards, tax laws can nevertheless be turned to competitive advantage under expert guidance. This requires intimate knowledge of both tax laws and administrative practices around the world. Because legislation is subject to constant amendment, it is also necessary to continually monitor savings and deferral opportunities in order to take immediate advantage of potential benefits and avoid needless liabilities.

HHI maintains international tax committees in the world's major economic regions. They are composed of planning specialists, including international tax partners who provide expert advice to all affiliates in each region. HHI tax planners seek not only to minimize the liabilities of existing operations, but also continually look for ways to exploit new opportunities – such as recommending changes in corporate structure to take advantage of international tax treaties.

Beyond the intricacies of taxation, the HHI network offers a variety of management advisory services that is as broad and sophisticated as the network's clientele.

An important area of activity is the design and implementation of electronic data processing and other computer-based information systems. Sophisticated information systems have become essential in modern business, providing day to day controls that are often vital to competitive survival. But while the right EDP system can provide enormous benefits, the wrong one can cripple a company with unnecessary costs and delays.

The first step towards a truly effective management information system is a feasibility study. HHI experts perform these studies for all types of businesses, including, wherever necessary, analyses of alternative systems to determine which will yield the best results at the least cost. Drawing on extensive experience, they also prepare recommendations on equipment and software, and then personally oversee implementation of the recommended plan. This last step is the most important, and the one which best reflects HHI's practical orientation. The ultimate objective of the entire process is to assist the client company to become self-sufficient in information processing, rather than depending on outside resources.

D

Eli Lilly and Company
A diversified, multinational corporation manufacturing quality pharmaceuticals for over 100 years as well as agricultural, cosmetic, and medical electronic products.

258 A

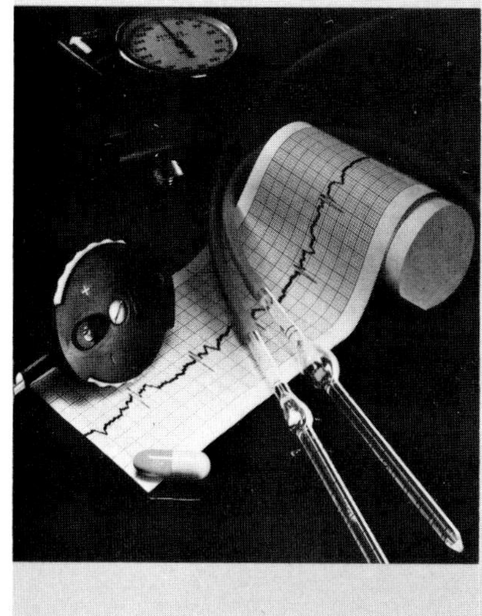

Pharmaceutical Division
Markets over 300 pharmaceutical products within the United States through Lilly and Dista sales organizations.

B

Eli Lilly International Corporation
Markets and distributes products in over 130 countries around the world, with production facilities in 18 countries.

C

258 A-C
Robert L. Willis, Richard E. Beck Art Directors
Design Associates/Indianapolis Agency
Eli Lilly and Company Client

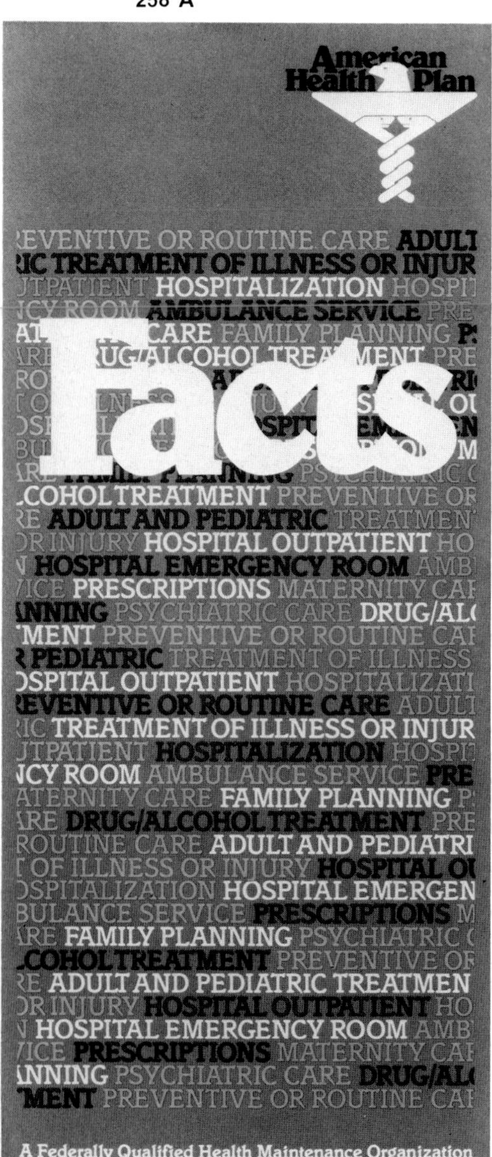

American Health Plan
Facts
A Federally Qualified Health Maintenance Organization

259
Michael Wolk, Ross Wittenberg Art Directors
Lisa Adams, Otis Sweat Illustrators
Joseph Piatti, Michael Wolk, Ross Wittenberg Designers
Piatti/Bornstein/Wolk & Associates, Inc. Agency
American Health Plan, Inc. Client

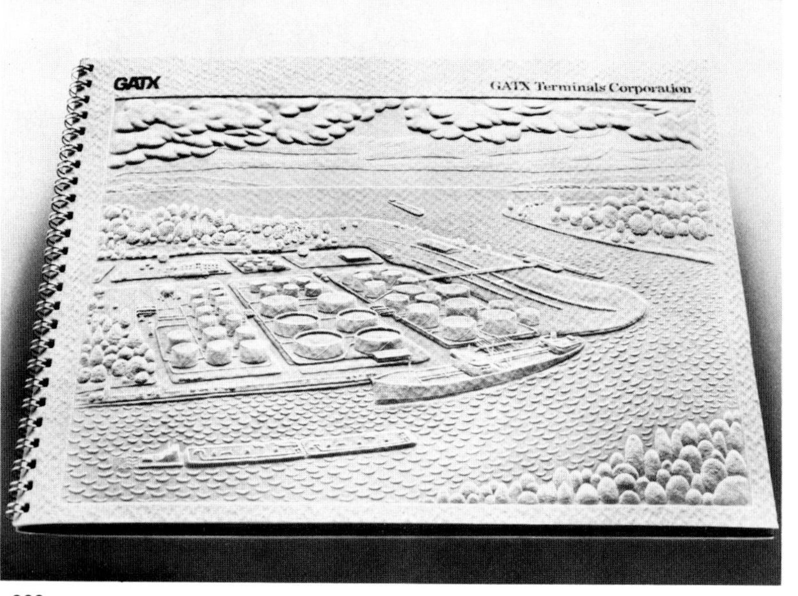

260

268
Steven Sessions Art Director
Joe Baraban Photographer
Baxter & Korge Inc. Agency
Schlumberger Client

269
Christer Holmquist Art Director
HLR/BBDO Agency
Foreningen for Blodavsjuka I Sverige Client

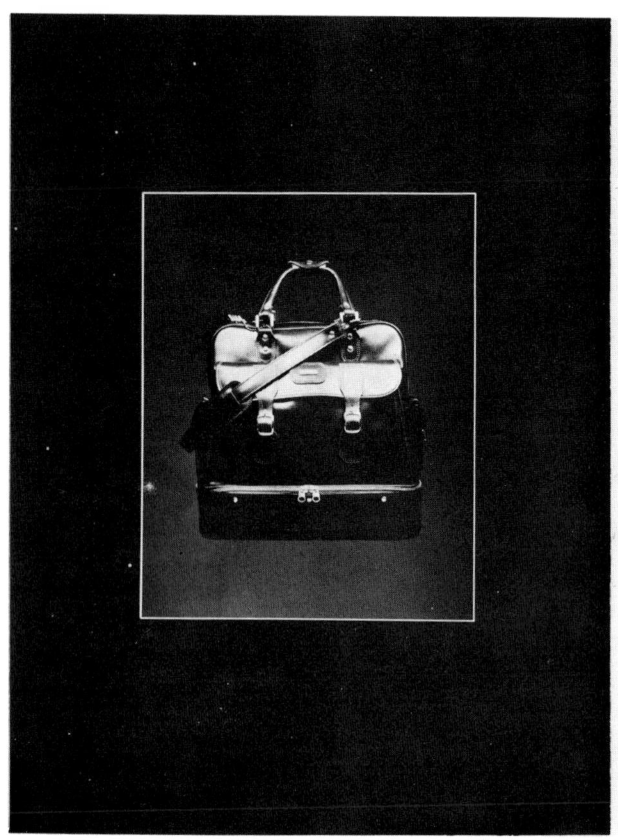

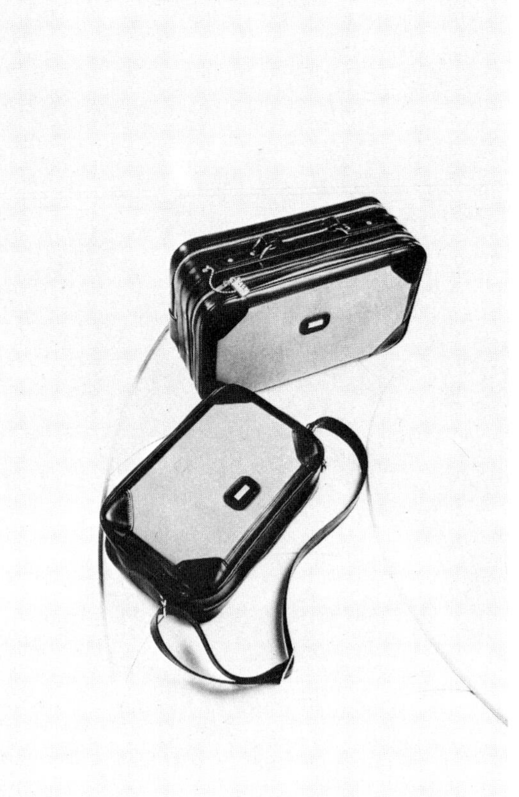

270
Alex Tsao Art Director
Neil Selkirk Inc. Studio
Epstein Raboy Advertising Inc. Agency
Invicta-York Luggage Client

271
William B. Stewart, Dennis Suplina Art Directors
Al Karp Photographer
North Studios Agency
Coopers & Lybrand Client

273
Steve McDonald Art Director
Linda Laffitte Illustrator
University of South Carolina Instructional Services Center Agency
Robert Sumwalt III—Pilot Client

274
Bob Pellegrini, David Kaestle Art Directors
Madelene Lees Designer
Pellegrini & Kaestle, Inc. Agency
Mobil Oil Corporation Client

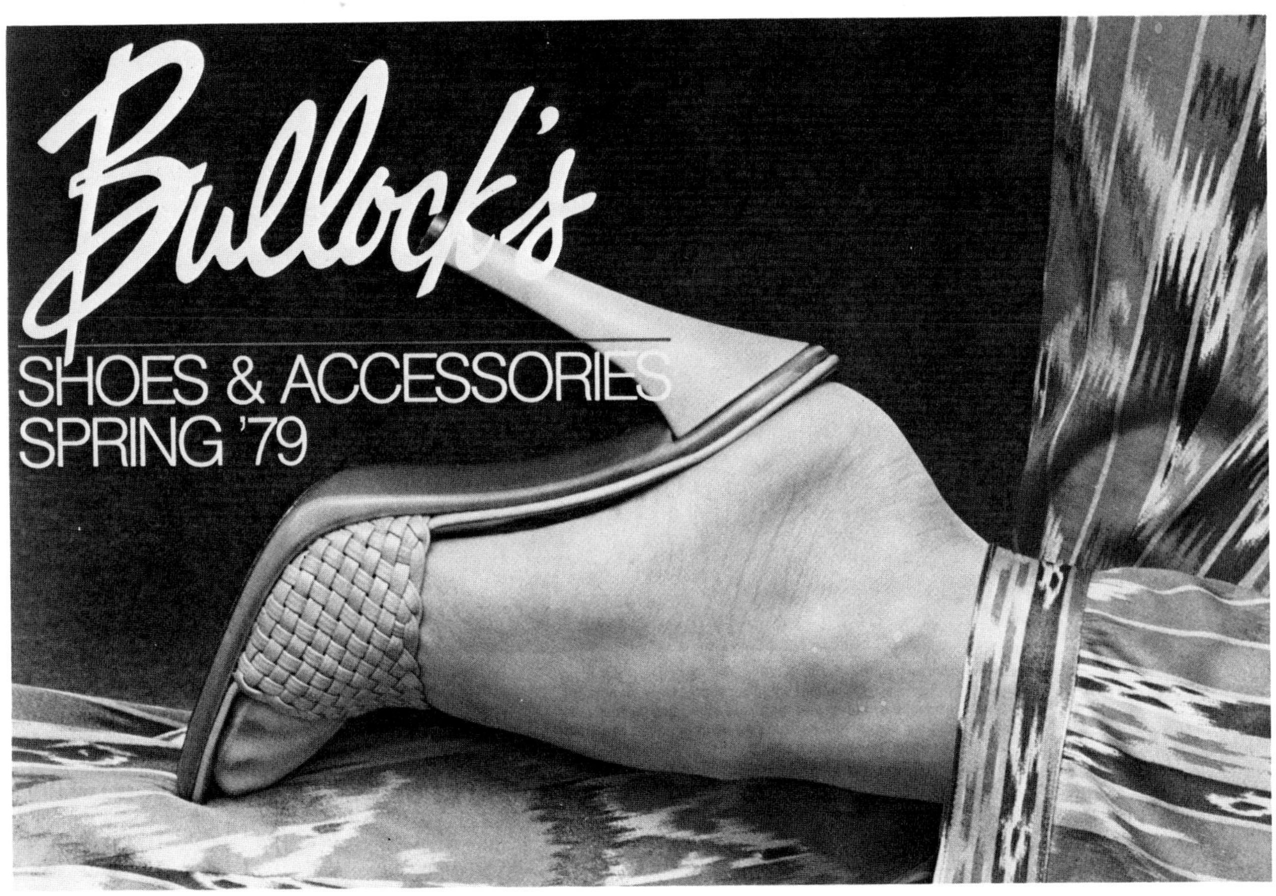

272
Pierre Camps Art Director
Brian Leatart Photographer
Bullock's Client

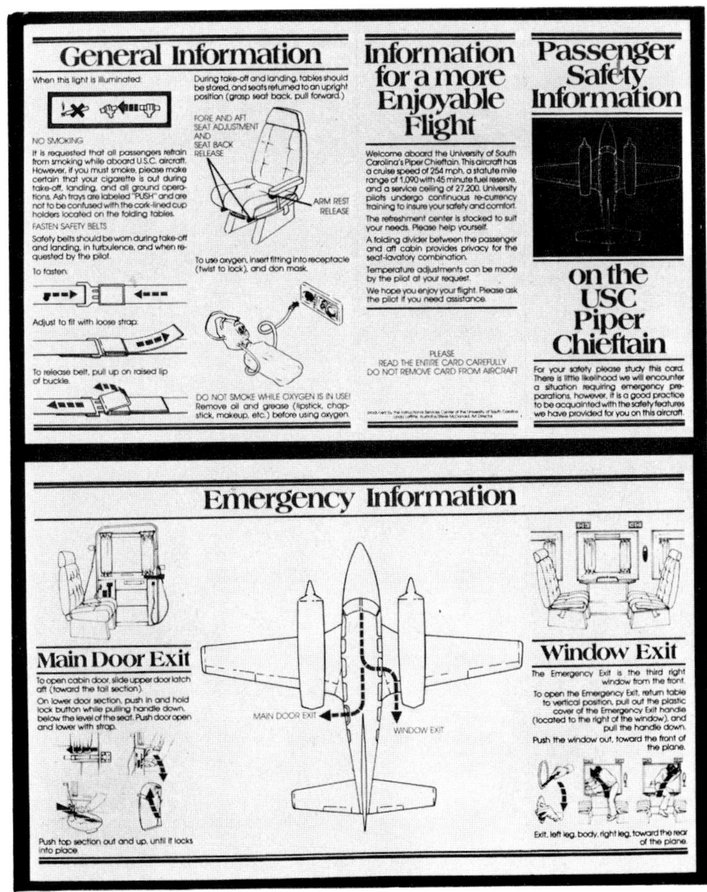

General Information

When this light is illuminated:

NO SMOKING

It is requested that all passengers refrain from smoking while aboard U.S.C. aircraft. However, if you must smoke, please make certain that your cigarette is out during take-off, landing, and all ground operations. Ash trays are labeled "PUSH" and are not to be confused with the cork-lined cup holders located on the folding tables.

FASTEN SAFETY BELTS

Safety belts should be worn during take-off and landing, in turbulence, and when requested by the pilot.

To fasten:

Adjust to fit with loose strap:

To release belt, pull up on raised lip of buckle.

During take-off and landing, tables should be stored, and seats returned to an upright position (grasp seat back, pull forward.)

FORE AND AFT SEAT ADJUSTMENT AND SEAT BACK RELEASE

ARM REST RELEASE

To use oxygen, insert fitting into receptacle (twist to lock), and don mask.

DO NOT SMOKE WHILE OXYGEN IS IN USE! Remove oil and grease (lipstick, chapstick, makeup, etc.) before using oxygen.

Information for a more Enjoyable Flight

Welcome aboard the University of South Carolina's Piper Chieftain. This aircraft has a cruise speed of 254 mph, a statute mile range of 1,090 with 45 minute fuel reserve, and a service ceiling of 27,200. University pilots undergo continuous re-currency training to insure your safety and comfort.

The refreshment center is stocked to suit your needs. Please help yourself.

A folding divider between the passenger and aft cabin provides privacy for the seat-lavatory combination.

Temperature adjustments can be made by the pilot at your request.

We hope you enjoy your flight. Please ask the pilot if you need assistance.

PLEASE
READ THE ENTIRE CARD CAREFULLY
DO NOT REMOVE CARD FROM AIRCRAFT

Passenger Safety Information on the USC Piper Chieftain

For your safety please study this card. There is little likelihood we will encounter a situation requiring emergency preparations, however, it is a good practice to be acquainted with the safety features we have provided for you on this aircraft.

Emergency Information

Main Door Exit

To open cabin door, slide upper door latch aft (toward the tail section).

On lower door section, push in and hold lock button while pulling handle down, below the level of the seat. Push door open and lower with strap.

Push top section out and up, until it locks into place.

MAIN DOOR EXIT

WINDOW EXIT

Window Exit

The Emergency Exit is the third right window from the front.

To open the Emergency Exit, return table to vertical position, pull out the plastic cover of the Emergency Exit handle (located to the right of the window), and pull the handle down.

Push the window out, toward the front of the plane.

Exit, left leg, body, right leg, toward the rear of the plane.

273

274

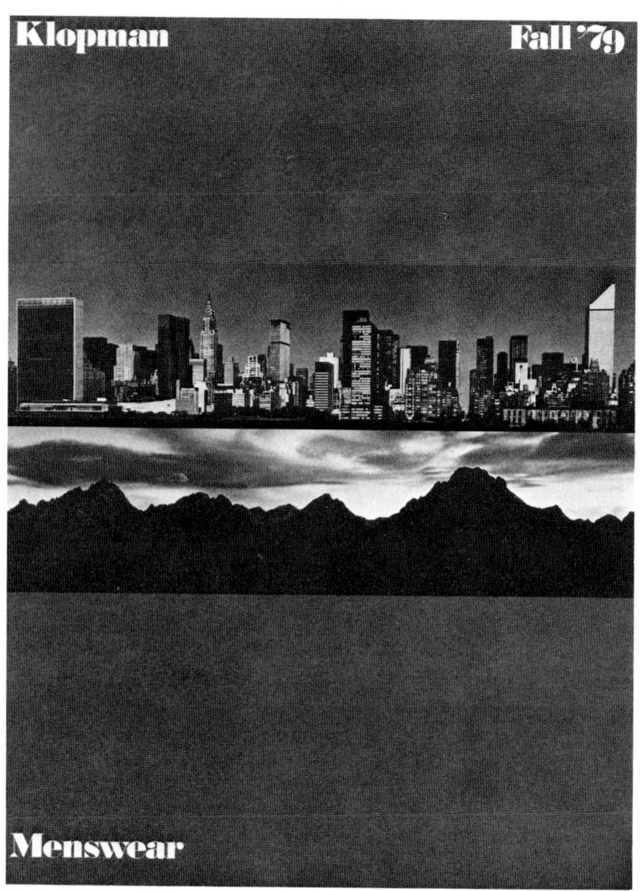

275
Bob Saipeter Art Director
Lopez Saipeter, Inc. Agency
Klopman Mills Client

276 A-C
Ktell Strahle, Anders Borgstrom
Art Directors
Hera Information Agency
Fiat Svenska AB Client

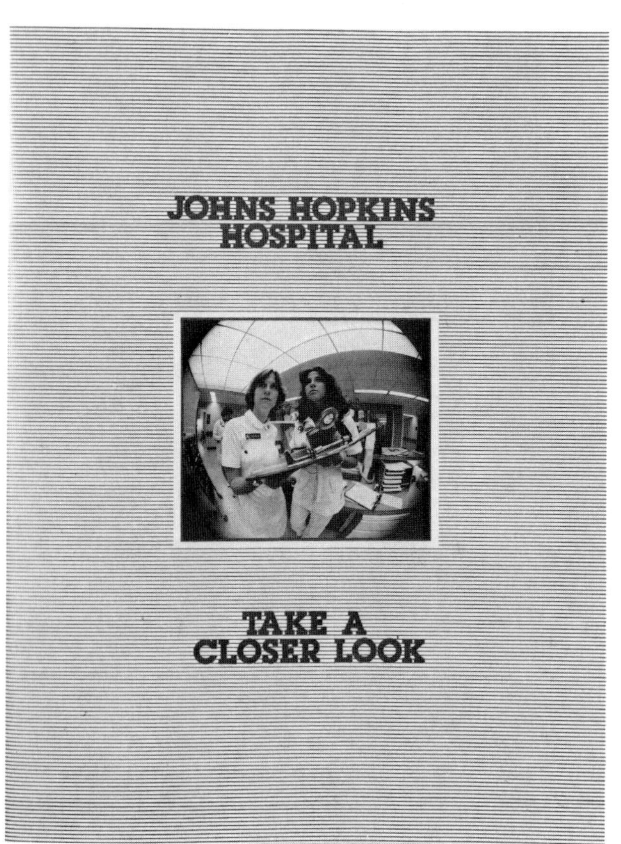

277
Robert Cunningham Art Director
Joe Sullivan Photographer
World Wide Agency, Inc., Advertising Agency
John Hopkins Hospital Client

278
William Naegels Art Director
Kenneth McGowan Photographer
Graphitti Agency
Warner Brothers Records Client

FIAT 127

Urban Granström är skogsförman vid Domänverket i Norrbotten. För en tid sedan köpte han och familjen en ny Fiat 127. De är Fiat-frälsta sedan fyra år tillbaka. – Bättre bil kan inte vi tänka oss, säger Urban bl. a. på nästa uppslag.

276 B

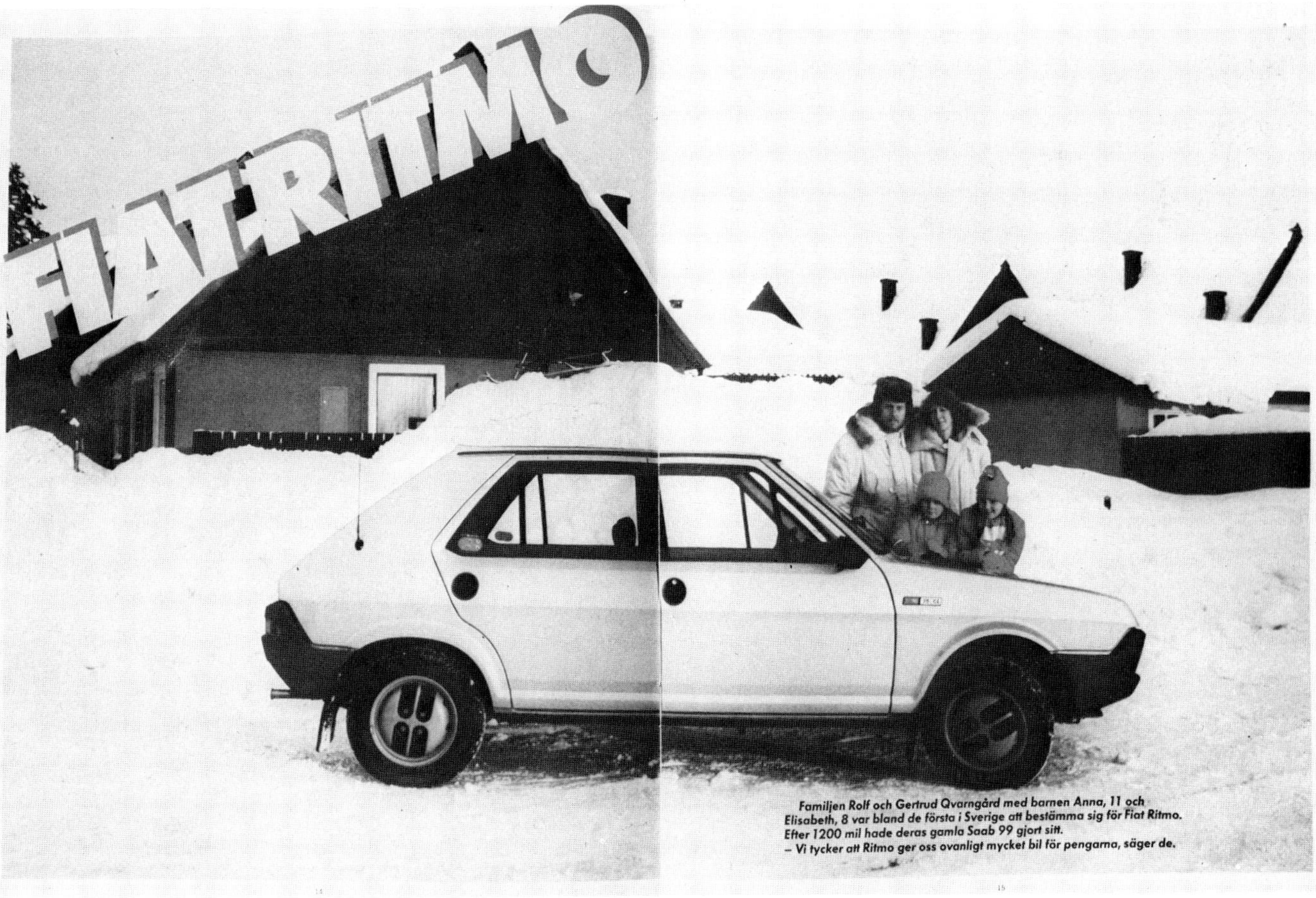

FIAT-RITMO

Familjen Rolf och Gertrud Qvarngård med barnen Anna, 11 och Elisabeth, 8 var bland de första i Sverige att bestämma sig för Fiat Ritmo. Efter 1200 mil hade deras gamla Saab 99 gjort sitt.
– Vi tycker att Ritmo ger oss ovanligt mycket bil för pengarna, säger de.

C

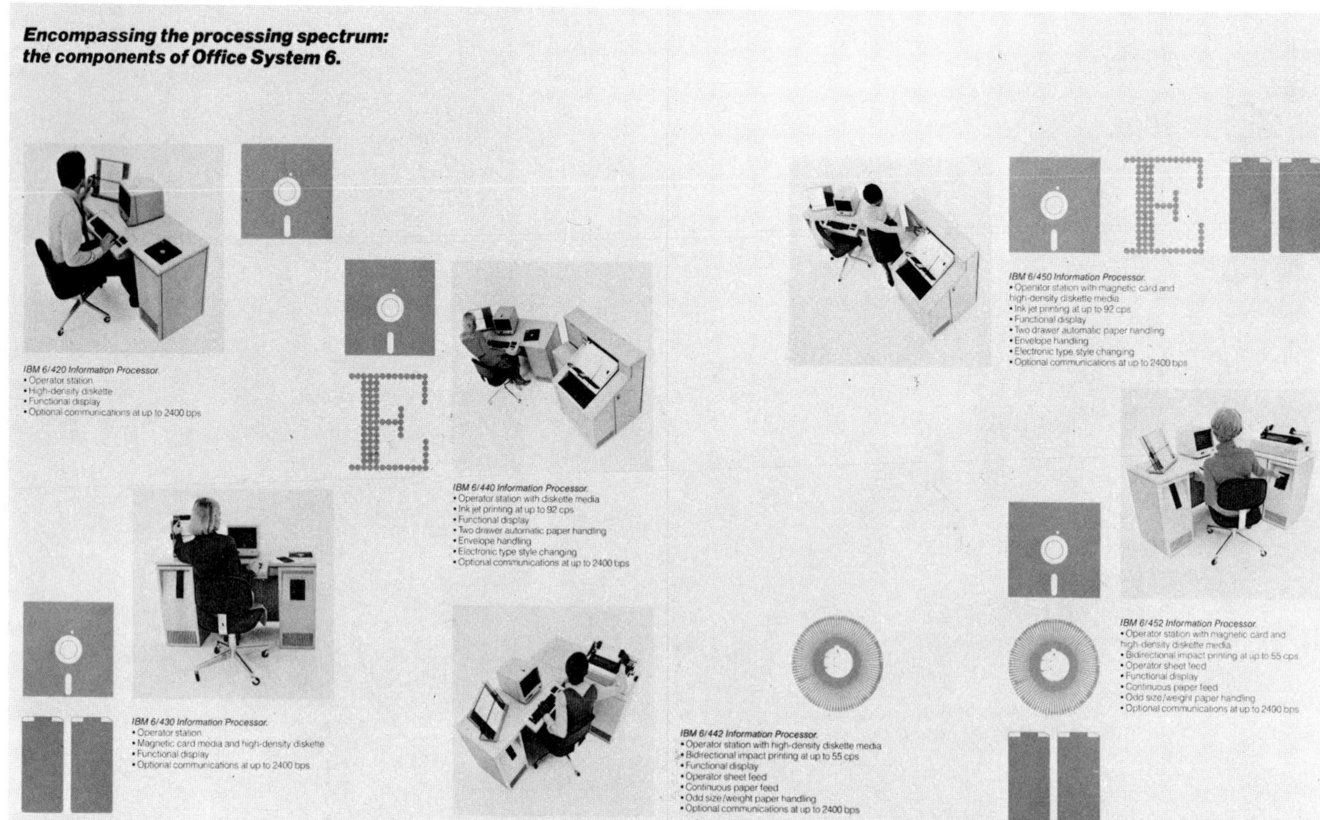

A

279 A-B
Peter McGuggart Art Director
Jim Broderick Photographer
Compton Advertising, Inc. Agency
IBM-OPD Client

IBM

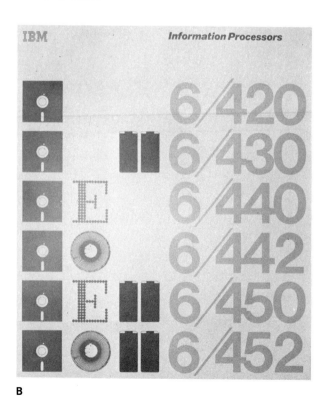

Information Processors

6/420
6/430
6/440
6/442
6/450
6/452

B

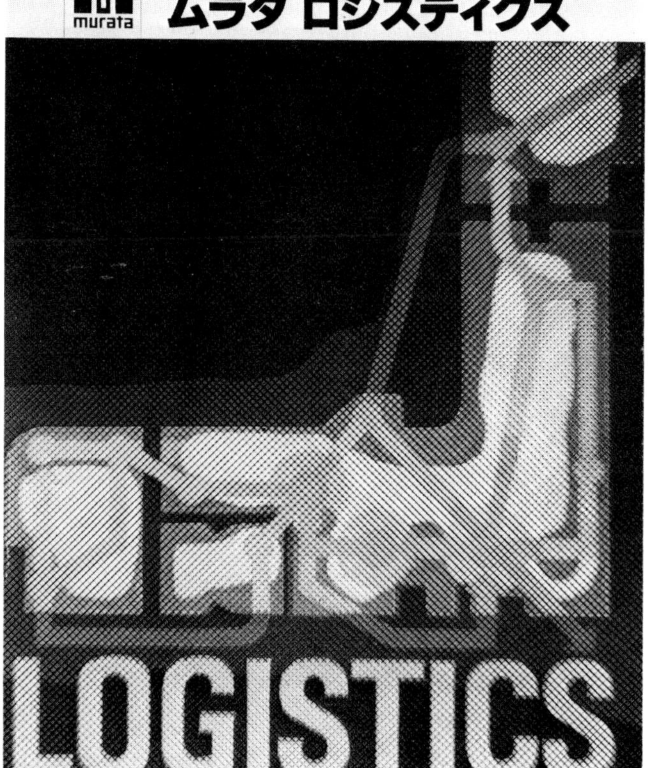

これからのビジネス戦略に効果を上げる —— Murata Logistics
murata
ムラタ ロジスティクス
LOGISTICS

A

280 A-C
Yutaka Matsushita Art Director
The Design House, Inc. Agency
Murata Machinery Ltd. Client

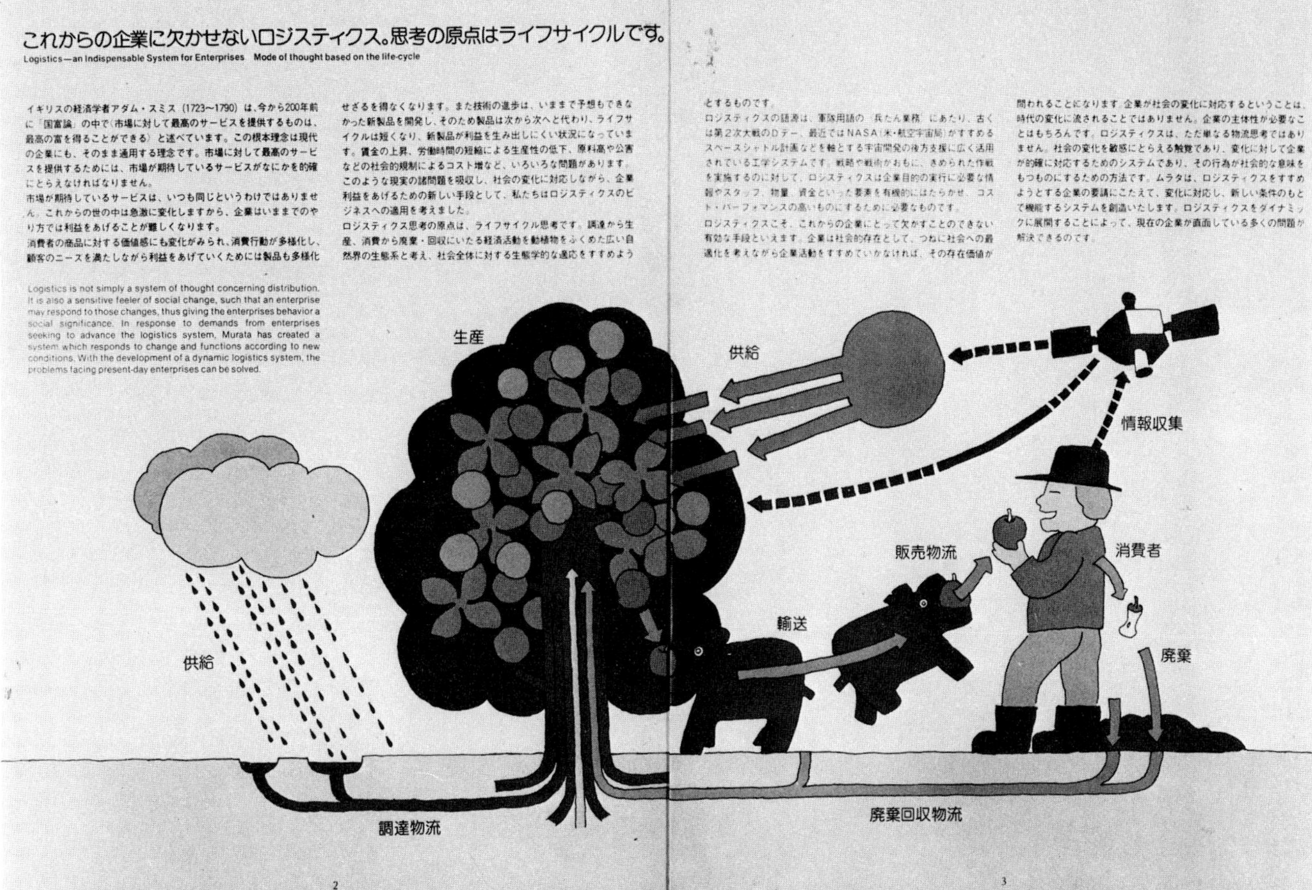

これからの企業に欠かせないロジスティクス。思考の原点はライフサイクルです。

Logistics—an Indispensable System for Enterprises   Mode of thought based on the life-cycle

イギリスの経済学者アダム・スミス（1723〜1790）は、今から200年前に「国富論」の中で〈市場に対して最高のサービスを提供するものは、最高の富を得ることができる〉と述べています。この根本理念は現代の企業にも、そのまま通用する理念です。市場に対して最高のサービスを提供するためには、市場が期待しているサービスがなにかを的確にとらえなければなりません。
市場が期待しているサービスは、いつも同じというわけではありません。これからの世の中は急激に変化しますから、企業はいままでのやり方では利益をあげることが難しくなります。
消費者の商品に対する価値感にも変化がみられ、消費行動が多様化し、顧客のニーズを満たしながら利益をあげていくためには製品も多様化せざるを得なくなります。また技術の進歩は、いままで予想もできなかった新製品を開発し、そのため製品は次から次へと代わり、ライフサイクルは短くなり、新製品が利益を生み出しにくい状況になっています。賃金の上昇、労働時間の短縮による生産性の低下、原料高や公害などの社会的規制によるコスト増など、いろいろな問題があります。
このような現実の諸問題を吸収し、社会の変化に対応しながら、企業利益をあげるための新しい手段として、私たちはロジスティクスのビジネスへの適用を考えました。
ロジスティクス思考の原点は、ライフサイクル思考です。調達から生産、消費から廃棄・回収にいたる経済活動を動植物をふくめた広い自然界の生態系と考え、社会全体に対する生態学的な適応をすすめようとするものです。
ロジスティクスの語源は、軍隊用語の「兵たん業務」にあたり、古くは第２次大戦のDデー、最近ではNASA（米・航空宇宙局）がすすめるスペースシャトル計画などを軸とする宇宙開発の後方支援に広く活用されている工学システムです。戦略や戦術がおもに、きめられた作戦を実施するのに対して、ロジスティクスは企業目的の実行に必要な情報やスタッフ、物量、資金といった要素を有機的にはたらかせ、コスト・パーフォマンスの高いものにするために必要なものです。
ロジスティクスこそ、これからの企業にとって欠かすことのできない有効な手段といえます。企業は社会的存在として、つねに社会への最適化を考えながら企業活動をすすめていかなければ、その存在価値が問われることになります。企業が社会の変化に対応するということは、時代の変化に流されることではありません。企業の主体性が必要なことはもちろんです。ロジスティクスは、ただ単なる物流思考ではありません。社会の変化を敏感にとらえる触覚であり、変化に対して企業が的確に対応するためのシステムであり、その行為が社会的な意味をもつものにするための方法です。ムラタは、ロジスティクスをすすめようとする企業の要請にこたえて、変化に対応し、新しい条件のもとで機能するシステムを創造いたします。ロジスティクスをダイナミックに展開することによって、現在の企業が直面している多くの問題が解決できるのです。

Logistics is not simply a system of thought concerning distribution. It is also a sensitive feeler of social change, such that an enterprise may respond to those changes, thus giving the enterprises behavior a social significance. In response to demands from enterprises seeking to advance the logistics system, Murata has created a system which responds to change and functions according to new conditions. With the development of a dynamic logistics system, the problems facing present-day enterprises can be solved.

2

3

280 B

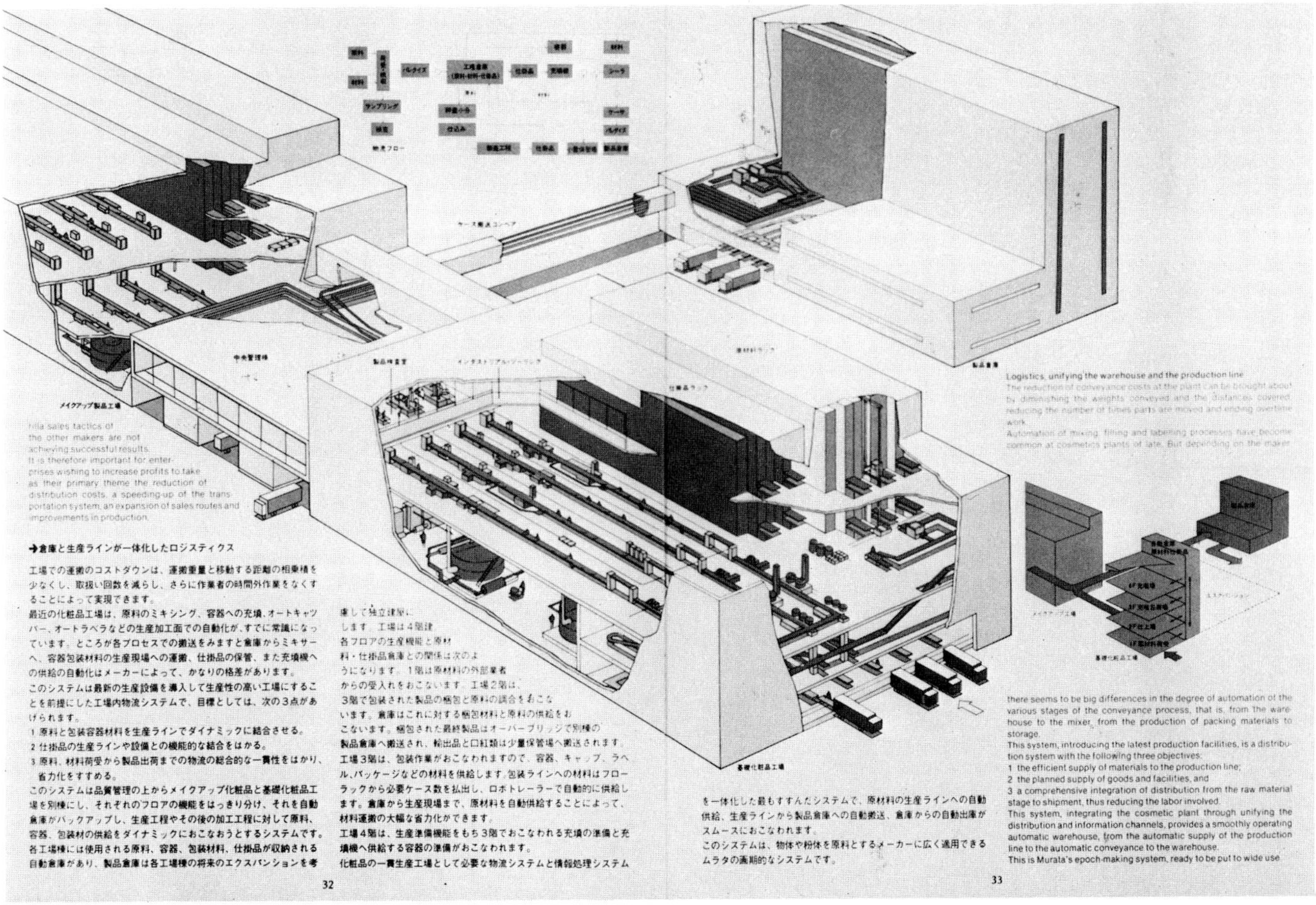

nila sales tactics of the other makers are not achieving successful results. It is therefore important for enterprises wishing to increase profits to take as their primary theme the reduction of distribution costs, a speeding-up of the transportation system, an expansion of sales routes and improvements in production.

→倉庫と生産ラインが一体化したロジスティクス

工場での運搬のコストダウンは、運搬重量と移動する距離の相乗積を少なくし、取扱い回数を減らし、さらに作業者の時間外作業をなくすることによって実現できます。
最近の化粧品工場は、原料のミキシング、容器への充填、オートキャッパー、オートラベラなどの生産加工面での自動化が、すでに常識になっています。ところが各プロセスでの搬送をみますと倉庫からミキサーへ、容器包装材料の生産現場への運搬、仕掛品の保管、また充填機への供給の自動化はメーカーによって、かなりの格差があります。
このシステムは最新の生産設備を導入して生産性の高い工場にすることを前提にした工場内物流システムで、目標としては、次の3点があげられます。
1 原料と包装容器材料を生産ラインでダイナミックに結合させる。
2 仕掛品の生産ラインや設備との機能的な結合をはかる。
3 原料、材料荷受から製品出荷までの物流の総合的な一貫性をはかり、省力化をすすめる。
このシステムは品質管理の上からメイクアップ化粧品と基礎化粧品工場を別棟にし、それぞれのフロアの機能をはっきり分け、それを自動倉庫がバックアップし、生産工程やその後の加工工程に対して原料、容器、包装材の供給をダイナミックにおこなおうとするシステムです。
各工場棟には使用される原料、容器、包装材料、仕掛品が収納される自動倉庫があり、製品倉庫は各工場棟の将来のエクスパンションを考慮して独立建屋にします。工場は4階建
各フロアの生産機能と原材料・仕掛品倉庫との関係は次のようになります。1階は原材料の外部業者からの受入れをおこないます。工場2階は、3階で包装された製品の梱包と原料の調合をおこないます。倉庫はこれに対する梱包材料と原料の供給をおこないます。梱包された最終製品はオーバーブリッジで別棟の製品倉庫へ搬送され、輸出品と口紅類は少量保管場へ搬送されます。工場3階は、包装作業がおこなわれますので、容器、キャップ、ラベル、パッケージなどの材料を供給します。包装ラインへの材料はフローラックから必要ケース数を払出し、ロボトレーラーで自動的に供給します。倉庫から生産現場まで、原材料を自動供給することによって、材料運搬の大幅な省力化ができます。
工場4階は、生産準備機能をもち3階でおこなわれる充填の準備と充填機へ供給する容器の準備がおこなわれます。
化粧品の一貫生産工場として必要な物流システムと情報処理システムを一体化した最もすすんだシステムで、原材料の生産ラインへの自動供給、生産ラインから製品倉庫への自動搬送、倉庫からの自動出庫がスムースにおこなわれます。
このシステムは、物体や粉体を原料とするメーカーに広く適用できるムラタの画期的なシステムです。

32

Logistics, unifying the warehouse and the production line

The reduction of conveyance costs at the plant can be brought about by diminishing the weights conveyed and the distances covered, reducing the number of times parts are moved and ending overtime work.
Automation of mixing, filling and labelling processes have become common at cosmetics plants of late. But depending on the maker, there seems to be big differences in the degree of automation of the various stages of the conveyance process, that is, from the warehouse to the mixer, from the production of packing materials to storage.
This system, introducing the latest production facilities, is a distribution system with the following three objectives:
1 the efficient supply of materials to the production line;
2 the planned supply of goods and facilities, and
3 a comprehensive integration of distribution from the raw material stage to shipment, thus reducing the labor involved.
This system, integrating the cosmetic plant through unifying the distribution and information channels, provides a smoothly operating automatic warehouse, from the automatic supply of the production line to the automatic conveyance to the warehouse.
This is Murata's epoch-making system, ready to be put to wide use.

33

C

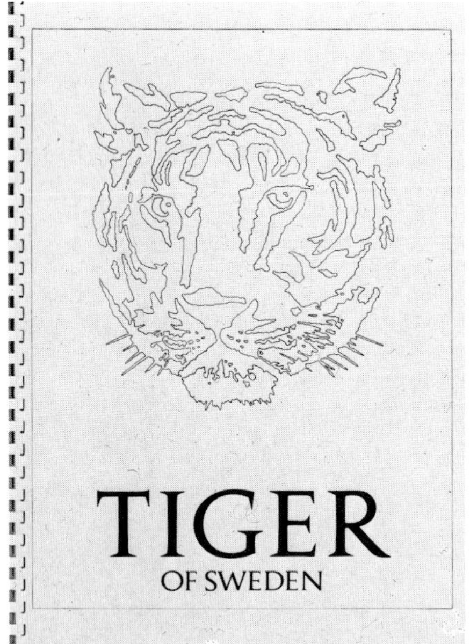

281 A

B

C

D

E

281 A-E
Torbjorn Winckler Art Director
Olle Bogren Photographer
Stendahls/Vasagatan Agency
Tiger/Rang AB Client

284
Jerry Bonar, Keith Bright Art Directors
Bruno Schreckf, Holly Ahlberg Photographers
Kara Blohm, Julie Rieffler Designers
Bright & Agate Inc. Studio
The Dreyfus Co. Agency
Vivitar Corporation Client

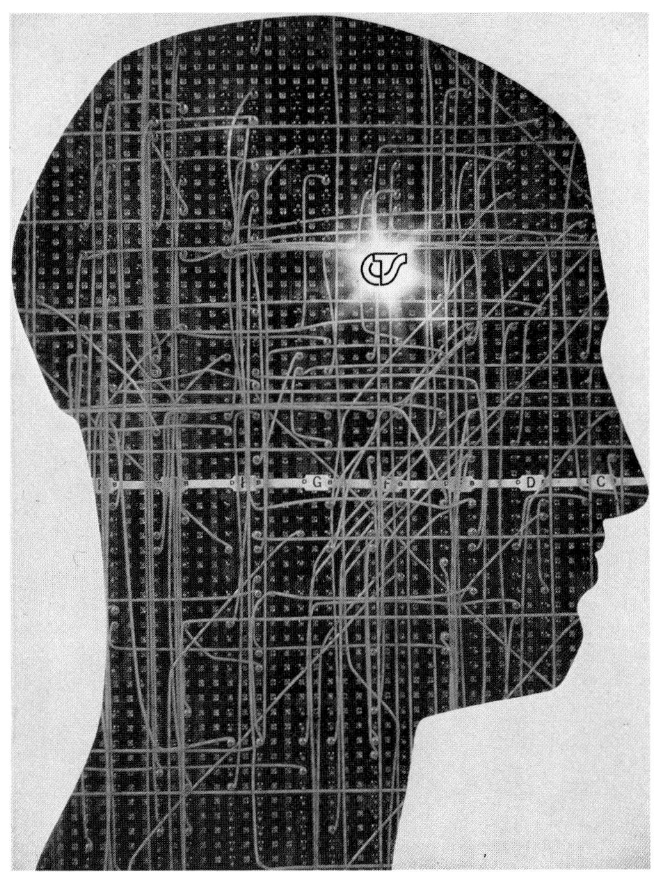

282
David Zeigerman Art Director
Allan R. Wahler, Steve Klausen Copywriters
Corporate Design Group, Inc. Agency
Cardinal Type Service, Inc. Client

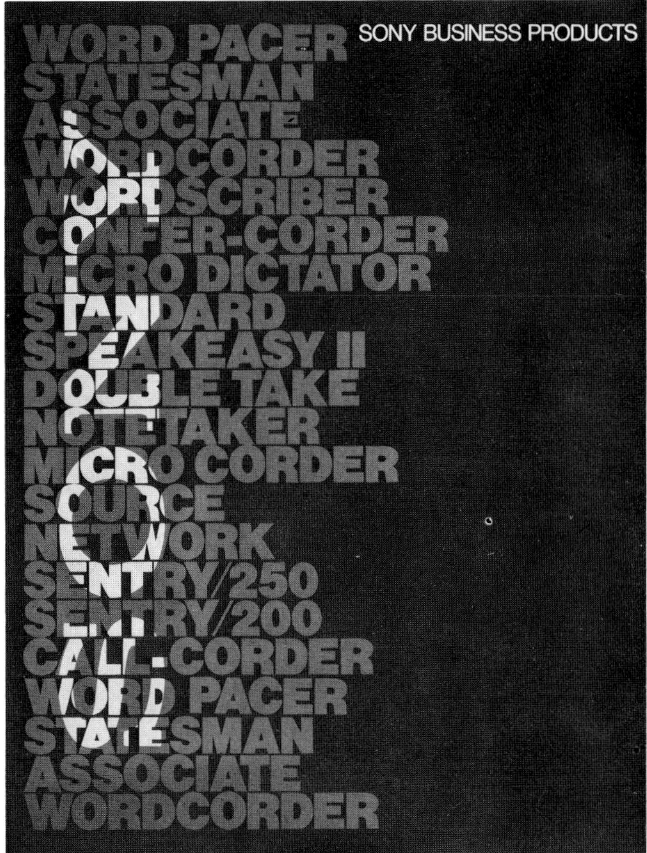

283
Michael Tedesco Art Director
Francis & Shaw, Inc. Agency
Sony Corporation Client

284

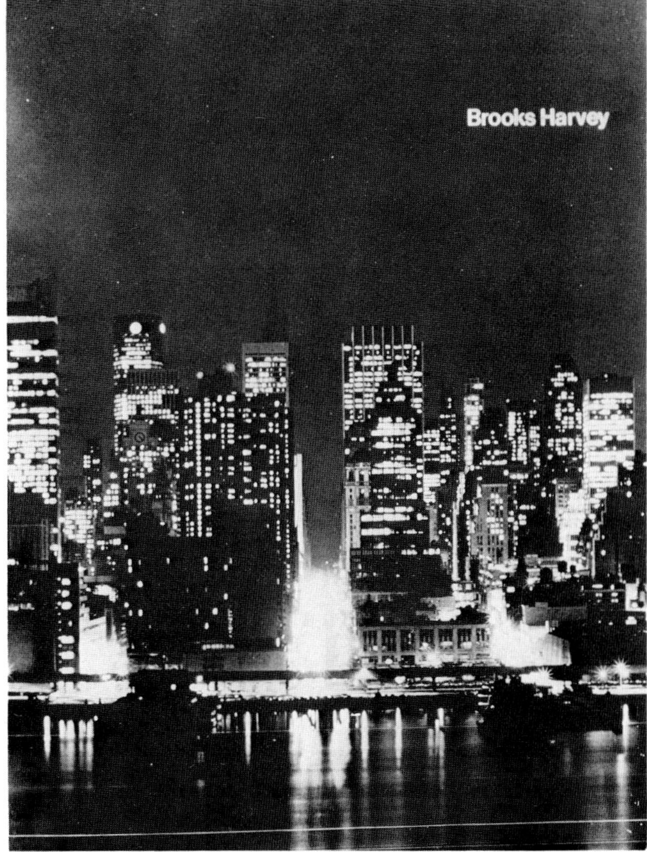

285
Evelyn Goutas Art Director
Harry Moshier Associates, Inc. Agency
Brooks, Harvey & Co. Inc. Client

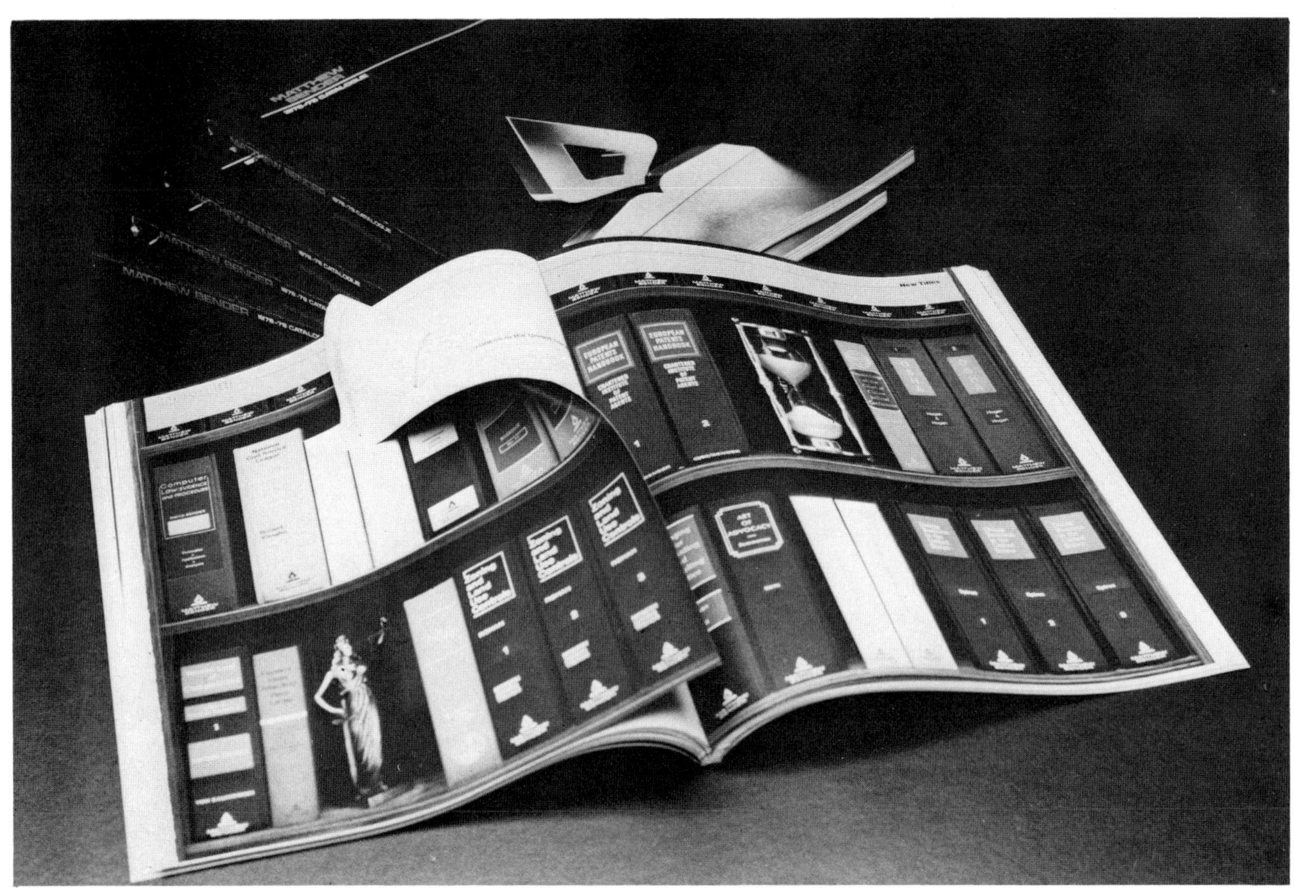

286
Thomas S. Bencze Art Director
Bill Ashe Photographer
Michael Shor Copywriter
Thomas S. Bencze, Andrew Didora Designers
Taylor & Ives, Inc. Agency
Mathew Bender Client

287
Jane Zash Art Director
Atelier International, Ltd. Client

A

Land of the Incas

25 days/Departing June 8

Peru and Ecuador, the fascinating "Indian countries" of South America, are set amidst the world's most extensive high mountain system, exceeded in elevation only by the Himalayas. In the Andean highlands of these countries, the descendants of the many related tribes that were ruled by the all-conquering Incas still adhere to ancient folkways and dress. Seen against the majestic mountain backdrop, the traditional activities of the Indians – farming, weaving, selling their crafts and produce at colorful open-air markets – provide a wealth of exciting subject matter for the travel photographer.

In considering this tour, please keep in mind the high altitudes: 9,300 feet above sea level in Quito; 10,000 feet and more in the Huaylas Valley; 11,000 feet in Cuzco; and as high as 13,000 feet on some of the passes we cross. Consider, also, that some of the roads are rough and dusty, and a few of the hotels in remote areas – that's where the best pictures are! – are far from first-class. This is a rugged tour for adventurous travelers – but we know of few that offer richer photographic rewards.

IT8LA1TLLI Limited to 17 Passengers

TOUR PRICE	
Land Arrangements	$2330
Single Room Supplement (no singles in Ecuador outside of Quito)	$ 220
Internal Peru Air Fare	$ 33
Airport Taxes	$ 7
AIR FARE	
Miami to Miami 150 Day Excursion	$ 491

LAN-CHILE Chilean Airlines

74

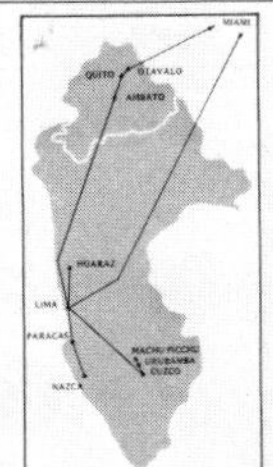

Itinerary

Our adventure begins in Lima, Peru, after an early Friday morning flight from Miami. We spend two days in the picturesque city that was capital of all Spanish colonial South America for nearly 300 years (*Lima Sheraton Hotel*).

By private motorcoach we cross Peru's coastal desert to Nazca, site of a highly developed civilization that flourished bewteen 400 and 800 A.D. (*Montecarlo Hotel*). A morning flight takes us over the Plains of Nazca, to photograph the huge geometric depictions of birds and animals whose purpose remains a mystery to modern archaeologists.

Our next stop is the beautiful beach resort of Paracas, where we cruise the sheltered islands of Paracas Bay, a nature reserve populated by millions of sea birds and herds of sea lions (*Paracas Hotel*).

Via colonial Pisco we return to Lima, and the next morning board a flight to 11,480-ft. Cuzco, hub of the mountainous Inca empire (*Libertador Marriott Hotel*). After touring the city and the Inca fortress of Sacsahuaman, we travel by train to fabulous Machu Picchu, "Lost City" of the Incas. Never invaded by the Conquistadors, Machu Picchu slumbered under cover of jungle until its discovery by Hiram Bingham in 1911. We spend an afternoon and the next morning photographing this awesome citadel of stone, with costumed Indian models to enhance our pictures (*Hotel Machu Picchu*).

Returning to Cuzco, we make a two-day excursion to the scenic Urubamba River valley, intensely farmed and framed by lofty peaks. We visit the villages of Chincheros and Pisac, and stay overnight in Urubamba (*Naranjachayoh Hotel*).

Back in Lima, we enjoy a day of leisure and visit the nearby pre-Inca ruins of Cajamarquilla before flying to Huaraz, in the heart of the Santa River valley (*New Huaraz Hotel*). For the following two days we will explore the scenic splendors of this spectacular region, visiting the Callejon de Huaylas, where crops are grown on terraces below the jumbled spires of the Black Cordillera on the west and the snow-crowned White Cordillera on the east; and mirror-like Lake Paron, nestled below the snow-crowned peak of Mt. Huandoy.

From Lima we fly along the White Cordillera to Quito, Ecuador, the world's second-highest capital city, where we board our private motorcoach for the drive south to the little city of Ambato (*Miraflores Hotel*). After morning coverage of the famous outdoor market, one of the most colorful in all of South America, we visit the semi-tropical resort village of Banos, with its hot springs and "miraculous" shrine.

Returning to Quito through the scenic Central Valley, we visit another market in Latacunga and drive past the perfect cone of 19,482-ft. Mt. Cotopaxi, the world's highest active volcano.

The next two days will be devoted to the fascinating colonial highlights of Quito. We then drive north through thatch-roofed villages to Ibarra (*Hosteria Chorlavi*) and mingle with colorfully costumed Indians at the famous Saturday market of Otavalo.

We return to Quito, and have a day at leisure before leaving Monday morning on our return flight to Miami.

B

288 A-B
Nita Alvarez Art Director
Rick Ergenbright Photographer
Andrew Ayers Illustrator
New Breath Productions Studio
Thru The Lens Tours, Inc. Client

289 A-C
Barry De Lee Art Director
De Lee Productions Agency
Majestic Gifts Client

A

B

C

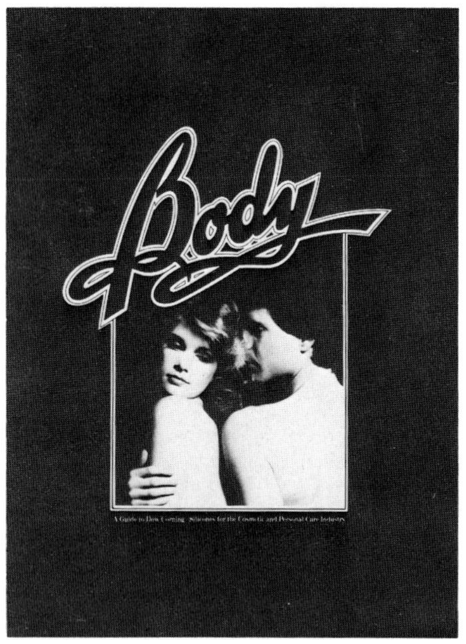

A

Skin

Skin. Soft.
Smooth. Sensuous.
And sensitive. Sensitive to climate, diet, emotions, age.

The skin is fragile. It needs special care and special protection. The same kind of special care and protection that Dow Corning silicones can give your skincare product formulations.

Dow Corning 200 fluid is a clear silicone polymer, and the most widely used silicone in skincare products. Typical uses include protective creams, hand lotions, waterless toilet soap, suntan lotions, aerosol shave creams, and aftershave lotions.

Although 200 fluid is available in viscosities from .65 to 100,000 cst, it is generally used in 100 cst viscosity when smooth feel and softness are required, and 350 cst for increased skin protection and water repellency without a trace of stickiness. Overall, Dow Corning 200 fluid gives non-oily lubricity, reduced surface tension, and increased efficiency to various preparations. In properly formulated products, Dow Corning 200 fluid spreads easily and assists rub-out characteristics. It forms a durable film with water repellency and soft feel, yet does not interfere with natural skin transpiration.

Dow Corning 556 fluid is a phenylmethylpolysiloxane fluid that has excellent solubility in alcohols and is compatible with most cosmetic materials, such as mineral oil. Overall, the fluid provides nonoily, easy-to-spread lubricity and allows natural skin transpiration through a soft, invisible film. It is typically used as a water-repellent additive, especially against water-borne irritants, and as an anti-stickiness additive in formulations for skin lotions and creams, suntan lotions and sprays, and preshave lotions.

Dow Corning 225 fluid provides similar benefits to formulations for skincare products, but is a low molecular weight polydimethylsiloxane fluid that is compatible with alcohol.

Silicone gylcol co-polymers Dow Corning 190 and Q2-7106 fluids are used in skin creams and lotions, preshave lotions, aerosol shaving lather, and perfumes and colognes to increase moisture attraction to the skin, to detackify, and to impart a non-oily smooth and silky feel.

These fluids provide good emolliency and are non-irritating and non-stinging. They insure smoother, wetter, and more stable foams for aerosol shaving preparations. Dow Corning silicone glycol co-polymers are compatible with water and alcohols.

Dow Corning 344,345, and Q2-1096 volatile silicone fluids are used as additives in skin lotions, stick products, sun products, bath oils, perfumes, colognes, pre- and post-shaving lotions, make-ups, and nail polishes. They impart the benefits of lubricity, feel, detackification, surface tension reduction, and leveling.

Dow Corning 344, 345, and Q2-1096 are essentially non-toxic and odorless, and tasteless. They may be used alone or blended together. Dow Corning 344 and 345 may be blended with alcohol or other cosmetic fluids to provide a fluid base for skincare products in solid or liquid form.

B

290 A-B
Joe Canciila Art Director
Ketchum MacLeod & Grove, Inc. Agency
Dow Corning Client

293 A-B
Jim Lienhart Art Director
Dan Morrill Photographer
Carol Blomstrand Copywriter
Murrie, White, Drummond & Lienhart Agency
The Ellerman Companies Client

294
Hoi Ling Chu Art Director
Marvin W. Schwartz, Somorkahan Pictures Corp. Photographers
Chermayeffe Geismar Agency
The Conservation Trust of Puerto Rico Client

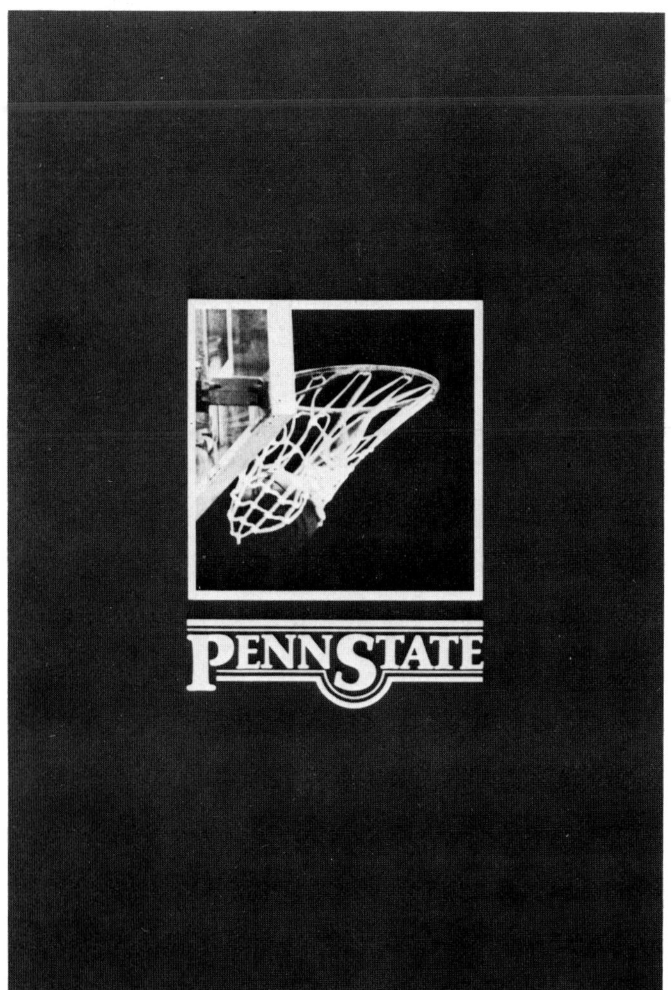

291
Larry Krezo Art Director
Alison Taggart, David Shelly, Patrick Little, Robert Beese, Bob Veltri Photographers
Salina Press Printer
Penn State Department of Publications Studio
Basketball Coaches Client

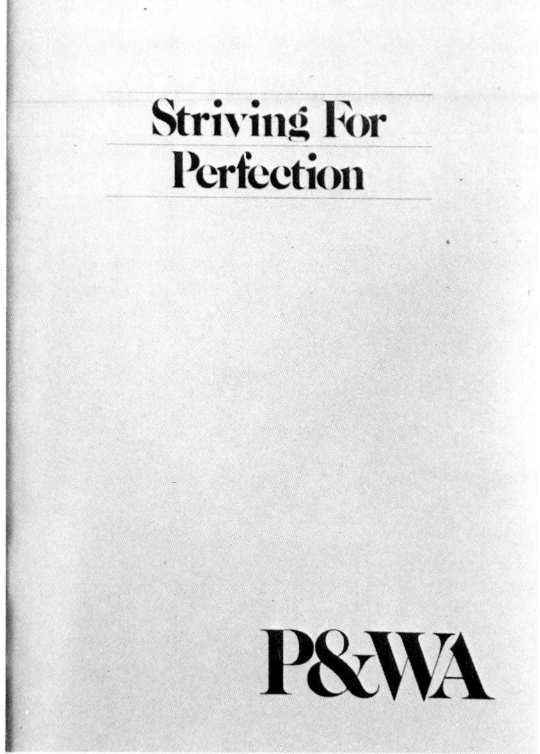

292
Bob Smith Art Director
Jack McConnell Photographer
Bob Smith The Artsmith Agency
Pratt & Whitney Aircraft Group Client

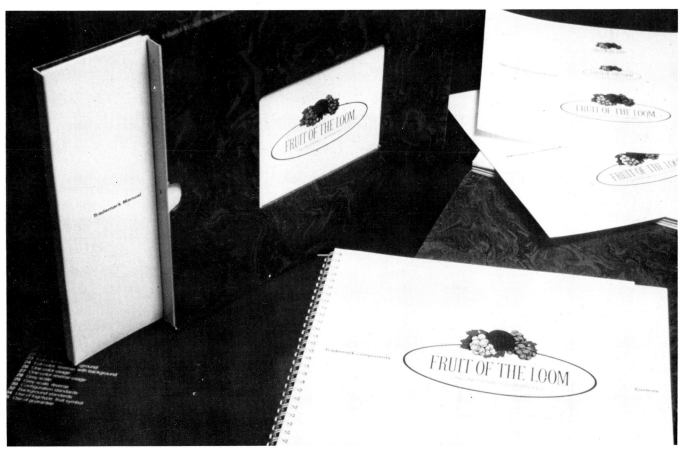

304
Ed De Martin Art Director
Wendy Oppel Designer
De Martin, Marona, Cranstoun, Downes, Inc. Agency
Northwest Industries, Robert Kurtzer Client

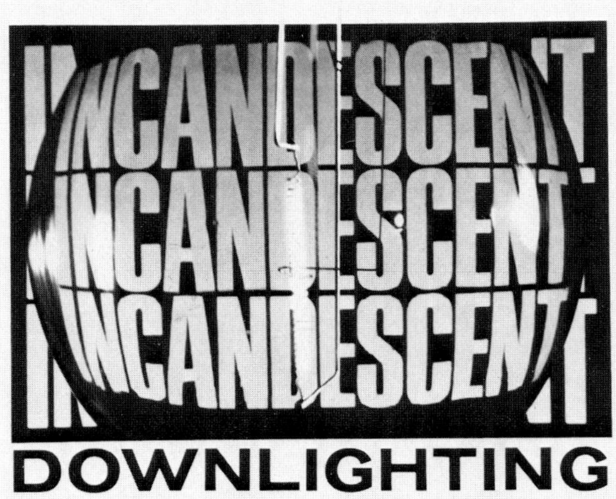

305
Al Intindola Art Director
Sal Merlo Photographer
Norman Peyser Designer
Lightolier Client

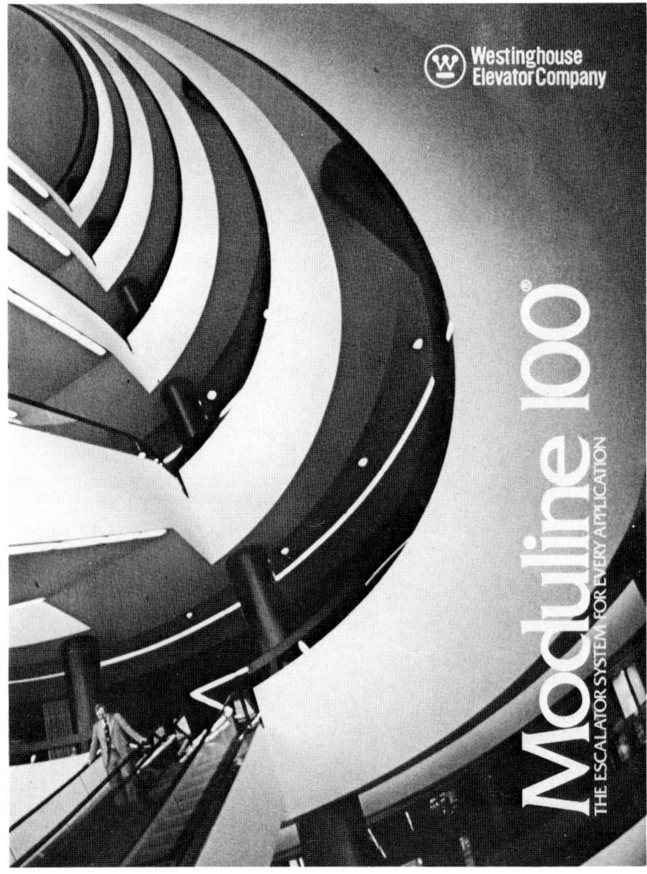

306
David Haynes Art Director
John Merhaut, Len Schugar, Harry Seawell, Chris Harris Photographers
Ketchum New York Agency
Westinghouse Elevator Client

307
Tim Ryan Art Director
Steve Myers Photographer
Kimble Pendleton Mead Illustrator
Tim Ryan Design Studio
Pratt Institute Client

308
Randee R. Rubin Art Director
Paul Elfenbein, Werner Wolff, Harold Sund, Erich Hartman, Charles Moore Photographers
James Orlandi & Associates Production House
U.S. Trust Company Of New York Client

309
Fred Wilinshurst, Randy Soper Art Directors
Gene Wolfshiemer Photographer
Randy R. Soper Designer
Art Type Production House
Security Bank Research Dept. Client

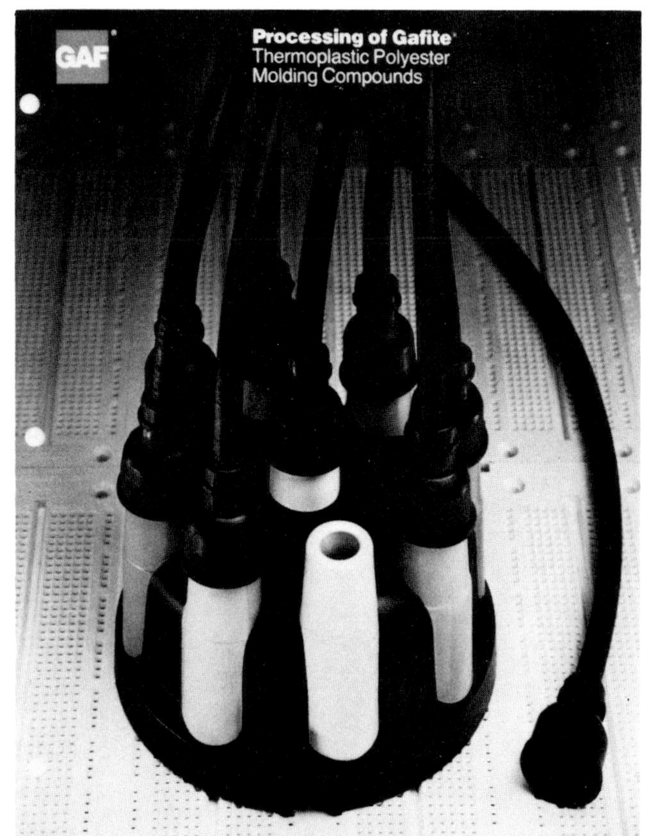

310
Paul D. Miller, Frank Marshall Art Directors
Larry J. Shmenco Photographer
Frank B. Marshall, Edward Spong Designers
Clarendon Press Production House
GAF Corporation Client

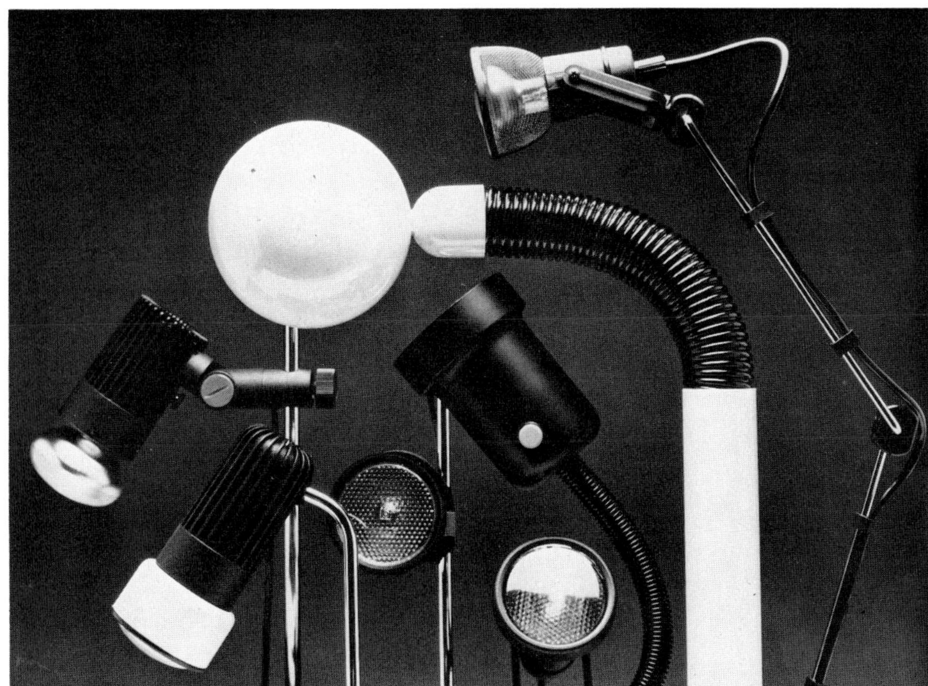

311
Fritz Haase Art Director
Nikolay Zurek Photographer
Haase & Knels, Bremen, D Agency
Brillantleuchten 78/79 Client

312
Terry R. Waln Art Director
Kazu Studio Photograpers
William Bohnhoff Designer
Bruce Offset Company Production House
Graphics Group Agency
Shaw/Walker Client

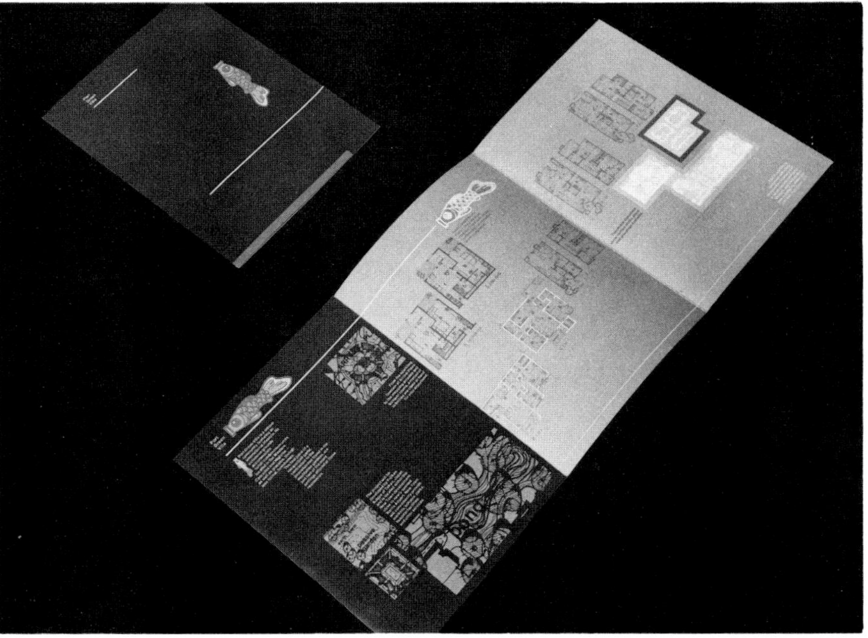

313
Jann Church Art Director
Jann Church, Lea Pascoe Designers
Jann Church Advertising & Graphic Design, Inc. Agency
AVCO Community Developers, Inc. Client

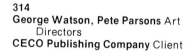

Play nine thousand holes of golf « Lunch in a foreign country « Take in a Broadway show « Sail America's longest freshwater shoreline « Visit with Picasso, Matisse, Andy Warhol & Van Gogh all in one afternoon « Roar with the Lions & Tigers « Fish & swim in over eleven thousand lakes « Have an evening lawn supper with your favorite star « Go to Hell & back « Ski a dozen slopes within an hour's drive « Board a steamer & cruise to an island of amusement « Buy fresh-picked flowers & vegetables at dawn « See where the lights first came on one hundred years ago « Dine atop one of the world's tallest hotels « Go from the motor capital of the world to a place no cars are allowed « Enjoy DETROIT PLUS

314
George Watson, Pete Parsons Art Directors
CECO Publishing Company Client

315
David Rushlow Art Director
Group 3hree Advertising Agency
Piper Aircraft Corporation Client

316
Siegried Gesk Art Director
P.B.A. & Associates Agency
Munising Paper Division, Kimberly-Clark Corporation Client

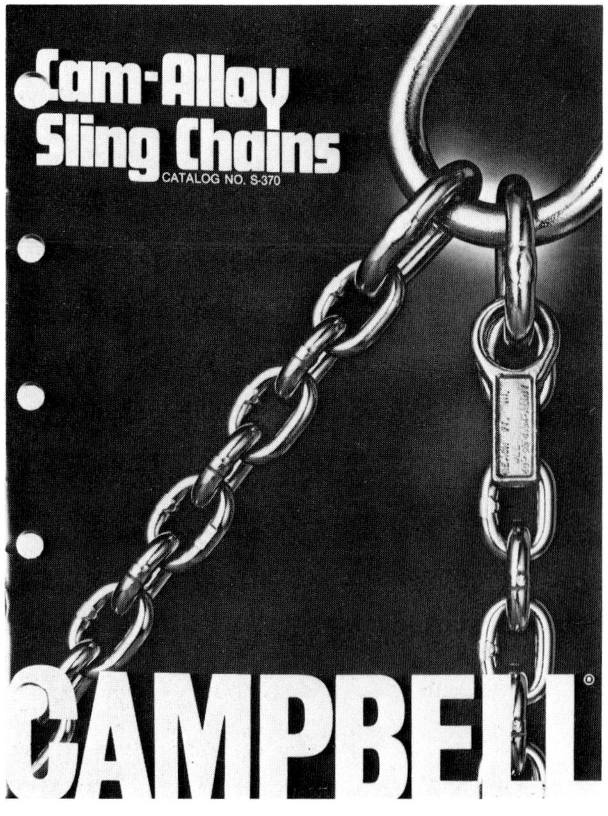

317
Scott W. Hershey Art Director
Bryson Leidich Photographer
Creative Concepts Advertising, Inc. Agency
Campbell Chain Co. Client

Play nine thousand holes of golf « Lunch in a foreign country « Take in a Broadway show « Sail America's longest freshwater shoreline « Visit with Picasso, Matisse, Andy Warhol & Van Gogh all in one afternoon « Roar with the Lions & Tigers « Fish & swim in over eleven thousand lakes « Have an evening lawn supper with your favorite star « Go to Hell & back « Ski a dozen slopes within an hour's drive « Board a steamer & cruise to an island of amusement « Buy fresh-picked flowers & vegetables at dawn « See where the lights first came on one hundred years ago « Dine atop one of the world's tallest hotels « Go from the motor capital of the world to a place no cars are allowed « Enjoy DETROIT PLUS

314
George Watson, Pete Parsons Art Directors
CECO Publishing Company Client

315
David Rushlow Art Director
Group 3hree Advertising Agency
Piper Aircraft Corporation Client

316
Siegried Gesk Art Director
P.B.A. & Associates Agency
Munising Paper Division, Kimberly-Clark Corporation Client

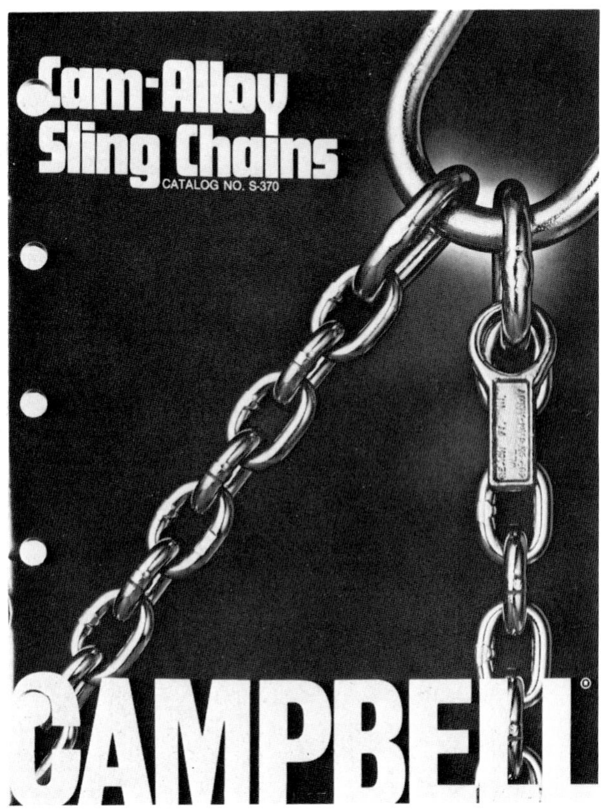

317
Scott W. Hershey Art Director
Bryson Leidich Photographer
Creative Concepts Advertising, Inc. Agency
Campbell Chain Co. Client

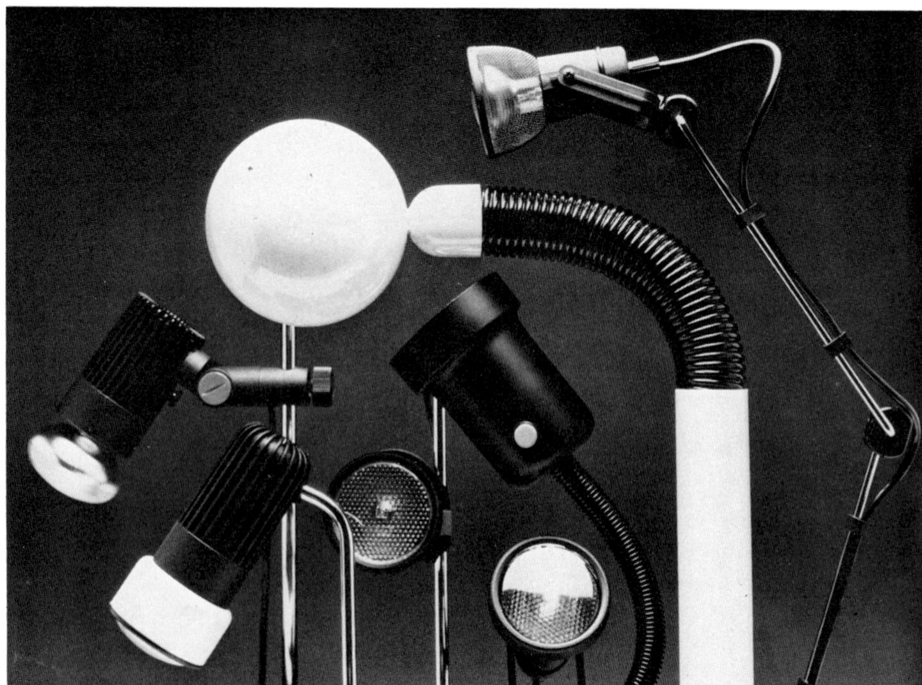

311
Fritz Haase Art Director
Nikolay Zurek Photographer
Haase & Knels, Bremen, D Agency
Brillantleuchten 78/79 Client

312
Terry R. Wain Art Director
Kazu Studio Photograpers
William Bohnhoff Designer
Bruce Offset Company Production House
Graphics Group Agency
Shaw/Walker Client

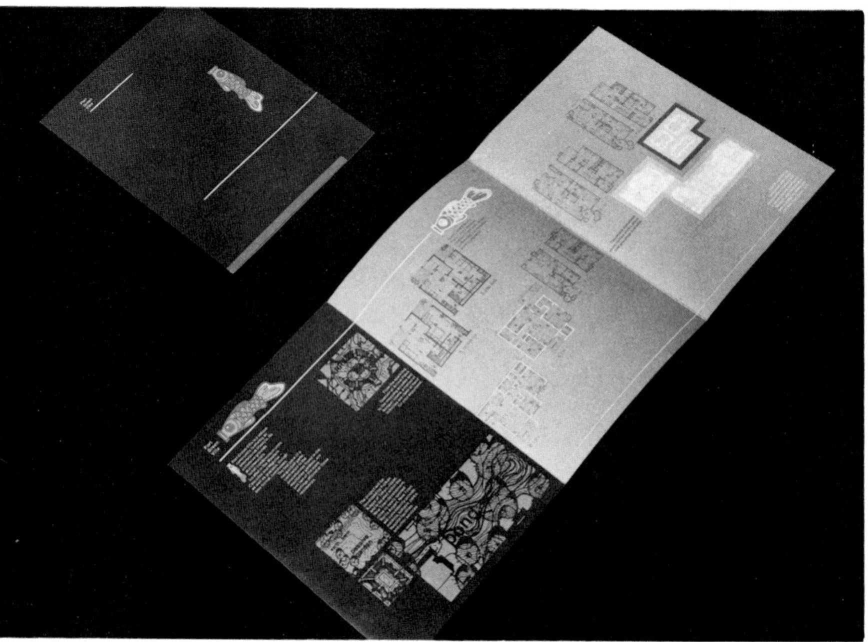

313
Jann Church Art Director
Jann Church, Lea Pascoe Designers
Jann Church Advertising & Graphic Design, Inc. Agency
AVCO Community Developers, Inc. Client

Magazine Covers

318
Frank De Vino Art Director
Peter Turner Photographer
Lynda Chyhai Designer
Omni Publications Client

319
Arie J. Geurts Art Director
Laboratorio de Diseno y Analisis de Mercado, Carton y Papel de Mexico S.A. Studio
Novum-Gebrauchsgrafik Client

320
George Coderre Art Director
Penton/IPC, Reinhold Publishing Company Agency
Progressive Architecture Client

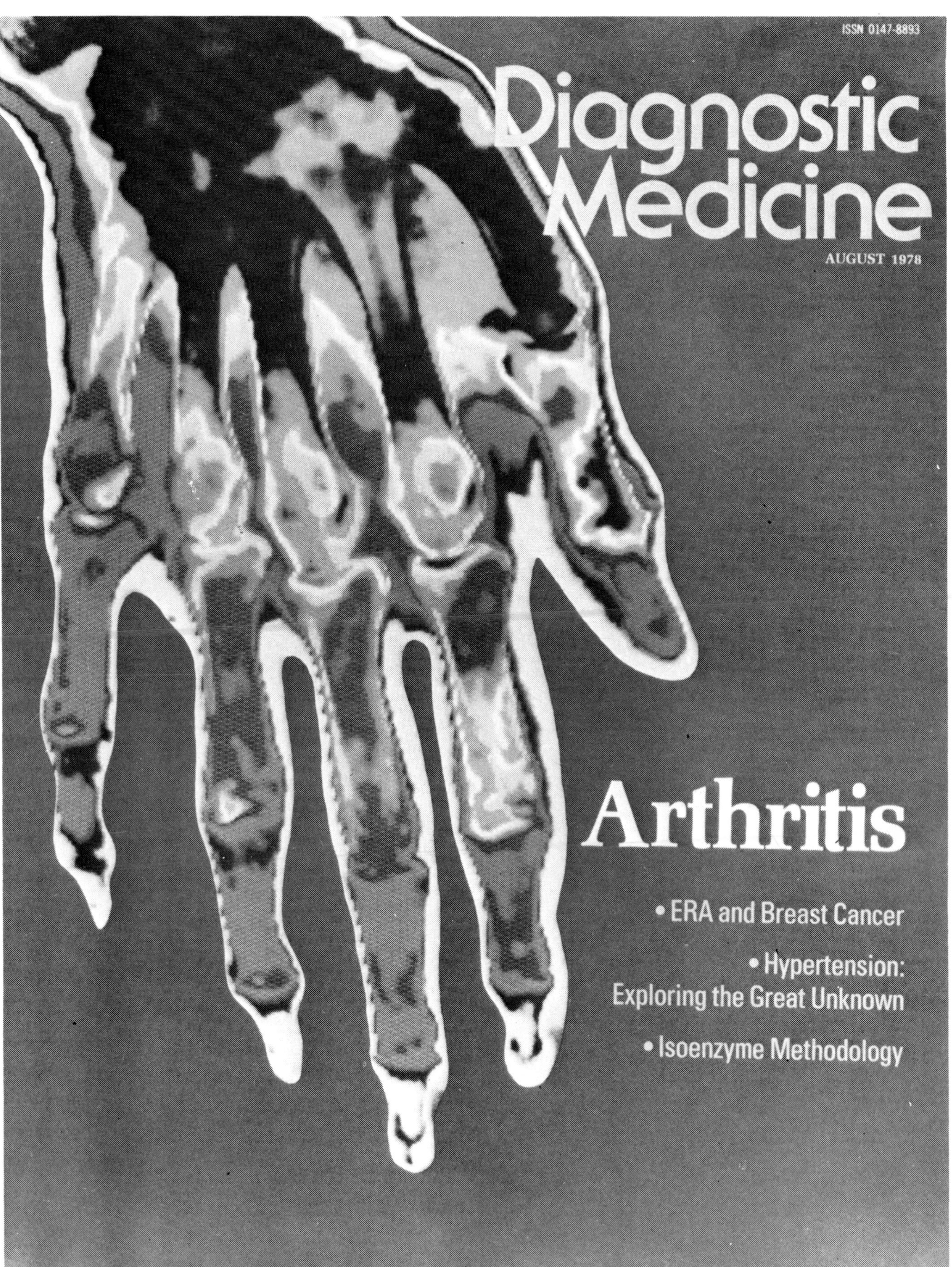

321
Albert M. Foti Art Director
Howard Sochurek Photographer
Diagnostic Medicine Magazine Client

323
Ellen Blissman Art Director
Jean-Claude Suares Designer
New York Magazine Client

322
Dave Boss Art Director
Stan Caplan Photographer
Don Weller Illustrator
The Weller Institute for the Cure of Design Agency
National Football League Properties Client

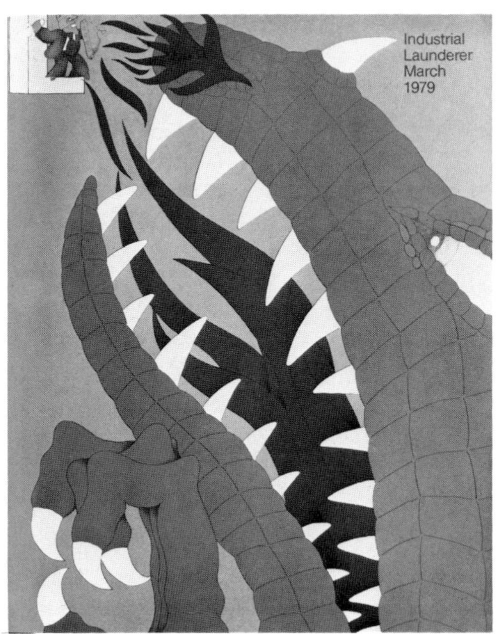

324
Jack Lefkowitz Art Director
Jack Lefkowitz, Inc. Agency
Industrial Launderer Magazine Client

323

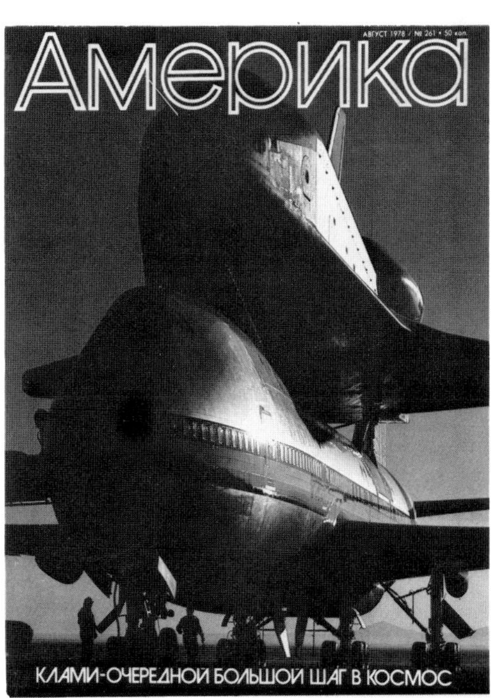

325
Dorothy Fall, David Moore Art Directors
Christopher Springmann Photographer
Dorothy Fall Designer
U.S. International Communication Agency Agency
America Illustrated Magazine Client

SANTA
BARBARA
MAGAZINE
WINTER/$2.00
WINGS: THE MONARCH BUTTERFLY MIGRATION
COMMERCIAL FISHERMEN: PROUD HUNTERS OF THE SEA
NOVELIST THOMAS SANCHEZ ON CALIFORNIA,
COYOTES AND OTHER WONDERS

326
Mark Oliver Art Director
George Lepp Photographer
Mark Oliver Associates Agency
Santa Barbara Magazine Client

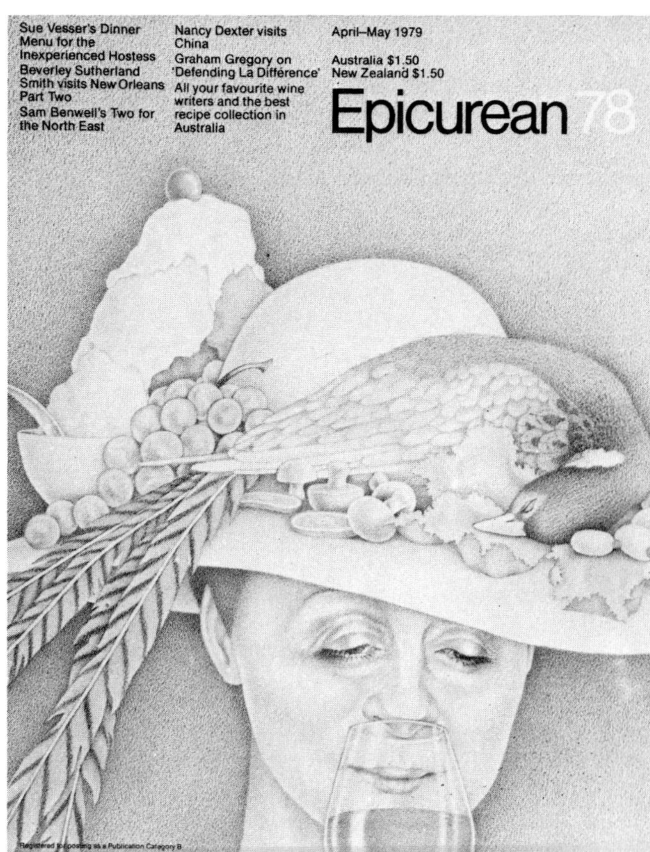

327
Ken Cato Art Director
John Humphrey Associates P/L
Photographers
Maire Smith Illustrator
Cato Hibberd Design Pty Ltd. Studio
Lawrence Publishing Co. Pty Ltd. Client

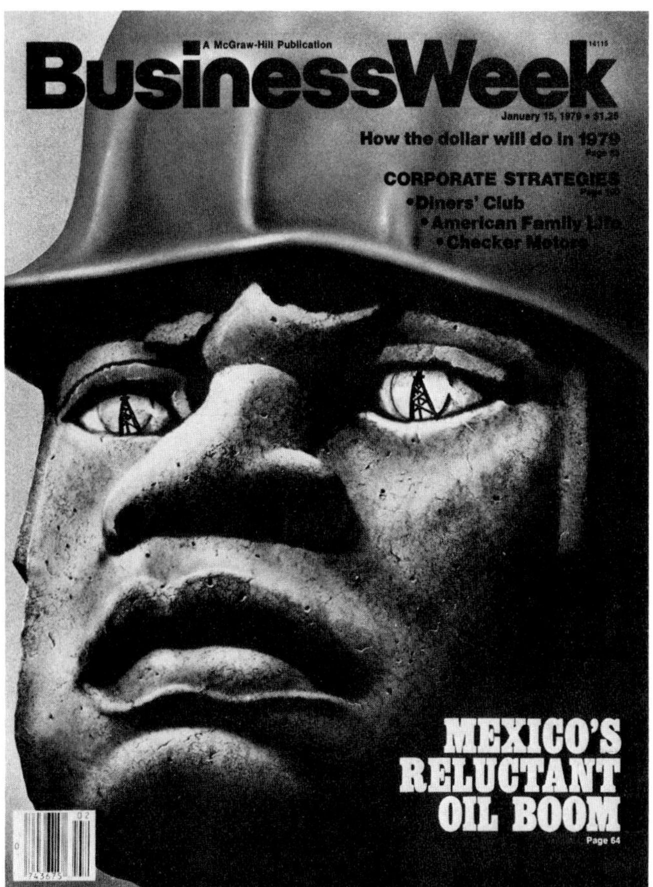

328
Judith Adel Art Director
Stanislaw Fernandes Illustrator
Business Week Client

329
Georges Haroutiun Art Director
Tim Saunders Photographer
Rod Della-Vedova Designer
Madame Au Foyer Client

330
Arthur Paul Art Director
Arthur Paul, Tom Staebler Designers
Playboy Enterprises, Inc. Client

331
Roger B. Carpenter Art Director
Stephan Harvey Photographer
Rod Dyer, Inc., Los Angeles Agency
12x12 Inside Client

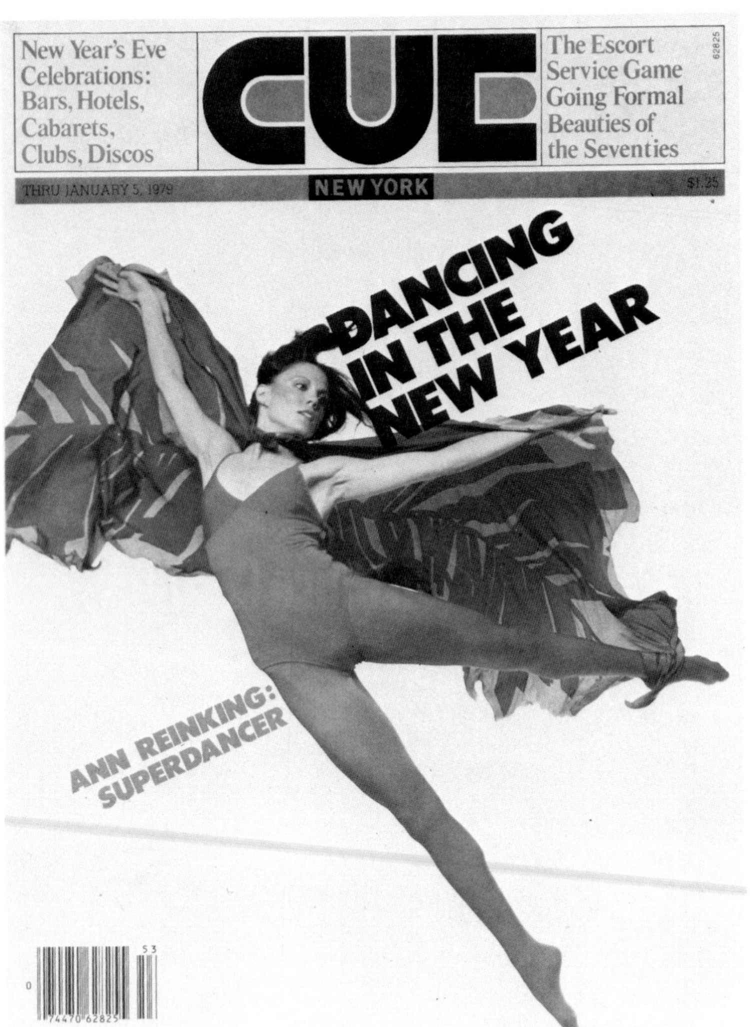

New Year's Eve
Celebrations:
Bars, Hotels,
Cabarets,
Clubs, Discos
CUE
The Escort
Service Game
Going Formal
Beauties of
the Seventies
THRU JANUARY 5, 1979
NEW YORK
$1.25
DANCING
IN THE
NEW YEAR
ANN REINKING:
SUPERDANCER

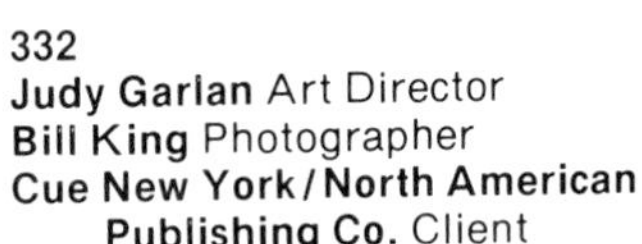

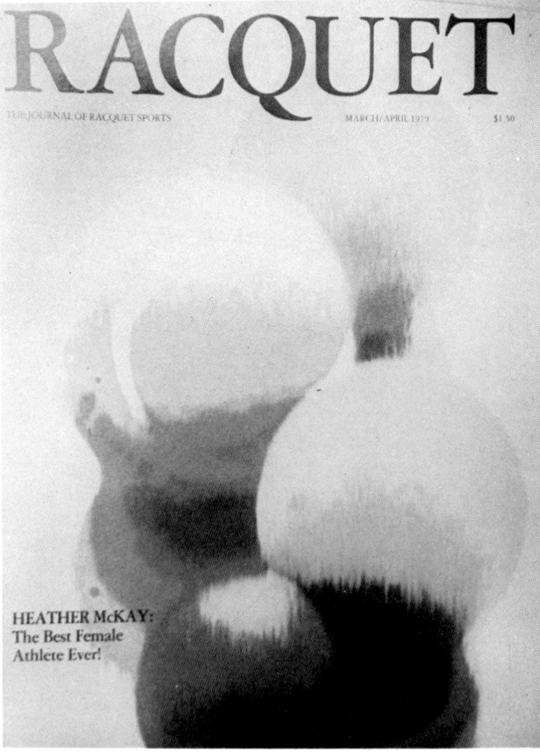

RACQUET
HEATHER McKAY:
The Best Female
Athlete Ever!

333
Andrea Da Riff Art Director
Geoffrey Gove Photographer
Racquet Magazine Client

332
Judy Garlan Art Director
Bill King Photographer
Cue New York/North American Publishing Co. Client

MAY 1979
Marine
Business
How dealers
sell today's
high prices
A heart attack almost
killed his business
Close more sales; train
prospects to say, "Yes!"
Buyers go crazy
at their annual sale
Contents, page 3

334
Ken Silvia Art Director
Norman C. Dow Photographer
United Marine Publishing Client

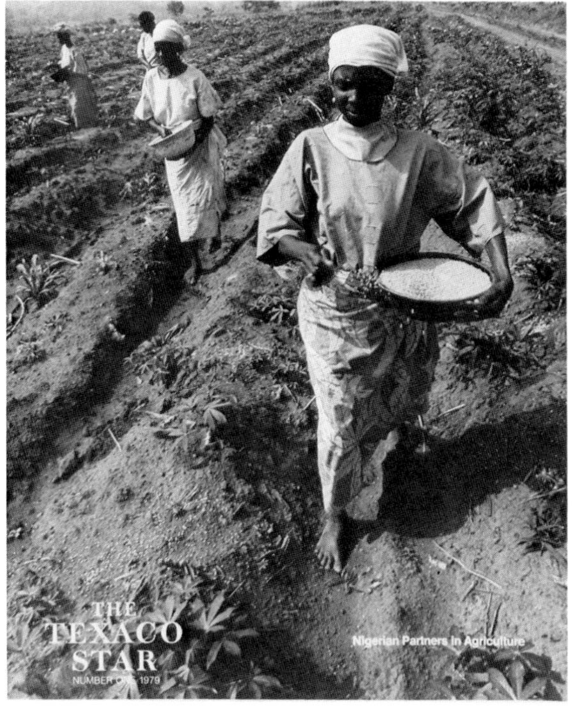

335
Leslie Segal Art Director
Ashvin Gatha Photographer
Corporate Annual Reports, Inc. Studio
Texico Star Client

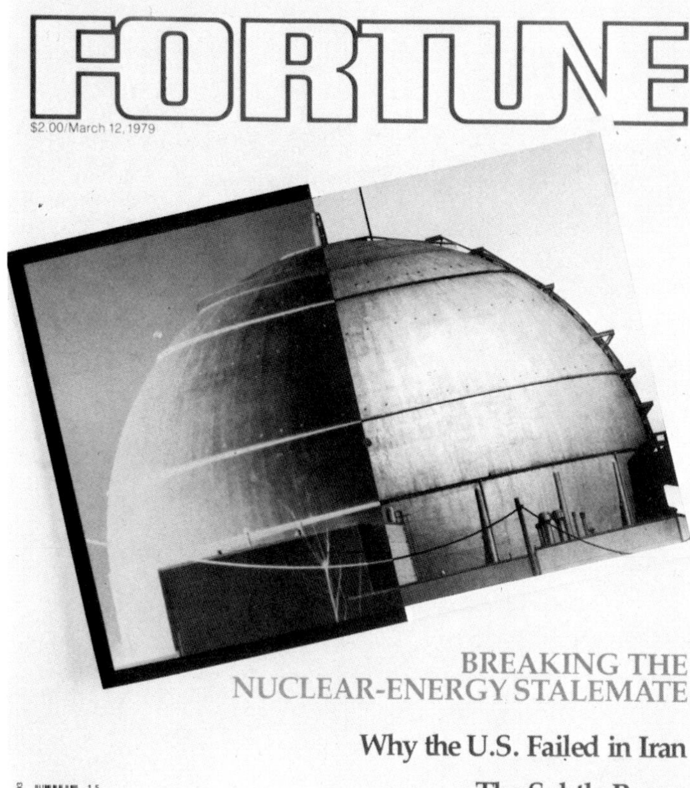

337
Ronald Campbell Art Director
Keith Godard, Works Designers
Fortune Magazine Client

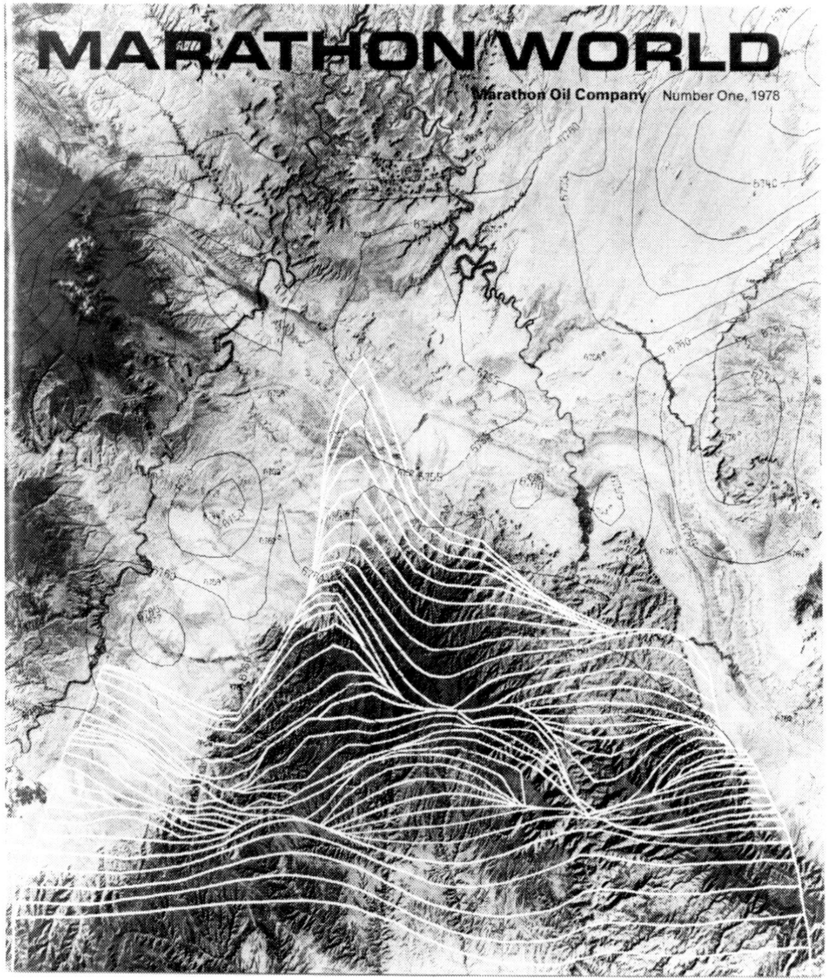

336
Stan Corfman Art Director
Marathon World Client

338
Byran Canniff Art Director
Ts'ai Chen-Hua Illustrator
Saturday Review Client

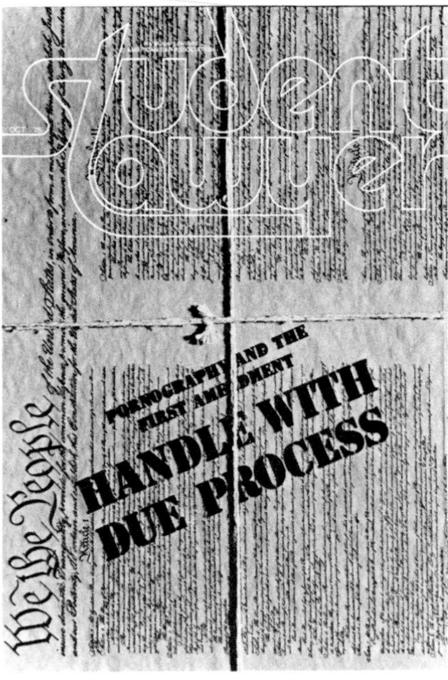

339
David Carothers Art Director
Henry Tyler Locke Photographer
Donna Tashjian Photo Editor
Jack J. Podell Creative Director
American Bar Association Press Client

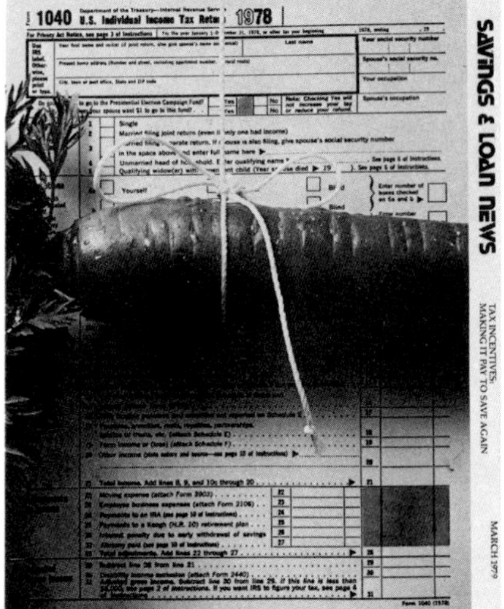

340
Jim Lienhart Art Director
Tom Vack Photographer
Murrie, White, Drummond & Lienhart Agency
Savings & Loan News Client

341
Walter Bernard, Rudy Hoglund Art Directors
Michael Doret Illustrator
Michael Doret Design Studio
Time Magazine Client

JANUARY 29, 1979 $1.25
TIME
Iran Without The Shah
THE COLOMBIAN CONNECTION
BILLIONS IN POT & COKE
DORET

342
John A. Kleiner Art Director
Art Wolfe Photographer
John A. Kleiner, Jeannie L. Kleiner Designers
John A. Kleiner Graphic Design Inc. Studio
ARCOtravel Club, Inc. Client

343
Howard E. Paine Art Director
Thomas J. Abercrombie Photographer
W. E. Garrett Designer
National Geographic Society Client

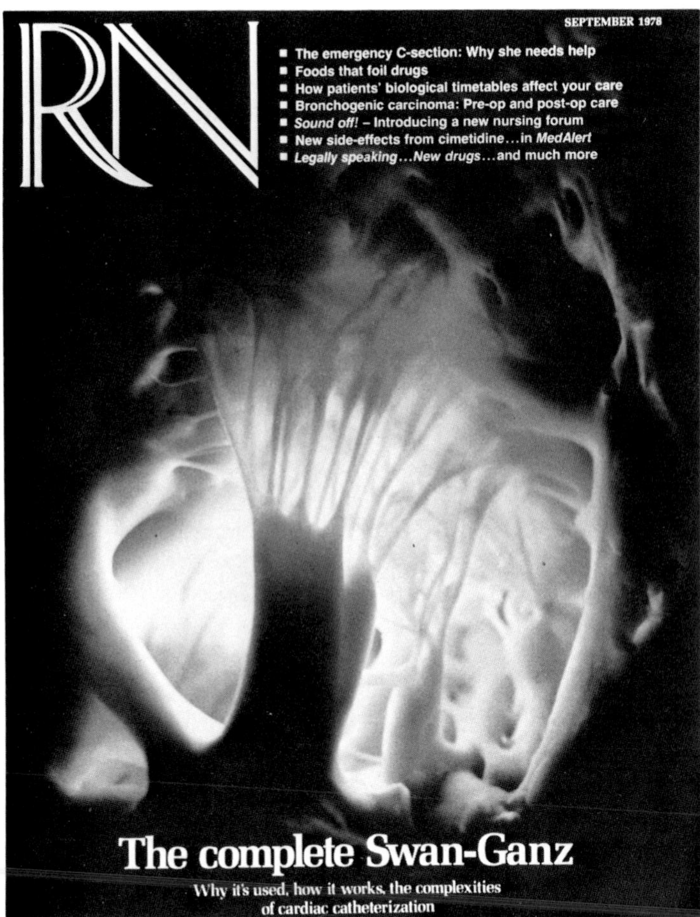

RN
SEPTEMBER 1978
■ The emergency C-section: Why she needs help
■ Foods that foil drugs
■ How patients' biological timetables affect your care
■ Bronchogenic carcinoma: Pre-op and post-op care
■ Sound off! – Introducing a new nursing forum
■ New side-effects from cimetidine...in MedAlert
■ Legally speaking...New drugs...and much more
The complete Swan-Ganz
Why it's used, how it works, the complexities of cardiac catheterization

344
Albert M. Foti, Barbara Silbert Art Directors
Lennart Nilsson Photographer
Barbara Silbert Designer
Medical Economics Company, RN Magazine Client

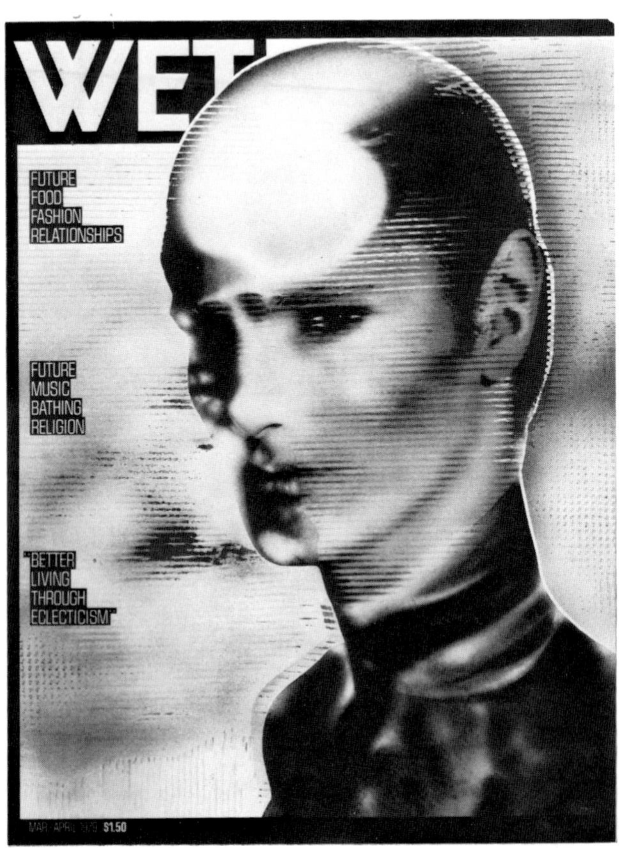

345
Lisa Powers, Taki Ono Art Directors
Amnesia Studio Agency
Wet Magazine Client

346
Rodney C. Williams Art Director
Jim Jindra, Joel Snyder Photographers
Chicago Magazine Client

347
Jessica M. Weber Art Director
Larry Couzens Photographer
The Int'l Review Of Food & Wine Client

348
Nickolas Dankovich Art Director
Charlie Company-Charlie Coppins Photographers
The Plain Dealer Magazine Client

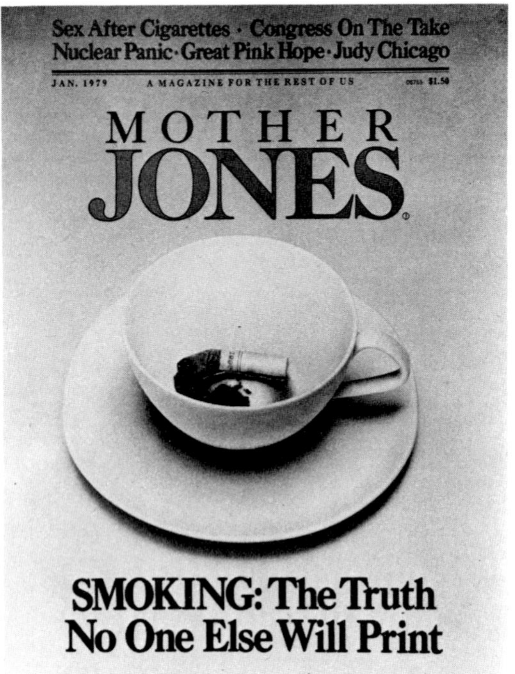

349
Louise Kollenbaum Art Director
Richard Hickson Photographer
Mother Jones Magazine Client

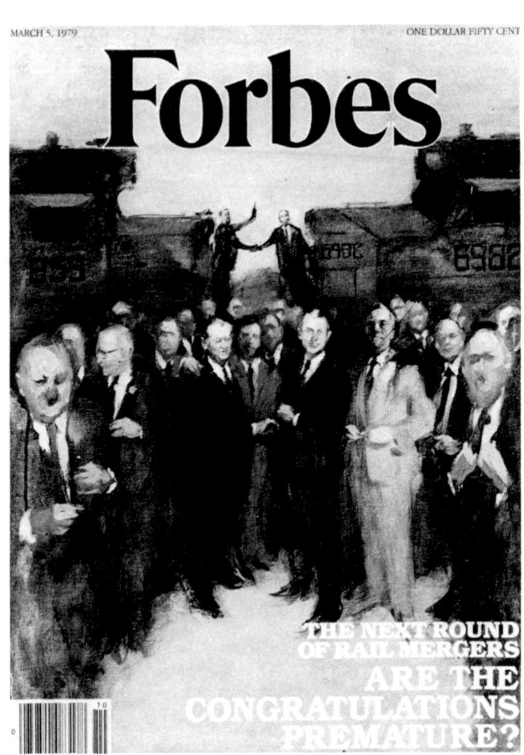

350
Everett Halvorsen Art Director
Skip Liepke Illustrator
Forbes Magazine Client

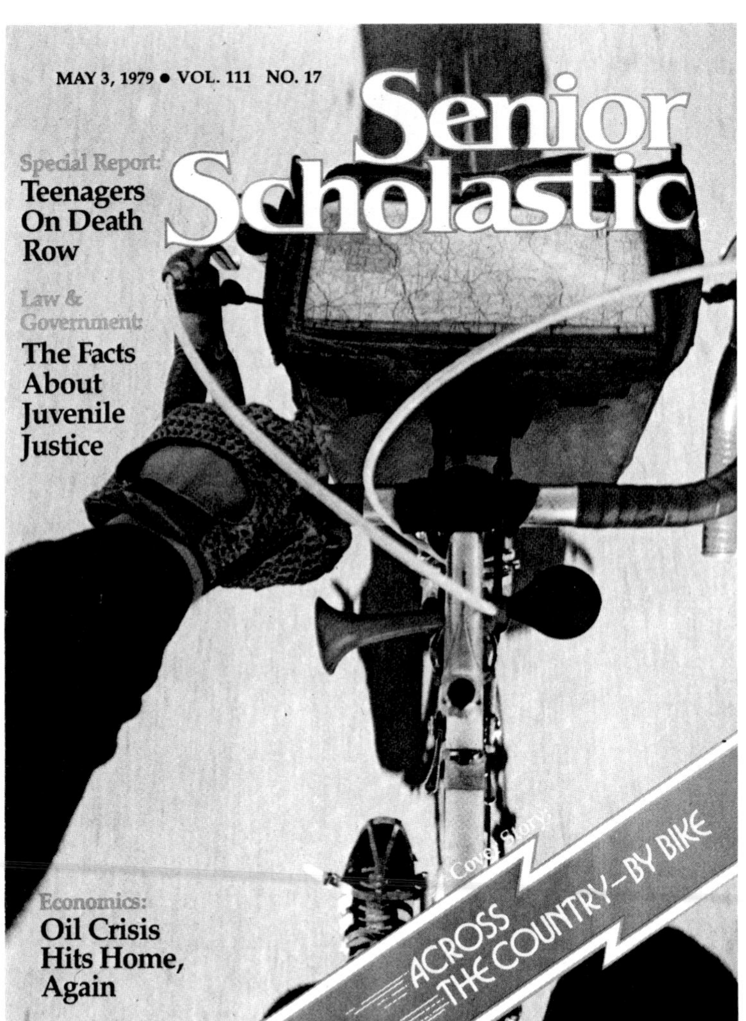

351
Dale Moyer Art Director
Mike Seresko Photographer
Dale Moyer, Jeff Derecki Designers
Scholastic Magazines Client

Book Jackets

352
Rinaldo Cutini Art Director
Armando Armando, Publisher Client

353
Diana Graham Art Director
Research Reports Picture Research
Diana Graham, Graphic Design Studio
Hagstrom Company Client

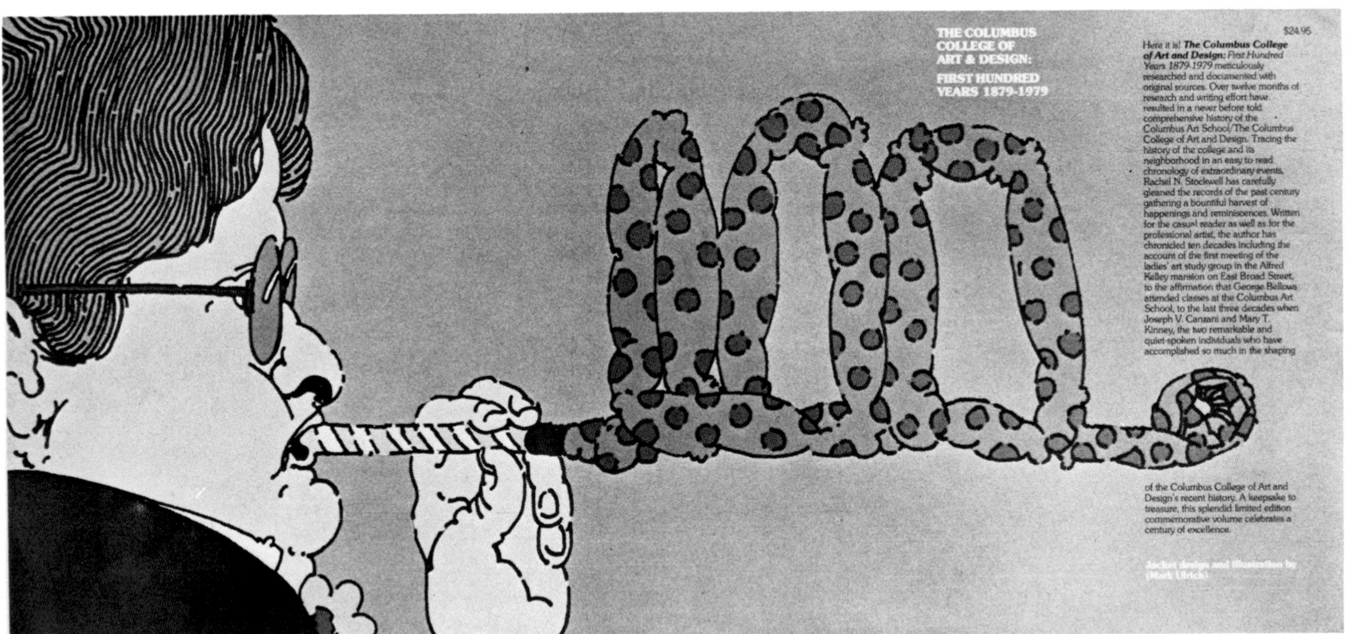

354
Mark Ulrich, Paul Moorehead
Art Directors
Columbus College of Art & Design
Client

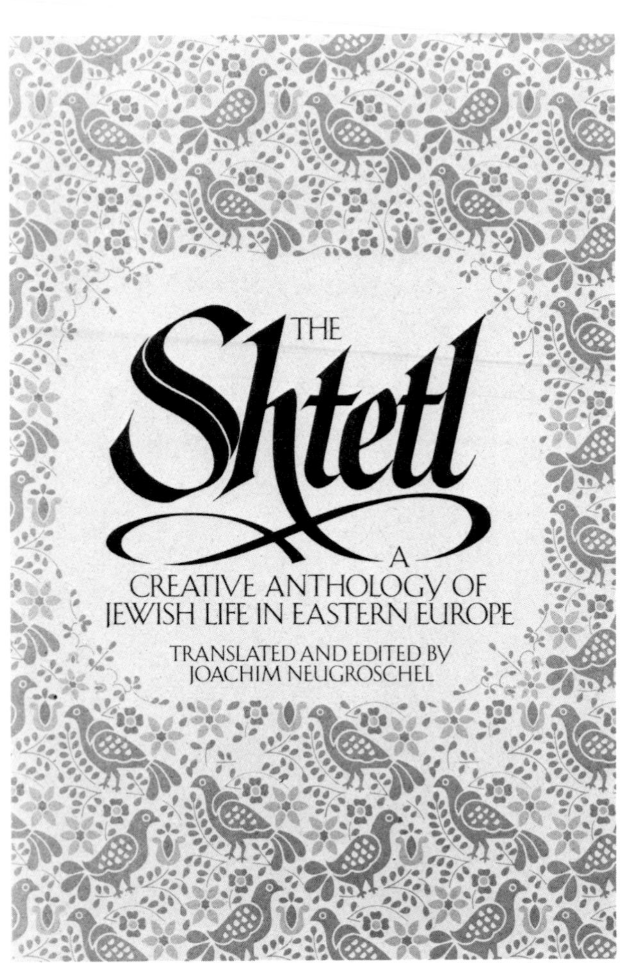

355
Lynn Hollyn Art Director
Lynn Hollyn, Muriel Nasser Designers
Richard Marek Publishers Client

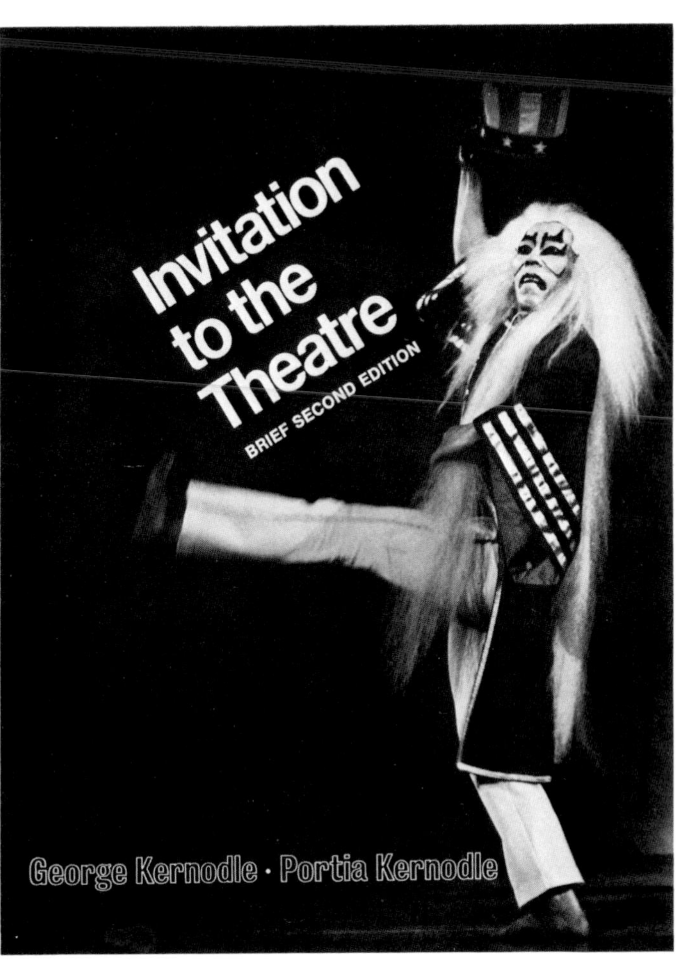

356
Anna Kopczynski Art Director
Van Williams Photographer
Harcourt, Brace, Jovanovich, Inc.
Client

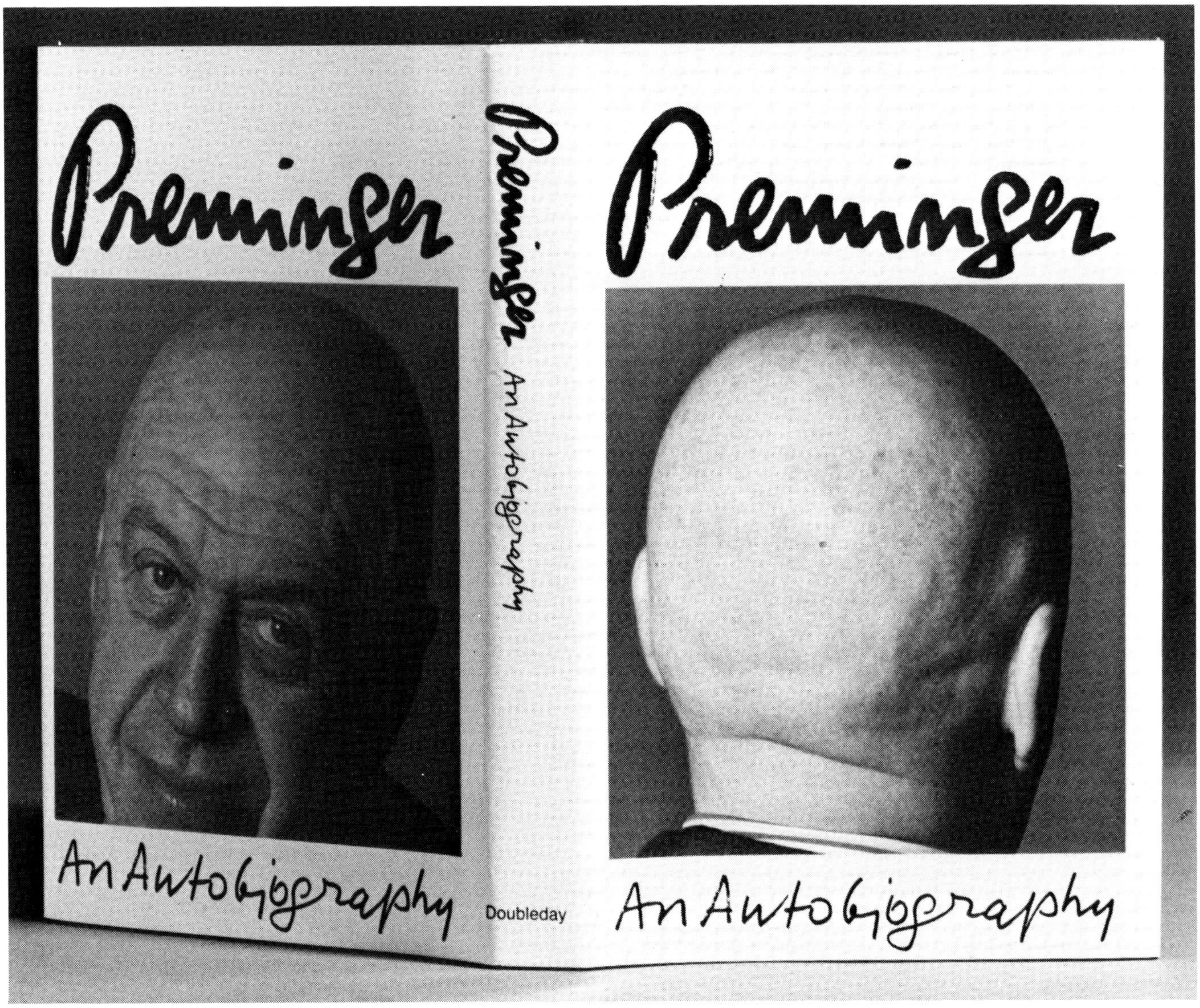

357
Art Goodman Art Director
Burt Glinn, Magnum Photographers
Saul Bass, Herb Yager Designers
Bass/Yager & Associates Agency
Doubleday Client

358
Sybil Broyles Art Director
Pat Berry Photographer
Mediatex Communications Corp. Client

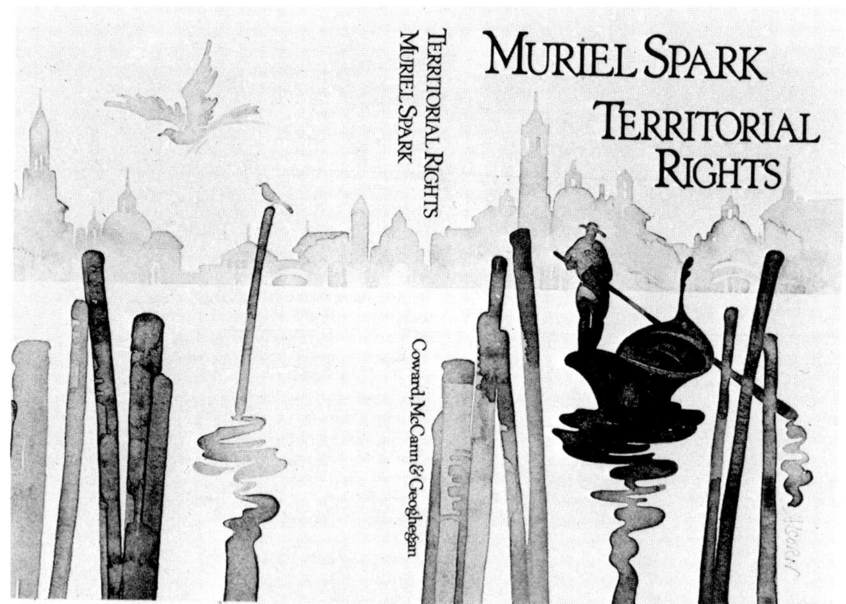

359
Lynn Hollyn Art Director
John Alcorn Designer
Coward, McCann & Geoghegan Client

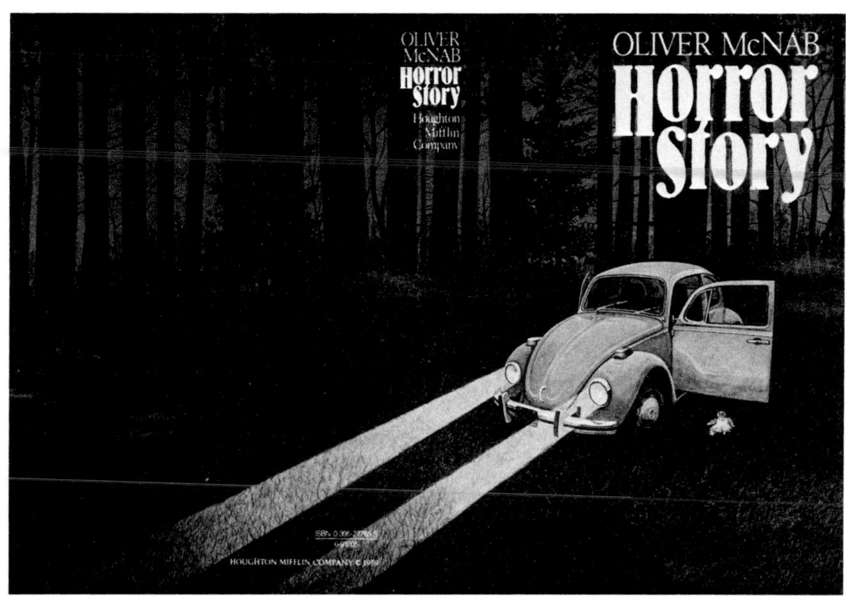

360
Louise Noble Art Director
Wendell Minor Illustrator
Wendell Minor Design Studio
Houghton Mifflin Co. Client

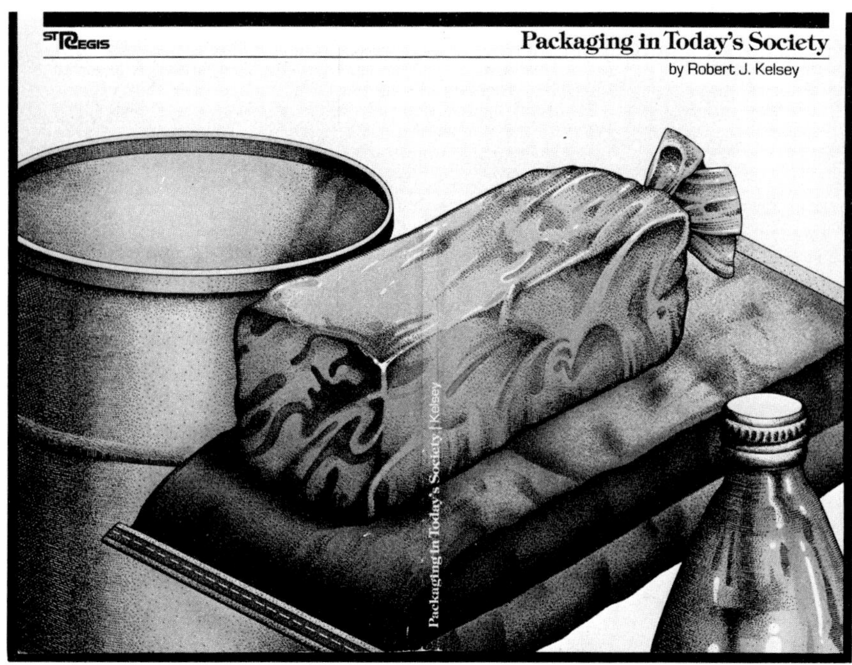

361
Kay Sabinson Art Director
Ed Lindlof Illustrator
Burson-Marsteller Agency
St. Regis Client

362
Milton Charles Art Director
Magic Image Inc. Photographers
Milton Charles, Matthew Tepper Designers
Pocket Books Client

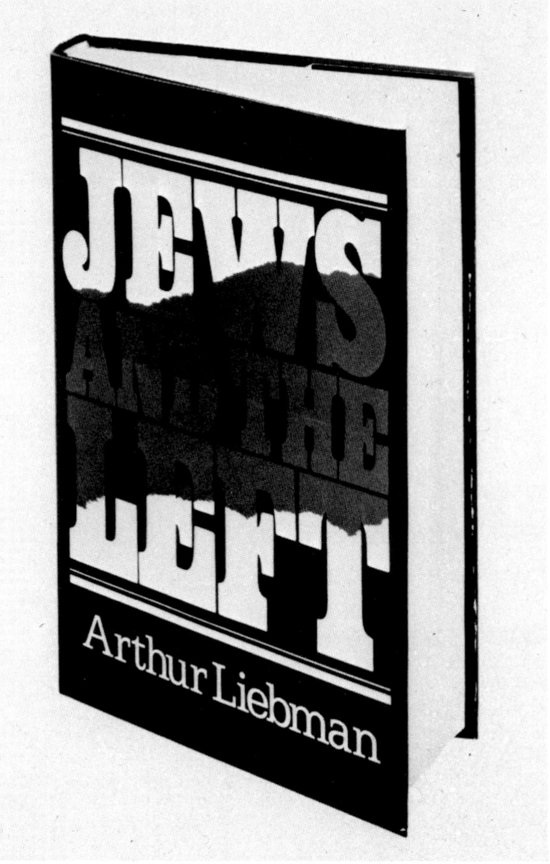

363
Barbara Gendler Soll Art Director
605 Advertising Group Agency
Wiley-Interscience Client

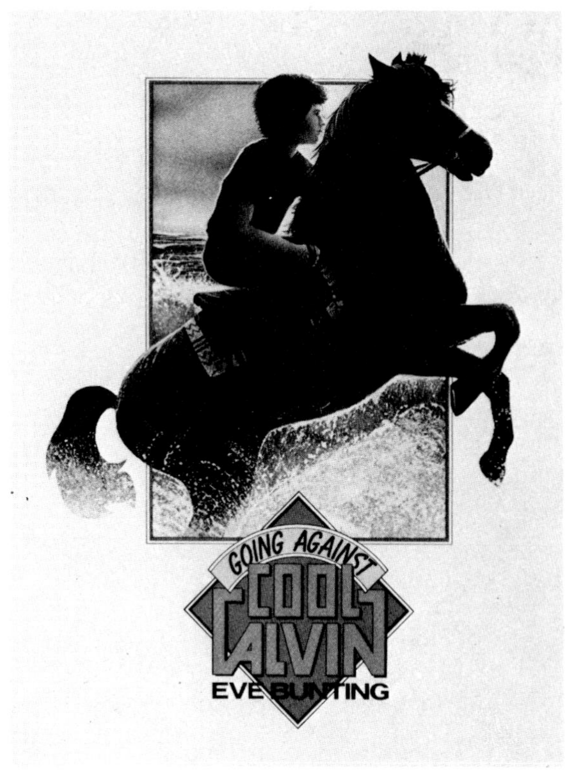

364
Skip Sorvino Art Director
Don Brautigam Illustrator
Stephanie Zuras Designer
Scholastic Magazines Client

365
Deborah Daly Art Director
Martin Geller Illustrator
Martin Geller Design Studio
St. Martins Press Client

366
T. Courtney Brown Art Director
Doug Taylor Illustrator
Michael Doret Designer
Doret & Taylor Studio
Stonehill Publishing Client

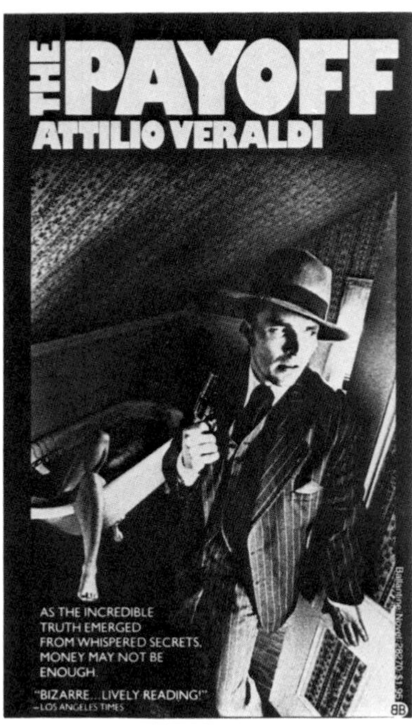

367
Don Smith Art Director
Ron F. Tunison Photographer
Ballantine Books Client

368
Jo Jones Art Director
Al Green Photographer
McGraw-Hill Book Co. Client

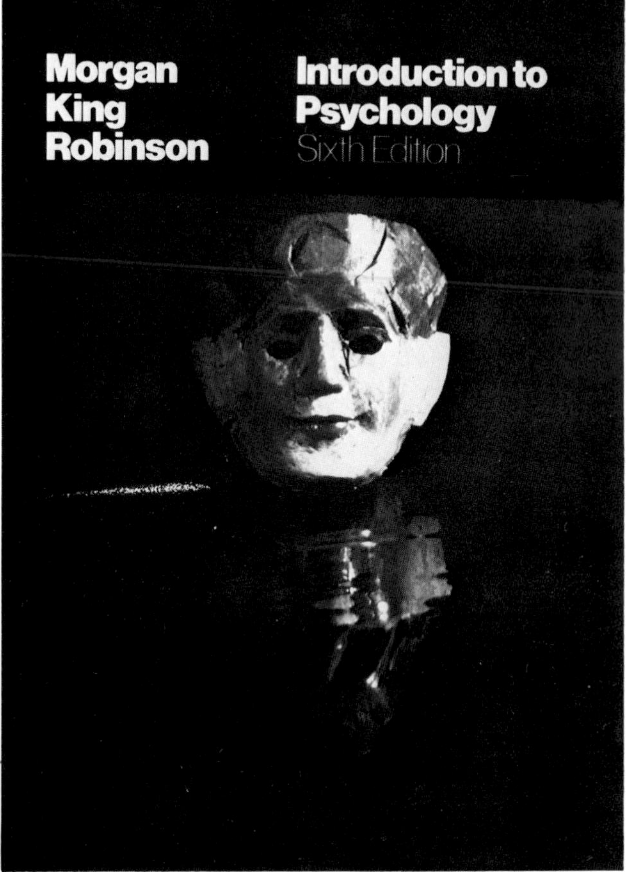

369
Merrill Haber Art Director
Ben Kann Designer
McGraw-Hill Book Co. Client

371
Cheryl Asherman Art Director
Marjory Dressler Photographer
Honi Werner Designer
William Morrow & Co., Inc. Client

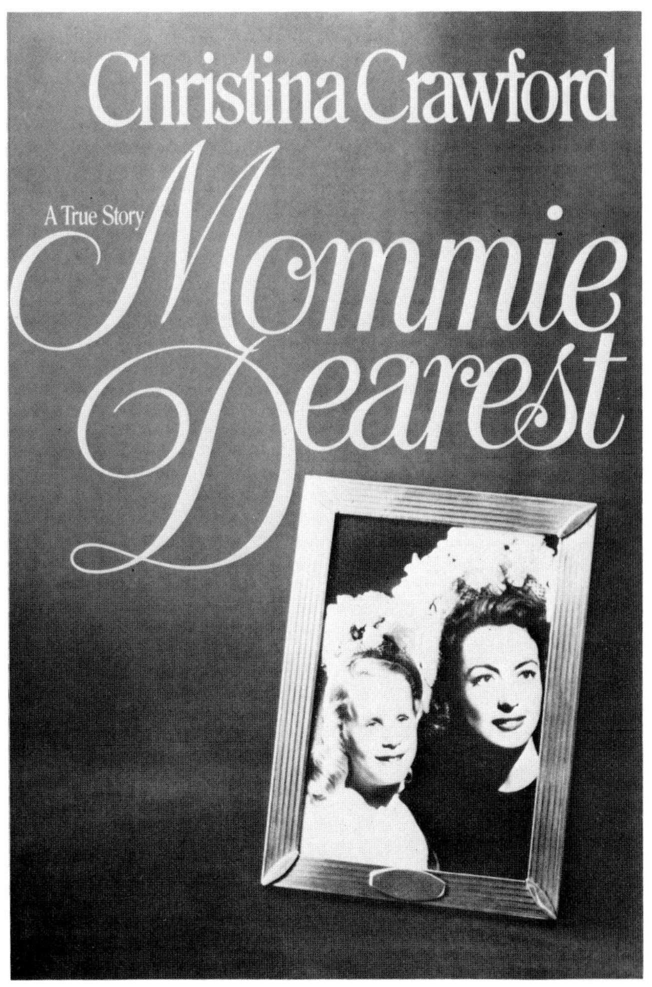

370
Jack W. Davis Art Director
Jack Davis Graphics Studio
University Of Illinois Press Client

372
Nicholas Krenitsky Art Director
McGraw-Hill Book Co. Client

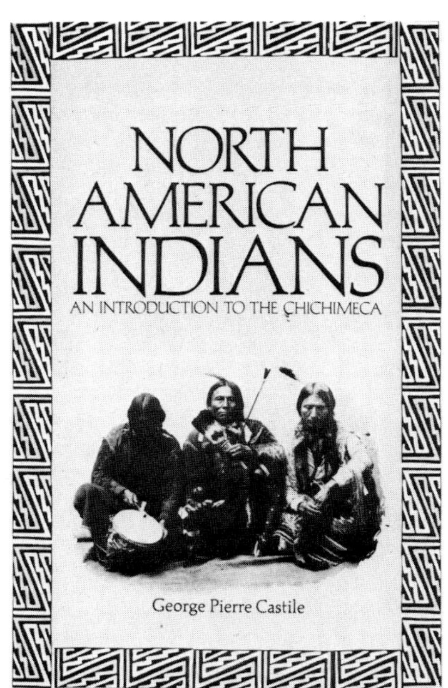

373
Joan O'Connor Art Director
McGraw-Hill Book Co. Client

374
Joan O'Connor Art Director
Carla Bauer Illustrator
McGraw-Hill Book Co. Client

375
Lynn Hollyn Art Director
Stan Zagorski Designer
Richard Marek Publishers Client

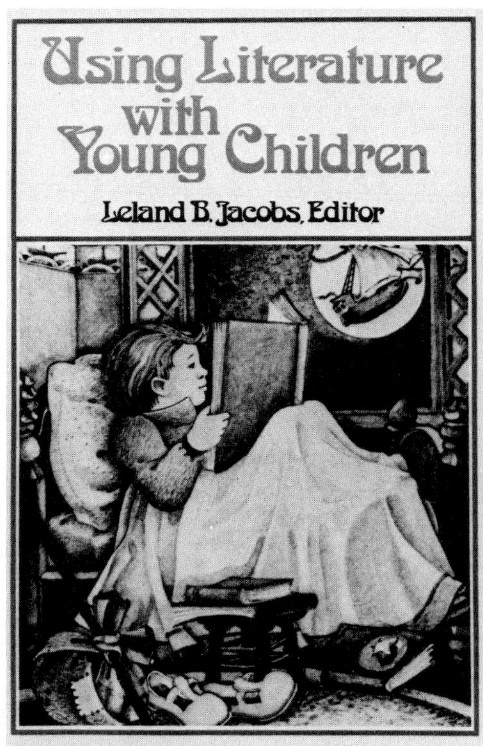

376
Frank B. Marshall III Art Director
John Wallner Illustrator
Frank B. Marshall III Designer
Teachers College Press—Columbia University Client

377
Harry Williams Art Director
Colin Molyneux Photographer
Wales Tourist Board Client

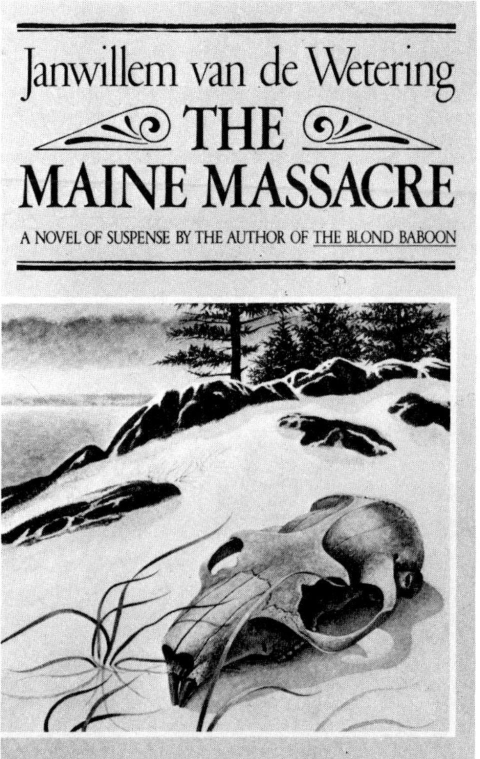

378
Louise Noble Art Director
Wendell Minor Illustrator
Wendell Minor Design Studio
Houghton Mifflin Co. Client

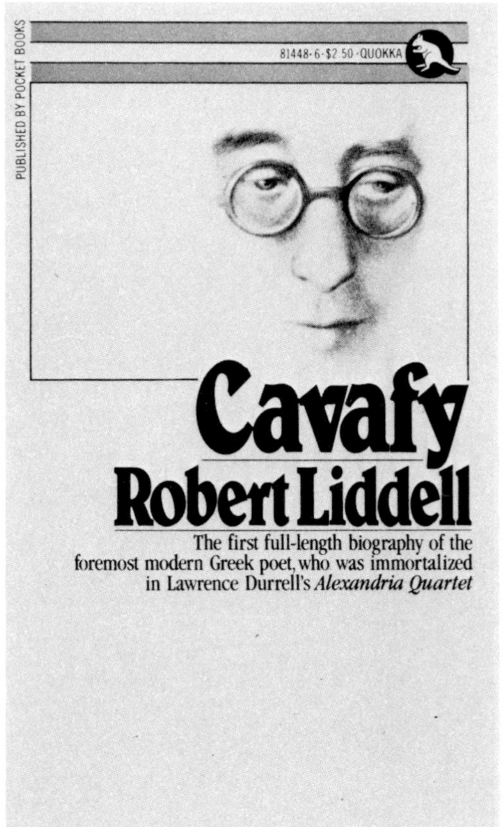

379
Milton Charles Art Director
Gillian Hills Illustrator
Milton Charles, Matthew Tepper Designers
Pocket Books Client

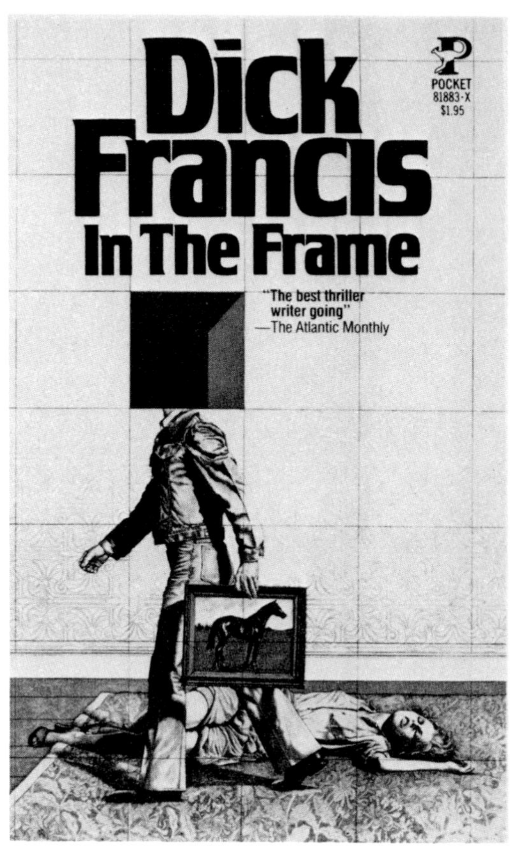

380
Milton Charles Art Director
Richard Smith Illustrator
Pocket Books Client

381
Saul Bass Art Director
Saul Bass, Art Goodman Designers
Bass/Yager & Associates Agency
Harcourt, Brace, Jovanovich, Inc. Client

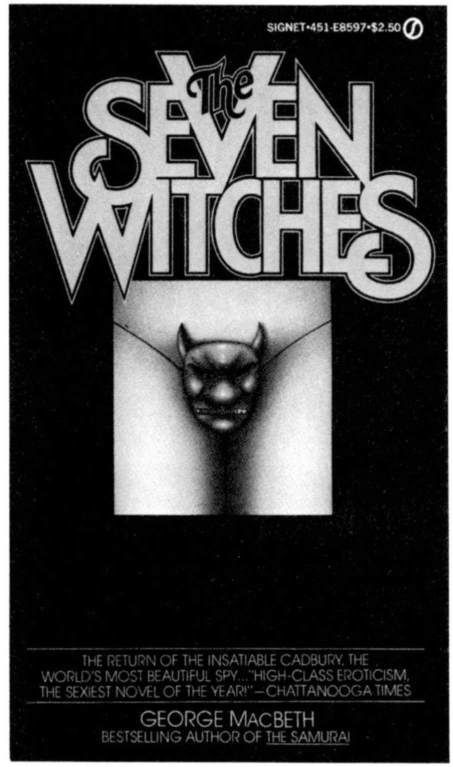

382
Jim Plumeri Art Director
Don Brautigan Illustrator
Richard Rossiter Designer
New American Library Client

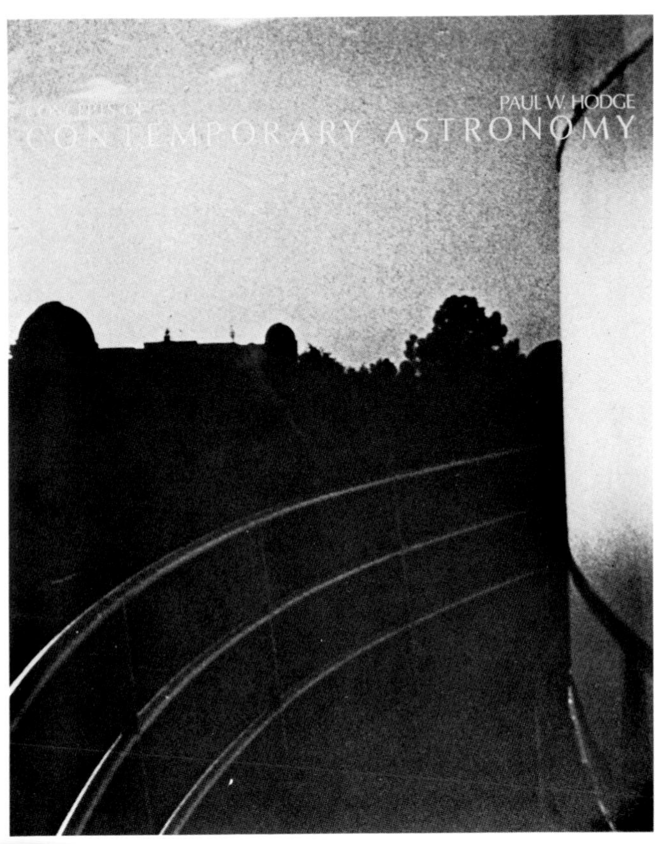

383
Chuck Carson Art Director
McGraw-Hill Book Store Client

384
Craig Butler Art Director
Wolin-Semple Studio Photographers
Butler Advertising Agency
L.A. Workbook Client

385
Daniel Haberman Art Director
Isadore Seltzer Illustrator
Royal Composing Room Client

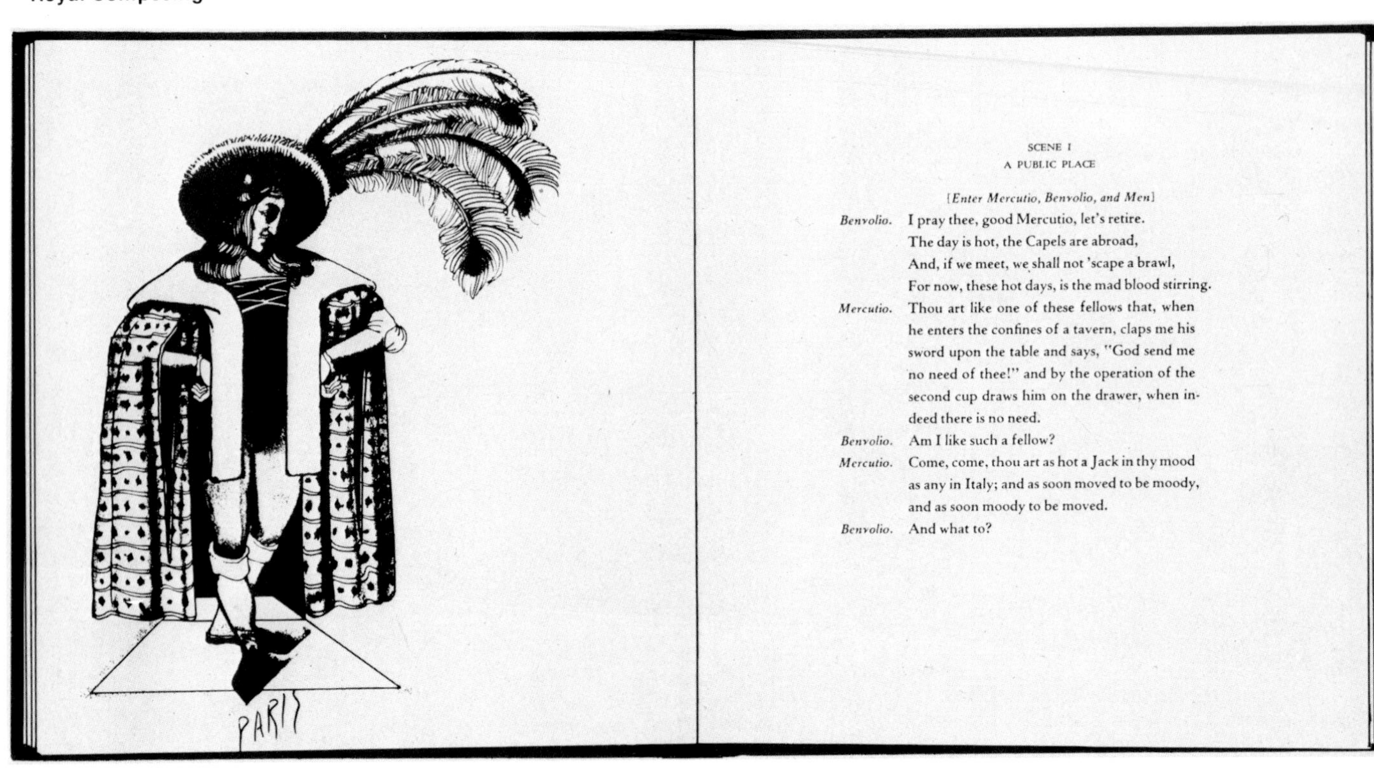

SCENE I
A PUBLIC PLACE

[*Enter Mercutio, Benvolio, and Men*]

Benvolio. I pray thee, good Mercutio, let's retire.
The day is hot, the Capels are abroad,
And, if we meet, we shall not 'scape a brawl,
For now, these hot days, is the mad blood stirring.

Mercutio. Thou art like one of these fellows that, when he enters the confines of a tavern, claps me his sword upon the table and says, "God send me no need of thee!" and by the operation of the second cup draws him on the drawer, when indeed there is no need.

Benvolio. Am I like such a fellow?

Mercutio. Come, come, thou art as hot a Jack in thy mood as any in Italy; and as soon moved to be moody, and as soon moody to be moved.

Benvolio. And what to?

Record Albums

386
Phil Carroll Art Director
Frank Safranek Photographer
Kris Johnson Designer
Fantasy Records Client

387
Robert Burns, Heather Cooper Art Directors
Heather Cooper, Carmen Djunko Designers
Paul Walker Type
Burns, Cooper, Hynes Limited Agency
SQN Records Client

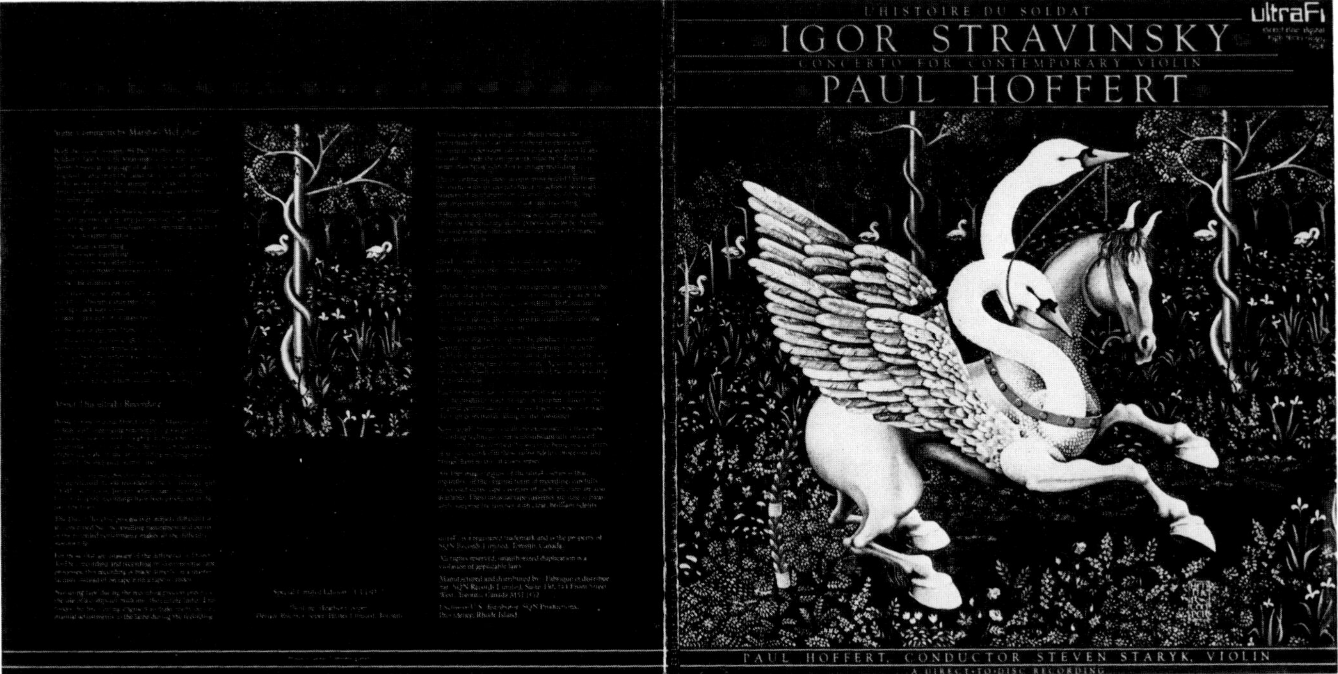

388 A-C
David Hogan Art Director
Mikel Covey Photographer
Jim Osborn Illustrator
Hot Graphics Studio
RCA Records Client

A

389
Phil Carroll Art Director
Lucinda Cowell Designer
Fantasy Records Client

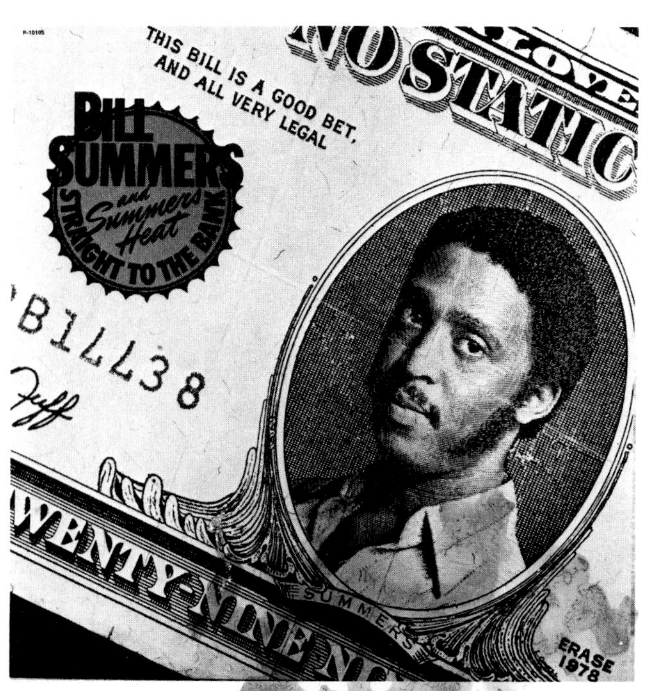

390
Phil Carroll Art Director
Phil Bray, Ron Michaelson
Photographers
Lucinda Cowell Designer
Fantasy Records Client

388 B

C

391
Ron Coro Art Director
Elliot Gilbert Photographer
Elektra/Asylum Records Client

392
Phil Carroll Art Director
Roy Decarava Photographer
Kris Johnson Designer
Fantasy Records Client

393
Phil Carroll Art Director
Larry Keenan, Jr. Photographer
Dennis Gassner Designer
Fantasy Records Client

394

395

396

396
George Osaki Art Director
Claude Mougin Photographer
Ria Lewerke Designer
R.I.A. Images Production House
L.K. Productions, Inc./MCA Records Client

397
Ron Coro Art Director
Bo Overlock Photographer
David Wilcox Illustrator
Ron Coro, Johnny Lee Designers
Elektra/Asylum Records Studio
Elektra/Asylum Records Client

398
Alwyn Clayden Art Director
John Shaw Photographer
Polydor Ltd. Client

397

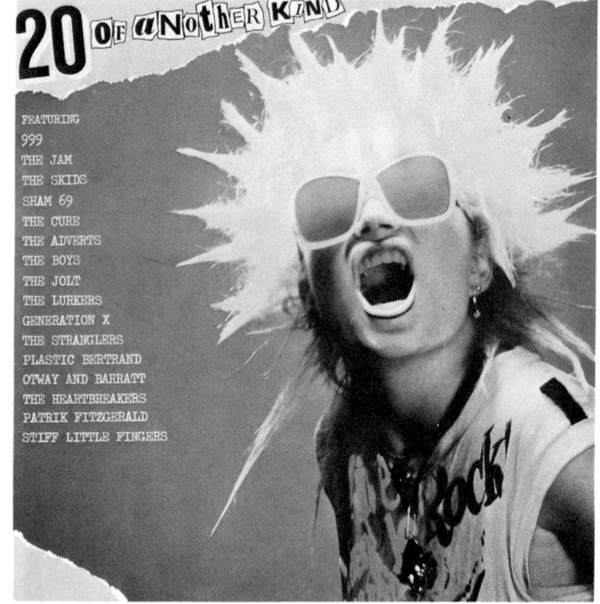

398

394
Phil Carroll Art Director
Elizabeth Lennard Photographer
Kris Johnson Designer
Fantasy Records Client

395
Phil Carroll Art Director
Phil Bray Photographer
Jamie Putnam Illustrator
Fantasy Records Client

399
Michael Mendel Art Director
Hal Wilson Photographer
Jim O'Connell Illustrator
Roadshow Graphics Studio
United Artists Records Client

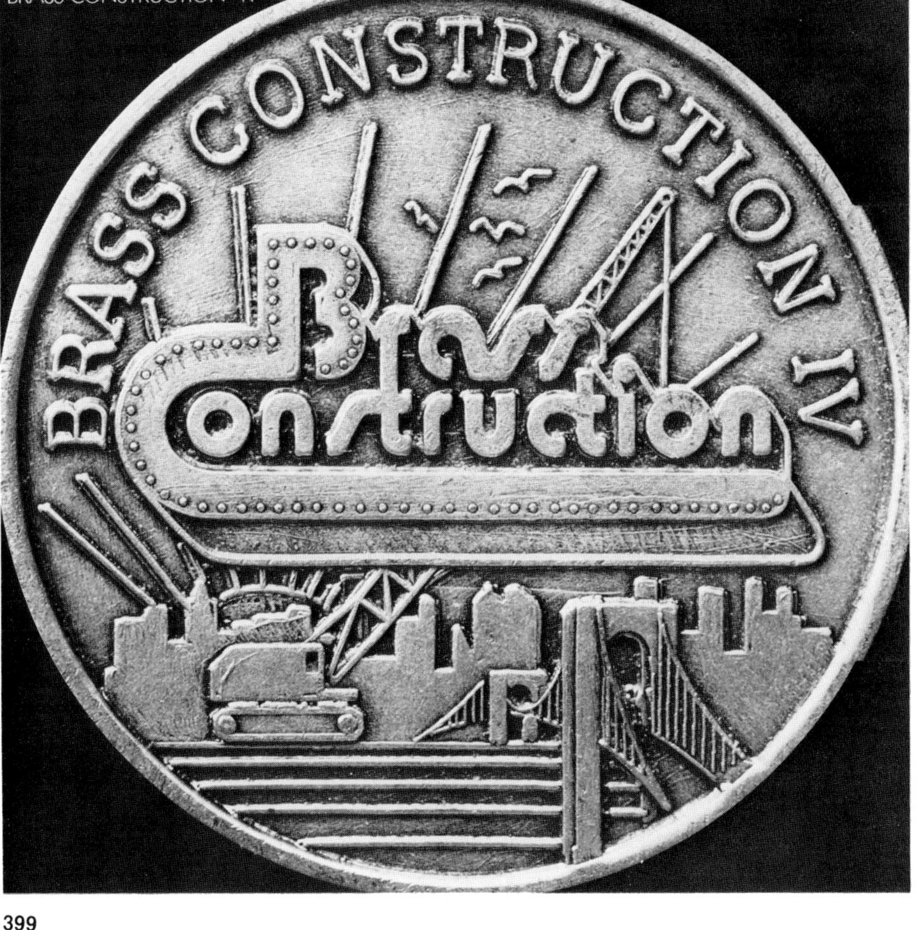

399

400
Jo Mirowski Art Director
Veronique Skawinska Photographer
Vangelis Designer
Polydor Ltd. Client

400

401
Roland Young Art Director
Mark Hanauer Photographer
Junie Osaki Designer
A & M Records, Inc. Client

401

402
Michael Mendel Art Director
Ruth Mendel Illustrator
51 West Records & Tapes Client

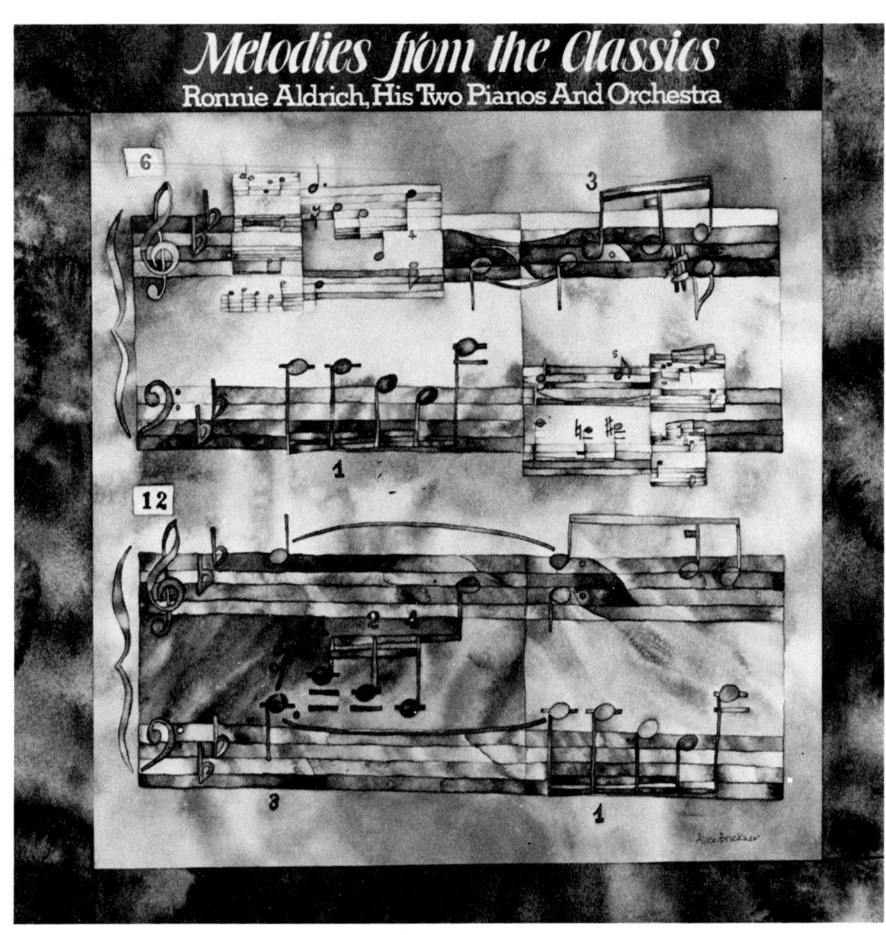

403
Lucy Kleps Art Director
London Records Client

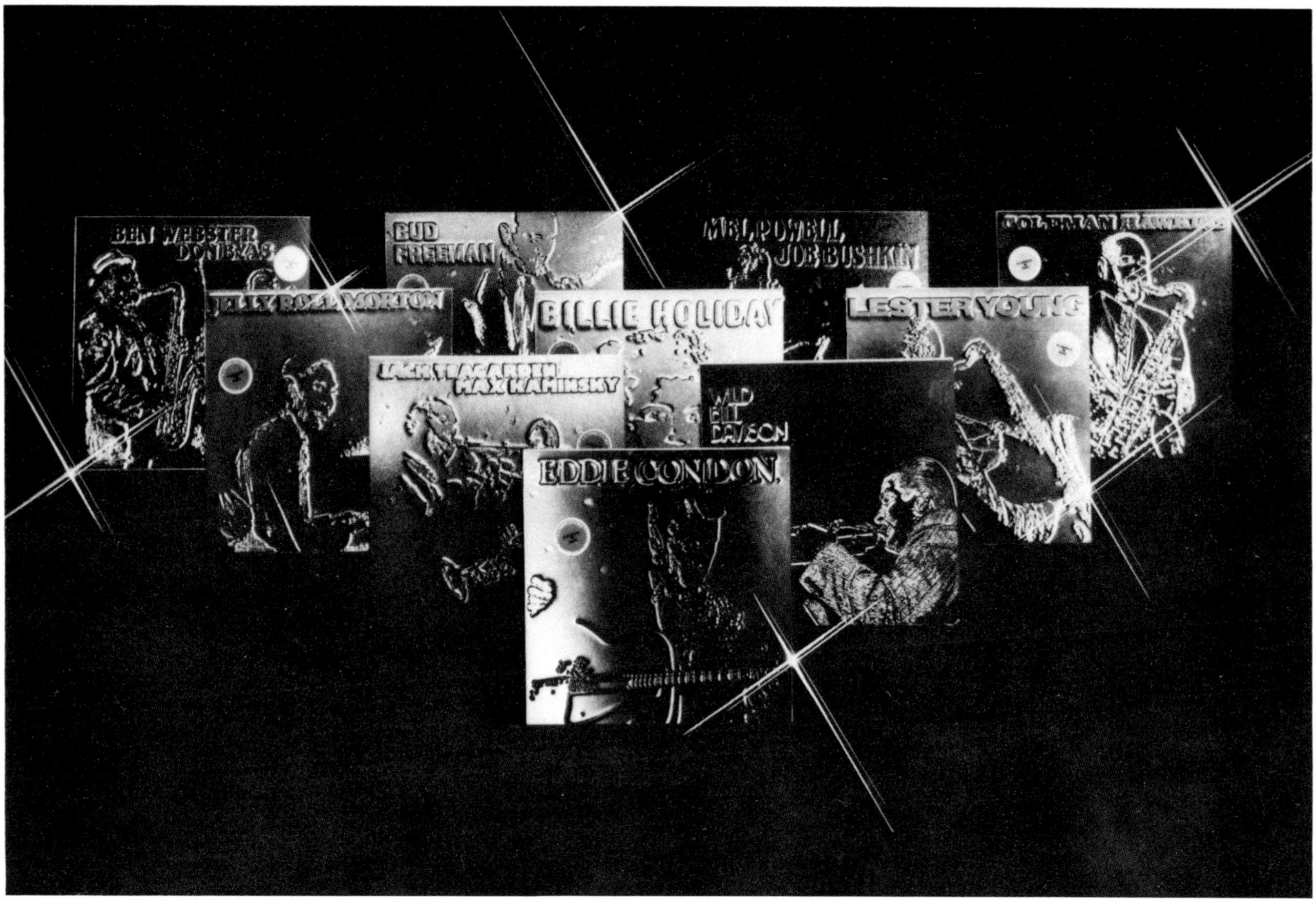

404
Ely Besalel Art Director
Besalel Ltd. Studio
CBS Records, Client

405
Roland Young Art Director
Mark Hanauer Photographer
Junie Osaki Designer
A & M Records, Inc. Client

406
Phil Carroll Art Director
Phil Bray Photographer
Georgia Gillfillan Designer
Fantasy Records Client

Package Design

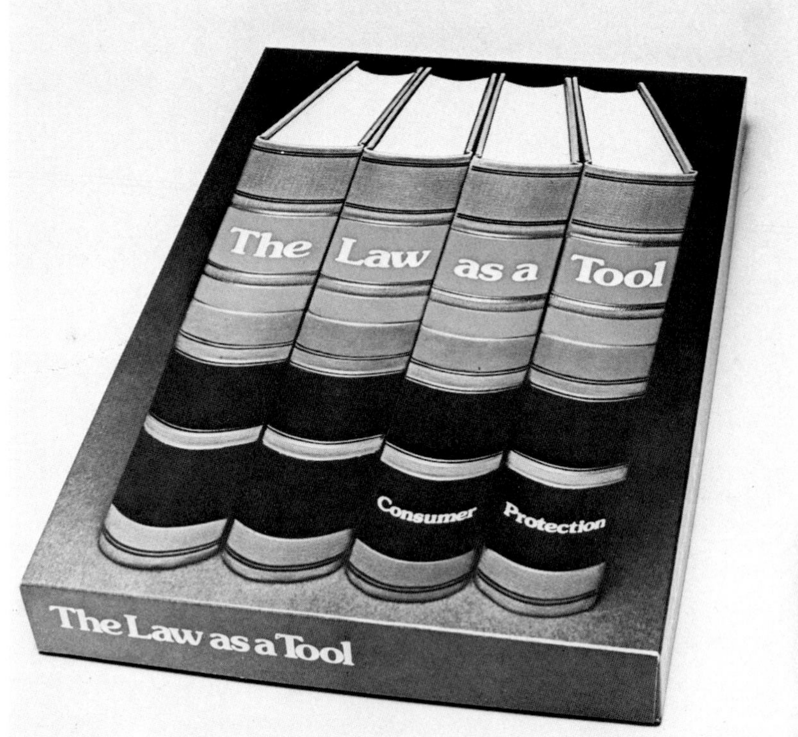

407
Ed Brodsky Art Director
Steve Eisenberg Photographer
Nina Manger Illustrator
Peggy Haney Copywriter
Brodsky Graphics Inc. Agency
J. C. Penney Company Client

408
Charles E. Norton Art Director
Manuel Denner Photographer
Joel Kaden Typographer
General Foods Corporate Design Center Agency
General Foods Corporation Client

A

409 A-B
Art Goodman Art Director
Saul Bass, Art Goodman Designers
Bass/Yager & Associates Agency
Burry's Client

410
Joel Bronz Art Director
John Kanelous Photographer
Bronz and Kanelous Design Studio
Stolzer Products Corp. Client

409 B

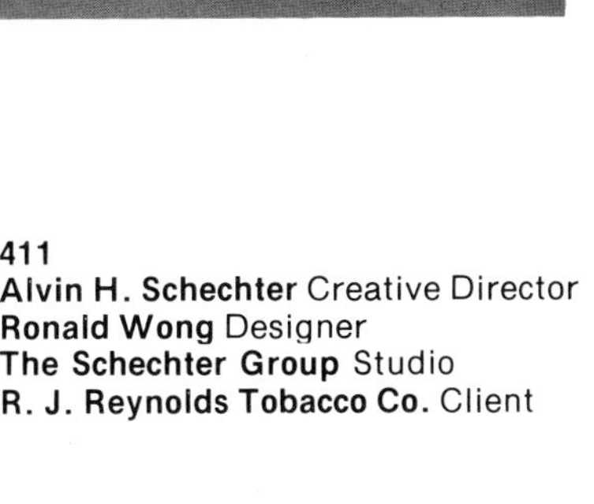

411
Alvin H. Schechter Creative Director
Ronald Wong Designer
The Schechter Group Studio
R. J. Reynolds Tobacco Co. Client

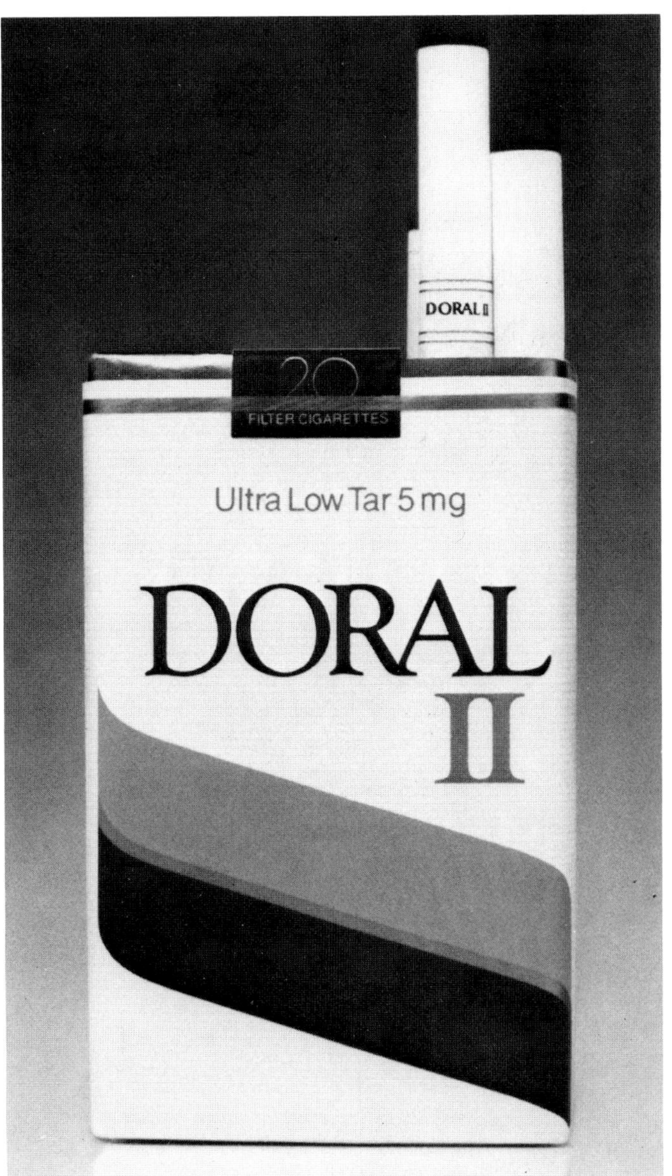

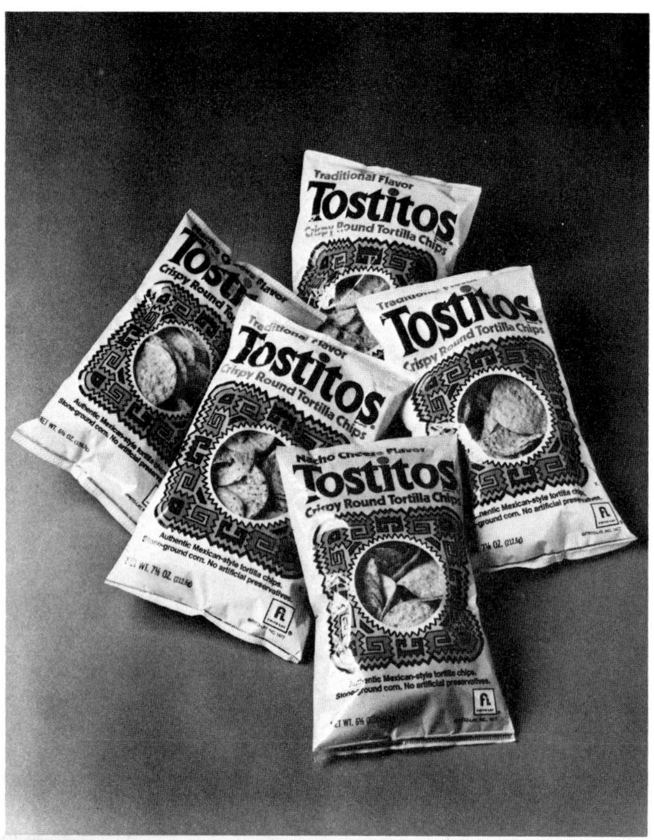

412
Juan Concepcion Art Director
Herbert M. Meyers Designer
Gerstman & Meyers Inc. Agency
Frito-Lay, Inc. Client

413
John DiGianni Art Director
Gianninoto Associates Inc. Studio
McCann Erickson Agency
Brown & Williamson Tobacco Corp. Client

414
Linda Powell Art Director
The Jones Colad Group Production House
Herman Miller, Inc. Client

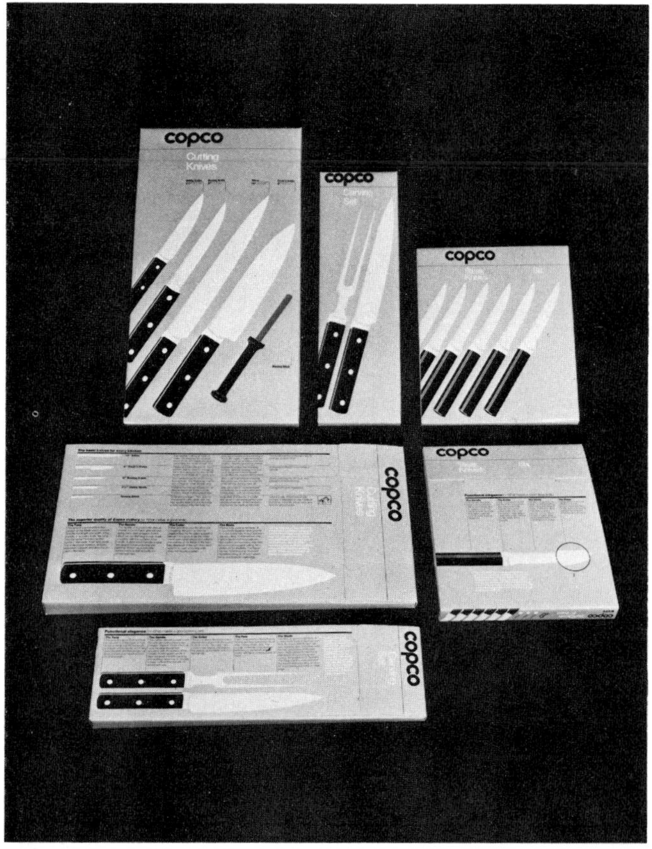

415
Marc-Albert Passy Art Director
Marc-Albert Passy, Marshall Harmon Designers
Passy Design Agency
Copco, Inc. Client

416
Gary Hinsche Art Director
Hinsche, Kay & Associates Agency
Healthways, Inc. Client

417
Rick Holeman Art Director
Kathy Hrouda Photographer
Ed Strong Designer
Rick Holeman, Art Director & Cowboy Agency
D. J. Enterprises Client

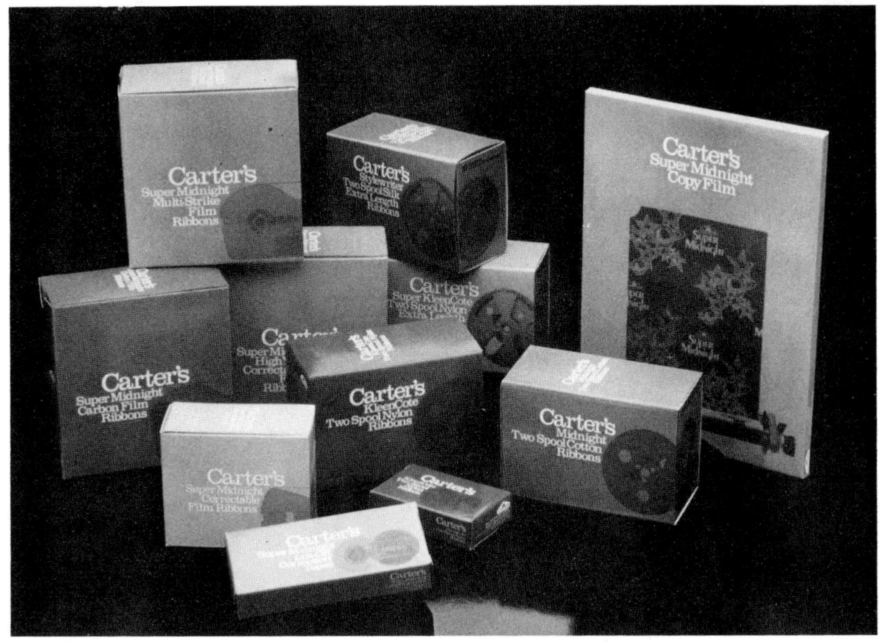

418
Cheryl Heller Art Director
Gunn Associates Agency
Carter's Ink Co. Client

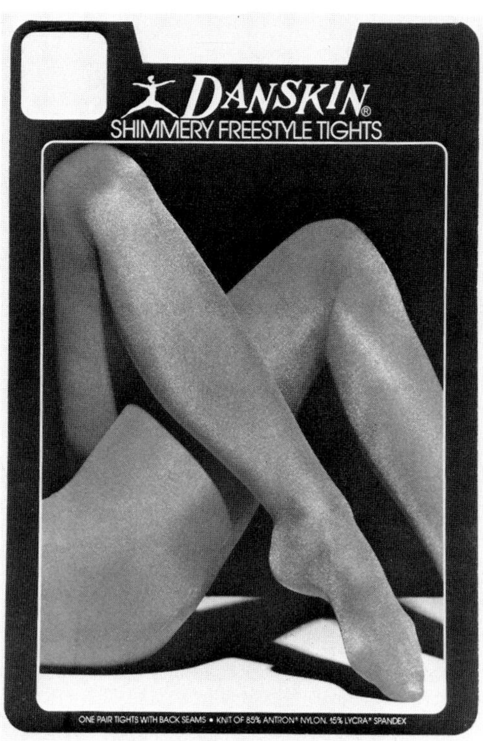

420
Sarah Melvin, Sky Underwood Art Directors
Gordon Munro Photographer
Susan Johnson Designer
Danskin, Inc. Client

419
Barbara Scharf Creative Director
Greenapple Sales Promotion, Inc. Agency
Almay Client

421
Lois M. Carlo Art Director
Lois M. Carlo, Jim Farmer Designers
Leber-Katz Partners Agency
M. Lowenstein & Sons Client

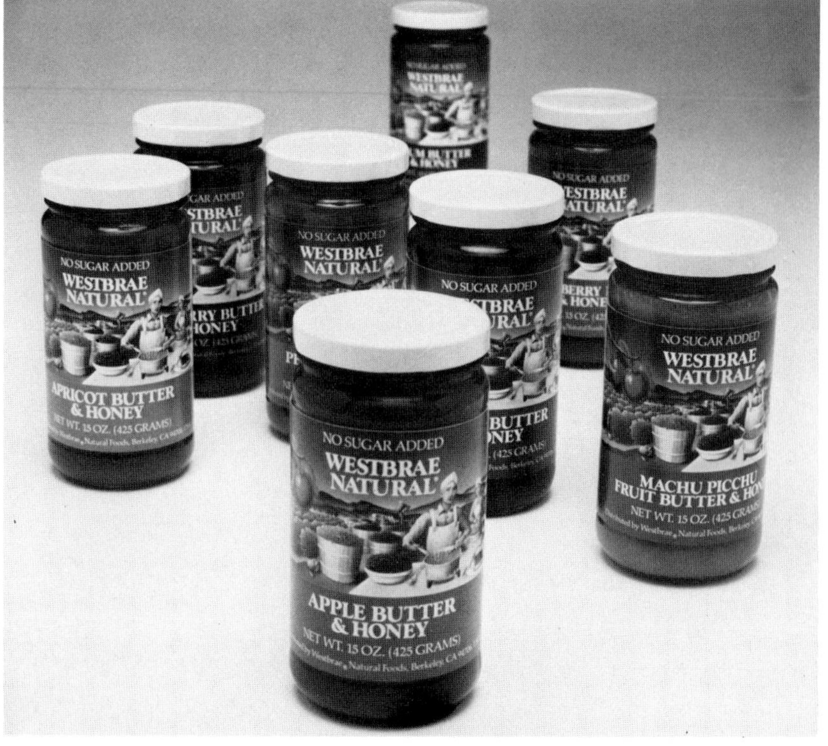

A

422 A-B
David Gauger Art Director
David Gauger, Paulette Traverso Designers
Gauger Sparks Silva Agency
Westbrae Natural Foods Client

423
Dennis Thompson, Jody Thompson Art Directors
Coming Attractions Agency
Somerset Wine Company Client

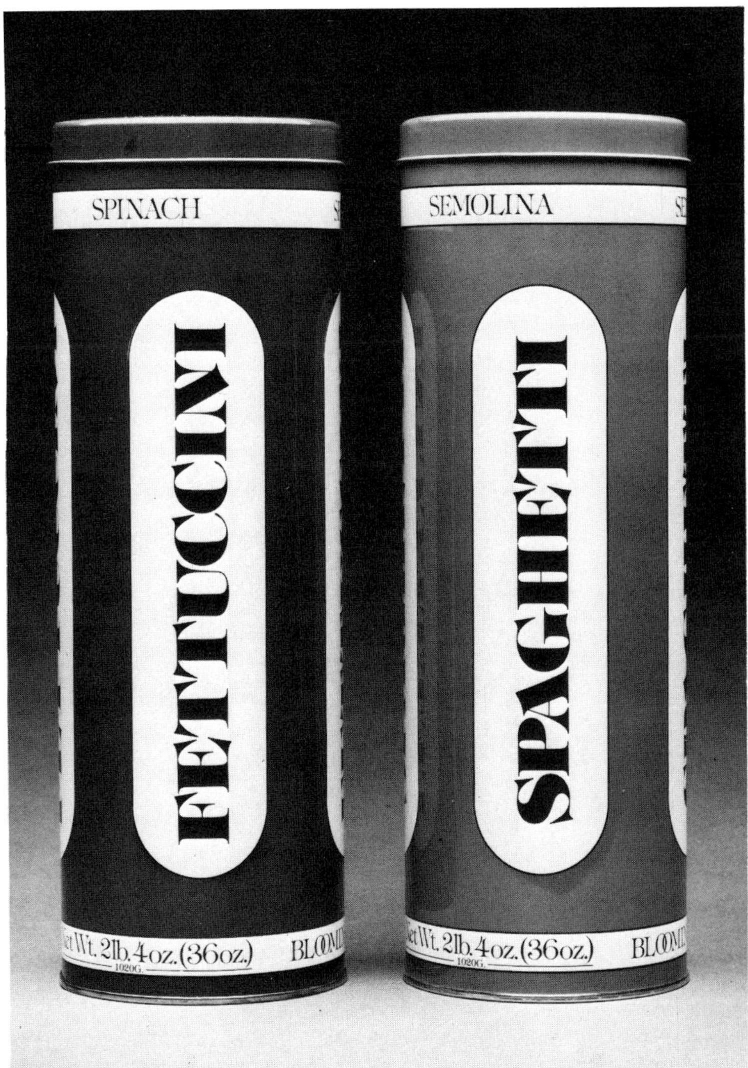

424
Steven Liska Art Director
Liska & Associates Agency
Bloomingdale's Dept. Stores Client

422 B

425
Stephen Laskoski Art Director
Dawne Barnes, Ruth Schweda Illustrators
Vicent Dutka Graphics, Stephen Laskoski Designers, Inc. Studios
McKim Agency
Kimberly-Clark Corporation Client

426
Bob Paganucci Art Director
Ed Gallucci Photographer
Bob Paganucci, Jane Cullen Designers
Ciba-Geigy Client

427
Jack Schecterson Art Director
Ray Diorio Studios Photographers
Barry Herstein, Jack Schecterson Designers
Jack Schecterson Associates, Inc. Agency
Buddy L. Corp. Client

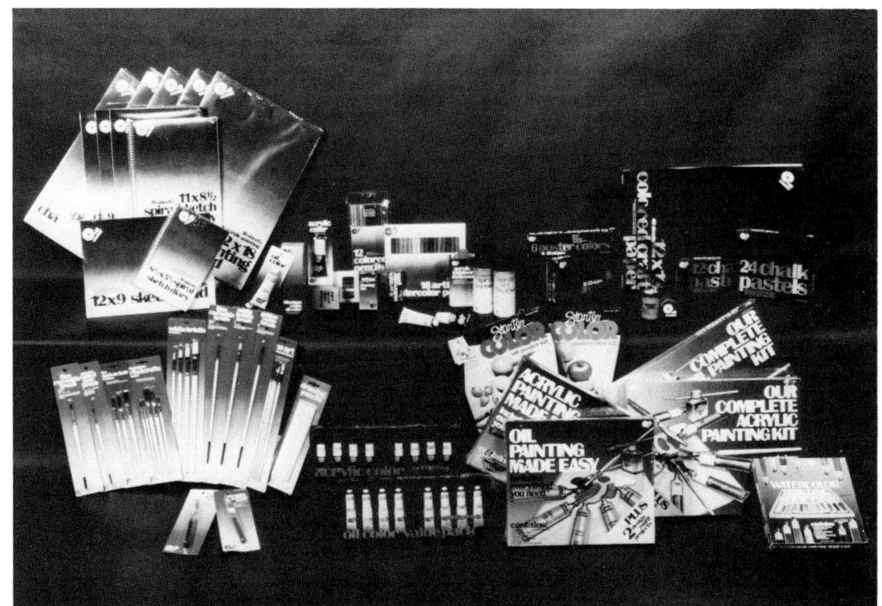

428
Richard P. Miller, Wells Moore
Art Directors
Maximum Graphic Design Associates
Agency
Craftint Corp. Client

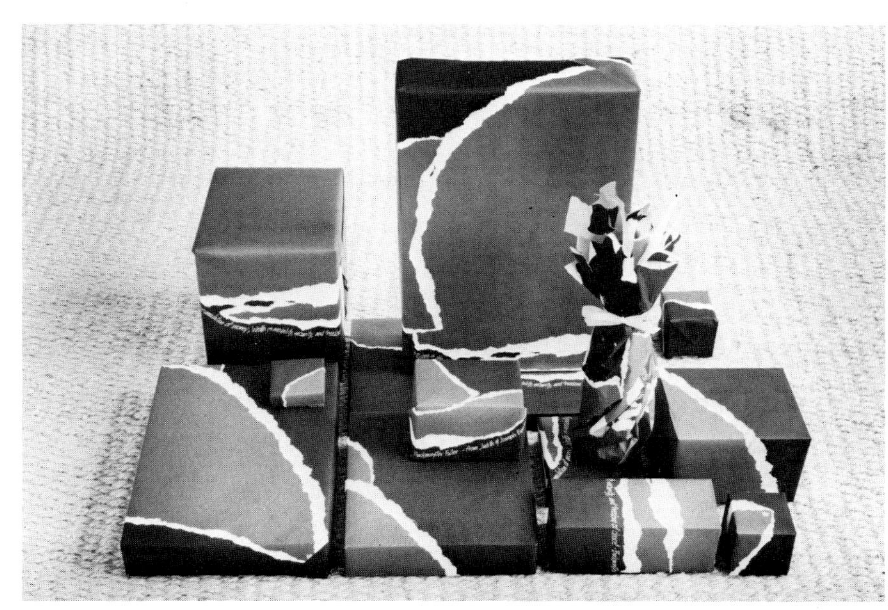

429
Joseph M. Essex Art Director
Burson-Marsteller/Design Group
Agency
Mr. & Mrs. Essex Clients

430
Steven Liska Art Director
Liska & Associates Agency
Bloomingdale's Dept. Stores Client

431
Graham Edwards, Arie J. Geurts Art Directors
Ruben Padova Photographer
Graham Edwards Illustrator
Laboratorio de Diseno y Analisis de Mercado—Carton y Papel de Mexico S.A. Agency
Ebesa Client

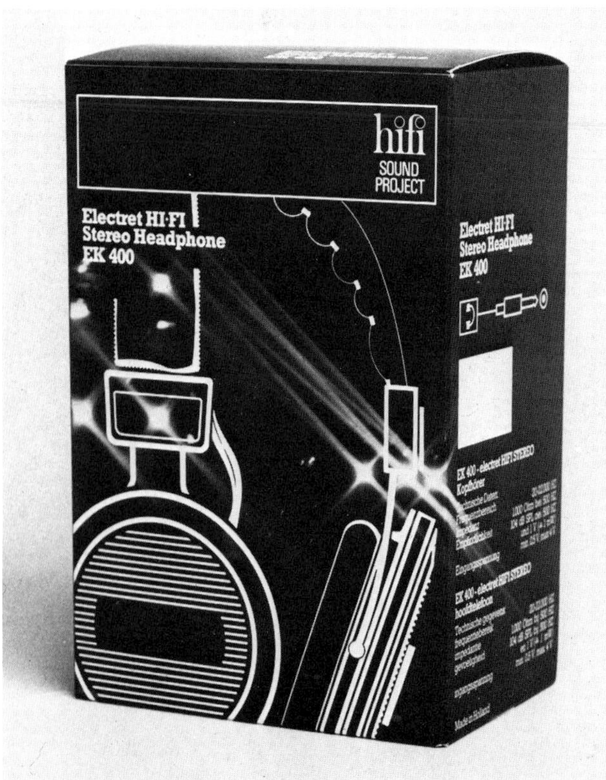

432
Jerome Bertrand Art Director
Bertrand Pack Design Agency
CIDC/N.V. Philips Gloeilampenfabrieken Client

433
Robert Burns Art Director
Tim Saunders Photographer
Heather Cooper, Carmen Djunko Designers
Burns, Cooper, Hynes Limited Agency
Yardley Client

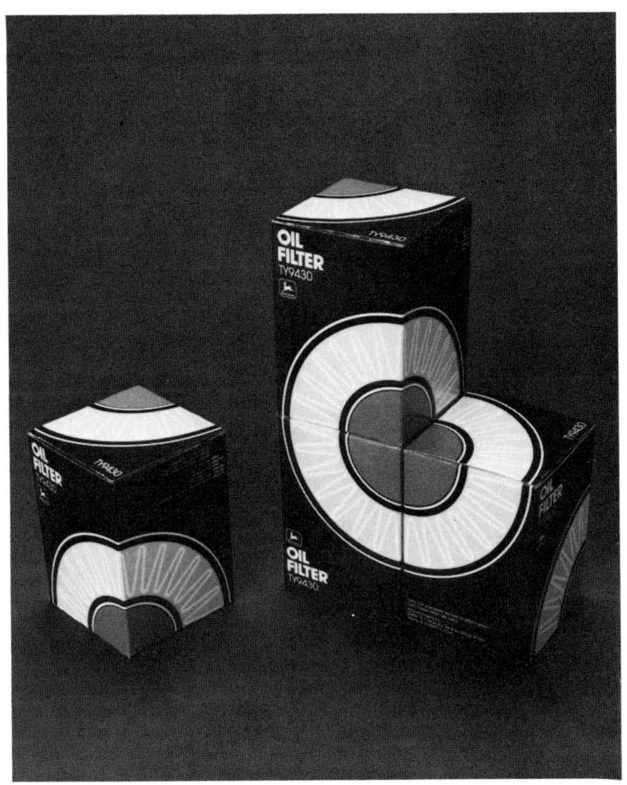

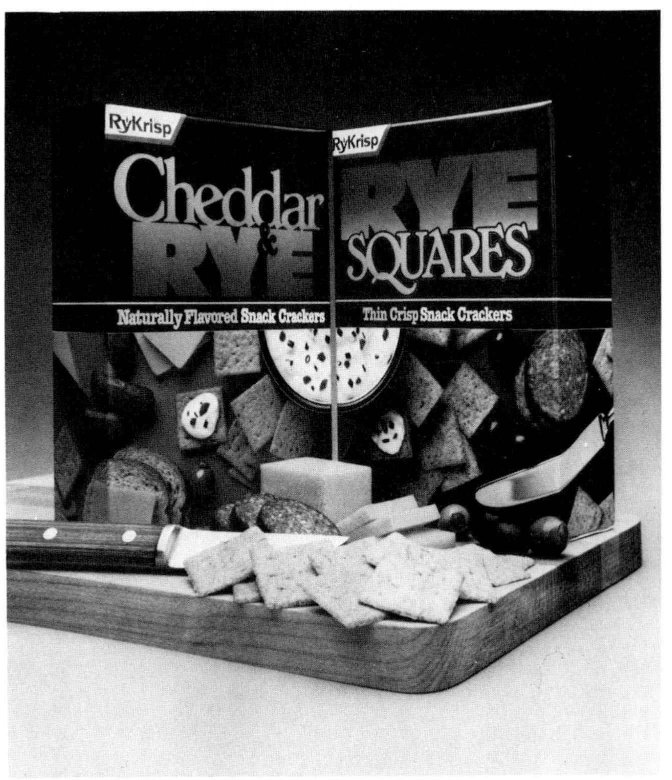

434
Roger L. Johnson Art Director
Ken Prestley Illustrator
Lant Elrod Designer
Hired Hand Visual Communications, Inc. Studio
Deere & Company Advertising Agency
John Deere Merchandise Division Client

435
Steve Morris, Steve Williams Art Directors
Jon Bruton Photographer
Vinyard & Lee & Willams Agency
Ralston Purina Company Client

436
Anne Shaver Art Director
George Parrish, Jr. Illustrator
Cargill, Wilson & Acree Agency
Bunker Hill Client

437

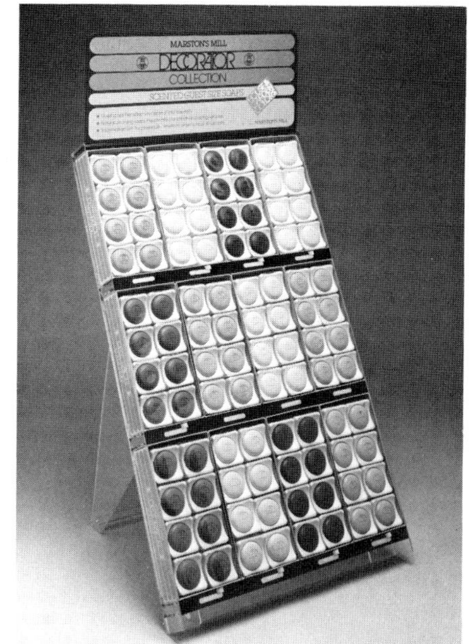

438

437
John DiGianni Art Director
Gianninoto Associates Inc. Studio
SSC&B, Inc. Agency
Thomas J. Lipton, Inc. Client

438
William R. Thauer Art Director
Curtis Packaging Structure
General Housewares Corp., Giftware Group Agency
Marston's Mill Client

439
Don Pflieger Art Director
Ashley Marilla Illustrator
Jack Speiller Copywriter
John Pistilli Designer
Sudler & Hennessey Agency
Stuart Pharmaceuticals Client

440
Jerome Gould, Ray Wood, Herb Weiland Art Directors
Gould & Associates, Inc. Studio
Masterfoods Of Australia Pty Ltd. Client

441
Warren A. Kass Art Director
Warren A. Kass Graphics, Inc. Agency
Austin, Nichols & Co., Inc./Baron Philippe de Rothschild Client

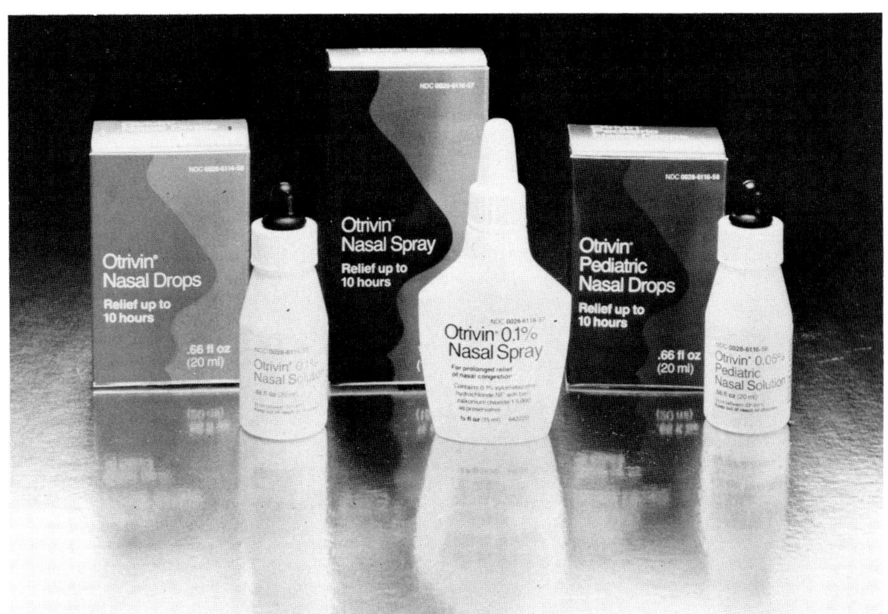

442
Bob Paganucci Art Director
Bob Paganucci, Jane Cullen Designers
Ciba-Geigy Client

443
Roger L. Johnson Art Director
Richard C. McNurlen Illustrator
John P. Traynor Designer
John Deere CP Marketing Client

444
Don Arnold Art Director
Steve Ewert Photographer
Jan de Goede Designer
de Goede & Others, Inc. Studio
Elkay Manufacturing, Inc. Client

445
Robert Lee Dickens Art Director
Allen Snook Photographer
Harold Hoffman Designer
Dickens Design Group Agency
Jeno's Inc. Client

446
Jennie Chien Art Director
Chien/Hori Agency
United Coffee Corporation Client

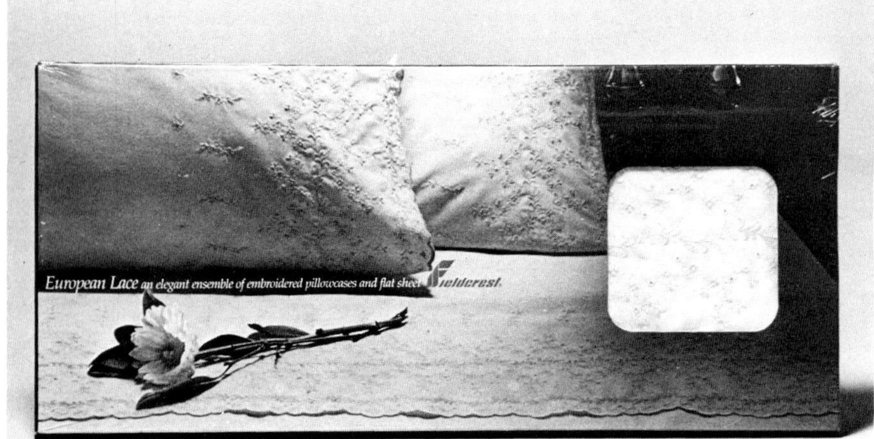

447
Fred Donoher Art Director
John Kanelous Photographer
Joel Bronz Designer
Bronz and Kanelous Design Studio
Fieldcrest Client

448
John Coy Art Director
John Coy Design Agency
Wally's Liquors/Sam Francis Client

449
Thomas A. Fraser Art Director
BFV & L, Inc. Agency
Bols Liqueurs & Brandies Client

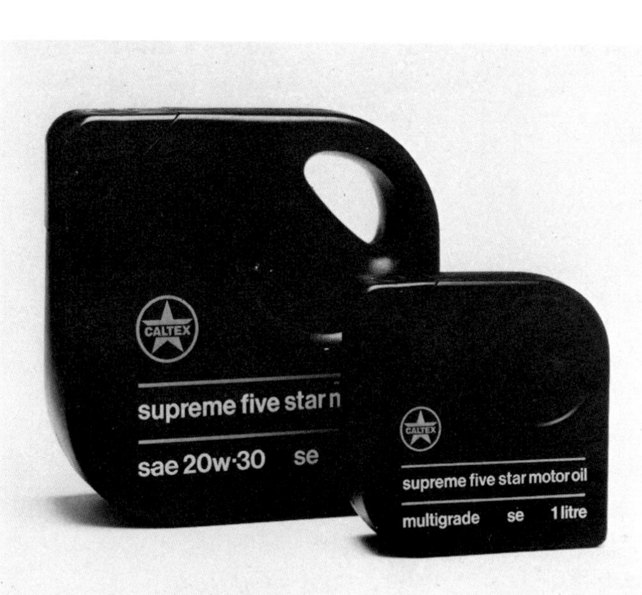

450
Jerome Gould, Herb Weiland, Ed Kysar
Art Directors
Gould & Associates, Inc. Studio
Caltex Oil Pty, Ltd. Client

451
Alan D. Wheeler Art Director
Marc Gobe Illustrator
David W. Evans Inc. Agency
Bendix Forest Products Corp. Client

452
James Stitt Art Director
James Stitt, Chuck Wertman Illustrators
James Stitt & Co. Design Firm Agency
Vichy Springs Mineral Water Corp. Client

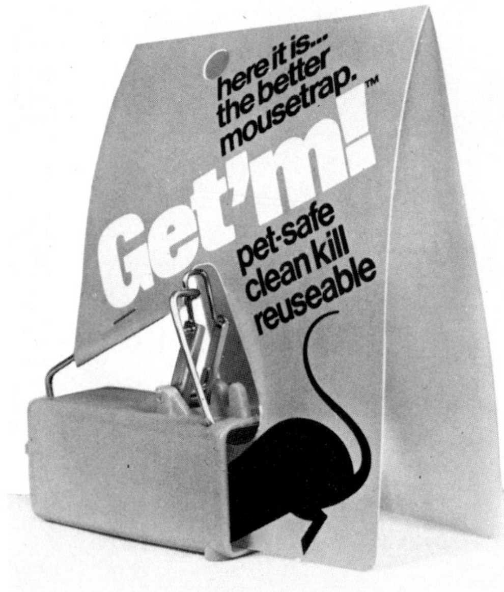

453
Joseph Selame Art Director
Joseph Selame, Richard Edlund Designers
Selame Design Associates Studio
Wicander Enterprises, Inc. Client

454
Susan Johnson Art Director
Danskin, Inc. Client

455
George Thornton Art Director
Sasha Warunkiw Illustrator
George Thornton & Associates Studio
John McNally & Associates Agency
Hillview Farms Client

456
Richard P. Miller Art Director
Blaine Waller Photographer
Maximum Graphic Design Associates Agency
Trio 3 Inc. Client

457
Randall Swatek, David Romanoff Art Directors
Swatek Romanoff Design Client

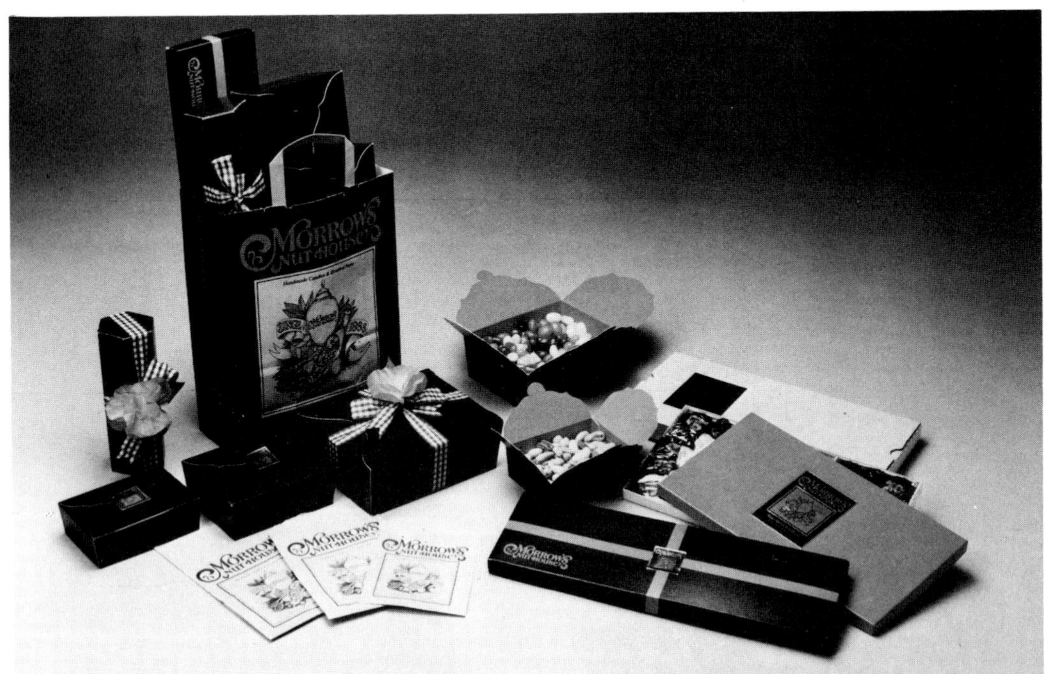

458
Jonathan Shook Art Director
Keith McConnell Illustrator
Zengo Yoshida, Jonathan Shook, Lynn Shook Designers
Morrow's Nut House, Herb Meyer Client

459
Douglas Boyd Art Director
Garry Sato Photographer
Gordon Tani, Scott A. Mednick Designers
Douglas Boyd Design Studio
K.D. Sports International Client

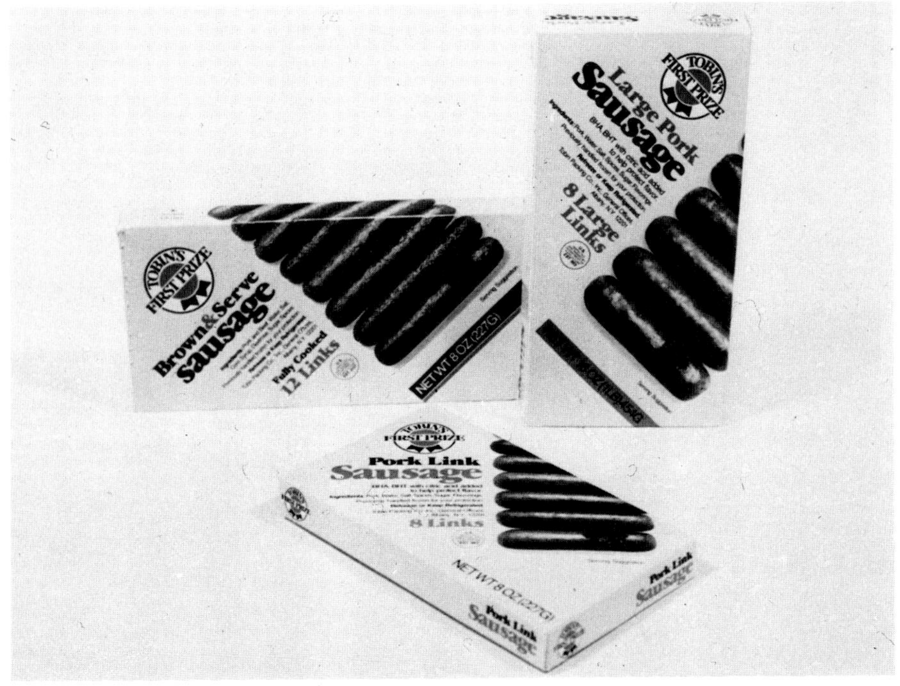

460
Toni Schowalter Art Director
Phil Koenig Photographer
Environments, Graphics & Goodies Agency
Tobin Packing Co. Client

COMPASS
FALL/WINTER EDITION
1978
Webb Institute: The Best and the Brightest
Peking Log
The Merciful Medics of North Sea Oil
Deadly Rogues of the Sea

A

461 A-B
Robert Cooney Art Director
R. A. Cooney, Inc. Agency
Marine Office of America Client

PEKING LOG

12

As reported by John A. Potts
Chairman and President of MOAC

13

Boating on Kunming Lake is a popular Chinese pastime. (Inset) The Continental Corporation delegation from left to right: John B. Ricker, Jr., John Buchanan, John A. Potts, Edward Matthews and Sebastian Lau.

On Sunday, June 25, an Iran Air jetliner took off from Tokyo Airport for a six-hour flight to Peking, the capital of the People's Republic of China. On board the aircraft with me were John B. Ricker, Jr., chairman and president of The Continental Corporation, who led our delegation; Edward Matthews, president of Continental Reinsurance Corporation; John Buchanan, Continental's Hong Kong-based resident vice president for Asia; and Sebastian Lau, managing director of the Asia Insurance Company (in which Continental owns a 10 percent interest). Sebastian, in addition to his knowledge of Chinese insurance operations, is fluent in Mandarin Chinese, a skill which would prove helpful to us during the next five days.

At a time when China is looking at the world with renewed interest, we had an official invitation to conduct exploratory business talks with The People's Insurance Company of China and its affiliate company, the People's Bank. Our purpose was to discuss how our respective companies might establish closer business relations.

The talks that we were to have with our Chinese counterparts over the next few days were uppermost in my mind as our plane winged its way northwest. Our flight would take us across the Sea of Japan, the Korean peninsula and the Yellow Sea into northern China. As we landed, our mood was one of anticipation because we were about to add a new and exciting dimension to Continental's international operations. Within minutes, we would be greeted by our Chinese hosts.

Leaving the plane, and stepping out into the extreme heat, we could not fail to notice a large flood-lit mural of Mao Tse-tung decorating the entrance to the terminal building. We introduced ourselves to the senior officers of the Chinese insurer. Included among them was Lin Chen-feng, whom I had met the year before at the Third World Insurance Conference in Manila. He had been most helpful to us in making this journey possible.

Our Chinese hosts had our passports and baggage cleared through customs and took us to our rooms at the Peking Hotel. Before leaving, they did everything they could to assure our comfort. During the remainder of the evening we drew up an agenda that would focus our discussions which were to begin the next morning at 9:30.

The People's Republic of China, long

B

A Tribute to JOE LOUIS

Though he held the heavyweight championship 12 years—longer than any man—the rest of his years were rent by tragedy. But he never stopped giving all he had to others

By TIM TYLER

462
Phyllis Cayton Art Director
Skip Liepke Illustrator
Sport Magazine Client

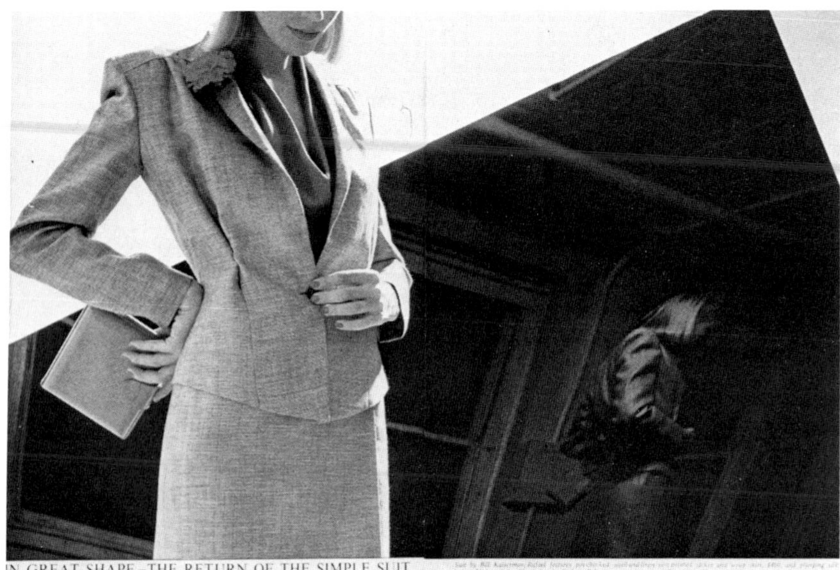

IN GREAT SHAPE—THE RETURN OF THE SIMPLE SUIT

463
Jean-Claude Suares Art Director
Dick Kranzler Photographer
Dick Kranzler, Inc. Studio
New York Magazine Client

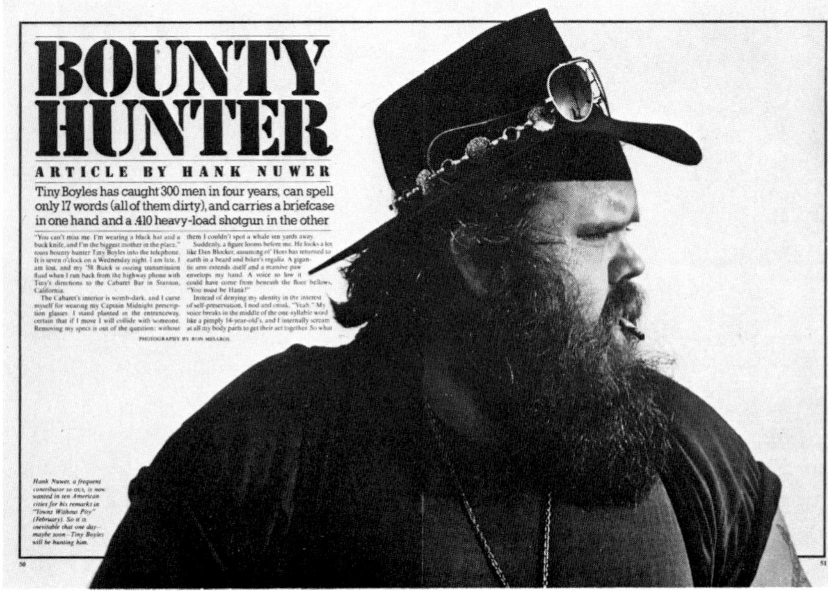

BOUNTY HUNTER

ARTICLE BY HANK NUWER

Tiny Boyles has caught 300 men in four years, can spell only 17 words (all of them dirty), and carries a briefcase in one hand and a .410 heavy-load shotgun in the other

464
Michael Brock Art Director
Ron Mesaros Photographer
James Kiehle Designer
Oui Magazine Client

ONLY THE STRONG SURVIVE

by Richard West

For three months I lived in the heart of the ghetto. Much of what I found there I expected: bitter poverty, crime, broken families, the dark underside of life. But I also found a community determined that life should win over death, hope over despair, pride over poverty. It's true that in the ghetto only the strong survive—and I don't mean just physical strength. I mean the strength that is in quick wits, friendship, family, religion, love, and hard work. Those two worlds—life at its worst and life at its best—exist side by side, beginning just outside my window.

Dawn in Houston's Fifth Ward on an autumn morning. The dark sky softens, lightens, the air warms with the rising sun as the day begins to breathe. Women in white uniforms and men carrying black lunch boxes already crowd the bus stops along Lyons Avenue and Liberty Road. The first yellow cabs arrive at Lovick's drugstore, delivering their drivers to coffee, pork chops, two over easy with country sausage, or rice and chili gravy, the favorite "bowl of soul."

On the side street beneath my upstairs apartment behind Lovick's, a group of black men—Grover,

465
Jim Darilek, Sybil Broyles Art Directors
Pat Berry Photographer
Mediatex Communications Corp. Agency
Texas Monthly Client

Fritz Goro:

Scientific Translations

Will Faller

When we asked Fritz Goro exactly how he came to scientific photography, he replied, "by accident." It was while on assignment for LIFE on Cape Cod. He received an urgent message delivered by a gas station attendant who flagged him down on the road inquiring if he was the photographer from LIFE Magazine. Fritz was sent to the Marine Biological Laboratory and Oceanographic Institute at Woods Hole where he completed his first science related assignment on the state of the art in marine biology and oceanography. That was in 1937. On November 9, 1978, in New York City Fritz was honored by the American Society of Magazine Photographers with its Life Achievement in Photography Award as the *Foremost Scientific Photographer*.

466
Victor Cevoli Art Director
Acme Printing Production House
Polaroid Corporation Client

THE SECOND BATTLE OF THE CORAL SEA

BY NEVILLE GREEN

Fishing for marlin Down Under is no game; it's an obsession.

Nobody saw the fish approach. Perhaps we were all lulled by the engines' droning, our senses dulled by the warmth and brilliance of the sun. Our first warning was the right-hand outrigger snapping like a pistol shot. I hit the alarm button next to the fighting chair and the reel raced in typical fashion with smoke streaming from it in a fine blue haze. I immediately called for water to cool it down. It was a big fish, all right. A very big fish. I could feel the mass of it when I thumbed the hot sides of the spool. The question that went unasked, but nonetheless hovered near the forefront of our thoughts was: *Is this the one?* No doubt we were dreaming an impossible dream: to hook and land a 2,000-pound black

467
Frank Rothmann Art Director
Chris Spollen Illustrator
Stewart Siskind Designer
Hearst Magazines Agency
Motor Boating & Sailing Magazine Client

A

B

468 A-B
Howard E. Paine Art Director
Ronald H. Cohn Photographer
W. E. Garrett Designer
National Geographic Society Client

A

B

469 A-B
Alfred Beck Art Director
Rocky Salskov, Mark Kreher Photographers
L.A. Times, Home Magazine Agency
L.A. Times Client

470 A

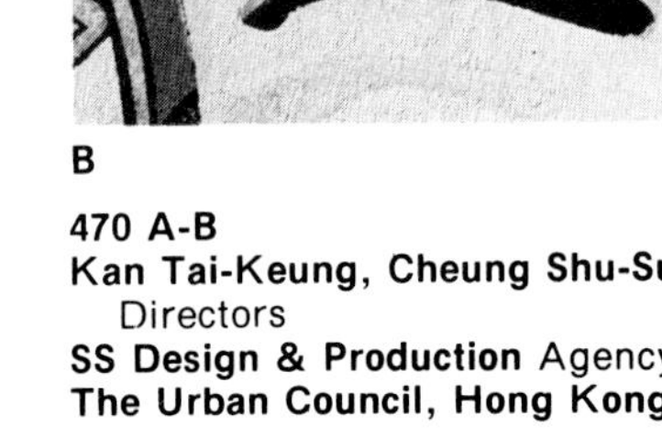

B

470 A-B
Kan Tai-Keung, Cheung Shu-Sun Art Directors
SS Design & Production Agency
The Urban Council, Hong Kong Client

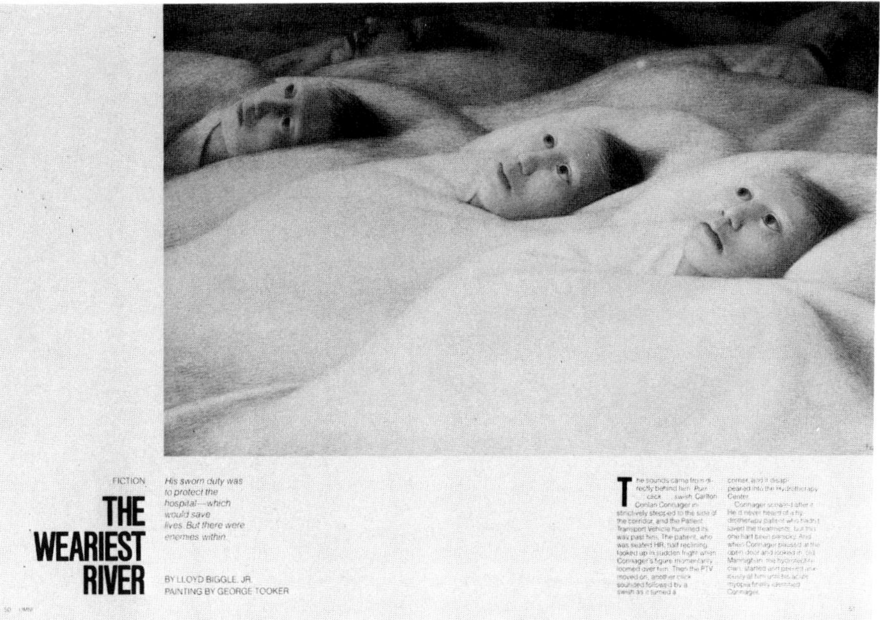

FICTION

THE WEARIEST RIVER

His sworn duty was to protect the hospital—which would save lives. But there were enemies within.

BY LLOYD BIGGLE, JR.
PAINTING BY GEORGE TOOKER

480
Frank De Vino Art Director
George Tooker Illustrator
Lynda Chyhai Designer
Omni Publications Client

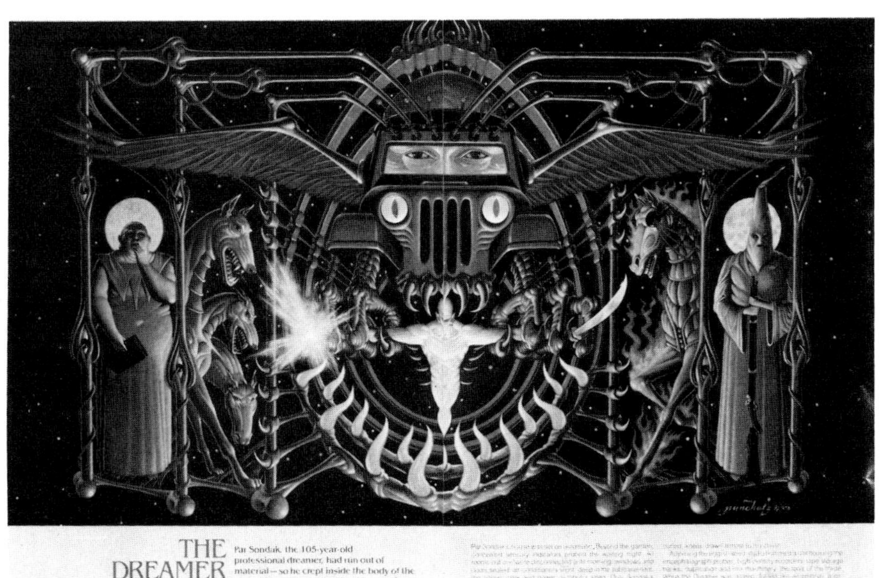

THE DREAMER

FICTION BY WILLIAM HJORTSBERG

Pat Sondak, the 105-year-old professional dreamer, had run out of material—so he crept inside the body of the young Nomad, turned on the Direct Experience Tapes, and curled up to sleep.

481
Joe Brooks Art Director
Penthouse International Ltd. Client

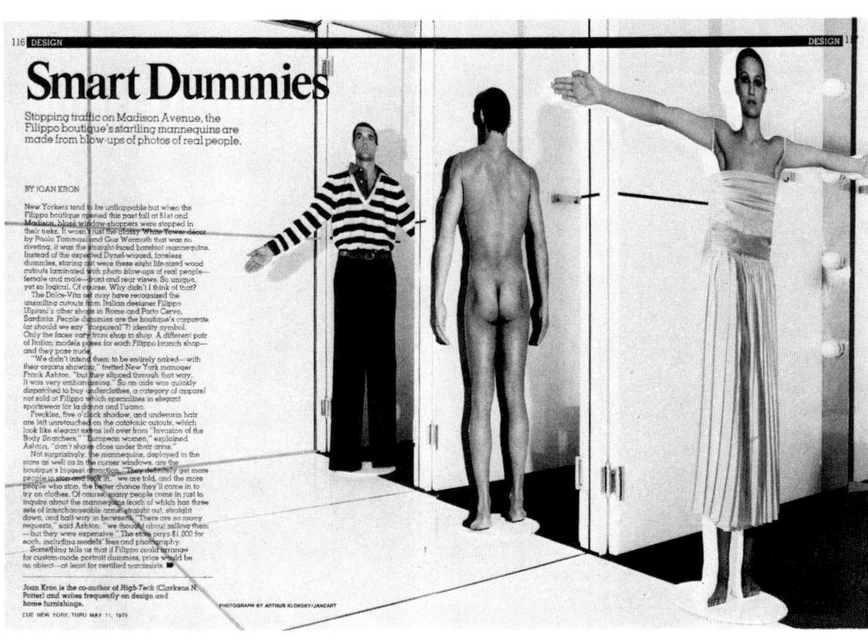

116 DESIGN

Smart Dummies

Stopping traffic on Madison Avenue, the Filippo boutique's startling mannequins are made from blow-ups of photos of real people.

BY JOAN KRON

New Yorkers tend to be unflappable but when the Filippo boutique opened this past fall at 81st and Madison, blasé window-shoppers were stopped in their treks. It wasn't just the glossy White Tower décor by Paolo Tommasi and Gus Wormuth that was so riveting; it was the straight-faced barefoot mannequins. Instead of the expected Dynel-wigged, faceless dummies, staring out were these eight life-sized wood cutouts laminated with photo blow-ups of real people—female and male—front and rear views. So unique, yet so logical. Of course. Why didn't I think of that?

The Dolce-Vita set may have recognized the unsmiling cutouts from Italian designer Filippo Ulpiani's other shops in Rome and Porto Cervo, Sardinia. People dummies are the boutique's corporate (or should we say "corporeal"?) identity symbol. Only the faces vary from shop to shop. A different pair of Italian models poses for each Filippo branch shop—and they pose nude.

"We didn't intend them to be entirely naked—with their organs showing," fretted New York manager Frank Ashton, "but they slipped through that way. It was very embarrassing." So an aide was quickly dispatched to buy underclothes, a category of apparel not sold at Filippo which specializes in elegant sportswear for la donna and l'uomo.

Freckles, five o'clock shadow, and underarm hair are left unretouched on the catatonic cutouts, which look like elegant extras left over from "Invasion of the Body Snatchers." "European women," explained Ashton, "don't shave close under their arms."

Not surprisingly, the mannequins, deployed in the store as well as in the corner windows, are the boutique's biggest attraction. "They definitely get more people to stop and look in," we are told, and the more people who stop, the better chance they'll come in to try on clothes. Of course, many people come in just to inquire about the mannequins (each of which has three sets of interchangeable arms: straight out, straight down, and half-way in between). "There are so many requests," said Ashton, "we thought about selling them—but they were expensive." The store pays $1,000 for each, including models' fees and photography.

Something tells us that if Filippo could arrange for custom-made portrait dummies, price would be no object—at least for certified narcissists. ■

Joan Kron is the co-author of *High-Tech* (Clarkson N. Potter) and writes frequently on design and home furnishings.

PHOTOGRAPH BY ARTHUR KLONSKY/JANEART

CUE NEW YORK, THRU MAY 11, 1979

DESIGN 117

482
Judy Garlan Art Director
Arthur Klonsky, Janeart Photographers
Cue New York Client

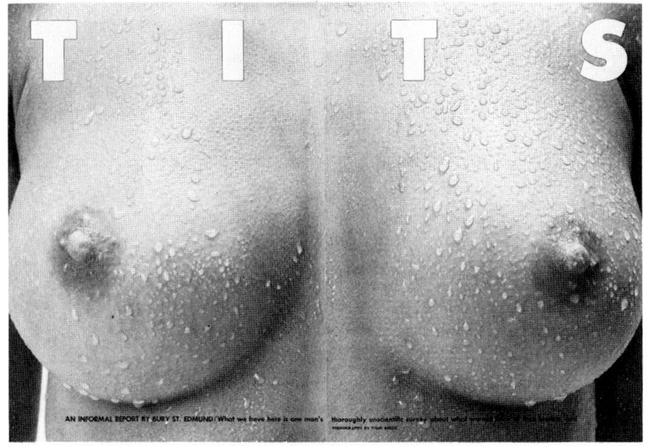

477
Michael Brock Art Director
Todd Smith Photographer
Oui Magazine Client

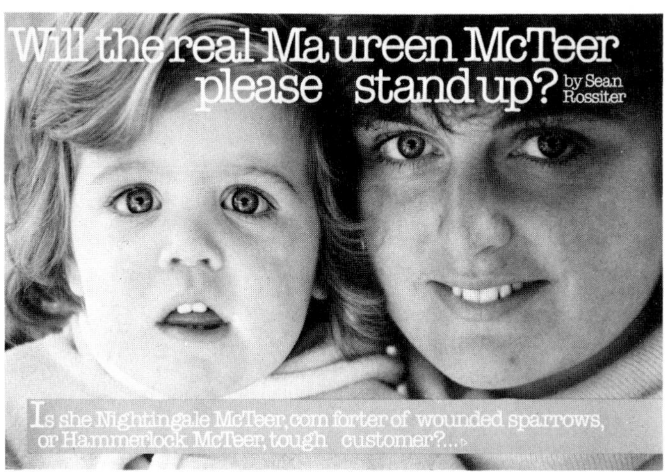

478
Richard M. Ference Art Director
George Barkentin Photographer
Bomac Batten Production House
Chatelaine Magazine Client

479
Mark Oliver Art Director
Peter D'Aprix Photographer
Mark Oliver Associates Agency
Santa Barbara Magazine Client

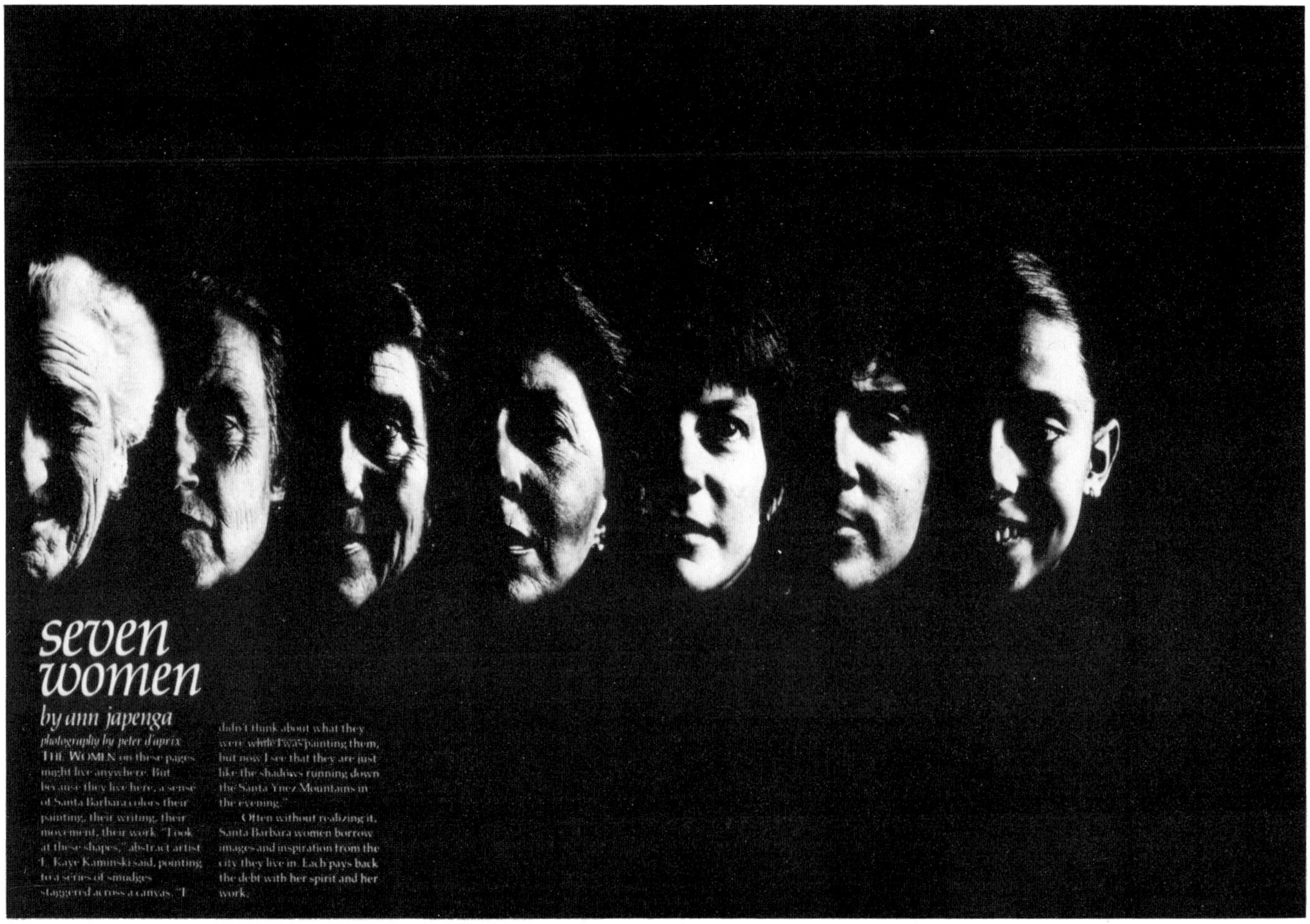

483
Georgia Candemeres, Tony De Vino Art Directors
Patrice Casanova Photographer
Georgia Candemeres Designer
McCall Pattern Company Client

484
Richard M. Ference Art Director
Jeremiah Chechik Photographer
Bomac Batten Production House
Chatelaine Magazine Client

485
David Moore Art Director
John Zimmerman Photographer
Patricia M. Gipple Designer
U.S. International Communication Agency Agency
America Illustrated Magazine Client

486
David Franek Art Director
Mark Heayn Photographer
Mark Heayn Studio Studio
Ashton Worthington Agency
DuPont Client

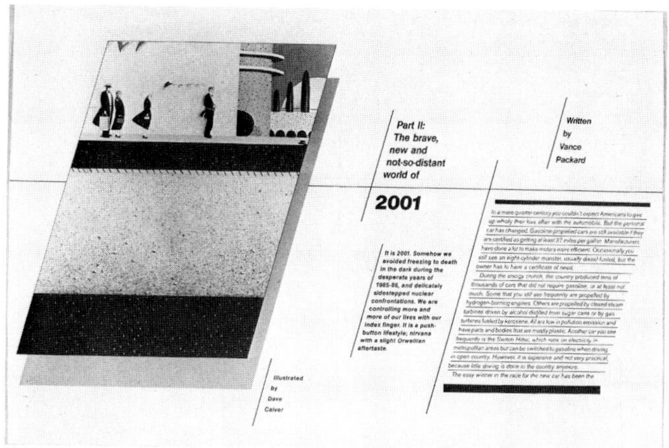

487
Greg Paul Art Director
Dave Calver Illustrator
Ohio Magazine, Inc. Client

488
Arthur Paul, Len Willis Art Directors
Dick Palladini Illustrator
Len Willis Designer
Playboy Enterprises, Inc. Client

489
Joseph A. Bruno Art Director
Catherine Perrot Illustrator
Connecticut Magazine Client

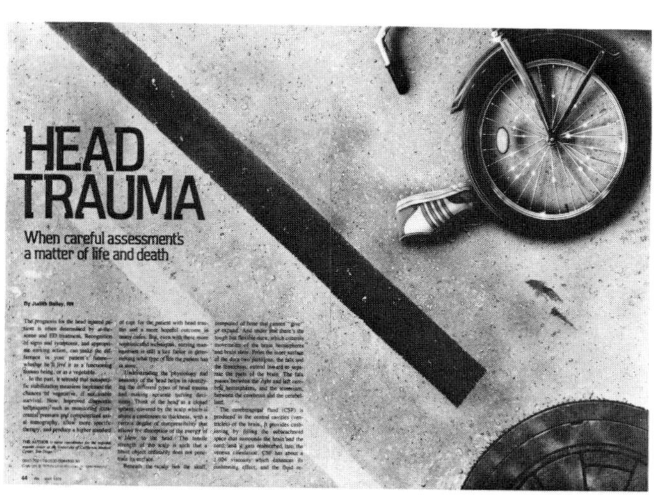

490
Albert M. Foti, Barbara Silbert, Art Directors
Don Brautigam Illustrator
Barbara Silbert Designer
Medical Economics Company Agency
RN Magazine Client

491
George Coderre Art Director
Penton/IPC [Reinhold Publishing Co.] Agency
Progressive Architecture Client

492 A-B
Georges Haroutiun Art Director
Myron Zabol Photographer
Rod Della-Vedova Designer
Comac Communications Agency
Homemaker's Magazine Client

Satin makes a nighttime statement with punch. Silver-gray classic-cut p-js by John Warden for Molyclaire, Montreal. About $55.
Rose-beige pyjama is part of a matched set of pants, "teddies" and jacket. Wayne Clark for Aline Marelle, Toronto; about $170.

A

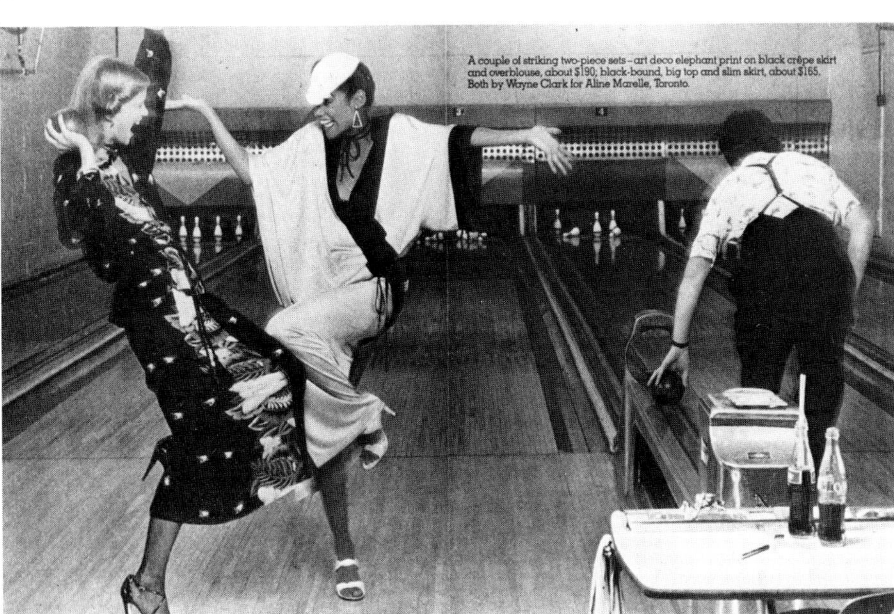

A couple of striking two-piece sets–art deco elephant print on black crêpe skirt and overblouse, about $190; black-bound, big top and slim skirt, about $165. Both by Wayne Clark for Aline Marelle, Toronto.

B

493
Brad Pallas Art Director
Francis Pelligrini Photographer
Linda Stillman Lettering
Hearst Corp. Agency
House Beautiful Client

By Naomi Barry

Robert Carrier plays host on a grand scale at Hintlesham Hall, serving England's finest food in an extraordinary setting.

Robert Carrier's *Avocado Mousse with Raw Mushroom Salad is shown with a collection of French copper and English steel molds in front of Hintlesham Hall, his restored Tudor manor house that is both restaurant and residence. Robert Carrier (opposite) composes a menu.*

A SQUIRE'S KITCHEN

Less than 20 years ago in Britain, the standard restaurant menu consisted of classical French cooking or traditional British fare: grilled steaks and chops, overcooked roasts with two "veg," and the ubiquitous steak-and-kidney pie. English gourmets now have a choice of dishes as varied as *brandade* of smoked trout, charcoal-grilled guinea fowl with juniper berries, rare beef with three sauces, lamb in Greek pastry, or German veal with almonds—if they dine at Carrier's Restaurant, that is.

The man behind this revolution in cooking is American-born Robert Carrier, whose five cookbooks (published in ten languages) are international best sellers and whose two famous restaurants, patronized by royalty, are "musts" on the list of every American visiting Britain this year.

According to distinguished restaurateur George Lang, "Robert Carrier is the only man to have changed singlehandedly the eating habits of an entire nation." Carrier admits, "Good cooking is fun . . . and ridiculously easy. I don't expect people to eat like Roman emperors three times a day. I prefer them to cook with me just once or twice a week when they want to cook for pleasure and for the sheer sensual enjoyment of good food."

Robert Carrier is indeed a sensualist. "An egotist and a showman, too," according to Michael Bateman, leading food critic of the London *Sunday Times*. "He is fussy, obsessive and hard to please, like most people in the food business who are worth their salt. The saints he honors are cookery writers and chefs down the centuries. The altar is his oven. His credo is a firm belief in the sensual qualities of cream and butter and olive oil and garlic and herbs, all magically used to enhance the flavors of meats and game and fish."

Carrier comes from a food-loving family—his mother always encouraged her three sons to help with the cooking. But it was not until the late 1950s that his interest in food

A

494 A-C
Diane Kavelaras Art Director
John Stewart Photographer
Cuisine Magazine Client

495 A-D
Arie J. Geurts Art Director
Frederick Catherwood Illustrator
Daniela San Jose Coordinator
Ing. Mario de la Torre Editor
Luis Olvera Production
Litografos Unidos Printing
Laboratorio de Diseno y Analisis de Mercado, Carton y Papel de Mexico Client

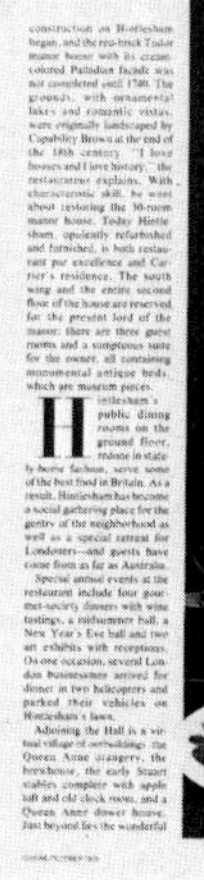

B

C

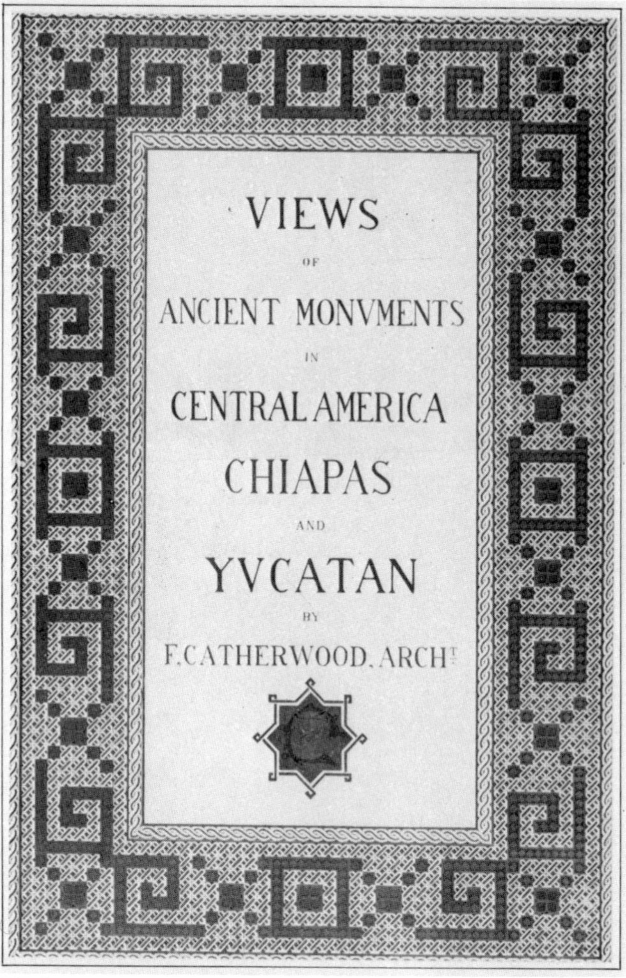

495 A

Pasamos (en Nohcacab) una calle larga bordeada de chozas con techos de palma habitadas sólo por indígenas....
Al fin había una capilla con altar adonde los habitantes ofrecían sus oraciones.
We passed through a long street having on each side thatched huts, occupied exclusively by Indians ... at the end was a chapel and altar at which the inhabitants of the village might offer up prayers.

Por leguas alrededor sólo hay agua en estos pozos (las norias de Nochcacab) todos los indígenas construyen sus residencias en el pueblo cerca de los pozos.
For leagues around there is no water except that furnished by these wells. All the indians have their huts or places of residence in the village within reach of the wells.

El edificio (Codz Pop de Kabah) mide 46 mts. de frente y al momento de verlo nos quedamos sorprendidos de la estraordinaria riqueza del ornamento de la fachada.
The building is 151 feet front, and the moment we saw it we were struck with the extraordinary richness and ornament of its façade.

El interior consiste de dos cámaras paralelas... ésta se comunica con una puerta al centro.
The interior consists of two parallel chambers... communicating by a door in the center

Casa No. 3. Cuando llegamos se veía tan bella cubierta de árboles que nos dolió tener que arrancarselos.
Casa No. 3. When we first came upon it was so beautifully shrounded with trees, that it was painful to be obliged to disturb them.

Esta fachada (en Las-Monjas de Uxmal) la adornan dos serpientes colosales entrelazadas; éstas recorren y enmarcan casi todos los ornamentos en toda la extensión del edificio.
This facade ... is distinguished by two colossal serpents entwined, running through and encompassing nearly all the ornaments throughout its whole length.

B

C

D

Photographer, costume, stage and film designer [My Fair Lady], painter, memoirist, decorator and dedicated gardener – a visit with celebrated

Cecil Beaton

By PATRICK O'HIGGINS

496 A-C
Brad Pallas Art Director
Ira Bass Designer
House Beautiful, Hearst Corp. Clients

496 A

Cecil Beaton

B

Cecil Beaton

C

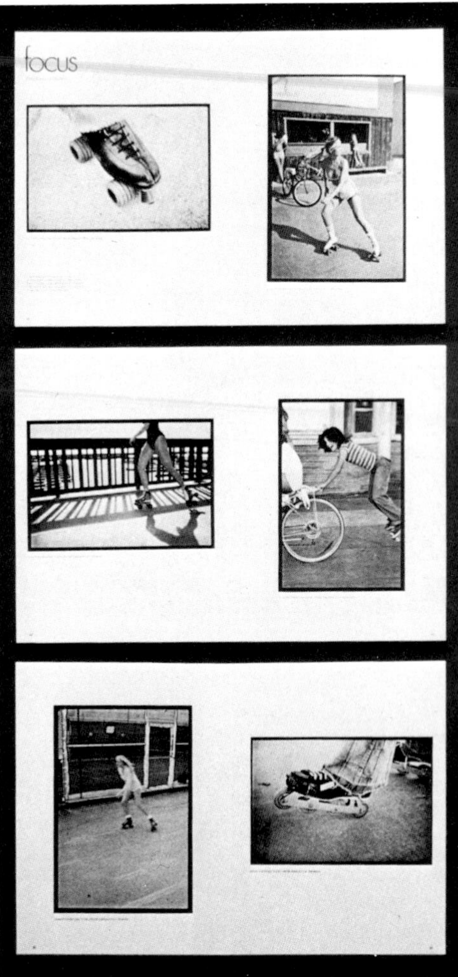

497
Paul Randolph Haven Art Director
Guy Motil Photographer
Roller Skating Magazine Client

498 A

B

C

498 A-C
David Moore Art Director
Yale Joel Photographer
Patricia M. Gipple Designer
U.S. International Communication Agency Agency
America Illustrated Magazine Client

499 A

499 A-C
Emma Landau Art Director
Antonio Frasconi Illustrator
Massimo Uignelli Design Consultant
American Heritage Magazine Client

B

C

ELEGANCE FOR THE EIGHTIES

five emerging designers create look-ahead looks especially for playboy

attire **by DAVID PLATT**

After a somewhat subdued post-Vietnam period, male attire has progressed to richly creative and liberated designs. With liberation comes redefinition, and PLAYBOY asked five emerging design talents to create for us their interpretations of the term elegance as they see it for the Eighties. Their predictions? A trend to relaxed dressing, with an emphasis on fine natural fabrics coupled with a looser silhouette. In other words, nothing very uptight. Our prediction? Tomorrow's styles should be terrific!

ALAN ROSANES

Alan Rosanes, a talented fabric designer, often gets his inspirations from rugged outdoor wear. Here, he casts his eye on the future with a variation on a poplin fishing vest worn over a knit shirt and multihued wool worsted slacks. Rosanes also favors fabrics that have a country flavor that can be adapted to city comforts: canvas, corduroy and flannel, for example. He sees this combination as "the new American mood." One that "explores the unexpected."

209

A

B

C

500 A-C
Arthur Paul, Bruce Hansen Art Directors
Martin Hoffman Illustrator
Bruce Hansen Designer
Playboy Enterprises, Inc. Client

501 A-B
David Moore Art Director
James L. Amos, Regene Radniecki, Will Quinn, Ron Sherman Photographers
Patricia M. Gipple Designer
U.S. International Communication Agency Agency
America Illustrated Magazine Client

A

B

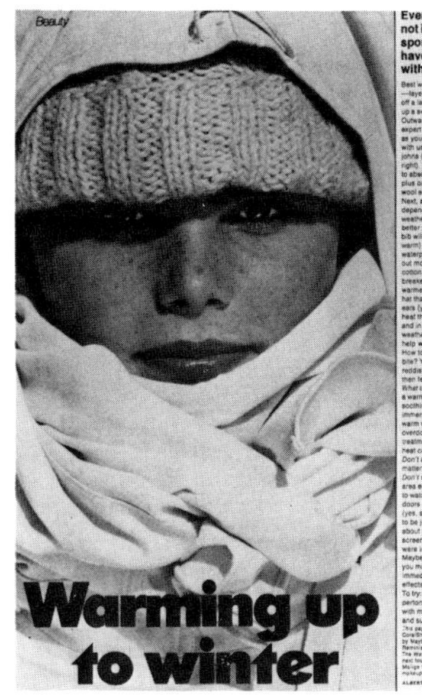

Beauty

Even if you're not into winter sports, you'll have to cope with the cold...

Best way to keep warm—layering. "Just take off a layer when working up a sweat," says Outward Bound survival expert Bob Bick, "add one as you cool off." Start with underwear and long johns (like our girl at right). Wear cotton socks to absorb perspiration, plus one or two pairs of wool socks for warmth. Next, a sweater (or two, depending on the weather) and pants, or better yet, overalls (the bib will keep your chest warm). After all that, waterproof boots to keep out moisture, a nylon or cotton/Dacron windbreaker, mittens (they're warmer than gloves), a hat that snugs over the ears (you lose a lot of heat through your head), and in really cold weather, a face mask—to help ward off frostbite. How to recognize frostbite? Your skin will turn reddish blue, then white, then feel sort of numb. What to do: Wrap up with a warm blanket, have a soothing hot drink, and immerse frozen area in warm water, without overdoing the heat treatment—too much heat can damage the skin. Don't apply snow—no matter what you've heard. Don't massage frozen area either. Another thing to watch for if you're outdoors a lot—sunburn (yes, sunburn). You have to be just as careful now about wearing a sunscreen or block as you were in the summer. Maybe more so, since you may not be immediately aware of the effects of the sun's rays. To try: Sun Gēr by Coppertone. Also lip color with moisturizer and sunscreen (see left).

Warming up to winter

ALBERT WATSON

A

Whatever your favorite winter sport, there's no reason you can't look great

Above: On bright, snowy days, snow reflects 100 percent of the sun's rays. So wear gray, green, or mirrored lenses to block glare, avoid eyestrain. Near right: Nails need special care too. Keep moisturized to prevent breakage. And try a wintry-white frost polish on nails, with creamy white on tips.

Above: When the weather turns frosty, your body needs liquid and food to keep warm. Delicious way to satisfy both needs—a cup of steaming hot chocolate. The milk and/or water supplies liquid; the sugar supplies fuel. *Top right:* If you're into snow sports, opt for a waterproof mascara. After applying, comb through lashes to remove excess, get a more natural look. *Bottom right:* To add moisture and cover dark circles and shadows, dot on creamy white makeup as shown; smooth in; cover with foundation.

ALBERT WATSON

doing it. Here, some great white accessories—for special cold-weather needs

Top left: Even though skin's drier in winter, extra-oily areas (like your forehead, nose, and chin) can still get oily. To cope—a dusting of powder. *Center left:* To untangle wind-whipped hair—a big, white wide-toothed comb. *Bottom left:* To prevent chapping and sunburn, use a lip balm with sunscreen. *Top right:* Watch out for sunburn when you're on the slopes. Use a heavy-duty protector, and for those super-sensitive spots, smear on the zinc oxide. *Bottom right:* Use highlighter for shine.

B

502 A-B
Tamara Schneider Art Director
Albert Watson Photographer
Seventeen Magazine Client

503 A-C
Frank Rothmann Art Director
Phil Dean Photographer
Stewart Siskind Designer
Hearst Magazines Agency
Motor Boating & Sailing Magazine Client

Often bypassed for the "glamour" of Nassau and Grand Bahama, these far-flung cays typify the tranquil beauty of the Bahama Out Islands.

EXUMAS

They string down across the Tropic of Cancer like the frozen wake of some God-skipped stone, a delicate tracery of islands, cays and countless, nameless rocks. Sun baked. Cooled by tropical breezes. Tenuous outcroppings of submarine reefs, rolling hills, hummocks and hillocks of pine and palm, casuarina and agave. And all intersticed with brilliant beaches and protected coves. They are the Exumas. As with all the Bahama Out Islands, the Exumas tender an otherworldliness, a time warp of simple accommodation with a generous and gracious landscape. Place names bespeak a contentment unknown to many outsiders: Happy People Marina; Hotel Peace and Plenty. Or, a casual deference bordering on indifference: Outyonder Cay (where else?). No freshwater rivers trundle silt down to the ocean's edge, leaving Bahamian waters among the purest and clearest on earth. Nowhere is this more profoundly seen than along the turquoise rim of the Exumas. The shallow Bahama Bank, fabled nursery for bonefish and permit, lies to leeward. And hard by is

Photographs by Phil Dean

Local sailboats compete in the Out Island Regatta at Georgetown every April (top); Pipe Creek (above) offers unexcelled beaches.

A

EXUMAS

No freshwater rivers trundle silt down to the ocean, so these Bahamian waters are among the purest and clearest on earth. Nowhere is this more profoundly beheld than in the Exumas.

the fathomless Tongue of the Ocean, the great natural fish trap for the bruising pelagic species of marlin and sail. To windward is the equally deep and productive Exuma Sound. For a hundred miles more or less they stretch through the tropical underbelly of the Atlantic, from uninhabited Sail Rocks to the north near New Providence Island, to the lesser appendages of Little Exuma. Along and along are some of the finest cruising waters available to North American yachtsmen. Most of the scattered population is weighted toward the larger more commodious islands of Great and Little Exuma in the extreme south, but there are charming outposts that make rappelling down the map a delight: Norman's Cay, Sampson Cay, Staniel Cay, Rudder Cut Cay, Rolleville and on into Georgetown with its lovely and protected Elizabeth Harbour, site of the Out Island Regatta every April. Although sparsely inhabited, there are many quiet, picturesque anchorages throughout the chain. Great Exuma is the commercial center for the islands, but Staniel Cay is

B

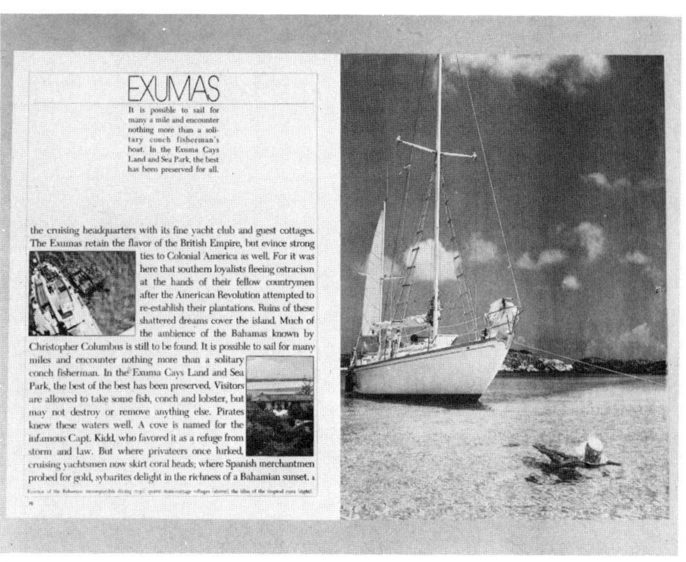

EXUMAS

It is possible to sail for many a mile and encounter nothing more than a solitary conch fisherman's boat. In the Exuma Cays Land and Sea Park, the best has been preserved for all.

the cruising headquarters with its fine yacht club and guest cottages. The Exumas retain the flavor of the British Empire, but evince strong ties to Colonial America as well. For it was here that southern loyalists fleeing ostracism at the hands of their fellow countrymen after the American Revolution attempted to re-establish their plantations. Ruins of these shattered dreams cover the island. Much of the ambience of the Bahamas known by Christopher Columbus is still to be found. It is possible to sail for many miles and encounter nothing more than a solitary conch fisherman. In the Exuma Cays Land and Sea Park, the best of the best has been preserved. Visitors are allowed to take some fish, conch and lobster, but may not destroy or remove anything else. Pirates knew these waters well. A cove is named for the infamous Capt. Kidd, who favored it as a refuge from storm and law. But where privateers once lurked, cruising yachtsmen now skirt coral heads; where Spanish merchantmen probed for gold, sybarites delight in the richness of a Bahamian sunset.

C

504
Howard E. Paine Art Director
Joseph J. Scherschel Photographer
W. E. Garrett Designer
National Geographic Society Client

Forbes

If there were no economists, where would we all go for economic certainty? "To gypsies, probably," says one of their number. But the gypsies never had it so good.

Cheerful Days In The Dismal Science

By Lawrence Minard

505
Everett Halvorsen, Roger Zapke Art Directors
Milt Kobayashi Illustrator
Forbes Magazine Client

By Thomas Sanchez

Coyotes of the Cañada

When I was a boy in California the fear residing deep in our native souls was *earthquake*, the force capable of rising like an awakening prehistoric monster, shrugging from its crusty shoulders all man's feeble structures. I recall a morning when I was 12 years old in Catholic boarding school near Mission San Juan Bautista. At 6 a.m. the long dormitory hall sleeping 70 boys in bunks began to tremble like the topmost limb of a redwood tree. The trembling grew to a clattering as the building shook, rattling rows of windows until the dormitory seemed a speeding boxcar hurtling on broken track. Then the force was gone, leaving only a few cracks etched along the

"Ho, ho, ho! You can never kill us Coyotes! We live forever."
–from "Indian Tales" by Jaime De Angulo

506
Mark Oliver Art Director
Mark Oliver Associates Agency
Santa Barbara Magazine Client

507

508 A

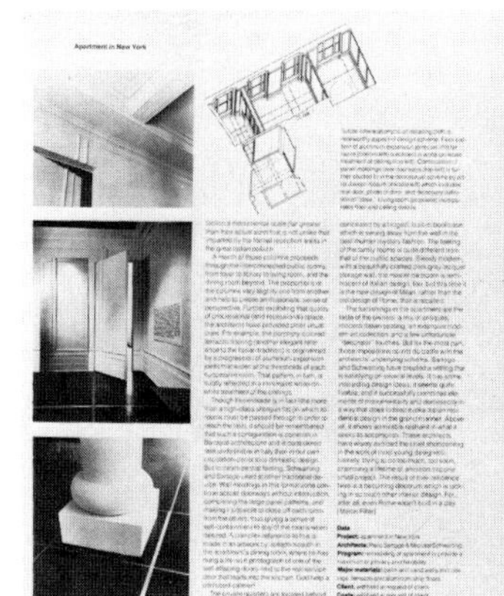

B

By John F. Coppola

NEW VIEWS OF MEDICAL SCIENCE

The trouble with talking about new medical technology is that it's moving into use faster than it's being accepted into the public consciousness. Outdated images keep getting in the way.

The white-coated doctor with a stethoscope—listening, probing, examining, then making a diagnosis—is not quite a picture of the past, but increasingly doctors are using sophisticated, computerized equipment in their work.

Computerized axial tomography, thermography, biostereometrics, complicated machines and processes with strange-sounding names—these are some of the diagnostic tools that the medical profession is now using to quantify and depict graphically the human body's functions and malfunctions.

This new technology, the subject of a photo essay on the following pages, puts new diagnostic tools in doctors' hands. They can use one of these tools, called computerized axial tomography (or CAT), to peer deep inside the patient's body without resorting to exploratory surgery; in a matter of seconds CAT scanners can provide cross-sectional pictures of the body which show even the soft tissues that X rays miss. Another new tool is biostereometrics, or bodygrams (photo at right) that depict the contours of the body. These contours can be used to document deformities or growth patterns and are also valuable in fitting artificial limbs properly. Doctors can use thermograms—or heat maps of the skin—to locate vascular conditions, inflammatory diseases or malignant tumors.

In addition to these new techniques—to mention just a few of the many that are now being applied in medicine—improvements on older techniques are also making an impact on the modern practice of medicine. For example, a computer-linked cardiograph records any evidence of disruption in the heart's activity, even silent abnormalities that the conventional electrocardiogram might never detect.

The new medical technology has made possible great advances in treatment as well as diagnosis. A portable artificial kidney is already being used to replace the complicated and costly dialysis process. An artificial heart has been developed and awaits testing in humans.

This new technology, of course, is not without its detractors. Some argue that it creates an impersonal gap between the doctor and the patient. Others criticize its cost. And still others question whether too much technology may in some cases prolong survival but not meaningful life. Nonetheless, no one questions the fact that physicians using the new technology are saving more lives than doctors have ever been able to save before and that the result has been an extension of life expectancy and a decline in infant mortality. Likewise, no one doubts that medicine's technological revolution is here to stay. In short, the art of healing has become the science of medicine. And in Dan McCoy's pictures on the following pages the science of medicine has been dramatized by the art of photography. In more ways than one, they provide us with new views of medical science.

In biostereometrics, a technique developed by the Baylor College of Medicine, a computer turns two-dimensional photographs of the body into "contour maps" that help reveal deformities, posture problems and curvature of the spine. Right, a bodygram (as it is also known) of a face is superimposed over the face itself in a striking union of human and computer vision.

Photographs by Dan McCoy

44

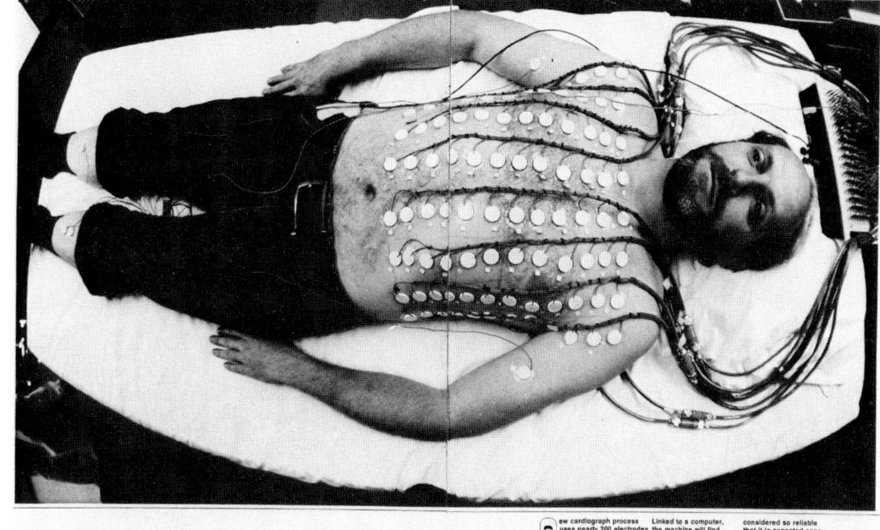

New cardiograph process uses nearly 200 electrodes to monitor the heart. Linked to a computer, the machine will find evidence of any disruption in the heart's pattern; and it is considered so reliable that it is expected soon to make the old process of the electrocardiogram obsolete.

509 A

A new type of artificial arm, shown below without cosmetic covering, was developed at the University of Utah's Project and Design Laboratory. The arm responds to electrical signals from the wearer's shoulder muscles in much the same way as brain signals trigger normal arm movements. Another newly developed artificial organ, a heart created by Medtronics, a leading manufacturer of medical devices, is shown in a sterile environment (insert). It is awaiting testing in humans.

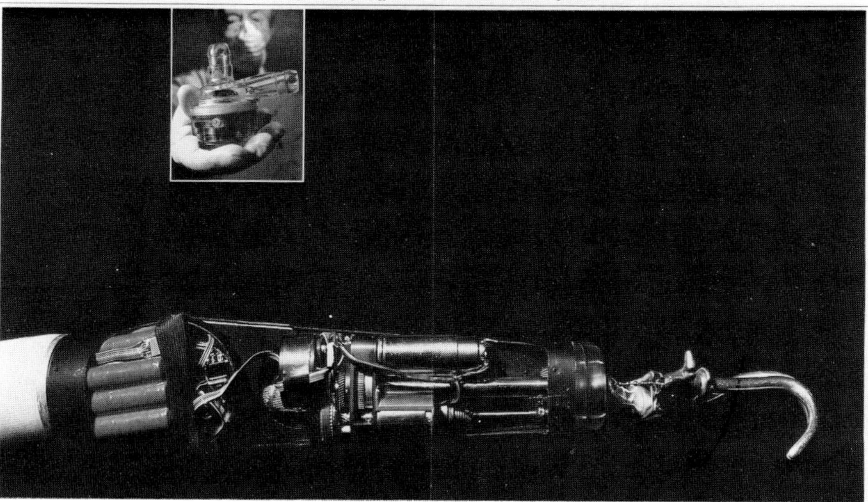

B

C

509 A-C
Joseph Morgan Art Director
Dan McCoy Photographer
Ellen Toomey Picture Editor
International Communication Agency Agency
Horizons USA Client

507
Howard E. Paine Art Director
Joseph J. Scherschel, Des & Jen Bartlett, Robert W. Madden Photographers
Roy Andersen Illustrator
W. E. Garrett Designer
National Geographic Society Client

508 A-B
George Coderre Art Director
Penton/IPC, Reinhold Publishing Company Agency
Progressive Architecture Client

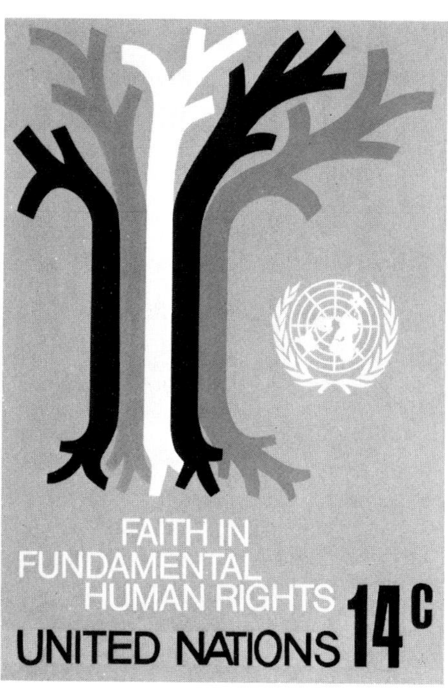

FAITH IN
FUNDAMENTAL
HUMAN RIGHTS
14c
UNITED NATIONS

510
Gerd F. Setzke Art Director
Kunstchule Alsterdamm Agency
United Nations Client

Trademarks & Logotypes

511
Minoru Morita Art Director
Japan Design Center Client

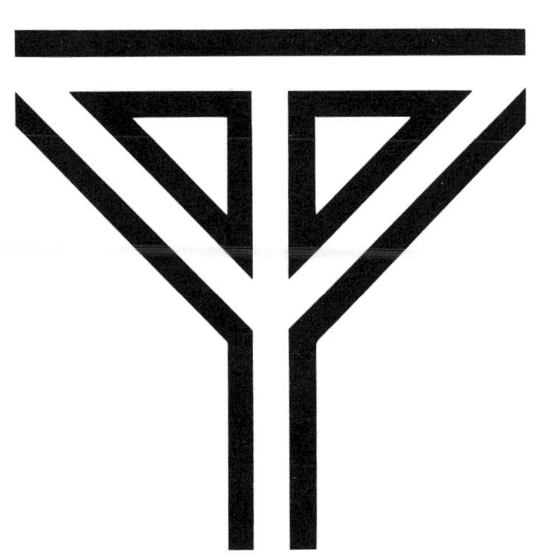

512
Hal Frazier Art Director
Frazier Design Associates Agency
Turner Young Construction Co. Client

513
Robert D. Ebstein Art Director
Graphic Ink Agency
Disctronics Client

514
Steve Erenberg Art Director
Ad Team, Inc. Agency
Force Field Furnace Client

515
David E. Carter Art Director
David E. Carter Corporate Communications Agency
Kentucky Electric Steel Client

516
Regina Ecklund Art Director
Opera House Graphics Client

517
Spyros Dellaportas Art Director
S. Dellaportas Advertising & Graphic Design Agency
Copan Client

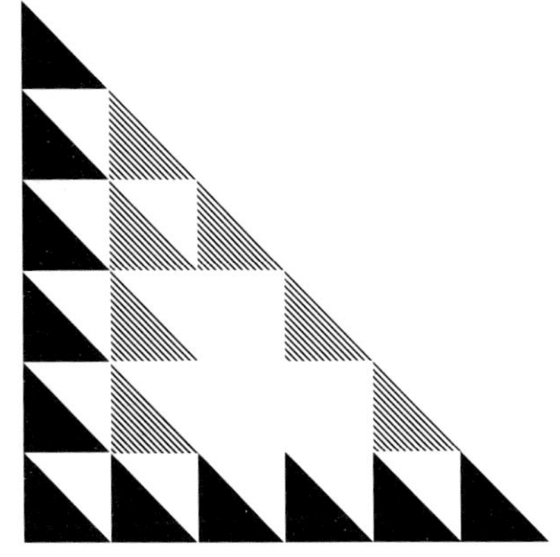

518
Nelu Wolfensohn Art Director
Lavalin Inc. Studio
Lamarre-Arcand et Associes Client

519
Lori L. White Art Director

520
Tom Walsh Art Director
Tom Walsh Graphic Design Studio
Chez-Paul Client

521
Jann Church Art Director
Jann Church Advertising & Graphic Design, Inc. Agency
State Mutual Savings & Loan Client

522
Jim Lienhart Art Director
Murrie, White, Drummond, Lienhart Agency
Allan Cox & Associates Client

523
Micheal Richards Art Director
Michael Mabry Designer
University of Utah Graphic Design Agency
University of Utah Bookstore Client

524
Oskar Blotta Art Director
Badillo/Compton, Inc. Agency
Asoc. de Radio Difusores Client

525
Bruce Wilmoth Art Director
Bruce Wilmoth, Art Direction Agency
Praxis, Inc. Client

526
Ralph E. Brown Art Director
Jack of Arts Production House
Colorado Woodsmiths Client

527
Robert Fernandez Art Director
Paul Pease Advertising Agency
Proteus Industries Client

528
Jane Sanders Art Director
Frank/James Productions Agency
Edison Brothers Client

529
Robert Burns Art Director
Ann Ames, Robert Burns Designers
Burns, Cooper, Hynes Limited Agency
Hunter Brown Ltd. Client

530
Jeff Lederman Art Director
Dr. Shen's Restaurant Client

531
Susan Jackson Keig Art Director
Commonwealth Preservation Council of Kentucky Client

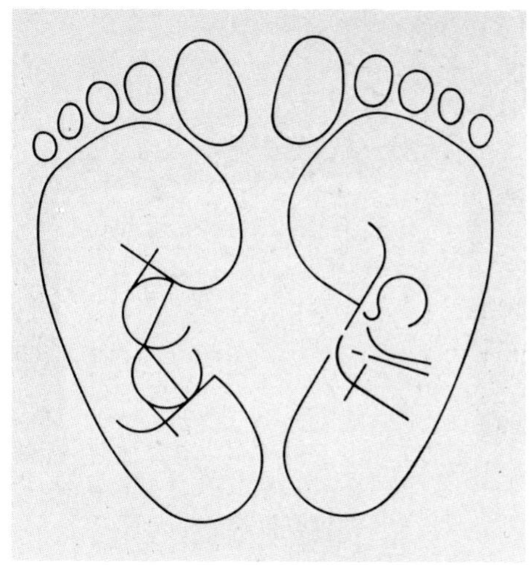

532
Charles Mosco Art Director
Charles Mosco Design Studio
Feet First Running Store Client

533
Joseph M. Essex Art Director
Burson-Marsteller/Design Group Agency
Society of Typographic Arts Client

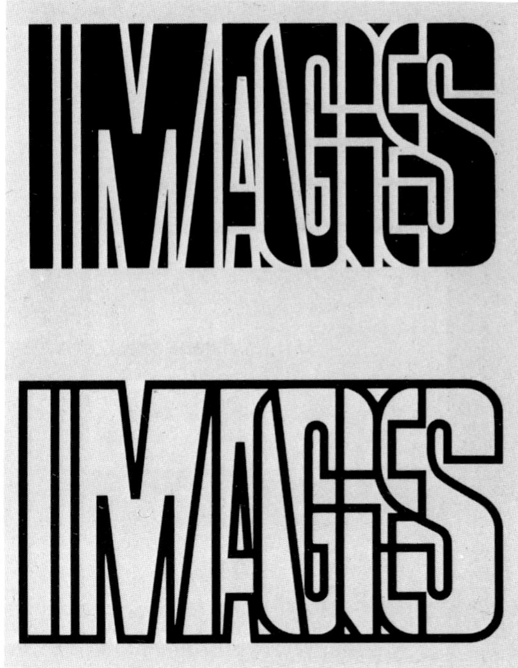

534
Arthur Eckstein Art Director
Arthur Eckstein & Associates Inc. Agency
Typographic Images Inc. Client

535
Neil Terk Art Director
Ray Cruz Designer
Ray Cruz Graphics Studio
Neil Terk & Co. Agency
Blimpie Client

536
Danny S. Chan Art Director
Canadian Broadcasting Corporation Agency
The Vancouver Canada Week Committee Client

537
John Jensen Art Director
Jensen Graphics Agency
Born Again Health Foods Client

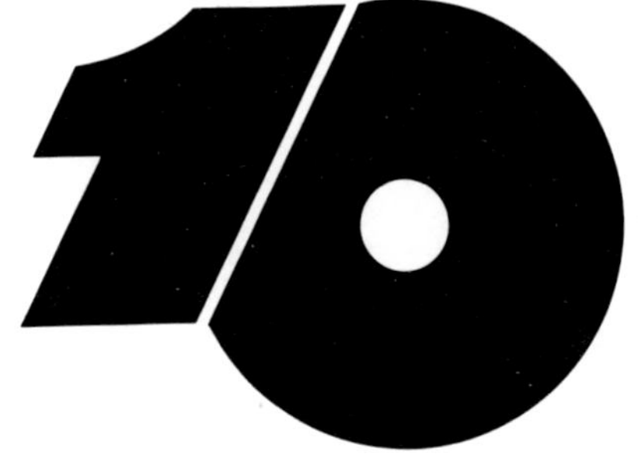

538
George McGinnis Art Director
Image Factory Agency
Corinthian Broadcasting Client

539
Ron Folsom Art Director
Folsom Graphic Design Studio
Foothill Civic Theatre Client

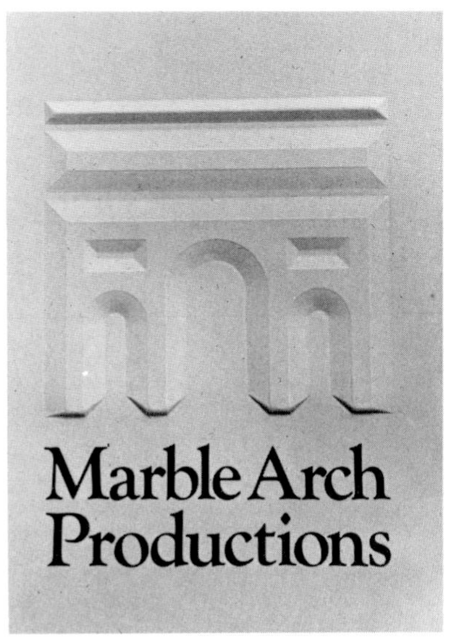

540
Phil Hatten Art Director
Phil Hatten Design Studio
Marble Arch Productions Client

541
Mike Mohamad Art Director
Tom Carnase, Ted Szumila Illustrators
Gene Kolomatsky Designer
NBC-TV Client

542
Linda Darnell Art Director
RJR Graphic Communications Agency
R. J. Reynolds Tobacco Co. Client

543
Primo Angeli Art Director
Mark Jones Illustrator
Primo Angeli Graphics Studio
Shorebird Restaurants Client

544
Mark Matsuno Art Director
Carl Ramsey Illustrator
Mark Matsuno Design Studio
Cornerstone Client

545
Joel Mitnick Art Director
William Hofstetter Inc. Agency
Sarava Associates Client

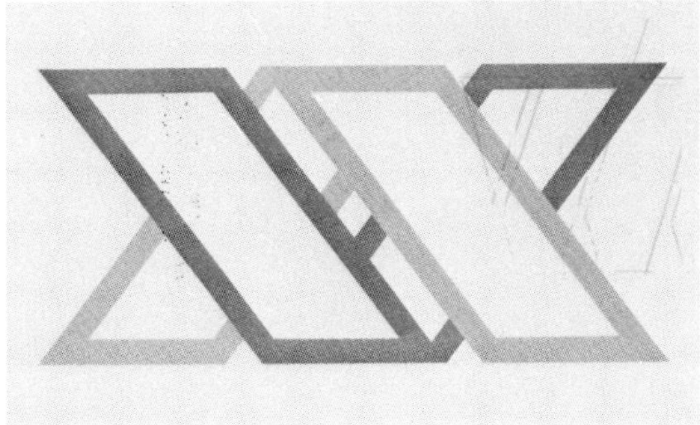

546
Hal Frazier Art Director
Frazier Design Associates Agency
Van Arnhem Films Ltd. London Client

547
Arthur Beckenstein Art Director

548
Fernando Medina Art Director
Zapatonian Client

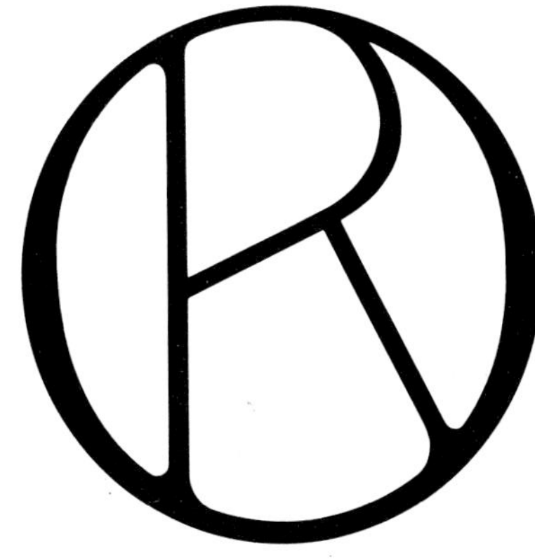

549
Denise Halpin Art Director
Rey Olsen Client

550
Kyosti Varis Art Director
Varis-Poteri-Veistola Agency
Suomen Kuvalehti Client

551
Kyosti Varis Art Director
Varis-Poteri-Veistola Agency
Espoo Golf Club Client

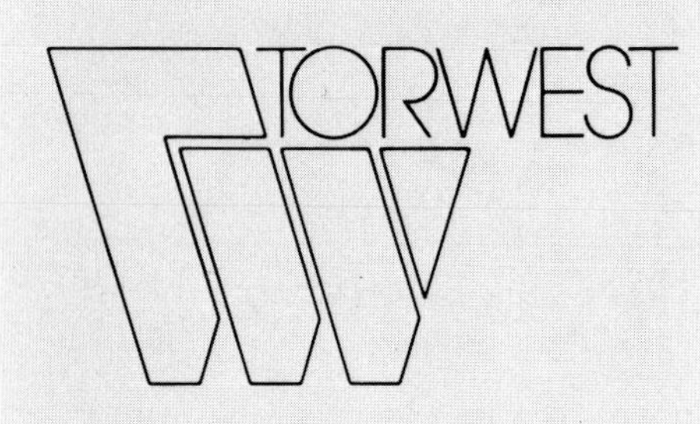

552
Carole L. Nervig Art Director
Carl A. Worthington Partnership Studio
Torwest Client

553
Arie J. Geurts Art Director
Laboratorio de Diseno y Analisis de Mercado, Carton y Papel de Mexico Studio
Gamesa, SA Client

554
Constance Kovar Art Director
Constance Kovar, Ltd. Studio
Group Fourmail, Inc. Client

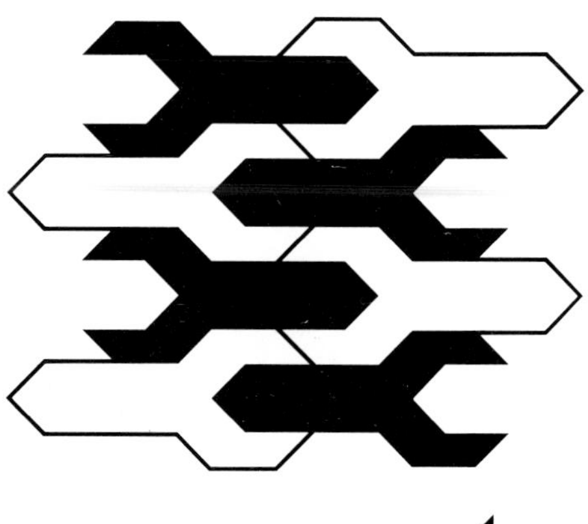

555
Clive Gay, Ernest Allen, Art Directors
Adam [Pty] Ltd. Agency
Propart Client

556
Sandy Williams Art Director
Sandy Williams, Melody Corbett Designers
Bill Lutz Graphics Studio
Nine Doors Restaurant Client

557
Asaf Mirza Art Director
Cabana, Seguin, Inc. Agency
Immeubles Simard Client

558
Fred Coe Art Director
Salvato & Coe Associates Studio
Bell Audio Systems, Inc. Client

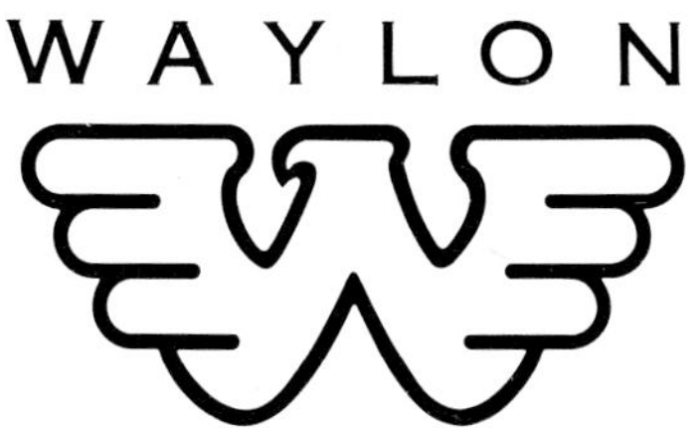

559
David Hogan Art Director
Hot Graphics Studio
Waylon Jennings/Utopia Client

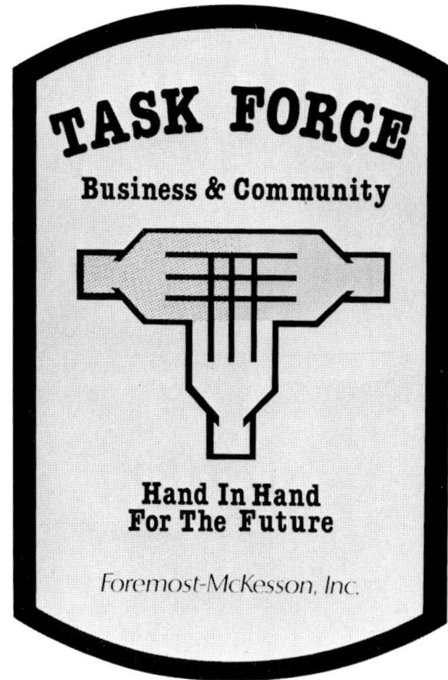

560
Steven Maxon Art Director
Foremost-McKesson Task Force Client

561
Ed Sobel Art Director
Kathie Broyles Designer
CBS Television Network Client

563
Jaime A. Sendra, Jack Hermsen Art Directors
Advance Design Center, Inc. Studio
Direccion Corporativa, S.C. Client

562
William R. Thauer Art Director
General Housewares Corp., Marston's Mill Client

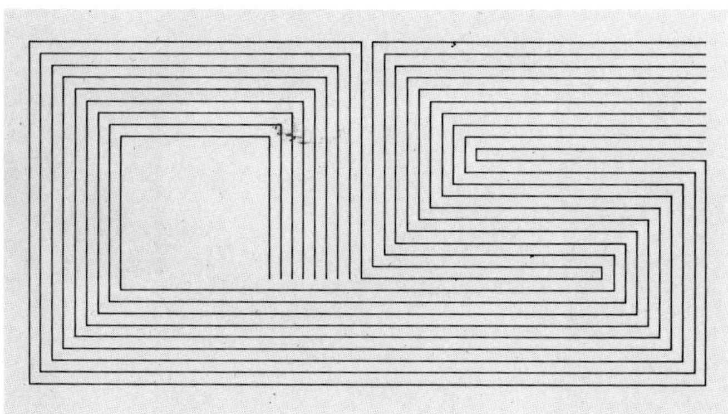

564
Mark D. Goldstein Art Director
The M & M Graphic Connection Studio
Opto-Systems, Inc. Client

565
Gina M. Palazzo Art Director
Gina M. Palazzo Client

Letterheads

566
Linda Powell Art Director
Linda Powell, Barbara Loveland Designers
Steketee-Van Huis, Inc. Production House
Herman Miller, Inc. Client

567
Robert Burns Art Director
Glynn Bell Technical Artist
Burns, Cooper, Hynes Limited Agency
Paul Epp Client

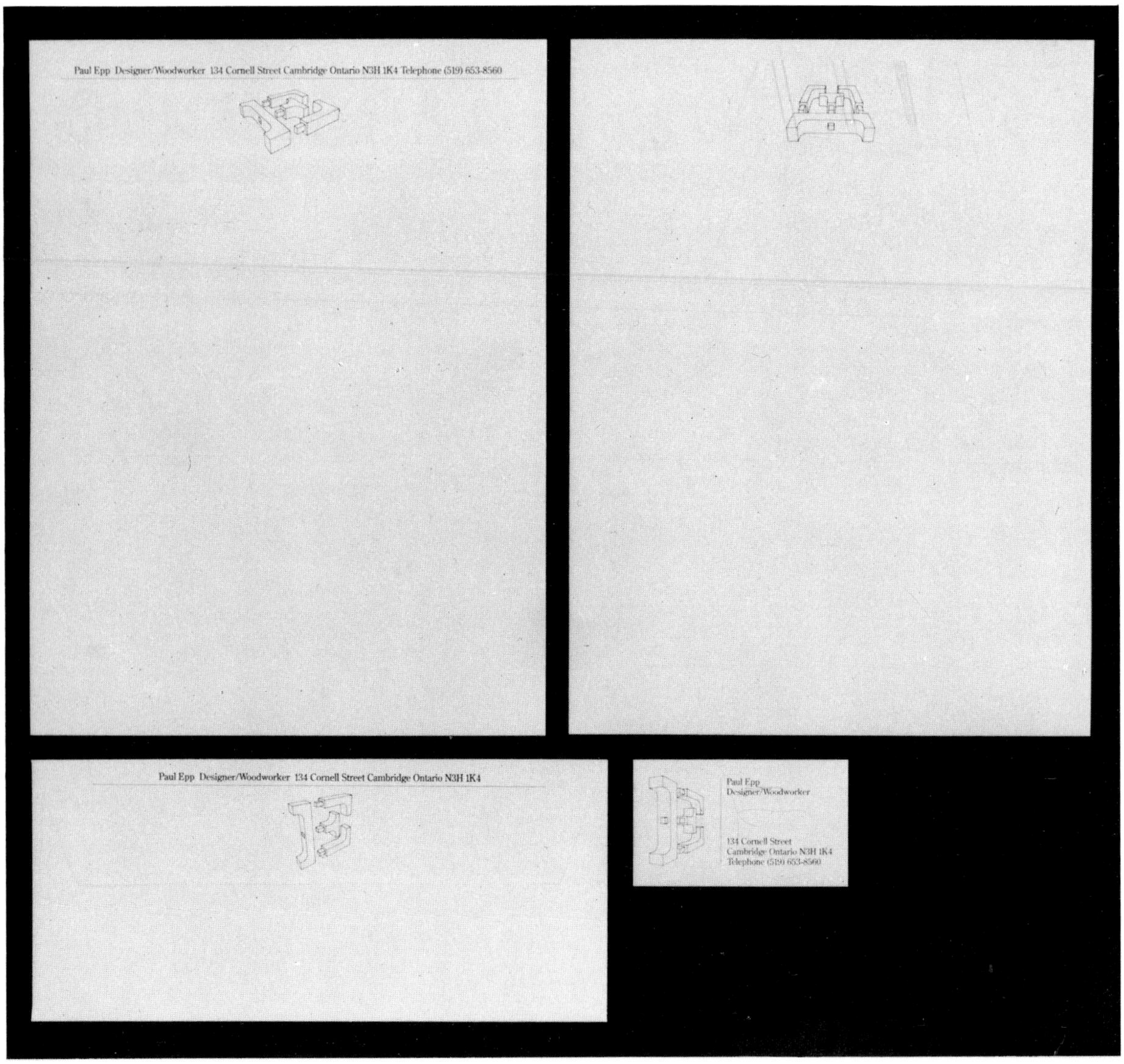

568
Robert Cipriani Art Director
Gunn Associates Agency
Lita Cipriani Client

569
Roberta Flechner Art Director
Carol D. Flechner Client

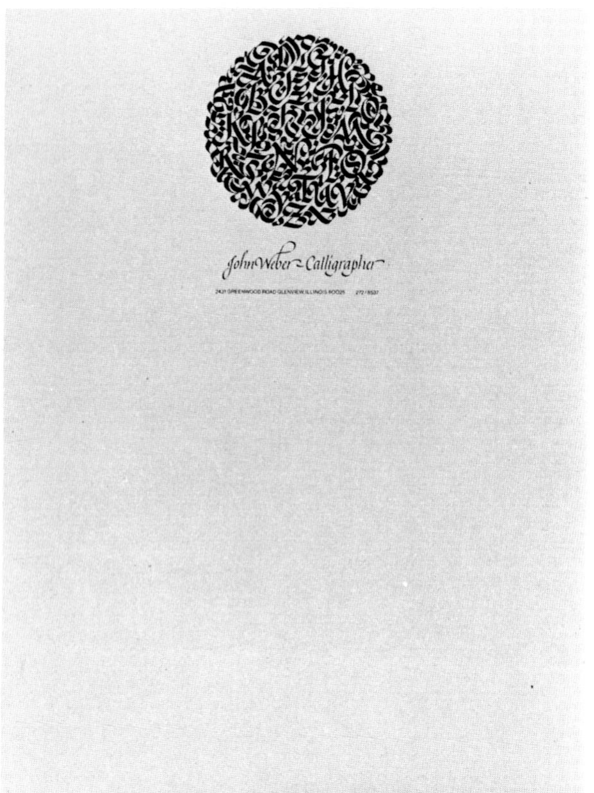

570
John Weber Art Director
Goldsholl Associates Agency
John Weber Client

571
Thomas Bodkin Art Director
Liza Lerner Client

572
Dale Lee Art Director
Innovations Studio
San Francisco Garment Delivery Service Client

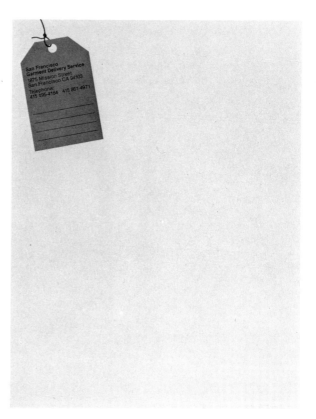

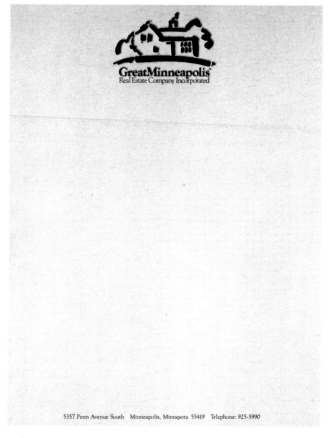

573
Barbara and Patrick Redmond Art Directors
Barbara and Patrick Redmond Design Agency
Great Minneapolis Real Estate Company, Inc. Client

574
Adam Starchild Art Director
Estate Bank & Trust Ltd. Client

575
Clive Gay, Doug Story Art Directors
Adam [Pty] Ltd. Client

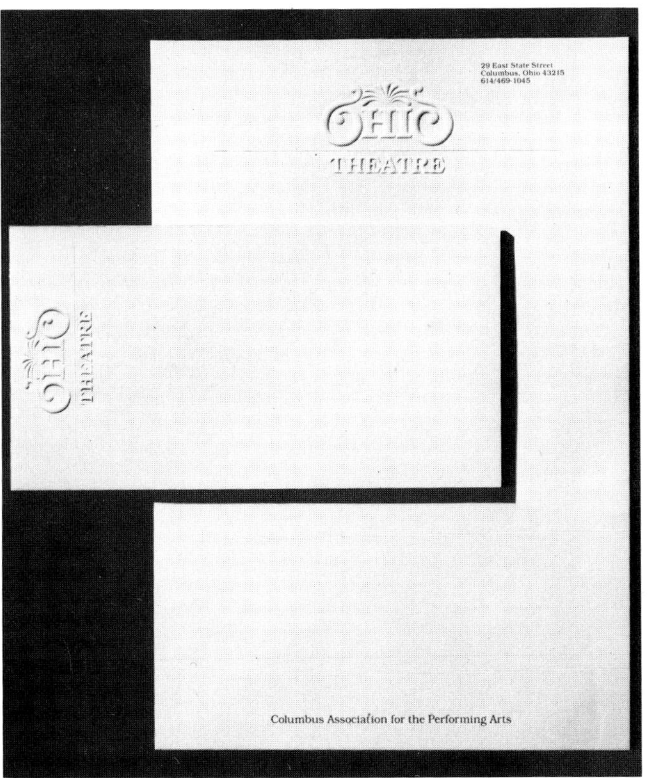

576
Fred Coe Art Director
Salvato & Coe Associates Agency
Columbus Association for the Performing Arts Client

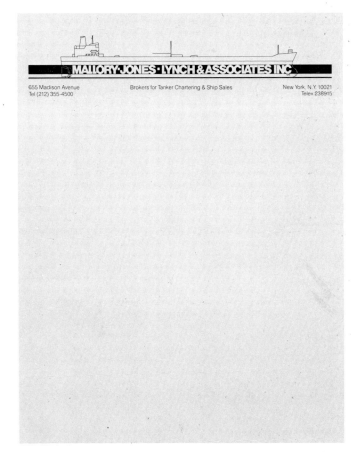

577
Michael Sabanosh Art Director
Hathaway/de la Chapelle Ltd. Studio
Mallory, Jones, Lynch & Associates, Inc. Client

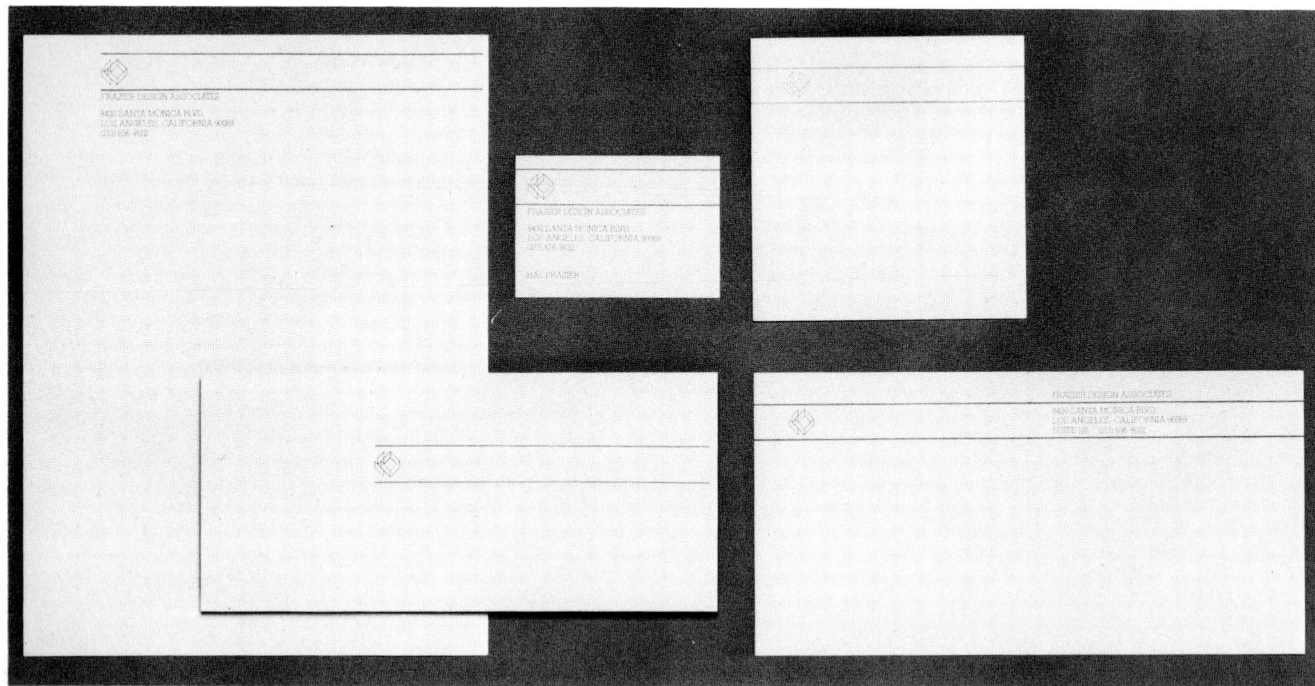

578
Hal Frazier Art Director
Courtney Reeser Designer
Frazier Design Associates Client

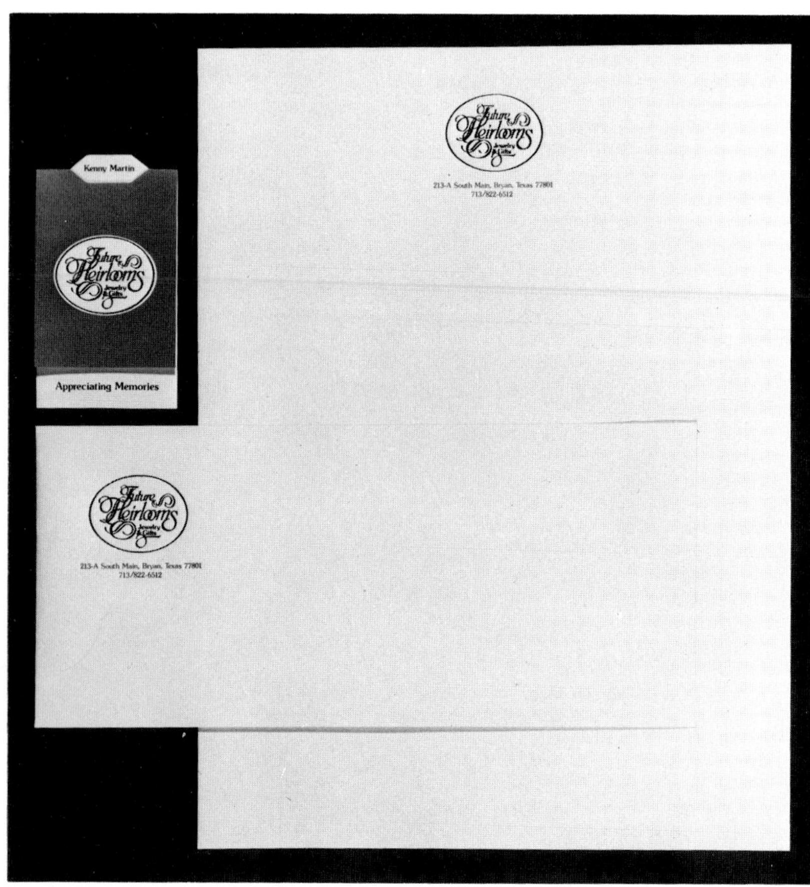

579
Ron Martin Art Director
Ron Martin Graphic Communications Agency
Future Heirlooms Client

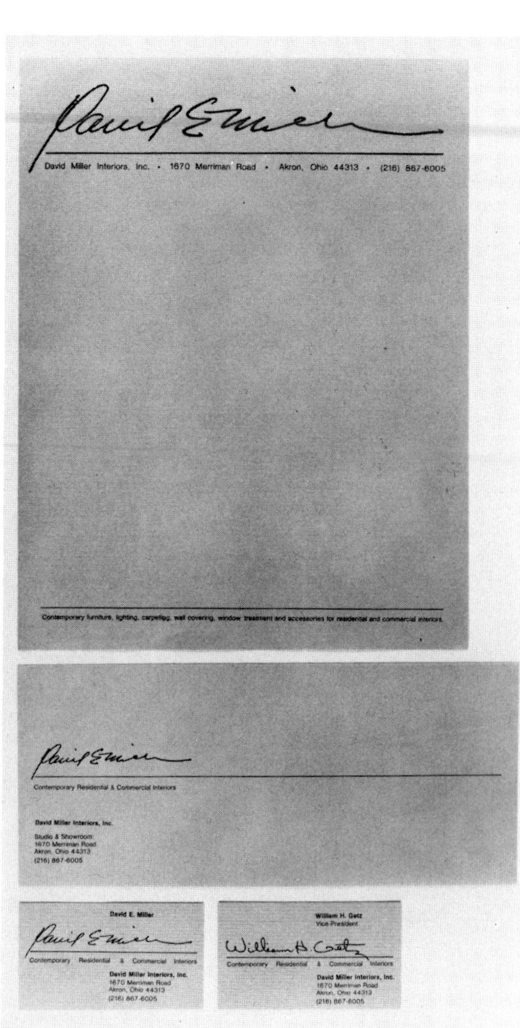

580
J. Brett Buchanan Art Director
J. Brett Buchanan, J. Charles Walker Designers
Tarragon Graphics Agency
David Miller Client

581
Arie J. Geurts Art Director
Laboratorio de Diseno y Analisis de Mercado, Carton y Papel de Mexico S.A. Client

582
Marianne Tombaugh Art Director
Culler Associates Inc. Client

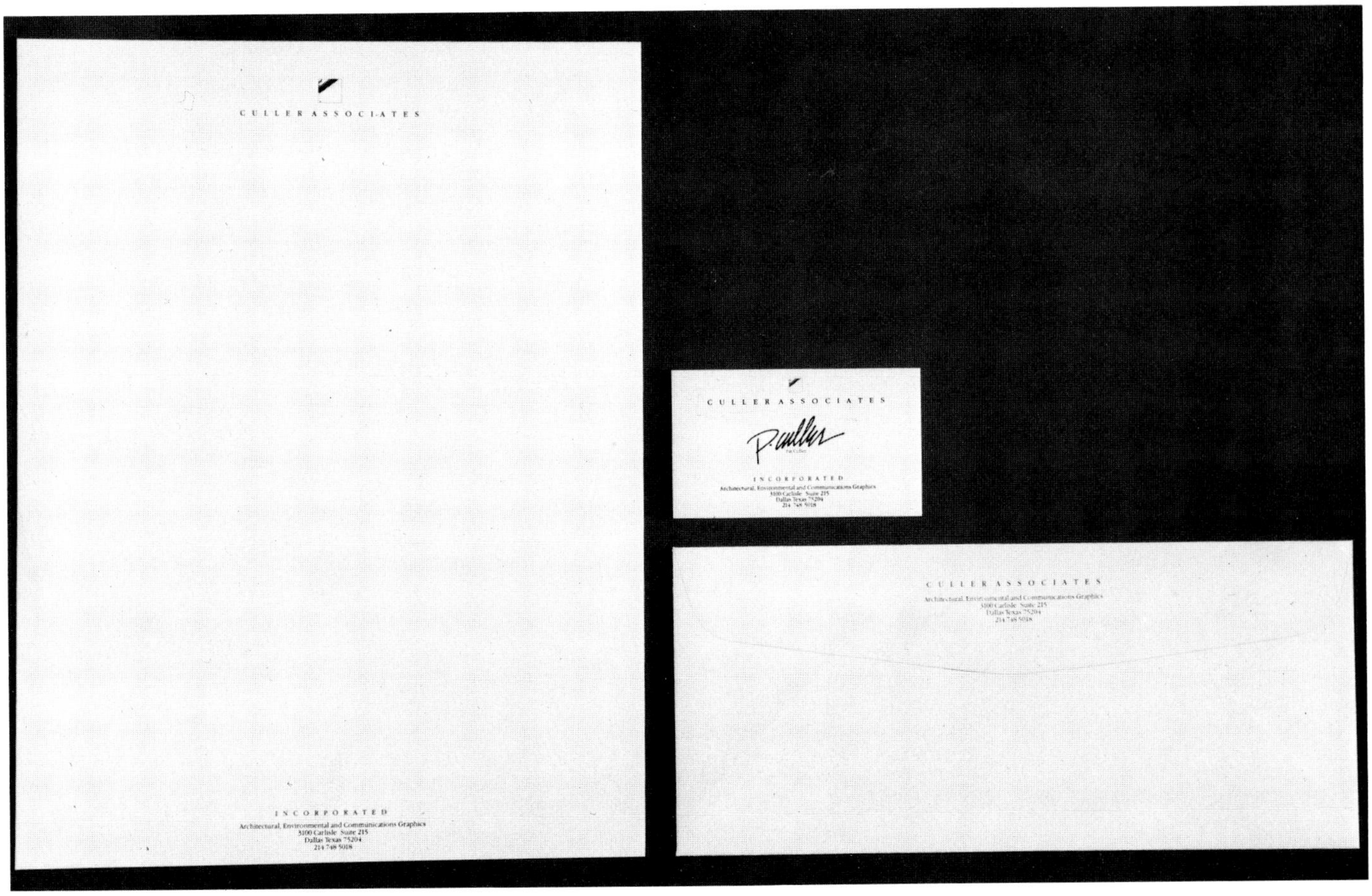

CULLER ASSOCIATES

INCORPORATED

CULLER ASSOCIATES

INCORPORATED

CULLER ASSOCIATES

583
Serge Bevil Art Director
Serge Bevil Designs Inc. Studio
Rent-A-Chef Client

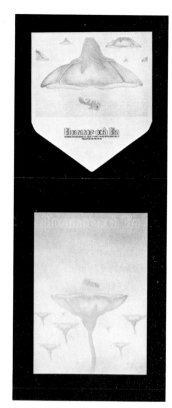

584
Gunnel Jonsson Art Director
Faltman & Malmen Agency
Blommor Och Bin Client

585
Marty Neumeier Art Director
Marty Neumeier Design Studio
The Garth De Cew Group Agency
Brokers Trust Client

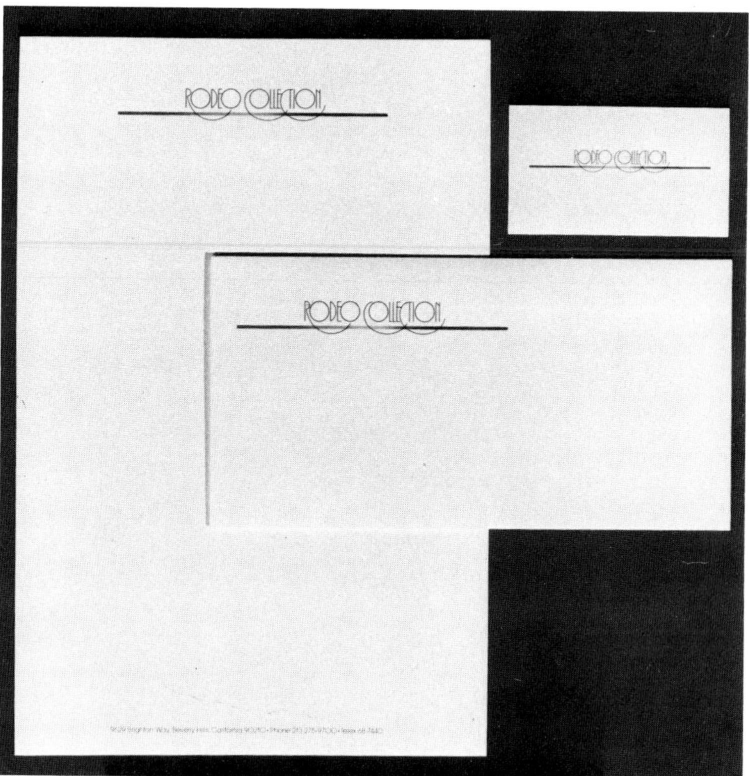

586
Saul Bass Art Director
Art Goodman, Vahe Fattal Designers
Bass/Yager & Associates Agency
Pacific Triangle Development Corp.
Client

587
Oswaldo Miranda Art Director
Miran Estudio Studio
Oswaldo Miranda Client

ARCADE TRAVEL

The Arcade / Suite 450
401 Euclid Avenue, Cleveland, Ohio 44114 / Phone (216) 241-3600
"High Atop the Old Arcade"

588
Rick Holeman Art Director
Karabinus & Associates Photographers
Ed Strong Designer
Rick Holeman, Art Director & Cowboy Agency
Arcade Travel Client

589
Frank M. Addington Art Director
Frank M. Addington Client

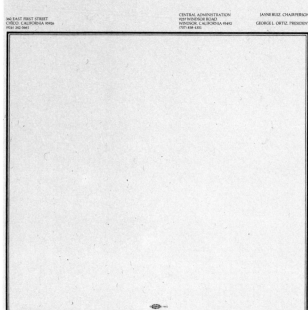

590
Pelle Lindberg Art Director
Hera Information Client

591
Wayne Gibb Art Director
California Human Development Corp. Client

592
David Gauger Art Director
David Gauger, Paulette Traverso Designers
Gauger Sparks Silva Agency
Chris Nater, Ad Agency Client

593
Kay Sabinson Art Director
Burson-Marsteller Agency
Owens-Corning Client

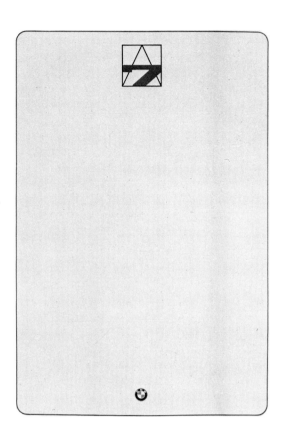

594
Erkki Ruuhinen Art Director
Anderson & Lembke Oy Agency
Ritta Ruuhinen Client

595
Frans Jacobs, Ian Coetser Art Directors
Frans Jacobs Illustrator
Ian Coetser Associates [Pty] Ltd. Agency
BMW [SA] Client

596
Jim Lienhart Art Director
Murrie, White, Drummond, Lienhart Agency
Allan Cox & Associates Client

597
Michael Wolk, Lisa Adams Art Directors
Wolk/Adams Agency
Old Post Office Client

Eugene Cheltenham
2224 Silver Ridge Avenue, #4
Los Angeles, California 90039
(213) 665-4631
Advertising

598
Eugene Cheltenham Art Director
Eugene Cheltenham Advertising Client

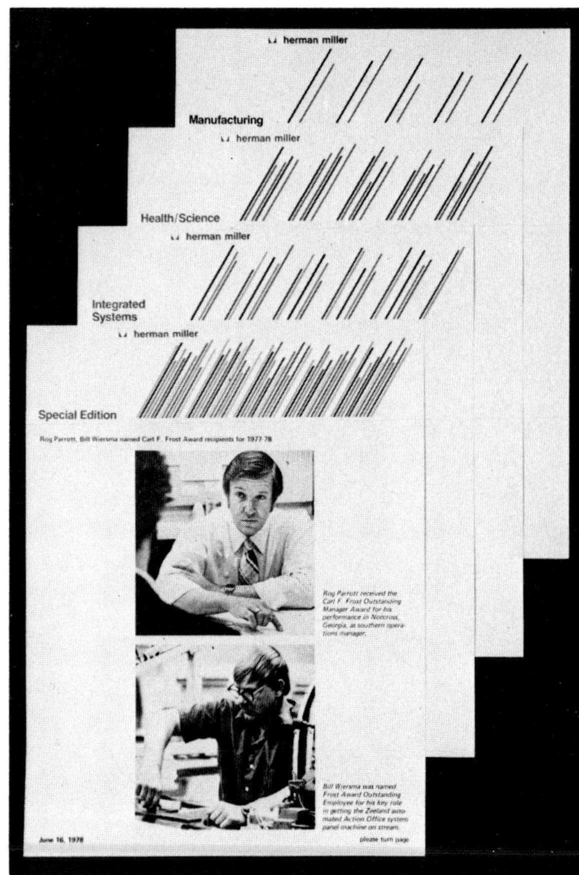

599
Barbara Loveland Art Director
Herman Miller, Inc. Client

600
Robert Cooney Art Director
R. A. Cooney, Inc. Agency
Richard Levy Client

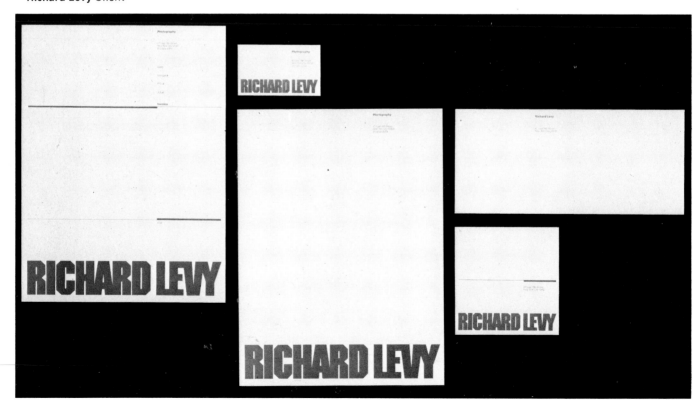

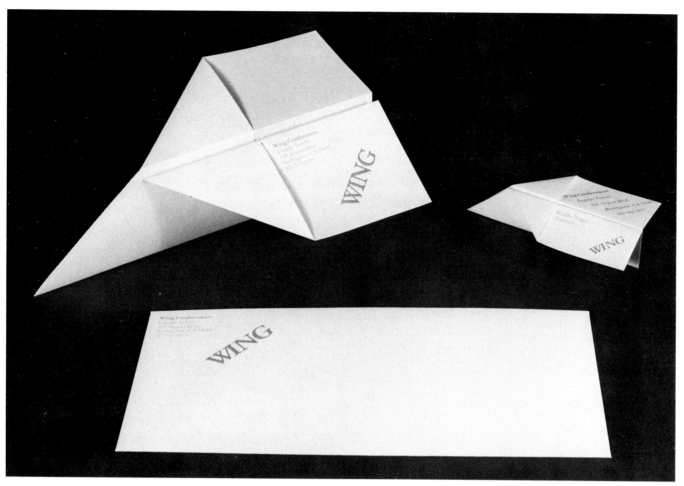

601
Debra Placzek Norby Art Director
Debra Placzek Norby, Jerry Haworth Designers
Placzek & Haworth Design Agency
Wing Conferences Client

602
Lynn Shook Art Director
Lynn Shook, Jonathan Shook, Mark Wood Designers
Shook & Associates Agency
Shermer Cockran Client

Promotionals

603
Ford, Byrne & Associates Art Directors
INA Client

604
Bruce Krug Art Director
Larry Mickey Copywriter
Frank/James Productions Agency
Rockwell/Sabreliner Client

605
Howard Vaughan, Jerry Takacs Art Directors
State Farm Insurance Companies Client

Unpacking Instructions

606
Charles Mosco Art Director
IBM Client

607
Oswaldo Miranda Art Director
Ernani Buchmann Copywriter
Estudio 700 Agency
Lidio Murara Client

A

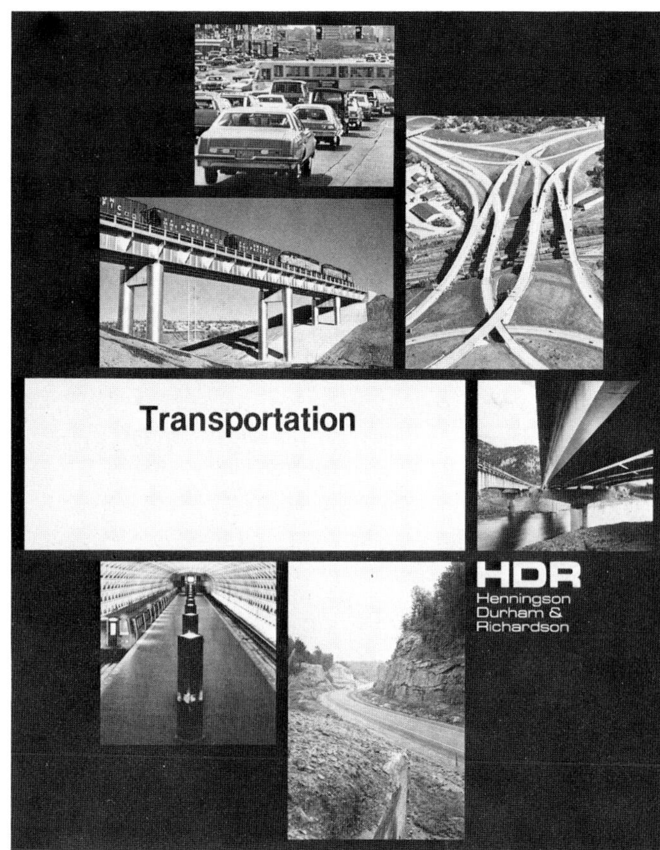

B

608 A-G
Ray Dotzler, Jr. Art Director
Gary J. H. Gerding Photographer
HDR/Communications Group Agency
Henningson, Durham & Richardson
Client

C

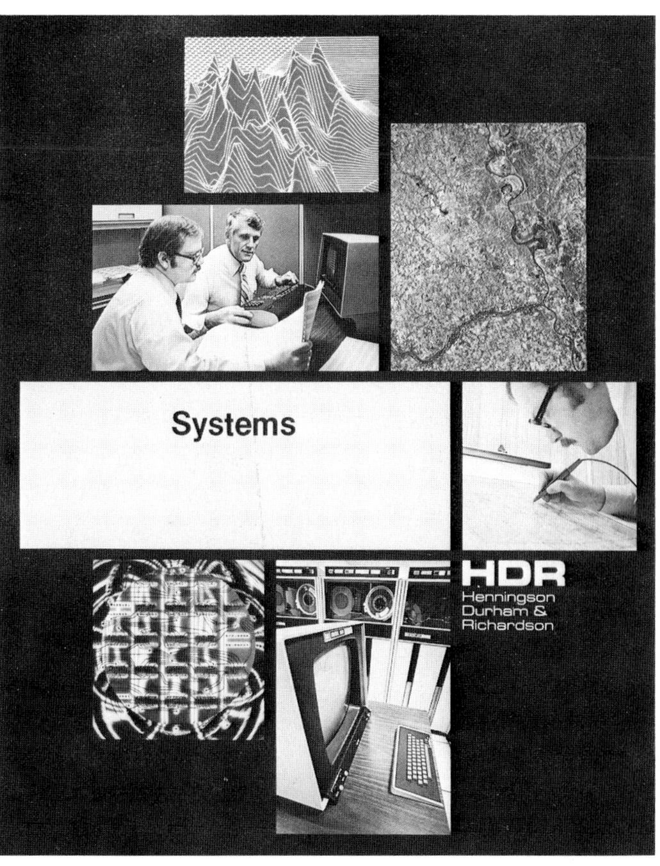

D

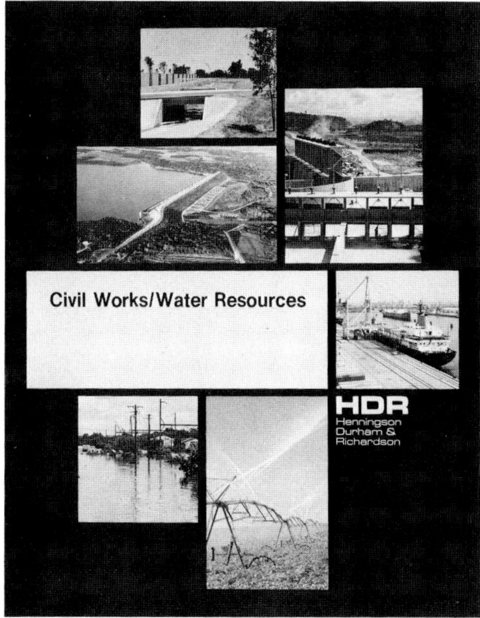

Civil Works/Water Resources
HDR
Henningson
Durham &
Richardson

E

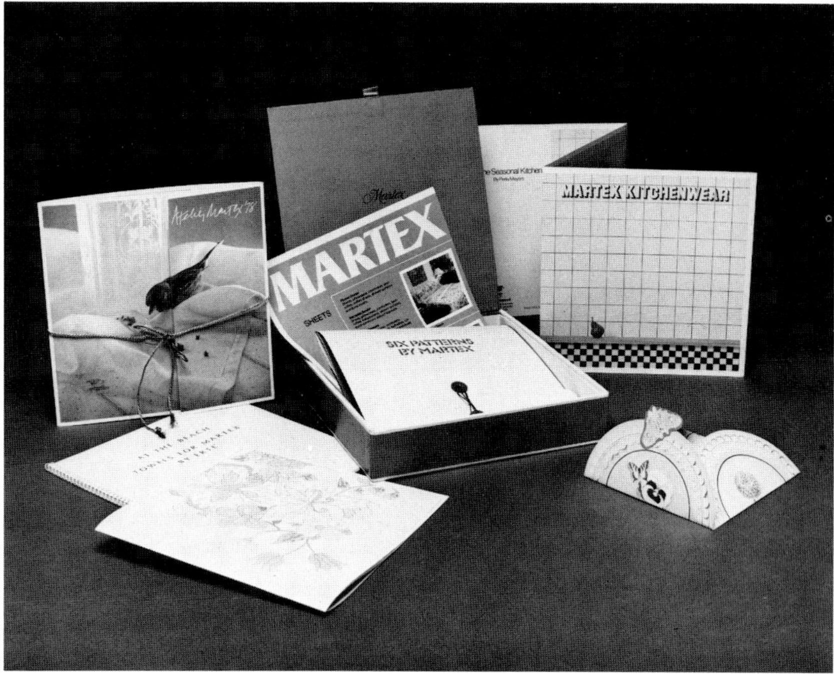

609
Molly Epstein Art Director
Paul Kopelow Photographer
RD Graphics Graphic Production
Martex/West Point Pepperell Client

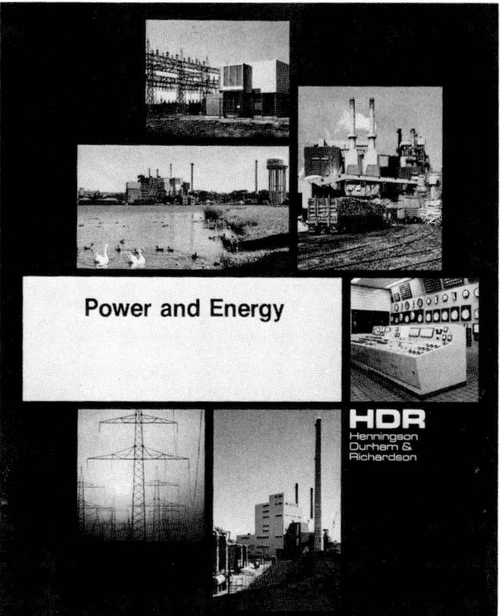

F

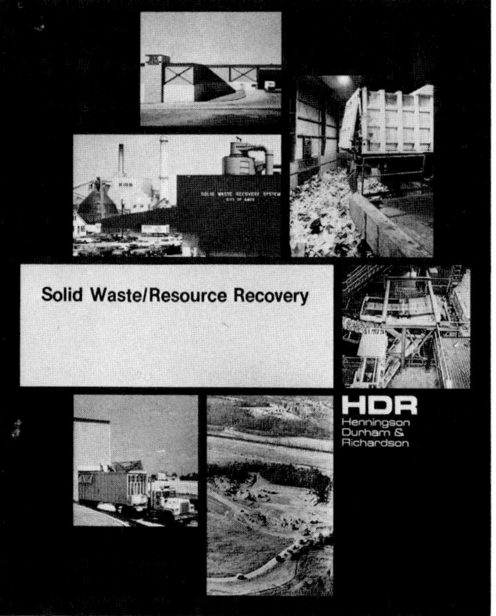

Solid Waste/Resource Recovery
HDR
Henningson
Durham &
Richardson

G

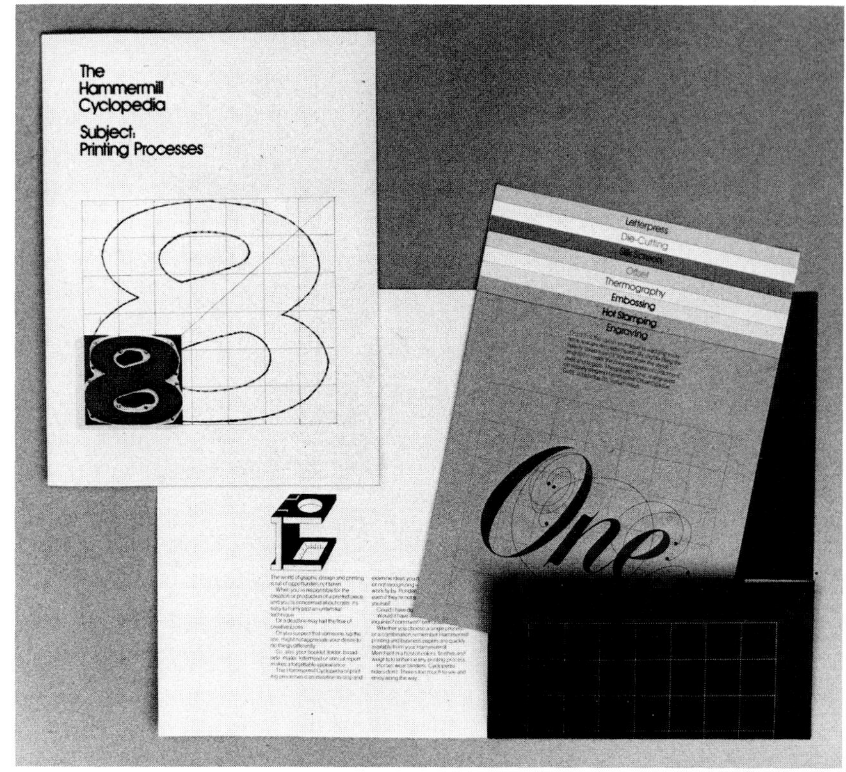

610
James Halt Art Director
Halt, James, Graphic Design Agency
Hammermill Paper Company Client

611
Bill Murphy Art Director
Ron Slenzak Photographer
Rod Dyer, Inc. Agency
Columbia Pictures Television Client

612
Jack Odette Art Director
Paul Katz Photographer
Herman McCray Designer
Citibank Client

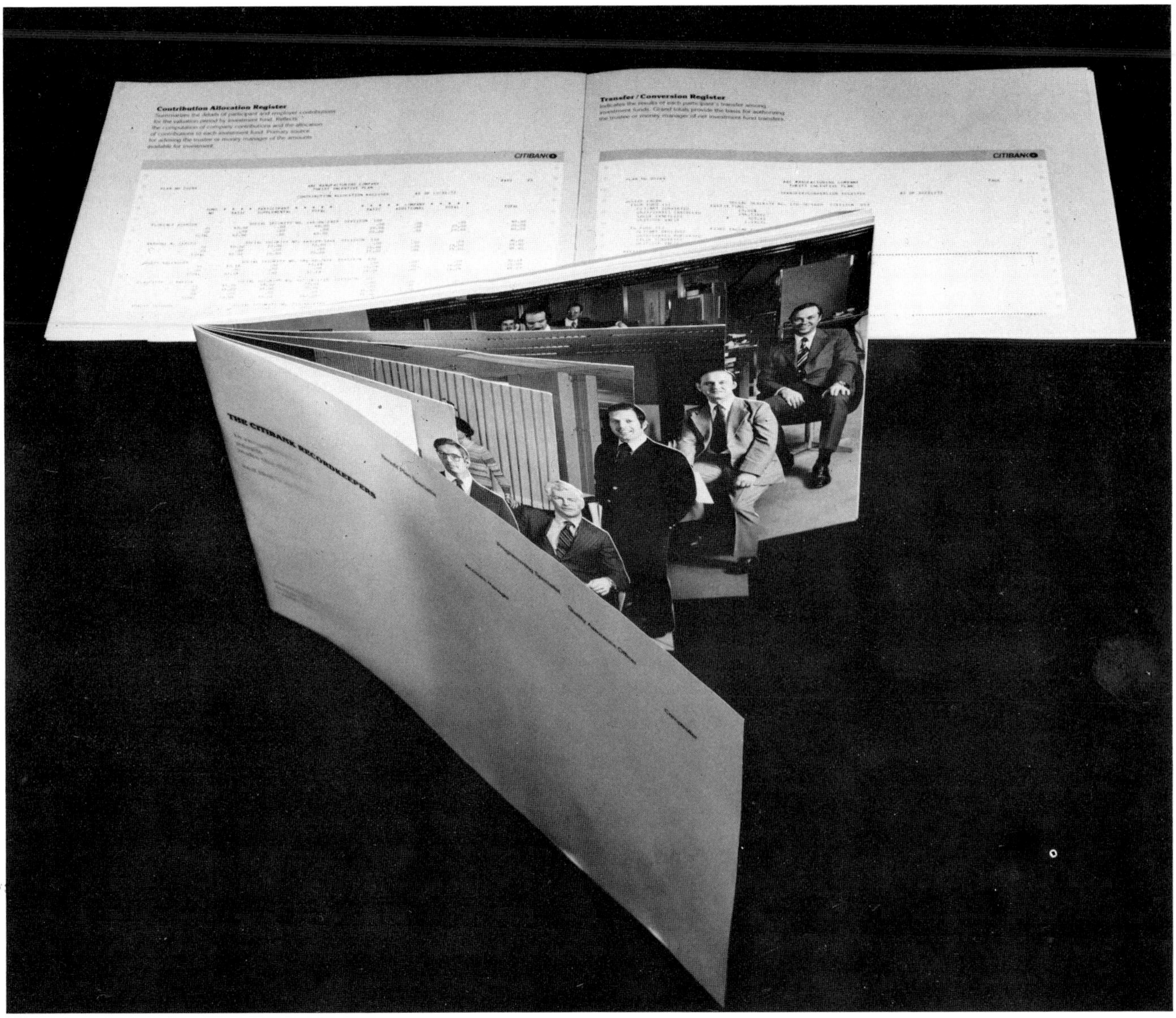

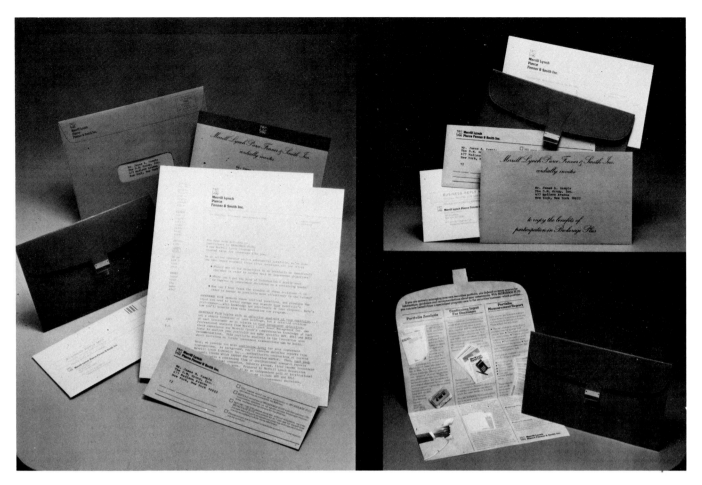

613
Maurice Grunfeld Art Director
Dennis Gottlieb Photographer
Laura Solomon Designer
The DM Group, Inc. Agency
Merrill Lynch Pierce Fenner & Smith Client

614
Glenn Ross Art Director
Girard & Mandel Production House
RSO Records Client

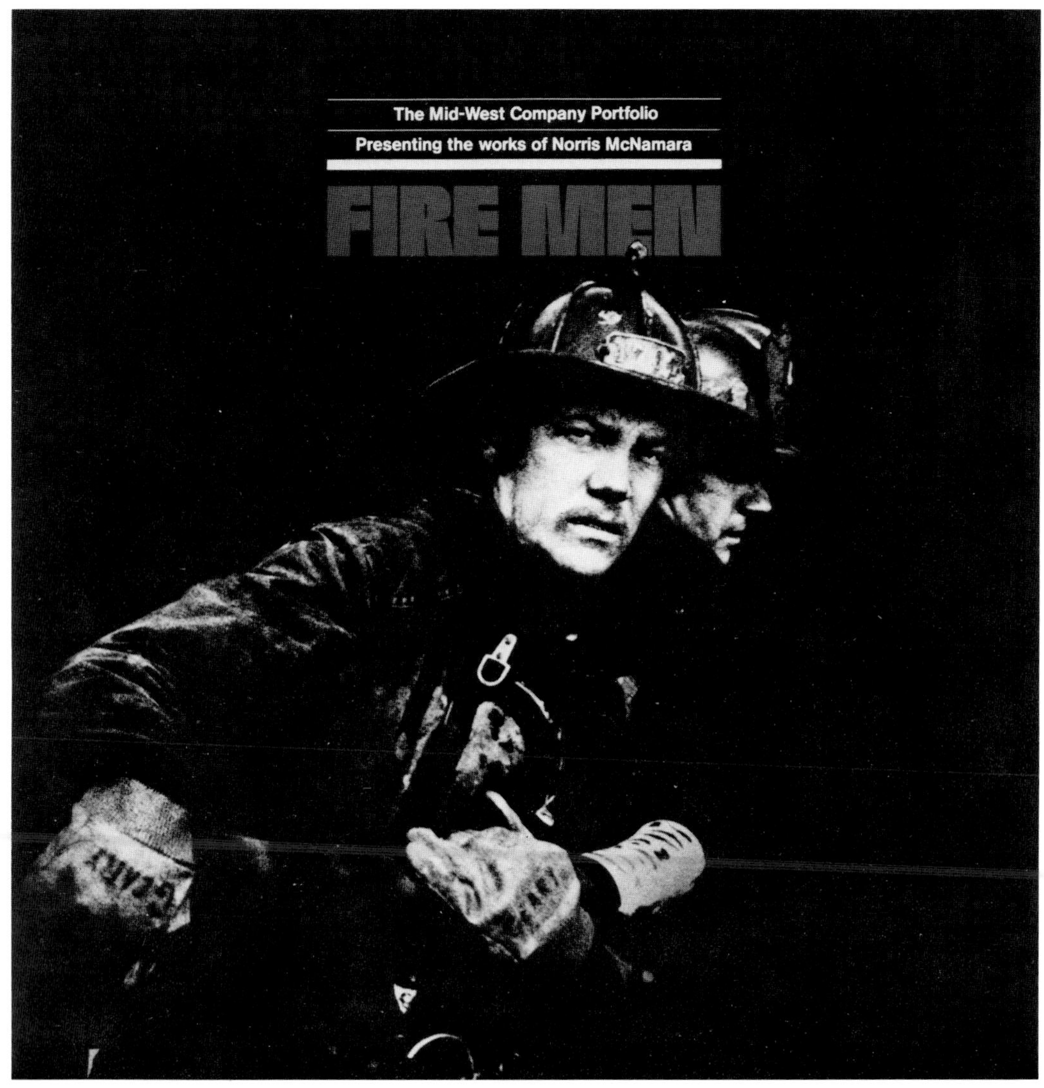

A

615 A-B
Gene Rosner Art Director
Norris McNamara Photographer
Marc Posner Copywriter
Gene Rosner Designer
Aztec Typography, Inc. Typography
Brown & Rosner Studio
Selz-Seabolt & Associates, Inc. Agency
The Mid-West Company Client

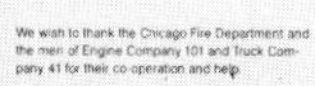

B

cuoio

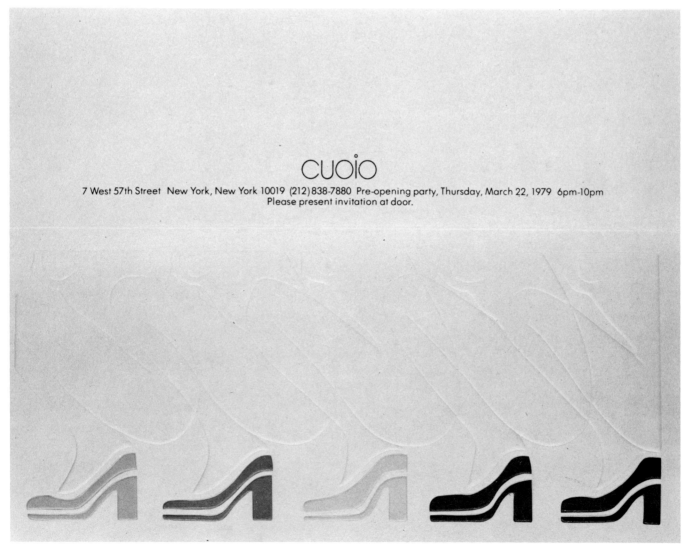

7 West 57th Street New York, New York 10019 (212) 838-7880 Pre-opening party, Thursday, March 22, 1979 6pm-10pm
Please present invitation at door.

616
Mark Kent, Joanne Hetherington Art Directors
The Graphic Supermarket Agency
Cuoio Client

617
Charles Blake Art Director
Frank Reilly Illustrator
Elaine Zeitsoff Designer
NBC-TV Client

618
Rick St. Vincent Art Director
L. P. McDonnell Photographer
Herlin Press Production House
St. Vincent, Milone & McConnell Advertising Agency
ITT Flygt Corporation Client

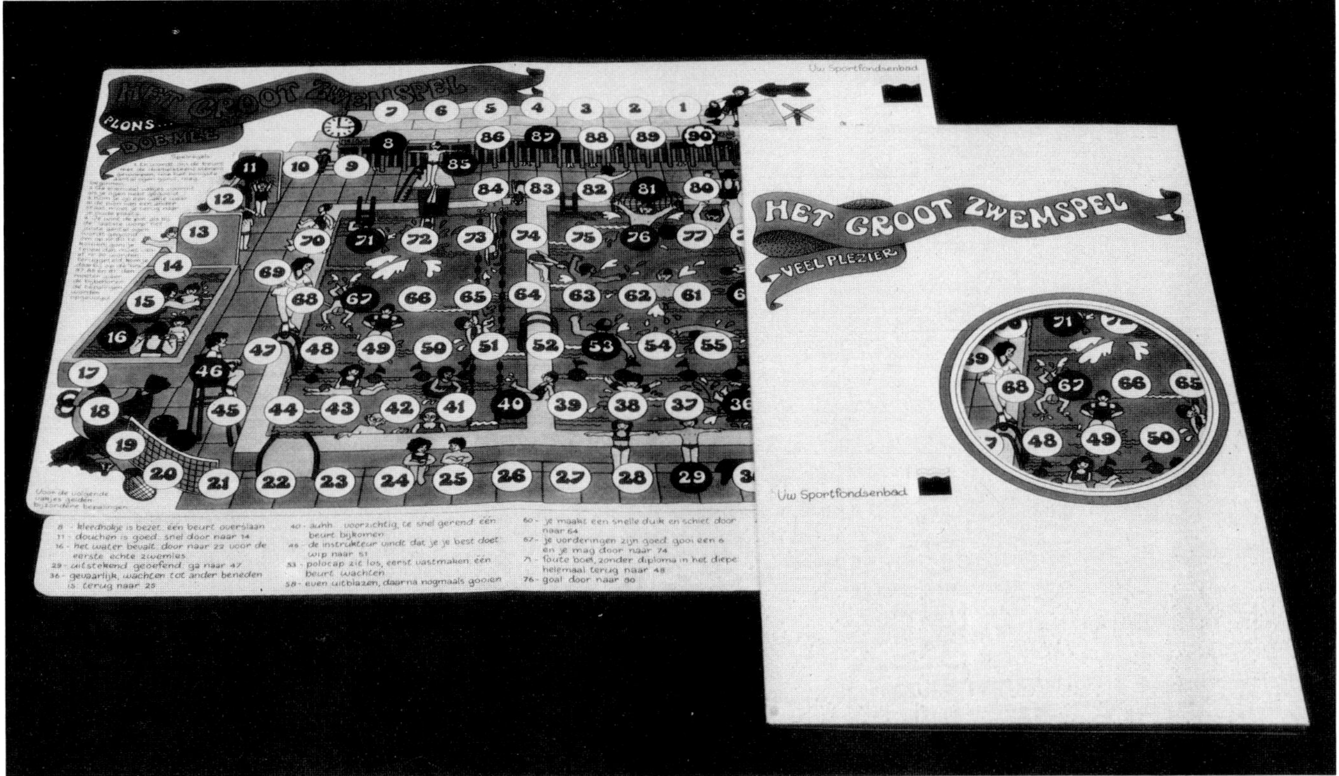

619
Jack De Lange Art Director
DLS Communications BV Agency
Sportfondsen Nederland BV Client

620
Michael Hay Art Director
Ehrenstrahle & Co. AB Agency
SKF Steel AB Client

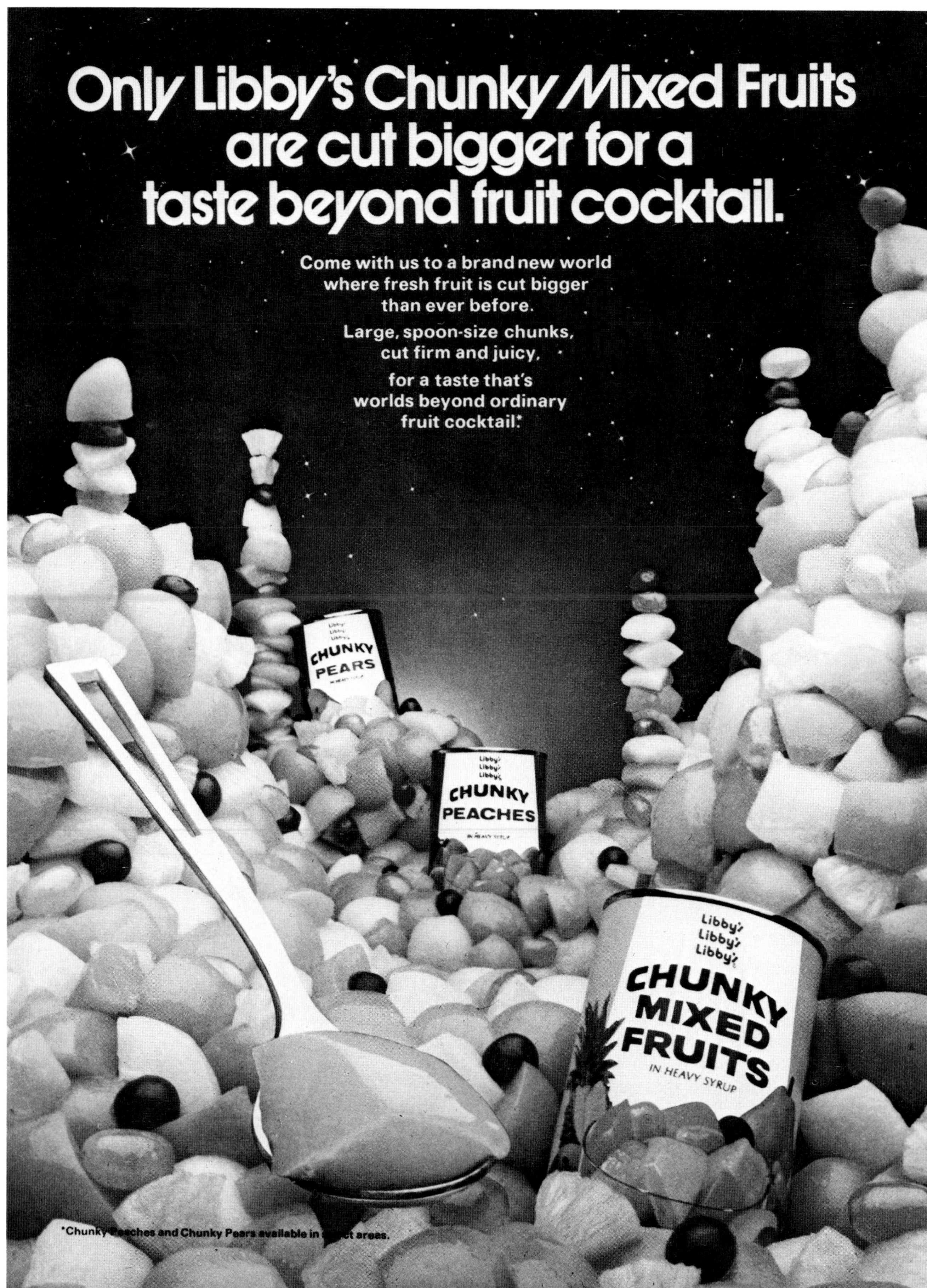
Only Libby's Chunky Mixed Fruits are cut bigger for a taste beyond fruit cocktail.
Come with us to a brand new world where fresh fruit is cut bigger than ever before.
Large, spoon-size chunks, cut firm and juicy,
for a taste that's worlds beyond ordinary fruit cocktail.*
CHUNKY PEARS
Libby's Libby's Libby's
CHUNKY PEACHES
Libby's Libby's Libby's
CHUNKY MIXED FRUITS
IN HEAVY SYRUP
*Chunky Peaches and Chunky Pears available in

621
Tom Gigante Art Director
Richard Foster Photographer
Gail Davis Copywriter
Tathum Laird & Kudner Agency
Libby, McNeil & Libby Client

FIRST BAPTIST CHURCH
BIBLE STUD
EVERY TU ESDAY HE RE
SUNDAY SERVICES
N KATY FWY
April 1 2 3 4 5 6 7 8 9 10 11 12 13 14 15 16 17 18 19 20 21 22 23 24 25 26 27 28 29 30 Typeworks, Inc.
May 1 2 3 4 5 6 7 8 9 10 11 12 13 14 15 16 17 18 19 20 21 22 23 24 25 26 27 28 29 30 31 3333 Eastside, Houston
June 1 2 3 4 5 6 7 8 9 10 11 12 13 14 15 16 17 18 19 20 21 22 23 24 25 26 27 28 29 30 31 (713) 527-9900

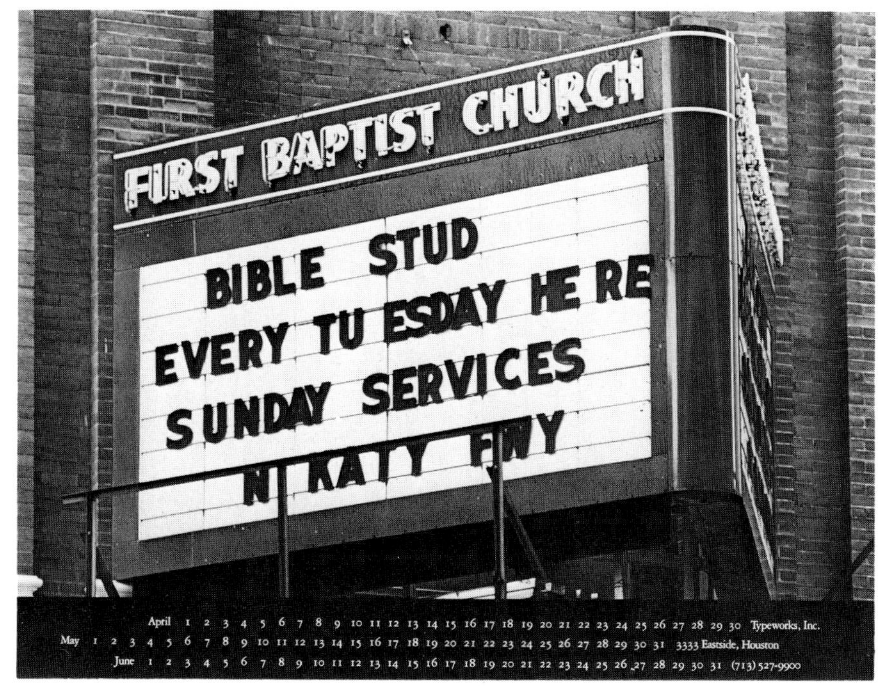

622
Jerry Herring Art Director
Joe Barbaran Photographer
Herring Design Agency
Typeworks, Inc. Client

623
Jerry Herring Art Director
Joe Baraban Photographer
Herring Design Agency
Typeworks, Inc. Client

1810
R
FREE PAKING
January 1 2 3 4 5 6 7 8 9 10 11 12 13 14 15 16 17 18 19 20 21 22 23 24 25 26 27 28 29 30 31 Typeworks, Inc.
February 1 2 3 4 5 6 7 8 9 10 11 12 13 14 15 16 17 18 19 20 21 22 23 24 25 26 27 28 3333 Eastside, Houston
March 1 2 3 4 5 6 7 8 9 10 11 12 13 14 15 16 17 18 19 20 21 22 23 24 25 26 27 28 29 30 31 (713) 527-9900

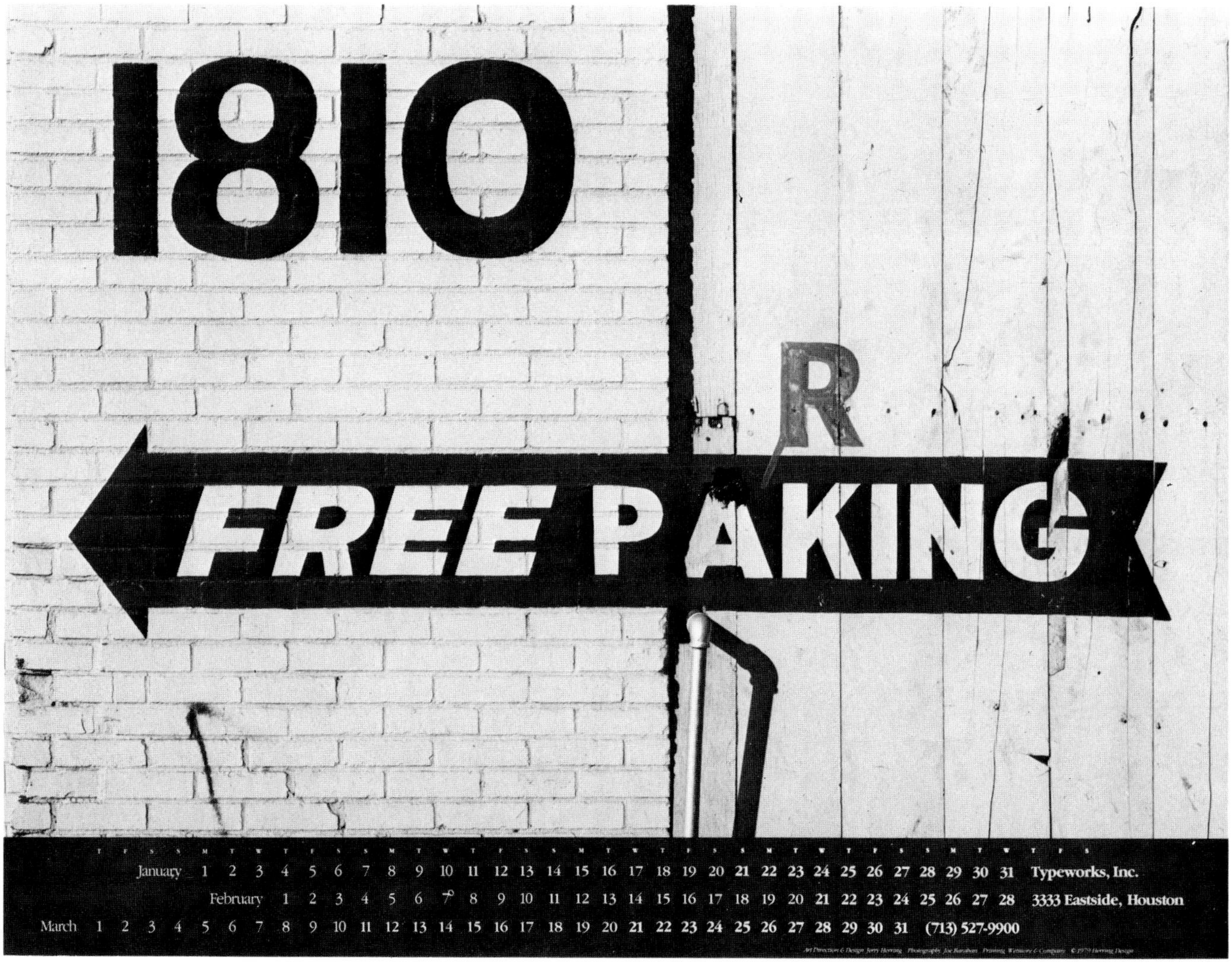

A

624 A-E
Albert Leutwyler, Oscar Schnider Art Directors
Kelly Kao Illustrator
Leutwyler Schnider Agency
Benihana Restaurant Client

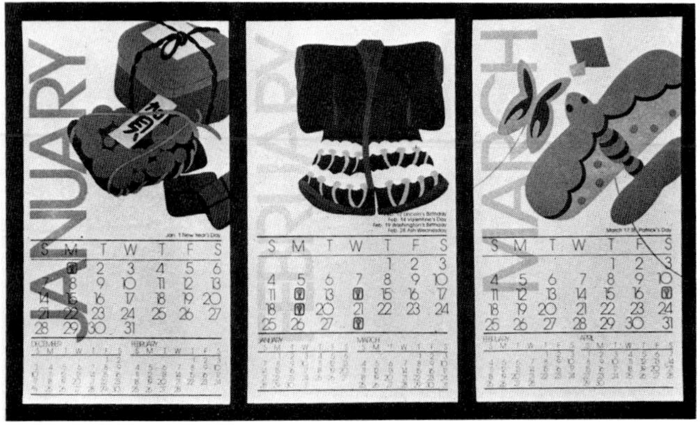

B

C

D

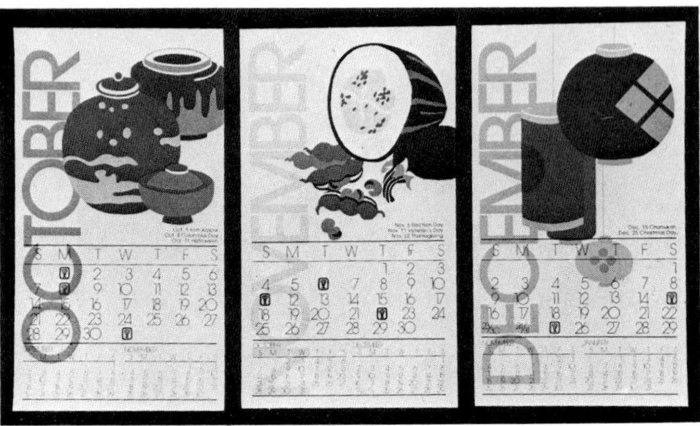

E

625
Robert Y. Williamson Art Director
Hill and Knowlton, Inc. Agency
Netherlands Info Office Client

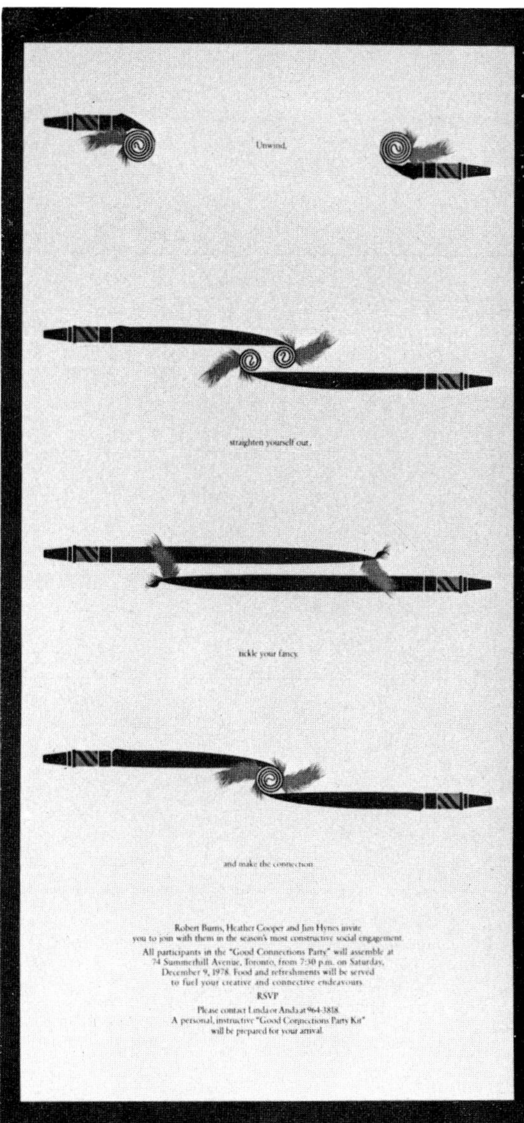

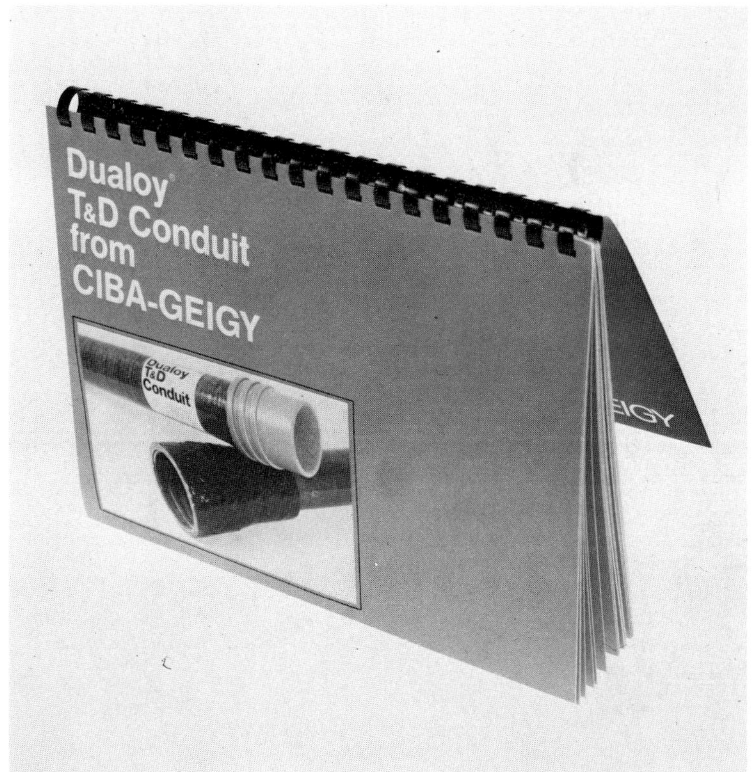

627
Tycho Weil Art Director
Marquardt & Roche Agency
Ciba-Geigy Client

626
Robert Burns Art Director
Heather Cooper Illustrator
Burns, Cooper, Hynes Limited Client

628 A-B
Tom Lewis Art Director
The Design Quarter Agency
San Diego Historical Society Client

San Diego Historical Society Title Insurance and Trust Collection

There's a part of history in every day life. Even the ordinary becomes extraordinary when we look back.

A

B

his *Memoirs*: "Our life there was of strict garrison duty, with plenty of leisure for hunting and social entertainments." Sherman even took up painting in 1842. It was rumored that Lt. Braxton Bragg relieved his boredom by writing memoranda to himself; as quartermaster, for instance, he would complain of bad beef to Bragg-the-commander. In 1843 there were

a half-dozen lieutenants and captains at the post who would later become generals: W. T. Sherman, Braxton Bragg, John F. Reynolds, Thomas W. Sherman, E. D. Keyes, and George H. Thomas.

Although the fort's routine varied little from year to year, individuality did not disappear. Edgar Allen Poe, famous poet and writer of ingenious short stories, spent over a year at Fort Moultrie. In 1827, young Poe left his foster father and in Boston enlisted for 5 years in Company H of the 1st U.S. Artillery. He signed his name "Edgar Allen Perry"; a recruiter added 4 years to his age and entered him as 22 years old. In November, Company H was transferred from Massachusetts to Fort Moultrie, and the literate "Private Perry" landed a job as commissary clerk. The next summer, a few months before Company H moved on to Virginia's Fort Monroe, Poe was promoted to the job of artificer (weapons repairman).

While stationed at Fort Moultrie, Poe made good use of his time. He began to write his longest poem, "Al Aaraaf", here and gathered material for later stories. "The Gold Bug," an intricate tale of pirate treasure, depends greatly on its Sullivans Island setting:

This island is a very singular one. It consists of little else than the sea sand, and is about three miles long. Its breadth at no point exceeds a quarter of a mile. It is separated from the mainland by a scarcely perceptible creek, oozing its way through a wilderness of reeds and slime, a favorite resort of the marsh hen. The vegetation, as might be supposed, is scant, or at least dwarfish. No trees of any magnitude are to be seen. Near the western extremity, where Fort Moultrie stands . . . may be found, indeed, the bristly palmetto; but the whole island, with the exception of this western point, and a line of hard, white beach on the seacoast, is covered with a dense undergrowth of the sweet myrtle so much prized by the horticulturists of England. The shrub here often attains the heights of fifteen or twenty feet, and forms an almost impenetrable coppice, burdening the air with its fragrance.

Poe also mentions Fort Moultrie at the end of his story "The Balloon Hoax," in which eight passengers aboard *Victoria* have allegedly crossed the Atlantic in 75 hours:

It was nearly dead calm when the voyagers first came in view

Braxton Bragg

John F. Reynolds

Erasmus D. Keyes

George H. Thomas

Edgar Allan Poe used Sullivans Island as the setting for several of his stories.

46

47

A

Constant Defender

The Story of Fort Moultrie

Mount Pleasant

Sullivan's Island

North Sand Head

Fort Moultry

Lower Middle

B

629 A-B
Steve Quine Art Director
Peter Larnish, Marge Alexander Designers
E. James White Company Agency
U.S. Park Service Client

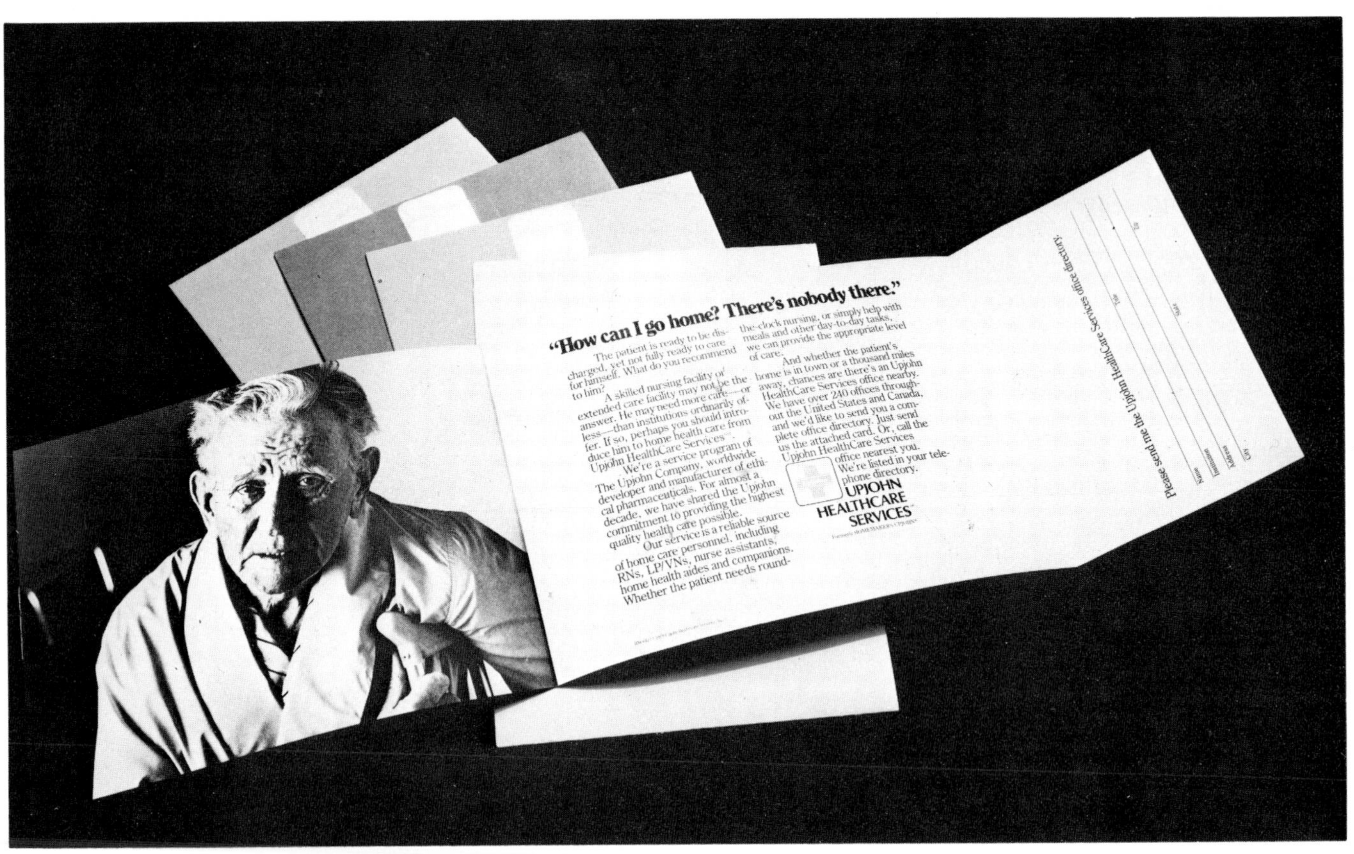

630
Dan A. Bixler Art Director
Jim Powell Photographer
Juhl Advertising Agency Agency
Upjohn Healthcare Services Client

631
Henry Epstein Art Director
Ken Petretti Illustrator
Tipp Gilbert Copywriter
Ken Petretti, Bill Duevell Designers
Sanders Printing Production House
ABC Television Network Client

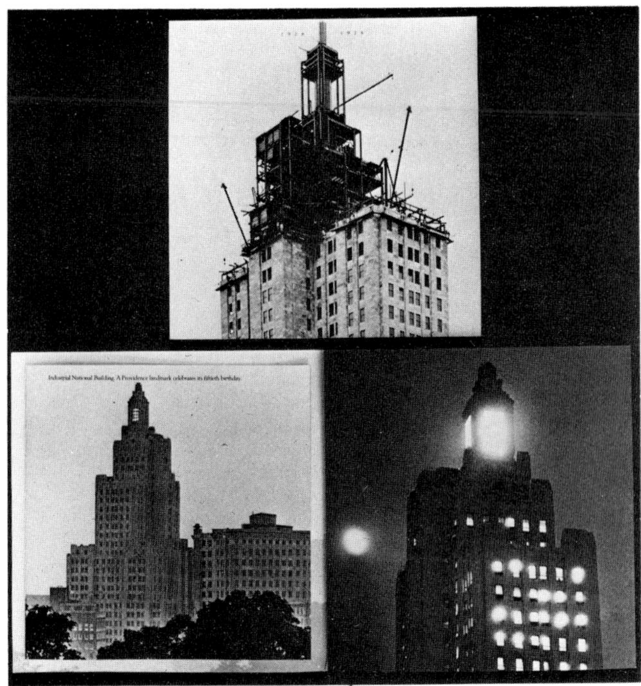

632
Tyler Smith Art Director
Chris Maynard Photographer
Tyler Smith, Art Direction Inc. Agency
Industrial National Bank Client

633
Constance Kovar Art Director
Constance Kovar, Kate Thompson Designers
Constance Kovar, Ltd. Studio
The J. N. Company Agency
Ralston Purina Company Client

634
Richard Vasquez Art Director
Christine Anderson Calligrapher
Vasquez Visuals Studio
Carol Moberg Communications Agency
Schieffelin & Co. Client

635
Walt Strubczewski Art Director
Art Direction, Inc. Designers
Kircher, Helton & Collett, Inc. Agency
Howard Paper Mills Client

635

636
Les Affonso Art Director
Bill Wagner Photographer
Gianettino & Meredith, Inc. Agency
WNEW-FM Client

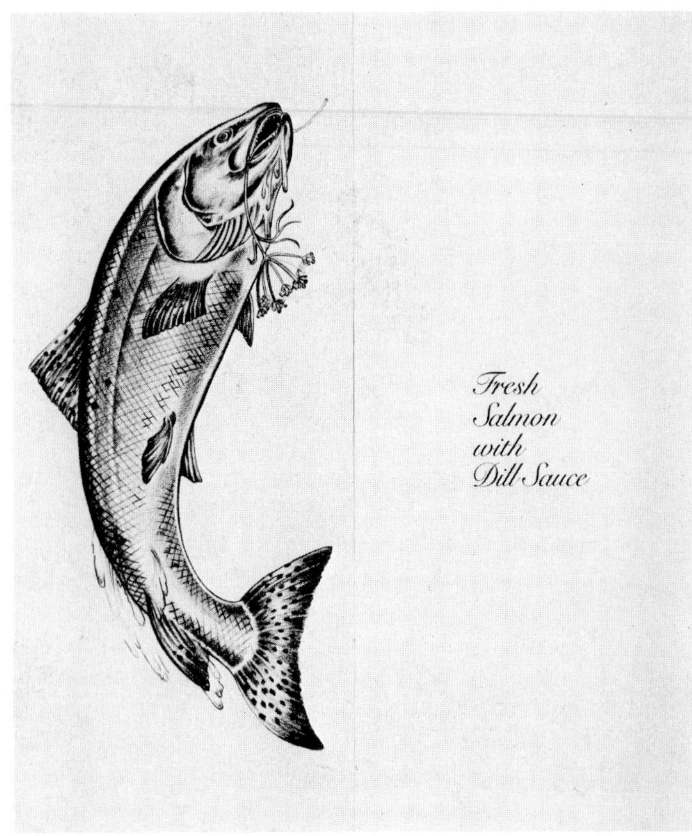

637
Herbert M. Rosenthal Art Director
Barbara Moore Illustrator
Institutional Investor Client

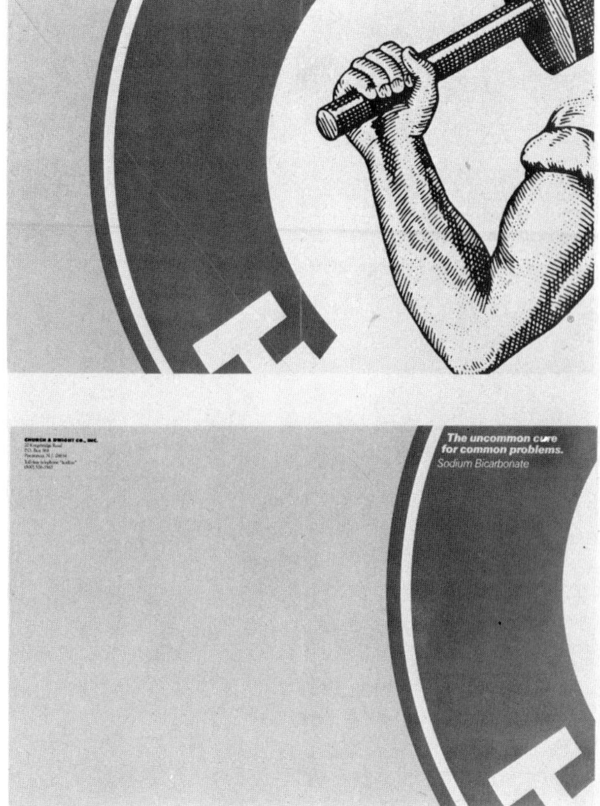

638
Joseph M. Essex, Ron Girman Art Directors
Ron Girman Designer
Burson-Marsteller/Design Group Agency
Church & Dwight Client

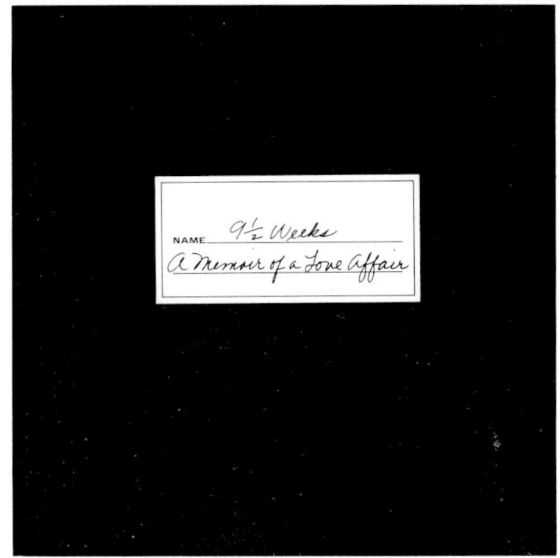

A

B

639 A-B
Tom Starace Art Director
Berkley Publishing Corp. Client

640
Joseph Hutchcroft Art Director
Container Corporation of America Client

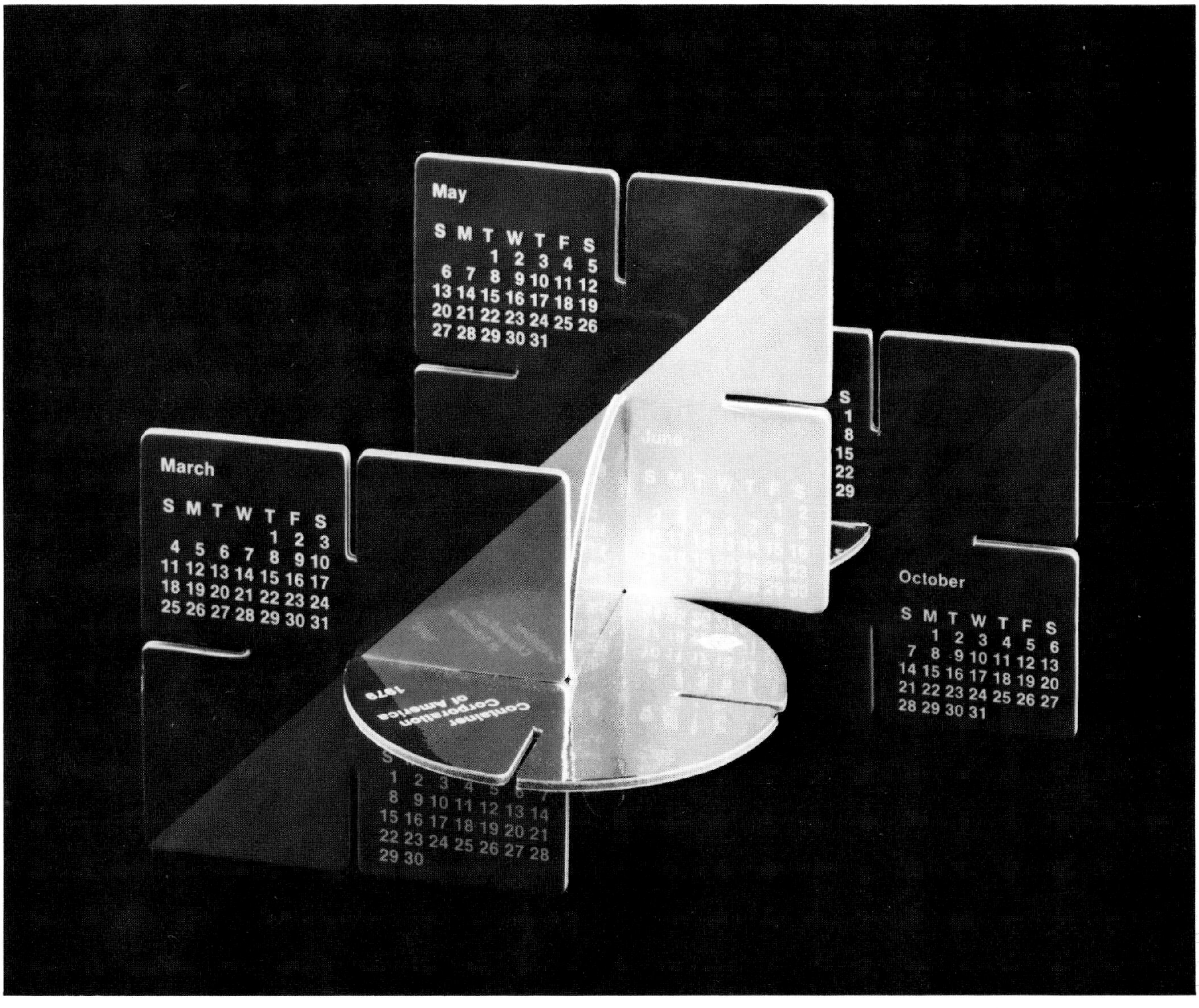

For years, we've been breaking ground.

Today, we break with tradition.

You've known us as Sanders Campbell & Company. A product of two innovative leaders. Founder Sanders Campbell and president Richard Mullen.

Today, we're Campbell/Mullen. A product of success.

As Campbell/Mullen our growth promises to uphold the tradition built by Sanders Campbell & Company. Because when it comes to real estate development, we will continue to break records.

CAMPBELL/MULLEN

641
Cap Pannell Art Director
Allday! Associates Agency
Campbell/Mullen Client

642
Doug Morrall Art Director
Brand Advertising, Inc. Agency
Safety-Kleen Corporation Client

643
Jerry Dadds Art Director
Alain Jaramillo, Dallas Weigel, Greg Pease, Craig Kenney Photographers
Richard Waldrep Illustrator
Jerry Dadds, Nancy Urbanski Designers
Charles Maltbie Associates, Inc. Production House
Eucalyptus Tree Studio Inc. Agency
City of Baltimore, Mayor William Donald Schaefer Client

642

643

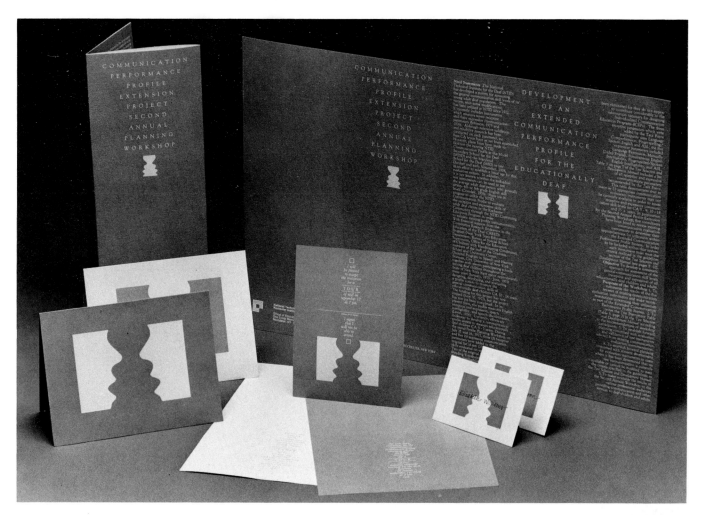

644
Thomas J. Castle Art Director
Mark Benjamin Photographer
L. Dean Woolever Designer
Media Production Department/NTID Studio
National Technical Institute for the Deaf
Dr. Donald D. Johnson Client

645
Tomas Gonda Art Director
Tomas Gonda, Charles Steiner, Miho, Bruce Davidson Photographers
Champion Papers Client

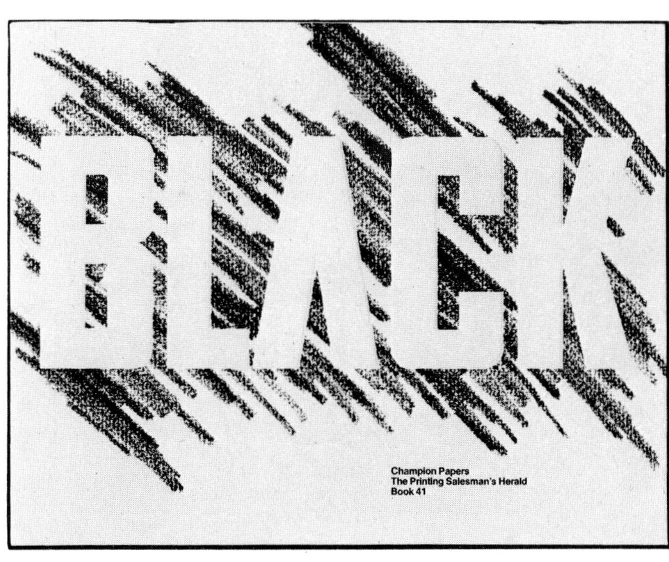

The Best of Gannett 1978

646
Robert Meyer Art Director
Ted Kawalerski Photographer
Gannett Co. Inc. Client

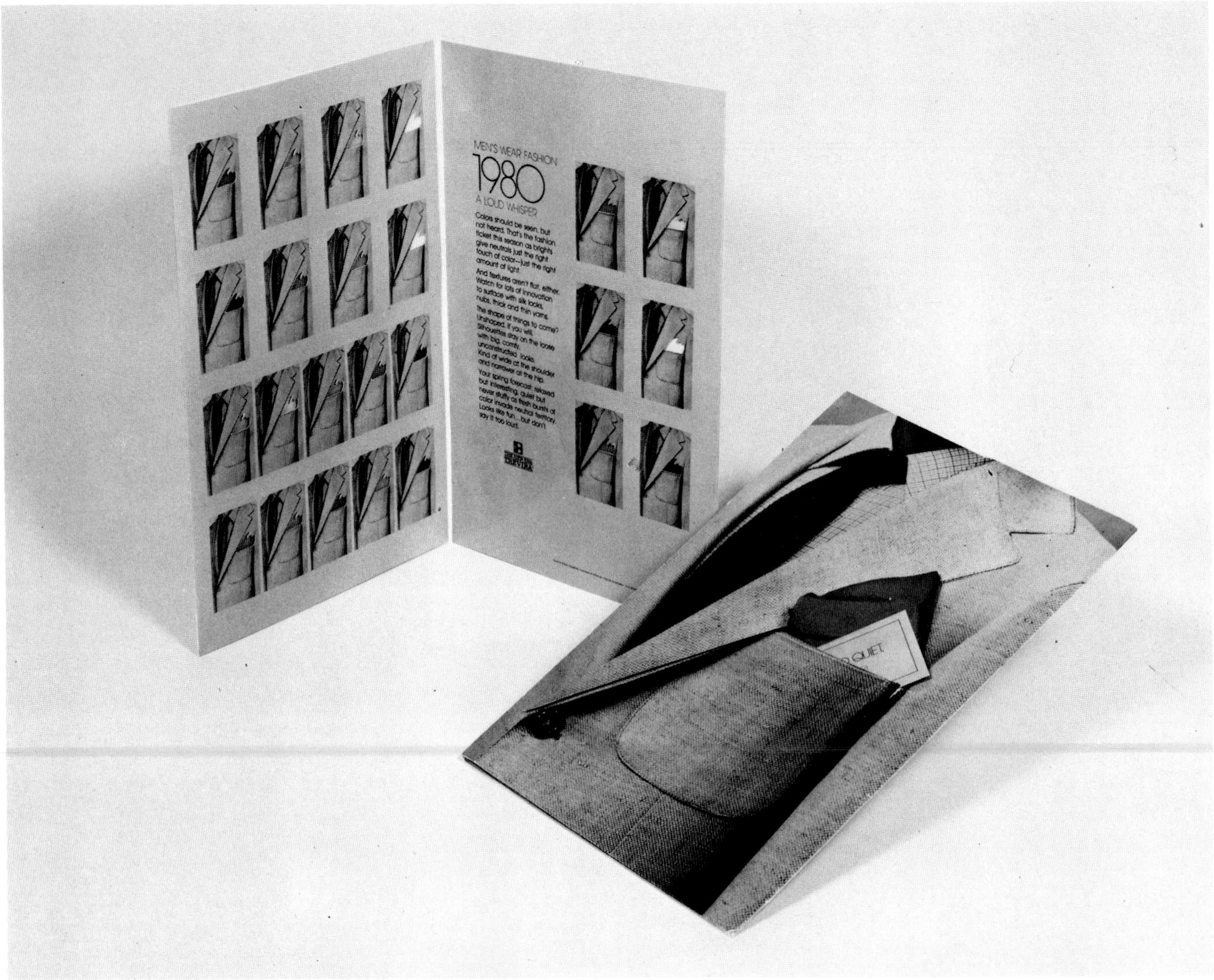

A

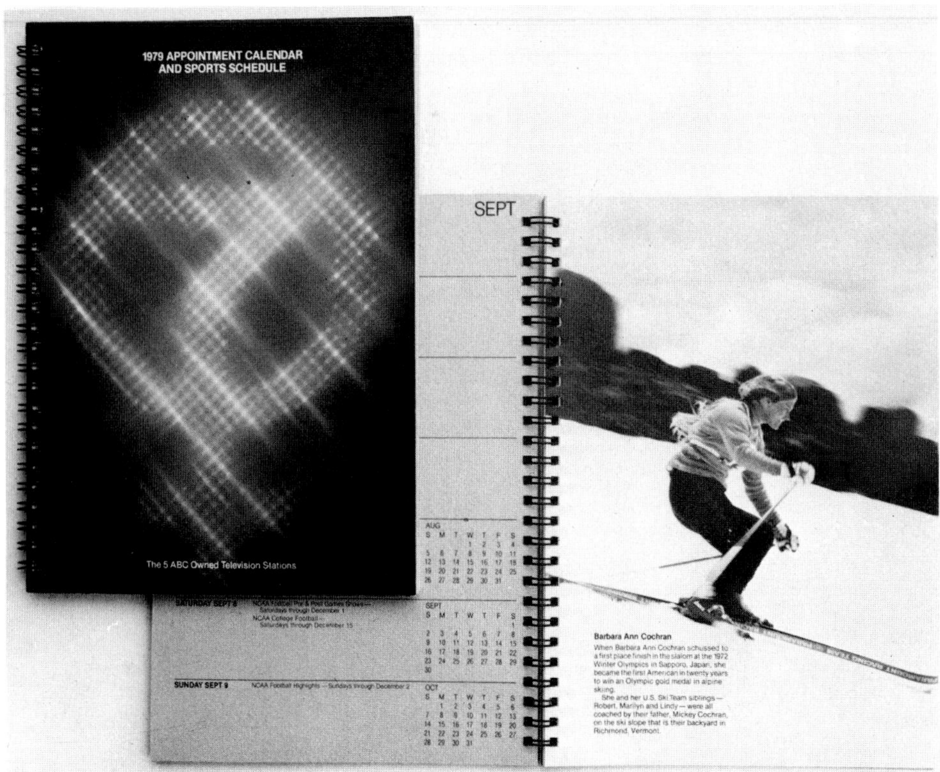

647 A-B
Joseph Barbera, Ike Millman Art Directors
Merchandising Workshop Agency
Hoechst Fibers Industries Client

648
Susan Heydt Art Director
Ong & Associates, Inc. Agency
ABC Television Spot Sales, Inc. Client

647 B

649
Glenn Ross Art Director
RSO Records Client

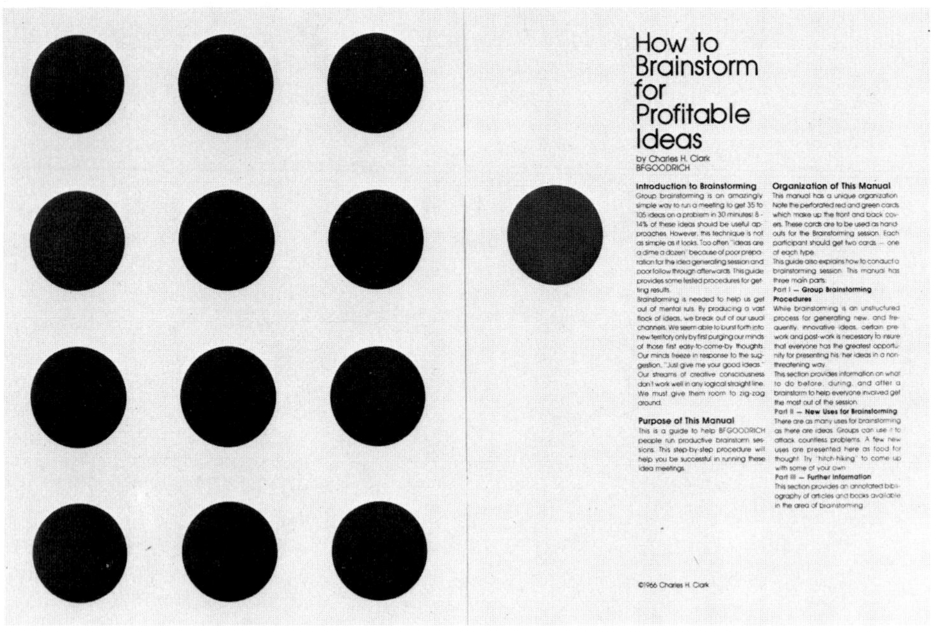

How to Brainstorm for Profitable Ideas

by Charles H. Clark
BFGOODRICH

Introduction to Brainstorming

Group brainstorming is an amazingly simple way to run a meeting to get 35 to 105 ideas on a problem in 30 minutes! 8 - 14% of these ideas should be useful approaches. However, this technique is not as simple as it looks. Too often "ideas are a dime a dozen" because of poor preparation for the idea generating session and poor follow through afterwards. This guide provides some tested procedures for getting results.

Brainstorming is needed to help us get out of mental ruts. By producing a vast flock of ideas, we break out of our usual channels. We seem able to burst forth into new territory only by first purging our minds of those first easy-to-come-by thoughts. Our minds freeze in response to the suggestion, "Just give me your good ideas." Our streams of creative consciousness don't work well in any logical straight line. We must give them room to zig-zag around.

Purpose of This Manual

This is a guide to help BFGOODRICH people run productive brainstorm sessions. This step-by-step procedure will help you be successful in running these idea meetings.

Organization of This Manual

This manual has a unique organization. Note the perforated red and green cards which make up the front and back covers. These cards are to be used as handouts for the Brainstorming session. Each participant should get two cards — one of each type.

This guide also explains how to conduct a brainstorming session. This manual has three main parts:

Part I — **Group Brainstorming Procedures**

While brainstorming is an unstructured process for generating new, and frequently, innovative ideas, certain pre-work and post-work is necessary to insure that everyone has the greatest opportunity for presenting his/her ideas in a non-threatening way.

This section provides information on what to do before, during, and after a brainstorm to help everyone involved get the most out of the session.

Part II — **New Uses for Brainstorming**

There are as many uses for brainstorming as there are ideas. Groups can use it to attack countless problems. A few new uses are presented here as food for thought. Try "hitch-hiking" to come up with some of your own.

Part III — **Further Information**

This section provides an annotated bibliography of articles and books available in the area of brainstorming.

©1966 Charles H. Clark

650
J. Charles Walker Art Director
J. Charles Walker, J. Brett Buchanan, David Middleton, Patricia Job Designers
Tarragon Graphics Agency
B. F. Goodrich Client

651
Dan Bittman Art Director
Corson Hirschfeld Photographer
Maurice Delegator Illustrator
Sive Associates Agency
The Art Director Club Show Client

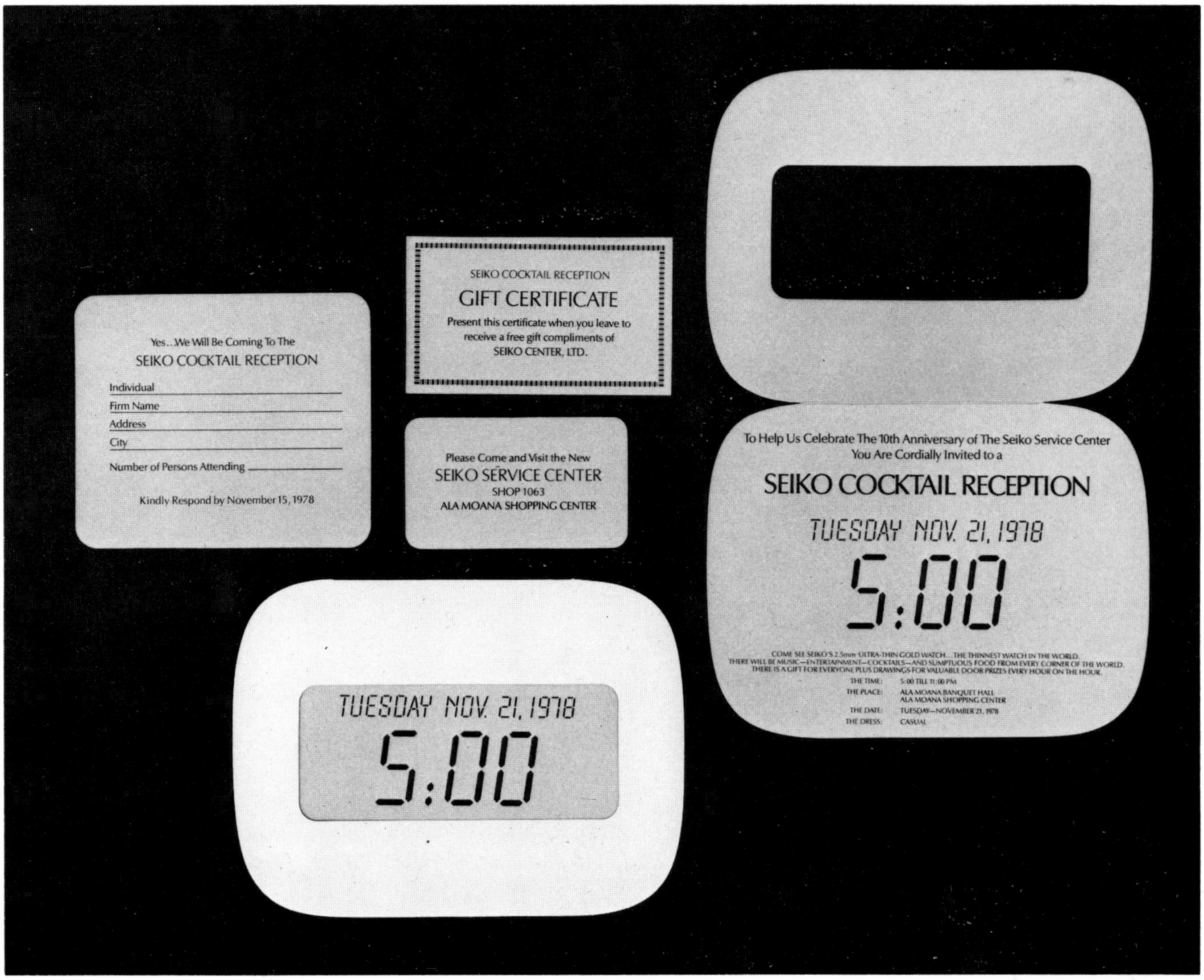

652
Barbara Scharf Creative Director
Greenapple Sales Promotion Inc. Agency
Seiko Time Corporation Client

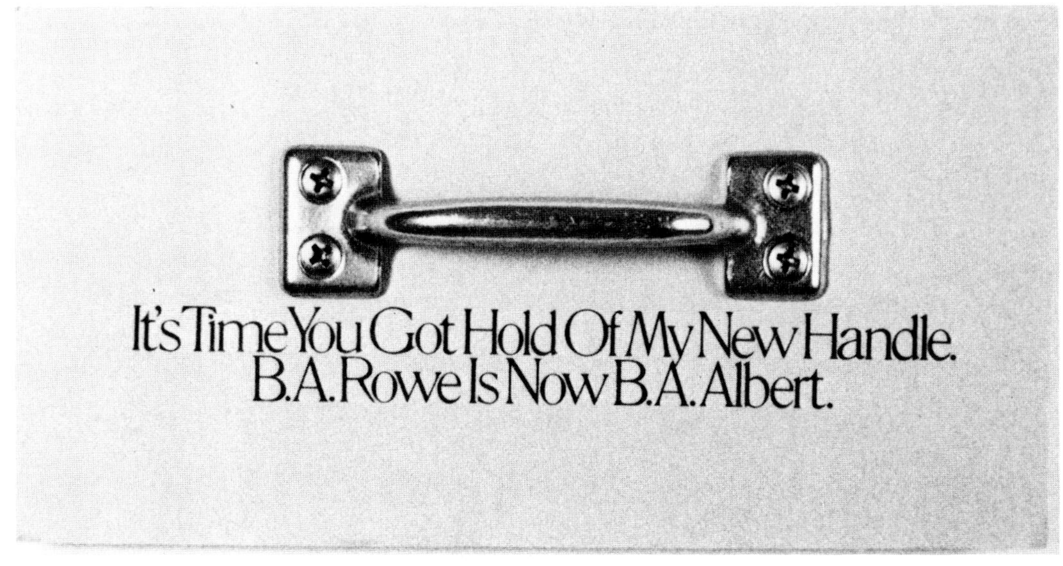

653
B. A. Albert Art Director
Burton-Campbell Agency
B. A. Albert Client

654
Russell G. Luedke Art Director
Design Directions, Inc. Agency
Neenah Paper Co. Client

Help A Hurt
Give to the 1978 Crusade of Mercy
Although we can't make the hurt go away, we can ease the pain a little through our contributions to the Crusade of Mercy.
Each year, the Crusade helps hundreds of charitable agencies—helping the hurts of blind people, flood victims, homeless babies, families of disabled veterans, retarded children, the handicapped, the aged and the ill.
By giving to the Crusade, you are helping to build a better community in which to live, work and raise your family.
Help the hurt. Pledge your fair share to the 1978 Crusade of Mercy.

Public Service Advertising

656
Jeff Barnes Art Director
Container Corporation of America Client

657
Valerie K. Newton Art Director
John Lawlor Photographer
Sister Mary Corita Illustrator
Imagemakers, Inc. Agency
National Center for Voluntary Action Client

658 A-B
Joe Hutchcroft, Paul Schulte Art Directors
Stan Jorstad Photographer
Paul Schulte Designer
Accurate Silkscreen Studio ,
Container Corporation of America Client

658 A

B

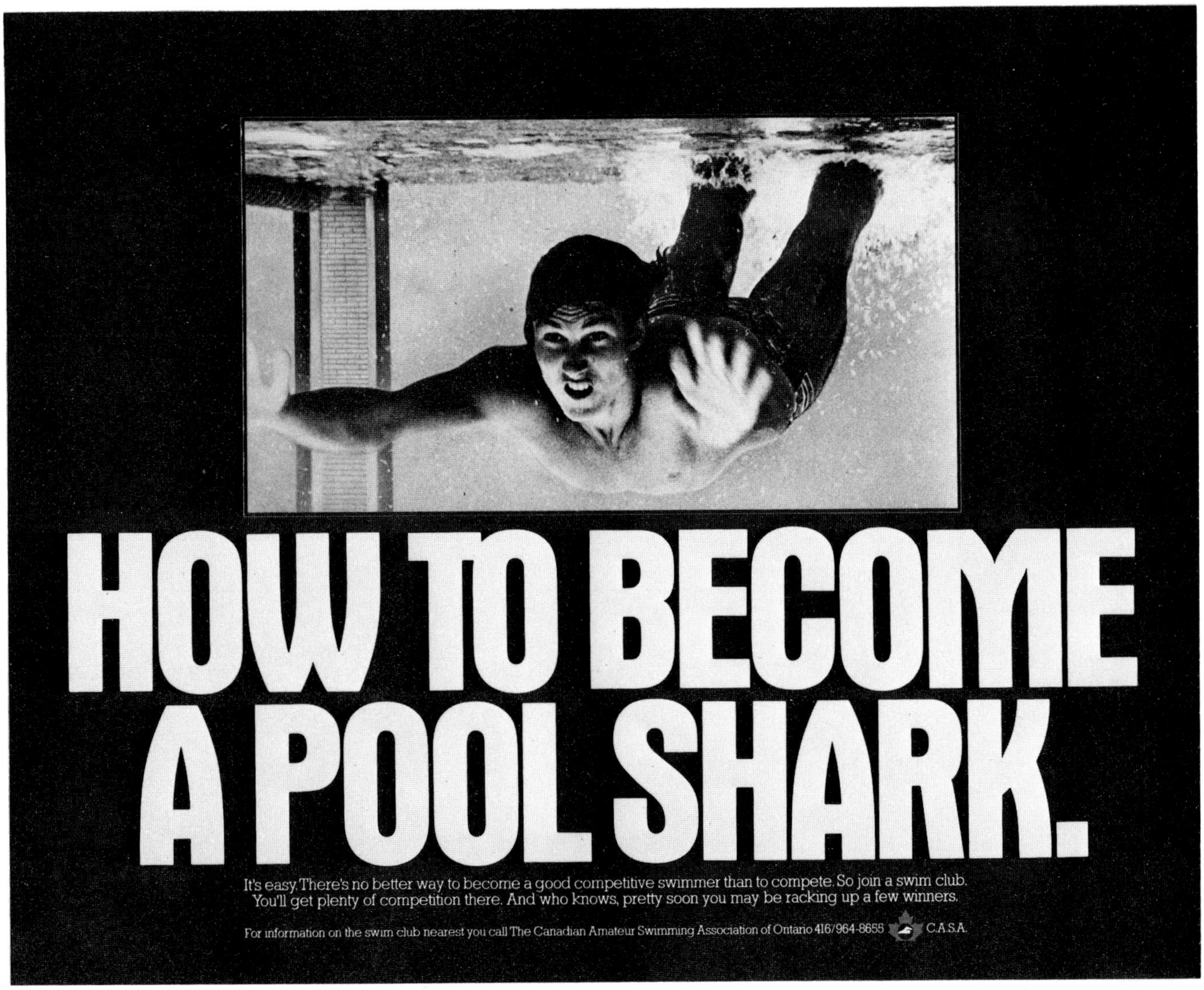

HOW TO BECOME
A POOL SHARK.
It's easy. There's no better way to become a good competitive swimmer than to compete. So join a swim club.
You'll get plenty of competition there. And who knows, pretty soon you may be racking up a few winners.
For information on the swim club nearest you call The Canadian Amateur Swimming Association of Ontario 416/964-8655
C.A.S.A.

659
Joe Shyllit Art Director
Tony Duffy Photographer
Kuleba & Shyllit Creative Services Agency
Canadian Amateur Swimming Association of Ontario Client

THE BANK,
POLITICS AND YOU
UCB PRACTICAL
POLITICS PROGRAM

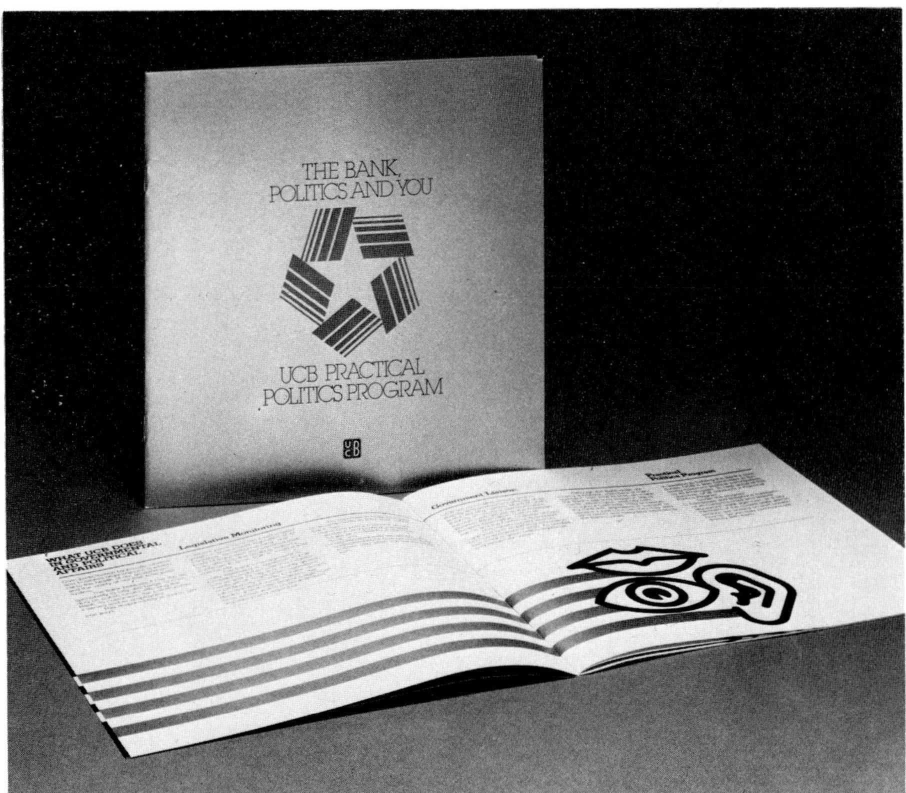

660
Richard Ikkanda Art Director
Frank Mediate Illustrator
Richard Ikkanda Design Group Agency
United California Bank Client

The main way that Cenikor has changed my life is my outlook on life.

My outlook is now positive and bright. My thought patterns have changed and my demands and expectations of my self are far greater than they ever were.

Vern, head of kitchen,
with Cenikor three years.

If you have a drug or behavioral problem you're serious about solving, or if you'd like to help someone who has, contact Cenikor.

Cenikor works.

In Houston: 228-4447
In Ft. Worth: 332-1044
In Denver: 234-1288

661
Jerry Herring Art Director
Joe Baraban Photographer
Herring Design Agency
Cenikor Foundation Client

663
Marianne Soufas Art Director
Chernoff/Silver and Associates Agency
Donald Stewart for U.S. Senate Client

HELP WANTED

UNITED STATES SENATOR

Immediate opening for an experienced legislator with a record of fighting and winning tough battles. Applicant must have proven ability to take on big special interests such as utility companies and loan sharks. Prefer someone who has not been part of insulated Washington network of politicans, bureaucrats, and lobbyists. Must be willing to travel across Alabama meeting the people and learning first-hand about their problems and needs. Must be informed on the tough political issues confronting Alabama and the nation and able to debate them with political foes. Final selection will be determined by the people of Alabama on Tuesday, September 26, at the polls.

Donald
Stewart
U.S. Senate

Authorized and paid for by the "Friends of Donald Stewart" Committee, William Head, Dothan, Treasurer, Post Office Box 2274, Anniston, Alabama, 36201

662
Clare Francis Art Director
Clare Francis Design Agency
Amnesty International, Gail McCloskey Client

'Red Terror'
November 1977–June 1978
Addis Ababa
Ethiopia Human Rights Campaign
Amnesty International November 1978–January 1979
For further information contact:
Ethiopia Coordinator
Amnesty International
2112 Broadway
New York, N.Y. 10023

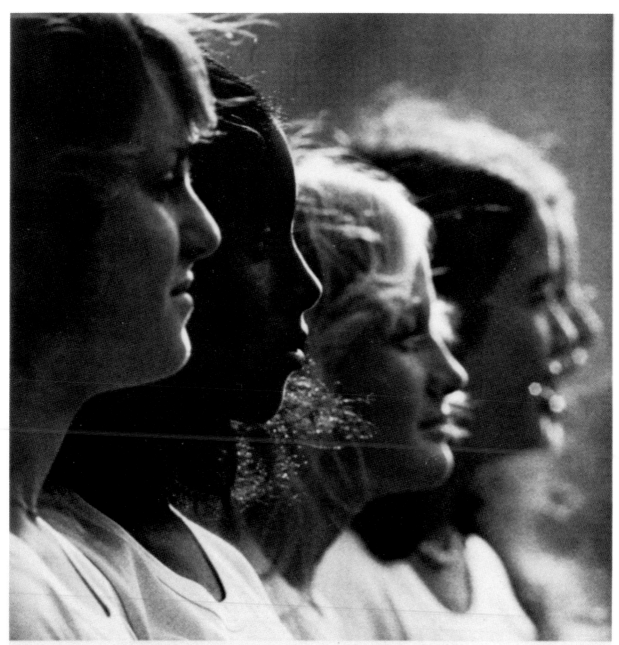

The new face of Girl Scouting

664
Saul Bass Art Director
Arnold Schwartzman, Art Goodman, Vahe Fattal Designers
Bass/Yager & Associates Agency
Girl Scouts of the USA Client

665
Susan Jackson Keig Art Director
James L. Ballard Photographer
John Weber Calligrapher
Frank J. Bussone Coordinator
Susan Jackson Keig, Designer Studio
Robert Russell & Associates, Inc. Agency
The Dirksen Center Client

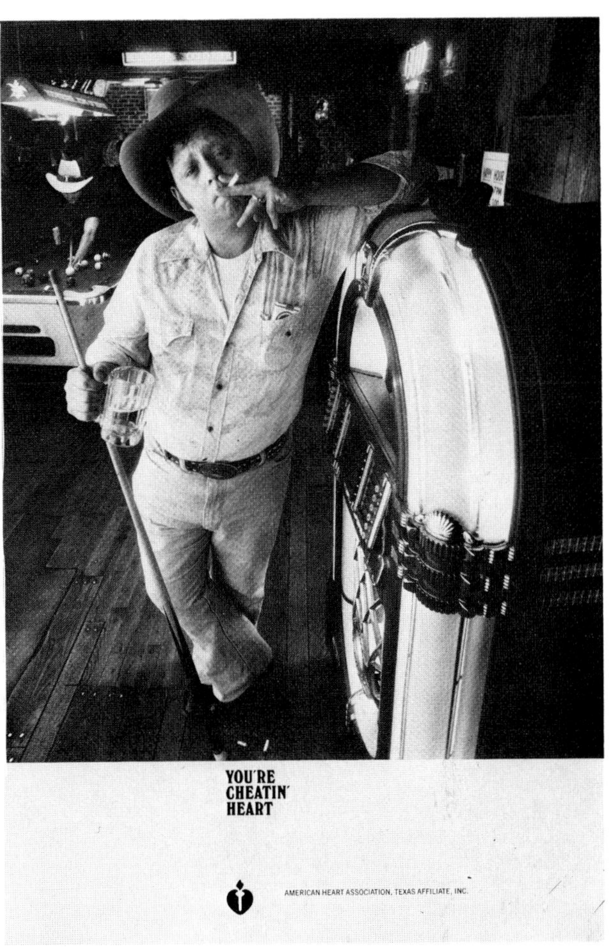

666
Steven Sessions Art Director
Chuck Untersee Photographer
Joe Romano Retoucher
Kenny Ragland Copywriter
Baxter + Korge, Inc. Agency
American Heart Association Client

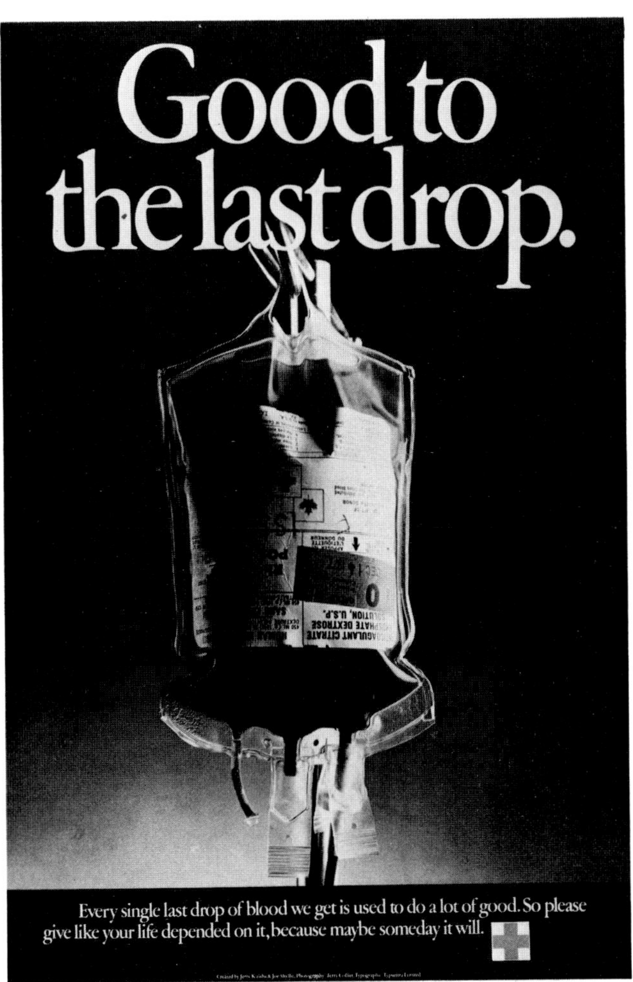

Good to
the last drop.
Every single last drop of blood we get is used to do a lot of good. So please give like your life depended on it, because maybe someday it will.

667
Joe Shyllit Art Director
Terry Collier Photographer
Kuleba & Shyllit Creative Services Agency
Canadian Red Cross Society Client

APPRENTICESHIP OPPORTUNITY

are offering an opportunity to school Leavers of Fifth Form standard to undertake an apprenticeship in Fitting and Machining.

Please apply in writing giving personal details academic achievements and a brief statement as to why you wish to become a Fitter and Turner.

Forty percent of the kids leaving school in Bundoora can't read this.

Industry is becoming more technical all the time.

So a kid who can't count, read or write has to be just about unemployable.

Tony Cree has been a teacher for ten years.

For five of them he's taught here in Bundoora.

Tony Cree is also a realist.

So he's been saying loud and long there's something fundamentally wrong with an education system that fails so completely.

For Tony Cree there's only one answer.

Forget about the fancy theories and go back to teaching the 3Rs.

Reading, writing and 'rithmetic.

And that way your kids will have been given a proper chance.

If you agree, vote for Tony Cree– he's our Liberal Candidate.

Vote for Tony Cree–and give your kids a chance.

Authorised by N. R. Hughes, 104 Exhibition St., Melbourne
For more information call the Bundoora Electorate Committee Rooms, 18 Dennison Mall, Bundoora Shopping Centre–or phone 467 6211.
Remember polling stops at 6 pm.

668
Kim Mukerjee Art Director
Mark Linhart Designer
Brand Management Agency
Bundoora Liberal Party Client

Public Service Campaigns

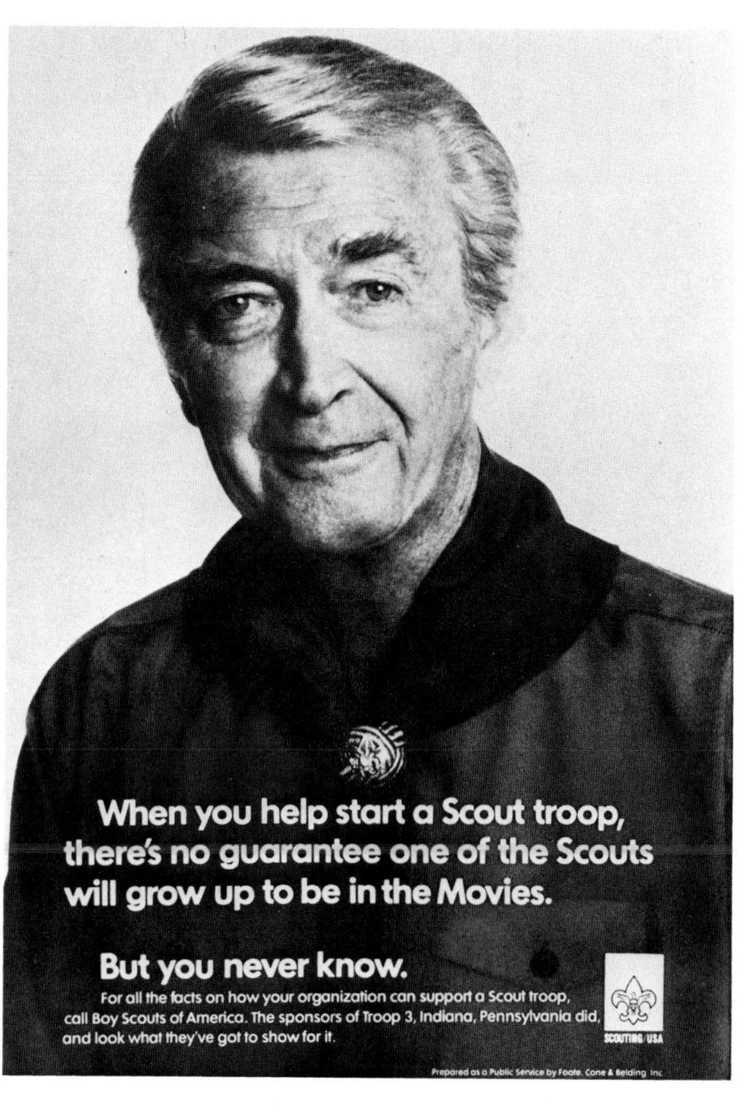

When you help start a Scout troop, there's no guarantee one of the Scouts will grow up to be in the Movies.
But you never know.
For all the facts on how your organization can support a Scout troop, call Boy Scouts of America. The sponsors of Troop 3, Indiana, Pennsylvania did, and look what they've got to show for it.
SCOUTING/USA
Prepared as a Public Service by Foote, Cone & Belding Inc.

669
Arnie Blumberg Art Director
Dick Stone Photographer
Foote, Cone & Belding Agency
Boy Scouts of America Client

670
Mark Nussbaum, Kevin Young, Albert Chiang Art Directors
Michael Halsband, Robert Goldstein, Stewart Martin, Alan Zindman Photographers
Frank Young, Regina Ovesey Creative Directors
David Frieberg, Steven Landsberg Copywriters
Public Service Advertising/School of Visual Arts Agency
1978 President's Campaign for the Handicapped Client

Carlos Martinez is determined to move ahead at Manufacturers Hanover Trust. He has Muscular Dystrophy.

Carlos Martinez was born in Puerto Rico. When his older brother started to fall repeatedly and have difficulty getting up, his parents did not know what was wrong. When the whole family moved to New York, both brothers were checked by doctors. "But," Carlos says, "they didn't have the equipment they have now. There weren't any muscular dystrophy clinics. The disease was difficult to diagnose, and they didn't know what we had until eight years later."

Carlos studied accounting at Long Island University, one of the most accessible schools for the handicapped. The Office of Vocational Rehabilitation sponsored his college education. With the help of a job placement counselor at the Institute of Rehabilitative Medicine, he got the interview which led to his present job as term loan analyst at Manufacturers Hanover Trust. He checks up on the finances of companies seeking loans from the bank for both the national and metropolitan divisions.

Carlos has applied for the management training program. He hopes eventually to hold an executive position in the bank. "Certainly being in a wheelchair hasn't helped me any," says Carlos. "You definitely have to strive harder than the average person."

Carlos does volunteer work for the Muscular Dystrophy Association. Right now he is co-ordinating a special project for the Association's Lower Manhattan Task Group, encouraging people with muscular dystrophy to discuss issues that affect them and to write letters to their representatives urging affirmative action. "I guess our position is analogous to the blacks in the civil rights struggle," says Martinez. "We're fighting to make other people aware that we have the same desires as they do, that we're not really different."

President's Committee on Employment of the Handicapped Washington, D.C. 20210

The School of Visual Arts Public Advertising System

THE 1978 PRESIDENTIAL CAMPAIGN FOR THE HIRING OF THE HANDICAPPED.

At 35, Max Cleland is the youngest man ever to head the Veteran's Administration. Cleland brings to his role as Veteran's Administrator a unique sensitivity to the problems of veterans, disabled veterans in particular. Cleland, a former high school basketball star and college honor student, lost both legs and his right arm in Vietnam.

Once one of the VA's severest critics, today Cleland is trying to change those things that were most frustrating to him. He can empathize readily with the disabled veteran. "About 12 months after I came back," Cleland says, "I really hit bottom. I spent a lot of time asking, 'Why me?' Finally I came to the realization that this is the way life would be, and I would have to move on."

In 1970, just out of the VA hospital, Cleland ran an energetic campaign for Georgia State Senate. As a state senator, he introduced Georgia's first bills to make public buildings accessible to the disabled, and worked closely with then-governor Jimmy Carter on veteran's affairs.

"The VA alone," Cleland says, "employs 38,000 disabled people, including nearly 15,000 disabled veterans. The disabled have the highest unemployment rate among veterans. Primarily, it's a skill problem, a lack of education. That's why we spare no resources in helping the disabled veteran receive the schooling or training he needs."

Cleland suggests that employers focus on the handicapped veteran's abilities, not his disabilities. "People have to see that a handicap may be just an inconvenience. At least we're making a start. The disabled are moving out of the backrooms and into the boardrooms."

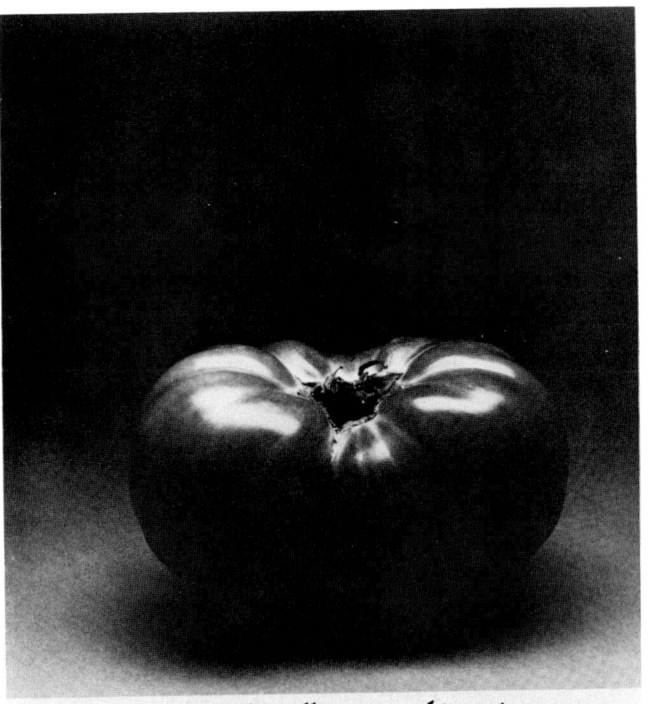

Tuskegee's well-managed tomato.

The tomato grower's cooperative was losing money. About $140,000 a year. Then a team from Tuskegee Institute arrived. They showed the growers not how to grow, but how to <u>manage</u> their business. The next year's profit was $500,000.

An unusual service for a college? Perhaps. But Tuskegee is more than a college. It is a unique national resource. It is 100 years of services such as this, combined with the educational process, which have earned us this reputation.

As we begin our second century, the veil of ignorance is raised, but not yet fully lifted. To cast it off, we need your help. During this, our centennial era, please give.

Invest in a unique national resource.

The Tuskegee Centennial Era Fund.

671 A

It pays to go to Tuskegee.

Every year, about 500 companies come to Tuskegee to recruit our graduates. In the engineering school, for example, there are about five jobs waiting for every graduate. Seven jobs for every veterinarian. Often at higher salaries than those offered to graduates of other schools. Because Tuskegee graduates are better prepared for jobs in the real world.

A Tuskegee education pays for students, obviously. But also for employers. And for the nation. And it's been that way for almost 100 years. Which is one reason why Tuskegee has been called a unique national resource.

As we begin our second century, the veil of ignorance is raised, but not yet fully lifted. To cast it off, we need your help. During this, our centennial era, please give.

Invest in a unique national resource.

The Tuskegee Centennial Era Fund.

B

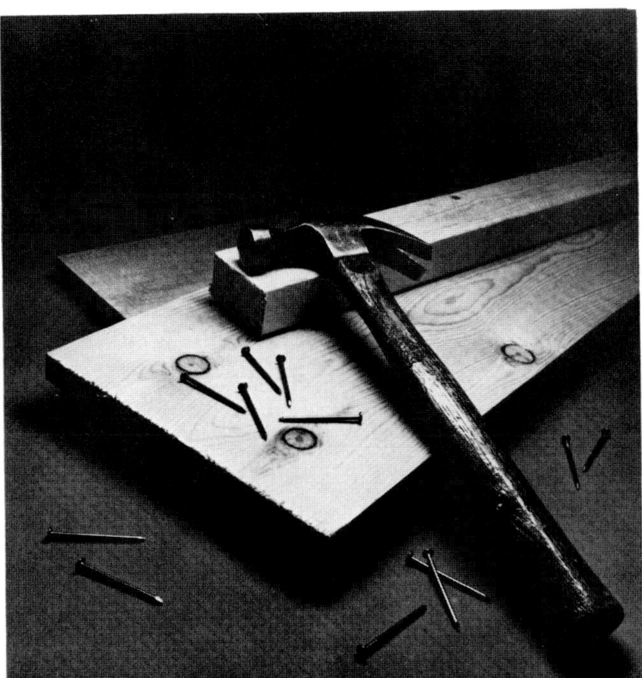

Welfare, Tuskegee style.

Perhaps the most impoverished people in the United States today are the rural poor. Here in Alabama, it was discovered a few years ago that 36% of them not only had no indoor plumbing, they had no outhouses. Welfare is one way to help, but at Tuskegee Institute, we would rather help them to help themselves. We teach them how to build their own houses. And how to earn a decent living.

Why is a college doing this? For one thing, our own students learn by teaching. No other institution anywhere is quite like it. It's been that way for 100 years. And that's just one reason why we've been called a unique national resource.

As we begin our second century, the veil of ignorance is raised, but not yet fully lifted. To cast it off, we need your help. During this, our centennial era, please give.

Invest in a unique national resource.

The Tuskegee Centennial Era Fund.

C

Tuskegee's new peanut.

In many minds, Tuskegee Institute is synonymous with George Washington Carver's pioneering work with the peanut. Nearly 100 years later, Tuskegee has grown far beyond its agricultural beginnings. There are now major programs in engineering, veterinary medicine, science, business and more. But Dr. Carver's work goes on. Today, Tuskegee is working similar miracles with the sweet potato. And, perhaps, developing a new Southeastern wine industry around the native Muscadine grape.

It is programs like this that help make Tuskegee far more than a college. That make it a unique national resource. Who knows? Someday a sweet potato farmer may be president.

As we begin our second century, the veil of ignorance is raised, but not yet fully lifted. To cast it off, we need your help. During this, our centennial era, please give.

Invest in a unique national resource.

The Tuskegee Centennial Era Fund.

D

671 A-D
Ozzie Hawkins Art Director
Miguel Martin Photographer
Bill Irvine Copywriter
J. Walter Thompson Agency
Tuskegee Institute Client

672 A

B

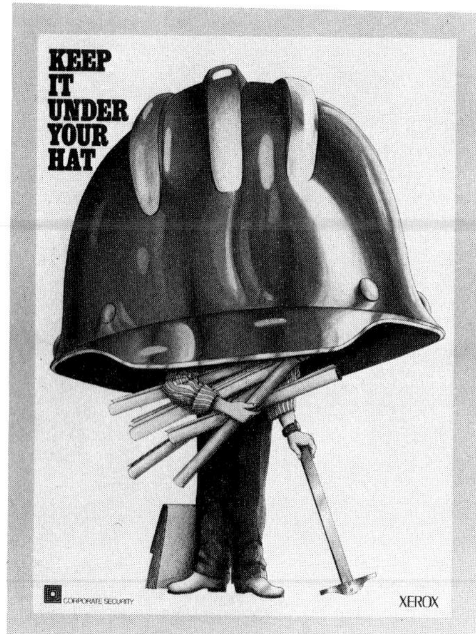

C

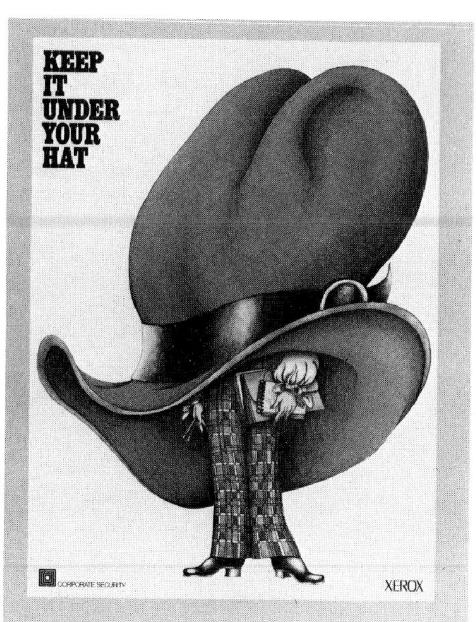

D

E

F

672 A-F
Bob Byrd Illustrator
Ford, Byrne & Associates Studio
Xerox Corporation Client

TELEVISION/FILM

Consumer Commercials

673 A

B

C

673 A-E
David Edwards Art Director
John Sturner Photographer
Stephanie Martin Copywriter
Durona Productions Production House
Sive Associates Agency
Hudepohl Brewing Company Client

D

Hudy
DELIGHT
BEER
Hudepohl Brewing Co. Cinti., Ohio
The Full Flavored
Light Brew From

E

674 A

B

C

674 A-E
Frank Burns Art Director
MB Communications, Inc. Agency
Milton Bradley Company Client

D

E

675 A

B

C

D

E

675 A-E
Gregg Snazelle Photographer
Snazelle Films, Inc. Production House
San Francisco Newspaper Agency Agency
San Francisco Chronicle Client

676 A

B

C

676 A-E
George Wyland Art Director
Hamster Films-Paris Production House
Dr. Rudolf Farner, Werbeagentur AG, BSR Agency
Renault S.A. Client

D

E

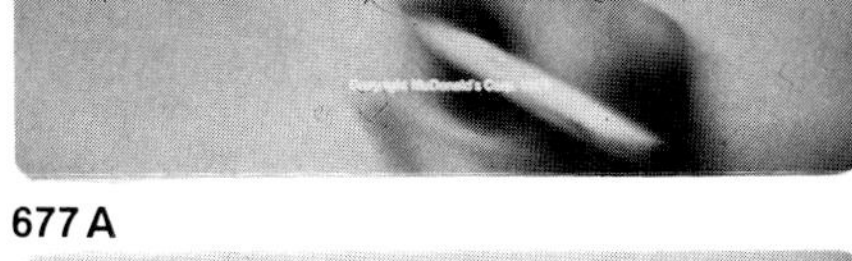

677 A

B

C

D

E

F

G

H

I

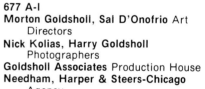

677 A-I
Morton Goldsholl, Sal D'Onofrio Art Directors
Nick Kolias, Harry Goldsholl Photographers
Goldsholl Associates Production House
Needham, Harper & Steers-Chicago Agency
McDonald's Corporation Client

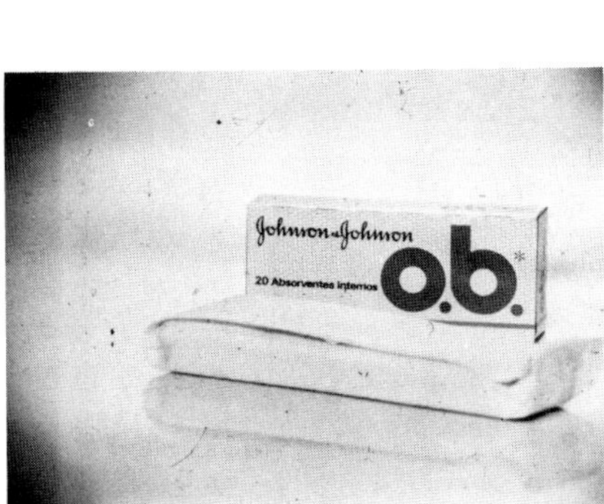
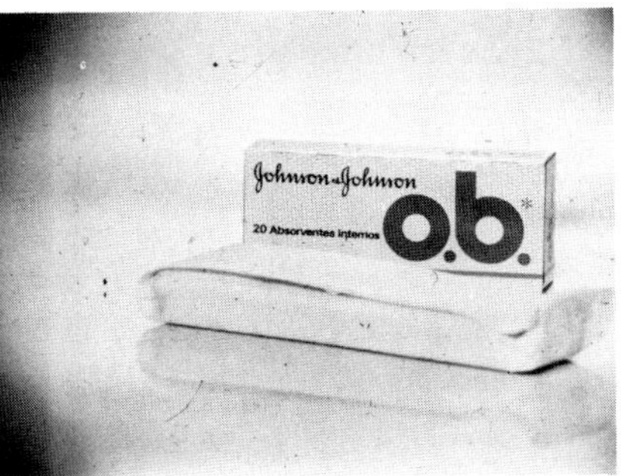

A

B

678 A-E
Jose Zaragoza, Neil Ferreira Art Directors
Fathon Filmes Production House
DPZ Propaganda S/A Agency
Johnson & Johnson Client

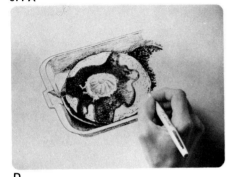

C

D

E

A

B

C

D

E

F

679 A-F
Jose G. Molinari Art Director
Pedro Juan Lopez Photographer
Guastella Film Producers Production House
Badillo/Compton, Inc. Agency
F & M Schaefer Brewing Co. Client

A

B

C

680 A-E
Bob Pearson Art Director
Tray Adair Productions Production House
Case Associates Advertising Ltd. Agency
Spalding Canada Client

D

E

A

B

C

D

E

681 A-E
Susan Wood Art Director
David Dee Director
David Dee Productions, Inc. Production House
BBDO, Inc. Agency
General Electric Client

A

B

C

D

E

682 A-E
Hal Goluboff Art Director
Mathieu, Gerfen & Bresner Agency
Elmhurst Dairies/Le Shake Client

683 A

B

C

684 A-E
Kent Eggleston Art Director
Lew Cady Copy Director
George Koblasa Cinematographer
EUE Screen Gems Production House
Broyles, Allebaugh & Davis Agency
Johns-Manville, Residential Division Client

684 A

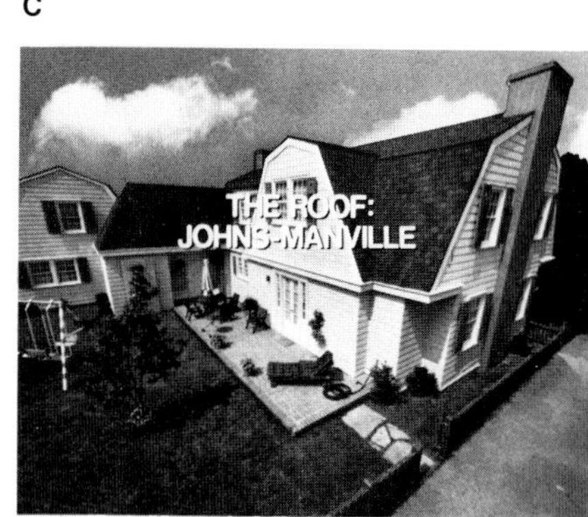

B

685 A

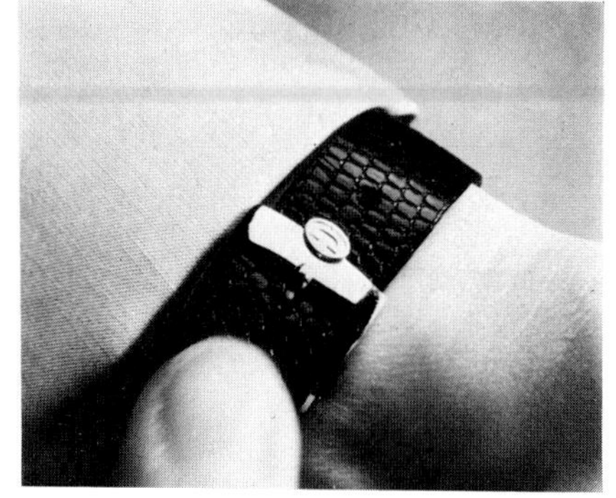

B

C

686 A-E
Norman Grey Art Director
Tom McNeer Copywriter
Tibor Hirsch Director
Bozell & Jacobs-Atlanta Agency
C & S Bank of South Carolina Client

686 A

B

687 A

B

C

D

E

690 A-E
Washington Olivetti, Francisco Petit Art Directors
DPZ Propaganda S/A Agency
Olivetti do Brasil S/A Client

C

D

A public service message
from
and the Newspaper Readership Project
np

E

D

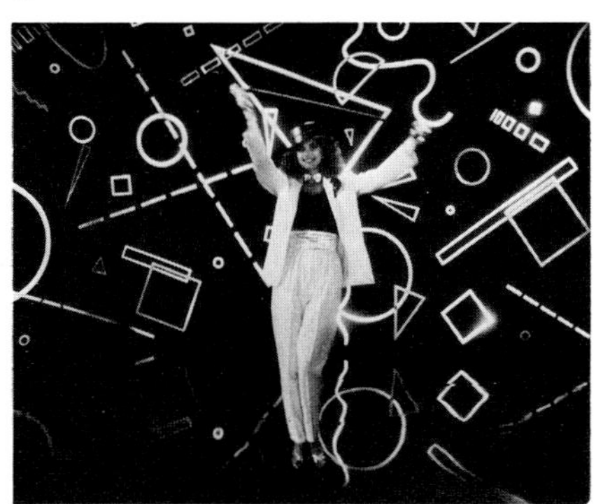

E

692 A-E
Mitchell Brisker Art Director
Richard Corbin, Ross Kelsey, Richard Cohen Photographers
Tom Steele, Pater Sato Illustrators
Duncan Majoribanks, Russ Moony Animators
Robert Abel & Associates, Inc. Production House
Dentsu Advertising Agency
Renown Clothing Client

C

D

E

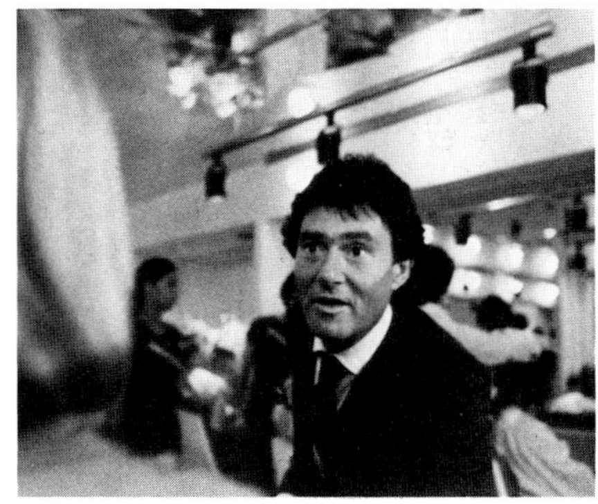

D

E

694 A-E
Len Favara Art Director
Heni Abrams Copywriter
Melvin Sokolsky Director
Sunlight Pictures Production House
Peter Rogers Associates Agency
Vidal Sassoon Client

What should your family do in the dark, America?

LYRICS: Dangle

your

dingle,

dangle your dingle and shine!

It's not out of sight

to be out of sight

anywhere you're going

where there is no light

I dangle my dingle

And I'm not just any dude. When you look beyond

695
Valerie K. Newton Art Director
John Lawlor Photographer
Editors Corner Production House
Imagemakers, Inc. Agency
Dimension Weld Client

696 A

B

C

D

E

F

G

H

696 A-H
Jose G. Molinari Art Director
Pedro Juan Lopez Photographer
Guastella Film Producers Production House
Badillo/Compton, Inc. Agency
Pepsi Cola Bottling Co. Client

697 A

B

C

D

E

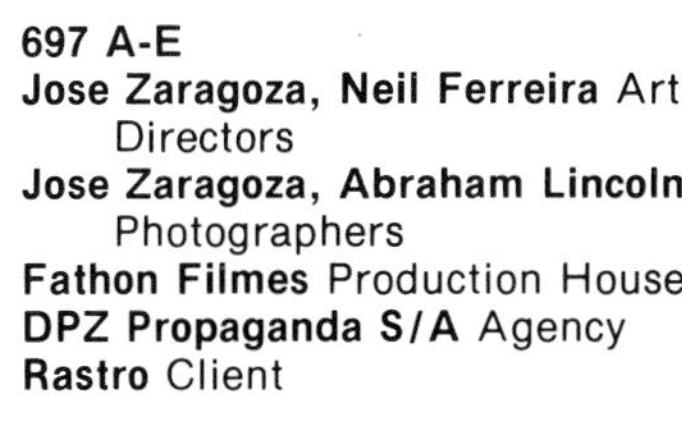

697 A-E
Jose Zaragoza, Neil Ferreira Art Directors
Jose Zaragoza, Abraham Lincoln Photographers
Fathon Filmes Production House
DPZ Propaganda S/A Agency
Rastro Client

698 A

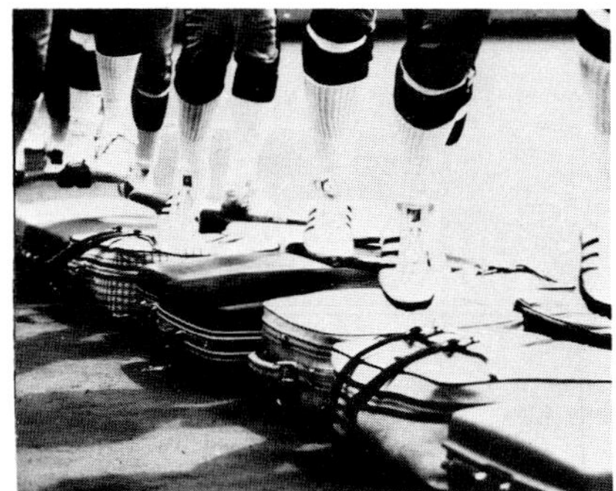

B

C

699 A-E
P. R. Christensen Art Director
Peach, Wemyss, Astor Studio
Brown, Christensen & Associates, Ltd. Agency
Keith Hay Ltd. Client

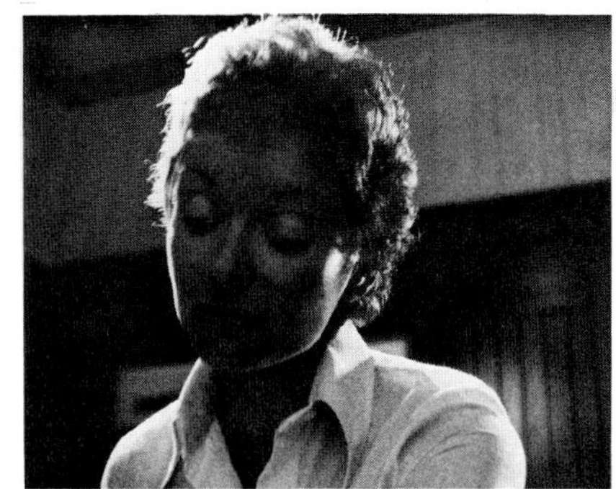

699 A

B

700 A

B

C

701 A-E
Barry Campbell Art Director
Brian Thomson Cinematographer
Ken Takasaki Director
Take One Productions Toronto Production House
F. H. Hayhurst Co. Ltd. Agency
Andres Wines Ltd. Client

B

702 A

B

C

698 A-E
John Kamerer Art Director
J. Walter Thompson Agency
Samsonite Luggage Client

D

E

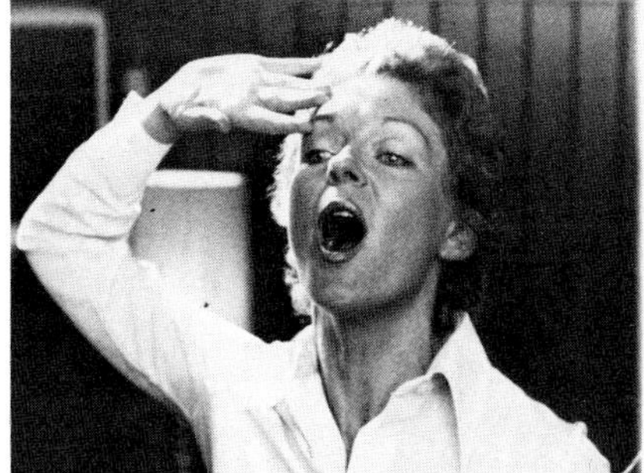

C

D

E

D

E

700 A-E
Ben van Damme Art Director
Bev Roberts Photographer
Julian Graddon Illustrator
Jill Brooks Animator
Ben van Damme, Ron Meijer Designers
Charlie Jenkins Director
Trickfilm Studios Ltd. Studio
McCann-Erickson [Nederland] BV Agency
Van den Bergh & Jurgens BV Client

C

D

E

D

E

702 A-E
John Salzinski, Mike Waterkotte Art Directors
Edit Chicago Studio
Riegert & Sweas, Chicago Agency
WABC Radio, New York Client

703 A

B

C

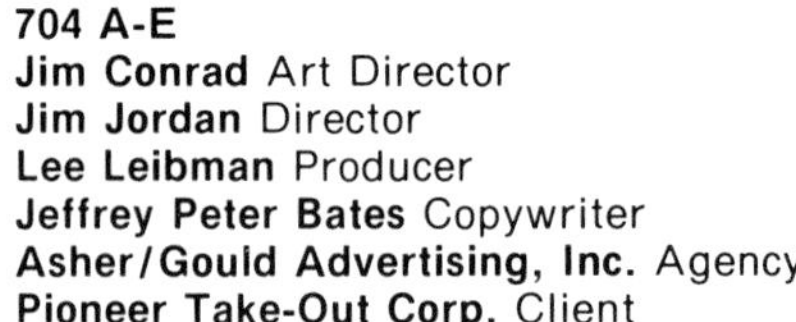

704 A-E
Jim Conrad Art Director
Jim Jordan Director
Lee Leibman Producer
Jeffrey Peter Bates Copywriter
Asher/Gould Advertising, Inc. Agency
Pioneer Take-Out Corp. Client

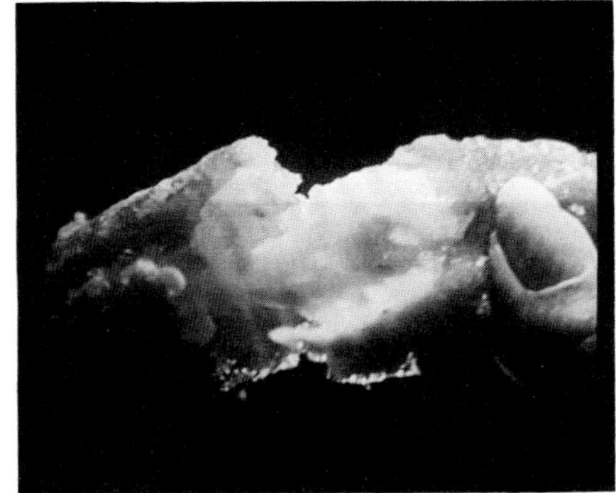

704 A

B

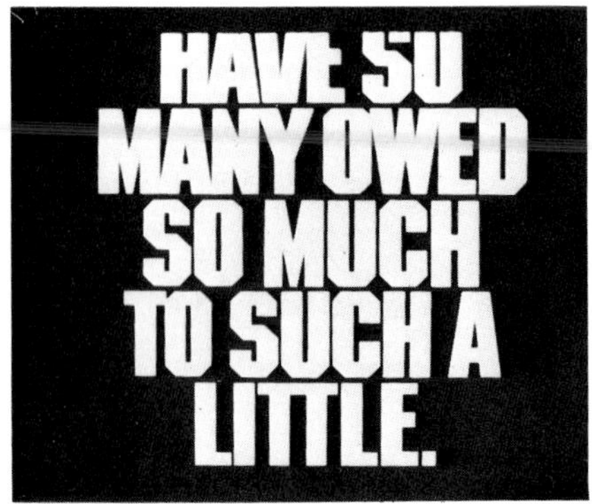

705 A

B

C

706 A-E
Josh Spencer Art Director
Mike Allcock, Bob Brown Illustrators
James Garrett and Partners Studio
J. Walter Thompson SA Agency
Combined Foods Client

706 A

B

707 A

B

C

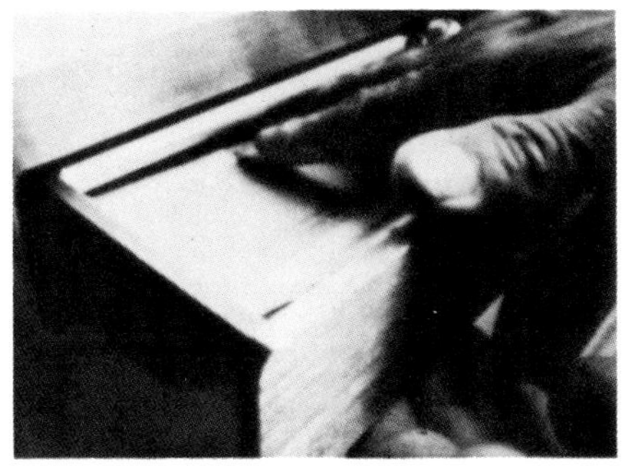

D

E

703 A-E
John Porter Art Director
Bob Fugate Copywriter
Wilson-Griak/Minneapolis Production House
Campbell-Mithun Agency
Northwestern Banks Client

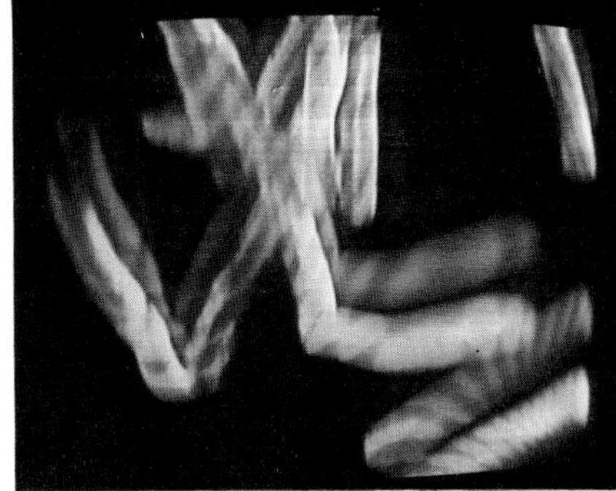

C

D

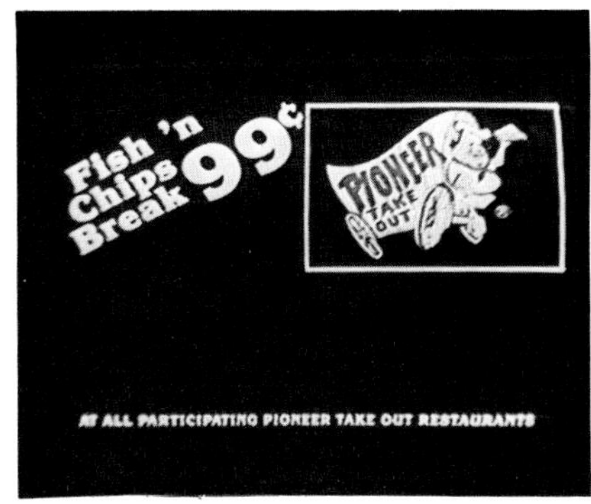

E

D

E

705 A-E
Mark Simkins Art Director
Chris Marrington Copywriter
Grey-Phillips, Bunton, Mundel & Blake Agency
Bristol Myers [Pty] Ltd. Client

C

D

E

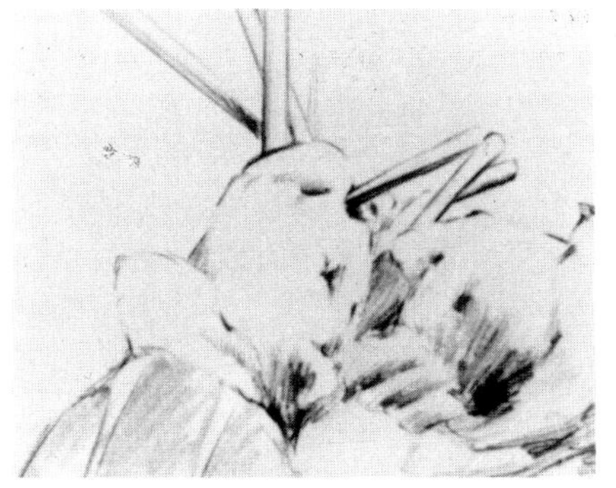

D

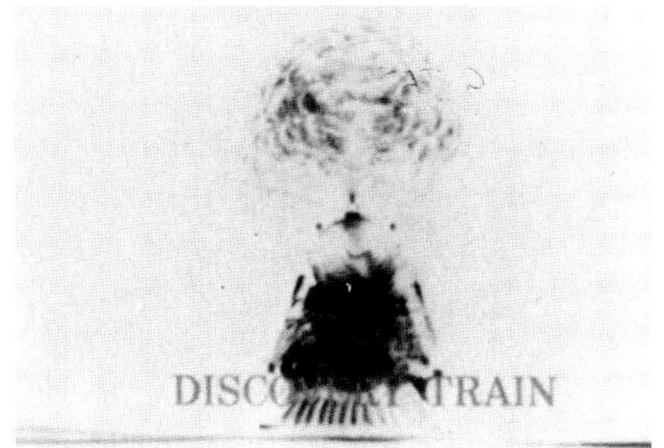

E

707 A-E
Bruce Dowad Art Director
Vickers & Benson Ltd. Agency
National Museums of Canada Client

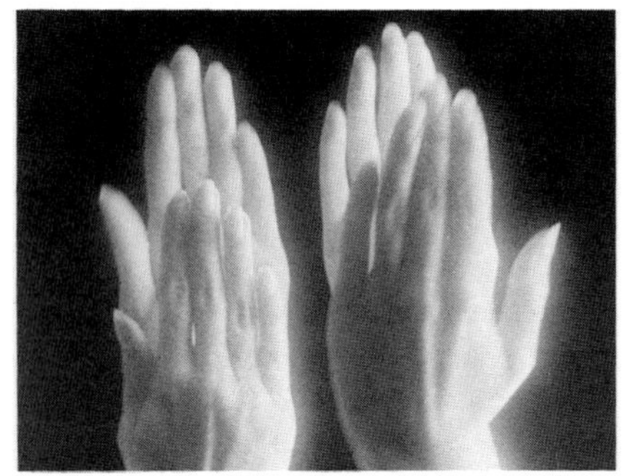

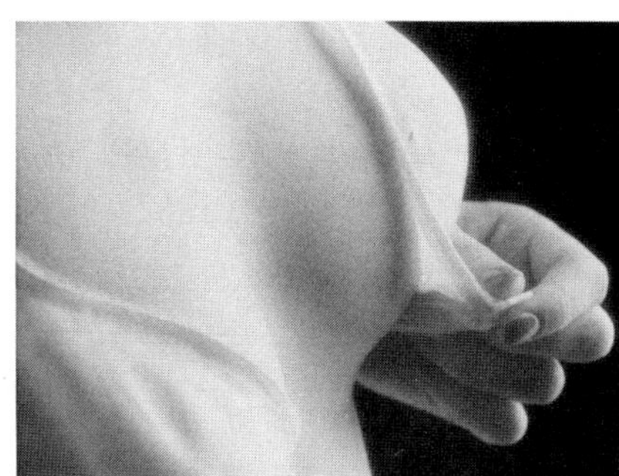

708 A B C

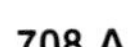

D

708 A-E
Dieter F. Kaufmann Art Director
Bob Lyons Director
Syd Kessler Music
Rabko Productions Production House
Anderson Advertising Agency
Lovable Bra Company Ltd. Client

E

709 A B C

D

E

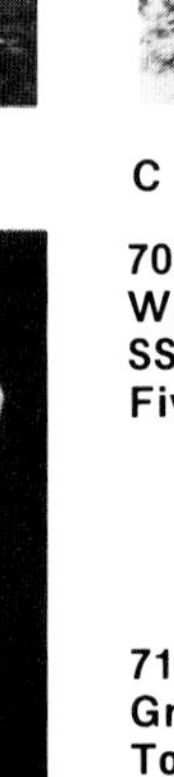

709 A-E
Warwick Keene Art Director
SSC&B: Lintas South Africa Agency
Five Roses Tea Client

711 A-F
Grace Kent Sage Art Director
Tony Brooke Photographer
Richard Merrell Designer
Harrison Productions Production House
Grace Kent Sage Advertising Agency
El Greco Shoes Client

710 A

B

C

D

710 A-E
Mark Howard, Syd Goldberg Art Directors
Dave Bruce, Peter Longauer, Mark Howard Animators
Mark Howard, Syd Goldberg Designers
Howard Graphics Inc. Studio
MCI Direct Marketing Agency
Rolling Stone Client

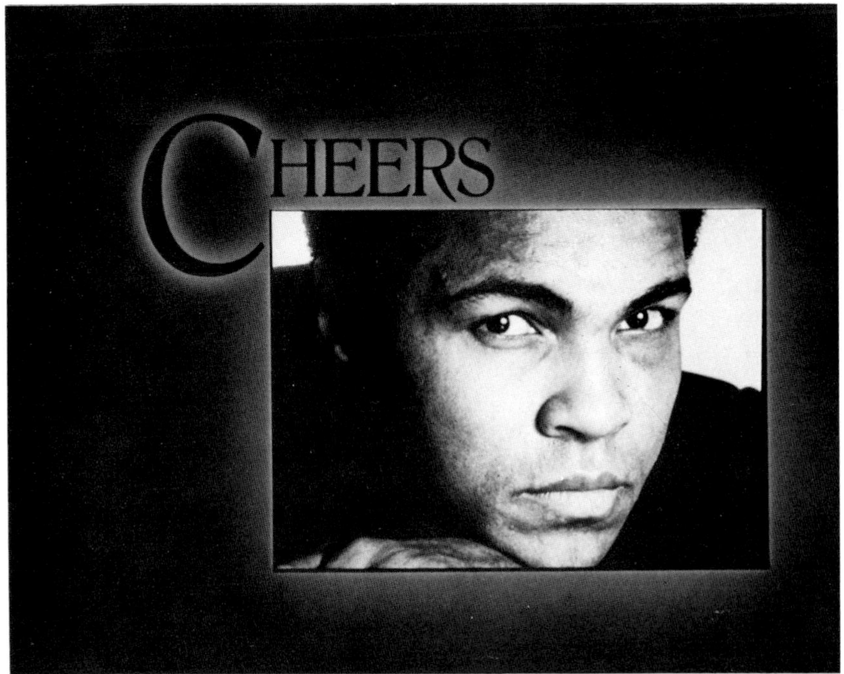

E

711 A

B

C

D

E

F

712 A

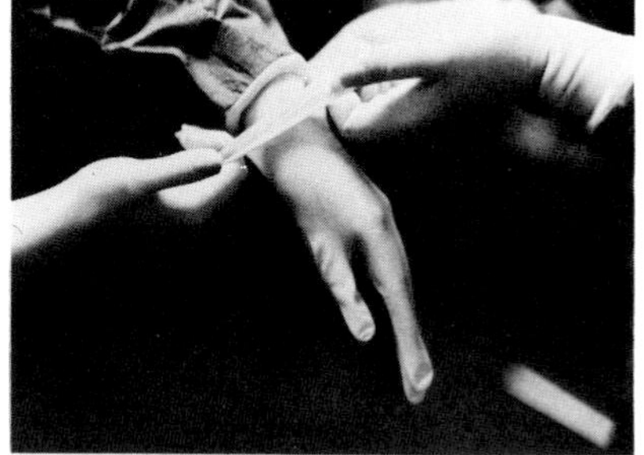

B

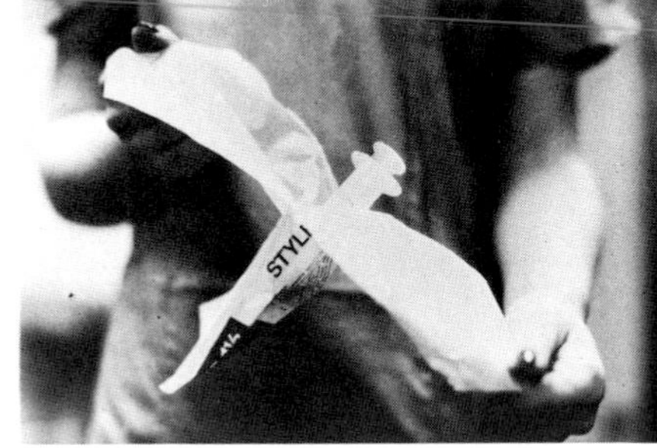

C

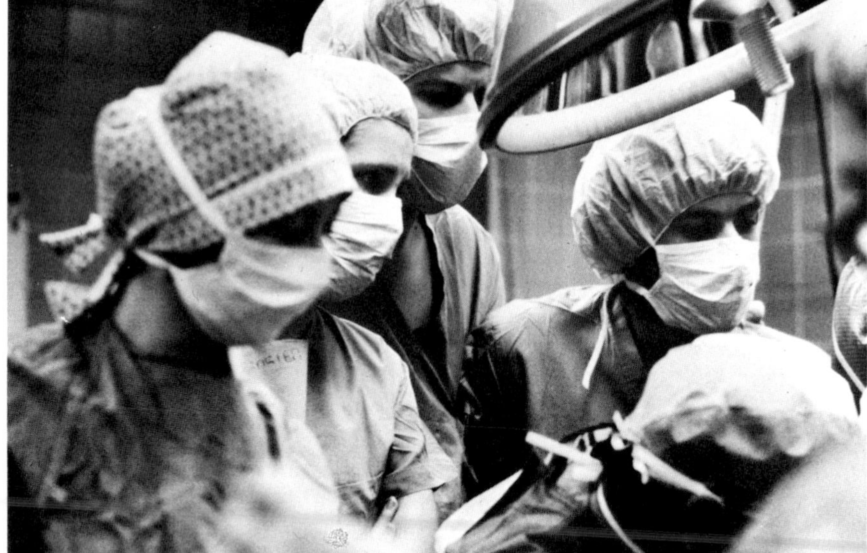

D

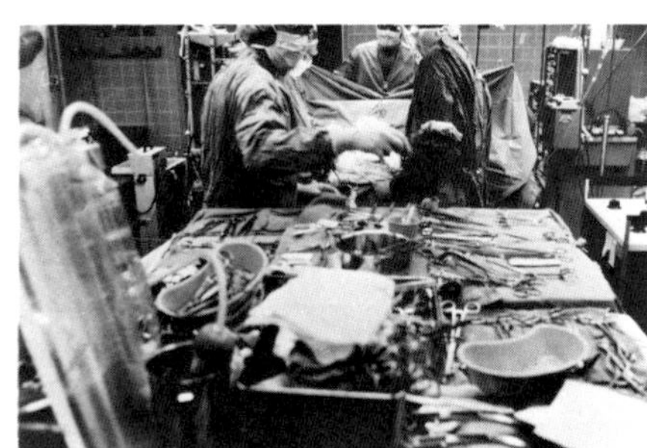

E

712 A-E
Kerry Bierman Art Director
Joe Sterling Photographer
Hal Rein Animator
Teletronics, Inc. Studio
American Hospital Supply Corp Client

713
Roger Flint Art Director
Lewis Schwartzberg Photographer
Eric Vose Illustrator
Brian Shepard Animator
Roger Flint Productions Production House
K-EARTH Radio Client

713

Consumer Campaigns

714 A

B

C

D

E

F

G

H

I

J

714 A-J
Rick Cowan Art Director
Cockfield Brown & Company Agency
Air Canada Client

715 A

B

C

D

E

F

G

H

715 A-H
Marvin Fireman Art Director
James Lawson Copywriter
Barbara Barrow Producer
Fucci Stone Productions Production House
Doremus & Company Agency
East River Savings Bank Client

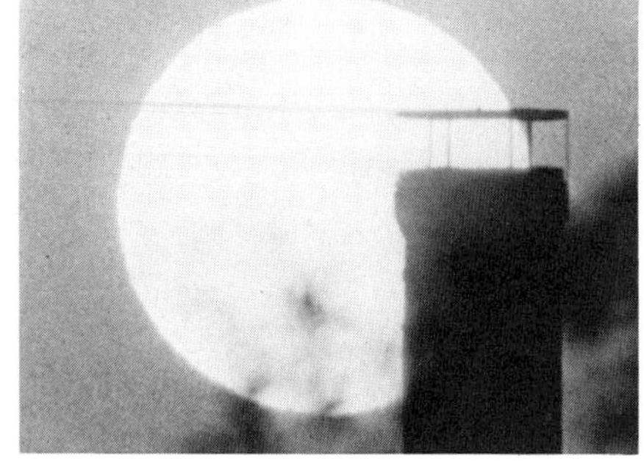

716 A

B

C

D

E

716 A-E
Don Harbor Art Director
Bruce Mansfield Copywriter
Jayan Film Productions Production House
Lawler Ballard Little Agency
Norfolk Redevelopment & Housing Authority Client

717 A

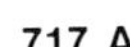

B

C

D

E

F

G

H

I

J

K

L

M

717 A-M
Bruce Dowad Art Director
Ousama Rawi Director
Candy Conacher Producer
Rabko Productions Production House
Vickers & Benson Ltd. Agency
Master Charge Client

718 A

B

718 A-O
Frank Kirk Art Director
Bob Cox Creative Director
Peter Murphy Copywriter
Vera Samama Producer
Jenkins-Covington Production House
Needham, Harper & Steers Advertising, Inc. Agency
American Honda Motor Company, Inc. Client

F

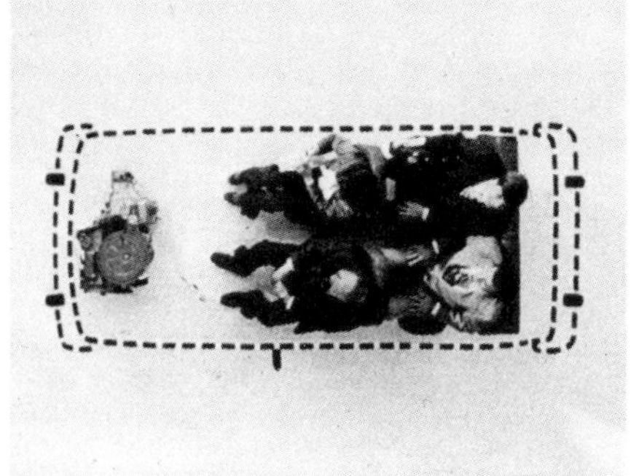

G

K

L

719 A

B

C

720 A-E
Jose Zaragoza, Neil Ferreira Art Directors
Cena Filmes Production House
DPZ Propaganda S/A Agency
Walita Electro Domesticos Ltda. Client

720 A

B

C

D

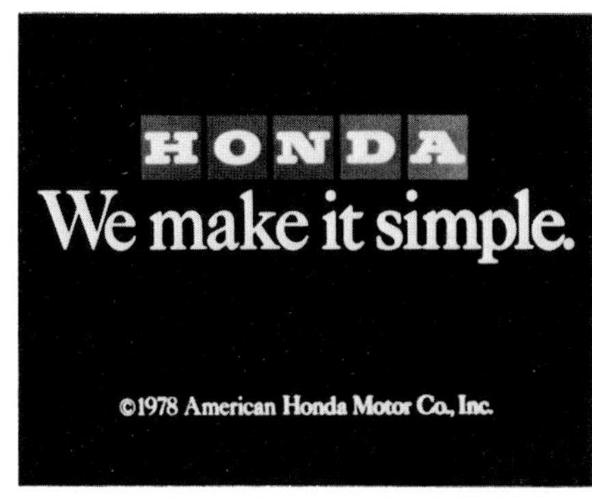

E

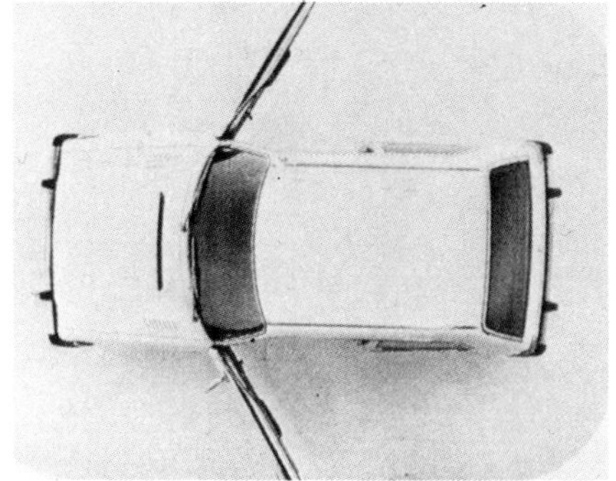

H

I

HONDA
We make it simple.
©1978 American Honda Motor Co., Inc.

J

M

N

O

D

E

719 A-E
Hal Goluboff Art Director
Mathieu, Gerfen & Bresner Agency
Great Waters of France/Perrier Client

C

D

E

Public Service Commercials

721 A-C
Richard Brown Art Director
Andreas Zahler Director
Susan MacMurchy Copywriter
Jenkins-Covington Production House
D'Arcy, MacManus & Masius Agency
National Guard Client

721 A

B

C

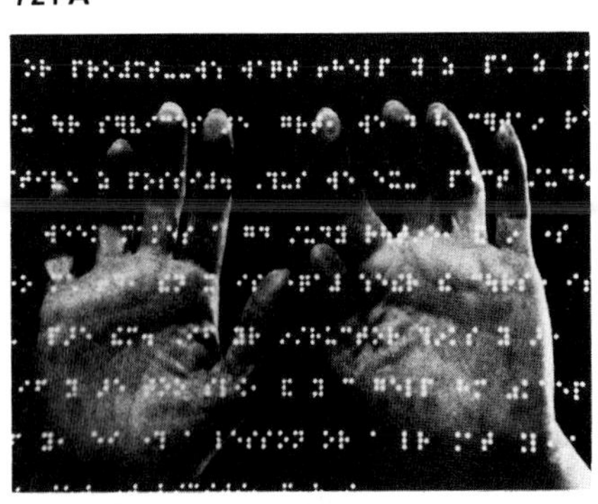
722 A

B

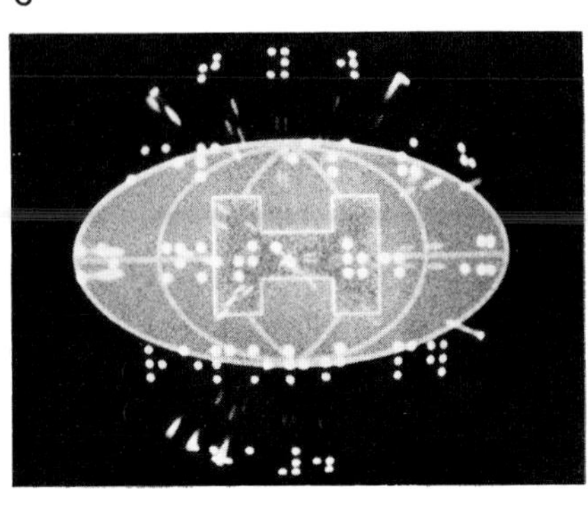
C

722 A-E
Millie Goldsholl Art Director
Harry Goldsholl Cameraman
John Follmer, Marie Cenkner Illustrators
Hugh Valentine Animation
Goldsholl Associates Production House
Hadley School for the Blind Client

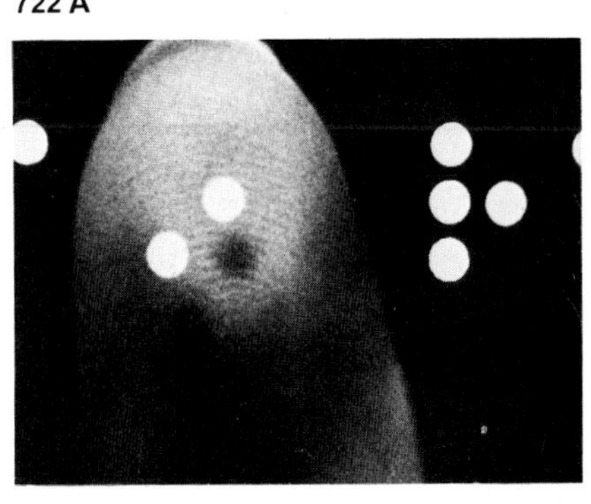
D

E

723 A-C
Reuben V. Valdez Art Director
Albuquerque Public Schools Client

723 A

B

C

724 A

B

C

D

E

724 A-E
Deborah Addison Art Director
Tom Trahan Photographer
Al Buono Copywriter
Holly Hartz Producer
"F" Troop Productions Production House
W. B. Doner & Company Agency
YMCA Client

(BACKGROUND SFX: SCREECHING SIREN, SCREAM)
ANNCR: This Memorial Day (July 4, Labor Day, Weekend) is going to be a real fun weekend.

(SFX: SQUEAL THEN BUMP OF A BUMPER CAR AND LAUGH, MUSIC)
Everybody's going to be anxious to get where they're going.

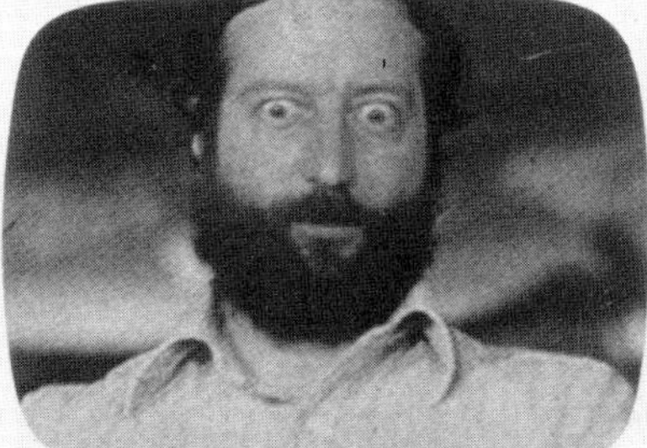

Some people will drink a little too much.
(SFX: BUMP)

Others will be just totally fed up.
(SFX: BUMP)

This Memorial Day (July 4, Labor day, Weekend) Drive seriously.

Don't get bumped off.

725

725
Bill Lemorande Art Director
Lemorande Production Co. Production House
Governor's Office of Highway Safety Client

726 A

B

STOP
Stop at the stopsign.

C

D

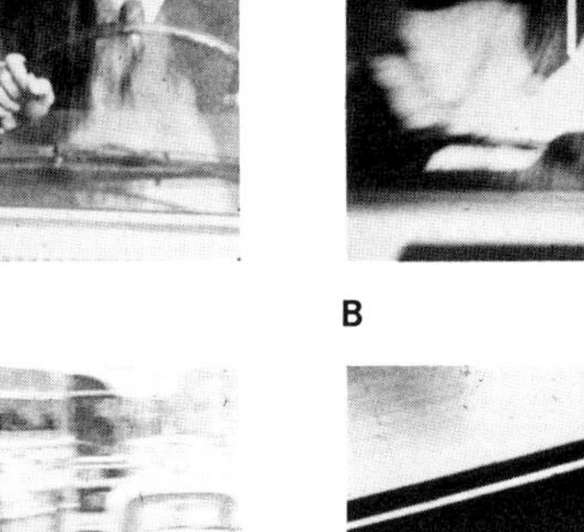

E

F

G

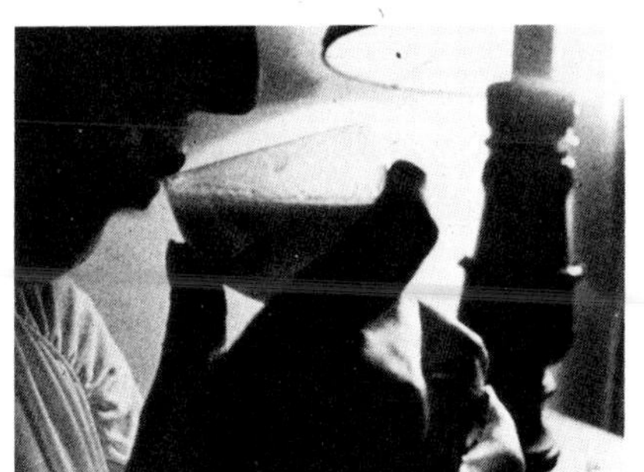

H

I

J

K

L

M

N

726 A-N
Francisco Petit, Washington Olivetto Art Directors
DPZ Propaganda S/A Agency
Comp. de Engenharia de Trafego Client

727 A

B

C

D

E

727 A-E
T. Flynn Art Director
Mike Jones Animator
Bajus-Jones Production House
Kircher, Helton & Collett, Inc. Agency
Gem City Savings Client

728 A

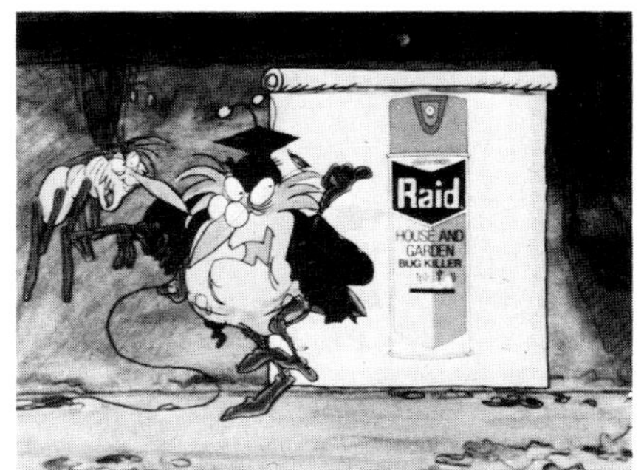

B

C

D

E

728 A-E
Peter Weis Art Director
Foote, Cone & Belding Agency
S. C. Johnson and Son, Ltd. Client

Show Openings/TV Graphics

729
Beverly Littlewood Art Director
Roy Ruan Designer
NBC NewsCenter 4 Client

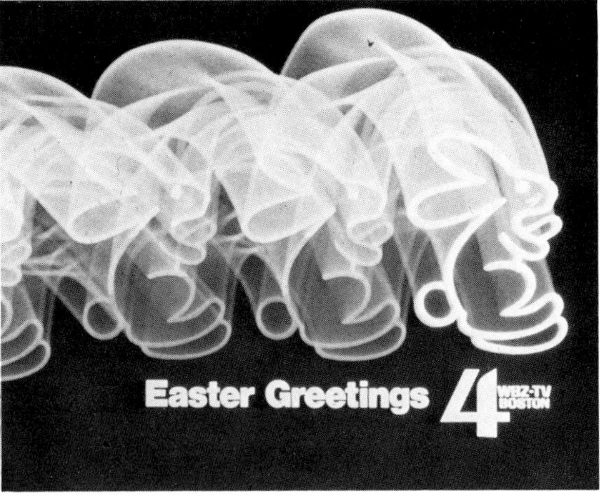

730
Ernest Legee Art Director
WBZ-TV Graphics Department Studio
WBZ-TV Client

731
Beverly Littlewood Art Director
James Gayles Illustrator
NBC NewsCenter 4 Client

732
Beverly Littlewood Art Director
Gary Teixeira Designer
NBC NewsCenter 4 Client

733
Lee Stausland Art Director
James Santiago Photographer
Network News Graphics Agency
The Today Show Client

734
Beverly Littlewood Art Director
Roy Ruan Designer
NBC NewsCenter 4 Client

735
Beverly Littlewood Art Director
Martin Geller Illustrator
NBC NewsCenter 4 Client

736
Beverly Littlewood Art Director
Eara Jordon Designer
NBC NewsCenter 4 Client

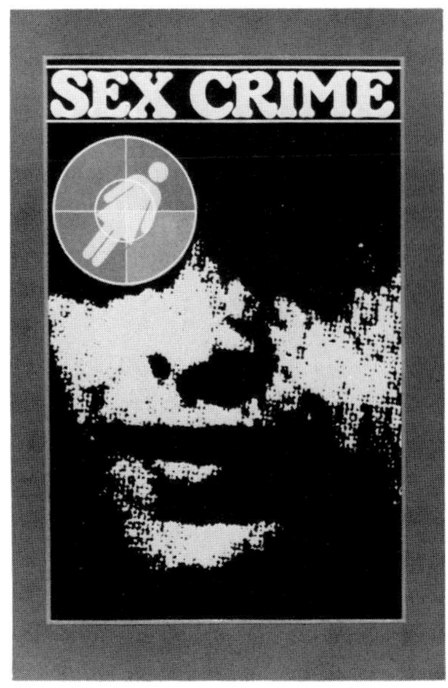

737
Milo Hess Art Director
WCBS-TV News Client

738
Gil Cowley Art Director
WCBS-TV News Client

739
Kenneth Dyball Art Director
WCBS-TV Client

740
Percy Powers Art Director
WLBT-TV Client

741
Jim Denney Art Director
WTAE-TV Client

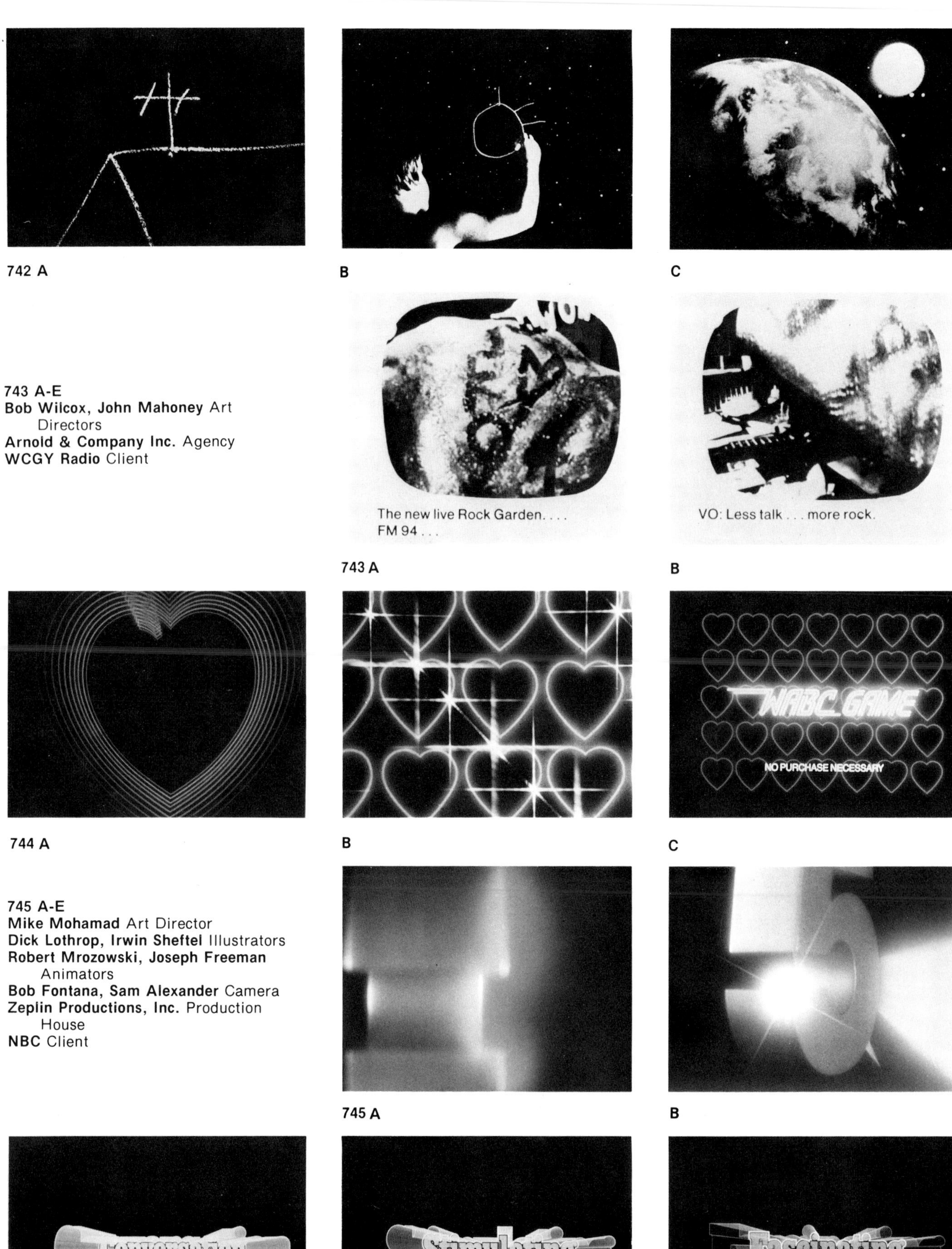

742 A
B
C

743 A-E
Bob Wilcox, John Mahoney Art Directors
Arnold & Company Inc. Agency
WCGY Radio Client

743 A
B

744 A
B
C

745 A-E
Mike Mohamad Art Director
Dick Lothrop, Irwin Sheftel Illustrators
Robert Mrozowski, Joseph Freeman Animators
Bob Fontana, Sam Alexander Camera
Zeplin Productions, Inc. Production House
NBC Client

745 A
B

746 A
B
C

D

E

742 A-E
Saul Bass Art Director
Saul Bass Films Production House
Bass/Yager & Associates Agency
NBC, Greg Garrison Productions Client

So . . .

C

you could win your very own imitation suede parrot . . .

D

DISC JOCKEY: Hey kids . . . if you're the 85th caller to Wild Man Steve . . .

E

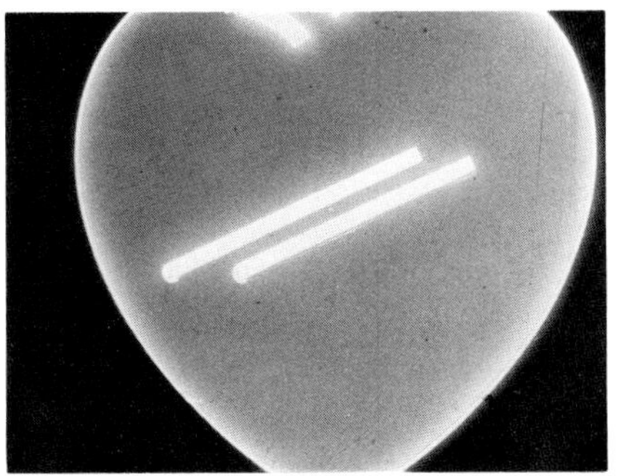

D

E

744 A-E
Rebecca Singer Art Director
Rebecca Singer Studio Inc. Studio
WABC Music Radio 77 Client

C

D

E

D

E

746 A-E
Rebecca Singer, Joanne Arnette Art Directors
Richard Phillips Copywriter
Rebecca Singer Studio, Inc. Studio
Young & Rubicam Agency
People Magazine Client

747 A

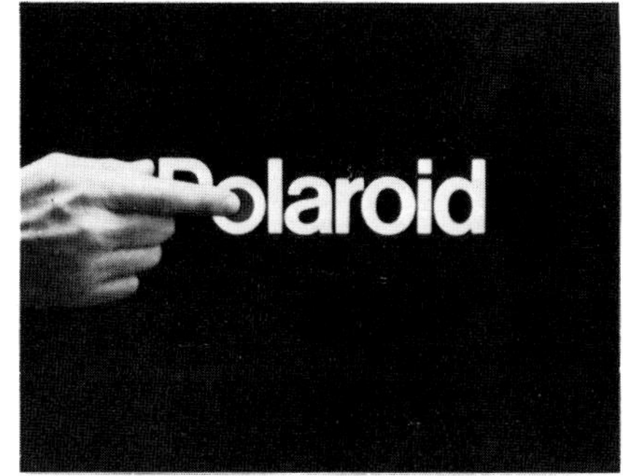

B

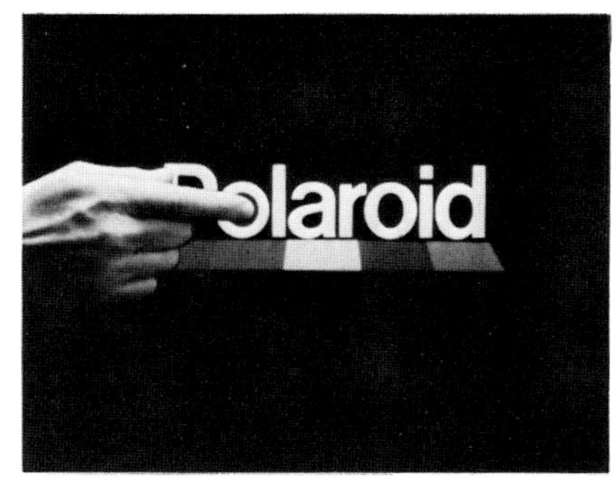

C

D

E

747 A-E
Charles Abrams Art Director
Image Factory Production House
Doyle Dane Bernbach Agency
Polaroid Corporation Client

748 A

B

C

D

E

748 A-E
Elinor Bunin Art Director
John Carter & Assoc. Film Editor
Elinor Bunin Productions, Inc. Production House
Airtime, Inc. Client

749

749
Richard W. Deardorff Art Director
Overlock Howe & Company Agency
KETC Channel 9, Public Television/St. Louis Agency

CONCEPT/DESIGN

Art/Illustration

750
John E. Fitzgerald, Iska Rothovius Art Directors
Daniel Schwartz Illustrator
New York Telephone Client

751
Frank De Vino Art Director
Samuel Bak Illustrator
Lynda Chyhai Designer
Omni Publications Client

FICTION

It was a prime corpus, complete with reconditioned heart, lungs, and enriched glands.

BODY GAME

BY ROBERT SHECKLEY

Dear Senator, I'm writing to you because you are our senior Senator and because you said at election time last year that you were our servant and that we should write to you immediately if we had any grievances. You were very definite, and you even got a little huffy and said it was actually a citizen's duty to write to his Senator and let him know what was going on. Well, Senator, I thought about that a lot. Naturally, I didn't believe the part about you being our servant, what with you earning 50 times, or 100 times, or for all I know 1000 times what we do. But the thing about writing to you, which you were so insistent on, that part got to me.

Your words puzzled me at first when you said we should let you know what was going on here. I mean, you were raised in this city same as me, and a man would have to be blind, deaf, dumb, and stupid not to know what's happening here. But I decided that I was being unfair; you've got to spend a lot of your time in Washington, so maybe you are out

PAINTING BY SAMUEL BAK

77

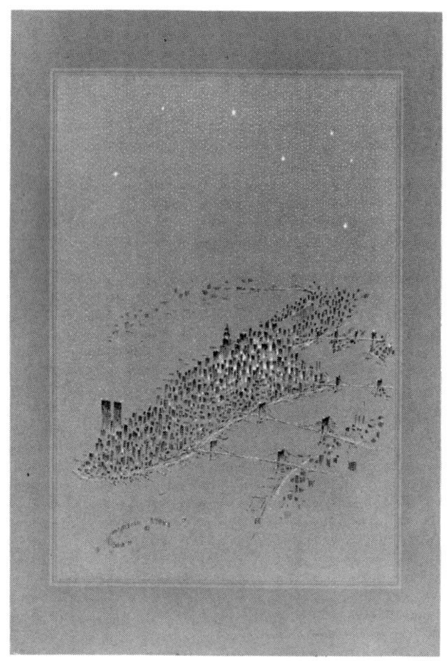

752
Brice Belisle Art Director
Redler, Inc. Client

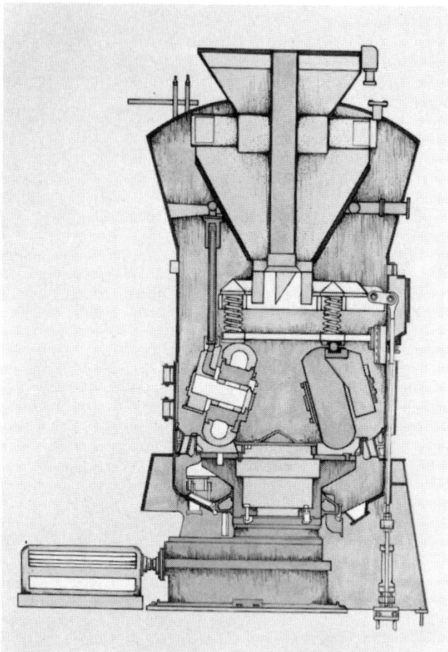

753
Diana Bruner Art Director
Babcock & Wilcox Corp. Client

Superscope, Inc. 1978 Annual Report

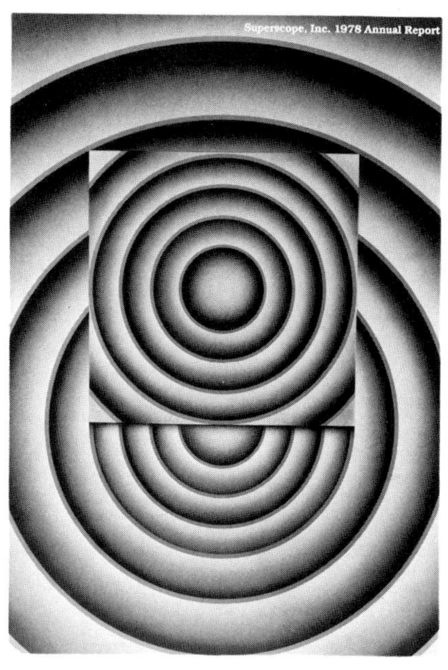

754
Dennis S. Juett Art Director
Bill Imhoff Illustrator
Tara Thomas Copywriter
Dennis S. Juett & Associates, Inc. Agency
Superscope, Inc. Client

755
Eileen Hedy Schultz Art Director
Bob Peak Illustrator
The Society of Illustrators Client

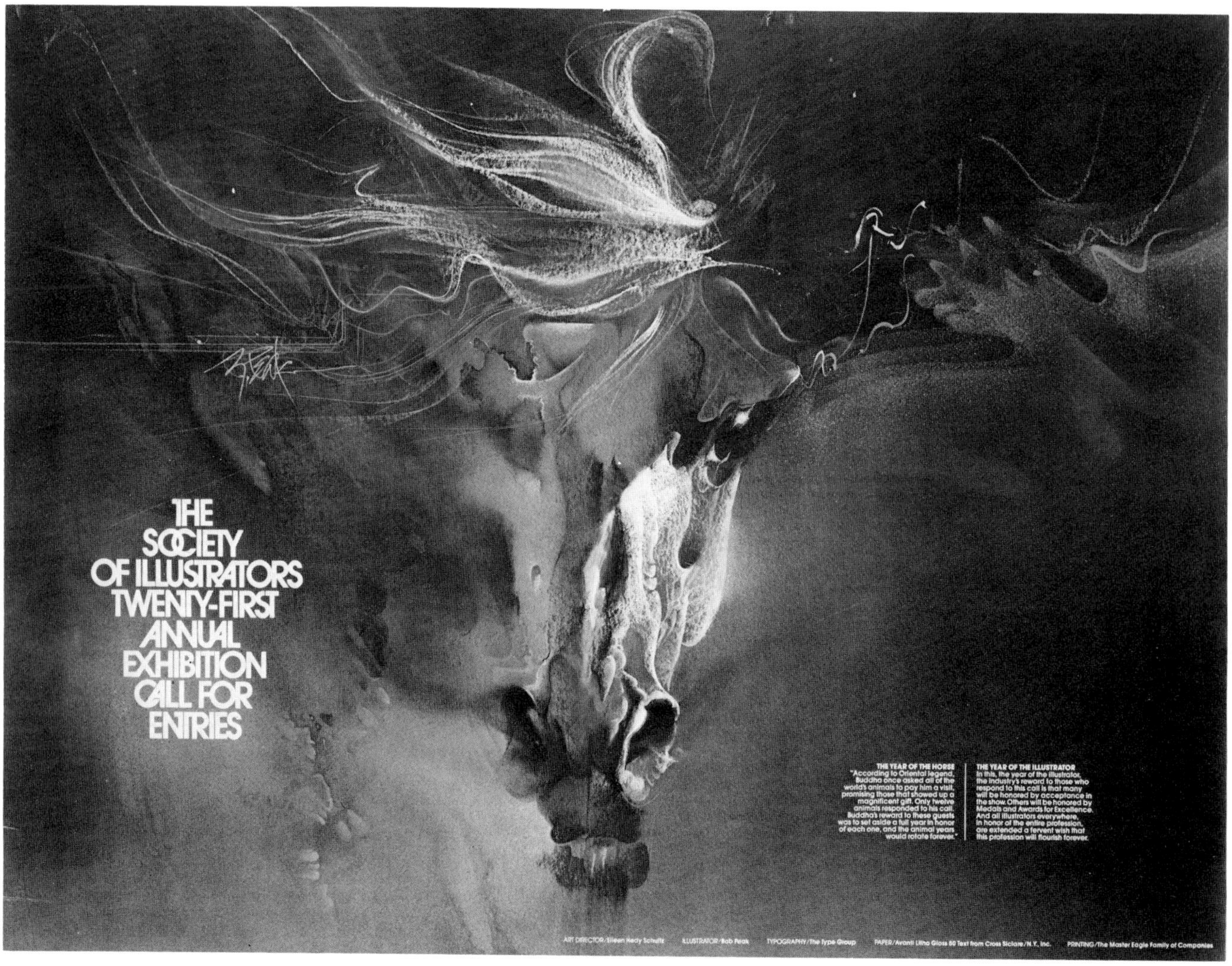

THE SOCIETY OF ILLUSTRATORS TWENTY-FIRST ANNUAL EXHIBITION CALL FOR ENTRIES
THE YEAR OF THE HORSE
"According to Oriental legend, Buddha once asked all of the world's animals to pay him a visit, promising those that showed up a magnificent gift. Only twelve animals responded to his call. Buddha's reward to these guests was to set aside a full year in honor of each one, and the animal years would rotate forever."
THE YEAR OF THE ILLUSTRATOR
In this, the year of the illustrator, the industry's reward to those who respond to this call is that many will be honored by acceptance in the show. Others will be honored by Medals and Awards for Excellence. And all illustrators everywhere, in honor of the entire profession, are extended a fervent wish that this profession will flourish forever.
ART DIRECTOR/Eileen Hedy Schultz
ILLUSTRATOR/Bob Peak
TYPOGRAPHY/The Type Group
PAPER/Avanti Litho Gloss 80 Text from Cross Siclare/N.Y., Inc.
PRINTING/The Master Eagle Family of Companies

756
Dean Gerrie Art Director
Greg Fulton Photographer
Robert Blissmer Designer
Dean Gerrie Design Agency
Ratel Electronics Client

THESE ARE THE ARMIES OF THE NIGHT.
They are 100,000 strong. They outnumber the cops five to one.
They could run New York City. Tonight they're all out to get the Warriors.
THE WARRIORS
Paramount Pictures Presents A Lawrence Gordon Production "THE WARRIORS"
Executive Producer Frank Marshall Based Upon the Novel by Sol Yurick
Screenplay by David Shaber and Walter Hill Produced by Lawrence Gordon
R RESTRICTED
Directed by Walter Hill
Read the Dell Book

757
Ed Brodkin Art Director
Ed Harridsleff Designer
David Jarvis Illustrator
Diener Hauser Bates Agency
Paramount Pictures Client

758
Heather Cooper, Robert Burns Art Directors
Heather Cooper Illustrator
Burns, Cooper, Hynes Limited Agency
Yardley of London Limited Client

THE DEVIL & BILLY MARKHAM

By Shel Silverstein

The Devil walked into Linebaugh's on a rainy Nashville night
While the lost souls sat and sipped their soup in the sickly yellow neon light.
And the Devil, he looked around the room, then got down on his knees.
He says, "Is there one among you scum who'll roll the dice with me?"
Red, he just strums his guitar, pretending not to hear.
And Eddie, he just looks away and takes another sip of beer.
Vince, he says, "Not me. I'll pass. I've had my share of hell,"
And kept scribbling on a napkin, some song he was sure would sell.
Ronnie just kept whisperin' low to the snuff queen who clutched at his sleeve,
And somebody coughed—and the Devil scoffed—and turned on his heel to leave.
"Hold on," says a voice from the back of the room, " 'fore you walk out that door.
If you're lookin' for some action, friend, well, I've rolled some dice before."
And there stood Billy Markham, he'd been on the scene for years,
Singin' all them raunchy songs that the town didn't want to hear.
He'd been cut and bled a thousand times, and his eyes were wise and sad,
And all his songs were the songs of the street, and all his luck was bad.
"I know you," says Billy Markham, "from many a dark and funky place,
But you always spoke in a different voice and wore a different face.
While me, I've gambled here on Music Row with hustlers and with whores,
And, hell, I ain't afraid to roll them devilish dice of yours."
"Well, then, get down," says the Devil, "just as if you was gonna pray,
And take these dice in your luckless hand and I'll tell you how this game is played.
You get one roll—and you bet your soul—and if you roll *thirteen* you win,
And all the joys of flesh and gold are yours to touch and spend.
But if that thirteen *don't* come up, then kiss your ass goodbye
And will your useless bones to God, 'cause your goddamn soul is *mine!*"
"Thirteen?" says Billy Markham. "Hell, I've played in tougher games.
I've loved ambitious women and I've rode on wheelless trains.
So gimme room, you stinkin' fiend, and let it all unwind
Nobody's ever rolled a thirteen yet, but this just might be the time."
Then Billy Markham, he takes the dice, and the dice feel as heavy as stones.
"They should, they should," the Devil says, " 'cause they're carved from Jesus' bones."
And Billy Markham turns the dice and the dice, they have no spots.
"I'm sorry," says the Devil, "but they're the only dice I got."
"Well, shit," says Billy Markham. "Now, I really don't mean to bitch,
But I never thought I'd stake my roll in a sucker's game like this."
"Well, then, walk off," says the Devil. "Nobody's tied you down."
"Walk off where?" says Billy Markham. "It's the only game in town.
But I just wanna say 'fore I make my play, that if I should chance to lose,
I will this guitar to some would-be star who'll play some honest blues,
Who ain't afraid to sing the words like damn or shit or fuck

ILLUSTRATED BY BRAD HOLLAND

759 A

I've rolled your dice, I've rolled 'em twice. Now I hear my loved ones cry,
And before I play that game again, I'll stay here in hell and fry."
"You sure are a grouch when you wake up," says the Devil, "but don't take it out on me.
In the misty worlds of heaven and hell, Bill, everything's done in threes."
"Well, you can take three kisses of my burning bum," says Billy, layin' back and closing his eyes,
"And I'll piss on your shoe, if ever you come near me again with them flyshit dice."
"Dice? Dice?" says the Devil. "Who said dice? Anybody hear me say dice?
Hey, imp, pour my buddy here a cool glass of water, and throw in a nice big chunk of ice."
"And since when," says Billy, raisin' up, "do you go around handing out gifts,
Except pokes from your burning pitchfork or mouthfuls of boiling shit?"
"Well, it's Christmas," says the Devil, "and all of us down here below,
We sort of celebrate in our own sweet way, and this year *you're* the star of the show.
Why, just last night I was up on earth and I seen that lovers' moon,
And I said to myself, 'Hey, I bet old Billy could use a little bit of poon.' "
"Poon?" says Billy Markham. "Last thing I need is poon.
Talk about gettin' my ashes hauled, hell, I'll be *all* ashes soon."
"*Damn, damn!*" the Devil screams. "He's been too long on the fire.
I told you imps to *fry him slow*, now you gone and burned out his *desire*.
You gotta leave 'em some hope, leave 'em some dreams, so they know what hell is for,
'Cause when a man forgets how sweet love is, well, hell ain't hell no more.
So just to refresh your memory, Billy, we're gonna send you back to earth
And I'll throw in a little Christmas blessin' to remind you what life is worth.
For exactly thirteen hours you can screw who you wanna screw
And there ain't no creature on God's green earth who's gonna say no to you.
While me and all these burning souls and all my imps and fiends,
We're gonna sit down here and watch you on that big twenty-four-inch color screen.
And we'll see each hump you're humping, and we'll hear each grunt you groan,
And we'll laugh at the look upon your face when it's time to come back *home*."
"Well, you're much too kind," Billy Markham says. "And you treat me much too well.
You gonna give me somethin' just to take it back—you sure know how to run a hell.
Well, a game is a game," Billy Markham says, risin' off his bed of coals.
"But what if one *won't* ball me, what if one I want says no?"
"No?" says the Devil. "What if one says no? Ain't nobody gonna say no.
Nobody quits or calls in sick when the Devil calls the show.
Not *man* nor *woman* nor *beast!*" screams the Devil, "and no laters or maybes or buts,
And before one soul says no to you, I'll see these hell gates rust.
But *if* anyone refuses you, I say, anyone you name,
Then you'll be free to stay on earth.
Now get out and play the game!"
Then a flash of light and a thunderclap and Billy's back on earth once more
And the asphalt sings beneath his feet as he weaves toward Music Row.
First he stops at the Exit Inn to seduce the blonde on the door,
Then the RCA receptionist he takes on the office floor.
He nails the waitress down at Mack's, the one with the pear-shaped breasts,
And four of the girls from B.M.I. right on Frances Preston's desk.
He screws his way from M.C.A. to Vanderbilt's ivy walls.
And he pokes everything that giggles or sings or whimpers or wiggles or crawls.
First Debbie, then Polly, then Dotty, then Dolly, then Jeannie, and Jessie, and Jan,
Then Marshall and Sal and that redheaded gal who takes the tickets at Opryland.
Then Hazel and Carla and an ex-wife of Harlan's, then Melva and Marge and Marie,
And three *fat* Gospel singers who all came together in perfect three-part harmony.
And Brenda and Sammy and Sharon and Sandy, Loretta and Buffy and Mae,
And Terri and Lynne at the Holiday Inn and Captain Midnight's fiancée.
Then Sherry and Rita, Diane and Anita, Olivia, Emmy and Jean,
And Donna and Kay down at Elliston Place—right there in the pinto beans.
He crashes a session in Studio B, where he humps both Janet and June
On John Gimble's fiddle, right in the middle of a Porter Wagoner tune.

B

"Hey, it's easy to talk of savin' ass," says Billy, "forgiveness is easy to say,
But when the shame burns worse than Hades' fires—how do you talk *that* away?"
"Shame?" laughs the Devil. "She's only a woman—she did what she had to do.
And right or wrong, she needs no curse from a hypocrite lame like you. . . .
She shall rule with me in this Kingdom of Flame, she shall sit next to me on my throne,
While you live with the truth—that the Devil's heart has more pity than your own."
"Hey, wait a minute," says Billy Markham. "I can't believe what you just said,
You givin' me this whole philosophy shit just 'cause you like the way she gave you head.
Why, you poor closet romantic, that chick was suckin' for her *life*.
Just wait see what kinda head you get *after* you make her your wife."
Or is it the sound of the wedding feast that the demons below have begun?
As the Devil, he sits with his betrothed and they pledge their love in the steam,
While halfway up the silken cord,
Billy Markham *screams!*

Billy Markham's Wedding

The trumpets of hell have sounded the word like a screeching clarion call.
The trumpets of hell have sounded the word and the word has been heard by all.
The trumpets of hell have sounded the word and it reaches the heavenly skies,

"In Hell," shouts the Devil, "that's blasphemy! I should burn you to dust where you stand,
But the venom you're carryin' in your heart, that's torture enough for any man.
So get your ass up that silken rope, climb back to your promised land,
And hold your illusions of momma and daughter tight in your sweatin' hand.
But you'll see that they're just bitches like she, and you'll scream when you find it's true,
But stay up there and scream to God—Hell's gates are *closed* to you."
And Billy Markham, clutching his loves, climbs upward toward the skies,
And is it the sharp night wind that brings the tears to Billy's eyes?
Or is it the swirling sulphur smoke or the bright glare of the sun?
Come angels, come demons, come half-breeds, too, the Devil is taking a bride,
And out of the Pearly Gates they come in a file two by two,
For when the Devil takes a bride, there's none that dares refuse.
And Jesus himself, he leads the way down through the starless night,
With Virgin Mary at his left side and Joseph on his right.
And then comes Adam and then comes Eve and the saints move close behind
And all the gentle and all the good, in an endless column they wind.
Down, down to the pits of hell, down from the heavens they sift
Like fallen stars to a blood-red sea, each bearing the Devil a gift.

C

759 A

THE DEVIL & BILLY MARKHAM

By Shel Silverstein

The Devil walked into Linebaugh's on a rainy Nashville night
While the lost souls sat and sipped their soup in the sickly yellow neon light.
And the Devil, he looked around the room, then got down on his knees.
He says, "Is there one among you scum who'll roll the dice with me?"
Red, he just strums his guitar, pretending not to hear.
And Eddie, he just looks away and takes another sip of beer.
Vince, he says, "Not me. I'll pass. I've had my share of hell,"
And kept scribbling on a napkin, some song he was sure would sell.
Ronnie just kept whisperin' low to the snuff queen who clutched at his sleeve.
And somebody coughed—and the Devil scoffed—and turned on his heel to leave.
"Hold on," says a voice from the back of the room, " 'fore you walk out that door.
If you're lookin' for some action, friend, well, I've rolled some dice before."
And there stood Billy Markham, he'd been on the scene for years,
Singin' all them raunchy songs that the town didn't want to hear.
He'd been cut and bled a thousand times, and his eyes were wise and sad,
And all his songs were the songs of the street, and all his luck was bad.
"I know you," says Billy Markham, "from many a dark and funky place,
But you always spoke in a different voice and wore a different face.
While me, I've gambled here on Music Row with hustlers and with whores,
And, hell, I ain't afraid to roll them devilish dice of yours."
"Well, then, get down," says the Devil, "just as if you was gonna pray,
And take these dice in your luckless hand and I'll tell you how this game is played.
You get one roll—and you bet your soul—and if you roll *thirteen* you win,
And all the joys of flesh and gold are yours to touch and spend.
But if that thirteen *don't* come up, then kiss your ass goodbye
And will your useless bones to God, 'cause your goddamn soul is *mine!*"
"Thirteen?," says Billy Markham. "Hell, I've played in tougher games.
I've loved ambitious women and I've rode on wheelless trains.
So gimme room, you stinkin' fiend, and let it all unwind
Nobody's ever rolled a thirteen yet, but this just might be the time."
Then Billy Markham, he takes the dice, and the dice feel as heavy as stones.
"They should, they should," the Devil says, " 'cause they're carved from Jesus' bones."
And Billy Markham turns the dice and the dice, they have no spots.
"I'm sorry," says the Devil, "but they're the only dice I got."
"Well, shit," says Billy Markham. "Now, I really don't mean to bitch,
But I never thought I'd stake my roll in a sucker's game like this."
"Well, then, walk off," says the Devil. "Nobody's tied you down."
"Walk off where?" says Billy Markham. "It's the only game in town.
But I just wanna say 'fore I make my play, that if I should chance to lose,
I will this guitar to some would-be star who'll play some honest blues,
Who ain't afraid to sing the words like damn or shit or fuck

ILLUSTRATED BY BRAD HOLLAND

B

I've rolled your dice, I've rolled 'em twice. Now I hear my loved ones cry,
And before I play that game again, I'll stay here in hell and fry."
"You sure are a grouch when you wake up," says the Devil, "but don't take it out on me.
In the misty worlds of heaven and hell, Bill, everything's done in threes."
"Well, you can take three kisses of my burning bum," says Billy, layin' back and closing his eyes,
"And I'll piss on your shoe, if ever you come near me again with them flyshit dice."
"Dice? Dice?" says the Devil. "Who said dice? Anybody hear me say dice?
Hey, imp, pour my buddy here a cool glass of water, and throw in a nice big chunk of ice."
"And since when," says Billy, raisin' up, "do you go around handing out gifts,
Except pokes from your burning pitchfork or mouthfuls of boiling shit?"
"Well, it's Christmas," says the Devil, "and all of us down here below,
We sort of celebrate in our own sweet way, and this year *you're* the star of the show.
Why, just last night I was up on earth and I seen that lovers' moon,
And I said to myself, 'Hey, I bet old Billy could use a little bit of poon.' "
"Poon?" says Billy Markham. "Last thing I need is poon.
Talk about gettin' my ashes hauled, hell, I'll be *all* ashes soon."
"*Damn, damn!*" the Devil screams. "He's been too long on the fire.
I told you imps to *fry him slow*, now you gone and burned out his *desire*.
You gotta leave 'em some hope, leave 'em some dreams, so they know what hell is for,
'Cause when a man forgets how sweet love is, well, hell ain't hell no more.

So just to refresh your memory, Billy, we're gonna send you back to earth
And I'll throw in a little Christmas blessin' to remind you what life is worth.
For exactly thirteen hours you can screw who you wanna screw
And there ain't no creature on God's green earth who's gonna say no to you.
While me and all these burning souls and all my imps and fiends,
We're gonna sit down here and watch you on that big twenty-four-inch color screen.
And we'll see each hump you're humping, and we'll hear each grunt you groan,
And we'll laugh at the look upon your face when it's time to come back *home*."
"Well, you're much too kind," Billy Markham says. "And you treat me much too well.
You gonna give me somethin' just to take it back—you sure know how to run a hell."
Well, a game is a game," Billy Markham says, risin' off his bed of coals.
"But what if one *won't* ball me, what if one I want says no?"
"No?" says the Devil. "What if one says no? Ain't nobody gonna say no.
Nobody quits or calls in sick when the Devil calls the show.
Not *man* nor *woman* nor *beast!*" screams the Devil, "and no laters or maybes or buts,
And before one soul says no to you, I'll see these hell gates rust.
But *if* anyone refuses you, I say, anyone you name,
Then you'll be free to stay on earth.
Now get out and play the game!"
Then a flash of light and a thunderclap and Billy's back on earth once more
And the asphalt sings beneath his feet as he weaves toward Music Row.
First he stops at the Exit Inn to seduce the blonde on the door,
Then the RCA receptionist he takes on the office floor.
He nails the waitress down at Mack's, the one with the pear-shaped breasts,
And four of the girls from B.M.I. right on Frances Preston's desk.
He screws his way from M.C.A. to Vanderbilt's ivy walls,
And he pokes everything that giggles or sings or whimpers or wiggles or crawls.
First Debbie, then Polly, then Dotty, then Dolly, then Jeannie, and Jessie, and Jan,
Then Marshall and Sal and that redheaded gal who takes the tickets at Opryland.
Then Hazel and Carla and an ex-wife of Harlan's, then Melva and Marge and Marie,
And three *fat* Gospel singers who all came together in perfect three-part harmony.
And Brenda and Sammy and Sharon and Sandy, Loretta and Buffy and Mae,
And Terri and Lynne at the Holiday Inn and Captain Midnight's fiancée.
Then Sherry and Rita, Diane and Anita, Olivia, Emmy and Jean,
And Donna and Kay down at Elliston Place—right there in the pinto beans.
He crashes a session in Studio B, where he humps both Janet and June
On John Gimble's fiddle, right in the middle of a Porter Wagoner tune.

C

"Hey, it's easy to talk of savin' ass," says Billy, "forgiveness is easy to say,
But when the shame burns worse than Hades' fires—how do you talk *that* away?"
"Shame?" laughs the Devil. "She's only a woman—she did what she had to do,
And right or wrong, she needs no curse from a hypocrite lame like you. . . .
She shall rule with me in this Kingdom of Flame, she shall sit next to me on my throne,
While you live with the truth—that the Devil's heart has more pity than your own."
"Hey, wait a minute," says Billy Markham. "I can't believe what you just said,
You givin' me this whole philosophy shit just 'cause you like the way she gave you head.
Why, you poor closet romantic, that chick was suckin' for her *life*.
Just wait see what kinda head you get *after* you make her your wife."
Or is it the sound of the wedding feast that the demons below have begun?
As the Devil, he sits with his betrothed and they pledge their love in the steam,
While halfway up the silken cord,
Billy Markham *screams!*

Billy Markham's Wedding

The trumpets of hell have sounded the word like a screeching clarion call.
The trumpets of hell have sounded the word and the word has been heard by all.
The trumpets of hell have sounded the word and it reaches the heavenly skies,

"In Hell," shouts the Devil, "that's blasphemy! I should burn you to dust where you stand,
But the venom you're carryin' in your heart, that's torture enough for any man.
So get your ass up that silken rope, climb back to your promised land,
And hold your illusions of momma and daughter tight in your sweatin' hand.
But you'll see that they're just bitches like she, and you'll scream when you find it's true,
But stay up there and scream to God—Hell's gates are *closed* to you."
And Billy Markham, clutching his loves, climbs upward toward the skies,
And is it the sharp night wind that brings the tears to Billy's eyes?
Or is it the swirling sulphur smoke or the bright glare of the sun?
Come angels, come demons, come half-breeds, too, the Devil is taking a bride.
And out of the Pearly Gates they come in a file two by two,
For when the Devil takes a bride, there's none that dares refuse.
And Jesus himself, he leads the way down through the starless night,
With Virgin Mary at his left side and Joseph on his right.
And then comes Adam and then comes Eve and the saints move close behind
And all the gentle and all the good, in an endless column they wind.
Down, down to the pits of hell, down from the heavens they sift
Like fallen stars to a blood-red sea, each bearing the Devil a gift.

756
Dean Gerrie Art Director
Greg Fulton Photographer
Robert Blissmer Designer
Dean Gerrie Design Agency
Ratel Electronics Client

THESE ARE THE ARMIES OF THE NIGHT.
They are 100,000 strong. They outnumber the cops five to one.
They could run New York City. Tonight they're all out to get the Warriors.
THE WARRIORS
Paramount Pictures Presents A Lawrence Gordon Production "THE WARRIORS"
Executive Producer Frank Marshall Based Upon the Novel by Sol Yurick
Screenplay by David Shaber and Walter Hill Produced by Lawrence Gordon
R RESTRICTED
Directed by Walter Hill
Read the Dell Book

757
Ed Brodkin Art Director
Ed Harridsleff Designer
David Jarvis Illustrator
Diener Hauser Bates Agency
Paramount Pictures Client

Yardley

758
Heather Cooper, Robert Burns Art Directors
Heather Cooper Illustrator
Burns, Cooper, Hynes Limited Agency
Yardley of London Limited Client

759 A-C
Arthur Paul, Kerig Pope Art Directors
Brad Holland Illustrator
Kerig Pope Designer
Playboy Enterprises, Inc. Client

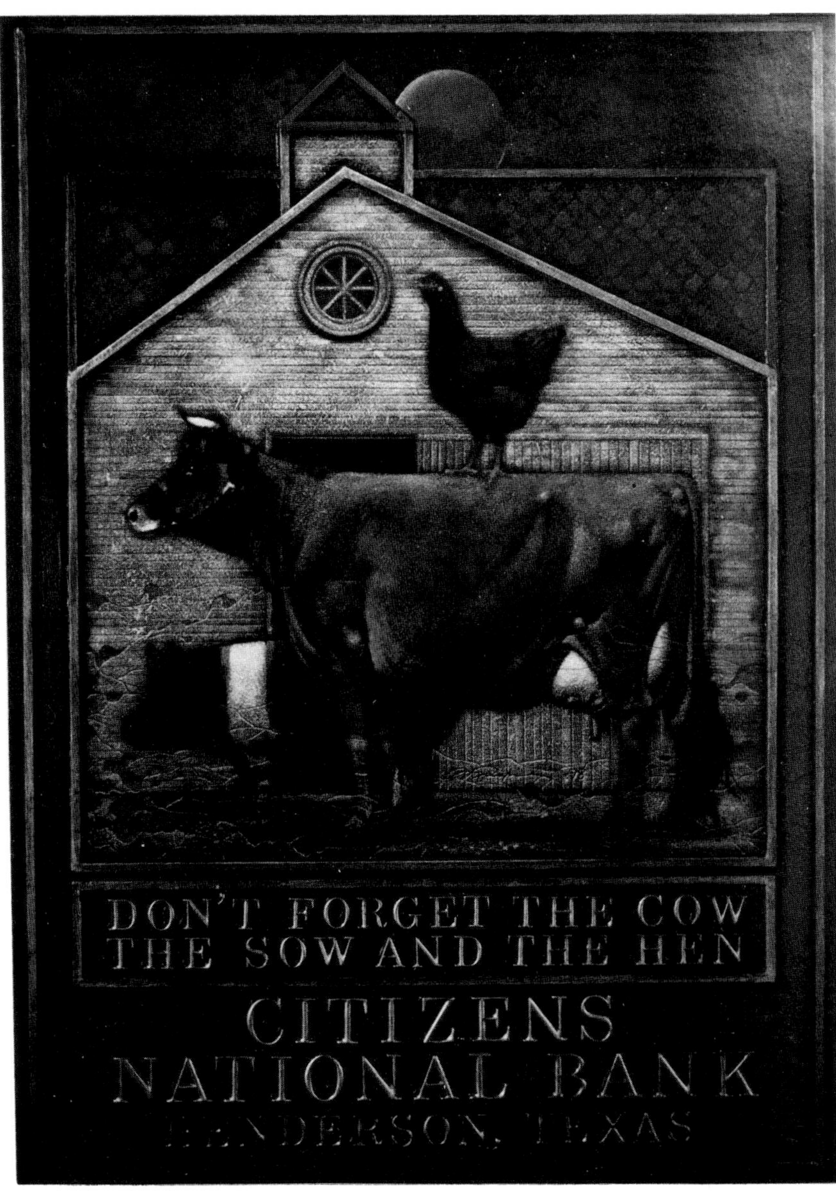

760
James Wilkins Art Director
Mark English Illustrator
William F. Finn & Associates, Inc. Agency
Citizens National Bank Client

SAUTERNE

A

TERN OF EXPRESSION

B

761 A-B
Michael C. Witte Illustrator
Penguin Books Client

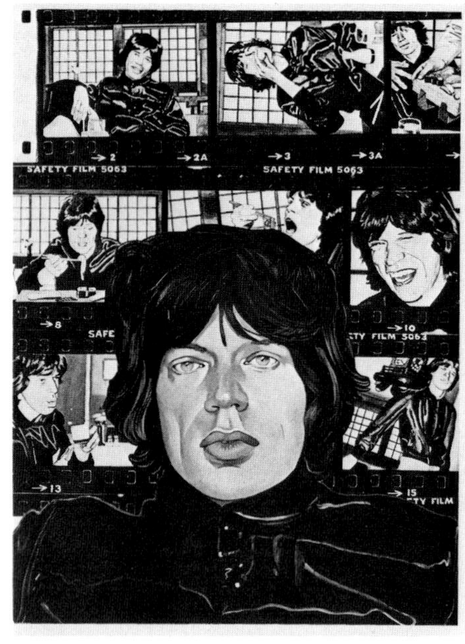

A CONVERSATION WITH

MICK JAGGER

King Monkey Punk jumps off the Empire State Building, bats away sputtering paparazzi, lays blitzkrieg to the rock press, stumbles into an Eastside Japanese restaurant and tries to eat our reporter.

INTERVIEW BY JOE JEROME · ILLUSTRATION BY JULIAN ALLEN 71

762
Michael Brock Art Director
Julian Allen Illustrator
Oui Magazine Client

Who Says the Poor Need Lawyers

Only our lawmakers see the need for needless litigation

The central problem suffered by poor people is their lack of money, a truism that generally eludes the understanding of those who make our laws. What can better explain the multitude of federal, state, and local programs intended to provide the poor with everything but money?

The long list of such programs includes food stamps; housing projects and subsidies; free medical care; until recently, government-paid abortions; and a variety of others—all providing what the government thinks the poor should have. Then there is the federal legal services program, as glaring an example as one can find of social paternalism toward the poor. Mistaken in conception, the program once had the virtue of being small and inexpensive, but recently its budget has grown to more than $200 million—an increase of nearly 2,000 percent in only 12 years, which is a healthy rate of growth by bureaucratic standards. It employs more than 3,000 lawyers across the country, a number legal services supporters intend to increase sharply within the next few years.

(Please turn to page 48)

by Stephen Chapman
Freelance writer, Washington, D.C.

Jean-Claude Lejeune/William Walker mural

29 million Americans are too poor to afford legal help

Bill Stephens graduated from law school 26 years ago. He now runs a law office in Tennessee—the state where his grandfather was a circuit-riding judge. Stephens and his fellow attorneys keep up that tradition, traveling throughout an eight-county area to counsel and represent their clients. But Stephens also uses techniques for reaching clients that his grandfather never dreamed of—a weekly radio show and a monthly television program on the law.

Pamela Isackes and Diana Greene are employment law specialists. They practice in New York City, but recently joined Baltimore attorneys Alan Davis and Richard North in a five-week federal trial challenging a labor union's training program on racial discrimination grounds. Preparation for the trial was grueling: there were 365 stipulations to prepare, 200 exhibits, 30 witnesses and four expert witnesses for the plaintiffs alone. Isackes, who finished law school four years ago, was lead counsel. She and Greene are now working on their next case: a major

(Please turn to page 49)

by Tim Ayers
Associate Director, Office of Public Affairs Legal Services Corporation

46 47

763
David Carothers Art Director
Jean-Claude Lejeune Photographer
American Bar Association Press Client

A CONVERSATION WITH

LINA WERTMULLER

This time, let's talk about Lina. Self-indulgent film maker. Political radical. Defender of the orgasm. And one pushy little broad. Ready to get swept away?

ILLUSTRATION BY JOHN COLLIER 71

764
Michael Brock Art Director
John Collier Illustrator
James Kiehle Designer
Oui Magazine Client

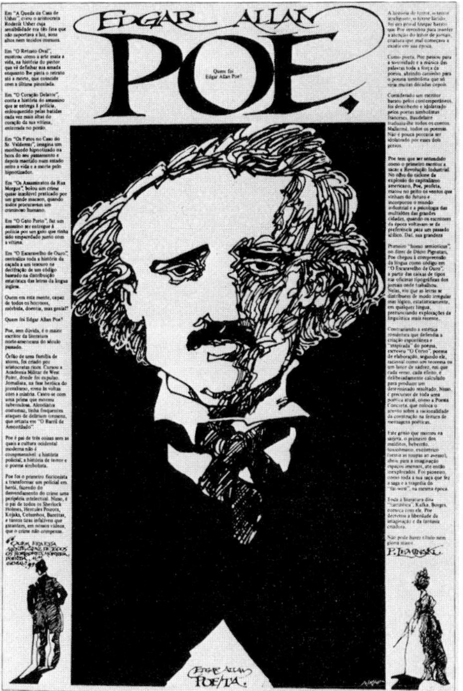

765
Oswald Miranda Art Director
Newspaper Diario do Parana Client

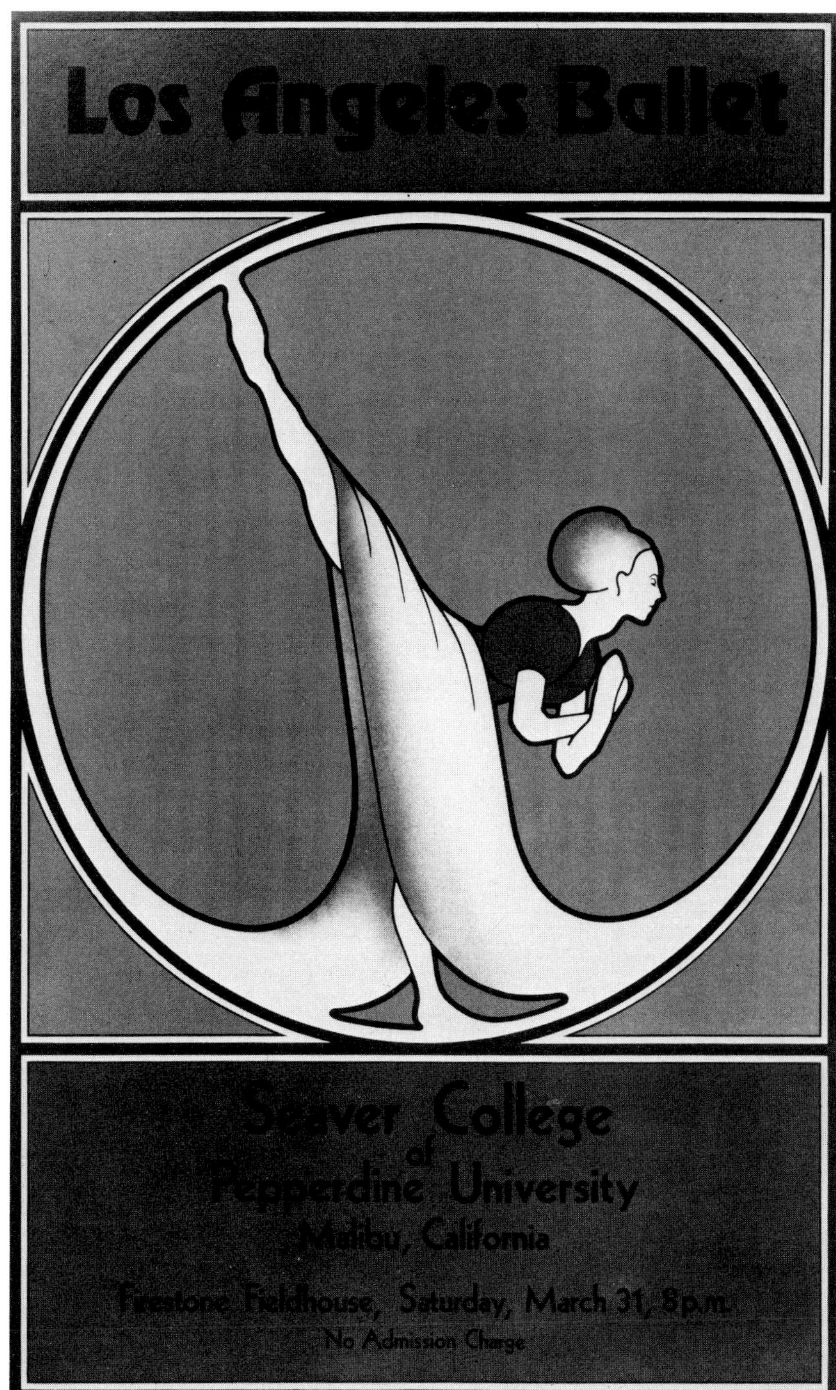

767
Frederick Mollner Art Director
Pepperdine University Publications Dept. Production House
Los Angeles Ballet Client

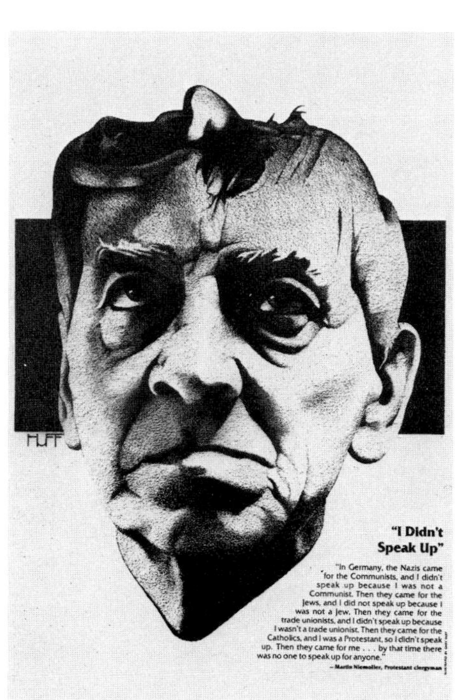

766
Harry Knox Art Director
Gary R. Huff Illustrator
Harry Knox & Associates Agency
Liberty Magazine Client

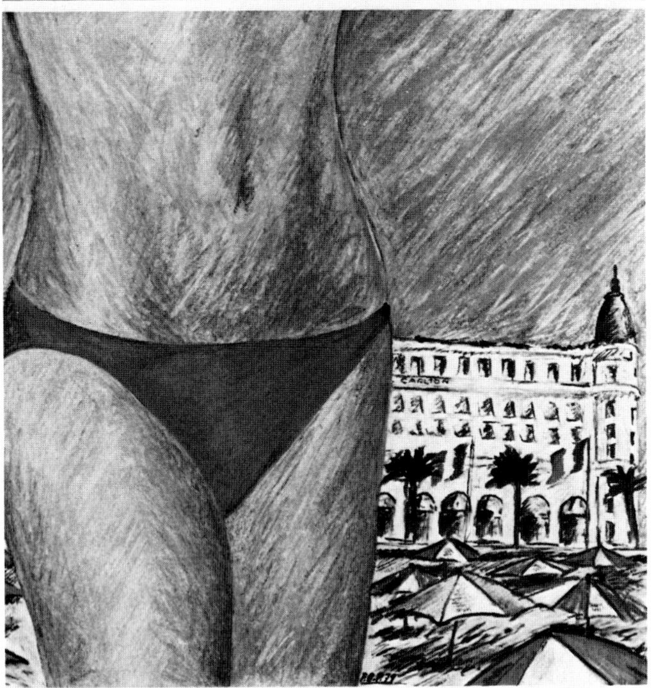

768
April Heater Art Director
Pierre Picot Illustrator
The Hollywood Reporter Client

769
Joseph Stelmach Art Director
Catherine Harris-Perrot Illustrator
RCA Records Client

770
Christopher Garland Art Director
David B. Garland Illustrator
Four-Star Graphics Studio
Zoetrope Client

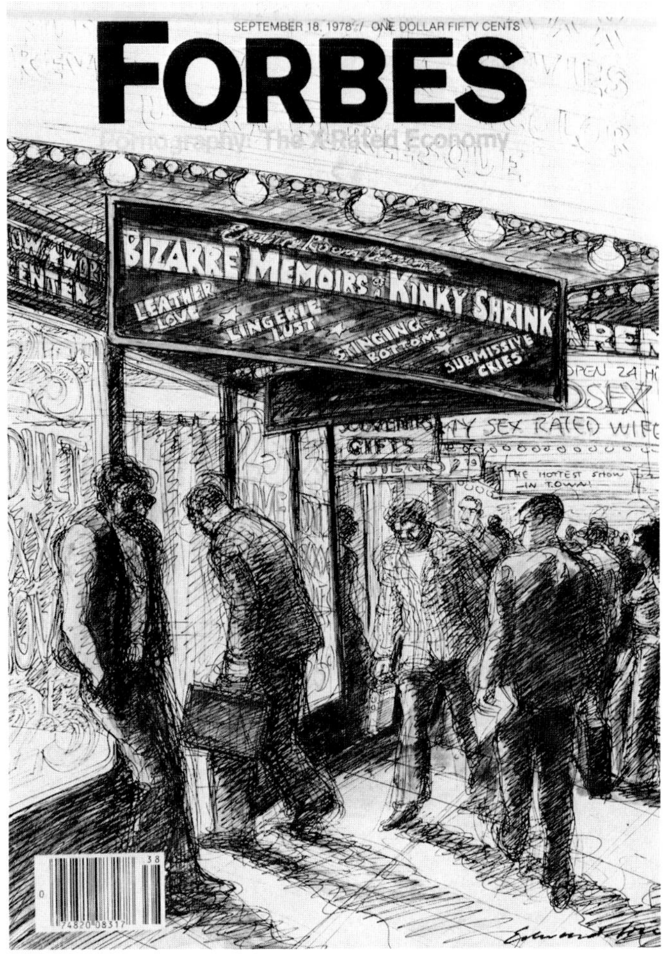

771
Peter Palazzo Art Director
Edward Sorel Illustrator
Everett Halvorsen Designer
Forbes Magazine Client

772
Jim Denney Art Director
WTAE-TV Public Affairs Department Agency
Public Service for Juvenile Justice Ctr. Client

773
Corinne Desarzens Illustrator

774
Ben Blank Art Director
Anthony Accurso Illustrator
ABC-TV World News Tonight Client

775
Judy Fendelman Art Director
Jean-Claude Suares Designer
New York Magazine Client

776
Ned Steinberg Art Director
Ellen Denton Illustrator
CBS News Client

777
Juan Jose Estevez Art Director
A. Ramon Gonzalez Teja Illustrator
"El Pais" Client

778 A-C
Jack Lund Art Director
Franklin McMahon Illustrator
Chicago Magazine Client

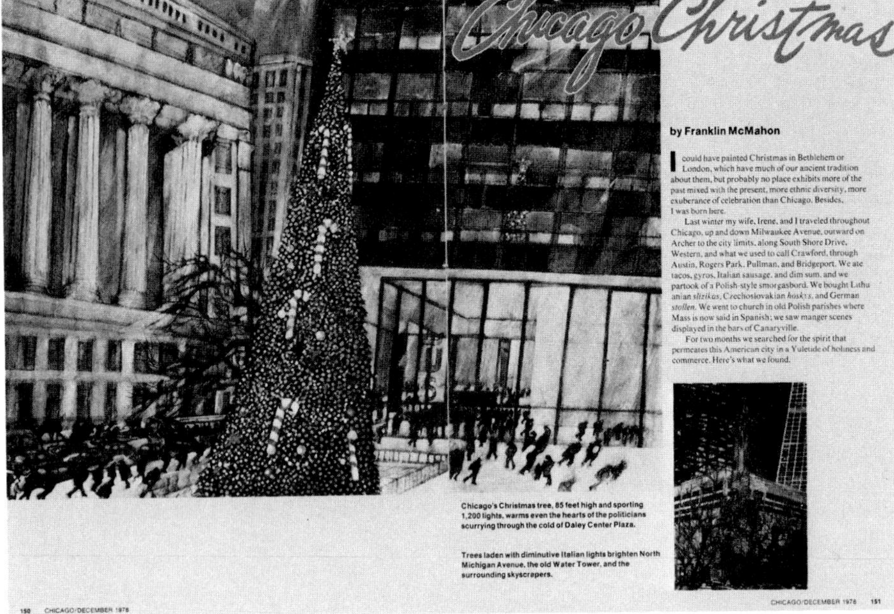

Chicago Christmas

by Franklin McMahon

I could have painted Christmas in Bethlehem or London, which have much of our ancient tradition about them, but probably no place exhibits more of the past mixed with the present, more ethnic diversity, more exuberance of celebration than Chicago. Besides, I was born here.

Last winter my wife, Irene, and I traveled throughout Chicago, up and down Milwaukee Avenue, outward on Archer to the city limits, along South Shore Drive, Western, and what we used to call Crawford, through Austin, Rogers Park, Pullman, and Bridgeport. We ate tacos, gyros, Italian sausage, and dim sum, and we partook of a Polish-style smorgasbord. We bought Lithuanian *slizikas*, Czechoslovakian *hoskys*, and German *stollen*. We went to church in old Polish parishes where Mass is now said in Spanish; we saw manger scenes displayed in the bars of Canaryville.

For two months we searched for the spirit that permeates this American city in a Yuletide of holiness and commerce. Here's what we found.

Chicago's Christmas tree, 85 feet high and sporting 1,200 lights, warms even the hearts of the politicians scurrying through the cold of Daley Center Plaza.

Trees laden with diminutive Italian lights brighten North Michigan Avenue, the old Water Tower, and the surrounding skyscrapers.

150 CHICAGO/DECEMBER 1978

CHICAGO/DECEMBER 1978 151

778 A

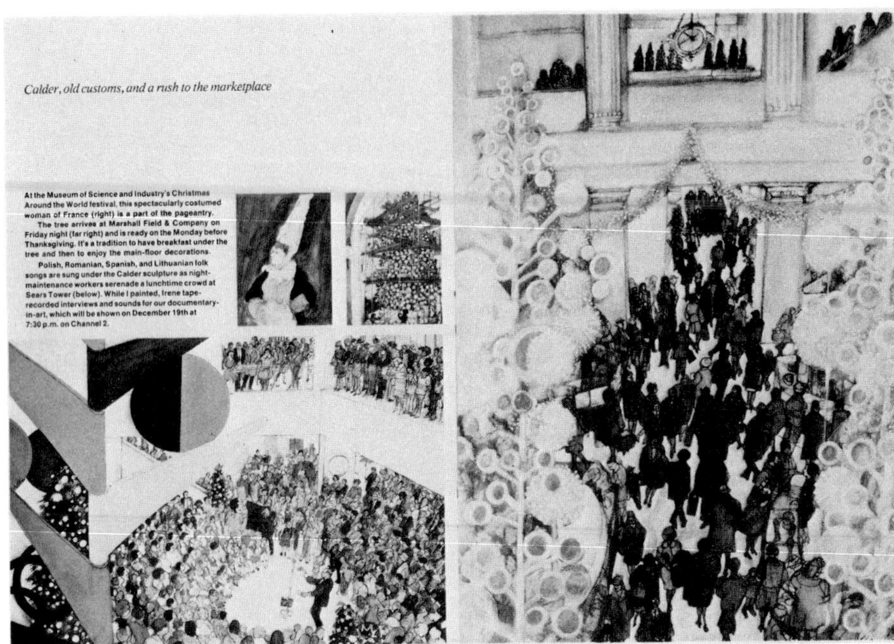

Calder, old customs, and a rush to the marketplace

At the Museum of Science and Industry's Christmas Around the World festival, this spectacularly costumed woman of France (right) is a part of the pageantry.

The tree arrives at Marshall Field & Company on Friday night (far right) and is ready on the Monday before Thanksgiving. It's a tradition to have breakfast under the tree and then to enjoy the main-floor decorations.

Polish, Romanian, Spanish, and Lithuanian folk songs are sung under the Calder sculpture as night-maintenance workers serenade a lunchtime crowd at Sears Tower (below). While I painted, Irene tape-recorded interviews and sounds for our documentary-in-art, which will be shown on December 19th at 7:30 p.m. on Channel 2.

B

New light, Sullivan, and a world full of song

Carson Pirie Scott & Company's Louis Sullivan façade (left) adds its own ornate Chicago tradition to the shopping scene at State and Madison. And a great crowd (below) visits the Christmas bazaar on 47th Street.

I like seeing Christmas trees in the windows of high-rise buildings and wreaths on the doors of prairie bungalows. But it is the drawings of people that best express the spirit of the city.

"We heard beautifully sung Afro-American spirituals, chants from the Middle East, and four performances of Handel's *Messiah*," said Irene, "and discovered something new to us, a Swedish Lucia celebration on North Elston (right). There was coffee, a bazaar, glögg, and a bake sale. The Vårblommans Childrens Club sang folk songs, and a white-robed girl with a crown of candles sang *Sankta Lucia*."

CHICAGO/DECEMBER 1978 155

C

779
Dale Moyer Art Director
Terry Steadham Illustrator
Jeff Derecki Designer
Scholastic Magazines Client

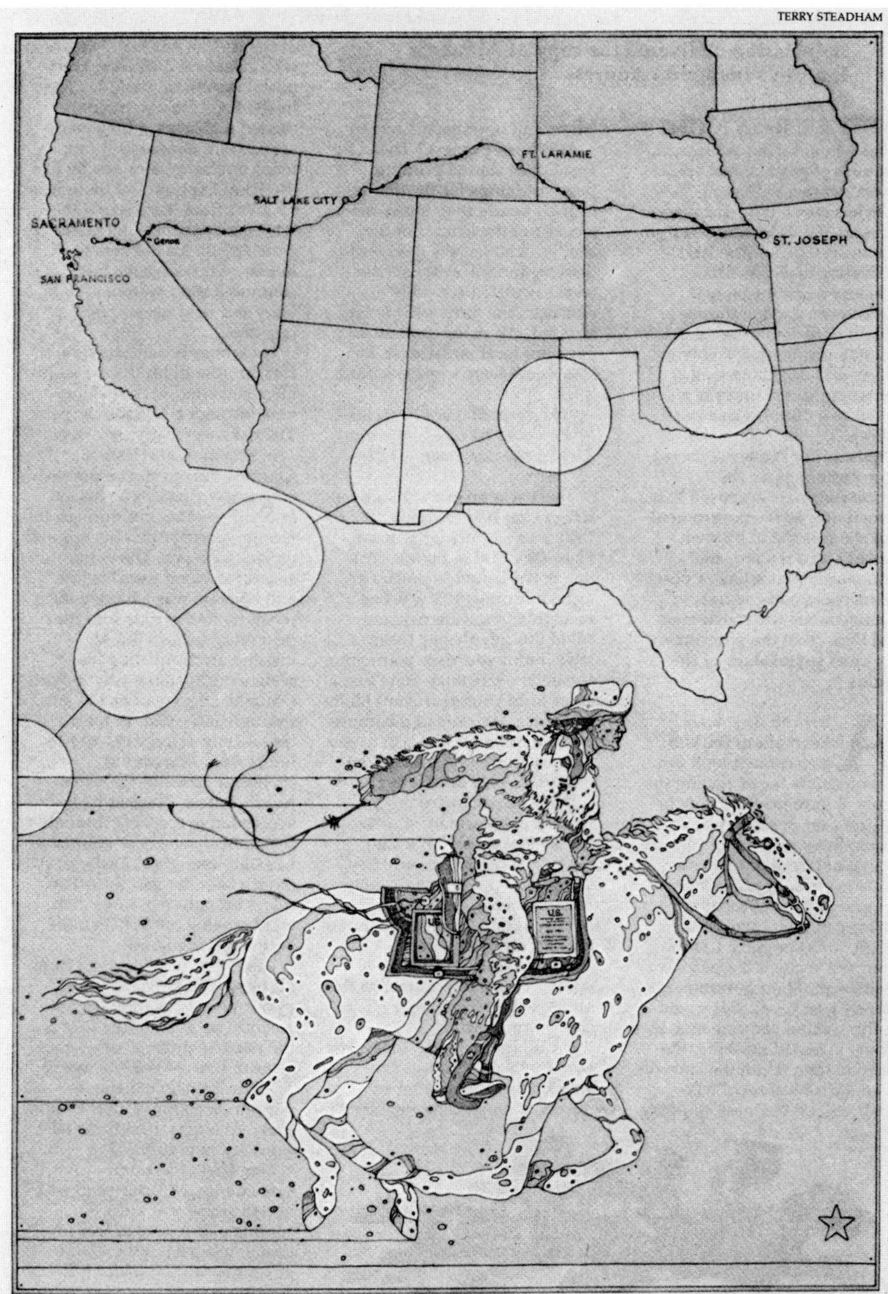

780
Beverly Littlewood Art Director
Andrew Wright Photographer
NBC NewsCenter 4 Client

781
Howard E. Paine Art Director
Roy Andersen Illustrator
W. E. Garrett Designer
National Geographic Society Client

782
Ricardo Rey Art Director
Ricardo Rey Studio, Inc. Studio
Colegio de Contadores Client

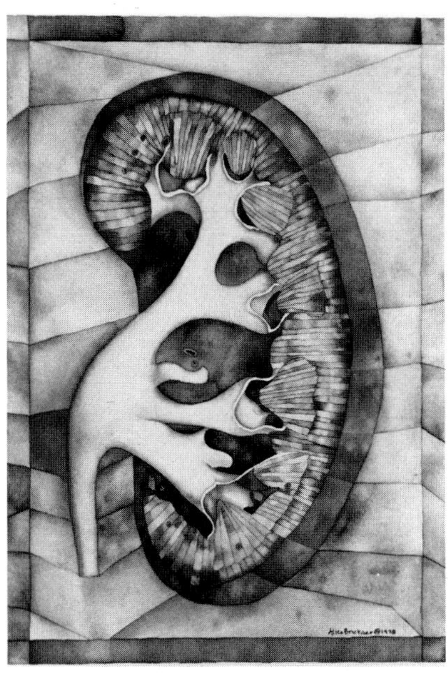

783
Tina Adamek Art Director
Alice Brickner Illustrator
McGraw-Hill Inc. Client

784
Jukka Veistola Art Director
Varis-Poteri-Veistola Agency
Suomen Palontorjuntaliitto Client

785
Joanna R. Van Kampen, Anita L. Ament Art Directors
Handmade Graphics Agency
La Mesa Blueprint Client

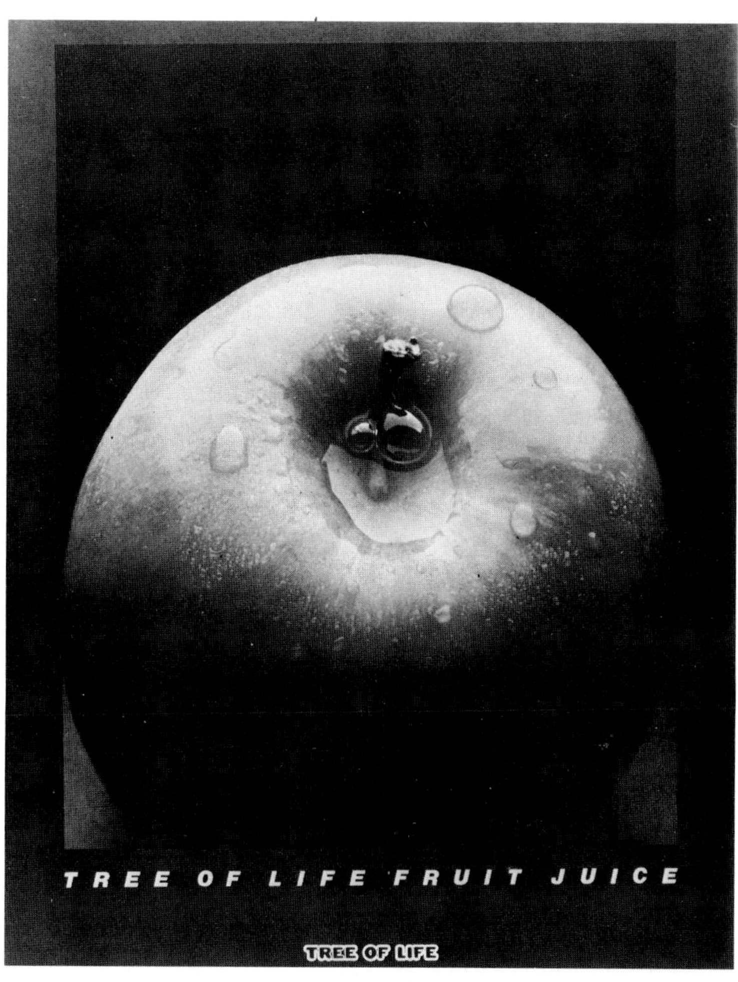
TREE OF LIFE FRUIT JUICE
TREE OF LIFE

Photography

786
Phil Marco, Morris Shriftman Art Directors
Phil Marco Photographer
Phil Marco Productions Studio
The Morris Shriftman Company Agency
Tree of Life Client

787
Ellen Blissman Art Director
Jean-Claude Suares Designer
New York Magazine Client

The past recaptured: *In his workroom, Charles James posed three weeks before his death with a model wearing his "taxi" dress—it looks graceful even when the wearer gets out of a cab.*

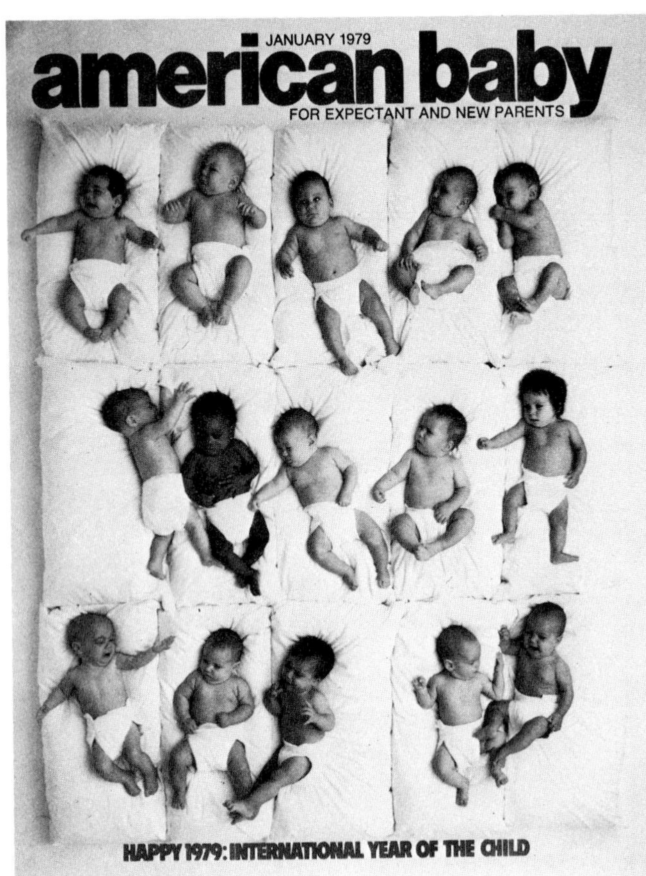

788
Jeanne Dzienciol Art Director
Michel Tcherevkoff Photographer
American Baby Magazine Client

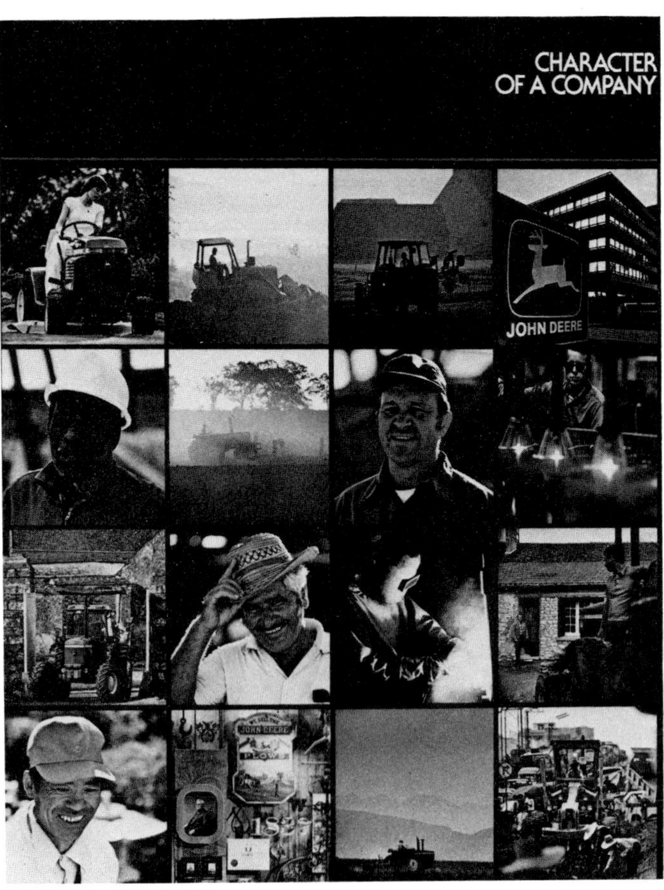

789
Peter Toth Art Director
Richard Tunison Photographer
Paul Meeden Copywriter
Deere & Company Client

790

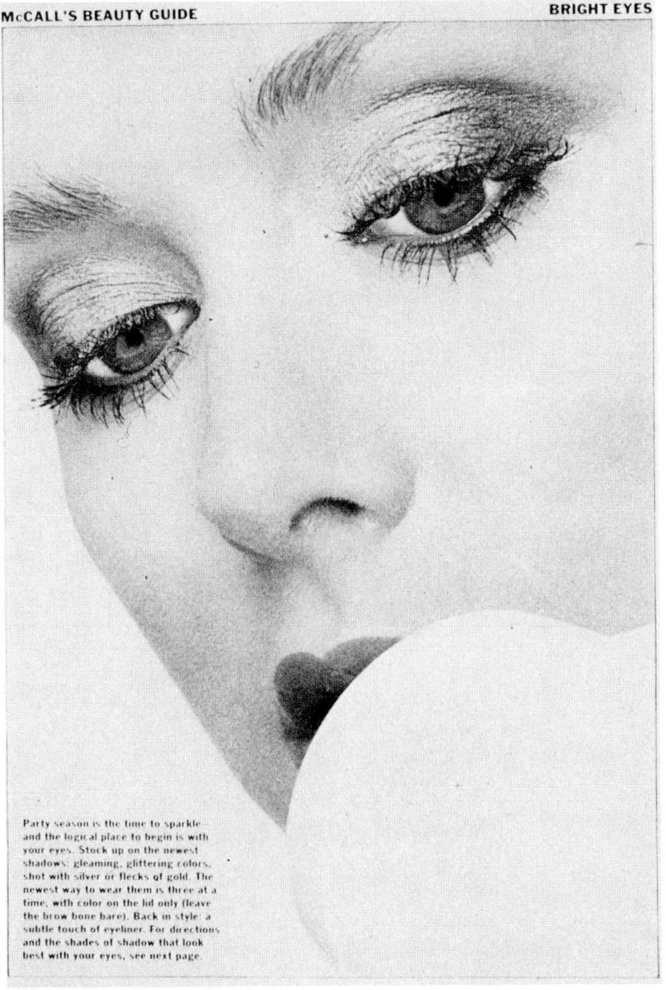

McCALL'S BEAUTY GUIDE
BRIGHT EYES
Party season is the time to sparkle and the logical place to begin is with your eyes. Stock up on the newest shadows: gleaming, glittering colors, shot with silver or flecks of gold. The newest way to wear them is three at a time, with color on the lid only (leave the brow bone bare). Back in style: a subtle touch of eyeliner. For directions and the shades of shadow that look best with your eyes, see next page.

791 A

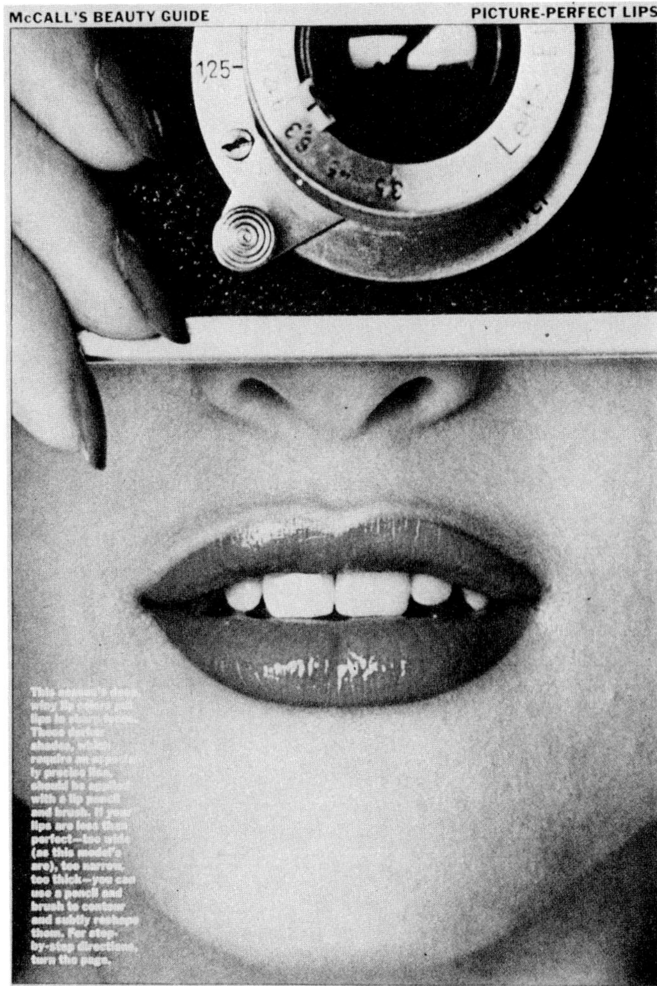

B

790
Tom Smith Art Director
David L. Simpson, Simpson/Flint, Inc. Photographers
Simpson/Flint, Inc. Studio

791 A-E
Alvin Grossman Art Director
Henry Wolf Photographer
Henry Wolf Productions Studio
McCalls Magazine Client

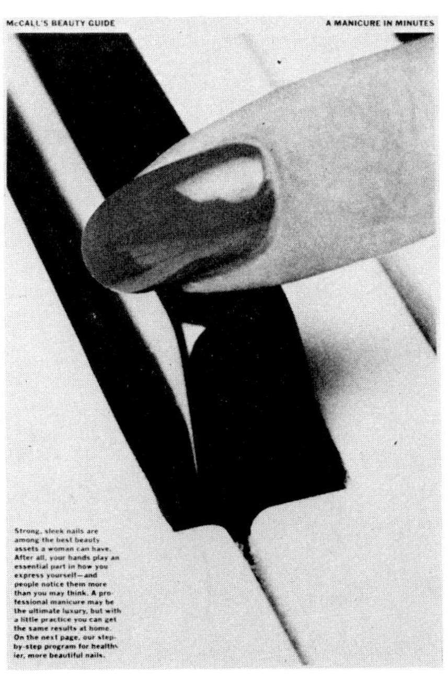

McCALL'S BEAUTY GUIDE
A MANICURE IN MINUTES
Strong, sleek nails are among the best beauty assets a woman can have. After all, your hands play an essential part in how you express yourself—and people notice them more than you may think. A professional manicure may be the ultimate luxury, but with a little practice you can get the same results at home. On the next page, our step-by-step program for healthier, more beautiful nails.

C

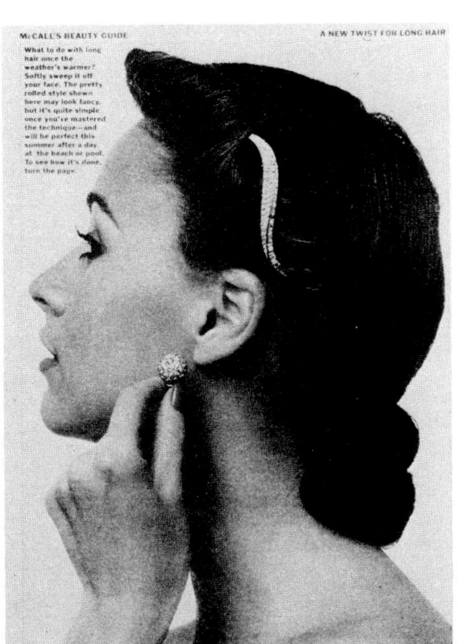

McCALL'S BEAUTY GUIDE
A NEW TWIST FOR LONG HAIR
What to do with long hair once the weather's warmer? Softly sweep it off your face. The pretty rolled style shown here may look fancy, but it's quite simple once you've mastered the technique—and will be perfect this summer after a day at the beach or pool. To see how it's done, turn the page.

D

McCALL'S BEAUTY GUIDE
HAIR REPAIR: A HOT-OIL TREATMENT
It can happen to anyone—the sun, wind or overbleaching leads to dry, brittle hair. Seriously damaged hair needs more than the usual quick conditioning. Beauty salons recommend hot-oil treatments to soak softness and shine back in. But in a half hour, before you shampoo, you can give yourself the same oil treatment at home. Try the method on the next page once a week until your hair is healthy and gleaming again.

E

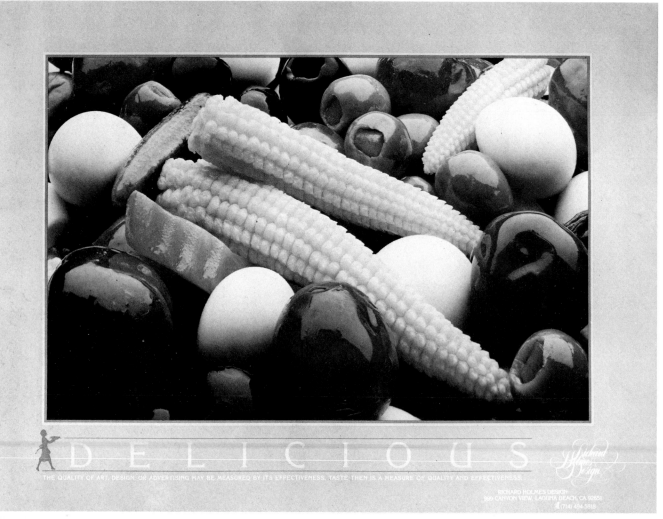

792
Richard Holmes Art Director
Herb Kravits Photographer
Richard Holmes, Jeanne Parker Designers
Richard Holmes Design Client

793
Kerry Peterson Art Director
Marvy! Advertising Photography, Inc. Studio
Minnetonka Labs Client

794
David Moore Art Director
David Muench Photographer
William McMillan Designer
U.S. International Communication Agency Agency
America Illustrated Magazine Client

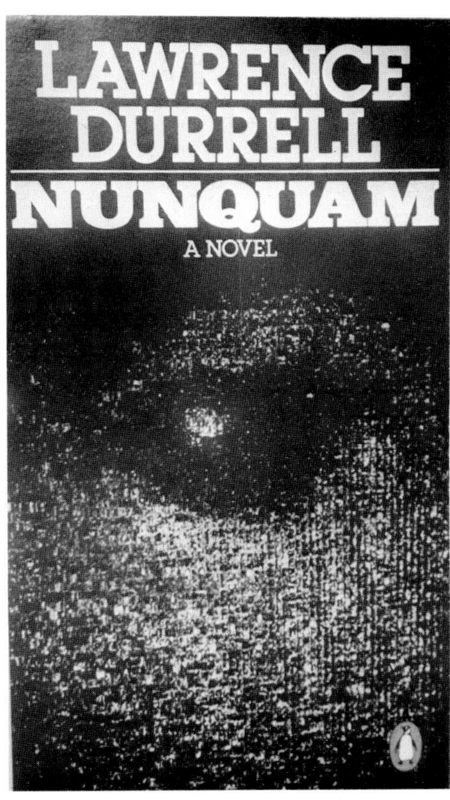

795
Neal Stuart Art Director
Geoffrey Gove Photographer
Penguin Books Client

just beyond the horizon
INDONESIA

796
Hans Hoefer Art Director
Hans Hoefer, Brent Hesselyn Photographers
APA Productions [Pte] Ltd. Client

LIVING IN ONE ROOM

Decorating by the Inch

By Molly Siple

"... Consider the furnishings we show you here: flexible storage systems, seating that hangs up or hides in a closet..."

The first step in decorating your one-room apartment is to give everything you don't use to the Salvation Army. Next, carefully watch how you spend your hours at home and don't make room for things you suspect you won't do... like serving sit-down dinners for eight.

Also, consider the furnishings we show you here: flexible storage systems, furniture that incorporates storage space, seating that folds and unfolds, stacks, rolls, and hides in a closet.

To expand your space visually, stay with light walls and light, unpatterned fabrics. Be consistent with colors and patterns, and don't divide your space into separate decorative themes. Wall-to-wall carpet and large rugs work best. And in choosing furniture, look for airy, see-through designs—a director's chair, say, or a glass coffee table.

Take heart. Follow some of these tips, and living in one room doesn't have to cramp your style.

Out of sight: These classic Alvar Aalto stools, 17½ inches high, store away in a closet, ready for a party. The stool in birch, $46; $52 with black or red Formica top. Art et Industrie, 132 Thompson Street.

Abracadabra: This sofa yields a bed and side tables. In quilted or non-quilted fabric, $850–$1,050. Design Research, 53 East 57th Street.

Built to scale: Super Erecta shelving comes in graduated lengths. This combination, 5 by 5 by 2 feet, about $250. The Professional Kitchen, 18 Cooper Square. Flower arranger Mimi Hermine was once a Munchkin.

Light 'n' lively: This lamp, with fabric panels that bend into (and hold) various shapes, divides space and illuminates, $275. Art et Industrie.

Extra! Extra! New Copco Gridworks add storage space. Grid, $16; racks, $9–$14; extra hooks, $2. Bloomingdale's.

74 NEW YORK/NOVEMBER 13, 1978

Photographed by Peter M. Fine

NOVEMBER 13, 1978/NEW YORK 75

797
Ellen Blissman Art Director
Peter M. Fine Photographer
Jordan Schaps, Jean-Claude Suares, Ellen Blissman Designers
New York Magazine Client

798
Darrel Fiesel Art Director
Ken Pace Photographer
Foto-Graphics, Inc. Studio
Foote, Cone & Belding Agency
Jenn-Air Corporation Client

The Biltmore Hotel

The Galleria, a through-block passage a level above the main lobby, is a showcase for the painting originally executed by Giovanni Smeraldi and recently touched up by his student A.T. Heinsbergen. In the music room (above), the apparently wood carved ceiling is actually hand-painted cast plaster. In the Gold Room (below) murals evoke the 1920s movieland quality with idiosyncratic charm.

A

799 A-B
George Coderre Art Director
Hedrich-Blessing Photographers
Progressive Architecture Client

The Biltmore Hotel

Interiors gradually shift from old but refurbished spaces to newly renovated as one goes from the lower public floors upstairs to the hotel rooms. The Crystal Ballroom downstairs has its hand-painted ceiling (right, top) intact. Hotel corridors have new carpeting, lighting, paint, and other details and furnishings. Similarly, the bedrooms, which come in a range of monochromatic color schemes, retain only the wood molding as a sign of former lives. Now dominant is the bold artistry of Jim Dine, who was commissioned to execute prints, wall friezes, paintings, even lamps and rugs. Downstairs in the lobby restaurant (bottom, left) old and new styles mesh, with original columns and ceiling left intact. An upstairs suite (bottom, right) shows mixing of wainscoting and molding with Jim Dine artwork, modern furniture.

B

800 A-C
Sybil Broyles, Jim Darilek Art Directors
Nicolas Russell Photographer
Texas Monthly Client

WORKING THE RIGS

Photography by Nicolas Russell

The job is tough, but so are the men who do it.

No one really likes the work. No one really likes getting out in the Texas sun and skinning his knuckles on heavy sections of steel pipe or wrestling with a spinning chain or climbing to the top of a rig where a single slip can lead to a ninety-foot fall or mixing drilling mud that gets in work clothes and combines with the grease, sweat, and oil to make a smell that no amount of washing can remove. No one likes to put up a rig in one isolated spot then take it down later only to put it up again in another isolated spot miles away. And no one likes the long hours and graveyard shifts and the endless driving back and forth to the job and coming home, as one roughneck put it, to "warmed over coffee and an asleep old lady."

Then why do people do it? They may like the money: when there's plenty of work, as there is today, roughnecks can make $15,000 to $25,000 in a year. They may like the people they work with. They may take pride in their toughness and satisfaction from knowing they can do a particular dirty and dangerous job better than the next man. And they may like the life that surrounds the oil rigs—the high school football games, the fishing trips in a pickup with a camper on the back, the beers on Saturday night, the long Sunday dinners after a morning in the Baptist church. But no one really likes the work.

Here's a bad situation. The roughneck in the center has lost control of the spinning chain used to tighten two sections of pipe, and he's trying to hang on. That's a good way to lose a finger. The other man has put his head down for protection.

A

"My dad drank an awful lot then. We literally lived in bars. I remember sitting under the table when I was just a little bitty thing, beer bottles would be flying through the air so thick you couldn't get up. I'd reach up on top of the table and rake change off and put it in my pocket.

"They'd party all night long, then they'd get up the next morning and go to work. I don't know how they did it. I know as a grown man now, I can't. I could last two days and then I'd go down."

Mickey Gaines
Roughneck
Odessa

The drillers on this solitary rig are "out of the hole," as you can tell by the sections of pipe on the left side of the rig.

The derrickman controls one end while floorhands stab one section of pipe into another. Sometimes he has to stretch farther so he removes his harness.

With the concentration of a gourmet over wine, a well-tester smells gas from a well.

B

"I was born and raised in Mississippi. I come from oil country over there. That's how I met Tommy. I was working in a little old Dairy Queen. We met each other. I knew everybody in the oil field and helped him find work. Back then the oil field was a lot harder. If you missed a day you needn't go back the second day 'cause you didn't have a job.

"My husband has been in the field twenty-two years now. It's buttered my bread many a day. I love it.

"I have two sons in it. They work with their daddy. And I have another son sixteen. That's what he's going to do when he comes of age.

"When we go on a rig we all like to take a part in it. We like to have cookouts and invite everybody. We like it sort of like a big family. Meet a lot of people. Some good people and some ain't worth a damn."

Eula Jones
Oil-field wife
Rusk

Benton Earl Downey and family; he started in the fields 20 years ago. He was 15.

Inside the toolpusher's shed: he is the boss and can take a few minutes to relax.

A sweet tooth and a dirty hand: on the rigs roughnecks eat cakes, soda pop, candy, and anything else with lots of sugar.

C

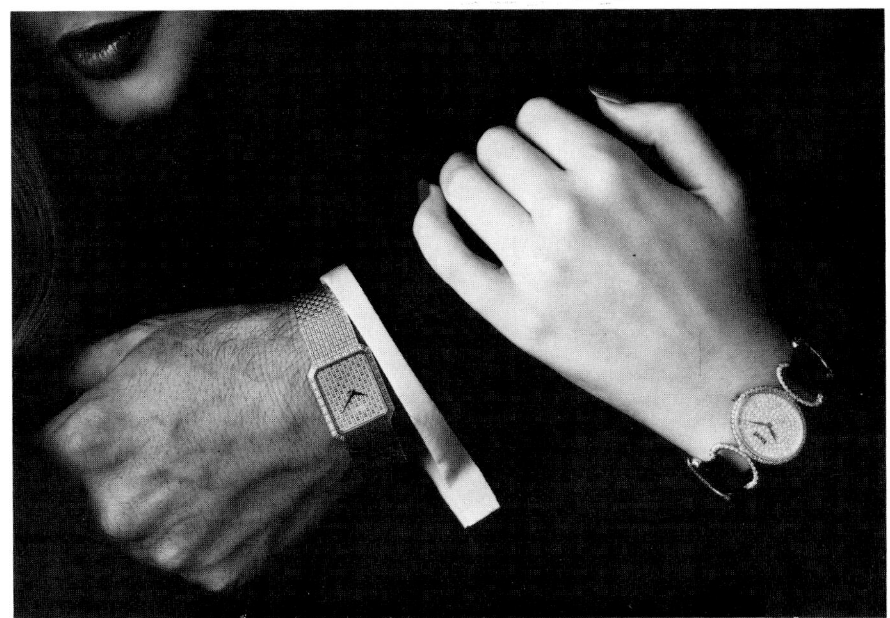

A

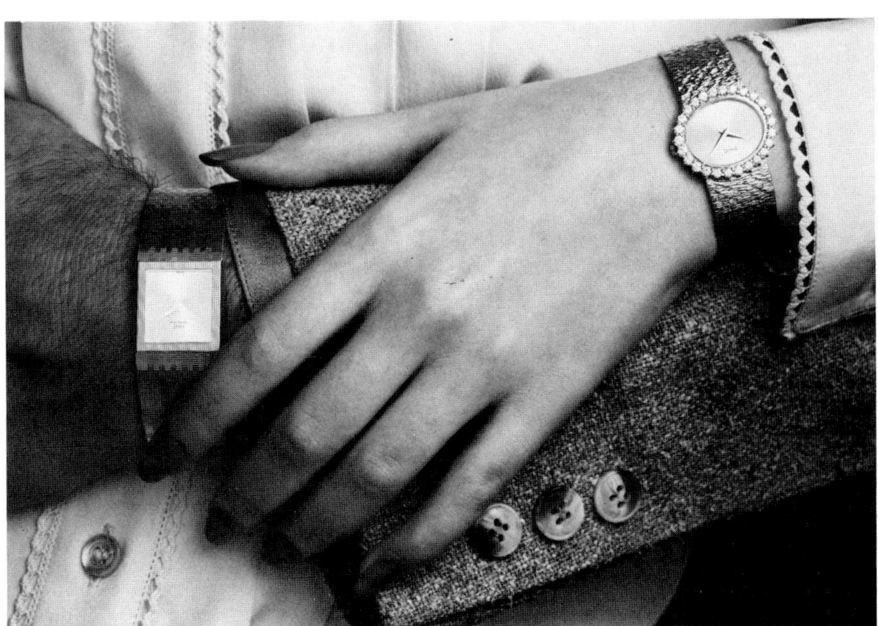

B

C

801 A-C
Charles Davidson Art Director
Mike O'Neill Photographer
Harry Viola Advertising Agency
Piaget Client

802
Howard E. Paine Art Director
Al Giddings Photographer
W. E. Garrett Designer
National Geographic Society Client

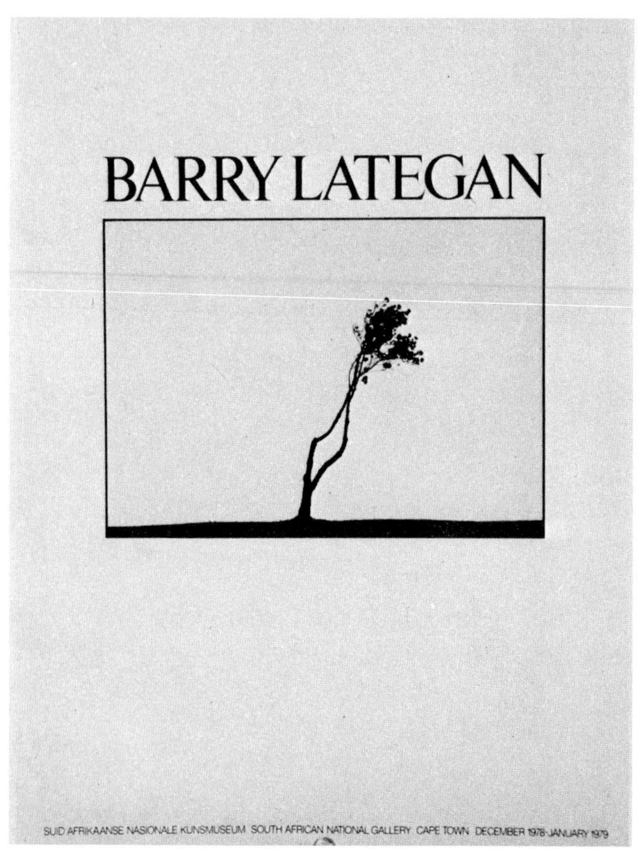

BARRY LATEGAN
SUID AFRIKAANSE NASIONALE KUNSMUSEUM SOUTH AFRICAN NATIONAL GALLERY CAPE TOWN DECEMBER 1978-JANUARY 1979

803
Barry Lategan Photographer
Derek Forsythe Partnership Production House
Barry Lategan Studio Client

804
Jose Zaragoza Art Director
Duailibi, Petit, Zaragoza Propaganda Agency
Rastro Client

Expo Rastro Fotos. MASP. 29 de novembro a 5 de dezembro. Fotos:
José Zaragoza, Abraham Lincoln, Moacir Lugato, Silvana Tinelli.
RASTRO

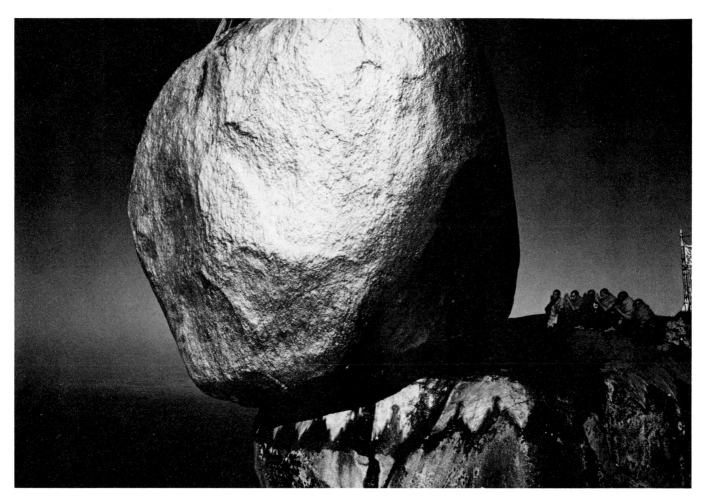

805
Tomiyasu Shiraiwa Art Director
Hiroji Kubota Photographer
Magnum Photos, Inc. Studio
Toppan Printing Co. Production House
DOI Group Client

806
Jessica M. Weber Art Director
Allen H. Lieberman Photographer
Allen Lieberman Associates Inc. Studio
Int'l Review of Food & Wine Client

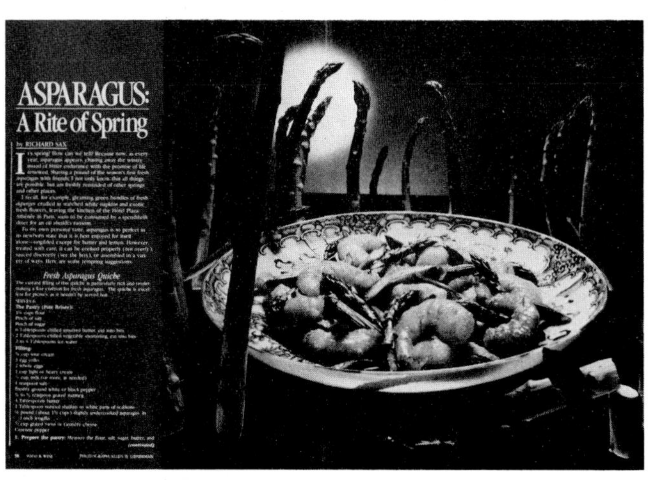

807
Edyce Hall Art Director
Tony Boring Photographer
R. J. Reynolds Industries, Inc. Client

A small circle of friends: The women for whom Mr. John has created hats and clothes have remained loyal friends and clients through all of his fashion epochs. On a recent Sunday, Mr. John and a few of his admirers gathered for a group portrait in the baroque confines of his Central Park West apartment. Clockwise, from the left of Mr. John (in sunglasses, center), his clients are: Annie Owen, Hildegarde, Mrs. Richard Ney, Mrs. Paul Kollsman, Mrs. Lorenzo Alvary, Monique Van Vooren, Mrs. H. Donald Sills, Mrs. Jack Dempsey, Ruth Warrick, Mrs. Orson D. Munn, Mrs. Mortimer Salomon, Julia Meade, Mrs. Henri Bendel, Adelle Dillingham, formerly Lady Beatty.

808
Ellen Blissman Art Director
Barbra Walz Photographer
Jean-Claude Suares Designer
New York Magazine Client

809
Chuck Rogers Photographer
Chuck Rogers Studio Studio
Nike Client

810
Peter Harrison Art Director
Randee Rafkin-Rubin Designer
James Orlandi & Associates Production House
Harrison Associates Agency
Mead Paper Client

Private Gardens

SangerHarris

A

An artful arrangement is created by
Ralph Montenero for Blanche
Lingerie. Luscious lace enriches the
body-skimming chemise silhouette
and accents the daring side slit of the
gown, 33.OO. To toss over, a
gossamer robe edged in lace, 3O.OO.
Both are nylon, sizes P-S-M, in
raspberry ice or black. Viewpoint
Intimate Apparel, Dept. 44O.
Send the gown at 33.OO in size
color ____, the robe at 3O.OO in
size ____ color ____ Texas
residents please add 5% tax. Inside our
delivery area, add 1.75 if your total
purchase is less than 4O.OO. Outside
our delivery area, add 2.3O for
handling up to 3 lbs.
Charge ____ Check ____
Acc't No.
Name
Address
City ____ State
Zip ____ Phone
SangerHarris

B

811 A–B
Wayne Scott Art Director
Constance Ashley, Bob Goodman, Francis Shepherd Photographers
Constance Ashley Studio Studio
Sanger-Harris Client

812
Don Adamec Art Director
Allen Vogel Studio, Inc. Photographers
Stan Carp Inc. Agency
Fritz & La Rue Co., Inc. Client

813
John Clayton Art Director
John Clayton Photography Studio

Emanuel
Ungaro
vous souhaite une
Belle Année
2 avenue montaigne paris

815
Denis Rodier Art Director
Jean Larcher Designer
Hollenstein Agency
Emanuel Ungaro Client

819
Brad Nims Art Director
WJLA-TV Public Service Client

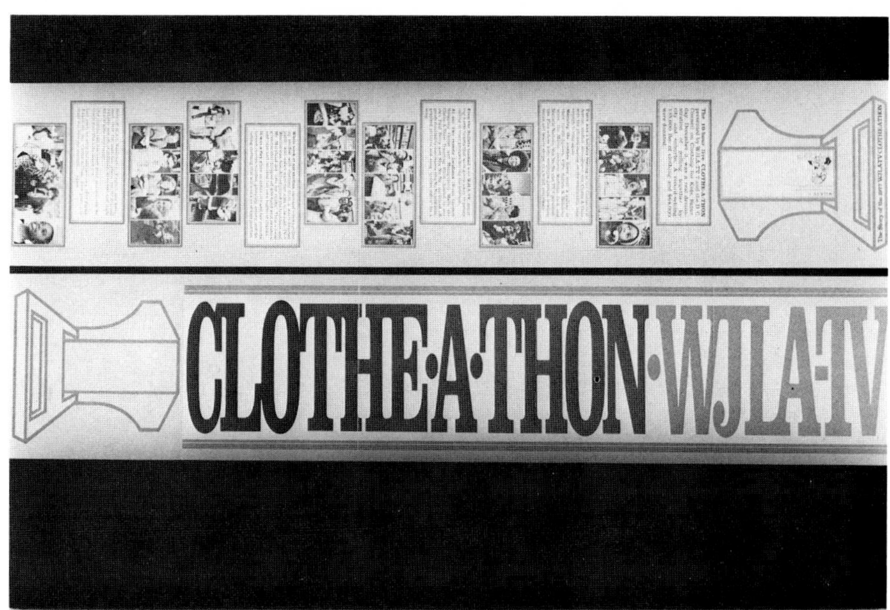

820
Michael Fountain Art Director
Michael Doret Designer
Rumrill-Hoyt, Inc. Agency
Remington Arms Co., Inc. Client

821
B. A. Albert Art Director
Neil Jordan Copywriter
Burton-Campbell Agency
Callaway Gardens Client

WHAT WILL YOUR GROUP DO ON THE OUTING YOU PLAN?

SPLASH. And swim in sparkling Robin Lake.
TOAST. On the mile long sandy white beach that runs 'round the lake.
CHEER. For the Florida State Flying High Circus with their jugglers, clowns and trapeze artists.
PADDLE. 'Round Robin Lake on the river boat Robin E. Lee. Or 'round Chickadee Lake in paddle boats and canoes.
THRILL. To daring feats of skill at the Water-ski Spectacular.
SING. With the Spirit of America Entertainers performing from their 1890's bandwagon.
WHISTLE. Along with our steam engine train, the Whistlin' Dixie.
TROMP. Over miles of nature trails.

822

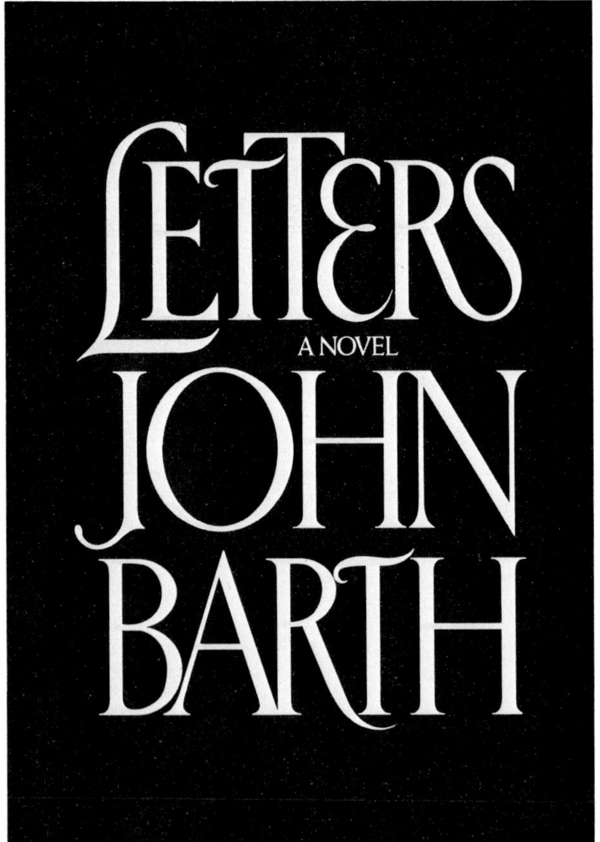

823

822
Ray Dotzler Jr. Art Director
Henningson, Durham & Richardson Client

823
Lynn Hollyn Art Director
David Gatti Typographer
G. P. Putnam's Sons Client

824
Henry Epstein, Bill Duevell Art Directors
William Duevell, ABC Visual Communications Department Photographers
ABC Corporate Art Department Studio
ABC Television Network Client

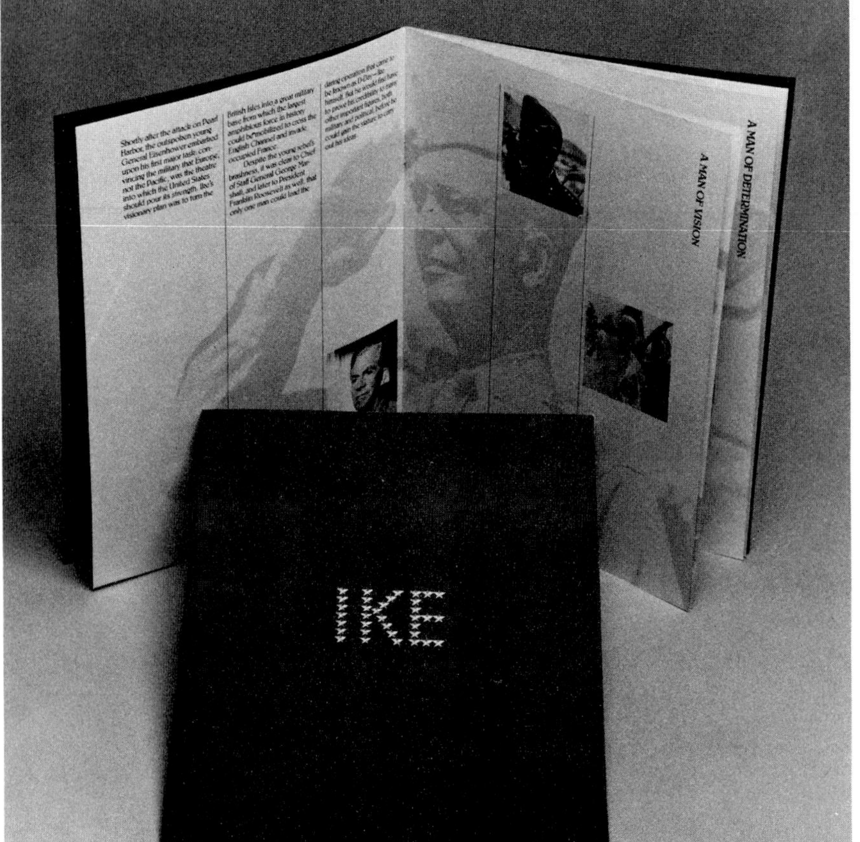

824

827
George E. Turnbull Art Director
Clementino, Turnbull & Company Agency
DeNormandie Research Client

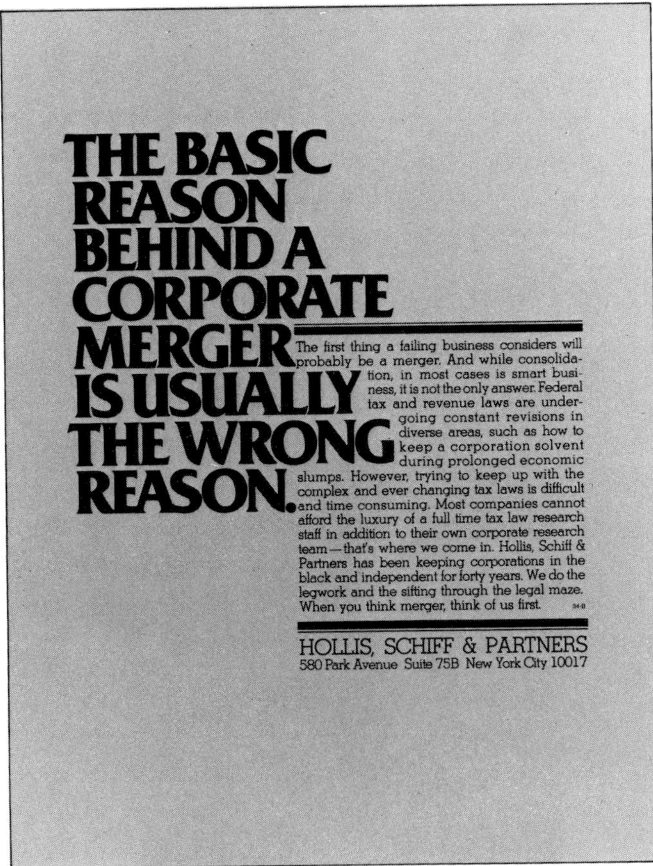

THE BASIC REASON BEHIND A CORPORATE MERGER IS USUALLY THE WRONG REASON.
The first thing a failing business considers will probably be a merger. And while consolidation, in most cases is smart business, it is not the only answer. Federal tax and revenue laws are undergoing constant revisions in diverse areas, such as how to keep a corporation solvent during prolonged economic slumps. However, trying to keep up with the complex and ever changing tax laws is difficult and time consuming. Most companies cannot afford the luxury of a full time tax law research staff in addition to their own corporate research team—that's where we come in. Hollis, Schiff & Partners has been keeping corporations in the black and independent for forty years. We do the legwork and the sifting through the legal maze. When you think merger, think of us first.
HOLLIS, SCHIFF & PARTNERS
580 Park Avenue Suite 75B New York City 10017

825
Richard Schneider Art Director
Schneider Studio Studio
Lansdown Advertising Agency
Hollis, Schiff & Partners Client

826
Joseph Rozon Art Director
Farquharson & Associates Agency
Ontario Association of Architects Client

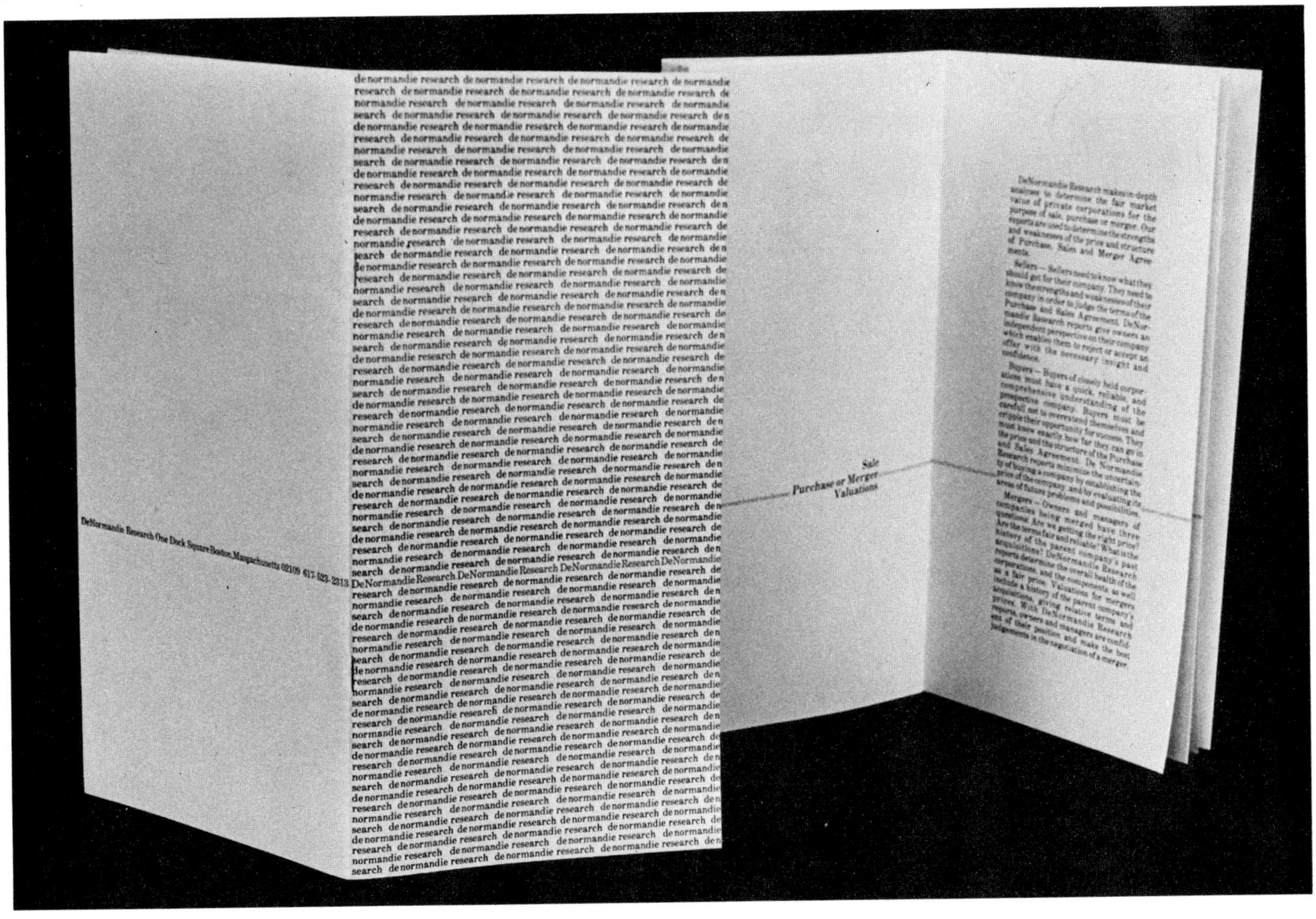

827

828
Jane Lewis Art Director
Hank Gans, Claude Furones Photographers
Merrill Lynch Client

829
Michael Sabanosh Art Director
Sabanosh Studio Studio
The Saloon Client

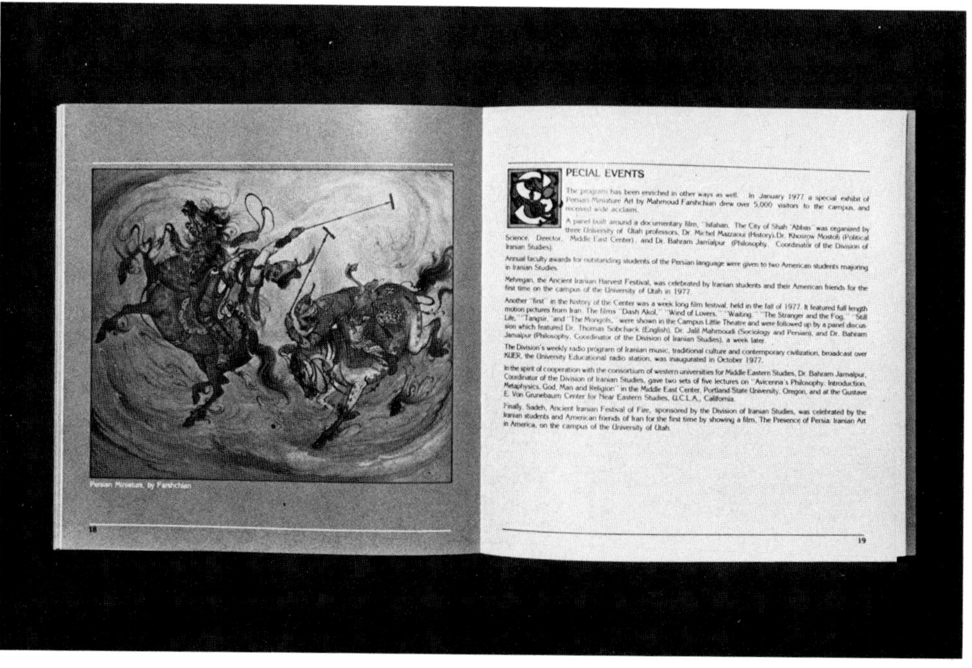

PECIAL EVENTS

The program has been enriched in other ways as well. In January 1977 a special exhibit of Persian Miniature Art by Mahmoud Farshchian drew over 5,000 visitors to the campus and received wide acclaim.

A panel built around a documentary film, "Isfahan, The City of Shah 'Abbas" was organized by three University of Utah professors, Dr. Michel Mazzaoui (History), Dr. Khosrow Mostofi (Political Science, Director, Middle East Center), and Dr. Bahram Jamalpur (Philosophy, Coordinator of the Division of Iranian Studies).

Annual faculty awards for outstanding students of the Persian language were given to two American students majoring in Iranian Studies.

Mehregan, the Ancient Iranian Harvest Festival, was celebrated by Iranian students and their American friends for the first time on the campus of the University of Utah in 1977.

Another "first" in the history of the Center was a week long film festival, held in the fall of 1977. It featured full length motion pictures from Iran. The films "Dash Akol," "Wind of Lovers," "Waiting," "The Stranger and the Fog," "Still Life," "Tangsir," and "The Mongols," were shown in the Campus Little Theatre and were followed up by a panel discussion which featured Dr. Thomas Sobchack (English), Dr. Jalil Mahmoudi (Sociology and Persian), and Dr. Bahram Jamalpur (Philosophy, Coordinator of the Division of Iranian Studies), a week later.

The Division's weekly radio program of Iranian music, traditional culture and contemporary civilization, broadcast over KUER, the University Educational radio station, was inaugurated in October 1977.

In the spirit of cooperation with the consortium of western universities for Middle Eastern Studies, Dr. Bahram Jamalpur, Coordinator of the Division of Iranian Studies, gave two sets of five lectures on "Avicenna's Philosophy: Introduction, Metaphysics, God, Man and Religion" in the Middle East Center, Portland State University, Oregon, and at the Gustave E. Von Grunebaum Center for Near Eastern Studies, U.C.L.A., California.

Finally, Sadeh, Ancient Iranian Festival of Fire, sponsored by the Division of Iranian Studies, was celebrated by the Iranian students and American friends of Iran for the first time by showing a film, The Presence of Persia: Iranian Art in America, on the campus of the University of Utah.

Persian Miniature, by Farshchian

18 19

830
Lucas R. Visser Art Director
James Paulsen Illustrator
Total Design Agency
University of Utah Client

831
Emilio Sanchez, Fred Wilmshurst Art Directors
Gloria Kramer Photographer
Floyd Uyehara Letterer
Emilio Sanchez Designer
Security Pacific Bank Client

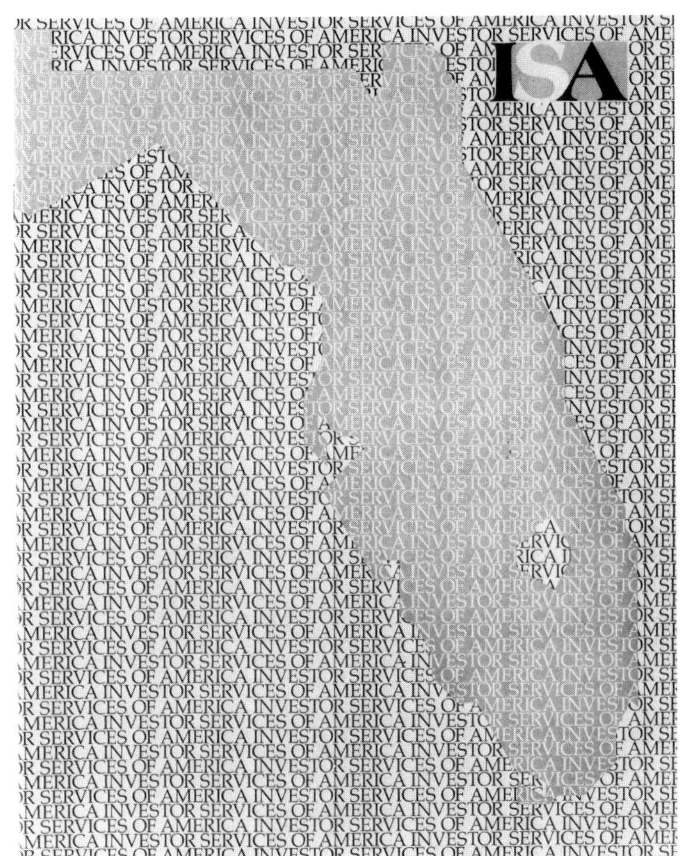

832
Stephen Bornstein, Ross Wittenberg Art Directors
Ross Wittenberg Photographer
Otis Sweat Illustrator
Piatti/Bornstein/Wolk & Associates, Inc. Agency
Investor Services of America, Inc. Client

833
Henry Epstein, Girish Patel Art Directors
Girish Patel Designer
ABC Art Department Studio
ABC Television Network Client

834
Milton Charles Art Director
Matthew Tepper Designer
Pocket Books Client

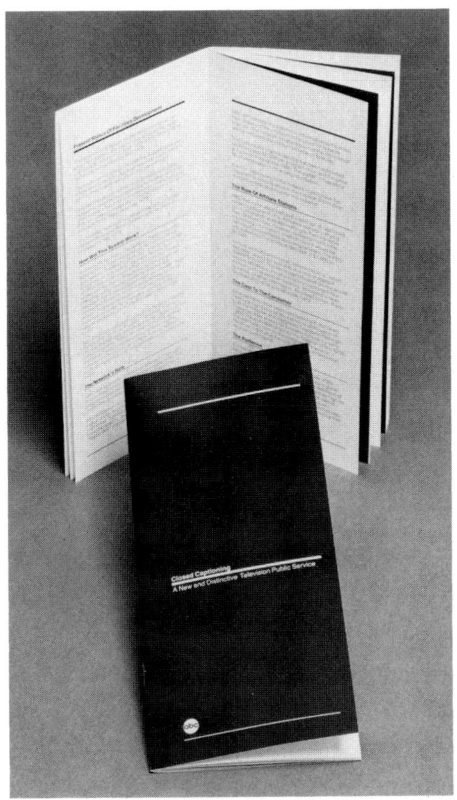

833

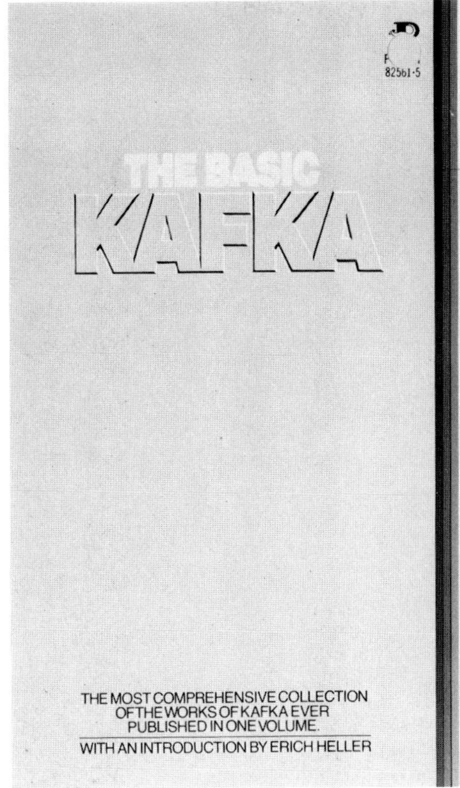

834

la banque provinciale du canada

abcdefghij
klmnopqrs
tuvwxyz
àâçéè ëê
îïôùûü 123
4567890 &
()/-:,

835

L 1 2 3 4 5 6 7 8 9 10 11 12 14 15 16

BRONZ AND KANELOUS
DESIGN INC.
CORDIALLY INVITE YOU
TO HELP MARK
THEIR BEGINNING.
FIVE TO NINE
THURSDAY,
MARCH 1, 1979
192 LEXINGTON AVE., N.Y.C.
(212) 683/2453

836

835
Asaf Mirza Art Director
Cabana, Seguin, Inc. Agency
La Banque Provinciale du Canada Client

836
Alain Filiz Art Director
Joel Bronz, Alain Filiz Designers
Bronz and Kanelous Design Client

837 A

837 A-B
Paul DiMartino Art Director
Graphics Group Inc. Agency
Allied Products Inc. Client

Dear Mr. Drexler,

For those who deal with the mechanics of agriculture and industry the future holds a growing, and even crucial, importance. Earth's population, now at a record-breaking 4 billion, is still expanding. Lately, to be sure, the rate of population growth has been slowing down, but we will surely see 6 billion on Earth by the year 2000, and a peak of possibly 8 billion in the course of the 21st Century.

How is there to be enough food grown to feed these billions, and how is that food to be transported from the point of production to the point of consumption? In view of the fact that we already have trouble feeding today's population, and the gloomy predictions that food production will not increase much beyond the present level, the proper functioning and expansion of food-related industries may be what will stand between civilization and the chaos of breakdown.

Clearly, the great concern of the present is just how we are to prepare for the future—and that means deciding just what the future will be.

There was once a time when the future could take care of itself; when technological advance was so slow that one could assume that the next century would conduct its business and its life much as the past century had. It was then not necessary to take change into account and one could safely "muddle through".

But the rate of technological change increases steadily. It became a whirlwind with the Industrial Revolution and since 1945 it has been a hurricane. We have in our own lifetimes passed through a series of changes—the "Television Age", the "Jet Age", the "Space Age", and the "Computer Age".

It is no longer possible to plan operations without taking into account the rapid change in the level of technology and the rapid responses of society to those changes. Every aspect of life is changing rapidly and will continue to do so, and to predict the nature, or even the direction, of those changes is difficult indeed.

Yet such prediction must be attempted. Forthcoming change must be assayed or no industrial project makes sense. And since those involved with food are in the forefront of the struggle to survive, it is most important for them to foresee from what direction change will come, where the dangers will appear, what shape the crisis will take—if they are to move intelligently with the change, to withstand the danger and defeat the crisis.

Isaac Asimov

Since Dr. Asimov wrote his first book in 1950, there are over 200 books today which carry his by-line. They range from non-fiction science subjects, history and geography to his "GUIDE TO THE BIBLE." He is an associate professor of biochemistry, Boston University, School of Medicine.

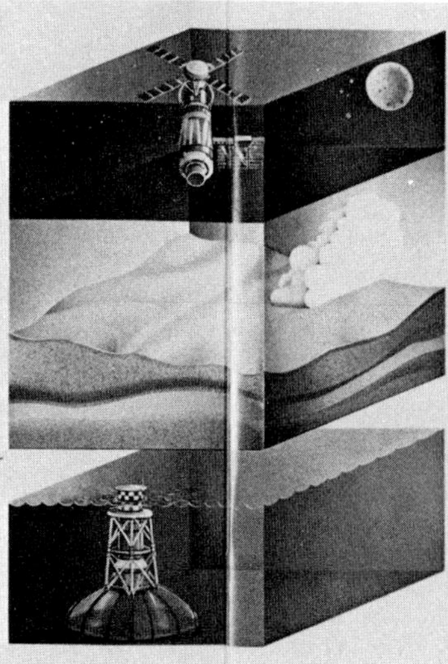

TO OUR SHAREHOLDERS, CUSTOMERS AND EMPLOYEES:

In Dr. Isaac Asimov's letter regarding the future, he stated, "...Clearly, the great concern of the present is just how we are to prepare for the future—and that means deciding just what the future will be." This was the top priority for Allied during 1978. We closed or are in the process of closing and/or liquidating five businesses, divested ourselves of six additional operations, and foresee turning around six others in an attempt to strengthen our foundation, and to position ourselves for the future. Without these operations Allied would have earned significantly more for the year.

Notwithstanding an anticipated slowdown in the economy, all groups expect improved results in 1979 versus 1978, largely due to the turnaround and/or elimination of the company's problem operations, higher farm income, coupled with increased export demand for our farm equipment, and continued strength and downsizing in the automotive industry. New products were introduced and new markets and channels of distribution were, and are, being penetrated which should also aid our 1979 results.

The year 1979 may be a difficult one for the economy and the company. It will be a year that will test the mettle of each of us as managers and leaders. During 1979 we are attempting to consolidate our investment as much as possible in view of the extremely high cost of working capital and the contemplated downturn in the economy in the second half of 1979.

Our production facilities are not specialized plants, but flexible ones which can be used for general purpose manufacturing, thereby adaptable to product changes as the future dictates. Along with our manufacturing resources, we feel that in our present management group we possess the human resources, the creativity and the ingenuity necessary to meet the challenges that lie ahead and to fulfill our financial and planning objectives.

For the Board of Directors
March 13, 1979

S. S. Sherman
Chairman of the Board

Lloyd Drexler
President & Chief Executive Officer

B

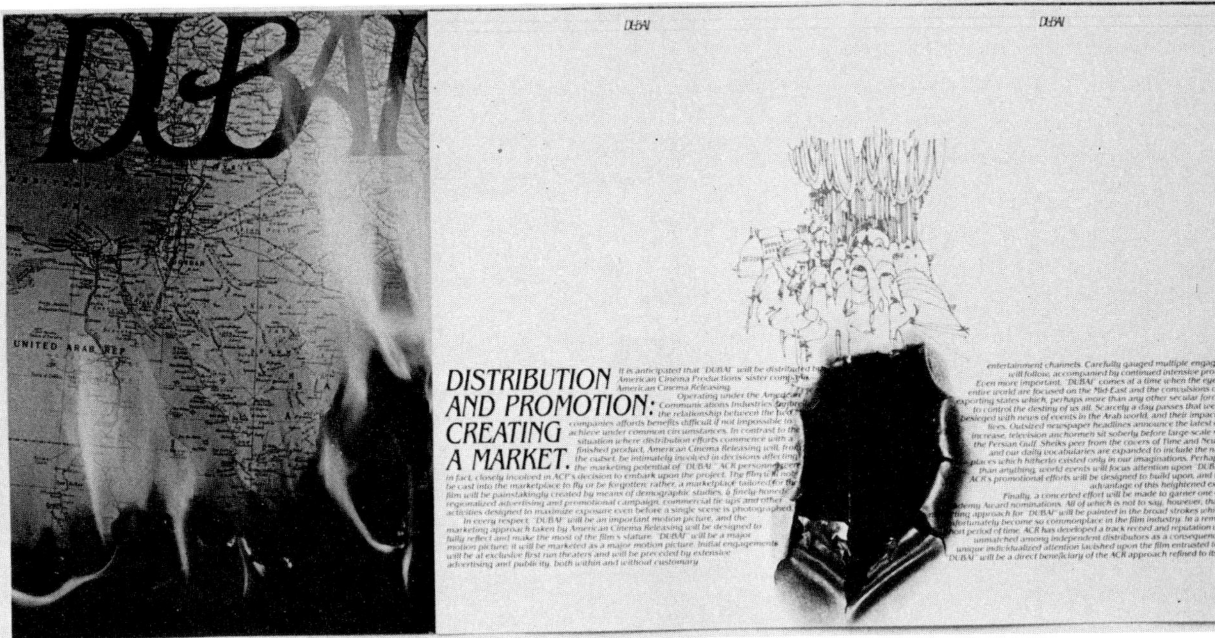

838 A

838 A-B
Tom Lewis Art Director
Michael Denny Photographer
Robert Watts Illustrator
The Design Quarter Agency
American Communication Industries Client

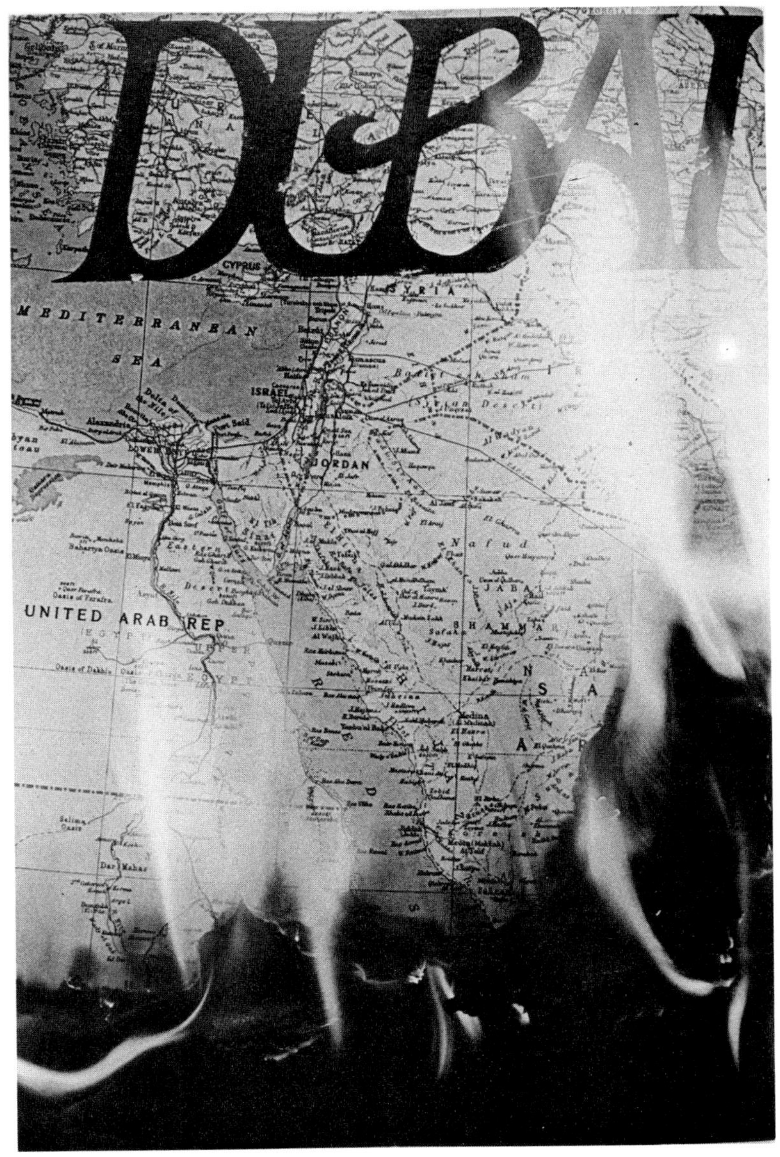

B

839
Edward Pessoa de Mello Art Director
Nilson Muller Photographer
Pessoa de Mello Propaganda Agency
Gip Imoveis Client

c. 1683-4*

BY A TYPOGRAPHER... I do not mean a printer, as he is vulgarly accounted, any more than Dr. Dee means a carpenter or a mason to be an architect, but BY A TYPOGRAPHER, I mean such a one, who by his own judgement, from solid reasoning with himself, can either perform or direct others, from the beginning to the end, all the handy-works and physical operations relating to TYPOGRAPHIE.

**Mechanick Exercises, Joseph Moxon*

**Royal Composing Room

387 Park Avenue South, New York, N.Y. 10016/889 6060

More than just a typographer

840

Martin Solomon Art Director

Royal Composing Room Client

INDEX

A

B

C

D

E

F

G

H